EXAMPLES&EXPLANATIONS

Intellectual
Property

Intellectual Property

Sixth Edition

Stephen M. McJohn
Professor of Law
Suffolk University

Wolters Kluwer

Printed in the United States of America.

1 2 3 4 5 6 7 8 9 0

ISBN: 978-1-4548-9198-7

Library of Congress Cataloging-in-Publication Data

Names: McJohn, Stephen M., 1959- author.
Title: Intellectual property : examples and explanations / Stephen M. McJohn, Professor of Law, Suffolk University.
Description: Sixth edition. | New York : Wolters Kluwer, [2018] | Includes index.
Identifiers: LCCN 2018033734 | ISBN 9781454891987
Subjects: LCSH: Intellectual property — United States. | LCGFT: Study guides.
Classification: LCC KF2980 .M42 2018 | DDC 346.7304/8 — dc23
LC record available at https://lccn.loc.gov/2018033734

About Wolters Kluwer Legal & Regulatory U.S.

Wolters Kluwer Legal & Regulatory U.S. delivers expert content and solutions in the areas of law, corporate compliance, health compliance, reimbursement, and legal education. Its practical solutions help customers successfully navigate the demands of a changing environment to drive their daily activities, enhance decision quality and inspire confident outcomes.

Serving customers worldwide, its legal and regulatory portfolio includes products under the Aspen Publishers, CCH Incorporated, Kluwer Law International, ftwilliam.com and MediRegs names. They are regarded as exceptional and trusted resources for general legal and practice-specific knowledge, compliance and risk management, dynamic workflow solutions, and expert commentary.

For Lorie, Ian, and Corn

Summary of Contents

PART IV. TRADE SECRET 511

PART V. THREE STATE LAW THEORIES AND PREEMPTION 577

Contents

Chapter 3   Copyright Does Not Protect Ideas, Functional Aspects, Infringing Material, Government Works   69

Chapter 4   Obtaining Protection and Licensing: Ownership, Formalities, Duration   111

Chapter 5   Exclusive Rights: Their Enforcement and Limitations   169

PART II. PATENT   247

Chapter 6   Patentable Subject Matter: Products and Processes   249

PART III. TRADEMARK

Chapter 10 Subject Matter of Trademark Law

Chapter 11 Substantive Standards for Protection: "The Source-Distinguishing Ability of a Mark"

Chapter 12 Obtaining Protection and Licensing: Using, Registering, Licensing, and Losing a Trademark 441

Chapter 15 Getting Protection Through Reasonable Security Measures and Losing Protection Through Public Disclosure **535**

Chapter 16   Misappropriation and Remedies   559

PART V. THREE STATE LAW THEORIES AND PREEMPTION   577

Chapter 17 Three More State Law Theories and Federal Preemption   579

Contents

Preface

This book provides tools for learning the fundamentals of intellectual property (IP) law. It is written for law students taking the Intellectual Property survey class—or for anyone else seeking an introduction to IP law. The book covers the four primary areas of IP law: copyright, patent, trademark, and trade secret. Although "intellectual property" is a term for related but distinct areas of the law, basic principles run through all the areas. Students (or lawyers) can prepare to handle IP issues skillfully by learning to focus on these common issues: the subject matter of protection, the steps necessary to secure protection, the scope of protection (and conversely, the right of others to use ideas and works unencumbered by IP claims), the process of licensing, and the remedies for infringement. The final chapter of the book touches on three related areas of law—contract law, the tort of misappropriation, and the right of publicity—and discusses how federal law can preempt state law affecting IP rights.

The text follows the method of the Examples and Explanations series. Each section first gives a short account of the law. It concentrates on the basic rules and concepts. In general, the text does not cover specialized areas, such as the copyright rules governing cable television transmissions or the patent rules on testing of generic pharmaceuticals. To keep things clear and short, such matters are left to more specialized texts.

The examples and explanations that follow the text in each section give substance to the rules and guide students in applying them to other sets of facts. The examples are drawn from many sources: judicial opinions, news reports, student questions, and daily life. The examples provide fact patterns to work with. Learning the law is not merely learning the legal rules. Learning the law means learning to apply those rules to a variety of cases. By working with concrete examples and explanations, active readers will develop that understanding.

The examples can also be used to review the concepts. Readers can work through the examples in a section without rereading the text. Readers can also change the facts in an example and ask whether the result would be different—or ask how the facts would have to change for the result to change in a specific way. For example, where the explanation states that the maker of a movie infringed copyright by copying certain elements from a book, ask what the result would be if the elements copied had been slightly different—or ask how the facts would have to change for there to be no infringement.

Preface

I greatly appreciate help from many quarters: from students and colleagues; from the readers who generously provided comments on drafts; from the creators, inventors, consumers, scholars, lawyers, pirates, and others who make the field more interesting every day; from Wolters Kluwer and associates (especially Carol McGeehan, Barbara Roth, Mei Wang, Lisa Wehrle, and, joining for the subsequent editions, Troy Froebe, Tony Perriello, Kathy Yoon, Peter Skagestad, Rebecca Logan, and Susan McClung); from the students at the *Northwestern Journal of Technology and Intellectual Property* (material first published in our annual surveys of IP law helps keep this book up to date); and, above all, from my family.

Intellectual Property

CHAPTER 1

The Contours of
Intellectual Property Law

This chapter uses a single case to outline four areas of intellectual property law.[1] Pendragon, a leading mathematician, devised a mathematical formula that could be used to draw nonrepeating patterns. Pendragon published his formula in mathematics journals, along with several examples of patterns drawn using the formula. By plugging different numbers into the formula, one can draw any number of different nonrepeating patterns. Pendragon's invention (or perhaps discovery) of Pendragon tiling was a significant advance in mathematics. Mathematicians have long worked hard to find such nonrepeating patterns. Many people took up further study and use of Pendragon's ideas. Mathematics departments all over the world began to teach about Pendragon patterns, and mathematicians deepened their research in advancing the area.

Pendragon patterns next moved beyond the world of mathematics. An engineer at Keening Paper read about Pendragon patterns in an article in *Science This Week*. The engineer realized that nonrepeating patterns could have a very useful application in making paper products. When paper is sold on rolls, one hazard of putting patterns on the paper is that the paper may stick to the roll if matching patterns are placed one on top of each other. The use of nonrepeating patterns could reduce this production flaw. Some

---

1. The example is based loosely on a case that was filed by Sir Roger Penrose against the Kimberly-Clark Corporation.

nonrepeating patterns would also reduce air spaces, reducing the size of the paper roll. Shortly thereafter, a design identical to a design in one of Pendragon's scholarly articles began to appear on rolls of paper towels made and sold by Keening. That particular design is just one of millions that could be made by using Pendragon's formula. Later on, other Keening products appeared with Pendragon patterns. These designs were not the same as those previously published by Pendragon. Rather, Keening apparently had used Pendragon's formula to draw additional designs, rather than simply copying designs from the work of Pendragon or others.

Almost two years after Keening started selling such products, Pendragon learned of this use of his work and consulted his lawyer. He asked her whether the law prevented the copying of the particular pattern that Keening had chosen and whether he had the right to prevent Keening from using his formula to draw other patterns and use them on their products.

COPYRIGHT

Copyright applies to original works of authorship as soon as they are fixed in any tangible medium of expression. The author of the work initially owns the copyright, although she may transfer her rights to others. If the work is created by an employee (a work made for hire), the author is deemed to be the employer. The copyright term lasts for the life of the author plus 70 years (or a fixed term of 95 years for works made for hire and some other categories of works). The copyright owner has the exclusive rights to make copies of the work, distribute copies to the public, adapt the work, display the work publicly, and perform the work publicly.

Pendragon's scholarly articles and his diagrams of Pendragon tiling qualify for copyright protection. They qualify as original works of authorship because they originated with him and easily meet the minimal standard of creativity required. Pendragon did not register his copyright. But copyright does not depend on complying with formalities, such as registering the copyright, depositing copies with the Library of Congress, or using copyright notices on copies of the work. Such practices are permitted and offer practical advantages, but they are not necessary to create the copyright. Rather, an author owns the copyright in any original work of authorship as soon as she fixes it in some tangible form (writes down a poem, takes a photograph, records a song, makes a sculpture).

Keening Paper apparently did infringe the copyright in one of Pendragon's designs. It copied the design from his article and sold copies to the public, thereby infringing the rights to make copies and to distribute those copies to the public. Keening might contend that there was no proof that it actually copied the design. But there is sufficient evidence to support an inference of copying, as opposed to Keening having made the design independently: The design had been published, an identical design appeared on Keening's paper product after Keening took an interest in Pendragon patterns, and the odds that the designs would coincidentally be identical were very low.

But Pendragon cannot use the copyrights in his articles and designs to prevent Keening from using Pendragon's mathematical formula to make its own patterns. Even if Keening admits that it copied Pendragon's formula from his work and used it to draw the designs, Keening would not be liable for copyright infringement. Copyright only protects creative expression. It does not protect ideas, principles, theories, and the like. One can freely copy from copyrighted works, if one only copies unprotected material. So it is not copyright infringement to copy the facts from a history book or to copy the way a computer program works.

PATENT

An inventor of a product or process has the right to seek a patent on his invention from the U.S. Patent Office. The patent gives the inventor the right to exclude others from making, using, offering to sell, selling, or importing the invention during the term of the patent. The patent term begins when a patent is issued and endures until a date 20 years from the date that the inventor applied for the patent.

Pendragon did not apply for a patent on his formula, so he cannot exclude others from using it. Even if Pendragon had applied for a patent, his formula would probably fall outside the scope of patentable subject matter. The scope of patentable products and processes is very broad. But certain things are not patentable, such as the laws of nature, physical phenomena, and abstract ideas. Pendragon's formula likely would fall into the category of nonpatentable abstract ideas. Pure mathematics and other abstractions are not patentable. Rather, to be patentable, an invention must produce a useful, concrete, and tangible result. Pendragon might argue that his formula does produce such a result because it can be used to draw interesting-looking patterns. But when the formula is not tied to any particular application but instead can be used to draw millions of patterns that could be used for any number of purposes, the formula would be deemed too abstract to be patentable.

Keening, however, did apply the formula to a useful, concrete, and tangible result. Although Keening did not invent the formula, an invention may consist of the application or improvement of someone else's work. Keening used the formula to make paper products that were less likely to stick to the roll. This invention might have qualified for a patent. Keening would have been subject to substantive standards for patentability. These require that the invention be new, useful, and nonobvious. Keening might well have met the requirement of nonobviousness, if paper engineers would not have been likely to make the leap that Keening's engineer did. Likewise, the invention was sufficiently useful, if it indeed would reduce the problem of paper sticking to the role. But Keening would not now meet the requirement that the invention be new. This requirement has two aspects. The invention was new when Keening first created it, in the sense that it was unprecedented. But it is no longer new in the other legal sense, which requires that Keening apply for a patent no later than one year after the invention is published or in public use. Because Keening has been selling the product for almost two years, the company has lost its right (if any) to patent it.

TRADEMARK

Trademark law comprises several related doctrines that serve a common purpose: to allow buyers to reliably distinguish a source of goods or services. A trademark is a symbol used by a person in commerce to indicate the source of her goods or services and to distinguish them from those sold or made by others. The trademark owner acquires trademark rights by making bona fide use of the mark in commerce. There is no time limit on the duration of the mark. Rather, the owner retains ownership of the mark until she abandons use of it. Trademark registration offers a number of legal and practical advantages, but registration is not necessary to create a trademark right. Unauthorized use of a trademark in a manner that is likely to confuse consumers about the source of goods or services infringes the trademark. Trademark law also provides causes of action beyond trademark infringement: false designation of origin; false advertising; dilution of famous trademarks; and impermissible registration, use, or trafficking in Internet domain names that are similar to the trademarks of others.

In this case, Keening did not use Pendragon's name or any other symbol that falsely indicated an affiliation with Pendragon. Keening did use one of Pendragon's designs and also used his formula. But neither were so closely associated with Pendragon as to confuse consumers about the source of the paper products or to imply Pendragon's endorsement. With respect to the formula, it is not protectable as a trademark in any event. Trademarks do not protect functional matter, and the formula plays a functional role in creating nonrepeating patterns.

TRADE SECRET

A trade secret is information that has economic value from not being known to or readily ascertainable by those who could gain value from its use or disclosure and is the subject of reasonable security measures. Typical trade secrets are customer lists, manufacturing processes, computer programs, and blueprints for machines, where such information is kept secret using reasonable security measures. Pendragon's formula is not a trade secret. Rather than being kept from others through the use of security measures, the information was freely published.

Like Pendragon, Keening did not take any security measures and therefore cannot have trade secret rights in its application of Pendragon's formula to paper products. Keening could have tried to exploit the information as a trade secret. It could have used the formula to produce the nonrepeating patterns without disclosing that it was using the formula. For the information to qualify as a trade secret, it would have to be valuable because it was unknown to Keening's competitors and also not readily ascertainable. The information was valuable because it made the paper less likely to stick to the roll and reduced the roll size. So the question is whether Keening's competitors could have readily figured out that Keening was using Pendragon's formula. They may well have been able to do so. If the competitors could discern that Keening had nonrepeating patterns on its products, a little research might have led them to the widespread knowledge among mathematicians that Pendragon patterns would produce such nonrepeating patterns.

This discussion shows just the bare outlines of intellectual property law. The succeeding chapters survey the basic principles of each area.

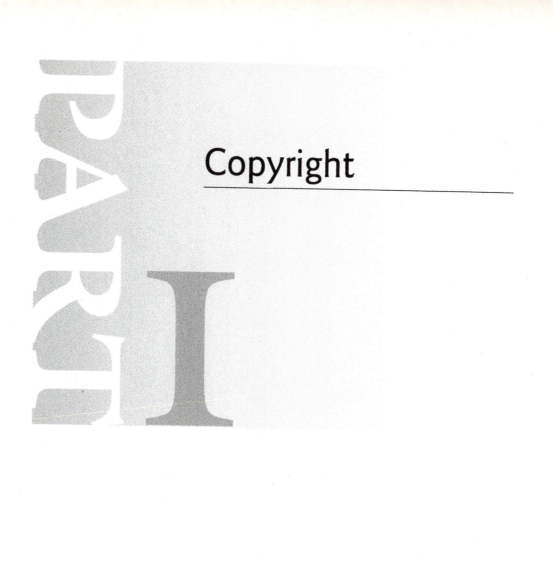

Copyright

PART I

Subject Matter: Creative Expression, "No Matter How Humble, Crude, or Obvious"

Do you have copyright in your class notes? Very likely. Copyright once applied only to maps, books, and charts, but now reaches every area of creative endeavor. Copyright applies to books, movies, software, and songs — but also advertisements, statues, blueprints, computer programs, T-shirt designs, diaries, warning labels, databases, fingerpaintings. . . . Copyright applies to any original work of authorship, fixed in a tangible medium of expression. This chapter addresses those three requirements: what qualify as works of authorship; what it takes to meet the originality requirement; and when a work is fixed, triggering copyright protection. Copyright is a statutory area of the law, enacted by Congress and signed by the President, after much lobbying by interested parties, such as publishers and entertainment companies. The Copyright Act creates copyrights for authors.

Suppose Ozzie authors a novel (or sculpture or song or dance or computer program or database or photograph or movie or biography or pantomime or painting or letter or . . .). As soon as she writes it, she holds the copyright in the work. The copyright will last her life plus 70 years. (If it were a work made for hire, her employer would own the copyright, and it would last 95 years.) To obtain copyright protection, she need not register the copyright with the Copyright Office or put "© 2009 Ozzie" on published copies of the work. She may register the copyright and use a copyright notice because they provide practical advantages. Among other things, the remedies for infringement are greater and proving infringement is easier where the work was registered before infringement. But she doesn't have to register in order to hold copyright and benefit from the set of exclusive rights it provides. As copyright holder, under section 106 of the Copyright Act, she possesses the exclusive right to:

1. reproduce the copyrighted work in copies or phonorecords (often called the *reproduction right* or the *right to make copies*);
2. prepare derivative works based on the copyrighted work (*adaptation right*);
3. distribute copies or phonorecords of the copyrighted work to the public by sale or other transfer of ownership, or by rental, lease, or lending (*public distribution right*);
4. perform the copyrighted work publicly (*public performance right*); and
5. display the copyrighted work publicly (*public display right*).

People might infringe on Ozzie's copyright by doing such things as the following without Ozzie's permission:

- making or selling copies of the novel
- copying creative elements of the novel into another book
- making a movie based on the novel
- publicly performing a scene from the novel
- downloading the text of the novel

But they might also be protected by various limitations on Ozzie's rights. Certain elements of the work would not be protected by copyright, such as ideas (such as the plot of the novel), elements not created by the author (facts about Chicago that Ozzie puts in the book), and functional elements (such as the rules of a game or the functions that software performs, not an issue with most novels). So other authors may freely copy a clever idea for a novel, or facts uncovered through research, or rules of an accounting system. Moreover, even copyrighted elements may be used under such limitations as fair use. Fair use might permit writing and selling an unauthorized parody of Ozzie's novel, or handing out photocopies of a chapter to a class, or including portions in a book review.

Ozzie's exclusive rights give her control over several types of commercial uses of the work: printing and selling the novel, selling chapters online, performing the work, etc. She also controls (subject to fair use and the nonprotection of ideas) how the work is adapted into other forms, such as sequels, translations, and other offshoots. So the basket of exclusive rights allows the author not just to exploit the work commercially, but also to control its public life (to a limited extent—she cannot dictate how critics review it or whether the public pays attention to it). An author can control the artistic uses of the work, such as by licensing performance of a play, subject to restrictions ("You cannot change the ending, or stage it as a parody"). Copyright also can be used to prevent dissemination of a work. An author may prevent a work from being published (such as an unfinished novel or a diary), which can protect artistic values and even privacy interests. But the hazard exists that authors will use copyright to censor or to limit the flow of information, such as by claiming copyright in e-mails discussing important issues, or even in a cease-and-desist letter threatening a lawsuit. Copyright law must often balance incentives to authors and protection of author's artistic creations against legitimate expressive interests of others.

Ozzie may sue an infringer in federal court. She may get remedies like damages, an injunction, and impoundment of infringing copies. If she had registered the copyright before the infringement, she may choose statutory damages rather than actual damages, and may also seek attorney's fees.

JUSTIFICATIONS FOR COPYRIGHT LAW

Copyright law can prohibit such activities as distributing copies of music, writing plays based on novels, performing songs in concert, publishing letters by famous authors, and selling artworks. One might argue that all of these activities are of a kind that the law should encourage, not deter. What is the purpose of a law that specifically prohibits some uses of creative works? The reasons for copyright law are often grouped into two sets: economic justifications and philosophical justifications.

Economic Bases for Copyright

Samuel Johnson said, "No man but a blockhead ever wrote, except for money." Copyright is usually justified as providing an incentive for the creation of works. The incentive-to-create theory draws its legal basis from the Constitution:

> The Congress shall have Power . . . to Promote the Progress of Science and the useful Arts, by securing for limited Times to Authors and Inventors the exclusive Right to their respective Writings and Discoveries.

U.S. Const. art. I, §8, cl. 8. Under this view, copyright exists in order to overcome the free-rider problem with public goods. Without copyright law, authors have a diminished incentive to produce works. A potential author might not spend all the time and money required to write a book or make a movie if others could freely make and sell copies. Copyright law gives them an exclusive set of rights in their works, and that set of rights is an incentive to create. The language of several Supreme Court cases is consistent with the incentive-to-create approach.

The benefits conferred by copyright do not come without costs. Costs of copyright can include transaction costs (hiring lawyers, negotiating for permission to use works, locating authors, and asking permission), rent-seeking (the use of copyright to get revenue from nonprotected elements or even making frivolous claims for their settlement value), dead-weight losses (uses of works that do not take place because of copyright, such as where an author does not write a book or song because of inability to get the necessary permission from certain copyright holders, or where a copyright holder chooses to sell fewer copies at a higher price), and distorted incentives (channeling resources toward copyrightable works). The Supreme Court has recognized that copyright protection can discourage innovations in distributing works: "The more artistic protection is favored, the more technological innovation may be discouraged; the administration of copyright law is an exercise in managing the trade-off." *MGM Studios Inc. v. Grokster, Ltd.*, 125 S. Ct. 2764, 2775 (2005). In deciding how much copyright protection to provide, the incentive-to-create approach might counsel balancing the benefits against the costs. For example, in considering how broad fair use is, one could balance the benefits of the proposed use against the costs in decreased incentives to authors.

Copyright law doctrine has not been strictly limited by the incentive rationale; the scope of copyright law is much broader. Copyright applies to *any* creative work as soon as it is fixed in a tangible form, including works that are created without the incentive of copyright, such as personal letters, school projects, and legal memoranda. Moreover, there are many incentives other than copyright for people to produce creative works. Diarists may write for catharsis, artists create for art's sake, scientists may write to gain peer recognition, professors may write to get tenure, and software developers write free software. The urge to create is instinctual. In William Faulkner's words, "An artist is a creature driven by demons. He doesn't know why they choose him and he's usually too busy to wonder why." Even nonblockheads creating for money can find others sources of revenue from their creations: musicians sell concert tickets, gag writers get salaries, artists sell the original work (a copy of a Picasso does not get the same price as the original). Finally, copyright's duration (life of the author plus 70 years) is longer than necessary to spur creation of works. The present value of royalties 70 years in the future is negligible, even for the few works that have such long-lasting commercial value. So the incentive-to-create theory provides a strong argument for copyright generally, but not one that closely matches the particular copyright law that we have, which is much broader than the incentive rationale alone would support. In some areas, lack of intellectual property protection may mean that freedom to copy speeds innovation. Perhaps because fashion design has little copyright protection, designers rapidly come out with new designs to maintain market leadership. *See* Kal Raustiala & Chris Sprigman, *The Piracy Paradox: Innovation and Intellectual Property in Fashion Design*, 92 Va. L. Rev. 1687 (2006).

The other leading set of economic theories of copyright have been called *property theories* or *ex post theories*. *See* Mark A. Lemley, *Ex Ante Versus Ex Post Justifications for Intellectual Property*, 71 U. Chi. L. Rev. 129 (2004) (skeptical). Rather than looking to copyright as simply providing an incentive to create works, they look to copyright as providing an incentive to efficiently exploit works. An analogy is made to real property law. If someone owns a home and yard, she has an incentive to expend resources to manage, maintain, and improve the home efficiently, because she gets the benefits. If she paints it, fixes things that break, and tends the garden, she can get the benefits of those costs (whether she lives there, rents it out, sells it, or lets her kids use it). She can decide how much costs to expend, in view of the benefits she will get. But without property rights, anyone could use the home and yard. No one would have much incentive to manage, maintain, and improve things, because others would get the benefit. Why fix everything up if that would just attract strangers to come in and live there? This is the well-known "tragedy of the commons." In economic terms, property serves to avoid externalities—situations where a decision maker does not bear the resulting costs or benefits.

Some apply the real property analogy to copyright to support arguments for very broad copyright protection. *See* Lemley, *supra*. By making works into private property, we give an incentive to manage, maintain, and improve the works. Copyright holders will preserve copies of old works (like delicate films), devise ways to improve works (like making sequels or other spin-offs), and seek new markets for works (bring them to a wider audience). So unlike the incentive-to-create approach, which counsels balancing the costs of protection against the benefits of providing incentives, the property approach leads some to say, "the more protection the better."

The two approaches can lead to different views about copyright law. Take fair use as an example. Fair use allows the use of copyrighted works without permission for such uses as education, criticism, research, and the creation of other works. An incentive-to-create theory of fair use might measure the costs (decreased incentives to authors) against the benefits (the favored use). A property theory might counsel that the copyright owner should generally decide how the work is used, so fair use would be applicable only where transaction costs or other obstacles to negotiation would prevent getting permission from the copyright owner. So the property approach would lead to a narrow view of fair use (and, in general, to broader copyright protection).

There are differences between real property and intellectual property that undermine the analogy. The key difference is the danger of overuse. *See* Lemley, *supra*. If land is open to all, it may be overused. If everyone can graze their cattle in the common, it may be overgrazed (and no one has incentives to plant, because other people's cows will eat the crop). Likewise, if everyone can use the house, no one has the incentive to maintain it. But information is not subject to that hazard. If everyone can read an author's book, so much the better. Rather, the key is to get the author to write it to start with—the problem addressed by the incentive-to-create approach. Having said that, the property approach, which supports broader copyright protection, may better reflect the broad copyright protection that we have.

"Public choice," another kind of political/economic theory, might explain why copyright protection is so broad. Copyright law is created by Congress. Legislation is often more affected by particular interests than broad public policy. Copyright law affects everyone, but the people (from authors to various industries) who own copyrights tend to be the most involved in creating copyright legislation. As a result, it may be that copyright leans toward authors, as opposed to the users of works. As always with politics, opinions differ about that.

Economic analysis of law has recently paid increasing attention to norms: informal, nonlegal standards of behavior. Some see copyright as the legal version of the norms that condemn plagiarism or even theft. Others view copyright as going beyond relevant norms. When the social standard of behavior differs from the legal standard, the law may not accomplish its goals, especially where the purpose of a law is to provide incentives for behavior. Some have questioned whether copyright law is rapidly diverging from norms about use of creative works — in short, whether copyright prohibits acts that are considered socially acceptable, even beneficial. This arises especially in such areas as music downloading or artistic uses of commercialized works.

Philosophical Justifications for Copyright

Copyright may also be supported by philosophical theories. These come in many varieties. For simplicity's sake, one could divide them into "personality" theories and "natural rights" theories.

Under the personality approach, an artist's personality is seen as linked to the works she has created. Anyone who makes use of the work indirectly affects the person of the author. Authors should control the uses of their work, and especially be entitled to prevent distortion or destruction of the work, or misattribution of authorship. Under this approach, copyright might be as broad as necessary to protect the author. There might be broader protection for categories of works that are more closely linked to the author: a work of art might get more protection than a commercial advertisement.

Under the natural rights approach, an author has a natural right to what she has created through her labor. It may be limited by the fact that in creation, she has reduced the resources available to others and also relied on elements created by others. So her rights should also let others likewise make some use of what she has created. Cf. Wendy J. Gordon, *A Property Right in Self-Expression: Equality and Individualism in the Natural Law of Intellectual Property*, 102 Yale L.J. 1533 (1993); Alfred C. Yen, *Restoring the Natural Law: Copyright as Labor and Possession*, 51 Ohio St. L.J. 517 (1990).

These views get less explicit recognition in U.S. law than economic theories. But they may influence the sense of fairness of judges, lawmakers, and commentators, even where they do not show up in judicial opinions or statutory language. They are also more widely accepted in other countries, and international/comparative law is increasingly influential in copyright. Indeed, the copyright statute even grants some artworks rights against distortion, destruction, and misattribution, in a provision adopted with international treaties in mind.

The particular doctrines or case outcomes supported by philosophical theories can, of course, vary widely along with the many varieties of the theories. But they provide a good framework for analyzing the issues.

Intellectual property law draws on our intuitive understandings—for better or worse. Origin stories in every culture assign meaning to institutions, provide an explanation and justification of social arrangements, and support cultural unity through common belief. Courts often look to the original language, or original purpose of the rule, or how it responded to a problem, or how the rule's author viewed the rule, such as with legislative history or the Federalist Papers. Intellectual property law provides a special twist on origin stories, by assigning control of information to the author or inventor that originated the information. Jessica M. Silbey, *The Mythical Beginnings of Intellectual Property*, 15 Geo. Mason L. Rev. 319 (2008). Similarly, cognitive science tells us that "the mind understands every entity in terms of four causes: who or what brought it about; what it's made of; what shape it has; and what it's for." Steven Pinker, *The Stuff of Thought* 61 (2007). Intellectual property mirrors this cognitive structure, giving legal rights to the party that brought the information about. *See* Lorie Graham & Stephen McJohn, *Cognition, Law, Stories*, 10 Minn. J. L. Sci. & Tech. (Winter 2009).

THE LEGAL STRUCTURE OF COPYRIGHT

The U.S. Constitution authorizes Congress to grant copyrights and patents:

> The Congress shall have Power . . . To promote the Progress of Science and useful Arts, by securing for limited Times to Authors and Inventors the exclusive Right to their respective Writings and Discoveries.

U.S. Const. art. I, §8.

Pursuant to this power, Congress has enacted the Copyright Act, which grants authors exclusive rights in their writings: copyrights in original works of authorship. "Authors" is very broadly understood to mean those who make many kinds of creative work; it does not refer only to writers. "Writings" is likewise read broadly to encompass many categories of creative works, provided they are fixed in some tangible medium of expression. The copyright owner has the exclusive rights to make copies of the work, to distribute copies of the work to the public, to prepare derivative works, to perform the work publicly, and to display the work publicly, along with other protections in the statute. Pursuant to the Constitution's language that the rights be granted for "limited times," copyright has a term specified by statute.

As suggested by the language of the Constitution, copyright provides an incentive to authors. Suppose an author is considering spending two years writing a novel. Without copyright protection, once she published the novel, others could simply make copies and sell them. Facing such a prospect, some would-be authors and publishers would choose other activities. But the exclusive rights provided by copyright provide the author means to exploit her work that are unavailable to others. In addition to providing an incentive, copyright serves the idea that authors deserve some control over works that they have created—both to reward the author and because misuse of the work may cause an intangible injury to the author.

Under *Eldred v. Ashcroft*, 537 U.S. 186 (2003), Congress has considerable latitude in shaping intellectual property law. The issue in *Eldred* was the constitutionality of the Copyright Term Extension Act of 1998, which added 20 years to the terms of existing copyrights—extending the copyrights in works dating back to the 1920s. *Eldred* rejected the argument that Congress had exceeded its power to grant copyrights for "limited Times" in order to "promote the Progress of Science." That clause, the plaintiffs argued, implies that Congress's authority is limited by the incentive-to-create rationale. If the purpose of copyright protection is to provide an incentive to create works, nothing Congress did in 1998 could provide an incentive to create works in the 1920s. But the Court held that the Constitution left it to Congress to choose the intellectual property regime that best serves the purposes of the clause. Likewise, *Golan v. Holder*, 565 U.S. 302 (2012), held that Congress did not overstep its bounds when it restored copyrights to foreign works, where U.S. copyright had been lost due to failure to comply with the formalities formerly required under U.S. law.

Comparing U.S. copyright law to other copyright regimes can be instructive. U.S. copyright law is generally pretty similar to copyright law in most other countries, in part because so many are party to Berne and the Trade-Related Aspects of Intellectual Property (TRIPS) Agreement. But U.S. law still differs in a number of respects. Notable examples include fair use (more broadly defined in the United States); formalities (the United States is unique in having a Copyright Office with extensive functions, such as registering copyrights and recording transactions involving copyrights, and U.S. law strongly encourages copyright registration, deposit of works, and use of copyright notices); moral rights (U.S. copyright law gives authors fewer moral rights, such as rights of attribution and protection of works from distortion), work-made-for-hire doctrine (under U.S. law, an employer has the copyright in a work created by an employee in the scope of employment—other jurisdictions have narrower rules), and statutory damages (in the United States, infringement of a registered work gives $750 to $150,000 in damages, even without showing harm).

Congress could limit copyrights to specific types of works. A copyright statute could be limited to books, or to fine art, or to works that met high standards of creativity. The first version of the copyright statute in 1790 applied only to maps, charts, and books. Until as recently as January 1, 1978, federal copyright law applied primarily to published works.[1] But the present copyright statute applies much more broadly:

> Copyright protection subsists, in accordance with this title, in original works of authorship fixed in any tangible medium of expression, now known or later developed, from which they can be perceived, reproduced, or otherwise communicated, either directly or with the aid of a machine or device.

17 U.S.C. §102(a). So the broad reach of copyright law applies to any work that meets three requirements: The work is an

1. original
2. work of authorship
3. fixed in a tangible medium of expression.

A broad range of works is protected by copyright. Copyrighted works include novels, music, artworks, and films, but also less elevated works, such as e-mail messages, doodles, love letters, souvenir T-shirts, shampoo bottle labels, computer programs, belt buckle designs, maps, yellow page phone books, advertisements, class notes, and pantomimes.

ORIGINALITY

A copyright in "We Shall Overcome" (a slightly revised version of the song "We Will Overcome," which is now in the public domain) was registered in 1960 and renewed in 1988. The copyright holders exercised considerable power over the work for decades. But in a declaratory judgment action brought by filmmakers, the court in 2017 held that "We Shall Overcome" lacked sufficient new creative elements to qualify for copyright:

> More specifically, the changes of "will" to "shall" and "down" to "deep" and the melodic differences in the opening measures and the seventh measure, do not create a distinguishable variation. These differences represent "variations of the piece that are standard fare in the music trade by any competent musician."[2]

---

1. The statute did provide for registration of specified types of unpublished works.
2. We Shall Overcome Found. & Butler Films v. Richmond Org., Inc. (TRO INC.), No. 16cv2725(DLC), 2017 U.S. Dist. LEXIS 146228, at *36 (S.D.N.Y. Sept. 8, 2017) (citation omitted and "citation omitted" omitted). The parties later settled. *See* Christopher Mele, *'We Shall Overcome' Is Put in Public Domain in a Copyright Settlement*, New York Times (Jan. 26, 2018), https://www.nytimes.com/2018/01/26/business/media/we-shall-overcome-copyright.html.

A work is not protected unless it is *original*: created by the author with at least a minimal spark of originality. 17 U.S.C. §102(a). Under *Feist Publications v. Rural Tel. Serv. Co.*, 499 U.S. 340, 369 (1991), originality has two distinct requirements. To be original means that a work is "independently created by the author (as opposed to copied from other works) and that it possesses at least some minimal degree of creativity." Feist Publications, unable to reach an agreement with Rural, simply copied the listings into its own regional directory. The Supreme Court held that Feist did not copy material that is protected by copyright, because there was no creativity in making the listings. *Feist* held that originality is required not just by the copyright statute, but by the Constitution. Congress has the power to grant exclusive right to "Authors" in their "Writings." Such words "presuppose a degree of originality."

The originality requirement has two important effects. First, a work that lacks originality is not protected by copyright (although it is pretty easy to show the necessary originality). A white pages phone listing, a list of customers, a mechanically produced copy of an eighteenth-century pirate map all lack originality and so are not copyrighted. But a hack novel, a clumsy drawing, or an awful song are all sufficiently creative to be copyrighted. Likewise, creative additions to preexisting material qualify for copyright. So a creative arrangement of the list of customers or a creative 2009 adaptation of the eighteenth-century map is copyrighted. Second, nonoriginal elements of a work are not protected. A book may be copyrighted. But nonoriginal elements (such as facts and elements in the book not created by the author) may be freely copied without infringing the copyright. One could freely copy the names of the customers or the data from the underlying map, just not the creative additions of the author.

Independent Creation

The first requirement, independent creation by the author, bars claims to the authorship of the works of others. If Homeowner discovers an unpublished short story in a dusty cabinet, he would not thereby own the copyright in the story. He did not write it. Likewise, if Plagiarist copies the work of another, she would not have any copyright in the copied material. Originality does not require novelty. Originality does not require that a work be unique or that it be different from preceding works. Suppose Painter paints an abstract painting today. By coincidence, the painting closely resembles another painting created decades ago. But Painter had never seen or heard of the first painting. Painter's painting would be original because it originated with him.

Here copyright differs from patent law. If Inventor invents a machine that, unbeknownst to her, is just like a machine that is already in public use, then Inventor is not entitled to a patent. Even though she came up with the invention herself, she would not meet the novelty required by patent law. In copyright, by contrast, it is no bar to protection that someone has already created a similar work.

Courts may nevertheless look at other works in deciding the question of originality. In *Acuff-Rose Music v. Jostens, Inc.*, 155 F.3d 140 (2d Cir. 1998), a songwriter claimed copyright infringement. His song used the phrase "you've got to stand for something or you'll fall for anything," which he alleged had been copied by defendant. The court considered the fact that similar phrases had been used in many different sources: "the Bible, Abraham Lincoln, Martin Luther King, Malcolm X, Ginger Rogers, and a chaplain of the U.S. Senate, and others that simply refer to it as an 'old saying.' Moreover, in 1985, popular songwriter and singer John Cougar Mellencamp recorded an album that included a song called 'You've Got to Stand for Somethin' featuring the lyrics, 'You've got to stand for somethin'/Or you're gonna fall for anything.' " *Id.* at 144. In light of the widespread use of the phrase, the court held that plaintiff had failed to show that he had originated the phrase, as opposed to copying it from someone else. Note that the court did not deny him protection on the basis that he was not the first one to use such a phrase. Rather, it determined that he failed to show that he came up with the phrase independently.

The requirement of independent creation also bars copyright protection in facts and other phenomena, even to the person who discovers them first. Discovery is not creation. If Biologist discovers that elephants can understand sign language, Biologist cannot claim copyright in that information. Even if she was the first to discover or the first to publish the fact, she did not originate the fact. Likewise, if Biologist weighs every elephant in every zoo in the United States, she has no copyright protection in the facts of their respective weights. Originality requires that one be the "maker" or "originator," not merely one who discovers and records a fact. So facts of all stripes — scientific, historical, biographical, news of the day — are unprotected by copyright. Likewise, one that discovers a beautiful gem, flower, or geological formation has no copyright in it.

Examples

1. *Discovered letter.* Historian, sifting through thousands of old documents purchased from a scrap paper dealer, finds a long-lost letter. The letter is covered in grime, making it impossible to read. Nevertheless, Historian imaginatively identifies it as potentially valuable, relying on various subtle clues and her own rich experience. Using great care and skill, Historian spends days cleaning the letter and restoring its colors. The handwriting is atrocious and idiosyncratic. Historian nevertheless manages to decipher it, using creative powers of reasoning, together with lots of research. The letter is anonymous but evidently was written around 1965. The letter describes 1960s life in Seattle, with many evocative details and creative turns of phrase. Historian types up the text of the

letter to make it easy for others to read. Historian claims copyright in the letter. If the purpose of copyright is to provide an incentive for the distribution of works, Historian argues, then she is entitled to copyright in the letter. Otherwise, she may turn her hand to writing trashy historical novels. Does she meet the originality requirement?

2. *Picture this.* Suppose Historian decides to make a photograph of the letter for archival purposes. She carefully positions several lights so that every facet of the letter is shown in the photograph. She also chooses a level of lighting that, together with a colored filter on her camera, lends a somber mood to the picture. Does her photograph meet the requirements of originality?

3. *Peeple's rock.* Peeple discovers a balancing rock, worn into mystic shapes by the elements. With great care and much consideration of lighting and angles, he takes a photograph of the rock and publishes it in a newsletter. A week later, Big-City Paper asks him where the rock is so it can send out a photographer. Peeple refuses to tell the secret desert location. Paper then publishes a copy of his photo. Paper argues that it did not violate copyright because Peeple discovered the rock; he did not independently create it. Has Peeple met the originality requirement?

4. *Souvenir.* Tourist arrives in Chicago and takes a photo of Wrigley Field, the stadium of the Chicago Cubs. Tourist frames the stadium, selects an angle that gives a pleasing shape to the structure, and waits for the moment when the sunlight falls on the stadium as clouds pass overhead. The photo Tourist produces is quite similar to a number of photos that have already been published. Indeed, Tourist can point to nothing that distinguishes her photo from the many thousands of photos that have been taken of Wrigley Field. Is Tourist's photo original?

5. *World heritage.* Anthropologist discovers a number of ancient designs carved into rocks. She painstakingly makes exact copies by skillfully rubbing over specially designed paper, placed on the designs. Does she have a copyright in the designs?

Explanations

1. Copyright protection requires that the work be original to the author. The author of the letter does meet the *Feist* standard of originality (independently created by the author and at least a minimal level of creativity). The letter itself is clearly creative and original. But Historian did not write the letter, so it was not original to her. Historian expended great resources, coupled with both historical and material expertise, to locate, restore, and make legible the contents of the letter. Much of her work did require creative thinking, which might meet the second requirement. She also put in a great deal of work and applied considerable skill. But

none of those substitutes for meeting both requirements of originality. The letter was written by someone else, so it was not independently created by Historian.

2. The photograph did originate with Historian, so it meets the first requirement. Unlike Example 1, Historian did not claim copyright in the work of another but has created a new work (the photograph). The issue is whether it meets the second requirement, a minimal level of creativity. One might argue that she was simply making a "slavish copy"—that all her work and all her decisions were geared not toward creativity but toward making as accurate a copy of the letter as possible. That is the theory used when copyright is denied to works such as digital reproductions of public domain paintings. But Historian went beyond making a copy. She also made creative choices about lighting and color to set a mood for the photograph. So Historian does have a copyright in the photograph. Her copyright protects only the expressive elements that she added to the preexisting work.

3. Peeple did not independently create the rock, but he independently created the photograph. This case illustrates the fact that an author can make an original work that portrays preexisting material. Peeple exercised ample creativity in considering lighting and angles. His photograph meets the originality requirement. In copying the photo, Big-City Paper necessarily copied original elements of Peeple's work.

4. Tourist's photo meets the originality requirement. This case illustrates the fact that originality does not require novelty, uniqueness, or any other high standard. A work need not be unprecedented to qualify for copyright protection. If the work originates with the author and is at least minimally creative, it is original. Tourist did not copy from the other photos, even though her product was similar. The work originated with her. She also made a number of creative choices in making the photo, satisfying the second requirement of originality, so her photo qualifies for copyright protection. An author may create an original work even though she uses preexisting material such as the subject of the work (in this example), facts or a previous work of authorship (as in the examples above), or other preexisting material. The issue is whether the author adds her own creative expression to the preexisting material.

   Does that mean that the next person to take a photo of Wrigley Field infringes Tourist's copyright? No. As the infringement chapter discusses, infringement requires copying. If the next tourist does not copy Tourist's photo, there is no infringement—even if the photo happens to be identical to Tourist's photo.

5. Although Anthropologist used considerable skill, she did not use creativity in making the rubbings. She has no copyright in the rubbings. On

the other hand, she has the rubbings, and as yet controls access to them. Copyright is not the only way in which information can be limited—for better or worse.

Note that the same issue may apply where preexisting designs are used for other purposes. If tattoo artist made an exact copy of a Maori design, there would be no copyright in the tattoo. If the artist used some creativity in adapting the design to a tattoo, then there could be copyright. That issue arose with respect to boxer Mike Tyson's tattoo, which was featured in the movie *The Hangover: Part II* and its advertising.

A Minimal Spark of Creativity

In addition to independent creation, originality requires creativity on the part of the author. *Feist* emphasized that this is a low standard. The "originality requirement is not particularly stringent," requiring only "some minimal level of creativity." 499 U.S. at 358. Originality will be found in all but a "narrow category of works in which the creative spark is utterly lacking or so trivial as to be virtually nonexistent." 499 U.S. at 359. Originality does not require that the work be innovative or surprising, only that it be more than "so mechanical or routine as to require no creativity whatsoever." 499 U.S. at 379. "The vast majority of works make the grade quite easily, as they possess some creative spark, 'no matter how crude, humble or obvious' it might be." 499 U.S. at 345 (quoting *Nimmer on Copyright*). As the legislative history put it, this "standard does not include requirements of novelty, ingenuity, or esthetic merit." House Report No. 94-1476. A second grader's T-shirt design (the word "Hi" on the front with a smiley face and the word "bye" on the back with a frowny face) met the requirement.[3]

Feist shows just how uncreative the author must be to fail to qualify for protection. The telephone book publisher simply listed the subscribers in alphabetical order. This tried and true arrangement of the information has long been used in telephone books. It was not a creative selection or arrangement of the information. The raw data was not original to Rural. Rather, that information existed before Rural ever gathered and published it. Rural Telephone did not have copyright in the raw data because of the first requirement (independent creation), and did not have copyright in the selection and arrangement of the data because of the second requirement (a minimal degree of creativity). Therefore, anyone could copy Rural's non-copyrightable listings. So, facts are not copyrightable. But a compilation of facts may be, if the selection, coordination, or arrangement of facts reflects the necessary creativity.

---

3. I.C. ex rel. Solovsky v. Delta Galil USA, 2015 U.S. Dist. LEXIS 132052 (S.D.N.Y. Sept. 29, 2015).

Subsequent cases have shown that even telephone listings can be sufficiently original to be copyrightable. One compiler selected New York City area businesses of interest to Chinese Americans and arranged them using categories devised to be of interest to that community. *See Key Publications v. Chinatown Today Publications Enterprises*, 945 F.2d 509 (2d Cir. 1991). Alternatively, someone could add creativity to the individual listings. An Icelandic white pages listing is original. Traditional names and the uses of patronyms and matronyms result in many identical names. A substantial portion of the male population is named Magnus Magnusson. So to identify subscribers, Icelandic phone books often include creatively chosen personal information (Magnus Magnusson, the golfing fan, drives an old Volkswagen Beetle).

The author need not show that she engaged in a lengthy creative process, or that she made notably creative decisions. The author need not meet any high standard of artistic creation. Indeed, creativity may be the result of accident. A painter may find that her work did not turn out how she intended or is marked by some accidental brushstrokes. But if she adopts the result as her own, it can be sufficiently creative. Here again copyright law differs from patent law, where an inventor is only entitled to a patent if the invention was not obvious, in light of the state of the art in the relevant field. By contrast, in copyright, even the author who turns out obvious but original works is entitled to protection.

The requirement of creativity is so low that most works meet it quite easily. But there have been cases where courts found too little creativity — usually cases where the plaintiff strained to find some original element in order to prevent others from copying material that was largely nonprotectable. In *Matthew Bender & Co. v. West Publg. Co.*, 158 F.3d 693 (2d Cir. 1998), for example, West published reports of judicial decisions. West had no copyright in the judicial opinions, because they were not created by West, rather by the judges and their clerks. West did add original, creative elements to its editions, such as summaries of points of law, but the defendant did not copy those elements. The defendants did copy the page numbers in the West volumes, in order to allow users to cite to the page in the West volume. West claimed that the page numbers were its original expression, and therefore protected by copyright. The court rejected that argument on the basis that giving sequential numbers to pages in a book is not even minimally creative (just as in *Feist*, where arranging the listings in a phone book alphabetically is not even minimally creative). The court also noted that West did not have copyright protection in corrections it made to the punctuation and spelling in the opinions, because such changes were too trivial to meet the creativity requirement. In a similar vein, photographs lacked originality, where plaintiffs did not "identify any conscious choices they made regarding lighting or camera angles for the purpose of being "original."[4]

---

4. Rigsby v. Erie Ins. Co., 2015 U.S. Dist. LEXIS 31711 (W.D. Wis. Mar. 16, 2015).

Courts have used the creativity requirement to frustrate other attempts to, in effect, use copyright to protect nonoriginal material. In one such case, plaintiff hired a builder to build a slightly customized house. Plaintiff took the builder's standard architectural drawings and marked a few places where plaintiff's house would be different. The house was built, and plaintiff was quite proud of it. Plaintiff was then dismayed to see that the builder had used the amended drawings to build an identical house for another customer. Plaintiff sued for copyright infringement, claiming that the changes to the drawings were sufficiently creative to qualify for copyright. The court rejected that argument, characterizing them as mere editorial changes. *Watkins v. Chesapeake Custom Homes, L.L.C.*, 330 F. Supp. 2d 563, 573 (D. Md. 2004). Plaintiff's real complaint was that the builder had built an identical home for someone else. But where the builder had not copied any creative elements originating with plaintiff, there was no copyright infringement. The originality requirement prevents copying alone from giving rise to infringement liability.

Courts have likewise rejected attempts to claim copyright in standard product features. Suppose a printer has a popular line of stationery for small business, with envelopes having labels such as "Addressee" and "Sender" and memo pads with such lines as "From:" and "To:." A competitor copies the envelopes, memo pads, and other products. Printer claims copyright infringement. A court is likely to hold that there is no copyright in standard labels, because they lack the necessary creativity. Similar issues arise when vendors copy the labels on products. If a ketchup maker uses a picture of a tomato on its goods, a court may hold that it lacks even the minimal creativity required for copyright, meaning there is no infringement if a competitor uses a similar tomato. But where there is any creativity to be found—in how the tomato is drawn, or how several tomatoes are grouped—then that may suffice for copyright protection (which would, however, give protection only against quite literal copying).

Similarly, legal forms that borrow standard language do not qualify for copyright simply because of a few changes in syntax or addition of a few words, done without any independent analysis or legal research:

> Even though word arrangements have been altered, they are at best merely a paraphrasing of earlier forms. There is nothing recognizably different from the language used in form books or earlier business forms. Elementary legal words and phrases are in the public domain, and no citizen may gain monopoly thereover to the exclusion of their use by other citizens.

M. M. Business Forms Corp. v. Uarco, 472 F.2d 1137, 1140 (6th Cir. 1973). This is not to say that blank forms never qualify for copyright. If there is creativity in selecting the categories of questions, or in designing the aesthetics of the form, or in drafting the language of the questions, then the originality requirement may be met.

Because the originality standard is somewhat vague, there have been several attempts to make per se rules to guide authors and courts. The

Copyright Office regulations bar registration for certain categories of works that are nonoriginal:

> Works consisting entirely of information that is common property containing no original authorship, such as, for example: Standard calendars, height and weight charts, tape measures and rulers, schedules of sporting events, and lists or tables taken from public documents or other common sources.

37 CFR 202.1(d). The Copyright Office regulations also bar registration for "words and short phrases such as names, titles, and slogans." This rule is frequently justified on the basis that such short phrases lack sufficient originality for copyright protection.

Examples

1. *Hyperborean?* The AudioQuest K2 terminated speaker cable is available on Amazon.com for a mere $8,450 a pair. This offer has spurred a number of reviews, the most popular beginning: "We live underground. We speak with our hands. We wear the earplugs all our lives. . . . We cannot maintain the link for long. . . . DO NOT USE THE CABLES! . . ." Is the Amazon review a copyrighted work?

2. *Prosaic?* Would the following paragraph qualify for copyright?
   "Contains about as much caffeine as a cup of coffee. Limit caffeine products to avoid nervousness, sleeplessness, and occasionally rapid heartbeat. You may experience a Niacin Flush (hot feeling, skin redness) that lasts a few minutes. This is caused by Niacin (Vitamin B3) increasing blood flow near the skin."

3. *Creative?* Nova adapts a design for Holiday Inn Express hotel. Nova adds a floor; enlarges the meeting area; changes the closet and door placements in rooms; and changes the size of the pool, exercise, and laundry areas. Nova makes these changes after receiving suggestions, along with graphic designs, from the client. Does Nova's work show sufficient creativity to qualify for copyright?

4. *Pro Forma?* Meds sells forms for use during an office visit with a doctor. The forms provide blanks for various categories of specified information: name, date of birth, sex, and ailment. Then for each ailment, the forms provide information to be obtained: "history of the present illness, a review of systems, medical and social history, physical exam, medical decision making, clinical impressions, and finally, consultation, disposition, and instructions." The forms list the common answers for many questions, to speed filling out the forms. Meds learns that Formulaic has copied Meds' forms and sold them. Copyright infringement?

5. *Haters gonna infringe.* Would singer Taylor Swift be liable for copying the phrases "playas . . . gonna play" and "haters . . . gonna hate" from one of the many songs playing on those themes?

Explanations

1. The review is a copyrighted work. It is a literary work. It easily meets the requirement of a modicum of creativity. The next question might be, who owns the copyright. As discussed later in the book, that might depend on Amazon's terms of service.

2. Courts interpret the creativity requirement quite liberally. "Because the medical caution statements appearing on the energy shots have appreciable differences, and stylistic flourishes may be inserted in the statement, the medical caution label has the minimum level of originality necessary to warrant copyright protection as a matter of law." *Innovation Ventures LLC d/b/a Living Essentials Ltd. v. N2G Distributing Inc.*, No. 2:08-cv-10983-PDB-MJH (E.D. Mich. 2011).

3. Nova did not show creativity. The additions were all made at the prompting of the client, and were relatively routine. So Nova did not contribute creative elements. *See Nova Design Build Inc. v. Grace Hotels LLC*, No. 10-1738 (7th Cir. 2011).

4. The court held that the forms lacked even the minimal creativity to be copyrighted. Rather, they simply called for "for the same information that any responsible physician would ask a patient with the given ailment." *See Utopia Provider Sys., Inc. v. Pro-Med Clinical Sys., LLC*, 596 F.3d 1313 (11th Cir. 2010). Just as every white pages phone book lists all the phone holders in alphabetical order, so there was no creativity in selecting, arranging, or coordinating the information on the forms.

5. "In order for such short phrases to be protected under the Copyright Act, they must be more creative than the lyrics at issue here. [P]layers, haters, and player haters had received substantial pop culture attention prior to 2001. . . . In short, combining two truisms about playas and haters, both well-worn notions as of 2001, is simply not enough." *Hall v. Swift*, 2018 U.S. Dist. LEXIS 43575, at *22-23 (C.D. Cal. Feb. 13, 2018).

New Works (Especially Factual Works, Compilations, and Derivative Works) May Incorporate Nonoriginal Elements

Irish folk tales are too old to be protected by copyright, but a compilation of Irish folk tales could have copyright protection (in its original selection or arrangement). Shakespeare's *Romeo and Juliet* is too old to be protected by copyright. *West Side Story*, which retells Romeo and Juliet in twentieth century New York City, is copyrighted. Compilations and derivative works may be copyrighted by adding original elements to preexisting material.

"§103. Subject matter of copyright: Compilations and derivative works

(a) The subject matter of copyright as specified by section 102 includes compilations and derivative works, but protection for a work employing preexisting material in which copyright subsists does not extend to any part of the work in which such material has been used unlawfully.

(b) The copyright in a compilation or derivative work extends only to the material contributed by the author of such work, as distinguished from the preexisting material employed in the work, and does not imply any exclusive right in the preexisting material. The copyright in such work is independent of, and does not affect or enlarge the scope, duration, owner-ship, or subsistence of, any copyright protection in the preexisting material."

An author can take other types of nonoriginal material and, by adding her own original expression, qualify for copyright. In the landmark case of *Alfred Bell v. Catalda Fine Arts*, 191 F.2d 99 (2d Cir. 1951), plaintiff engraver made mezzotint engravings that were reproductions of classic paintings. The engraver did not seek simply to duplicate the paintings. Because the engraver had to make creative choices about the depth and shape of the engraving depressions, the work went beyond purely the mechanical to be original. Likewise, changing the size, spacing, and proportions of a graphic design could supply the necessary modicum of creativity. An original arrangement of even the most mundane elements can qualify for copyright. A video game might use only simple, familiar shapes, such as rectangles and squares, and familiar colors. But sufficient creativity could be shown in selecting the shapes and colors and devising the actions of those elements during play. *See Atari Games v. Oman*, 979 F.2d 242 (D.C. Cir. 1992).

Facts are not copyrightable, but works containing facts may be copy-rightable, because they contain other elements created by the author. As the Copyright Office regulations put it, "A fact or event, as distinguished from the manner in which it is described in a particular work, is not copyright-able." Compendium II: Copyright Office Practices 202.02(d). Drawing the line between unprotectable facts and copyrightable expression is not always so clear. For example, if a database consisted of the prices that cars had been sold for, those prices would be facts, information about the actual transac-tions that had occurred. But some courts have held that "blue book" listings of car values were not mere facts. *See CCC Information Services v. Maclean Hunter Market Reports*, 44 F.3d 61 (2d Cir. 1994). The listings were not reports of actual transactions, but were estimates of value. Although the estimates were based on the prices that cars had sold for, they also required consideration of various other factors. The price listings, therefore, included some elements that originated with the authors, as opposed to mere facts.

The Copyright Office has also addressed the issue of originality in compilations. "An author may have copyright in a work consisting entirely of unprotected elements (such as facts or works created by others), if she shows the requisite creativity in selecting, coordinating, or arranging those unprotected elements. The greater the amount of material from which to select, coordinate, or order, the more likely it is that the compilation will be registrable. Where the compilation lacks a certain minimum amount of original authorship, registration will be refused. Any compilation consisting of less than four selections is considered to lack the requisite original authorship."

So selecting four elements would be deemed insufficiently creative. But "[t]he selection and ordering of 20 of the best short stories of O. Henry would be registrable as a compilation." Compendium II: Copyright Office Practices 307.01. A compilation may also have originality in the coordination or arrangement of the elements. This means more than simply the format in which the items are printed. Rather it requires an "original ordering or grouping of the items." Id. at 307.03.

The amount of creativity required is not great. But, under *Feist*, nothing substitutes for creativity. The author cannot win protection by showing that he invested considerable resources (such as the work that went into gathering the information for thousands of telephone listings). Likewise, even if great skill or technical prowess is used, that does not make up for a lack of creativity. For example, courts have denied protection in cases in which all the author's efforts are geared toward copying a preexisting work as accurately as possible. It may be technically difficult to make such a "slavish copy," but doing so does not show the necessary creativity. But if the author adds creative elements in making her reproduction, such choices may meet the requirement of creativity.

An author may use a device in a creative way to produce an original work. *Burrow-Giles Lithographic v. Sarony*, 111 U.S. 53 (1884), rejected the argument that making a photograph was simply a mechanical process lacking in originality. The photograph at issue was a portrait of Oscar Wilde. Defendant argued that the photograph was simply an exact reproduction of the image of Oscar Wilde. But the photographer had made a number of creative choices: posing the subject, selecting and arranging the subject's clothes and other things in the picture, and choosing the lighting.

Courts have used the creativity requirement to frustrate other attempts to, in effect, use copyright to protect nonoriginal material. In one such case, plaintiff hired a builder to build a slightly customized house. Plaintiff took the builder's standard architectural drawings and marked a few places where plaintiff's house would be different. The house was built and plaintiff was quite proud of it. Plaintiff was then dismayed to see that the builder had used the amended drawings to build an identical house for another customer. Plaintiff sued for copyright infringement, claiming that the changes to the drawings were sufficiently creative to qualify for copyright. The court rejected that argument, characterizing them as mere editorial changes. *Watkins v. Chesapeake Custom Homes, L.L.C.*, 330 F. Supp. 2d 563, 573 (D. Md. 2004). Plaintiff's real complaint was that the builder had built an identical home for someone else. But because the builder had not copied any creative elements originating with plaintiff, there was no copyright infringement. The originality requirement prevents copying alone from giving rise to infringement liability.

Courts have likewise rejected attempts to claim copyright in standard product features. Suppose a printer has a popular line of stationery for small business, with envelopes having labels such as "Addressee" and "Sender" and memo pads with "From:" and "To:" lines. A competitor copies the envelopes, memo pads, and other products. The Printer claims copyright infringement. A court is likely to hold that there is no copyright in standard labels, because they lack the necessary creativity. Similar issues arise where vendors copy the labels on products. If a ketchup maker uses a picture of a tomato on his goods, a court may hold that lacks even the minimal creativity required for copyright, meaning there is no infringement if a competitor uses a similar tomato. But where there is any creativity to be found — in how the tomato is drawn, or how several tomatoes are grouped — then that may suffice for copyright protection (which would, however, give protection only against quite literal copying).

To repeat a key point, legal forms that borrow standard language do not qualify for copyright, simply because of a few changes in syntax or addition of a few words, done without any independent analysis or legal research:

> Even though word arrangements have been altered, they are at best merely a paraphrasing of earlier forms. There is nothing recognizably different from the language used in form books or earlier business forms. Elementary legal words and phrases are in the public domain and no citizen may gain monopoly thereover to the exclusion of their use by other citizens.

M. M. Business Forms Corp. v. Uarco, 472 F.2d 1137, 1140 (6th Cir. 1973). Some blank forms never qualify for copyright. Creativity in selection, arrangement or wording may meet the originality requirement.

Copyright Estoppel

Under the doctrine of "copyright estoppel," if an author represents information as factual (or otherwise noncopyrightable, such as representing it as the work of others), then she will not have copyright protection in the information — even if she actually originated it. *See Arica Institute, Inc. v. Palmer,* 970 F.2d 1067 (2d Cir. 1992). If an author concocted a story and presented it as fact, the events would be unprotected by copyright (as opposed to events in an avowedly fictional novel). Analogously, original theories could be treated as fact. In *Nash v. CBS, Inc.,* 899 F.2d 1537 (7th Cir. 1990), the author wrote a book about the gangster John Dillinger. The author reported that Dillinger had survived the famous shooting at the Biograph Theater in Chicago and lived out his life under another name in the West. Some television producers copied those elements, along with other specific facts reported by the author, and used them in making a television show. The author then sued for copyright infringement. The courts held that by presenting the information as factual, she had effectively waived any copyright protection.

Copying Unprotected Material Is Not Infringement

The originality standard is quite low, which means that copyright protection is not difficult to obtain. But copyright protection extends only to the original elements of the work. This reflects an important copyright principle. It is not infringement to copy nonprotected elements of a copyrighted work, such as nonoriginal elements, ideas, or functional elements. Infringement requires copying of original, expressive elements of the work. The rule that copyright protects only original elements supplies some balance.

Nonoriginal elements are especially common in two categories of works, derivative works (because they are adaptations of preexisting works) and compilations (which may be collections of facts or preexisting works). The statute expressly states that only the new elements are protected: "The copyright in a compilation or derivative work extends only to the material contributed by the author of such work, as distinguished from the preexisting material employed in the work, and does not imply any exclusive right in the preexisting material." 17 U.S.C. 103.

Suppose a database contains much factual information related to the city of Worcester, such as names of residents and streets, information about utility fixtures, and real estate taxes for properties. The database compiler selects and arranges the information in a creative way, making the database a copyrighted work. Someone who literally copied the entire database without permission would likely infringe the copyright, because she copied both the protected and nonprotected elements of the work. Suppose someone else copied only some of the factual information from the database, and did not copy the selection or arrangement of the information. The second copier would not infringe, because she copied only nonprotected information (the nonoriginal facts). So copying from a copyrighted work is not necessarily infringement; copying protected elements from a copyrighted work may be infringement.

Derivative works and compilations are especially likely to contain nonoriginal and hence noncopyrighted material. But all works must contain nonoriginal elements to be copyrighted.

The originality analysis, then, arises in two types of cases: cases involving copying of the entire work, and cases involving copying part of the work. Where the entire work is copied, the issue may be whether the work as a whole qualified for copyright protection. If the work was unoriginal, then it was not protected by copyright and even copying of the entire work would not be infringement. More commonly, the issue of originality arises where defendant copied only certain elements from plaintiff's work. Defendant contends that the elements that were copied were not original, and therefore there was no infringement.

A useful practical distinction is often made between works with thin protection and works with thick protection. A work with thin protection is made of mainly of nonprotected elements. Factual works (like telephone directories, books of sports statistics) have thin protection. This means that broad literal copying (such as copying the entire directory) is likely infringement, because it would include copying the creative elements, such as the selection and arrangement of data. Highly creative works (like an imaginative novel) have thick protection, because there would be infringement not just from literal copying, but also nonliteral copying (copying not the exact words, but the sequence of events and various characters). Because copyright hinges on creativity, creative works receive greater copyright protection.

A practical problem can be identifying which elements of the work are not protected. Nonoriginal elements are not protected. But the author is not required to identify which elements of her work are original. Imagine there was a 1910 book about the Civil War. Publisher has the only extant copy. Publisher scans the book, then has an employee edit and supplement the book, perhaps adding a paragraph here, a chapter there. Publisher publishes the updated book, with a foreword explaining that some elements have been added, but not specifically identifying the new elements. Publisher would have copyright protection in the new creative elements, but everything from the original 1910 book would be unprotected by copyright. But a reader might be unable to distinguish between the protected and unprotected elements, meaning that copying would risk infringement. The same problem arises in many other types of work. A song may have an original, protected melody, or may have copied it from another. A drawing in an advertisement may be new or copied from an old master. So the originality requirement leaves unoriginal material legally unprotected, but does not always provide the key to using it.

Examples

1. *Translation.* Historian translates the letter into Spanish. For many of the words and phrases, there are numerous potential Spanish equivalents. Historian seeks to produce a translation that is accurate and pleasing to the ear. She claims a copyright in the translation of the letter. Is her translation original?

2. *Folk songs.* An old New England fisherman learned many local folk songs during his years at sea. His younger colleagues prefer other diversions, such as watching videos and listening to recorded contemporary music.

Concerned that oral tradition will no longer suffice to pass along the songs, he decides to preserve them. He selects a number of good exemplars and selects the order and grouping for a book of songs. He composes arrangements for the songs and also invents melodies and words for some that he cannot remember. He also visits fishermen in Newfoundland and records them singing their local folk songs. He publishes sheet music of his arrangements of the New England songs and his recordings of the Newfoundland songs. A large music publisher then starts to sell identical copies of the sheet music and the recordings. The publisher argues that it has not copied protected expression because none of the works were original to the fisherman. Rather, they were traditional folk songs, many generations old. Were the new arrangements and recordings original to the fisherman?

3. *Just the facts.* Editor spends years compiling her encyclopedia of sports trivia. She pores through newspapers, books, and other sources to find some of the facts. Other facts she digs up herself from interviews with retired athletes. She uses several innovative techniques to compile the information, devising several new categories and new ways of grouping sports information. She also makes deliberate choices about what information to include, based on numerous factors. Shortly before publishing her book, she learns that facts are not protected by copyright. Does copyright offer her any protection?

4. *Original mint condition?* Medallica makes and sells metallic replicas of U.S. coins and paper currency. Medallica makes three-dimensional silver versions of U.S. folding money. In making each note replica, Medallica makes choices about how to translate color contrasts into a silver medium, how to represent the intricate background detail of U.S. Treasury notes, whether certain features should be dull silver or highly polished silver, and whether certain features should be engraved or set off in bas relief. Medallica also makes three-dimensional replicas of U.S. coins. Its replicas are larger versions of the U.S. coins, made from similar materials. Medallica does not have access to the U.S. mint materials and therefore faces a number of difficult technical issues in making the coin replicas: what materials to use, the correct manufacturing process, constructing plates that will give the correct images. Medallica's engineers and technicians exhibit enormous skill and expertise in managing to produce astonishingly exact replica coins. Are Medallica's replicas original, for the purposes of copyright law?

5. *Mapmaker, mapmaker.* Mapmaker spends several years gathering information about Boffin Island. Mapmaker researches such sources as geological surveys, satellite photographs, interviews with residents, and Mapmaker's own surveying expeditions. Drawing from this huge amount of information, Mapmaker produces a variety of maps of Boffin Island, both maps

of the entire island and of various regions. Some maps emphasize geological information; others show points of historical interest. Rival makes exact copies of Mapmaker's maps and sells them, arguing that the maps are not original. First, they include only facts, which are unprotected by copyright. Second, maps are intended to be exact copies of Boffin Island and therefore lack creativity. Is Rival violating copyright law?

6. *Odd numbers.* Autoparts Manufacture uses a part-numbering system. A particular type of carburetor, for example, bears the number 03-11-62. The first pair of digits refers to the category of product, the second pair refers to the particular style of engine, and the third refers to the specific dimensions. Although Autoparts Manufacturer devised the system, it did not choose the specific combination of numbers for each part. Rather, the specific numbers are generated by using the system. Autoparts Manufacturer discovers that a competitor uses some of the numbers in its service manuals. Are the numbers copyrighted?

7. *"The most beautiful woman in the world."* In a local folktale, a young boy loses his mother. Naturally, he tells searchers that she is the most beautiful woman in the world. Villagers check with all the local beauties, but none is missing her child. Finally, the mother appears—not striking to any but her son. Scriptwriter hears of the story and uses it as the basis for a movie, adding many plot twists, bits of dialogue, and other elements. Novelist sees the movie and writes a novel based on the basic plot. Novelist only copies the elements taken from the folktale. All the other elements of the novel (such as the setting, the dialogue, various incidents that carry the story forward) are different than the film. Is the movie sufficiently original to be copyrighted? If so, did Novelist infringe the copyright?

8. *Butterfly chaos.* Nabokov, a lepidopterist, collects all the information he can about butterflies. Through his own fieldwork and library work, he amasses as many facts relating to butterflies as he can. He then arranges the facts according to his own categories, thereby creating a taxonomy of butterfly information. He publishes a book in which all the information is arranged in various categories Nabokov has devised. Is Nabokov's work copyrightable—or has he failed to exercise sufficient creativity because he has included every fact he could find?

9. *A book about a show about nothing.* A book called *The Seinfeld Aptitude Test* (SAT) contains questions about the television show *Seinfeld.* For example:

   1. To impress a woman, George passes himself off as
     (a) a gynecologist
     (b) a geologist
     (c) a marine biologist
     (d) a meteorologist

2. What candy does Kramer snack on while observing a surgical procedure from an operating-room balcony?

3. Who said, "I don't go for those nonrefundable deals. . . . I can't commit to a woman . . . I'm not committing to an airline"?

The producers of *Seinfeld* sue for copyright infringement. In defense, the authors of *The SAT* argue that they have simply copied unprotected facts, the things that the characters did and said during the show. Have the defendants copied original expression or facts?

10. *GNU twist.* Some software developers decide to write a new version of Unix, a widely used operating system. The first order of business is to think of a name for the software. They hit upon the name GNU Project. GNU is pronounced "guh-noo" and stands for "GNU is not Unix." The G in GNU stands for GNU, the name itself. They decide to register copyright in the phrase "GNU Project" (just the phrase itself, not the software). The Copyright Office denies registration on the basis that the word is not sufficiently original. First, there is an animal called the "gnu." Second, words or short phrases are not sufficiently original for copyright protection. Is "GNU Project" original, for purposes of copyright law?

11. *Battle of the forms.* Kregos sells a "pitching form," for use by baseball fans. The form lists nine items. Two of the items apply to the entire season: won/loss record and earned run average. Three of the items relate to the opposing team at the site of the game: won/lost record, innings pitched, and earned run average; and four of the items are based on the pitcher's last three games: won/lost record, innings pitched, earned run average, and men on base average. The purpose of the form was to provide information with which a baseball fan could use her own knowledge to predict the likely performance of the pitcher.

Each item was a type of statistic that was not original to Kregos, but no form had ever listed all these nine items of information together. Some forms had listed some of the items along with other items not on Kregos's form. The information to fill out the forms could be gleaned from publicly available information. The Associated Press began publishing a form copied from Kregos's form, listing the same nine categories of information. The Associated Press claims Kregos has no copyright, because he simply listed preexisting statistical categories. Are the forms sufficiently original for protection?

12. *Tradition.* Lifvon Guo is an elder of the Ami, an indigenous group in Taiwan. He travels to Europe with a group of performers. Unknown to him, someone records him singing the "Song of Joy," a traditional Ami song. The recording is subsequently combined with a twentieth-century dance beat, and released by the group Enigma, as "Return to Innocence." The song sells millions of copies and is used in advertisements for the

Olympic games in Atlanta. Does Lifvon have a copyright in "Return to Innocence"? Does Enigma?

13. *True fact?* The Bible is copyrighted.

14. *Based on a true story.* Dranker, a forensic psychiatrist in Boulder, writes a book telling the story of her career and of her many cases. She publishes the book, which has quite modest sales. One night, she watches a television show, *FSI: Boulder*, which features fictional forensic psychiatrist with a background very similar to Dranker. The show revolves around a case much like one described in Dranker's book. As each new episode airs, the show repeatedly shows fictionalized stories based on Dranker's experience. The shows do not use any of the creative expression from Dranker's book, but readily plunder her store of facts without giving any credit to Dranker. Does she have an action for copyright infringement? Would it make a difference if Dranker had not published the book, but rather had recorded the stories in her diary which was lost and somehow wound up with the scriptwriters?

15. *Trick or treat.* Suppose that, in the last example, Dranker confessed that her story about her career and all the incredible cases she worked on were actually fabrications. Rather than a forensic psychiatrist, she was simply telemarketer with an active imagination. After confessing, she then decides to pursue her copyright action against the producers of *FSI: Boulder*. They did not copy unprotected facts, but did copy her creative, and therefore copyrighted, confabulations. Are her fictional facts copyrighted?

16. *Life, uncopyrighted.* Zippy Mart has a contractor install a security camera behind its cashier's station, in industry standard fashion. One evening, the camera captures inebriated celebrity Rome Sheraton arguing with his dramaturge. After an employee posts the footage on Thoutube, Zippy Mart claims copyright. Is the footage copyrighted?

17. *Digital sculptures or copies?* Meshwerks, under contract with Toyota, made digital models of Toyota vehicles with a two-step process. First, Meshwerks used robotic arms patched into a computer network to precisely measure the form of the vehicle. Second, Meshwerk's digital sculptors tailored the screen images and data points to make the models as accurate as possible. The digital models are very helpful to car designers, who manipulate the models to simulate the effects of design changes, both functional and aesthetic. After Toyota makes use of the models beyond the scope of the original contract, Meshwerks claims copyright infringement. Are the digital models copyrighted?

18. *Coloring book creativity.* Publisher copies a public domain map from a U. S. census publication, then adds colors, shading, and a new typeface. Is the spruced-up map copyrightable?

19. *Cease and desist posting that cease-and-desist letter.* Blogger posts a rant about Big Corp. Soon, Blogger receives a cease-and-desist letter from Big Corp's lawyers, alleging defamation and unfair trade practices. Blogger posts a copy of the letter online. Blogger soon receives another cease-and-desist letter, contending that Blogger is infringing the copyright in the cease-and-desist letter. Could a cease-and-desist letter be copyrightable? If so, would it be infringement for the recipient to post it online, to tell the world?

20. *Thousand words.* Photographer Harney took a photo of socialite Clark Rockefeller and his daughter leaving a Boston church. Not too long after, Rockefeller went on the run after being exposed as an impostor, Christian Karl Gerhartsreiter. The photo was published widely, including an FBI "Wanted" poster, as the police hunted Gerhartsreiter. A made-for-TV movie recounted the tale, using its own version of the photo (recreated with actors) without permission from Harney. Infringement to make a similar photo using actors?

Explanations

1. One might argue that Historian was simply making a slavish copy. But translation from one language to another is not a mechanical task; nor is it simply a matter of reproduction. The translator necessarily makes choices that affect the aesthetic quality of the translation. Author did not write the original letter, but many elements of the translation would meet both of the requirements of originality.

2. The folk songs are not original to the fisherman. But the arrangements and some of the melodies and words are. Likewise, his selection and ordering of songs in his book could have the requisite originality. So he could have a copyright in his versions of the New England songs and in the selection and arrangement of the contents of the book. Cf. *Italian Book v. Rossi*, 27 F.2d 1014 (S.D.N.Y. 1928).

   The recordings also qualify as sufficiently original. Because he recorded the songs, he did not add any elements such as arrangements, melodies, or new lyrics. But the recordings are original in the same sense as a photograph. Like a photographer, the recorder makes creative choices, such as what elements to include and where to position microphones.

3. The facts are not copyrightable. Whether Editor drew the facts from other sources or dug them up herself, the facts preexist Editor and are not original to her. But her selection and arrangement of the facts is protected by copyright. This compilation is different from the white pages telephone directory in *Feist*. The telephone directory simply listed subscribers alphabetically, following long-standing industry practice. Such arrangement and selection lacked even minimal creativity. But Editor creatively devised new ways of selecting and then arranging information. So the original

elements of her compilation are protected by copyright. Someone who copied only factual material, without copying her original selection or arrangement, would not infringe her copyright.

4. The designs of the U.S. notes and coins are not original to Medallica. But its designs of the replica notes probably do have sufficient originality. The designs copy many elements from the notes, but also include a number of elements beyond "slavish copying." The coin replicas, however, lack originality. Although great technical skill was used, it was used solely toward making as exact copies as possible. Cf. *Medallic Art Co. v. Washington Mint*, 208 F.3d 203 (2d Cir. 2000) (unpublished opinion).

5. Works such as maps can exhibit creativity, even though they serve to represent facts. In deciding which features to include on a map and how to represent them, the mapmaker makes creative choices. *See, e.g., United States v. Hamilton*, 583 F.2d 448 (9th Cir. 1978). Mapmaker could not recover from a rival mapmaker who only copied discrete pieces of information from her maps. But it would likely be infringement to copy the map wholesale, which would copy Mapmaker's selection and arrangement of factual information, together with any creative expression in its representation. This is an example of so-called thin copyright protection, which protects only against very literal, wholesale copying.

   The argument that the map is simply a copy of Boffin Island is inapplicable. The lack of originality for "slavish copying" applies to making a copy of a creative work. It does not bar copyright for using photography for capturing realistic images. The use of a map to represent facts is even less like making a duplicate.

6. The part numbers are not creative expression. They are dictated by the system, rather than by a creative choice of a human. So the numbers are not copyrightable. Cf. *Southco v. Kanebridge Corp.*, 390 F.3d 276 (3d Cir. 2004) (en banc). Note that numbers as such are not categorically non-protectable. A number is not copyrightable, but creative expression that is expressed in numbers may be. For example, the selection and arrangement of used car value listings would be protectable as a compilation.

7. The movie is protected by copyright even though it is not wholly original but based on a preexisting work. By adding original creative expression (the plot twists, dialogue, and other elements), Scriptwriter qualifies for copyright protection. But copyright protects only the original elements of the movie. Novelist did not copy original elements but copied only those elements from the folktale. So Novelist did not infringe the copyright in the movie. Cf. *Reyher v. Children's Television Workshop*, 533 F.2d 87 (2d Cir. 1975).

8. Nabokov has met the creativity requirement. The telephone book publisher in *Feist* published every listing it could identify, in alphabetical order. Nabokov did publish every fact he could find, so he may not have

exercised creativity in the selection of information. But he did not simply list the facts in alphabetical order. Rather, he exercised creativity in the coordination and arrangement of the information, because he devised the categories by which the information was organized. As the court that posed this hypothetical put it, "Facts do not supply their own principles of organization. Classification is a creative endeavor." *American Dental Assn. v. Delta Dental Plans Assn.*, 126 F.3d 977, 979 (7th Cir. 1997).

9. The defendant did copy original expression. As the court aptly put it: "*The SAT* does not quiz such true facts as the identity of the actors in *Seinfeld*, the number of days it takes to shoot an episode, the biographies of the actors, the location of the *Seinfeld* set, etc. Rather, *The SAT* tests whether the reader knows that the character Jerry places a Pez dispenser on Elaine's leg during a piano recital, that Kramer enjoys going to the airport because he's hypnotized by the baggage carousels, and that Jerry, opining on how to identify a virgin, said 'It's not like spotting a toupee.' Because these characters and events spring from the imagination of *Seinfeld*'s authors, *The SAT* plainly copies copyrightable, creative expression." *Castle Rock Entertainment v. Carol Publishing*, 150 F.3d 132, 139 (2d Cir. 1998).

   The *Castle Rock* court drew a sound distinction between what it called "true facts" and fictional facts. The reason that facts are not copyrighted is that facts (for purposes of copyright law) do not originate with their discoverer. Rather, facts are information that someone may find, but not that someone creates. But the "facts" in *Seinfeld* (such as Jerry placing a Pez dispenser on Elaine's leg during a piano recital) are indeed created by the authors of the show, as opposed to being information that existed beforehand and were later discovered (like facts about the extinction of dinosaurs).

10. This case presents issues as to both requirements of originality: independent creation and a modicum of creativity. Most authority would agree that a phrase as short as "GNU Project" is not copyrightable. The policy is sound, because otherwise no one could publicly mention the name of the project without risking infringement. Some ground the rule on the originality requirement, on the theory that coining a short phrase does not meet even the minimal requirement for originality. But this seems a little dubious, because the phrase is quite creative. A better rationale might be that a short phrase does not constitute a work of authorship, and therefore is not within copyrightable subject matter.

   If short phrases were copyrightable, then the next issue would be whether this one originated with the software developers, given that "gnu" is already a word. But their "work" was the phrase, "GNU Project." Like most literary works, it is composed of preexisting words, but nevertheless is itself something that originated with the author.

11. The forms are sufficiently original for protection. *See Kregos v. Associated Press*, 937 F.2d 700 (2d Cir. 1991). Although Kregos did not originate the

various statistical categories, he did originate the listing of those nine categories together. This selection and arrangement would meet the minimal standard of *Feist*.

12. This example, which highlights some troubling outcomes of the originality requirement, is drawn from Angela R. Riley, *Recovering Collectivity: Group Rights to Intellectual Property in Indigenous Communities*, 18 Cardozo Arts & Ent. L.J. 175 (2000) (analyzing the Ami "Song of Joy" case and other cases, and proposing modifications to copyright law to protect indigenous culture). Lifvon Guo does not have a copyright in the Ami's "Song of Joy," because he is not its author. It is a traditional song, so very likely its author (for copyright purposes) can no longer be identified. Moreover, the song is old enough that it would be out of copyright protection anyway.

   But Enigma does have a copyright in "Return to Innocence." Enigma did not author the "Song of Joy," so does not have a copyright in that musical work. But Enigma would have a copyright in the work based on the "Song of Joy" (assuming that adding the dance beat met the minimal requirement of creativity) and also the sound recording of the music. So Enigma would appear to have a copyright in music based on the traditional song, as well as the recording of "Return to Innocence." Indeed, even the person who recorded Lifvon Guo's performance probably has a copyright in that sound recording, assuming some creative choices were made in producing it. Such cases raise the question whether there should be adjustments to intellectual property law to address the fact that indigenous cultural material may be effectively privatized by others, while the indigenous people themselves may not have recognized rights in the material.

13. True. The Bible (reportedly the best-selling book of all time) is under copyright—or more accurately, various versions of the Bible are copyrighted. *See* Roger Syn, © *Copyright God: Enforcement of Copyright in the Bible and ReligiousWorks*, 14 Regent U. L. Rev. 1, 2-3 (2001-2002) ("All major English Bible translations, except the Authorised Version, are subject to copyright. Copyright also subsists in some standard editions of the ancient biblical manuscripts from which translations are made."). The original texts are in the public domain. But a publisher can use those texts as the basis for another work in several different ways: by translation, by annotation, by editing, by adding pictures, and so on. Provided that the required minimal creativity is met, the work would be subject to copyright (protecting only the new elements, of course). The ethics of claiming exclusive rights in such texts are another, somewhat controversial, matter.

14. Dranker does not have an action for copyright infringement. Cf. Malcolm Gladwell, *Something Borrowed*, New Yorker (Nov. 22, 2004) (relating the tale of a psychiatrist whose work with serial killers, along with a magazine article about her, was used without attribution in a play). Facts are not

protected by copyright, so there is no infringement for copying facts. Assuming that the scriptwriters copied only facts (a big assumption, because usually there is some creative expression mixed in with facts in a literary work), they could not be liable for copyright infringement. Copyright is different from the ethical proscription of plagiarism, which applies to the use of another's work without attribution.

The result would be the same even if Dranker had written the facts in a private diary. She would have the copyright, but it would not be infringed by copying facts. Of course, the copier would need access to the diary, which might violate some other law (trespassing, trade secret, or possibly rights of privacy).

15. A court would likely hold that Dranker did not have copyright protection in fictional events that she presented as facts. Under the copyright estoppel approach, the public is entitled to rely on the author's representation of what is factual material. Otherwise, any work could present a trap for the unwary. Someone who uses in good faith material that is presented as factual (and therefore unprotected) will not be liable for infringement.

16. This raises a question that will pop up more and more. As security cameras, personal cameras, communications technology, and virtual and online behavior all proliferate, the question arises as to whether the recorded information is copyrighted. *Madisonian.net*'s authors often acutely discuss such near future issues. The last chapter discussed the argument that often such information will not be a "work of authorship." A related argument is that the originality necessary for copyright is lacking. Mounting a security camera behind a cashier is a functional standard industry practice, no more creative than listing all the names in the phone book in alphabetical order. One can distinguish this example from the *Zapruder* case, in which a home moviemaker happened to capture a historic event. The moviemaker made various creative choices: "Zapruder selected the kind of camera (movies, not snapshots), the kind of film (color), the kind of lens (telephoto), the area in which the pictures were to be taken, the time they were to be taken, and (after testing several sites) the spot on which the camera would be operated." His intent was to film the Kennedy motorcade. Mounting a security camera in standard fashion could be deemed to lack originality. By contrast, if an artist mounted the same camera in the same alley to capture the occurrences over the course of a year, that would be well above the line of a "minimal spark of creativity." So the state of mind may make the difference where creativity is at issue. Even with a security camera, if some creative choices were made in deciding where to mount it or what it should capture, then it might meet the low standard required for creativity. Copyright is not the end of the story. The owner of a security camera (or cell phone, or permanent personal video recorder, or day care cam) may not have a copyright. But they do have the footage.

So unless they permit it to be released, they may still control its dissemination. A person does not have exclusive rights in her life story. But she may control what she discloses, and someone who wants to make a film or book about her may pay for the information.

Bonus (and preview) question: If the security footage were copyrighted, who would own the copyright? The camera was not put up by Zippy Mart or its employees, rather by an independent contractor. So if sufficient creativity went into that process, the author and copyright holder would be the contractor (unless Zippy got an assignment of the copyright in the contract!). The chapter on ownership discusses the rules.

17. The Tenth Circuit held that the digital models were not copyrighted, due to lack of originality. *Meshwerks, Inc. v. Toyota Motor Sales U.S.A., Inc.* (10th Cir. 2008). The digital models were copies (very good copies) of the cars, representing no independent creation. Despite the skill and even creativity required to create the models, they did not have any creative elements independent from their role as copies (in a different medium). Unlike a photograph, where the author makes choices about pose, positioning, and lighting, the models served only to accurately reproduce factual data about the configuration of the vehicles.

18. Merely adding commonplace elements such as colors, shading, and a new typeface to an existing map fails to show even the minimal creativity required for copyright. *Darden v. Peters*, 488 F.3d 277 (4th Cir. 2007) (upholding decision of Copyright Office to deny registration).

Darden makes one wonder about the copyrightability of such items as colorized black-and-white films, or remastered sound recordings. Such works certainly require technical skill but, if done in a way that did not include creative choices, would not qualify for a separate copyright (remember that copying such new versions could still infringe the copyright in the original). It would depend on showing that colorizing or remastering does not simply add standard elements, but rather requires creative choices. A court might also be sensitive to the hazard of a party capturing public domain material, as by colorizing a public domain film that has not been widely distributed, and effectively precluding others from using it.

19. A cease-and-desist letter could be copyrightable, if the author used some menacing creativity rather than just relying on a form letter or standard language. But Blogger's posting the letter online would surely qualify as fair use (to preview a key topic in copyright). Blogger was not seeking to cut into the market for a copyrighted work, rather to inform the public of the communication from the law firm. Fair use is a key First Amendment safeguard. The case might be different if defendant were copying the letter for a book of legal forms.

As this example illustrates, fair use may be used to permit parties to use copyrighted works, especially where the purpose of the use is not to exploit the creative expression, but to disseminate unprotected aspects (such as getting facts from a database, or using functional aspects of a work or communicating ideas). A party that has been threatened with legal action must be able to effectively communicate that to the public.

20. The court recognized the creativity in composing the picture, but held that Sony copied only unprotected facts: "Harney's creation consists primarily of subject matter—'facts'—that he had no role in creating, including the central element of the Photo: the daughter riding piggyback on her father's shoulders. . . . we do not see how subsequent events can fortuitously transform unoriginal elements of a visual work into protectible subject matter," 704 F.3d 173 (1st Cir. 2013).

WORK OF AUTHORSHIP

Copyright applies only to original "works of authorship." 17 U.S.C. §102(a). The category of "works of authorship" is very broadly construed. Copyright protection could have been limited to works of fine art or high literary merit. It could also have been limited to established categories, such as novels, short stories, poems, paintings, and the like. Likewise, copyright could include some genres (such as literary fiction, history, documentary) and deem others unworthy of protection (risqué works, detective novels, comic books).

To the contrary, copyright applies without regard to artistic merit. A work does not have to meet any standard of artistic merit to qualify as a work of authorship. Nor is copyright limited to particular categories of creative works. Creative expression takes many forms. Judges are ill-equipped to act as critics of art or literature. Any work that qualifies as an original work of authorship is copyrightable, irrespective of whether it is high art, popular art, commercial art, idiosyncratic doodling, or any other form of expression. *See Bleistein v. Donaldson Lithographing*, 188 U.S. 239 (1903).

Nor are the categories of protected works limited by the incentive purpose of copyright. Absent copyright, many works would not be produced. If authors had no exclusive rights, some books, movies, recordings, and artworks would not be created. On the other hand, absent copyright, many works would still be created. Many other reasons exist for people to create works. Even without copyright to protect their right to exploit the works, artists would still create art, academics would write articles, and people would write letters. Some categories of works do not rely on the exclusive rights of copyright for remuneration. An advertising agency creates original works but seeks payment from its client rather than from paying customers. Even authors who usually rely on copyright protection do not depend absolutely on copyright law. Books, movies, and music, for example, would still be produced without copyright. Creative impulses, desire for expression and recognition, and many other forces motivate the production of creative works. But copyright law does not limit protection to works that would not be produced absent copyright protection.

The requirement that something be a work of authorship does exclude some fruits of human creativity from copyright protection. Conversation often includes witty remarks, descriptions, or art criticisms.[5] Granting copyright to conversation or personal conduct would greatly inhibit human interaction. If such everyday activity were copyrighted, others would be excluded from repeating it. It would also be difficult to know when someone could claim copyright in such activity, if they needed to show only that it was original (and had been somehow preserved in a tangible form). To prevent such uncertainty, under the leading decision, it would "be required that the speaker indicate that he intended to mark off the utterance in question from the ordinary stream of speech, that he meant to adopt it as a unique statement and that he wished to exercise control over its publication." *Estate of Hemingway v. Random House*, 23 N.Y.2d 341 (1968).[6] Such a statement reserving rights is not a general requirement—a short story, letter, or painting is protected by copyright without any explicit claim by the author. But those works fall within the categories where one might expect copyright to apply. They also have natural boundaries that separate them from other communications. Explicit claims would be necessary only for claims to copyright in conversation or everyday behavior as a "work of authorship," where others would think it unrestricted. Likewise, the requirement that something be a "work of authorship" could be used to deny claims to copyright protection to such creative activities as crime sprees, tantrums, and practical jokes. Such "works" have the necessary originality, but would not be taken by others to be the creation of protected works.

The limitation of copyright to "works" can also exclude other creative expression. The U.S. Copyright Office takes the position that copyright is not available for words and short phrases, such as names, titles, and slogans. 37 C.F.R. §202.1. Several cases are in accord. The rule seems a necessary one—if a word or short phrase could be copyrighted, then any use of the word would be potential copyright infringement. Words or short phrases should receive, if anything, the more narrow protection of trademark law. "Coca-Cola" is a trademark, but one can still utter the word without infringing the trademark—only using the mark in ways that interfere with Coca-Cola's use to accurately identify its product to consumers is barred.

The rule denying copyright protection is often justified by stating that words or short phrases are not sufficiently original. But certainly even a

---

5. In practical terms, copyright in everyday activity is also usually unavailable because of the requirement that a work be fixed under the authority of the author (discussed below). But this may change as more and more of everyday activity is recorded by one means or another.
6. The case involved common law copyright, but indicated that the same principle would apply to federal copyright law.

single word could originate with the author and have much more than the requisite minimal spark of creativity—like such coinages as "copyleft," "copywrong," and "copy-broke." A broader rationale might be that a word or phrase does not constitute a work of authorship. Recall, however, that a copyrighted work may be made up of noncopyrightable elements. So although a short statement may not be copyrightable, a compilation of short statements (such as a book of short jokes or slogans) could be.

The limitation of copyright to "works of authorship" also implies an author. This means that a human created the work, using the requisite creativity. In a work made through a completely mechanical process, copyright might be denied on the basis that no one was the "author." Thus, if a security camera mounted in a lobby, recording 24 hours a day, captured a dramatic event, the video could be uncopyrighted. Computer-generated works also raise the issue of authorship: If works are generated automatically or are the product of some future artificial intelligence, there may be no human author. "Works" created by natural processes or by nonhuman animals would also not be "works of authorship." Nor does copyright apply to video made when a seagull stole the camera or to photos made by macaques monkeying around with an unattended camera. The Ninth Circuit looked at the structure of the Copyright Act as a whole in deciding that a monkey, which somehow took a selfie, did not have standing to sue when the photo went viral. "For example, the 'children' of an 'author,' 'whether legitimate or not,' can inherit certain rights under the Copyright Act. Also, an author's 'widow or widower owns the author's entire termination interest unless there are any surviving children or grandchildren of the author, in which case the widow or widower owns one-half of the author's interest.' The terms 'children,' 'grandchildren,' 'legitimate,' 'widow,' and 'widower' all imply humanity and necessarily exclude animals that do not marry and do not have heirs entitled to property by law." *Naruto v. Slater*, 2018 U.S. App. LEXIS 10129, at *12-13 (9th Cir. Apr. 23, 2018) (statutory citations omitted).

The Copyright Office has interpreted the statute to require a human author:

> In order to be entitled to copyright registration, a work must be the product of human authorship. Works produced by mechanical processes or random selection without any contribution by a human author are not registrable. Thus, a linoleum floor covering featuring a multicolored pebble design which was produced by a mechanical process in unrepeatable, random patterns, is not registrable. Similarly, a work owing its form to the forces of nature and lacking human authorship is not registrable; thus, for example, a piece of driftwood even if polished and mounted is not registrable.

Compendium II: Copyright Office Practices 503.03(a).

Copyright's exclusions for purely mechanical works and for everyday behavior and conversation are starting to overlap. Increasingly, what we say and do is recorded by various devices: security cameras, communications technology, virtual worlds, chat rooms. More than one person wears a camera intended to record his entire life—and wearable technology may soon do that for the average consumer. Are all those captured moments subject to copyright? One could well argue that they do not constitute works of authorship. In the same way that a conversation does not have boundary lines that mark it as a "work," so 24/7 automatic recordings of data lack the authorial intent and announcement that would stake a copyright claim. The incentive of copyright is not needed to encourage the creation of such collections of information—they are already created for other reasons. Without a showing that someone set out to create a work, courts should hesitate before affording copyright protection to such information.

Finally, a person's identity is also not a work of authorship. One might think of the *persona* of some people as their own creation, whether Muhammad Ali, Truman Capote, or Madonna. Someone's character, persona, or likeness is in part created by the person—but also by other factors (their genetic makeup and experiences, including the influences of others). More importantly, such elements are not embodied in a tangible form, which would set the boundaries of the protected work. *See Brown v. Ames,* 201 F.3d 654 (5th Cir. 2000). Someone can create a work imbued with their persona, such as an autobiography, self-portrait, or ballad. But the work, not the persona, would be copyrighted.

To sum up, the scope of "works of authorship" is broad indeed. It does, however, exclude such things as

- everyday conversation and behavior (unless the author does something to claim ownership and specifically mark it as a work);
- purely mechanical works;
- words and short phrases;
- a person's identity; and
- works with no human author.

Examples

1. *Story of my life.* Welles uses her phone to record video over hours, capturing people going through life in a city day. She edits it modestly into an untitled documentary. Copyrightable work of authorship?

2. *Coveted cover.* TV Land magazine sues a competitor magazine, alleging that the competitor infringed copyright by copying the cover of an edition of *TV Land.* The competitor did not literally copy the text and layout, but rather the size, shape, and graphic design of the cover. The design is composed of basic elements, composed into a pleasing package, likely to catch the eye of someone standing in line at a grocery checkout counter. Competitor argues that the design of a magazine cover is product packaging, not a work of authorship. Is the design of the magazine cover a work of authorship?

3. *Instant messaging.* Author and Writer carry on an extended interchange over a computer network via instant messaging. They carry on a far-ranging

discussion of literature, including many witty remarks and incisive analyses of famous works. Author subsequently claims copyright in her contributions to the conversation. Were her instant messages (either individually or together) works of authorship?

4. *Same product, different package.* Rather than having the instant messaging conversation, Author writes down her views in an essay, likewise composed of witty remarks and incisive analyses of famous works. Is her essay a work of authorship?

5. *Prepared remarks.* Literary Critic writes to Author, requesting a meeting to discuss Author's works. Anxious to come off well, Author sits down over several days and writes out a lengthy analysis of his own work. During the videotaped meeting, Author then delivers the analysis interview paragraph by paragraph, in response to questions posed by Literary Critic. Does Author have a copyright in his remarks?

6. *Whale songs.* Cetologist makes a number of recordings of humpback whales singing off the islands of Hawaii. Cetologist has studied the whales for years and draws on her experience in positioning the microphones, setting the recording levels, and deciding when to make the recordings. The recordings capture a number of noises made by the whales, with many musical qualities. Merchant gets access to the tapes, makes copies, and sells them to whale enthusiasts. When Cetologist claims copyright infringement, Merchant contends that the recordings are not works of authorship. Are the recordings works of authorship?

7. *Funded.* Herzog wishes to film a documentary about modern life in towns on the Mississippi River. Herzog receives a grant from the Philo Foundation, which fully funds the production of the film. Herzog sends copies of the film to a number of universities, hoping to encourage interest in the work. Several months later, Herzog learns that Movie House has been running Herzog's film for several weeks, making a nice profit. When Herzog seeks compensation, Movie House argues that the work is not copyrighted. Copyright exists to provide an incentive to produce works, and that rationale does not support copyright in works that are funded from the outset, argues Movie House. Does copyright apply to works that would be created anyway?

8. *Photoshopper.* Pixel has assembled a considerable collection of public domain photographs from around 1900, all of which are now in digital form. Using Photoshop, a popular piece of software for manipulating images, she creates a series of pictures. Although her pictures appear to be photos taken during 1900, they are actually made by cutting and pasting elements from many pictures. For example, one shows a boy wearing a policeman's uniform as a Halloween costume in conversation with a police officer. But Pixel had used Photoshop to take the various elements from a number of photos: The image of the boy was taken from a school picture; his bag was taken from a picture of a store; his uniform was taken from

a picture of a police officer, and then reduced in size; and the police officer was adapted from the image of a mail carrier. Photoshop automatically adjusts many aspects of the pictures to ensure that they do not look like cut-and-paste collages, but instead, like single images. After Vader Publishing uses some of the images without Pixel's permission, she sues for copyright infringement. Vader defends on the basis that the pictures were all made by Photoshop, not Pixel, and are therefore the product of software, not works of an author. Are the manipulated images works of authorship?

9. *Elephant see, elephant do.* Shawn, an elephant keeper, patiently teaches Romany the elephant how to paint. After considerable training, Romany learns to pick up a brush, dip it in the palette, and daub paint on a blank piece of paper. Encouraged with treats, Romany covers much of the paper. The zoo sells the painting at a charitable auction for a few dollars. The buyer then sells posters featuring Romany's quite abstract and messy painting. The zoo, feeling cheated, considers suing for copyright infringement. Is the painting copyrighted?

10. *What's a voggle?* Sitting in calculus class one day, Tango raises his hand and ask the instructor, "What's a voggle?" Having looked in the dictionary, Tango knows that there is no such thing. The closest is a Siberian language known as Vogul. So his question causes a certain confusion and a little respite from mathematical rigor. Other students adopt the same trick, asking "What's a voggle?" to English teachers, gym teachers, and even the security personnel. For no apparent reason, the phrase becomes extremely popular, and soon the catchphrase "What's a voggle?" appears online, on television and in the papers. Tango wonders if he should be receiving copyright royalties on the word voggle, and the phrase, "What's a voggle?" Should he?

11. *Performance anxiety.* Cindy Lee Garcia had a minor role in a film with the working title *Desert Warrior.* After that film was abandoned, the producer then used the footage of her scenes in an anti-Islamic film titled *Innocence of Muslims,* dubbing offensive lines over her performance. Garcia sued for copyright infringement, claiming copyright in her performance, as a work of authorship itself. Should she succeed?

Explanations

1. Welle's documentary is a work of authorship. None of the exclusions apply to her work. She is not claiming copyright in everyday behavior, rather in a film of everyday behavior. Copyright applies to many works that record noncopyrightable elements.

2. The design of a magazine cover may be a work of authorship. The layout of a magazine cover may not qualify to hang in an art gallery, and its purpose may be to attract readers' attention rather than to express artistic impulses. But the commercial character of a work does not bar it from

47

being a work of authorship. A cover design does fit within the definition of a "pictorial, graphic, or sculptural work" as a two-dimensional work of applied art. To receive copyright protection, it would also have to meet the requirements of originality. Even though the design employed nonoriginal components, the requisite creativity could be shown in the choices of how to put those components together. *See Reader's Digest Assn. v. Conservative Digest*, 821 F.2d 800 (D.C. Cir. 1987).

3. The issue is whether the instant messages are a "work of authorship." Very little case law exists ruling on this sort of issue. The basic question is whether instant messages qualify as everyday conversation (unprotected without explicit claims of rights) or as letters (protectable without requiring an explicit claim of right, as many cases have held). The interchange here more closely resembles a conversation, with a give and take in real time. As technology preserves more and more of our casual communications and daily activity, such copyright issues may proliferate.

4. The essay is a work of authorship. The requirement of an explicit claim of right applies only to things such as conversation or everyday behavior, which otherwise would not be separated out as works by others. Note that this rule arises not from the statute or a line of cases, but rather a single, well-known case. If such cases do become more common, courts may not necessarily adopt the explicit claim requirement, instead relying on the other requirements to play the gatekeeper role.

5. Whether the *discussion* qualifies as a work of authorship is a moot point. Author's written version of his analysis would qualify as an original work of authorship (specifically, a literary work). Anyone who made copies of the videotape would potentially infringe the copyright (subject to various limitations discussed in the infringement chapter).

6. The whales are also red herrings. Cetologist has created original works of authorship: the sound recordings. She made a number of creative decisions in how and when to make her recordings. She has created original works of authorship, just as if she had photographed the whales.

7. Herzog's film is copyright protected, even if the copyright's incentive was not necessary for its creation. Nothing in the copyright statute limits copyright in general to works that require the incentive of copyright.

8. The manipulated images are works of authorship. The computer program may do much of the work, but Pixel selects the elements and cuts and pastes them. That would be sufficient to make Pixel the author.

9. A painting by an elephant would not be copyrighted, because there is no human author.

10. Tango has no copyright in the word "voggle" or the phrase "What's a voggle?" The weight of authority denies copyright to words or short

phrases. One reason for the rule is that they do not show sufficiently originality (although it would seem that the requisite minimal creativity could be met by thinking up a new word or phrase). A better reason is probably that they are simply too short to qualify as works of authorship.

11. Garcia was not the author of the film. She may have performed creatively, but her performance was not a separable copyrighted work. "Take, for example, films with a large cast—the proverbial 'cast of thousands'—such as Ben-Hur or Lord of the Rings. The silent epic Ben-Hur advertised a cast of 125,000 people. In the Lord of the Rings trilogy, 20,000 extras tramped around Middle-Earth alongside Frodo Baggins (played by Elijah Wood). Treating every acting performance as an independent work would not only be a logistical and financial nightmare, it would turn cast of thousands into a new mantra: copyright of thousands." Garcia v. Google, Inc., 786 F.3d 733, 742-743 (9th Cir. 2015) (en banc).

CATEGORIES OF WORKS

The U.S. Copyright Act of 1790 covered only books, maps, and charts. Since then, Congress has exponentially broadened the scope of copyright. Now copyright covers books, movies, and songs—but also advertisements, blueprints, computer programs, diaries, dances, and finger paintings, T-shirt designs, sculpture, speeches. . . . The statute now provides that works of authorship include the following categories:

1. literary works;
2. musical works, including any accompanying words;
3. dramatic works, including any accompanying music;
4. pantomimes and choreographic works;
5. pictorial, graphic, and sculptural works;
6. motion pictures and other audiovisual works;
7. sound recordings; and
8. architectural works.

17 U.S.C. §102(a).

The categories are not mutually exclusive, so a work could fall into more than one category. A play may be both a literary work and a dramatic work. Nor is the list itself exclusive. A work that did not fit into any of the listed categories could still qualify for copyright if it were an original work of authorship. But the categories are illustrative, so the fact that a work appears to fall into one of the categories may influence a court in deciding whether the work is a work of authorship. In any case, the definitions of the categories (discussed below) are so broad that almost any creative work would fall into at least one category. If a work uses letters or numbers, it is a literary work. If it is in two or three dimensions, it is likely a pictorial, graphical, or sculptural work. That covers almost all potential works already.

The importance of the categories lies not in setting the boundaries of copyright but in applying other rules in the statute. As discussed later in the book, certain copyright rules are applicable only to specific categories of works of authorship. Some rules apply only to sound recordings or dramatic works or architectural works, and so on. To see if a work is subject to certain rules, one must determine which category the work falls into. The following paragraphs list the categories, provide definitions where applicable, and note some rules applicable to particular categories.

Literary Works

Finnegans Wake is a literary work. So is the software code for Minecraft. This category includes "works, other than audiovisual works, expressed in words, numbers, or other verbal or numerical symbols or indicia, regardless of the nature of the material objects, such as books, periodicals, manuscripts, phonorecords, film, tapes, disks, or cards, in which they are embodied." 17 U.S.C. §101.

Such a broad definition goes well beyond what is normally considered "literature" to include anything made with letters, numbers, or other symbols. Some examples of literary works are plays, short stories, novels, movie scripts, letters, e-mail messages, computer programs (whether in source code, object code, or other form), cooking recipes, souvenir T-shirt messages, mathematical proofs, and municipal zoning ordinances. As with all the categories, each of the foregoing would have to qualify as an original work of authorship to have protection.

An important type of literary work is a computer program, also known as software. Software is copyrightable, whether in source code, object code, or other form. This certainly takes the definition of "literary work" beyond its meaning in other contexts. Literature departments in universities are usually quite separate from the computer science program. Literary theory pays much more attention to poetry than computer code. At one time, it was widely debated whether computer programs should be subject to copyright at all. Copyright protects creative expression. Computer programs can be seen as functional works, as opposed to expressive works. They are also sets of instructions for machines, as opposed to creative works experienced by people.

Congress amended the Copyright Act in 1980 to define computer program, as "a set of statements or instructions to be used directly or indirectly in a computer in order to bring about a certain result." 17 U.S.C. §101. It also added §117, which imposed some limitations on the copyright of a computer program. The two amendments imply that computer programs are copyrightable. Since then, the issue has not been whether computer programs are copyrightable, but rather how broad the scope of protection is.

Example

Literary? A number of provisions of the Copyright Act apply to "literary works." Which of the following are literary works?

- A novel, published in book form
- A novel, available only online as an electronic book
- A set of instructions for assembling a swimming pool
- A computer program
- The book you are reading
- A warning label on an energy drink
- A tweet

Explanation

They are all literary works. A novel might be the only one that would be studied in a literature class, but the definition of literary work for copyright law is very broad: any work "expressed in words, numbers, or other verbal or numerical symbols or indicia," regardless of the form in which it is fixed. Literary work lawsuits have included warning labels, course syllabuses, legal briefs, letters, T-shirt statements, and more.

Musical Works, Including Any Accompanying Words

"Pretty Woman," "Blurred Lines," "Happy Birthday to You," and "We Shall Overcome" are examples of disputed musical works, as is "Pi Symphony." The category of musical works spans all genres, from a cappella to zigeunermusik. An important distinction exists between a musical work and a sound recording. A musician who composes music or writes a song is the author of a musical work. A producer who controls the recording of some sounds creates a sound recording, a separate category of work. A producer who makes a recording of a musician performing musical work is the author of a sound recording. If the recording is put on a compact disc, the CD is both a copy of the musical work and a phonorecord of the sound recording. Anyone who makes an unauthorized copy of the recording potentially infringes two copyrights: the musician's copyright in the musical work and the producer's copyright in the sound recording.

Example

Musing on musical works: Which of the following would qualify as "musical works," for the purposes of copyright law?

- "Happy Birthday to You"
- "Satisfaction" by Jagger and Richards
- An opera
- A symphony
- The background music for the video game Cut The Rope
- The theme music to Jeopardy
- A song written by some kids as their club's song
- A recording, available on iTunes, of Hamlet

Explanation

All would qualify as musical works, except the last. This illustrates the broad reach of copyright. The Hamlet example simply reminds that musical works may appear mixed with other works.

Dramatic Works, Including Any Accompanying Music

"Dramatic works" is not defined in the statute, but according to a leading treatise the category includes "any work in which performed actions, speech, or incident, or all three, convey theme, thoughts or character to an audience." Paul Goldstein, Copyright (2d ed. 1996) at 2:110. Examples of dramatic works would include "choreography, pantomimes, plays, treatments, and scripts prepared for cinema, radio, and television." Copyright Office Fl 119. The distinguishing characteristic of a dramatic work is that the actions are "intended to be performed," as opposed to being "narrated or described." An opera would be a dramatic work, whereas a novel would not (although many dramatic incidents may be described in the novel). The opera is intended to be performed onstage with the singers playing the roles of characters. A novel is intended to be read. Even some works that are performed in public (such as rock songs) are not dramatic, where they are not performed in character to act out the drama in the song. "Dramatic" refers to how the work is performed (in character), as opposed to whether its plot is exciting.

A dramatic work would likely fall into another category, such as literary work or musical work. The principal effect of a work qualifying as a dramatic work is that it is not subject to some of the limitations on copyright. For example, the compulsory license for musical works in §115 applies only to nondramatic musical works. Nondramatic literary and musical works are subject to use, without requiring permission of the copyright holder, in online education, in religious services, or at certain charitable functions, under §110.

Pantomimes and Choreographic Works

This category could include ballet, mime, jazz dance, or post-modern dance. Note an example of the overlapping categories. Many pantomimes and choreographic works also qualify as dramatic works. They could also be literary works if described by letters, numbers, or symbols. The Copyright Office has defined choreographic works as follows: "Choreography represents a related series of dance movements and patterns organized into a coherent whole." Compendium of Copyright Office Practices, Compendium II 450.03(a). "Choreography is the composition and arrangement of dance movements and patterns, and is usually intended to be accompanied by music. Dance is static and kinetic successions of bodily movement in certain rhythmic and spatial relationships. Choreographic works need not tell a story in order to be protected by copyright." Id. at 450.01. So it would appear that all preplanned routines (such as diagrammed football plays, choreographed professional wrestling matches, or a floor exercise routine in gymnastics) might not be choreographic works, if they were not dance.

Pictorial, Graphic, and Sculptural Works

This category includes "two-dimensional and three-dimensional works of fine, graphic, and applied art, photographs, prints and art reproductions, maps, globes, charts, diagrams, models, and technical drawings, including architectural plans." 17 U.S.C. §101. Recall that the 1790 Act covered only maps, books, and charts. Now maps are simply one item in one of the categories.

This is another very broad category. As interpreted by the courts, it includes not only such traditional categories as sculpture and paintings, but any two- or three-dimensional work. Courts have held that belt buckle designs, vodka bottles, lamps, and mannequins fall within the category. A family's vacation photos, the design of its treehouse, its toddler's finger painting, a scarecrow in its garden could all qualify (as always, subject to the requirements of originality).

Example

Overlap: Could a work fall into both "literary works" and "pictorial, graphic, and sculptural works"?

Explanation

There are many examples of such an overlap, where the letters or other symbols are made or arranged artfully. To name just a few: posters, signs, and concrete poetry, such as "Easter Wings" (not under copyright, being from 1663):

Lord, who createdst man in wealth and store,
Though foolishly he lost the same,
Decaying more and more,
Till he became
Most poore:
With thee
O let me rise
As larks, harmoniously,
And sing this day thy victories:
Then shall the fall further the flight in me.

My tender age in sorrow did beginne
And still with sicknesses and shame
Thou didst so punish sinne,
That I became
Most thinne.
With thee
Let me combine,
And feel this day thy victorie:
For, if I imp my wing on thine,
Affliction shall advance the flight in me.

Motion Pictures and Other Audiovisual Works

We know movies are copyrighted, from the FBI warning that starts each film. Movies fall into this category, but its reach is much broader. Audiovisual works are "works that consist of a series of related images which are intrinsically intended to be shown by the use of machines, or devices such as projectors, viewers, or electronic equipment, together with accompanying sounds, if any, regardless of the nature of the material objects, such as films or tapes, in which the works are embodied." 17 U.S.C. §101.

Video games, slide shows (including those using primarily text), and many types of conceptual art fall into the category of audiovisual works. An audiovisual work must have a visual component but need not have any accompanying sounds. The use of some machine or device is required. A play, puppet show, circus act, or other work that has great auditory and visual impact but relies on no device to show it is not an audiovisual work.

Example

Powerpoint? Into what category would a slide presentation fall?

Explanation

It would certainly be an audiovisual work (as "a series of related images that are intrinsically intended to be shown by the use of machines, or devices such as projectors, viewers, or electronic equipment"). If it used verbal or numerical symbols (alas, slideshows often use them to excess), it would be a literary work. It might also be a choreographic work, if shown to illustrate a dance, or a musical work. Unless intended to be acted out, it would not be a dramatic work. It could possibly be an architectural work (discussed below). It won't be a sound recording, because we will see that that definition excludes the sounds accompanying an audiovisual work. This example emphasizes that works may fall in multiple categories. It often matters only when there is a rule that applies only to specific categories (such as the compulsory license we will see for musical works).

Sound Recordings

Sound recordings are "works that result from the fixation of a series of musical, spoken, or other sounds, but not including the sounds accompanying a motion picture or other audiovisual work, regardless of the nature of the material objects, such as disks, tapes, or other phonorecords, in which they are embodied." 17 U.S.C. §101.

The most familiar sound recordings are recordings of music. But a sound recording could be a recording of birdcalls, a student's recording of a lecture, or a recording of the sounds of a hurricane. As noted above, an important distinction often must be made when a sound recording is made of the performance of another work. The author of a sound recording is the one who makes the creative choices about the content of the recording and who controls the making of the recording. The author of the sound recording may be a different person than the author or performer of the underlying work. There may be two separate works, with two different authors. If Producer records Musician singing Musician's new song, the recording captures a sound recording (authored by Producer) and a musical work (authored by Musician). Likewise, if Fan records Poet reading poetry, Fan is the author of a sound recording, with a separate copyright from Poet's copyright in the poem (as a literary work and perhaps also as a dramatic work).

As Chapter 5 discusses, sound recordings have more limited exclusive rights than other categories of works. The exclusive right to make copies extends only to reproductions of actual sounds (other works are protected also against nonliteral copying). The exclusive public performance right is limited to performance via a digital audio transmission. Various compulsory licensing provisions also apply to sound recordings.

Architectural Works

An architectural work is "the design of a building as embodied in any tangible medium of expression, including a building, architectural plans, or drawings. The work includes the overall form as well as the arrangement and composition of spaces and elements in the design, but does not include individual standard features." 17 U.S.C. §101.

An architectural work is the design of a building—before the building is built, and even if the building is never built. But the definition limits architectural works to the designs of buildings. Frank Lloyd Wright designed furniture, but furniture designed by an architect is not an architectural work. Not all structures are buildings. The design of a store inside of a shopping mall might not be deemed to be the design of a building (if the mall constitutes the building). The legislative history indicates that "buildings" include places that people enter (such as houses, temples, or schools), but not structures such as bridges and highways.

The exclusive rights in architectural works are subject to some specific limitations. 17 U.S.C. §120. If a building is visible from a public place, the copyright owner has no rights against the making, distribution, or display of images of the building. The owner of a building may alter or destroy it without obtaining permission from the owner of the copyright in the design of the building.

Examples

1. *Originality variations.* Would copyright protect the following?

   a. A researcher discloses many unprecedented facts about Madagascar hissing cockroaches: they sing mating calls, they form social clubs, they have nicknames for each other, along with many detailed facts from observation.

   b. A book written by the researcher disclosing and analyzing those facts.

   c. The researcher, after others have republished the "facts," reveals she ingeniously made them all up.

   d. The videos made by a worm researcher, cleverly planned, placed, and lighted to capture the day-to-day life of a worm.

   e. The worm researcher's descriptions of dozens of subjects, capturing their individual characteristics, but in a whimsical way (e.g., "Looks like Beethoven").

   f. The worm researcher's database, which is cleverly arranged and coordinated to facilitate searching and also by various comical categories.

   g. A kindergartener's drawing of a mousetrap.

   h. The list of names of students in a law school, arranged alphabetically by the registrar.

   i. The same list, arranged to sound as poetically as possible by the registrar.

   j. A video of a sunken ship in Lake Michigan, controlled remotely from the surface.

   k. A selection of violinist jokes, collected, selected, and arranged by a violinist.

   l. Valeria rewrites Shakespeare's *Merchant of Venice* as a political commentary on modern commercial society. She refashions the characters, puts the dialogue into modern idiom, adds topical humor, and tweaks the plot. Her work nevertheless copies thoroughly from the original.

Explanations

1. Under *Feist*, originality is a two-part requirement: (i) independently created by the author, and (ii) possessing at least some minimal degree of creativity.

   a. The facts are not created by the researcher, but instead are discovered. They are not original to her and so noncopyrightable.

   b. Her book would meet both requirements. Many elements of her text would originate with her and show the requisite creativity.

   c. If she represented fiction as fact, she would not have copyright in the material, under the copyright estoppel doctrine. Others are entitled to rely on an author's representation.

   d. The videos capture noncopyrighted facts about worms. But the videos themselves are made by the researcher and reflect a number of creative choices, so they would be copyrighted. Others could copy the facts, but not the expression without potentially infringing. Another researcher could use the facts in her book, but would potentially infringe if she made copies and sold copies of the video without permission.

   e. The descriptions may capture facts, but also have original, creative elements.

f. The facts in the database are not original, but creative selection, arrangement, and coordination of facts in such a compilation meet the originality requirement. Others could copy the facts but not the original arrangement and coordination.

g. Copyrighted. The kindergartener originated it, with the requisite creativity.

h. Neither the names (which the registrar did not originate) nor their arrangement (in alphabetical order, completely nonoriginal as in *Feist*'s telephone listings) are original.

i. The registrar's arrangement of the names would be sufficiently creative. Others could copy the names, but not this arrangement of them, without potentially infringing.

j. The facts of the ship are not original, but the making of the video would likely show the necessary creativity. The fact that a device actually fixed the work would not bar copyright, where a human made the creative decisions that directed it.

k. The jokes did not originate with the violinist. But she showed originality in her selection and arrangement of the compilation.

l. A work based on a preexisting work can be original if the author adds new creative elements. The adaptation of *Merchant of Venice* would handily clear the low hurdle of a "minimal spark of creativity."

Compilations (Works Created by Assembling Other Works or Information) and Derivative Works (Works Based on Existing Works) Are Also Copyrightable

Compilations

A "compilation" is defined as "a work formed by the collection and assembling of preexisting materials or of data that are selected, coordinated, or arranged in such a way that the resulting work as a whole constitutes an original work of authorship. The term 'compilation' includes collective works." 17 U.S.C. §101. Examples of compilations: a yellow pages telephone directory; a database of astronomical information; a collection of poetry; a CD containing photographs from *National Geographic*.

Compilations play an important role in copyright. A compilation may be composed of noncopyrightable elements, but the compilation itself may be protected by copyright. The key issues with compilations are often originality and scope of protection. To be protected by copyright, the compilation must be sufficiently original. It may be completely composed of nonoriginal elements (such as facts or preexisting works), but there may be sufficient originality in the selection, coordination, or arrangement of the elements. Under *Feist* (discussed previously), that requires just a minimal level of creativity. The scope of protection becomes an issue where there has been copying from the compilation, but the defendant contends that only nonprotected elements were copied. The question could be whether defendant copied the original selection and arrangement of the elements or copied only unprotected, nonoriginal elements.

Derivative Works

Derivative works raise a number of issues, which will be discussed in later chapters. The two key uses of the term: First, a derivative work is copyrightable. So although *Huckleberry Finn* is long out of copyright, a new work based on it (*Huckleberry Finn*, the musical, or *Huckleberry Swede—The Sequel*) would be copyrighted. Second, if a work is under copyright, then the copyright holder has the exclusive right to make derivative works. So the holder of the copyright in *Evil Genius* has the exclusive right to make sequels, adapt it into a musical, have it translated into Finnish. . . .

A "derivative work" is defined as a work based upon one or more pre-existing works, such as a translation, musical arrangement, dramatization, fictionalization, motion picture version, sound recording, art reproduction, abridgment, condensation, or any other form in which a work may be recast, transformed, or adapted. A work consisting of editorial revisions, annotations, elaborations, or other modifications which, as a whole, represent an original work of authorship, is a "derivative work." 17 U.S.C. §101.

Examples of derivative works based on *Gone with the Wind*: a film based on a novel, like the film *Gone with the Wind*; *Scarlett*, a sequel to the novel; *Tatt av vinden*, a translation into Norwegian; *The Wind Done Gone*, a parody; an annotated edition of *Gone with the Wind*; and a musical based on *Gone with the Wind*.

A derivative work may have its own copyright, provided it is sufficiently original. The work may be based upon another copyrighted work, or on a work that is in the public domain. But the copyright in the derivative work applies only to the new creative expression, not to elements copied from the underlying work.

As discussed in more detail later, derivative works raise a number of issues with respect to both copyright ownership and infringement. If a work is under copyright, the copyright owner has the exclusive right to make derivative works based on the copyrighted work. If someone else makes an unauthorized derivative work, it may infringe the copyright. In addition, there is no copyright protection for portions of the new work that use material illegally. But preparation of a derivative work without permission may not infringe; it may be authorized under the fair use doctrine, for example.

As later chapters will discuss, the derivative right also plays a role in a number of specific rules. When licenses are terminated, the licensee may retain the right to utilize derivative works. When copyrights are restored in foreign works that fell into the public domain due to failure to comply with the United States' formality requirements, the copyright may not apply to derivative works based on the formerly public domain work. Musical works are subject to a compulsory license that authorizes others to make cover versions, but not to prepare derivative works. The renewal, notice, registration, and remedies rules all have special provisions for derivative works.

Example

Spinoffs? What derivative works would be made from the novel, *The Catcher in The Rye?*

Explanation

The reclusive J.D. Salinger did not prepare or authorize any derivative works based on *The Catcher in The Rye* (other than its many translations). He never sold the movie rights (despite interest ranging from Marlon Brando to Jerry Lewis). But derivative works could have included sequels, prequels, translations, a movie (and its sequels), a radio drama, a stage play, a musical, abridgements, and annotated editions.

FIXATION

To be subject to copyright, a work must be fixed in a tangible medium of expression. 17 U.S.C. §102. The Constitution grants Congress the power to give copyrights in the "Writings" of authors, but copyright is not limited to written works like novels and textbooks. "Writings" is broadly construed to cover any form in which an author's work is embodied, such as books, recordings, notes, photographs, drawings, computer chips, sculpture, or any other tangible, stable form. The work need only be "fixed" in some tangible form to be copyrightable. The definition of "fixed" is broad:

> A work is "fixed" in a tangible medium of expression when its embodiment in a copy or phonorecord, by or under the authority of the author, is sufficiently permanent or stable to permit it to be perceived, reproduced, or otherwise communicated for a period of more than transitory duration.

17 U.S.C. §101. The work must be embodied in a copy or phonorecord to be fixed. "Copy" is likewise broadly defined to include almost any medium that can capture a work:

"Copies" are material objects, other than phonorecords, in which a work is fixed by any method now known or later developed, and from which the work can be perceived, reproduced, or otherwise communicated, either directly or with the aid of a machine or device.

17 U.S.C. §101. "Phonorecord" has a parallel definition, as the form in which sounds (other than those in audiovisual works) are fixed. 17 U.S.C. §101. These definitions are broad enough to clarify that the work need not be fixed in a form that humans can read. Pre-1976 Act cases had held that piano rolls (the rolls inserted into player pianos) were not covered by copyright because—unlike things such as music scores, paintings, and books—they were not readable by humans. The statute now encompasses piano rolls, as well as more modern forms of recordings such as CDs and DVDs. The definition of "fixed" refers to "embodiment in a copy or phonorecord." The definitions of "copies" and "phonorecords" cover all forms, whether accessible by humans or not.

Until the work is fixed, it is not protected by federal copyright. If a speaker gives a speech, or a songwriter creates a song, or a choreographer makes a dance, all without reducing the works to any tangible form, the work is uncopyrighted. Anyone else who sells copies of the speech, or sings the song in concert, or performs the dance publicly is not infringing copyright. For most authors, the fixation requirement is not difficult to meet: The speaker can simply write the speech down or record it; the songwriter could put the music in sheet music form or use a tape recorder; and the writer simply writes the story. Indeed, for writers, sculptors, photographers, and perhaps most authors, fixation occurs naturally as part of the creative process. For some authors, however, the fixation requirement is more difficult to meet: improvisational artists, such as jazz musicians, comedians, and dancers more often create works (or add elements to existing works) without fixing them in a tangible form. To gain federal copyright protection, they must take steps to fix the work. For example, the choreographer could make notations about or videotape or photograph the dance, and the comedian could make notes about or videotape a performance. Once the work is fixed, copyright protection attaches. Anyone who *subsequently* made copies (or did other things within the exclusive rights of the copyright holder) would be potentially infringing. Even silence can be fixed. The score of John Cage's composition, 4'33" simply instructs the performer not to play for four minutes and thirty-three seconds.

The author of the work need not personally fix the work in tangible form to gain copyright protection. Rather, the work can be fixed "by or under the authority of the author." If author dictates his novel to a stenographer, that suffices. By contrast, *unauthorized* fixation does not serve to trigger copyright. If Speaker gives her impromptu speech and is surreptitiously recorded by Bootlegger, copyright does not apply. But if Speaker writes the speech down, Bootlegger is potentially infringing if he made more copies or performed the work in public.

An open issue is whether authorization must be given before the fixation. If Bootlegger is the only one to record Musician's new song, can Musician meet the fixation requirement by subsequently ratifying the fixation, thereby authorizing it? The language of the statute seems to require that the fixation be authorized at the time. Moreover, courts generally consider issues of copyrightability as of the time of fixation. Subsequent authorization, then, may well be insufficient.

Fixation must be "sufficiently permanent or stable to permit it to be perceived, reproduced, or otherwise communicated for a period of more than transitory duration." 17 U.S.C. §101. So the work need not be etched in granite, but it must be in a stable form. Just how stable is not clear. An important issue (although it usually arises in the context of infringement, not initial protection) is whether a work is fixed when a computer makes a temporary copy in its memory (to run a program, look at an image, and so forth). Because such temporary copies are refreshed many times a second by the computer, some argue that they are transitory and not sufficiently stable to be copies. Recent amendments to the Copyright Act, however, seem to assume that even a temporary copy in a computer's memory is fixed.

The definition of "fixed" also addresses a potential loophole for bootleggers. Suppose that a television or radio program is being broadcast live. If a work must be fully fixed before it is protected by copyright, then during the broadcast the work would be unprotected by copyright. Someone who made a contemporaneous copy or performed the work in public would not be infringing. The definition closes this loophole:

> A work consisting of sounds, images, or both, that are being transmitted, is "fixed" for purposes of this title if a fixation of the work is being made simultaneously with its transmission.

17 U.S.C. §101. Another loophole for bootleggers is closed by protection for a category of unfixed works. Live musical performances receive special protection, even if the performance is not fixed under the authority of the author. The statute imposes liability for anyone who makes an unauthorized recording or transmission of such a performance, or who thereafter distributes recordings. 17 U.S.C. §1101.

Several rationales are commonly given for the fixation requirement, the rule that federal copyright will not apply unless a work has been embodied in some tangible form. One rationale is that the fixation requirement is required by the U.S. Constitution. The Constitution grants Congress the power to give copyrights in the "Writings" of authors. The word "writing" implies that the work be recorded in some form. Granting copyrights in unfixed works would exceed the power of Congress. Note that "Writings" has not been limited to its usual literal meaning, which might limit copyright is to written works like novels and textbooks. "Writings" is broadly construed to cover any form in which an author's work is embodied, such as books, recordings, notes, photographs, drawings, computer chips, sculpture, or any other tangible, stable form.

Another rationale given for the fixation requirement is that it sets boundaries. By putting the work in tangible form, the author defines what is included in the work. By setting such boundaries, the author informs others of the extent of the author's claimed rights. Just as fences may serve to show the boundaries of real property, the fixation requirement marks the author's intellectual territory. In turn, this facilitates transactions involving copyrights. Markets function better when rights are clearly defined, because that makes it easier to engage in transactions.

Fixation also plays an important role in enforcing copyright, insofar as it serves an important evidentiary function. In many areas of the law, the rules prompt parties to put things in writing. An oral contract, for example, may not be enforceable. A written contract provides better evidence that the parties had an agreement and what the terms of the agreement were. Likewise, enforcement of copyright in an unfixed work (like an improvised song or dance) would require determining just what the author, without the benefit of a recording, performed. It would be very difficult to determine whether expressive elements were copied from a work without a tangible copy of the work showing just what those expressive elements were.

It is important to note that copyright protection *attaches when the work has been fixed*. A novel, for example, may be copyrighted as soon as the author has put it in some tangible form: written it out on paper, typed it into a computer, even dictated it into a tape recorder. To obtain copyright protection, it is not necessary to register the work with the U.S. Copyright Office, or to put the little © on the work, or to publish the work, or to make more than one copy of the work, or even to let anyone know that the work exists.

The rule that fixation is the moment at which copyright protection attaches represents a considerable change in copyright law. Before 1978, federal copyright protection attached to a work when the work was published with a copyright notice (such as "© 1946 James Baldwin") on copies of the work. To obtain federal copyright protection, then, the author usually had to meet two requirements: publication and use of a copyright notice. Some unpublished work could be copyrighted by registration. At the time, most unpublished works were not subject to federal copyright, and even until 1989, works that were published without a copyright notice could forfeit their copyright and go into the public domain. Now, an author need only write the novel for copyright to attach, and remain attached.

Federal copyright law has expanded considerably: rather than applying primarily to published works, it now also applies to unpublished works of many types, including novels that do not find publishing contracts, private letters, art class projects, e-mails, and so on. While copyright infringement was usually thought of only where someone had copied a published work, it now is often claimed in litigation about such unpublished works.

Examples

1. *At what point in time.* In 2006, Concord creates a short story, "Lanes and Games." She spends several days working out most of the details in her head, then writes it all down over several days. She subsequently types the words into her computer and e-mails them to her publisher. The publisher soon prints 1,000 copies of the book (with a copyright notice on each one) and delivers them to various bookstores. The books are put on display and most are sold over the next few months. Meanwhile, just after the book is published, Concord registers the book with the Copyright Office. She downloads the form and mails it in, with the fee. Soon, she receives a certificate of registration.

    At what point does Concord have a copyright in the short story? What if all the events had occurred in 1966?

2. *Making a record.* Coauncord has an idea for another short story. Over several days, she devises an intricate plot and peoples the story with some complex characters. She does not have time to sit down and write out the story. Rather, she simply writes the title of the story, "Worm Tunnel," on a postcard and mails the postcard to herself. Does she have a federal copyright in the story? What if she had carried a tape recorder and dictated the story as she thought it up?

3. *Philosophical differences.* Thelma and Louise, two folk singers, write the song "Drumlin Farm," by improvising both tune and words while playing their guitars. When satisfied, they make an audiotape of themselves performing the song. After happily listening to it, they decide to read up on copyright law to figure out their rights. Soon, they are a little confused. Do they have a musical work? A sound recording? And is the tape a copy or a phonorecord?

4. *Improvable.* Nick and Tony are improvisational comedians. During their act, they take suggestions from audience members and improvise skits. They learn that some of their acts have been copied by local standup comedians. Can they get copyright protection without resorting to a scripted act?

5. *Dance.* Choreographer works over several weeks to create an intricate dance. She then spends hours rehearsing the dance with her troupe. They perform the dance to a large and appreciative audience. Choreographer then learns that another troupe, which surreptitiously recorded the performance, plans to perform it. Does she have a copyright in the choreography of the dance?

6. *Rats.* The musical *Rats* is greatly successful. The musical has a number of memorable characters drawn from a children's book about the various rats living under a restaurant. The musical has several popular songs and lots of funny banter. The Broadway production features creative makeup designs on the various actors' faces. Part of the attraction is that Producer bans the publication of photos of the made-up actors. Only those attending live performances see the makeup designs. Tabloid Photographer takes unauthorized photos of the actors by sneaking backstage. When Producer seeks an injunction against publication of the photos, Photographer argues that the makeup designs are not fixed and therefore are unprotected. Are the designs painted on the actors' faces sufficiently fixed to attain copyright protection?

7. *Written on face?* Suppose that none of the songs and dialogue in *Rats* had ever been recorded or written down. Rather, they had all been improvised over time. Another production of the musical starts up. Producer argues that the musical is fixed because the characters' makeup designs are painted on the actors' faces. Does that suffice?

8. *Screen display.* Omni creates a successful video game, Scramble. Omni sells the game in game cartridges. When a cartridge is put in a game console, on-screen cartoon characters perform various actions, subject to some control by the player. Competitor creates a strikingly similar game. Sued for copyright infringement, Competitor argues that Scramble is not copyrightable because it is not fixed but appears only in fleeting images on the screen. Is Scramble fixed?

9. *Unfixed?* Author writes a story and reads it in public. She then inadvertently destroys the only copy of the story. Moviemaker was at the reading, loved the story, and has a tremendous memory. He would like to copy the story into a script without Author's consent. Does Author lose copyright because her work is no longer fixed?

10. *Fixed?* Author prepares a lecture on literary theory, which sets forth her views in witty and incisive fashion. She does not write her remarks down. She delivers the lecture to an audience of two people. Author uses a tape recorder to record the lecture. Has she fixed an original work of authorship? Would it make a difference if the recording was never published or even played again?

11. *Authorized by author?* Poet composes a poem in his mind. He recites it privately to several friends, not realizing that one friend is videotaping the performance. When he is later informed of the taping, Poet says, "That's OK. You did me a favor by fixing it. Now I have copyright in the poem." Is he right?

12. *Unplugged.* Scribbler appears at a book signing to plug his latest collection of short stories. Before sitting down to sign copies of the book, he reads

one story from the book aloud to the assembled throng. The store offers to tape the reading, but he declines. One audience member tape-records the reading without permission and then soon sells copies to the public, advertising in various literary journals. Accused of copyright infringement, the entrepreneur argues that she tape-recorded an unfixed work (the reading) and cannot be infringing. Will that argument succeed?

13. *Ever-changing?* Kelly plants and tends that a "permanent Wild Flower Floral Display." The bed has aesthetic appeal, partly from how the flowers change with the season. Is the work copyrighted?

14. *Virtual fixation?* Firesabre "terraforms" islands in the virtual world Second Life. Is Firesabre's work fixed in a tangible medium, although in a virtual world?

Explanations

1. Concord has a copyright in the story when she fixes it in a tangible medium of expression. She did this when she wrote down the short story. None of the subsequent actions (putting it in a computer, printing, and publishing copies with a copyright notice) were necessary to receive protection under the current version of the statute.

   If all this had occurred in 1966, the answer would be different. Until 1978, federal copyright applied primarily to published works. So copyright would not attach until the work was published with a copyright notice. And if it had been published without a copyright notice, Concord would have lost her copyright and the work would be in the public domain, free for anyone else to copy.

2. Concord has a copyright in the story when she fixes it in a tangible medium of expression. She has not done this, so she has no copyright. Writing down the title alone does not fix the entire work. If, however, she dictated the story into a tape recorder, that would fix it in tangible form and she would have a copyright.

3. The authors have two copyrights: a copyright in the musical work, "Drumlin Farm," and a copyright in the sound recording, in the recording of them singing the song. The tape is both a copy of the musical work and a phonorecord of the sound recording.

4. Nick and Tony do not need to use a script to have copyright protection. Rather, they could record their act as they improvise it. That would fix it in tangible form, and they would then have copyright in the work.

5. Choreographer does not have a federal copyright in the dance. Her choreography is an original work of authorship, but it has not been fixed by or under the authority of the author. Even though she and her troupe have committed it to memory and performed it in public, copyright does

not attach without authorized fixation. The other troupe did videotape the dance, but that would have met the fixation requirement only if it had been authorized.

Choreographer is not out of luck. She can still fix the work (in notation, in videotape, or any other tangible form), thereby receiving copyright protection. As later chapters discuss, the other troupe would be liable if it subsequently made copies or performed the work publicly (although it can keep the videotaped copy it made before protection attached).

6. Copyright protection does not require the actor to wear the makeup permanently. Rather, fixation must be "sufficiently permanent or stable to permit it to be perceived, reproduced, or otherwise communicated for a period of more than transitory duration." 17 U.S.C. §101. The makeup on the actor's face is sufficiently stable to meet the fixation requirement. Cf. *Carell v. Shubert Organization*, 104 F. Supp. 2d 236 (S.D.N.Y. 2000).

7. Painting the actors' faces does fix the makeup designs. It does not fix the entire musical, which is a musical work (as well as a literary and a dramatic work). Fixation must embody the work in a tangible medium of expression, such that it may be "perceived, reproduced, or otherwise communicated." Simply showing the makeup designs on the actors' faces does not communicate the entire musical. Rather, Producer would have to write it down, videotape it, or otherwise fix the entire work. Once Producer did so, however, he could then exercise his exclusive rights and prevent the other production from publicly performing the work. Even if the other production fixed the work first, the other producers would have no copyright because the musical was not original to them.

8. Scramble is fixed in the game cartridges, which are clearly sufficiently stable. Although the game is viewed on the screen, fixation can be in any form. Likewise, a musical work may be fixed on a CD, even if it is usually experienced only in the fleeting sounds from the speakers. The game is fixed, even if the player can affect particular performances of the game. See *Stern Electronics v. Kaufman*, 669 F.2d 852 (2d Cir. 1982). Many types of works are affected by choices of the audience.

If the work did appear only on the screen, it probably would not qualify as fixed. Such a copy is not permanent or stable. The weight of authority now seems to be that temporary copies in computer memory are sufficiently stable, even though they are constantly renewed. A screen display is also refreshed many times a second (although not as frequently as memory). But the overall duration is much more fleeting than the temporary memory copy. The screen display changes in less than a second, while the memory copy sits there much longer.

9. Once fixed, the work is protected by copyright. The statute does not require that the work remain fixed. See *Peter Pan Fabrics v. Rosstex Fabrics*, 733

F. Supp. 174 (S.D.N.Y. 1990) (rejecting even the possibility of such an argument). So Author still has her copyright. But it may be difficult to enforce. To bring an enforcement action would requires registering the work, including depositing a copy of the work. Proving infringement would also require comparing the accused work against a copy of the work, likewise difficult if the only copy no longer exists.

10. Yes. By tape-recording the lecture, Author fixed a literary work. Fixation need take no particular form, so she need not transcribe the lecture or put it on paper in any way. The size of the audience is irrelevant. If she had simply tape-recorded the lecture with no one else present, it would have been fixed.

    Copyright no longer turns on publication, so whether a work is published or used in any other way does not affect whether it receives copyright protection. So if Author never publishes the recording, never plays it again, or promptly loses it, she is still entitled to copyright protection (although any of those would make it harder to register the work and to prove infringement, which, as discussed in subsequent chapters, requires proof that defendant copied from the protected work).

11. The videotaping was initially unauthorized and hence did not fix the poem. Poet is seeking to subsequently ratify the fixation, thereby retroactively authorizing it. This argument seems to lack support in the statute. Poet would be well advised to simply write the poem down or otherwise fix it himself (or authorize someone to do so).

12. The short story was fixed in tangible form when Scribbler wrote it. (It is also being sold in fixed form in the books.) Upon fixation, Scribbler had a copyright in the story. Audience member is making copies (and distributing them to the public, which also falls within the copyright holder's exclusive rights) and therefore is infringing.

13. The court, faintly echoing Chauncey Gardiner, held that the work was neither a work of human authorship nor fixed in tangible form: "A garden's constituent elements are alive and inherently changeable, not fixed. Most of what we see and experience in a garden—the colors, shapes, textures, and scents of the plants—originates in nature, not in the mind of the gardener. At any given moment in time, a garden owes most of its form and appearance to natural forces, though the gardener who plants and tends it obviously assists." *Kelley v. Chicago Park Dist.*, 635 F.3d 290 (7th Cir. 2011).

14. "Fixed" under the Copyright Act requires only that the work be "sufficiently permanent or stable to permit it to be perceived, reproduced, or otherwise communicated for a period of more than transitory duration." As long as Firesabre's work has a little creativity, it can be a copyrighted work. *FireSabre Consulting LLC v. Sheehy*, 2013 U.S. Dist. LEXIS 139550 (S.D.N.Y. Sept. 26, 2013).

CHAPTER 3

Copyright Does Not Protect Ideas, Functional Aspects, Infringing Material, Government Works

Suppose movie studio makes millions by copying a clever idea from a copyrighted short story. That would not be copyright infringement, though it may disappoint the story's author. Copyright protection is easy to obtain. The author need merely put a work in tangible form that has a modicum of creativity. But although the work is copyrighted, many aspects of the work may be freely copied. Nonoriginal aspects (such as facts and material from preexisting works) are not subject to copyright. As this chapter discusses, even certain elements created by the author are not subject to the copyright, because copyright does not apply to such things as the subject matter of copyright. The exclusions can make elements of a work or the entire work unprotected by copyright.

Copyright would not apply to a great idea for a book (or to the many ideas expressed in the book), a method of cloning mice, the rules of a game, an unauthorized sequel to *WALL-E* (unless making the sequel was fair use), or the Copyright Act itself. Copyright does not apply to ideas, functional matter, infringing material, or government works.

IDEAS AND FUNCTIONAL ASPECTS

Copyright does not protect ideas. That may be the easiest copyright rule to state and the hardest to apply. It is often difficult to distinguish noncopyrightable ideas from copyrightable creative expression of those ideas. The

69

rule is also one of the most important rules in copyright. Because copyright does not protect ideas, copyright should not restrict the free flow of ideas. Indeed, the noncopyrightability of ideas is important in making copyright, which restricts many types of speech, consistent with the freedom of speech mandated by the First Amendment.

Copyright does not protect ideas or other nonexpressive elements of a work. Copyright protects only the elements of the work that are creative expression, such as the particular ways an author expresses an idea. This central exclusion is set forth in 17 U.S.C. §102(b):

> In no case does copyright protection for an original work of authorship extend to any idea, procedure, process, system, method of operation, concept, principle, or discovery, regardless of the form in which it is described, explained, illustrated, or embodied in such work.

If an author has an idea for a short story, the idea is not protected by copyright — no matter how original the idea is. There is no copyright infringement if someone copies the unprotected idea. If the author confides her idea in a letter to a friend, and the friend uses the idea to write a story, there is no copyright infringement. If the author instead writes the short story, which is read by a famous author, who then takes the idea by using it in a short story, there is no copyright infringement. If a moviemaker steals the idea and uses it as for a blockbuster movie, there is no copyright infringement. Ideas are not copyrightable, and copying of unprotected elements is not copyright infringement.

Ideas of all sorts are excluded from copyright protection. A paper in a biology journal may propose a new interpretation of some fossils. The author's theory would be an unprotected idea. A legal brief may argue for the application of a statute to a particular case — likewise an unprotected idea. A movie's premise, like the Chicago Cubs winning the World Series and thereby triggering a new ice age, is an unprotected idea. An idea for a new product (picnic tables configured to confuse wasps), the idea that makes a joke funny, the idea that makes a song memorable, and the idea to write a play about the kidnapping of heiress Patty Hearst are all unprotected by copyright.

A copyrighted work may contain many ideas. The overall idea for the movie may be "what happens when the Cubs finally win a championship." But the movie may be built with many more ideas, such as the return of Al Capone and the effect of Lake Michigan freezing solid. A book of science will likely be chockful of ideas. None of the ideas are protected by copyright.

Copying ideas is not copyright infringement, even if the copying is deceitful, in breach of a confidence, or otherwise underhanded. Stealing an idea is not copyright infringement. Even if the obscure short story writer can prove that a famous author copied an idea from her story, that does not entitle her to collect for copyright infringement. Plagiarism (presenting the work of others as one's own) is not necessarily copyright infringement.

So copyright does not protect the most valuable aspects of creative works. As Justice Brandeis famously said, "The general rule of law is that the noblest of human productions — knowledge, truths ascertained, conception and ideas — become, after voluntary communication to others, free as the air to common use." At first blush, the nonprotection of ideas might seem contrary to the purpose of copyright. Copyright serves as an incentive to authors. By giving authors exclusive rights in their works, copyright gives the authors a reason to create and publish. An author need not fear that she will bear all the costs of creating the work while unscrupulous copiers garner the benefit. If others can freely copy the author's ideas, does that not decrease the incentive to produce ideas?

It might. There arguably would be a greater incentive to produce ideas if ideas were protectable by copyright. Perhaps not, because there are many other incentives to produce ideas. Moreover, copyright protection has costs, as well as benefits. If ideas were copyrighted, the flow of ideas would be greatly restricted. Anyone who wanted to use the ideas in a story, a scientific paper, a painting, or a computer program might need the permission of the copyright holder. So the rule denying protection to ideas, but granting protection to the particular way an author expresses her ideas, reflects a balance between the benefits of copyright (providing incentives to authors, and giving authors the right to control what they have created) and the costs of copyright (the increased costs on those who wish to use copyrighted works, the transaction costs of negotiating for agreements to use copyrighted works, and the deadweight costs where potential uses are not realized because of copyright concerns). The role of copyright, therefore, is not to provide the maximum incentive possible for authors. Rather, copyright protection is limited in order to balance the benefits to authors against the costs of copyright protection. By giving an author rights in her creative expression, copyright provides sufficient protection for the production of creative works. If an author can have the exclusive right to sell copies of her novel and to make a movie out of it, that may give her sufficient incentive to spend a year or two writing the book. Even if others can copy the idea behind a movie, the producers can prevent others from closely copying the movie. That is sufficient protection, evidently, for movie companies to spend millions of dollars on their works.

So the reason ideas are not protected by copyright has nothing to do with ideas being less valuable than expression or with Congress not wishing to provide incentives for the production of ideas. Quite the opposite. Ideas are too valuable to be copyrighted. Rather, the free flow of ideas is too important to permit the exclusive rights of copyright to control ideas. Sufficient incentive for the production of works exists by giving authors exclusive rights limited to the expression in the works. The rule does not necessarily hurt authors, even if it provides them less copyright protection.

Authors are also users. Every work uses ideas that have been created by others, to some extent.

The freedom to copy ideas is central to the constitutional role of copyright. If copyright prohibited copying of ideas, it would be difficult to square with the First Amendment's freedom of expression. The Supreme Court has recognized this. *Eldred v. Ashcroft* rejected a First Amendment challenge to extension of copyright terms. The plaintiffs had argued that adding 20 years to the terms of existing copyrights was an impermissible limitation on freedom of speech. The Court held, however, that copyright legislation was not normally subject to First Amendment scrutiny. Rather, copyright has "built-in First Amendment accommodations." Copyright does not prohibit the copying of ideas, and copyrighted works are subject to fair use for such purposes as education, criticism, news reporting, or research. The Court reasoned that copyright and the First Amendment actually serve the same goal. Copyright promotes freedom of expression by giving an incentive to produce works, while protecting freedom of expression by limiting protection to an author's expression, as opposed to the ideas in the work. *See also Golan v. Holder*, 565 U.S. ___ (2012) (upholding restoration provisions, which restored copyright to foreign works that had gone into the public domain in the United States due to failure to comply with the formalities required by U.S. law).

Examples

1. *Suggestions.* A *New Yorker* cartoon shows a box with two slots, fixed on an office wall. The sign on the box reads, "Suggestions. Or toast." A designer at Wacky Products sees the cartoon and uses it as the basis for a new novelty product, a toaster with "Suggestion Box" imprinted on the side. The toaster becomes a highly popular holiday gift that year. The cartoonist claims copyright infringement. Has Wacky Products infringed the copyright in the cartoon?

2. *Famillionaire. The Apprentice* is a "reality" television show. Each week, a team of aspiring businesspeople attempt an assigned business task, like marketing a new airline. The tasks are designed to test skills important in succeeding as entrepreneurs. The team members then are evaluated by Donald Trump, a quirky wealthy businessman. Some team members are summarily fired each week, until finally the remaining contestant is the winner. The show is highly successful. Imitation being the sincerest form of flattery, another network soon airs *The Rebel Billionaire*. In this show, team members attempt assigned tasks, like walking a tightrope between two hot air balloons. The tasks are designed to test such qualities as risk-taking and coolness under fire, qualities important for entrepreneurs. The team members are evaluated by Richard Branson, a quirky

wealthy businessman. Some team members are gently fired each week, until finally the remaining contestant is the winner. Does *Rebel Billionaire* infringe the copyright in *The Apprentice?*

3. *Ratz.* Mattel, the maker of Barbie dolls, develops an idea to follow up with a contrasting line of dolls—young, stylish, with exaggerated features, big heads, and attitude. A competitor learns the idea and markets Bratz dolls, with wild commercial success. Copyright infringement?

Explanations

1. Wacky has not infringed the copyright in the cartoon. Wacky copies the basic idea of the cartoon: that a suggestion box might double as a toaster, implying that suggestions will be flamed. But Wacky did not copy the expression of the idea. Rather, Wacky expressed the idea in quite a different way.

2. *Rebel Billionaire* did not infringe the copyright in *The Apprentice.* Rather, it copied the unprotectable idea of a reality show, where contestants perform tasks assigned by a quirky rich person. *The Rebel Billionaire* also copied some elements more specifically, such as eliminating contestants each week, but those elements would likely be unprotected as well, because they are necessary to implement the unprotected idea. If the second show had copied not just the idea, but more specific elements, such as the specific tasks that were performed, the result might be different.

3. No copyright infringement. An idea for a line of dolls is not protected by copyright. *See Mattel Inc. v. MGA Entertainment Inc.*, 616 F.3d 904 (9th Cir. 2010).

Idea vs. Expression: The Abstractions Test

Ideas are not protected by copyright, but the original way an author expresses the ideas is protected. The distinction between nonprotected ideas and protected expression is key to the scope of copyright protection. If an author writes a novel, her original expression is protected by copyright, but the ideas in the novel are not. The rule is simple to state, but difficult to apply. Literal copying (such as word-for-word copying of a novel, or a recording of a copyrighted song) is copying protected expression, likely infringement. Copying only the basic idea behind the work (the premise of a movie or the big idea in a novel) is copying unprotected ideas, not infringement. The more difficult cases are where the copying lies between those extremes. The distinction between protected ideas and unprotected expression arises frequently, in both advising and litigation. Suppose the comedy about the Cubs winning is a hit movie. Other producers will consider following in its footsteps. How closely may they copy without infringing? Would a film infringe if it copied the overall structure, substituting elements from another city? In another context, a publisher wishes to create a new biology textbook to compete with an established work. The new book cannot copy word for word without infringing. But may it copy the overall organization? The specific way that the material is divided into chapters? The selection of topics to cover and to exclude?

Neither the statute nor the case law defines "idea" or "expression." In fact, there is no true distinction between ideas and expression. Rather, the idea/expression distinction in copyright law is really a policy-based distinction about which elements of a work should be subject to the copyright holder's exclusive rights and which elements should be free for others (other authors and other users of the work) to copy. If a bootlegger sells posters of a copyrighted painting, word-for-word copies of a novel, or bit-by-bit copies of a computer program, that clearly constitutes copying an author's expression of his ideas. But copyright must do more than protect against such literal copying. Otherwise, another author could simply change the wording and still free-ride on the first author's work. On the other hand, copyright must permit some copying. If it were infringement to copy any element of a work, regardless of how general, copyright would effectively grant protection to the ideas as well as to their expression. But, if the protection against nonliteral copying is too strong, then it will effectively prohibit copying of ideas.

A leading treatise provides a helpful guide to the analysis. See Paul Goldstein, *Copyright*, §2.3.1. Ideas may be concepts, solutions, or building blocks. Copyright would not apply to ideas such as a parade with floats or a game show or contest, or the concept that items might be painted in rainbow colors. *Id*. Rather, such general concepts should be free for others to copy, as long as they do not copy the particular expression of the concept in specific parade design or game show production. Ideas can be solutions, like the design of forms necessary to implement an accounting system, or rules for a game. *Id*. Ideas can also be "building blocks," such as the plot and theme of a novel, colors and shapes in visual works, or rhythms and notes in musical works. *Id*. Such general elements are necessary for the creation of other works. By deeming them to be unprotected ideas, the law prevents a single author from controlling an entire genre of artistic expression. *Id*. Otherwise, the author of the first rap song or first situation comedy might claim the exclusive right to make works in that area. Seeing ideas as concepts, solutions, and building blocks is a useful way to see how the idea/expression distinction is really an exercise in balancing the author's rights against the costs of copyright protection on other authors, as well as consumers.

In deciding whether a defendant has copied protected expression, courts use the "abstractions test," first developed by Judge Learned Hand. *See Nichols v. Universal Pictures*, 45 F.2d 119 (2d Cir. 1930). Suppose plaintiff's work is a popular play, set in New York in the early 1900s. A young couple (one Jewish, one Irish Catholic) secretly marry. Their respective fathers become comically exercised and quarrel. The secretly married couple produces grandchildren. The fathers reconcile their differences. Such elements are unprotected ideas. Otherwise, the first playwright would be granted a virtual monopoly on a genre of works. One could express the same basic elements in innumerable ways. As Learned Hand put it, "A comedy based upon conflicts between Irish and Jews, into which the marriage of their children enters, is no more susceptible of copyright than the outline of Romeo and Juliet." *Id.* at 122. So no infringement results if a second author copies all those general elements but expresses them in a different form. The second author could write new dialogue, invent a new specific plot to follow the general outline, invent different characteristics to give the respective family members, change the neighborhood in which the story was set, and concoct a new scene that resolves the various conflicts. Provided the second author copies only the unprotected general ideas from the first work, she does not infringe.

To copy at a much more specific level is taking protected expression. Another author might copy not just the general story but the particular way it unfolded in plaintiff's play: the sequence of scenes, the plot mechanisms for revealing information to the characters, the dramatic series of acts and exchanges leading to the resolution. Such copying is infringement because it takes not just the general ideas but their expression. Copyright does not protect the outline of a play in which a woman poisons her lover but is acquitted due to the perjured testimony of a friend. But it is infringement to copy the main traits of the characters, much of the dialogue, and also the long series of detailed incidents and actions of the story, down to the level of gestures. *See Sheldon v. Metro-Goldwyn Pictures*, 81 F.2d 49 (2d Cir. 1936).

The same principles govern other types of works. For example, a famous cover from the *New Yorker* magazine shows the myopic worldview of a typical New Yorker. *See Steinberg v. Columbia Pictures*, 663 F. Supp. 706 (S.D.N.Y. 1987). The illustration showed Manhattan depicted in detail, a brown strip vaguely labeled "Jersey," then an anonymous square, with only a few spots labeled Las Vegas, Los Angeles, and Asia off on the horizon. The picture captures how a New Yorker thinks of the world as comprising New York, with a few other places only vaguely on the horizon. Another artist could copy the idea by depicting a view that echoes the primacy of Manhattan in the world. But it would be copying of expression if the second artist depicts the same vantage point, colors the sky similarly, copies details of buildings originally invented by the first artist, and copies other specific expressive elements.

Not all copying of specific elements is deemed copying of expression. Nonoriginal elements are not protected. Elements that necessarily follow from the unprotected ideas are also unprotected. If a play is set among immigrants in New York in the early 1900s, that setting largely determines such elements as dress, manners of speaking, elements of scenery, and so on. Likewise, if a detective story is set in a monastery, it likely will have several suspects who are monks. Similarly, under the "scenes a faire" doctrine, elements of a work may be unprotected if they are commonly found in works of that genre. If a detective story has some fairly stock thug characters (who were nevertheless created by the author, if somewhat unimaginatively), another author may use such characters in her story without infringing.

The more original the idea, the more this rule will come into play. The science fiction work *Dune*, for example, had the original premise of a world in which water has become truly scarce and must be conserved with heroic means. That idea is not protected by copyright. Another author would be free to write her own science fiction novel set on a planet with very little water. Of necessity, specific elements of her book might be similar to elements of *Dune*. Water would be fought over, individuals would carry devices to minimize water usage and wastage, the landscape would be more like a sandy desert than a plush rain forest. But even though such copying of specific elements would be at a relatively low level of abstraction, it would not be infringement. Otherwise, the idea underlying *Dune* would be effectively protected from copying.

A nice example is *Educational Testing Services v. Katzman*, 793 F.2d 533 (3d Cir. 1986). ETS alleged copyright infringement by Princeton Review's copying from multiple-choice questions. Princeton Review made slight changes to the questions, for example in a question on antonyms:

SAT Question

9. REPROBATE: (A) predecessor (B) antagonist (C) virtuous person (D) temporary ruler (E) strict supervisor

Princeton Review Question

9. REPROBATE: (A) antagonist (B) predecessor (C) virtuous person (D) temporary ruler (E) strict supervisor

ETS would not have copyright protection in such ideas as the meaning of "reprobate," or whether the opposite of "reprobate" is a virtuous person or an evildoer, or even in the idea of writing a multiple-choice question about the word "reprobate." But Princeton Review copied much more specifically than that. Likewise, Princeton Review copied the ETS math questions, making only minor changes in the numbers that made no real difference to the question. ETS has no copyright in mathematical rules or their use, but was accorded copyright in the particular questions it formulated to test knowledge of math. The key, with both, is that ETS did not get exclusive rights in mathematical rules or in the meaning of words—rather, Princeton Review and others were left with many other ways to test the same ideas with multiple-choice questions.

The scope of protection is also affected by the degree of originality in the work. One novel might be written in highly creative form, with unique characters, an inventive plot line, and imaginative prose. Another novel might be original, but composed of clichés, recycled plot turns, and derivative characters. Both are protected against word-for-word copying. But the first has greater protection against nonliteral copying. Similarly, a work that primarily conveys unprotected material (such as facts or theories) has more limited protection than a work that is principally creative expression. A book of history, then, may be copied more closely than a book of fiction. *Who Destroyed the Hindenburg?* details the history of that famous zeppelin and sets forth the theory that a particular member of the crew had sabotaged it. The book contains many elements that are nonprotected (being facts or theories based on those facts). A disaster film was made (without permission of the book's copyright owner) that copied many specific elements from the book, such as the age and birthplace of the saboteur, various specific pertinent details about the airship and its crew, a warning letter from a Mrs. Rauch, Germany's ambassador discounting threats of sabotage, even the smuggling of monkeys aboard another zeppelin in the fleet. Such specific copying from a largely fictional novel would have likely been infringement. But in this case, the details were not the product of plaintiff's creativity but rather facts and theories from his research. So with factual works (and other works largely composed of nonprotected subject matter), copying of protected expression can occur only at a much lower level of abstraction, closer to verbatim copying. *See Hoehling v. Universal City Studios*, 618 F.2d 972 (2d Cir. 1980).

Sometimes an idea can be expressed only one or a few ways. To the extent that the idea constrains its expression, the expression is unprotected. Courts have called this rule the "merger doctrine." The illustrations on the label of a product, for example, are often creative drawings that qualify for copyright protection. But the nature of the product often constrains the nature of the illustrations. A box of cinnamon tea is likely to bear pictures of cinnamon sticks or cinnamon toast. Such depictions are not protected by copyright. *See Yankee Candle v. Bridgewater Candle*, 259 F.3d 25 (1st Cir. 2001). The merger doctrine only limits protection to the extent of the relevant idea. It does not authorize copying that goes beyond that necessary to use the idea. Another tea seller would infringe if, in addition to the cinnamon stick, she copied in minute detail the box's expressive elements such as shading, exact forms, and arrangement of elements.

So how do you protect an idea? Try contract or secrecy or norms or attribution. An idea is not protected by copyright. An aspiring Spielberg or Edison or Gates has a great idea. How can she protect it from copying against others—especially if she has to get other's help to realize the idea (make the movie, sell the invention, start the business).

One device is contract. Before disclosing the idea, she can require others to sign a nondisclosure agreement (NDA). That contract will enforceable. But she may find that others are reluctant to sign. Movie studios, venture capitalists, and others often have a policy of not signing NDAs. They have legitimate concerns about signing an NDA then hearing an idea that they have already heard (or is obvious or would have come around anyway)—or being subject to a claim later that is broader than the idea actually disclosed. Someone requiring an NDA before disclosure may find no one willing to hear the pitch at that price of signing.

Secrecy may work for some ideas. Some ideas can be exploited without disclosing them to others. Software, manufacturing processes, customer lists, and other trade secrets can be kept confidential. But other ideas—the idea for a movie or product—must be disclosed at some point, in order to sell to the public. But secrecy may help gain lead time over competitors.

Attribution may help for some authors. Ideas may not be protected—but the originator of an idea is often accorded public and professional respect. Artists, academics, scientists, and business people often benefit from a reputation as an innovator.

Examples

1. *Stolen idea.* Pixie Studio is in the midst of producing an animated movie, *Pumpkin*. The title character is adopted by a little boy, who finds the orange kitty sleeping on a warm jack-o'-lantern late one Halloween night. A month before the movie is ready to open, a rival studio suddenly comes out with *Tango*, an animated tale about a boy who finds a stray kitten one Thanksgiving, sleeping in the boy's furry boots. Like *Pumpkin*, the movie has various scenes of an outdoor cat adapting to indoor life, encountering various household appliances for the first time, learning about the wonders of the food and water dishes. It turns out that the rival learned about the basic storyline of *Pumpkin* through industry gossip. Pixie's executives are livid about the blatant theft of their intellectual work. Can they sue for copyright infringement?

2. *Zooperman.* A cartoonist starts a new comic book series, Zooperman Comics. She copies a number of elements from the popular Superman cartoons. Like Superman, Zooperman is a journalist who hides his identity beneath everyday clothing but who periodically changes into a special costume and fights crime. Both costumes are tight-fitting acrobatic suits with flowing capes. Both cartoons show their heroes crushing guns in their powerful hands, stopping bullets with their bodies, ripping open steel doors, and making building-sized leaps in a city. Each is

described as the strongest man in the world who uses his powers to fight "evil and injustice." Each is vulnerable to a rare substance (kryptonite for Superman, festonium for Zooperman). Each retreats to a refuge in the Arctic occasionally for contemplation. The specific depictions are different in many details. Their capes and costumes are different colors. One hero catches bullets; one lets them bounce off him. One leaps over buildings; one leaps from building to building. Superman's Arctic refuge is a fortress; Zooperman's is a whalebone tent. Cartoonist argues that she has simply copied an idea (the strongest man in the world who hides his identity whenever he is not fighting crime). Has she copied only unprotected ideas or also protected expression?

3. "*I'll Fly Away.*" Freelance Writer spends several weeks writing a short story, "I'll Fly Away," about a prisoner who seeks solace in music. Serving time for youthful crimes, the young man writes songs describing his life and expressing his frustrations and dreams. He works with other prisoners to develop his music. Over time, they help each other learn many other life lessons. The story ends as he reenters the outside world, with the various possibilities in the balance.

   Writer submits the story to Magazine and receives a polite rejection. A few months later, Magazine publishes a story attributed to one of its editors. The basic story line is the same: A prisoner enters prison as a confused teenager, spends time writing music and songs, and emerges as a man. Other than the basic story line, all the elements are different. Magazine admits that Editor was inspired by Freelancer's story. Has Magazine copied protected expression?

4. "*Wings Tips over the Edge.*" Photographer creates "Wing Tips over the Edge," a photo taken from the point of view of a businessperson on the edge of a roof, looking down on a city street. The photo is in a book distributed to local advertising agencies. An advertising agency has the photo in mind when it makes its ad for a financial news service. The similarities are the point of view, that of a potential jumper looking past his shoes; the business attire of the jumper; and a city street below. The street and buildings are quite different, and all other details such as the background, perspective, lighting, shading, and color of the photographs are dissimilar. Has the advertising agency copied protected expression?

5. *One fine groundhog.* The novel *One Fine Day* is about a man trapped in a repeating day. The novel starts with an account of a typical day: He wakes up to his custom-rigged alarm saying, "Wake up, you lazy bustard"; he rides down the elevator with a red-headed woman; he sees a number of people and incidents on his way to work, where he has a number of contentious encounters; he then spends the evening listening to music and ignoring periodic phone calls. Before going to sleep, he changes the

tape to a more friendly message. The next morning, however, he again hears "Wake up, you lazy bustard." He sees the same woman in the elevator, the same people in the same places as he goes to work, and the same incidents occur over the course of the day in exactly the same way. The next day, everything repeats itself, with the exception of the changes that the man himself makes. The day repeats itself numerous times until it is fixed by a combination of witchcraft and divine intervention.

The novel serves, without permission, as the basis for the film *Groundhog Day*. A self-centered weatherman becomes trapped in Punxsutawney, Pennsylvania, on Groundhog Day. He wakes up every day to the same song from his clock radio, runs into the same characters on his way to work (the groundhog's hole), and experiences the same incidents, except as changed by his actions. The repeating characters and incidents in the film are quite different from those in the novel. As the man realizes the day is endlessly repeating, he uses the time to better himself in various ways—learning music, becoming empathetic toward others, and finally falling in love. The latter breaks the spell, and he wakes to a new day. Does the script use unprotected ideas or protected expression?

6. *Greetings.* SentiMental sells a popular greeting card. The cover has the message "I Miss You," and inside says "and you haven't even left yet." There is an accompanying picture of a boy crying forlornly while sitting on a curb next to his dog. Another card publisher copies the card, using the same words and a rather different picture of a weeping boy sitting on a curb next to his dog. Rival argues that it has simply copied the unprotected idea and that finding infringement gives SentiMental a monopoly over a rather mundane sentiment—a boy's doleful anticipation of the departure of a loved one. Has Rival copied protected expression or an unprotectable idea?

7. *I missed you.* Souvenirs sells a T-shirt to tourists in San Francisco. The shirt reads, "Someone went to San Francisco and got me this shirt because they love me very much." The shirt has simple illustrations of Bay-area staples: the Golden Gate bridge, Chinatown, and Fisherman's Wharf. Seeing how popular the shirt is, another vendor comes out with a shirt reading "Someone who loves me went to San Francisco and got me this shirt." The shirt also has several simple designs: the Golden Gate bridge, Chinatown, cable cars, sea lions, and Nob Hill. The overall arrangement of the elements in the two shirts is completely different. Did the second vendor copy protected expression?

8. *History mystery.* Lucky Jim writes a scholarly article, the fruit of his months of research in the Fort Wayne archives. The article describes his research activity in detail, relates numerous interesting facts gleaned from his readings, and argues that those facts refute the accepted version of the

history of Indiana. Kingsley Amiss, the editor of *History Journal*, reviews the manuscript and offers to publish it. Months pass by without the article appearing. Finally, the article does appear—but it appears, word-for word, in *Monthly History Revue*, with authorship attributed to Amiss. Sued for infringement, Amiss argues that he has stolen only ideas about history, which may be blameworthy but is not copyright infringement. Has Amiss copied protected expression? What if Amiss had written the essay in his own bombastic prose, copying only Lucky Jim's theories and some of the supporting facts, but still deceptively claiming credit for the work himself?

9. *Blues clues.* Punkt paints "Blue Moom," a four-by-five-foot painting, all basic blue. The painting is well received by critics and the public. Not long after, Vango paints "Aquatic," a painting exactly the same color, and about one-quarter larger. Vango freely admits that he copied from Punkt's work, but argues that he copied only the idea of a basic blue painting. Has Vango copied protected expression?

10. Pi. Erickson's Pi Symphony assigns a musical note to each digit in pi from 0 to 9. Blake's likewise makes What Pi Sounds Like, with different rhythms and harmonies. Infringement?

Explanations

1. Pixie would not be entitled to remedies for copyright infringement because the rival has copied only the unprotected idea of finding a stray kitten on a holiday together with elements that flow from that idea, such as various scenes of the outdoor cat adjusting to indoor life. This would be true regardless of how the rival learned of the idea, whether through gossip or even espionage (although the latter could give rise to liability under other theories, such as misappropriation of trade secret if the project was subject to security measures, or breach of contract if a Pixie employee were involved).

2. Cartoonist has copied protected expression, as well as unprotected ideas. She is free to copy the idea of a crime-fighting superstrong man who hides his identity and secret powers. Some other elements necessarily follow from the unprotected ideas: He likely would dispose of bullets fired by criminals and might have to rip open a few doors to get at them. But there are many ways that such an idea could be expressed. The hero need not leap around city buildings, specifically battle "evil and injustice," be vulnerable to a rare substance, or have an Arctic refuge. All those details express ideas that could be expressed differently. Cf. *Detective Comics v. Bruns Publications,* 111 F.2d 432 (2d Cir. 1940). For example, the superstrong man could have a vulnerability, but it need not be to some rare substance.

3. Magazine has copied only unprotected ideas. The elements copied were very general and represented only the bare bones of the story: a prisoner coming of age through working in music. The fact that the story was submitted directly to Magazine does not affect its protectability under copyright. Offering unprotected ideas does not confer copyright protection to the ideas.

4. The author of the second photo probably did not copy protected expression. The idea of the first photo is of a businessperson looking down on the street contemplating a leap. That idea is not protected by copyright. There are also a number of quite specific similarities. In other cases, copying such specific elements would constitute protected elements. But here a court likely would hold that the similarities follow from the idea — the point of view, the business attire, the city street below. So the second photograph did not copy protected expression. Cf. *Kaplan v. Stock Market Photo Agency*, 133 F. Supp. 2d 317 (S.D.N.Y. 2001). A counterargument is that the idea is more general — the idea of a businessperson contemplating suicide. The view of a city street from the ledge of a building, including the feet of the businessperson, is only one way of expressing that unprotected idea. Under this view, the many specific elements in the photo are protected expression.

5. Despite the copying of a number of specific elements, the author of the film probably has copied only unprotected elements — ideas and elements that necessarily flow from the idea. The general idea is a man caught in a repeating day. The copied elements flow closely from that idea. There are a number of ways that a repeating day could unfold, but the basic outline likely would involve waking up, going to work, encountering a number of people, and experiencing various incidents. The film does not copy elements that do not flow from the idea, such as the specific characters and incidents that occur during the day. Cf. *Arden v. Columbia Pictures Indus.*, 908 F. Supp. 1248 (S.D.N.Y. 1995). A counterargument is that the copying was more specific than necessary. The day always has the central character woken up by an alarm, meeting people on his way to work to generate comic incidents, and changing the repetition of action only from the man's intervention. A repeating day could be portrayed in many other ways, for example, by losing its repeating character. But deeming such elements to be protected probably would give too broad protection to the first work because it would encompass many variations on the basic plot idea of a repeating day.

6. This case probably involves copying of protected expression. Copyright does not protect the idea of feeling someone's absence before the actual departure — or even the more specific idea of telling someone that you miss him before he goes. But Rival copied more specifically than that. It

copied the exact words: "I Miss You . . . and you haven't even left yet," coupled with a picture of a weeping boy sitting on a curb by his dog. There are many other ways that a card maker could have expressed the same ideas. Cf. *Roth Greeting Cards v. United Card Co.*, 429 F.2d 1970 (9th Cir. 1970).

7. Only unprotected ideas were copied here. As in the last example, the second author copied a relatively mundane sentiment, coupled with appropriate images. But the second author did not literally copy the words of the message. The second author also did not use the same set of images. In addition, the various images likely would be treated as scenes a faire. When certain elements are commonly used in a particular genre, their copying is not deemed taking of protected expression. Icons of San Francisco on souvenir T-shirts are likely to fall into that category. Cf. *Matthews v. Freedman*, 157 F.3d 25 (1st Cir. 1998). This example reflects the lower scope of protection for works with limited originality.

8. Amiss copied protected expression, as well as unprotected ideas and facts. The article contained unprotectable ideas. But there are many ways in which such ideas could be expressed. A word-for-word copy captures the expression as well as the ideas.

   There is no infringement if Amiss copies only theories and facts. Taking unprotected material does not infringe the copyright, no matter how scurrilous the actions may be.

9. Art can often present puzzles for copyright law. Sometimes, as here, the idea behind a work is very difficult to define, and also to separate from the expression of the idea. One could say that the idea of a work is a basic blue painting, and therefore Vango copied only the unprotected idea. Or one could say that the idea is a painting of one color, and that Vango copied the particular expression of the idea. On policy grounds, a court is likely to hold that one painter cannot have the exclusive right to make blue paintings—and therefore that Vango copied only the unprotected idea.

10. In the court's words, "Pi is a non-copyrightable fact, and the transcription of pi to music is a non-copyrightable idea. The resulting pattern of notes is an expression that merges with the non-copyrightable idea of putting pi to music: assigning digits to musical notes and playing those notes in the sequence of pi is an idea that can only be expressed in a finite number of ways." *Erickson v. Blake*, 839 F. Supp. 2d 1132 (D. Or. 2012).

    Norms (rules of customary behavior, as opposed to rules of law) may also cut down on copying. A comedian's jokes may not be protected by copyright, but comedians may reduce copying through informal social sanctions. See Christopher Sprigman & Dotan Oliar, *There's No Free Laugh (Anymore): The Emergence of Intellectual Property Norms and the Transformation of Stand-Up Comedy*, 94 Va. L. Rev. 1787 (2008). Many professions and social networks have norms against copying.

Attribution may help for some authors. Ideas may not be protected, but the originator of an idea is often accorded public and professional respect. Artists, academics, scientists, and businesspeople often benefit from a reputation as an innovator.

Example

Ratz again. Bryant works for Mattel, designing fashion and hairstyles for high-end Barbie dolls. Bryant's contract provides: "I agree to communicate to the Company (Mattel) as promptly and fully as practicable all *inventions* (as defined below) conceived or reduced to practice by me (alone or jointly by others) at any time during my employment by the Company. I hereby assign to the Company . . . all my right, title and interest in such *inventions*, and all my right, title and interest in any patents, copyrights, patent applications or copyright applications based thereon." (Emphasis added.) The contract further provides: "the term 'inventions' includes, but is not limited to, all discoveries, improvements, processes, developments, designs, know-how, data computer programs and formulae, whether patentable or unpatentable." Bryant has an idea for a Bratz line of dolls, and makes some sketches and model. Bryant later leaves Mattel for a competitor, who makes and sells the Bratz dolls, reaping millions of dollars. Is Bryant liable for breach of contract?

Explanation

Bryant is not liable for breach of contract. He agreed to communicate and assign his rights to "inventions," as defined in the contract. An idea for a line of dolls did not fall within the contract's definition of invention. *See Mattel Inc. v. MGA Entertainment Inc.*, 616 F.3d 904 (9th Cir. 2010). So Mattel did not have the right to the multimillion dollar deal. This example illustrates that one can use contracts to control the rights of noncopyrightable ideas—but those contracts must be carefully drafted.

Functional Aspects of Works

Copyright does not protect the functional aspects of works. The statute specifically excludes both ideas and several categories of functional elements: Copyright does not protect any "idea, procedure, process, system, method of operation." 17 U.S.C. §102(b). There would be no copyright protection for an original safety *procedure* for scuba diving in caves, for an original *process* for domesticating wild berries, for an original *system* of operating a dental office, or for an original *method of operation* for steering a rocket ship.

Many functional elements, such as procedures, systems, or methods of operation, could simply be viewed as noncopyrightable ideas. But the functionality issue differs in an important way from the exclusion of such ideas as the concept for a story or a mathematical principle. Where the plot of a novel or the concept underlying an abstract painting is an uncopyrightable idea, the effect is likely to be that the idea is left in the public domain, free for others to copy. In general the idea/expression question revolves around whether elements should be copyrightable or left in the public domain.

With functional elements, the dividing line is a slightly different one. Functional elements, such as manufacturing methods or designs of machines, are not copyrightable—but they may be patentable. Patent law, unlike copyright law, protects functional elements. Indeed, patents on inventions can apply only to new and useful products or processes. So the basic issue in functionality is often whether an element is creative, and therefore belongs in the realm of copyright, or functional, and therefore belongs in the realm of patent. Some useful ideas are too abstract for patent protection. Like copyright, patent does not protect ideas. Rather, patent only applies to practical applications of ideas in useful inventions.

A work may be functional and still have protected creative expression. A lamp base functions to hold the lamp up, but a lamp base composed of a dancer statuette is protectable by copyright. *Mazer v. Stein*, 347 U.S. 201 (1954). A map functions to help navigation, but is protectable. Computer programs fulfill many functions, but are protected literary works. In each case, the key is to differentiate the protected expressive aspects from the unprotected functional aspects.

Baker v. Selden, 101 U.S. 99 (1879), sets the standards for functionality analysis. Plaintiff held the copyright on a book explaining an accounting system. The book contained an essay that explained how the system worked and forms to implement the accounting system. The accounting system was clearly unprotected (in the terms of the present statute, as a "process [or] system"). The essay explaining the system was protected expression because the essay was simply the way in which the author explained the system. Another author could explain it in quite different terms. The issue was whether there was copyright protection for the forms used to implement the system. The forms were held unprotected because use of such forms was necessary to use the system. To prevent copying of the forms would have the effect of protecting the system. Copyright does not protect elements that necessarily flow from unprotected ideas. *Baker* stands for the proposition that even expressive elements are unprotected when they are functional.

Even an explanation of a system could be unprotected. The lengthy essay in *Baker* could have been written quite differently. But some descriptions are largely dictated by the systems they describe. The rules of a sweepstakes competition, for example, set forth how the competition operates. To give copyright protection to the explanation of the sweepstakes could, in effect, give one competitor exclusive rights to hold such competitions. There are only a few ways to clearly say, "Entrants should print name, address, and Social Security number on a boxtop or on plain paper." *See Morrissey v. Procter & Gamble*, 379 F.2d 675 (1st Cir. 1967). Likewise, documents used to implement the corporate reorganization of insurance companies have little, if any, protection. For others to copy the plan of the reorganization, it is necessary to use similar wording. *See Crume v. Pacific Mutual Life Ins.*, 140 F.2d 182 (7th Cir. 1944). Many legal documents have little or no protection because the use of particular words and phrases is necessary to comply with applicable legal requirements.

Although courts frequently state that copyright does not protect functional aspects of works, perhaps the more accurate phrase is elements with a *utilitarian* function. Almost every creative element of a work performs some function in a broad sense. Witty lines amuse, dramatic plots cause suspense, music stirs many emotional responses, beautiful forms inspire. But such elements are exactly the sort of creative expression that receive protection.

Courts look to several guides in determining whether elements are functional. One approach asks whether it is necessary to copy the element to implement an unprotected idea. The scope of protection depends heavily on how broadly the unprotected idea is defined. Courts may also consider factors geared to the need for competitors to copy the element: such factors as whether the element in question increases the efficiency of the process, whether external factors favor adoption of the element in question, or whether the element has become a standard in the relevant industry or is necessary for compatibility with other works. Another approach concentrates on the specific categories listed in the statute: whether the elements constitute an unprotected procedure, process, system, or method of operation. Such words are subject themselves to broad or narrow interpretation.

The rule that copyright does not protect functional elements may play an increasing role in a world where everyday events and behavior are recorded by devices such as security cameras, personal video recorders, and gaming and virtual world software. Such collections of information may, in some cases, be regarded not as copyrightable works of authorship but rather simply functional and factual data.

Examples

1. *Fosbury flop.* In 1968, Dick Fosbury changed the sport of high-jumping. He introduced a radically new technique, jumping headfirst and facing the sky. The "Fosbury Flop" turned out to be the most efficient way for people to high-jump, from a combination of physics and physiology. It is now the standard technique. Could Fosbury have copyrighted the move?

2. *Theme song. The Flimpsons* is a weekly television show. Its catchy theme song, "Meet the Flimpsons," begins the show each week. The song wittily

introduces the main characters and the premise of the show and is also used to market the show. A local bar regularly plays the song without a license from the copyright owner, arguing that the song is functional and therefore not protected. Is the song an unprotected functional work?

3. *Kregos revisited.* Recall that Kregos sells a "pitching form" for use by baseball fans, listing nine items of baseball statistics. The purpose of the form is to provide information with which a baseball fan could use her own knowledge to predict the likely performance of a pitcher. We discussed earlier the fact that the form is sufficiently original to qualify for copyright protection, but should it be excluded from protection for another reason, namely functionality?

Explanations

1. Fosbury could not have copyrighted the move, because it is functional: the most efficient way to high-jump. Copyright did not protect a sequence of yoga poses. The sequence was functional, as opposed to a creative arrangement such as the choreography of a ballet (which could include creative leaps).[1]

2. The theme song is not functional in the sense of copyright law. The theme song does perform several functions in a modest dramatic sense. It introduces characters and the premise of the show. It may put the viewer in a proper mood to enjoy the show. It serves a marketing role as a reminder of a popular product. But such aspects of a creative work are not functional for the purpose of limiting copyright protection. The song is not an "idea, procedure, process, system, method of operation." Nor is it an element that has become an industry standard or is necessary for compatibility with other products (factors that some courts would consider). Protecting the theme song does not limit competitors in any substantial way: a rival TV producer can use its theme song to do whatever she pleases without fear of infringing the *Flimpsons'* theme song. Use of the song is not necessary to comply with industry standards or to efficiently create a television program. Therefore, none of the factors weighing toward functionality apply here.

3. The form is not denied copyright on the basis of functionality. It would be unprotected if it embodied a system for predicting the outcomes of baseball games. If Kregos had devised a formula for using specific statistics to predict outcomes, then the form would probably be denied protection under *Baker v. Selden*, as something necessary to implement the system. But Kregos's form makes a more modest claim, simply suggesting that those nine statistics might be helpful to the fan in making her own predictions.

---

1. Bikram's Yoga Coll. of India, L.P. v. Evolation Yoga, LLC, 803 F.3d 1032 (9th Cir. 2015).

Instructions and Rules

Words, pictures, and other symbols can be functional. The instructions for assembling a bicycle are utilitarian, in that they are intended to be used to bring about a result: the assembled bicycle. Many literary works are functional in this sense: cooking recipes, operating manuals for electrical devices, instructions for games, how-to books for home maintenance, and so on. Rules can also be functional in nature. The rules for playing card games, the rules for contests, or the safety rules for workers at a construction site are all functional, intended to be used to accomplish various goals.

The functional elements of such works are not protected. But their purely expressive elements are protected. In determining whether an element may be copied, a court is likely to rely heavily on *Baker v. Selden*. Suppose that defendant copied plaintiff's instructions for operating a digital camera. The court may first attempt to identify a clearly unprotectable functional element (the system for operating the camera). Then the court, in effect, will consider whether the elements that were copied were like the forms in *Baker v. Selden* (which were necessary to use the accounting system and therefore not protected) or like the essay explaining the system (which was protected, because there are many different ways that one could write an essay explaining the accounting system). In short, the question is whether there were alternative ways to implement the functional purpose of the work. So if there were many different ways to write the instructions to operate the camera, then plaintiff's set of instructions would be deemed to be protected expression. But if there is only one or a few ways to efficiently give a set of instructions, then the instructions would likely be deemed to be nonprotected.

The level of creativity in the work is likely to affect the issue of functionality. If the instructions are set forth in a simple, straightforward way, then it is more likely that they will be deemed functional, and hence nonprotected. But if the instructions clearly contain elements that are not necessary for instruction, rather serve other purposes (such as creative phrasing, jokes, or historical information), then the instructions are more likely to be deemed protected by copyright. In that event, however, only the creative aspects are protected. A party that copies only functional aspects (such as copying the information necessary to operate the camera without copying the jokes and historical information) would not infringe. Instructions and rules, therefore, may be protected, but would receive only thin protection.

Examples

1. *Voop.* Two kids invent Voop, a card game. They creatively combine various elements from card games like bridge, hearts, spades, and poker. Their combination results in a new game that is easy and fun to play. The kids write up the rules. Rather than a straightforward statement of the

rules, however, the kids use many puns, puzzles, and tricks to state the rules. They also include a number of stories and pictures, springing from events during various Voop games. All this material is included in their notebook entitled "Rules of Voop." Is it copyrightable? Suppose Yoyle read "Rules of Voop," figured out what the basic rules of Voop were, and wrote a concise statement of those rules. Would Yoyle infringe the kids' copyright?

2. *Rollerball.* Promoter invents rollerball, a new sport that combines various elements of hockey, speed skating, and lacrosse, together with a few new rules devised by Promoter. Promoter stages several matches, which turn out to be great spectacles as well as exciting athletic events. The number of fans increases quickly. Knowing he cannot copyright the rules of play, Promoter writes detailed accounts of the matches. Another promoter stages a rollerball match after she read some of Promoter's accounts. She simply uses the same rules without staging the same events during those games. Promoter then sues for copyright infringement, arguing that the match infringes the copyright in his written descriptions, which are protected literary works. Were protected elements copied?

3. *Draft evader.* The Law Society drafts a Model Right of Publicity Statute. The society is concerned that the right of publicity is a cause of action that varies widely from state to state, is created by statute in some states and common law in others (or both), and is subject to considerable difference in judicial application. To promote uniformity among states, the society drafts the model statute, which the society regards as a concise statement of the best view of the elements, defenses, and remedies of the cause of action. The drafters first agreed on the set of rules that should govern the right of publicity. They then, after several drafts, agreed on how to express those rules. They also arranged the rules in a comprehensive fashion. Finally, they drafted commentary and examples to guide interpretation of the rules. Unlike drafters of some model statutes, the society does not urge states to adopt the model statute as drafted, but rather to use it only for guidance in drafting statutes. No jurisdiction has enacted the model statute into law. Is the model statute (including the rules as written by the drafters, the arrangement of the rules in the outline, the commentary, and all examples) protected by copyright?

4. *Tetris.* In Tetris, developed in the USSR in the 1980s, players must align falling "geometric block pieces (called tetrominos)" to fill the horizontal lines. Mino wrote and sold code to reproduce Tetris: "the style of the pieces is nearly indistinguishable, both in their look and in the manner they move, rotate, fall, and behave. Similar bright colors are used in each program, the pieces are composed of individually delineated bricks, each brick is given an interior border to suggest texture, and shading and gradation of color are used in substantially similar ways to

suggest light is being cast onto the pieces." Infringement or permissible copying of a functional game?

Explanations

1. "The Rules of Voop," as written by the kids, is protected by copyright. To the extent the rules govern the play of the game, they are unprotectable functional elements. Even though a game is for recreation and playing the game serves no end in itself, the rules of a game are functional. They represent an unprotected idea, process, or system. If the kids had written the rules up in a straightforward way, their description would have no protection. Because card games are described by a standard terminology, there is only one way (or only a few ways) to succinctly state the rules. Accordingly, such statement is unprotected under the merger doctrine. Otherwise, giving protection to the description of the rules effectively protects the game itself. But the kids chose a creative way to express the rules of the game. Giving them exclusive rights to their particular description does not limit others from copying the functional aspects. For the very reason that the description is protected, its copyright is not infringed by Yoyle. Yoyle did not copy the creative, protected aspects of the description. Rather, Yoyle copied only unprotected functional aspects.

2. The rival promoter has not copied protected expression. Promoter does have copyright protection in his detailed descriptions of the rollerball games. The rules of rollerball are not protected (as an idea, system, or process). His descriptions, however, capture much more than the rules. They describe the events in particular games of rollerball, as well as other details like descriptions of players and the crowd. The rival promoter, however, did not copy the protected expression. Rather, by staging her own rollerball games, she simply copied the unprotectable rules of play.

3. The rules of a game have been deemed unprotected because copying the rules is necessary to implement the game, an unprotected procedure. One might then expect that a model statute setting forth the rules governing the right of publicity would also be unprotected. But (although authority on the subject is sparse), copyright has been generally recognized in model statutes. The model statute sets forth proposed rules, which in themselves are unprotected as ideas, systems, or procedures. But the model statute also contains creative elements, such as the arrangement of the rules, the wording chosen to describe particular rules, and the commentary and examples chosen to illustrate the rules. Only if the rules could be expressed in one (or a few) forms of expression would the draft statute be denied protection. Here, that is not the case. The

drafters found numerous possibilities to express individual rules. They arranged the rules for creative reasons, unconstrained by functional considerations. The examples would also be creative expression. An infinite number of examples could be devised to illustrate the application of broad-ranging rules.

4. Infringement: Mino copied not just the functional elements of how the game worked, but also its aesthetic elements. There "was no necessity for Mino to mimic Tetris's expression other than to avoid the difficult task of developing its own take on a known idea." *Tetris Holding, LLC v. Xio Interactive, Inc.*, 863 F. Supp. 2d 394 (D.N.J. 2012).

Software

By their nature, computer programs (also known as "software") are functional. The copyright statute defines "computer program" as "a set of statements or instructions to be used directly or indirectly in a computer in order to bring about a certain result." 17 U.S.C. §101. At one time, there was considerable debate about whether computer programs were subject to copyright at all, or rather were nonprotected functional works. The present statute, however, clearly implies that computer programs are eligible for protection as literary works. The question has shifted to determining the extent of protection for computer programs. In software infringement cases, the basic question is to identify which elements have been copied and determine whether those elements are protected.

Computer programs are quite different from things like novels because they are primarily functional. Programs do things. A computer program performs intellectual work. It might operate a video game, predict the weather, monitor credit card transactions for possible fraud, create architectural drawings, or anything else. It will get input (information from databases of customer information; other programs that it interacts with; automatic sensors; users via a keyboard, mouse, or joystick; etc.). It produces output (the video game display, the weather predictions, the fraud warnings, the drawings—not to mention things like prompts for more input and error messages). The software engineer will design how the program will receive the input and produce output. She is likely to make an overall design (which would be an outline, flowcharts, scribbled notes, or ideas in her head). She will then implement that design by writing the program in source code. The source code is then translated by a compiler into machine code. In other words, a compiler takes the source code as its input and produces machine code as its output. The machine code is the form of the program that is executed by the computer. Once compiled, the program can be run. It won't work perfectly the first time. Rather, it will be tested and revised many times, to remove bugs, to make other changes suggested by users, and to add other features. So in general terms, a computer program is likely to start as a design and then be written out in source code, a portion of which might look like this:

```
#include <time.h>
#include <limits.h>
#ifndef ACOS4
#include.<sys.types.h>
#endif
```

It then will be compiled into machine code, which can look like this (except it would go on for many more lines):

```
F0F0F3F5 F0F0F0F0 F0F0F0F0 7B899583 93A48485
F0F0F3F6 F0F0F0F0 F0F0F0F0 7B859584 89864040
F0F0F3F7 F0F0F0F0 F0F0F0F0 40404040 40404040
F0F0F3F8 F0F0F0F0 F0F0F0F0 A3A89785 84858640
F0F0F3F9 F0F0F0F0 F0F0F0F0 A3A89785 84858640
F0F0F4F0 F0F0F0F0 F0F0F0F0 A3A89785 84858640
F0F0F4F1 F0F0F0F0 F0F0F0F0 40404040 40404040
F0F0F4F2 F0F0F0F0 F0F0F0F0 615C40E2 E8D4C1D7
```

That pattern (design, source code, machine code) is common, but programs may be created other ways. Novels are often outlined, written, and edited, but some writers may simply write without outlining. Likewise, some software engineers may simply write the source code without much of an overall design. Moreover, automated development tools often do much of the coding today. In some instances, an engineer may write the program in machine code.

A program is a text that "behaves." Pamela Samuelson, Randall Davis, Mitchell D. Kapor, & J.D. Reichman, *A Manifesto Concerning the Legal Protection of Computer Programs*, 94 Colum. L. Rev. 2308, 2316-2317 (1994) (proposing new legal regime more suited to software). The difficulty in applying copyright law to software has been to separate its functional (not copyrightable) aspects from its aesthetic (copyrightable) aspects.

Copyright law must adapt to special concerns with software: functionality (software has creative aspects, but is largely functional), interoperability (software must often be adapted to work together with other programs or with devices), and network effects (the more people use a program, the more useful it is to others). *See, e.g.*, Stacey L. Dogan & Joseph P. Liu, *Copyright Law and Subject Matter Specificity: The Case of Computer Software*, 61 N.Y.U. Ann. Surv. Am. L. 203 (2005).

A very helpful case to understand the issues is the much-criticized *Whelan Associates v. Jaslow Dental*, 797 F.2d 693 (3d Cir. 1986). In *Whelan*, plaintiff held the copyright in a program used to administer a dental office. The defendant had not copied the program code line for line, but rather had copied the structure of the program. The court, recognizing that computer programs are literary works, analyzed the case much like a case involving copying of a novel. The court reasoned that the computer program's unprotected idea was to efficiently administer a dental office. There are many different ways to implement that idea. Therefore, the court reasoned, the particular program structure chosen by plaintiff was protected expression.

Courts and commentators have overwhelmingly rejected the *Whelan* approach, as based on a faulty analogy. A computer program is not like *Moby Dick*. Computer programs are indeed literary works, but not all literary works receive the same level of protection. As the last chapter discussed, factual works receive a thinner level of protection than creative fictional works. Likewise, computer programs, which are largely functional, should receive thinner protection. In particular, the *Whelan* court erred in assuming that a program had a single unprotected idea. Rather, computer programs have an overall function (like administering a dental office), but implement that through many less abstract functions (such as performing accounting tasks, sorting through patient records, or keeping track of appointments). All those elements make up the structure of the program, which *Whelan* had held protectable. In short, *Whelan* gave the plaintiff exclusive rights in its system for operating a dental office. This is exactly what *Baker v. Selden* warned against, using copyright to give patent-like protection to a system.

After *Whelan*, courts have accorded a much thinner level of protection to computer programs. Notably, the cases borrow considerably from the analysis of the idea/expression dichotomy in literary works, vindicating the first step *Whelan* took. But they use those tools to considerably decrease the scope of protection, as applied to computer programs.

The leading case for analyzing claims of infringement for nonliteral copying of a computer program is *Computer Associates Intl. v. Altai*, 982 F.2d 693 (2d Cir. 1992). *Computer Associates* set forth an abstraction-filtration-analysis, which focuses on identifying elements of a program that would not be protected. In this approach, the court first borrows from the abstractions test by identifying the structure of the program, from its highest level (the program's ultimate function, such as running the accounting system for a business), through midlevel (such as modules that update inventory, or sort the customers in alphabetical order) to its lowest level of abstraction (the literal code of the program).

The next step is to filter out nonprotected material. Such material would first include "elements dictated by efficiency." If there were only a limited number of ways to efficiently store the information or to update the financial records, then such methods would not be protected. The court also indicated that "elements dictated by external factors" would be functional, and nonprotected. It made analogy to the scenes a faire doctrine, which denies protection to stock characters in literary works. Likewise, many elements in the computing environment are standard, like the Windows operating system or the use of personal computers. So elements in the program used to meet such standards might not be protected. The final step is to filter out elements that did not originate with the program's author, such as code or algorithms copied from others.

Computer Associates emphasizes filtering out all the unprotected functional or nonoriginal elements, to see if any nugget of original, creative expression remains. In practice, this leads to a very thin level of protection. In general, the literal code of the program is likely to be held copyrightable, because there are many different ways to write code to implement the various nonprotected functional features of the program. But elements any more general than that are likely to be identified as functional, because they serve efficiency or external factors or borrow from the works of others. Although *Computer Associates* has been widely followed by courts in the United States and even abroad, some courts and commentators warn that it can lead to insufficient protection for software.

An approach that might lead to greater protection is exemplified by *Softel v. Dragon Medical and Scientific Communications*, 118 F.3d 955 (2d Cir. 1997). *Softel* made a key point missing from *Computer Associates*. It is not enough to go through the elements of a work individually and ask whether each element is protected expression, as the *Computer Associates* seems to do in its filtration approach. Rather, individual unprotected elements may be put together in a way that is protected. The individual facts in a database are not protected, but an original selection or arrangement of those facts may be protected. The individual words in a poem are not protected, but the arrangement of those words in the poem is protected. So courts should also consider whether unprotected functional elements in a computer program were put together in an original, nonfunctional way. A computer program might qualify for protection as a *compilation* of unprotected elements.

Computer Associates stands for one approach—looking at the software and filtering out all unprotectable elements, to see if a protectable nugget remains. *Softel*, on the other hand, suggests looking at what the software developers have done, to see if they have shown originality in compiling unprotected elements.

Computer Associates and *Softel* dealt with nonliteral copying. Defendants did not literally copy the code of the program, rather wrote their own program that did similar things. Literal copying of the code will usually be infringement, because there are usually many ways to write code that expresses the various functions of the program. But the question may be more difficult where there is literal copying, not of the code, but of other elements of the program, such words or pictures that the user sees.

The leading case is *Lotus Development v. Borland Intl.*, 49 F.3d 807 (1st Cir. 1995). Lotus 1-2-3 was an immensely popular spreadsheet program, a program that allowed users to perform accounting functions and other finance tasks on a computer. The program was so popular that it fueled the popularity of early personal computers. Borland, seeking to lure Lotus users to Borland's less popular program, copied Lotus's "menu command hierarchy." In other words, Borland copied the exact commands (such as Copy, Print, or Quit) that 1-2-3 employed, as well its menu command hierarchy. Lotus had "469 commands arranged into more than 50 menus and submenus." *Lotus* presented a close call on the functionality/expression issue. Each command by itself was functional. Lotus could not claim protection in such functional (not to mention nonoriginal) commands as Copy or Print. But Borland also copied the intricate arrangement of those commands in various menus and submenus. That menu hierarchy would seem creative. There are millions of ways to arrange the commands into menus, and many of them would function just as well as the Lotus arrangement. The reason that Borland copied was to allow Lotus users to switch to Borland without learning a new set of menus (and to allow users to copy over their macros, which they could write themselves to implement series of commands).

The courts struggled with *Lotus*. The trial court held that the menu command hierarchy was protectable expression, on the theory that Lotus had chosen just one of many ways of implementing the idea of a menu command hierarchy. On appeal, the First Circuit took a narrow approach to the issue. Rather than approaching it in general terms, the court held that the menu command hierarchy was a "method of operation," one of the specific exclusions from copyright in §102 of the Copyright Act. The menu command hierarchy, in this view, was the means by which users control and operate the Lotus program. When the Supreme Court decided to hear the case, the computer industry and copyright lawyers eagerly awaited guidance on applying the functionality doctrine to software. But the Court split 4-4, thereby simply affirming the appellate court and without a written opinion. So *Lotus* leaves the extent of protection for software an open issue.

Examples

1. *The examined life.* Bug is a very busy person. She works as an independent software developer, takes evening courses in law, and helps run a family with four kids. She uses some of her precious time to write a computer program to give her more time. The program runs a calendar, maintains an updated contact list (friends, kids' friends, doctors, teachers, coaches), schedules a car pool, sends out e-mails of reminders and thank-yous, and performs various other mundane yet critical tasks. Bug uses the program herself, then sells copies to a few dozen people in town. She learns that one buyer, Abel, made several copies and sold them. Another buyer, Babel, watched Abel using the program a number of times and wrote another program that performed all the same tasks. The overall structure of the program is similar, but the code written to implement that structure is quite different. Have Abel or Babel infringed Bug's copyright?

2. *An elegant solution.* At work one day, Bug takes on the task of writing a program that will use publicly available data from a weather satellite to calculate the amount of energy a particular area receives in the form of sunlight. Bug tries various approaches to the problem. Finally, she comes up with a brilliant solution and writes an extremely short program that performs the task, ingeniously using only about six lines of code. Does Bug have a copyright in her short but powerful program?

3. *Let a thousand flowers bloom.* Blossom Software sells Wypo, a popular photo processing program that consumers use to manipulate digitized pictures. Wypo presents a user with commands such as Stretch, Copy, Print, and Even Out Colors. The user can make sophisticated changes by using these rather simple commands. The commands are arranged in various menus, which pop up for different tasks. A competitor develops a new spreadsheet program. To lure customers who are using Blossom's program, the competitor copies the commands and the pop-up menu structure. This way, a Blossom user can switch to the new program without learning a new set of commands and menus. By copying those elements, the new program is also compatible with other Blossom software products, making it more attractive to Blossom users. Has the competitor copied unprotected functional elements or protected creative expression?

4. *APIs?* Google wanted to make Android phones work with the widely used Java language. Unable to agree on a license with Oracle, the owner of Java, Google decided instead to independently develop software that worked with Java. Google did not copy the code that runs Java, but did copy the "structure, sequence, and organization" of the code that runs Java. To do that, Google also copied Java's APIs (application programming interfaces). In order for Android developers to use Java functions, Android copied the names and headers for the Java modules. For example, Google would copy the header for a method that compares numbers, "java.lang.Math.max," and then write code that does the comparison and returns a result. Did Google copy creative expression, which is protected by copyright, or functional matter, which is not copyrightable?

Explanations

1. Babel is not liable for infringement. Babel watched how the program worked and wrote one that performed the same functions. That is not infringement.

   Abel is potentially liable. Abel made several copies and sold them. Presumably, Abel copied not just the unprotected functional elements but also the protected expression of those elements in the literal lines of object code.

The example does not ask about a more difficult case, where some-one looked at the source code of the program in detail and copied closely in writing his or her own code. Addressing that question would require more facts about the program itself and the specific elements that were copied. This example just shows that, in general, wholesale literal copy-ing of software is likely to infringe, but simply copying the function of a program does not.

2. Bug probably does not have a copyright. In general, computer programs are protected by copyright. But this program is so short and written so ingeniously that it is probably denied copyright under the merger doc-trine. "Short programs may reveal high levels of creativity and may pre-sent simple, yet unique, solutions to programming quandaries. Just as a mathematician may develop an elegant proof, or an author may express ideas in a spare, simple, but creative manner, so a computer program-mer may develop a program that is brief and eligible for protection. But unless a creative flair is shown, a very brief program is less likely to be copyrightable because it affords fewer opportunities for original expres-sion." *Lexmark Intl. v. Static Control Components*, 387 F.3d 522, 542-543 (6th Cir. 2004) (citation omitted). The functional aspects of Bug's program are so closely identified with its short text that it is not copyrighted. Otherwise, Bug might effectively have exclusive rights in the function-ality of the program. If, however, a program could easily be written that did the same thing using different code, the answer would be different.

3. This example is drawn from the *Lotus* case. Courts have differed on whether such elements of software are protected by copyright. A narrow view of functionality (as in *Oracle v. Google*, discussed below) would deem the menu-command hierarchy to be protected expression. The unpro-tected idea is the use of a hierarchical set of commands to implement the photo editing program. The particular set of commands and menus chosen is only one possible expression of that idea. Another software developer could have achieved the same function with a completely dif-ferent set of commands.

Another view, consistent with *Lotus v. Borland*, concentrating on inter-preting the specific categories in 17 U.S.C. §102(b), could be that the set of commands is an unprotected "method of operation." The user uses the program by responding to the menus the program presents. Likewise, the set of commands could be deemed an unprotected "sys-tem": The set of commands functions together to perform the functions of the program.

Yet another view would be to deem the set of commands to be functional, simply because it is necessary to achieve compatibility with other Blossom products. Consumers have become accustomed to using Blossom's set of commands. Copying the elements also allows the new

97

program to interact with other Blossom software products. A court could hold that such compatibility characteristics make the set of commands functional (or that fair use authorizes copying in order to copy nonprotected elements, as discussed later in the chapter).

4. This case has created a split among the Federal Circuits on the scope of copyright protection for software. Under *Lotus*, this would seem like permitted copying of functional matter. The hierarchy of methods and wording of headers sounds like the hierarchy of menus and wording of menus that were held unprotected in *Lotus*. But the Federal Circuit took a different approach. *Oracle Am., Inc. v. Google Inc.*, 750 F.3d 1339 (Fed. Cir. 2014). Like the trial court in *Lotus*, it focused on whether there were other ways to accomplish the same function. There were: Google could have used a different taxonomy of methods and used different headers to have its own program to implement a programming language (although it would not have been compatible with Java). The holding, however, was quite narrow. The court remanded to the trial court to determine if Google was protected by fair use. Spoiler alert: not fair use, according to the 2018 Federal Circuit opinion in the case, as discussed later in this book.

Useful Articles

One class of works has a specific test of functionality. If a "pictorial, graphic, or sculptural work" is a "useful article," it is protectable only if its aesthetic features are separable from its utilitarian aspects. This specific rule applies only to a "useful article," a narrower category: "an article having an intrinsic utilitarian function that is not merely to portray the appearance of the article or to convey information." Maps, computer programs, and clocks are all useful things but not "useful articles" because they convey information. One case held that a toy airplane is not a useful article because it serves to play the role of an airplane in child's play. *See Gay Toys v. Buddy L. Corp.*, 703 F.2d 970 (6th Cir. 1983). The counterargument would be that the toy plays a purely functional role: something to play with. Whether the work is a useful article can be important because the separability rule has been interpreted differently from the general exclusion of functionality from copyright. Computer programs, for example, raise issues of functionality, but are not useful articles.

Courts had used several approaches to define separability. Some courts require physical separability. A creative lamp design is not protectable because the shape of the lamp is not physically separate from its functional aspect. *See Esquire, Inc. v. Ringer*, 591 F.2d 796, 807 (D.C. Cir. 1978). Other courts require "conceptual" separability. This can be understood several ways. There may be conceptual separability if the article has a useful function but is also shown to be appreciated for its aesthetic appeal. A belt buckle design could have separability if the buckles produced from it served to buckle belts, but also were displayed as artworks in a museum, sold to art collectors, or featured in design magazines. *See Kieselstein-Cord v. Accessories by Pearl*, 632 F.2d 989 (2d Cir. 1980). Another approach is to ask whether an individual thinks of the aesthetic aspects of the work as being separate from its functional aspects. Yet another approach considers the design process: There is separability only if the designer is able to make aesthetic choices that are unaffected by functional considerations. A serpentine bicycle rack design is unprotected because every change in the shape made for aesthetic purposes affects the function of the bike rack. *See Brandir Intl. v. Cascade Pac. Lumber*, 834 F.2d 1142 (2d Cir. 1985).

Clothing would usually be a useful article. Even if it serves to portray its own appearance, it also serves the purely utilitarian functions of clothing (clothing the person wearing it, keeping them warm). But some clothing might not go beyond portraying its appearance. A costume worn over other clothing might serve only to portray its own appearance.

A clothing design, then, is copyrightable only if its aesthetic elements are separable from its function. Generally, this bars copyright for clothing designs. A change in the design for aesthetic reasons (for example, changing the hemline, narrowing the shoulders, or making the pants wider) will affect the way the work functions as clothing. Function and form are generally so intertwined that copyright protection is negligible. As a result, copyright gives fashion designers little protection against copying (as long as the copier does not infringe the relevant *trademark*, as opposed to copyright). Knock-off designs are freely sold. Some have proposed changes in the copyright statute to give special protection for fashion designs. Others argue that the lack of legal protection has made the field more dynamic, because designers must rely on constant change and building a reputation as a market advantage.

As of 2017, clothing received more protection under *Varsity Brands*, which seemed to adopt the conceptual approach to separability. Is the header to a Java application programming interface similar to a cheerleading uniform? The Supreme Court increased the copyright protection for functional works, holding that cheerleader uniform designs were not precluded from protection as functional. The Court upheld copyright in the design of cheerleader uniforms, which consisted primarily of ""combinations, posi-tionings, and arrangements of elements" that include "chevrons . . . , lines, curves, stripes, angles, diagonals, inverted [chevrons], coloring, and shapes." "Varsity Brands replaced a number of vague tests formulated by courts over the years with a single, if elusive, test: "In sum, a feature of the design of a useful article is eligible for copyright if, when identified and imagined apart from the useful article, it would qualify as a pictorial, graphic, or sculptural work either on its own or when fixed in some other tangible medium."

> Applying this test to the surface decorations on the cheerleading uniforms is straightforward. First, one can identify the decorations as features having pictorial, graphic, or sculptural qualities. Second, if the arrangement of colors, shapes, stripes, and chevrons on the surface of the cheerleading uniforms were

separated from the uniform and applied in another medium — for example, on a painter's canvas — they would qualify as "two-dimensional . . . works of . . . art," §101. And imaginatively removing the surface decorations from the uniforms and applying them in another medium would not replicate the uniform itself. Indeed, respondents have applied the designs in this case to other media of expression — different types of clothing — without replicating the uniform. The decorations are therefore separable from the uniforms and eligible for copyright protection.

The direct effect is more protection for fashion design, until now ripe for knock-offs. The Courts' decision could also be read broadly, to lead to more protection for other functional works, like computer programs.

To summarize the useful article analysis: The first question is whether the work is a useful article under the statutory definition. If it is a useful article, the next question is whether it has "pictorial, graphic, or sculptural features that can be identified separately from, and are capable of existing independently of, the utilitarian aspects." If it does have such separable aesthetic elements, it may be copyrightable. Otherwise, it is not. If the item does not fall within the definition of useful article, then it still must have original, creative elements to be protected, and its functional aspects will not be protected. A map, for example, is not a useful article. But whether a particular program is protectable depends on analyzing its elements to determine whether it has the necessary original, creative expression to qualify for protection.

The Copyright Office's regulations on the copyrightability of costume designs illustrate the analysis well, giving an example of the major variations on the theme:

> The examining practices with respect to masks will not treat masks as useful articles, but will instead determine registrability on the existence of minimum pictorial and/or sculptural authorship. Garment designs (excluding separately identifiable pictorial representations of designs imposed upon the garment) will not be registered even if they contain ornamental features, or are intended to be used as historical or period dress. Fanciful costumes will be treated as useful articles, and will be registered only upon a finding of separately identifiable pictorial and/or sculptural authorship.

Copyright Office, Library of Congress, Registrability of Costume Designs, 56 FR 56530 (1991). Under this view, masks are not useful articles, because they serve only to portray their own appearance. Garments are useful articles (worn to clothe the person), so they are subject to the separability rule — and generally will not have separable elements because each part of the garment usually plays a functional role. Fanciful costumes (like a Wookie costume) are also useful articles, subject to the separability analysis. But they will sometimes pass the separability test because they may have separable pictorial or sculptural elements.

Examples

1. *Useful articles?* Only "useful articles" are subject to the separability requirement to qualify for copyright protection. Which of the following are useful articles? Of those, which meet the separability requirement?
   a. Swiss army knife
   b. Instruction manual for a car
   c. A human dummy, used in anatomy classes
   d. A radiator cover, with an ornate design
   e. A car engine
   f. Design of an automobile body

2. *Mannequin.* Pad designs a human torso form, which is used to display clothing. In designing the form, Pad attempts to make it both realistic looking and well suited for draping clothing. The form works very well, and a number of stores and clothing designers seek to buy from Pad. Another designer, Sad, copies Pad's form exactly and offers a similar form at a lower price. Has Sad copied protected expression?

3. *Man again.* Tad creates a sculpture of a human torso. Tad's sculpture is quite realistic, capturing a form that is both lifelike and aesthetically appealing. Is the sculpture protected expression?

4. *Stolen act.* Ved the Magician devises ingenious ways to make pigeons appear from his sleeve, mice to disappear from boxes, and playing cards to pop up on demand. Roman attends Ved's shows, figures out the tricks, and incorporates them in Roman's act. Copyright infringement?

Explanations

1. A useful article is "an article having an intrinsic utilitarian function that is not merely to portray the appearance of the article or to convey information."
   a. A Swiss army knife is a useful article. It has numerous utilitarian functions (cutting, opening bottles, unscrewing screws, opening cans) and does not merely portray its own appearance or convey information.
   b. A car's instruction manual is useful but is not a "useful article." It has a utilitarian purpose, but that is to convey information.
   c. A human dummy, designed for use in anatomy classes, is not a useful article. It serves both to portray its own appearance and to convey information.
   d. The radiator cover is a useful article. It is ornamental but does not serve to "merely" portray its own appearance. Rather, it has other, utilitarian functions (hiding the radiator and preventing burns).
   e. A car engine is a useful article. It satisfies the statutory definition.

f. A car body is a useful article. Like the radiator cover, it has both aesthetic and utilitarian functions.

Of the useful articles, the designs of the Swiss army knife and the car engine are very likely unprotected because they lack utilitarian aspects separable from their aesthetic features. Whether the designs of the automobile body and radiator cover are protected depends on which test of separability the court employs. Both designs lack physical separability. The automobile body might also lack conceptual separability under the design process test because any change in the design would affect the functional aspects — if the shape were changed, that would affect the aerodynamics. But if the broader approach were used, the aesthetic aspects would be shown by displays in museums and in magazines. The radiator cover likely passes all the conceptual separability tests. The variations in design do not affect its function. It also had aesthetic features that make one appreciate it separately as an artwork.

2. The torso form is a useful article. It has a utilitarian function (to drape clothes) and does not serve to convey information. Accordingly, it is protected only if its aesthetic features are separable from its utilitarian aspects. The design lacks physical separability, so a court using that test would hold it unprotected. Because its design is geared solely toward its utilitarian role, it probably also lacks conceptual separability. Under the design process test, none of the design choices are free of functional considerations. Even under the broader approaches, separability is lacking. The aesthetic features still are linked to the utilitarian aspects. There is no suggestion that it can be appreciated simply as a work of sculpture. Cf. *Carol Barnhart, Inc. v. Economy Cover Corp.*, 773 F.2d 411 (2d Cir. 1985). The result would be different if the mannequin also had purely expressive features, not affected by its functional role, such as sculptural elements designed to give it a "hungry look." See *Pivot Point Intl., Inc. v. Charlene Products*, 372 F.3d 913, 931 (7th Cir. 2004).

3. Tad's sculpture of a human torso is probably protected. It is not a "useful article." As a sculpture, it has no utilitarian function. Therefore, it is not subject to the separability test. Rather, whether it is functional would be determined by the general functionality analysis (which varies from court to court, as discussed above). Under any approach, however, a pure sculpture likely is not functional.

4. No infringement, if Roman has copied only Ved's methods. See *Rice v. Fox Broad. Co.*, 330 F.3d 1170 (9th Cir. 2003). A magic trick is functional, because it accomplishes a specific task. As long as Roman did not copy Ved's patter or creative elements not part of the workings of the tricks, he would not infringe.

INFRINGING WORKS

Infringing works are barred copyright. Sylvester Stallone wrote and starred in three movies about a plucky boxer, Rocky Balboa. Anderson wrote a thirty-one page treatment for a proposed "Rocky IV" and met with Stallone's movie company, but no deal developed. Later, Anderson claimed copyright infringement, alleging that Stallone used the treatment in making *Rocky IV*. But Anderson's treatment infringed, as an unauthorized derivative work of the Rocky movies. Anderson could not sue Stallone for copyright infringement, because Anderson had no copyright to infringe. *Anderson v. Stallone,* 1989 U.S. Dist. LEXIS 11109 (C.D. Cal. Apr. 25, 1989).

Copyright does not protect material created by infringing another copyright. Under 17 U.S.C. §103(a), "protection for a work employing pre-existing material in which copyright subsists does not extend to any part of the work in which such material has been used unlawfully." In part, this rule reinforces the originality requirement. If Author's novel includes a chapter lifted word for word from another novel, Author has no copyright protection in that chapter because it was not original with her.

But the rule is broader than simply barring copyright to the copied material. The rule bars copyright for "any part" of a work in which infringing material is used. It bars copyright for original expression that was created by unlawful use of other works. Suppose Author takes another's short story and expands it into a novel. If Author only copies the unprotected ideas, of course, there is no infringement. But if Author copies protected expression, there is no protection for any part that used material from the short story.

This is different from patent law, where anyone may seek a patent on an improvement on a patented invention. The second inventor may not be able to practice the improvement without infringing, but the first inventor likewise cannot practice the invention without infringing the improvement patent. In copyright, one who builds on an existing work has no copyright in the parts using infringing material, meaning the first author can use those parts without infringing.

What constitutes a "part" of a work remains an open question. For example, every chapter of a book might make unauthorized use of material from another copyrighted book. A court could reason that because each chapter makes unlawful use of material, each chapter is not protected, making the entire work unprotected even if Author adds much original expressive material. Likewise, if Author instead makes a film closely based on the story, a court could deny copyright to the entire film. Another approach is for the court to separate out portions that do not use protected material and to hold those portions to be copyrightable.

Examples

1. *Guitar.* The musician sometimes known as Prince often refers to himself with an elaborate, unpronounceable, copyrighted symbol of his own devising. He gives permission to various entities to use the symbol on T-shirts and other products. An instrument maker fashions a guitar in the shape of the symbol and shows it to Prince. Soon, Prince appears in concert with a similar guitar. Is Prince liable for copyright infringement?

2. *Payback Day?* Suppose that the makers of the film *Groundhog Day* used ideas copied without permission from the novel *One Fine Day*. That does not constitute copyright infringement because ideas are not protected by copyright. The writer of *One Fine Day* obtains a copy of *Groundhog Day* and starts making copies and selling them to the public. The writer argues that *Groundhog Day* is itself not protected by copyright because the complete film is based on ideas taken without permission from another work. Is *Groundhog Day* unprotected by copyright?

3. *Free for all?* Andre writes a novel, *My Birthday*. Bootles unscrupulously copies in wholesale fashion from *My Birthday* in writing his novel, *Bad Dog Day*. Every part of *Bad Dog Day* makes ample use of original creative expression from *My Birthday*. Clever then makes and sells copies of *Bad Dog Day* without permission from Andre or from Bootles. Clever contends that her actions are not copyright infringement. *Bad Dog Day* is unprotected by copyright because it copies so much from *My Birthday*. Accordingly, Clever argues, it is not infringement to copy or sell copies of *Bad Dog Day*. Has Clever copied protected expression — and if so, whose?

Explanations

1. Prince is not liable for infringement. The guitar design was based on the copyright symbol. Assuming it was infringement to copy the symbol, there is no copyright in any part of the guitar design using the symbol. Assuming the entire design depended on the symbol, because it set the shape of the guitar, the entire design of the guitar would be noncopyrightable. There would be no infringement for copying it. *See Pickett v. Prince*, 207 F.3d 402, 406 (7th Cir. 2000). Note also that some elements of a guitar's design would be functional, and therefore noncopyrightable.

2. *Groundhog Day* is protected by copyright. The bar to copyright for works making unauthorized use of preexisting material applies only to "unlawful" use of such material. Copying of ideas is not unlawful. To the contrary, the nonprotection of ideas is intended to encourage the copying of ideas by authors. Copyright encourages the free flow of ideas by providing enough protection for the creation of works, but not so much protection to discourage the free use of ideas.

3. Clever has copied protected expression—from *My Birthday*. Every part of *Bad Dog Day* makes unlawful use of infringing material copied from *My Birthday*, so *Bad Dog Day* is denied copyright entirely. So copying *Bad Dog Day* does not infringe any copyright in *Bad Dog Day*. But anyone who makes literal copies of *Bad Dog Day* does copy protected expression from *My Birthday* (because that expression had been copied into *Bad Dog Day*). Therefore, such a copier infringes the copyright in *My Birthday*. So the fact that *Bad Dog Day* is not protected by copyright does not effectively put *My Birthday* into the public domain.

GOVERNMENT WORKS

The Copyright Act is not copyrighted. Copyright protection "is not available for any work of the United States Government." 17 U.S.C. §105. The statute defines a "work of the United States Government" as "a work prepared by an officer or employee of the United States Government as part of that person's official duties." 17 U.S.C. §101. This rule denies copyright to thousands of works produced by federal employees: court opinions, federal laws and regulations, administrative reports, official photographs, and much more. NASA, for example, produces many wonderful noncopyrighted photographs and videos.

The rule does not bar copyright if the author is an independent contractor, as opposed to a federal employee. So a photographer hired for a particular event would take copyrighted photographs. Nor does the bar apply to work by federal employees that is not part of their official duties. So a senator's diary or the personal photos taken by a soldier are copyrighted. Moreover, the provision authorizes the federal government to acquire ownership of copyrights—even if the government funded and directed the work, and required transfer of copyright as part of the contract. *See Schnapper v. Foley*, 667 F.2d 102 (D.C. Cir. 1981).

Several policies support the rule against copyright in U.S. government works. Copyright gives the copyright holder exclusive rights to copy, distribute, adapt, perform, and display the work. People need access to government works for many reasons: to obey the law, to participate in government programs, and so on. To permit the government to limit access to some official works would run contrary to the principles of due process. Moreover, copyright in government works would create a potential for censorship. Finally, the purpose of copyright is to provide an incentive to produce works. But if the government is funding and directing the work, the incentive rationale has less force.

The statute by its term applies only to works of the federal government. The United States has three sets of sovereigns: the federal government, the states, and Indian tribes. Relying on the due process rationale, courts have extended the rule to other legal documents that create legal obligations, such as state or tribal statutes and judicial opinions. But less settled is whether the rule applies to other government-produced documents, such as the reports of state or tribal administrative agencies, and governmental maps. In deciding whether copyright applies, courts can look to the basic purposes behind the bar: the notice required by due process of law, the incentive provided by copyright to create works, and issues of free speech. The Copyright Office has taken the position that

> [e]dicts of government, such as judicial opinions, administrative rulings, legislative enactments, public ordinances, and similar official legal documents, are not copyrightable for reasons of public policy. This applies to such works whether they are Federal, State, or local as well as to those of foreign governments.

Compendium II: Copyright Office Practices 305.08(d).

Another issue arises when a work created by a private party becomes part of the law. A private party could draft an ordinance that is adopted by a municipality. If Citizen made a copy of the ordinance, she would also be making a copy of the private party's draft code. Authority is split on whether adoption of the code by a government puts the text into the public domain.[2]

Examples

1. *Entitled to my opinion.* Handy, a federal judge, writes a draft of a blistering dissent in the case of *Soda v. Pop.* The draft sets forth Handy's unorthodox views on the doctrine of equivalents, interspersed with ad hominem attacks on the other judges on the panel. After reconsideration, Handy decides not to submit the opinion, but simply to join in the majority opinion. She thinks she has destroyed every copy of the draft. Much to her dismay, she learns that the *National Jaw Journal* has obtained a copy and plans to publish it. She seeks to prevent publication, claiming the copyright in the opinion. A draft opinion that was never submitted, she argues, does not have the force of law and therefore should not be treated as a government work. Is the draft opinion copyrighted?

---

2. The Fifth Circuit has held that when a model code was enacted into law, it became unprotected by copyright under the merger doctrine. *See Veeck v. Southern Bldg. Code Congress,* 293 F.3d 791 (5th Cir. 2002) (en banc); *see also Building Officials & Code Admin. v. Code Tech.,* 628 F.2d 730 (1st Cir. 1980) (expressing doubts about enforceability of copyright in privately authored building code) and *Practice Mgt. Info. Corp. v. Am. Med. Assn.,* 121 F.3d 516 (9th Cir. 1997) (holding governmental regulations requiring compliance with medical procedure code did not render copyright unenforceable).

2. *Article of impeachment.* Dandy, another federal judge, drafts an article about ceramics. The article has nothing to do with Dandy's duties but is written for purely personal purposes. The article argues that ceramics have played a hitherto unappreciated role in historical developments. The article is based more on Dandy's imagination than on historical research. Is the article a nonprotected U.S. government work? Would it make a difference if the article were actually written by Dandy's law clerk, acting on Dandy's orders, working in his office during normal office hours?

3. *Brief encounter.* Advo submits an amicus brief in the case of *Soda v. Pop*. Advo, a beverage lawyer, is deeply interested in the issues raised by the case and submits the brief to suggest to the court a resolution that balances various competing policies. Months later, Advo is surprised to see her brief reprinted in *Vending Machine Law Journal*. The editors of the journal tell Advo that they did not ask her permission for publication because a brief submitted in a federal case is a U.S. government work, unprotected by copyright. Did Advo produce an uncopyrighted work?

4. *Animal farm.* The U.S. Department of Agriculture decides to make an entertaining documentary about methane as an alternative energy source, intended for instructional use in high schools. It has a number of employees in its film production department, but they are all booked on other projects. The Department pays an independent contractor a lump sum to write and produce the film, leaving all the creative and production details up to the contractor. The contract stipulates that the copyright in the film belongs to the U.S. government. The film is completed and copies are distributed to a number of teachers. Gadfly, an activist, obtains a copy, and then makes and sells copies. Gadfly argues that the film is not protected by copyright because it is really a product of the federal government. Otherwise, Gadfly contends, the U.S. government could engage in the sort of limits on distribution of publicly financed works that the statute seeks to prevent. Is the film a U.S. government work?

5. *Slowpoke County maps.* Slowpoke County prepares "info maps," which provide lots of information about Slowpoke County. Slowpoke prepares the maps by having employees sift information from Slowpoke's public real estate and other records, as well as various sources of data in the local public library and online. The maps provide much information about the Slowpoke's economic and social makeup. Reading the map gives its viewer an overall picture of the businesses, schools, residences, farms, and other community-related organizations that make up the county. Slowpoke makes the maps to promote the county. Slowpoke sells the maps for a modest price to real estate agents, investors, tourists, historians, and various others interested in such data. Slowpoke's revenue from the maps almost exactly matches its costs. Indeed, without the revenue, Slowpoke's council well might not authorize the activity. Floyd, the local barber,

makes a copy of one of the maps and begins selling them to Slowpoke's usual buyers for half the price. Floyd argues that Slowpoke cannot claim a copyright in a government-produced work. Are the maps copyrightable?

6. *Copyright a patent?* Christopher invents an automatic macaroni-and-cheese maker. He drafts a patent application. The application has two principal parts: the written description, which artfully describes the device and how to make it, and the claims, which set the boundaries of his claimed rights. The U.S. Patent and Trademark Office allows the claims and issues a patent. The patent contains the written description and claims, which taken together define the scope of Christopher's rights.

   Andy, writing a book on patent law, considers including portions of Christopher's patent in a book on software law. A Patent Office regulation permits facsimile reproduction of the entire patent (37 1.71(e)), but that would take up too much space in Andy's book. Does Andy need Christopher's permission? Would it be different if Andy were writing a book about food technology?

7. *Monumental.* The U.S. government is holding a competition seeking a design for a monument to the Space Shuttle. Frank submits the winning design. In negotiations, Frank declines to assign the copyright to the government. He still gets the contract, and builds the monument. Is it copyrighted?

Explanations

1. The draft opinion is not subject to copyright. Handy is a federal employee, so any work she creates as part of her official duties is a noncopyrightable work of the U.S. government. The statute does not differentiate between categories of work but applies across the board. So whether the draft is submitted, has legal effect, or ever sees the light of day is irrelevant. The only question is whether Handy prepared it as part of her official duties. Had she vented her feelings in a personal diary, the result would be different. But preparation of draft opinions is well within the scope of a judge's official duties.

2. The article is not a U.S. government work, which is work prepared by a federal officer or employee within the scope of that person's official duties. A federal judge's official duties include presiding over cases, drafting opinions, and participating in the administration of the courts. An article on ceramics written for purely personal purposes does not qualify because it is a personal project.

   If the law clerk drafts it, the article is a nonprotected U.S. government work. The law clerk is a federal employee, and her duties probably include following the orders of her boss, including drafting the article. From her point of view (unlike Dandy), the writing is not a personal work but is a part of her job.

3. Advo is not a federal employee, so her brief is not a U.S. government work. Nor is it denied protection under the judicial doctrine denying protection to official legal documents. The brief may set forth Advo's view of the law, but it does not authoritatively establish law, unlike a judicial opinion or legislative edict. By custom, lawyers have rarely enforced copyright in briefs or other documents that are made part of the public record—and the fair use doctrine (discussed in Chapter 5) authorizes some uses of such works.

4. The film is not a U.S. government work. It is a copyrighted work, with the copyright owned by the U.S. government. The statute, by its terms, applies only to works prepared by U.S. officials or employees. The film was prepared by an independent contractor, who is neither an official nor an employee. The statute also specifically permits the United States to acquire ownership of copyrights. The statute contemplates that the United States will indeed have exclusive rights in some works, with the attendant ability to restrict their reproduction, distribution, and performance by others. Moreover, the work at issue does not raise the sort of censorship or due process issues that might arise if, for example, the United States commissioned contractors to prepare judicial opinions and then sought to restrict their distribution.

5. The maps probably would not be denied copyright, although they are government works. In deciding whether official legal documents should be noncopyrightable, courts look to whether individuals require access to the works to have knowledge of the law, and to the incentive rationale behind copyright. The maps contain much information, but no one requires access to the maps to comply with the law. The information is available in publicly accessible sources. In addition, the incentive rationale applies here. If not for the ability to raise revenue from the maps, Slowpoke might not produce them at all. Making such maps is not necessary for fulfillment of the county's basic governmental activities, so it is not an activity that would occur with or without copyright in the maps. A court might also consider whether granting copyright creates a risk of government censorship. When the information is freely available elsewhere (if in a less handy form), censorship would not appear to be a risk.

6. The patent is a U.S. government work, so is not copyrighted, but it includes material from a preexisting work—Christopher's patent application. The question would be whether Andy would potentially infringe the copyright (if any) in Christopher's patent application. Presumably, the patent application would be copyrightable as an original work of authorship. It would contain many functional elements but would likely easily meet the low standard of creativity required. The issue is what effect it has when the application is then largely copied into a patent issued by the U.S.

government, a document that has the legal effect of defining legal rights. There are several possible approaches a court might take.

Merger. Under *Veeck*, a court might reason that, like a privately drafted code adopted into law, the text is now inseparable from the law (an idea) and therefore unprotected. But that seems to take the *Veeck* approach too far, to strip copyright from every document with legal effect.

Official government work. A court might consider several policies: the notice required by due process of law, the incentive provided by copyright to create works, and issues of free speech. The court could reason that the public needs access to patents (to avoid infringement, etc.), that the patent right is plenty of incentive to draft patents, and that free discussion of patent rights requires they be uncopyrighted.

Fair use. The best result would allow a balancing of interests. A court might hold that Christopher does not lose his copyright, but the patent text is subject to broad fair use (discussed later in the book), such as inclusion in a patent law text. One might argue that using the description in a technology book is not a fair use, because it does not depend on the legal nature of the patent but rather is simply using Christopher's description. But one factor in fair use (to jump ahead a little) is the nature of the work. Christopher drafted the application hoping his text would wind up in a U.S. patent, so he might have expected to be subject to use of the text by others. This case would differ from a case where a novel became evidence in a precedential case (defamation, copyright infringement). In that case, the relevant portions of the novel would be fair use for legal discussion, but the author would not lose her entire copyright.

Estoppel. To throw in some more review: Just as one forfeits copyright protection by representing creative expression as facts, so too one might forfeit copyright by drafting something with the expectation that it be included in an official legal document. A party could implicitly consent to that by filing its application with the USPTO.

The USPTO allows an applicant to include a copyright notice, provided the applicant includes the following authorization:

> A portion of the disclosure of this patent document contains material which is subject to copyright protection. The copyright owner has no objection to the facsimile reproduction by anyone of the patent document or the patent disclosure, as it appears in the Patent and Trademark Office patent file or records, but otherwise reserves all copyright rights whatsoever.

7. The monument is copyrighted. It was created not by a federal employee but by an independent contractor. For the same reason (Frank is not an employee), the work made for hire doctrine does not apply. Frank owns the copyright. *See Gaylord v. United States*, 595 F.3d 1364 (Fed. Cir. 2010).

Obtaining Protection and Licensing: Ownership, Formalities, Duration

This chapter discusses ownership of copyright, licensing, duration of protection, and the formalities of notice, registration, and deposit.

INITIAL OWNERSHIP OF COPYRIGHT

Copywriters may not get copyrights. If an advertising agency's employee writes copy or draws graphics for an ad campaign, the copyright in the work will belong to the employer agency, not the employee—unless the agency has agreed in writing that the copyright will belong to the employee (unlikely) or to the client who paid for it (quite likely). Where several parties are involved in creating a work (whether paying for it, physically creating it, or contributing material), we may ask, which one owns the copyright? If the parties have agreed in writing as to who will own the copyright, then it will be assigned however they agreed. Well-advised parties always do this. But in many cases, creative works are made without alerting the lawyers. In the absence of agreement, copyright provides default rules that assign ownership.

Copyright subsists from the first time the work is created. 17 U.S.C. §302(a). The author initially owns the copyright. She may transfer any or all of her rights or may allow others to exercise those rights. To determine ownership of a copyright (or of some of the exclusive rights of the copyright), one needs to determine two things. Who is the author or authors (and therefore the initial owner of the copyright)? Has ownership of the copyright (or some of the rights of the copyright holder) been effectively transferred to someone else (and if so, was such transfer subsequently terminated pursuant to contract or a statutory right)?

Suppose Writer writes a story. The copyright vests initially in the author or authors of the work. 17 U.S.C. §201(a). The general rule is that the actual creator of the work is the author. If, however, Writer is an employee creating a "work made for hire," her employer is deemed to be the author and owns the copyright. If Writer is a reporter employed by a newspaper company, the newspaper company is the author of the stories written by Writer. By contrast, if Writer is an independent contractor and has not made a valid agreement that the work is a work made for hire, Writer is the author and initially owns the copyright. If a newspaper hires her as a freelancer to write a single story, Writer initially owns the copyright in the story. If she is a joint author, she is a co-owner of the copyright. If the work is a collective work, then the various copyright holders retain the copyright to their respective contributions, and the author of the collective work has a copyright limited to reproducing the entire work and its revisions. If Writer's story is included in an edition of the newspaper, the newspaper owns the copyright in the collective work (the edition of the newspaper), but Writer retains her copyright in the story (assuming again she has not signed the copyright over to the newspaper).

Ownership of the copyright has important consequences. Suppose business hires Software Developer to write a program that performs the accounting, inventory, and other functions for the business. The parties say nothing in the contract about ownership of the copyright. The copyright owner has the exclusive rights to copy, adapt, distribute, publicly perform, and publicly display the work. If it is a work for hire, the business owns the copyright. If it is not a work for hire, Software Developer owns the copyright. Business would presumably have implicit permission to make copies or adapt the program for the purposes of the contract. But Software Developer, not the business, owns the exclusive rights to sell copies to any similar business, adapt the program to other uses, and so on. If it is a joint work, they are co-owners of the copyright, and both can exercise the exclusive rights.

The rules assigning ownership are gap-filling rules. The parties can agree among themselves as to who will own the copyright. These days, most employees sign contracts assigning to their employer copyright in their works. Ownership of copyright should likewise be specified in contracts with consultants, freelancers, architects, actors, software consultants, and joint venture partners. A party hiring an independent contractor can secure an assignment of the copyright in the work. Joint authors can agree that the copyright in the work will belong to a single author or to a third party (such as a corporation formed by the joint authors). So the ownership assignment rules come into play only if the parties have not effectively addressed the issue. If the question is, Who owns the copyright?, the answer should be in the contract. If it is not, then we look to rules such as work made for hire and joint author.

Who Is the Author?

The copyright initially belongs to the author or authors of the work. When a work is created, one of the following situations will apply:

- *The author is an individual:* If the author is an individual, she initially owns the copyright.
- *The work is a work made for hire:* In this case, the hiring party owns the copyright. There are two types of works made for hire:
  1. works by employees within the scope of their employment; and
  2. certain specially order or commissioned works, where the parties expressly agree in writing that it is a work made for hire.
- *The work is by joint authors:* The joint authors are co-owners, with equal, undivided interests in the copyright.
- *The work is a collective work:* The author of the collective work will have a thin copyright in the work as a whole, but authors of individual portions may retain their separate copyrights.

Typical disputes over ownership include disputes between a hiring party and a hired creator; disputes over whether the work was a work made for hire; and disputes between the primary author of a work and another who contributed to the work, over whether the work was a joint work.

The ownership-assignment rules above are subject to transfers of the copyright. For example, if Scribbler has signed an agreement transferring copyright in her novels to Publisher, then Publisher will own the copyrights, even though Scribbler is the author of the novels. The copyright will initially vest in Scribbler and then be transferred to Publisher. So, if we ask who owns the copyright, the first place to check is whether the parties involved agreed in writing as to who would own the copyright. If not, the following rules govern.

Individual Works

The statute does not define "author." Usually, there is no question as to who could claim authorship. If Poet pens an ode, Mime choreographs a pantomime, or Crooner doodles a ditty, each owns the respective copyright (assuming none is working as an employee). Where more than one person produces the work, a single person may nevertheless be deemed the author of the work, even if he did not actually perform any of the hands-on labor in fixing the work. If more than one person claims to be the author, courts look to such factors as who initiated the work, who contributed original creative expression, who controlled the production of the work, whom the parties considered to be the author, and whom third parties recognized as the author. For example, the undersea filming of the wreck of the *Titanic* required the participation of many people who could man the surface ship and the submarine filming unit. But a single person could be the author if he did the following: directed the filming, specified the camera angles and shooting sequences, held daily planning sessions with the film crew to give them detailed instructions for filming, directed the crew's work from the surface, and screened the footage each day to see that it was satisfactory to him. *Lindsay v. The Wrecked and Abandoned Vessel* Titanic, 52 U.S.P.Q. 2d 1609 (S.D.N.Y. 1999).

Example

Image conscious. Paparazzi, a self-employed photographer, lingers outside the entrance to Celebrity's apartment building. When Celebrity emerges, Paparazzi takes a photo of Celebrity walking by a garbage can. When Paparazzi seeks to license the photo to various tabloids, Celebrity claims copyright in the photo. Celebrity argues that the photo has value only because of her hard work in establishing her fame, and therefore the right to exploit that fame belongs to Celebrity. Who owns the copyright in the photo?

Explanation

Paparazzi owns the copyright in the photo. Celebrity may have done all the work to establish the public interest in Celebrity, but the copyrighted work at issue is simply the photograph, with its image of Celebrity. Paparazzi is clearly the author of the photo. In deciding authorship, courts consider such factors as who initiated the work, who contributes creative expression, who controls the creation of the work, who makes the creative decisions, and who third parties would consider the author. All of those factors weigh toward Paparazzi being the author. Nor is it a joint work (discussed below), which requires (1) that each author contribute copyrightable expression and (2) that each author intend to be a joint author when the work is created. Celebrity would not meet either of those requirements. Note that Paparazzi's copyright does not give unlimited rights to use the photo; it confers only the exclusive rights of a copyright owner. Certain commercial uses of the photo would make Paparazzi liable under trademark law or right of publicity law.

Works Made for Hire

Suppose a hired party creates a sculpture, dance, book, software program, movie. . . . The contract between the parties should spell out who owns the copyright. If not, we first ask if it is a work made for hire.

If the work is a work made for hire, the employer is deemed to be the author and, unless the parties agree otherwise, owns the copyright. According to 17 U.S.C. §101, a work is a work made for hire if the following are true:

1. the work was prepared by an employee within the scope of her employment; or
2. the work
   a. is specially ordered or commissioned; *and*
   b. falls into one of nine specific categories (a contribution to a collective work, a part of a motion picture or other audiovisual work, a translation, a supplementary work, a compilation, an instructional text, a test, answer material for a test, or an atlas); *and*
   c. the parties sign an agreement designating it to be a work made for hire.

The first category applies to many works, vesting the copyright in the employer: manuals written by technical writers employed by a software company; advertisements (copy, visuals, and editing) created by employees of an advertising agency; a brief written by an associate at a law firm. The second category applies more narrowly because it requires a specific agreement and only applies to the specific categories. It applies when a newspaper agrees with a freelancer that a story constitutes a work for hire or if a movie producer hires a freelance scriptwriter and the parties agree that the script is a work for hire.

As in tax law and employment law, it is not always clear whether someone is an employee or an independent contractor. *Comty. for Creative Non-Violence v. Reid*, 490 U.S. 730 (1989), set the rule for determining whether a work is made for hire. In CCNV, a nonprofit organization hired a sculptor to create a sculpture of a homeless family. After the sculpture was complete, the parties disputed ownership of the copyright. The Supreme Court held that the classification of the hired party follows the common law of agency, looking to such factors as the following:

- the hiring party's right to control the manner and means by which the product is accomplished;
- the source of the instrumentalities and tools;
- the location of the work (such as the hiring party's place of business or the hired party's home);
- the duration of the relationship between the parties;
- whether the hiring party has the right to assign additional projects to the hired party;
- the extent of the hired party's discretion over when and how long to work;
- the method of payment;

- the hired party's role in hiring and paying assistants;
- whether the work is part of the regular business of the hiring party;
- whether the hiring party is in business;
- the provision of employee benefits;
- the tax treatment of the hired party.

Applying these factors, the Court held that the sculpture was not a work made for hire, so the sculptor owned the copyright. CCNV did direct the work to some extent, suggesting that the family be portrayed reclining on a steam grate and ensuring in other ways that the sculpture met their specifications. But the other factors weighed heavily in favor of holding that the sculptor was an independent contractor, as opposed to an employee. Working as a sculptor is a "skilled occupation." He supplied his own tools and worked in his own studio without daily supervision by CCNV. The contract was for only two months. CCNV had no right to assign other tasks to him. He had complete freedom in deciding "when and how long to work." The contract price was payable upon completion of the job, a typical way to pay independent contractors, as opposed to a typical employee's salary. Nor did CCNV "pay payroll or social security; taxes, provide any employee benefits, or contribute to unemployment insurance or workers' compensation funds."

Not everything an employee creates is a work for hire. It must also be within the scope of her employment. Courts also follow agency law here, considering several factors:

1. whether the work is of the type that the employee is employed to perform;
2. whether the work occurs substantially within authorized work hours; and
3. whether its purpose, at least in part, is to serve the employer.

A writer who writes an article at home outside office hours may nevertheless create a work for hire if he wrote on topics within his job description, coauthored and discussed the article with a fellow employee, and received reimbursement to present the paper at a symposium. See Marshall v. Miles Laboratories, 647 F. Supp. 1326, 1331 (N.D. Ind. 1986). Likewise, software may be a work made for hire, even though written by a chemist, if it performed functions within his general work responsibilities. See Miller v. CP Chemicals, 808 F. Supp. 1238 (D.S.C. 1992).

The second category of works for hire includes works made by non-employees. Usually, if an independent contractor creates the work, it is not a work made for hire, but the statute does permit the parties to agree that some such works will be treated as works made for hire. For example, if Publisher commissions Scholar to make a translation of a book, the parties can effectively agree that the translation will be a work made for hire. Publisher will therefore be the author and own the copyright.

Mere assignment of ownership is not the reason for the rule. The parties can always agree to a transfer of ownership of the copyright, so Publisher and Scholar could simply have agreed that Publisher would own the copyright. Likewise, for works that do not fall within the specific categories, the parties can still agree that the hiring party will own the copyright. Indeed, if they agree that it is a work made for hire, a court may simply treat that as an assignment of ownership.

But work made for hire status has other effects (discussed later in the book): the duration of copyright is different; for works of visual art, there are no moral rights under §106A; and there are no rights of termination. The latter is of the most practical importance. Those are not subject to change by agreement of the parties. So when Scholar agrees that the translation will be a work made for hire, Scholar effectively gives up any rights to terminate the transfer. Likewise, if the screenwriter, sound track composer, and director of a film all agree that their contributions will be works made for hire, they will have no rights to terminate the transfers.

Examples

1. *Go-getter.* Snaps has been a full-time employee of Tabloid for many years. Snaps's job is to take pictures of celebrities. Tabloid pays Snaps a regular paycheck (subject to withholding all relevant employee taxes, such as Social Security and income taxes) and offers participation in the company employee retirement plan. Tabloid assigns Snaps to photograph specified celebrities and also instructs Snaps to photograph celebrities if the opportunity arises by chance during another assignment. Tabloid also provides considerable support, including equipment, reimbursement of expenses, and help with logistics. Snaps discusses various matters with editors in general terms but has great discretion in fulfilling his duties. Snaps's work hours are largely set by Tabloid, although Snaps sometimes fits in jobs before or after the assigned hours. Snaps has signed a multiyear employment contract, which does not contain a clause assigning copyright in Snaps's photos to Tabloid. One photo target is Celebrity. Snaps, using considerable creativity, captures a great photo of Celebrity pushing aside a nonentity to get a taxicab. Who owns the copyright in the photo?

2. *Multitasker.* Tabloid requires Snaps to spend Monday mornings in his office at Tabloid to be available for meeting with editors. While sitting at his desk, Snaps borrows a pad of paper from a secretary and writes a short story about an adventurous celebrity photographer. Snaps writes the story purely for personal purposes, hoping vaguely to use it one day in a book. Just after finishing the story, Snaps learns that Laura Lawyer, a famous defense attorney, is having lunch in a nearby park. Snaps hurries

off, camera in hand, and leaves his new manuscript sitting on the desk. An editor picks it up and decides to publish it in Tabloid's *Sunday Magazine*. Snaps learns of this and demands an extra bonus. Who owns the copyright in the story?

3. *Opportunity knocks.* Snaps leaves his camera gear in the office one Monday while he goes for a stroll. Suddenly, he notices that Wobbly Allen, a reclusive filmmaker, is ambling toward him, hiding behind big sunglasses and a sombrero. Snaps grabs a camera out of the hands of Terry Tourist and quickly takes six pictures of Allen. Tourist then grabs back the camera and vanishes. Snaps learns that Tourist is peddling the photos to other tabloids. Tourist argues that because the photo was made with Tourist's camera, the copyright belongs to Tourist. Who owns the copyright in the photos?

4. *The new guys.* Foodko hires two eager employees to work in its meat packing area. They sign detailed employment contracts, are put on the payroll, and are subject to supervision by various bosses. The employees are actually television producers, full-time employees of Network, making an undercover investigation of food industry practices. The two producers covertly videotape their workplace, recording various unsavory and unsafe things done with meat intended for consumers. To suppress the making and distribution of the video, Foodko claims that Foodko owns the copyright because it was made by Foodko employees while working at their jobs in the meat packing area. Who owns the copyright in the video?

5. *The occasionals.* Two photographers work sporadically on the set of the *Harpoon* television talk show. The producers hire them for a few days a month to capture still photographs of the lively program. When not working at the *Harpoon* show, the photographers take other freelance assignments. The *Harpoon* producers pay them cash and do not treat them as employees for payroll, tax, benefits, or other purposes. The producers set up the set, select guests, and largely control the proceedings. The producers do not pay any attention to the photographers and do not consider the photographers when making various choices about how to stage the show. The photographers decide when and how to take photos, under no supervision by the producers (other than to stay out of the way). Who owns the copyright in the photographs?

6. *Informality.* A software developer takes on various projects for a start-up company. He works under the supervision and direction of the company; takes on additional tasks when assigned, and regards himself as an employee in his dealings with the company. But he is relatively independent. He works at home, not at the office. He sets his own hours and working conditions. He does not receive a salary, but is paid in

stock. Nor does the company list him as an employee for tax purposes or employee benefits. Is the software he writes a work made for hire?

7. *Terms of employment.* Stallman does occasional freelance consulting for Softco. The terms of their contract provide that Softco owns copyright in all the code Stallman writes for each project. But Stallman later contends he owns the copyright. He was an independent contractor: working sporadically; hired and paid for specific projects; completely in control of how, when, and where he worked; not listed as an employee for taxes or any other purpose. The contracts even listed him as Stallman Contracting. Who owns the copyright?

Explanations

1. The copyright in the photo belongs to Tabloid. A work is a work made for hire if it is made by an employee within the scope of his employment. Whether the hired party is an employee or is an independent contractor is governed by the factors listed in the text above. Almost every factor favors finding an employment relationship here. Snaps receives a regular paycheck; Tabloid withholds taxes consistent with an employment relationship; Tabloid provides Snaps employee benefits; Tabloid assigns jobs to Snaps and sets Snaps's hours; Tabloid also provides other support, such as reimbursing expenses and helping with logistics. The only factors at all tending toward a finding that Snaps is an independent contractor are that Snaps has considerable discretion in carrying out assignments and that he took the initiative in snapping the particular photo. But the weight of the other factors shows that Snaps is an employee, albeit one with some discretion.

   For the photo to be a work made for hire, it must also have been within the scope of the employee's employment. That is clearly met here; Snaps's job is to take pictures of celebrities, and here he did exactly that.

2. Snaps owns the copyright in the story. He is an employee, but the work is only made for hire if it is created within the scope of his employment—in this case, to take photos of celebrities. As the text above states, the relevant factors are:

   a. whether the work is of the type that the employee is employed to perform;

   b. whether the work occurs substantially within authorized work hours; and

   c. whether its purpose, at least in part, is to serve the employer.

   Here, only the second factor weighs in favor of it being within the scope of his employment—and very weakly so because he was simply biding time. Writing a story is well outside his job of taking pictures, and the purpose was purely personal. So the work is outside the scope of Snaps's employment and therefore not a work made for hire.

3. The copyright belongs to Tabloid. Snaps created the photo. Snaps made all the relevant creative decisions and controlled the production of the photo. He did make unauthorized use of Tourist's camera, but those are not relevant factors here. Snaps is an employee of Tabloid, working within the scope of his employment, so the copyright belongs to Tabloid.

   The foregoing applies only to the copyright. If Tabloid wishes to exploit its copyright, it may need access to the camera (or at least the card with the pictures). Personal property law would determine the ownership of the camera and card — and they presumably still belong to Tourist. So Tabloid owns the copyright, but Tourist owns the physical embodiment of the pictures. Neither can exploit their property without the other, which would encourage a mutual agreement.

4. Network owns the copyright. The producers were indeed employees of the food company — but the video was not made within the scope of their employment. It was made on Foodko premises on Foodko time, but the nature of their employment was far removed from making revelatory videos. The video was made by employees of Network within the scope of their employment. Network accordingly owns the copyright. Cf. *Food Lion v. Capital Cities/ABC*, 946 F. Supp. 420 (M.D.N.C. 1996).

5. The photographers own the copyrights in the photos. The photographers are not employees. Although they are paid by the producers, all the other factors weigh in favor of their being independent contractors rather than employees. They work only sporadically, are not paid out of the payroll, and are not treated as employees for purposes of benefits or other employment arrangements. The producers do control the set and proceedings of the show but do not exercise control over the making of the photographs.

   Producers might also argue that the photos are joint works. Arguably, the producers meet the first requirement, contribution of copyrightable expression. The producers control the staging of the set and the proceedings, so their creative decisions would contribute to the content of the photographs. But there must also be intent on the part of all parties to be joint authors, and that is not shown here. Cf. *Natkin v. Winfrey*, 111 F. Supp. 2d 1003 (N.D. Ill. 2000).

6. Courts are very leery where a company fails to treat a person as an employee for tax and other filing purposes, then claims the person as an employee, to claim ownership of the copyright. *JustMed, Inc. v. Byce*, 600 F.3d 1118 (9th Cir. 2010) took a more practical approach. The court emphasized that the dispute arose in a small, start-up company, where

there is often insufficient attention to formalities. The substance of the relationship was an employment relationship, and so the software was a work made for hire. JustMed shows that courts approach the issue with flexibility. It also emphasizes the practical point: the company should have had a signed writing agreeing that it would own the copyright in the software. Then, there would be no need to deal with the uncertainty of the work made for hire doctrine.

7. This example reminds us that the parties can assign ownership of the copyright by agreement (and generally should). The copyright was not a work made for hire. The copyright vested initially in Stallman—and instantly transferred to Softco, per the agreement. Ownership of the copyright depends on the work made for hire doctrine only when the parties have not already settled the matter.

Implied License, Where Contract Does Not Address Copyright

A family business hires a software consultant to write some software to handle accounting and inventory tracking. The contract between the parties does not address the question of who will own the copyright in the software. The consultant finishes the job, installs the software, and takes the agreed fee. The consultant is not an employee (the business does not pay her a salary, supervise her work, or treat her as an employee for tax or benefit). The software is not a work made for hire. The software consultant is the author and owns the copyright, including the exclusive right to make copies and adapt the work. Does that mean that the business now needs permission to use the software (which would involve making copies) or adapt it (which could involve preparing a derivative work)?

Courts hold that if a party is hired to create a work, if the parties do not address the copyright issue in the contract, there will be an implied, non-exclusive license for the hired party to use the work as contemplated by the parties' transaction. *See, e.g., Asset Mktg. Sys. Inc. v. Gagnon*, No. 07-55217 (9th Cir. 2008). So the family business would have an implied license to make copies and adapt the work, to the extent the parties expected the family business to use the work.

But the software consultant still owns the copyright, and the implied license is nonexclusive. So uses beyond the original plan would not be permitted. The software consultant would be able to market the software to other businesses, sell the copyright to a big software company, or adapt the software to other uses.

Whenever a party is hired to create a work, the parties should address the ownership of the copyright in the contract. Otherwise, the hiring party may end up with limited rights in the work they paid to have made.

Example

"Hollywood is a place where a man can get stabbed in the back while climbing a ladder." Studio commissions Faulkner to write a screenplay for *Meet the Snopes.* The agreement is informal and oral. Before too long, Faulkner hands over the text, and Studio hands over the check. Just as production is to begin on the film, Faulkner's attorney contacts Studio. Faulkner was not an employee. The screenplay was not a work made for hire. Faulkner, as author, owns the copyright and is offering to grant permission for Studio to make the film and distribute it — for a fee. Has Studio bought nothing more than a piece of paper because they did not get the copyright?

Explanation

Faulkner does own the copyright. But Studio will have an implied license to use the screenplay as contemplated by the parties. Where the parties neglect to address copyright ownership in the written agreement, the hiring party will get an implied, nonexclusive license to use the work. Studio can make the film and distribute it without permission from Faulkner.

But uses beyond the parties' implied agreement would infringe the copyright. This would depend on a showing of what the parties intended. But Faulkner could argue that Studio would infringe if it made a sequel, a novelization, or a Broadway musical. In addition, Faulkner would have the right to grant licenses to others. Studio should have addressed the ownership of copyright in the contract. The implied license rule will help it, but getting a clear assignment of copyright in the contract is much better.

Joint Authors

More than one person may qualify as the author. Authors of a joint work are co-owners of the copyright in the work. 17 U.S.C. §201(a). Joint authors have equal undivided interests in the copyright. Each has the right to use or to license the work without requiring permission from the other. The one obligation is to share any profits made. If Poe and Doe are joint authors of a novel, either one could authorize a publisher to print and distribute it or moviemaker to film it. She would then be accountable to her joint author to share the profits, if any.

A work is not a joint work simply because more than one person has input. A joint work is defined as "a work prepared by two or more authors with the intention that their contributions be merged into inseparable or interdependent parts of a unitary whole." 17 U.S.C. §101. Courts read that definition to set a high standard for showing joint authorship, requiring (1) that each author contribute copyrightable expression and (2) that each author intend to be a joint author when the work is created. *See, e.g.,*

Thomas v. Larson, 147 F.3d 195 (2d Cir. 1998). A person may contribute a considerable amount to a work without qualifying as a joint author. For example, in *Thomson v. Larson*, the author of the musical *Rent* worked with a dramaturge in revising the musical. The two worked together intensively on revising the work, which later became a commercial success. Larson had the sole decision-making authority, was consistently billed as the author (with credit to Thomson as dramaturge), and showed through other conduct and statements that he viewed himself as the sole author. In addition, all agreements with third parties characterized Larson as the author. Accordingly, there was no showing that he had the necessary intent for joint authorship. This rule avoids making a joint author of everyone who contributes to a work, which would result in numerous authors for works. Rather, to be a joint author, one must generally bargain for that status.

Examples

1. *When I nod my head, hit it.* Celebrity decides to enter the market for photos of Celebrity. She meticulously dresses herself and arranges furniture and artwork for a backdrop. She sets a camera on a tripod, picks a filter, sets the lighting, frames a shot, and focuses the camera. She asks Friendly Neighbor to help. Celebrity poses and gives a signal to Neighbor, who pushes the button to take the picture. Neighbor subsequently becomes less friendly and claims that the photo's copyright belongs to Neighbor or that both Neighbor and Celebrity are joint authors. Who owns the copyright?

2. *Muses.* Poet writes a series of poems about spring. Poet assigns the copyrights in the poems to Publisher for an agreed sum. Publisher commissions Musician to set the poems to music. Musician does so, resulting in a number of popular songs. When Poet hears how much revenue the songs are earning, she demands a share. She argues that the songs are joint works and that Poet is a joint author, entitled to a share of the profits. Are the songs joint works?

3. *Second thoughts.* Serving a lengthy sentence for stock fraud, Aaron decides to tell his story to the public. He contacts a friendly journalist, Roswell. They decide to have Aaron do a tell-all interview. They discuss the points they want to make and the effect they seek on the audience. They also discuss the role each will play, both in planning and execution. Aaron thinks of a sympathetic way to present his tale. Roswell thinks up lengthy questions that both serve as background and paint Aaron in a good light. They meet to discuss and revise their respective contributions. They then conduct the interview, recorded by a video recorder set up by Roswell. Everything goes according to plan, and they get precisely the interview they sought. But Aaron then rethinks his original plan and decides he would be better off remaining silent. Aaron claims authorship of the work and forbids Roswell from making copies, broadcasting the

interview, or doing anything else that falls within the copyright holder's exclusive rights. Does Aaron have the exclusive rights in the work?

4. *Separate ways:* Zach and Cody write a musical together, hoping for a Broadway hit. Their relationship sours. Zach is still seeking investors, when he learns that Cody has freely permitted various troupes to perform the work. Commercial opportunities fade for a work that is no longer new. Are the troupes liable, for performing the work without Zach's permission? Is Cody liable to Zach for infringement?

Explanations

1. The copyright belongs to Celebrity. In deciding authorship, courts consider such factors as who contributes creative expression, who controls the creation of the work, who makes the creative decisions, and who third parties would consider the author. Celebrity made all the artistic and technical decisions in producing the image. Neighbor played a purely mechanical role, hitting the button on cue from Celebrity.

   For the same reason, Neighbor does not qualify as a joint author. Under the standards most courts apply, joint authorship requires (1) that each author contribute copyrightable expression and (2) that the joint authors intend to be joint authors. Neighbor meets neither requirement. Neighbor simply pushed a button on cue, without contributing any original creative expression. Celebrity did not show any intent to make Neighbor a joint author. So Celebrity alone owns the copyright.

2. The songs are not joint works, even though they use Poet's creative expression. As courts now apply the rule, joint work status requires intent on the part of all authors, at the time of their respective contributions, to create a joint work. When Poet wrote her poems, she intended to create poems. The songs are musical works, incorporating preexisting material from Poet's poems. Had Poet not sold the copyright, making the songs, selling them, or performing them publicly would have infringed her copyright. But she sold the copyright to Publisher, who accordingly has the exclusive rights to make copies of the poems, adapt them, or perform them publicly.

3. Aaron is an author, but not the only one. Aaron and Roswell are joint authors. Each had the requisite intent to be a joint author and contributed copyrightable expression. They are co-owners of the copyright. Either can exercise the exclusive rights of the copyright owner without the permission of the other. Accordingly, Roswell can make copies, broadcast the tape, or do anything else without infringing Aaron's copyright.

   Not every interview would be a joint work. There are several possible permutations. Depending on the roles the parties played, one or the other could be the author. An interview could even be a compilation of separate individual works.

4. With a joint work, either joint author may authorize others to use the work. The joint author need only account to the other joint authors for a share of the profits. So Cody could independently authorize the troupes to perform the work. Zach's permission is not necessary. Neither the troupes nor Cody is liable for infringement. Cody must account to Zach for a share of the profits, but there were none to share. Failing to protect a joint author's ability to exploit a work is not copyright infringement. *See Severe Records LLC v. Rich*, No. 09-6175 (6th Cir. 2011). Joint authors are well advised to have a contract covering their relationship. Otherwise, each may be at the mercy of the other.

Collective Works

Collective works are distinguished from joint works. A collective work is "a work, such as a periodical issue, anthology, or encyclopedia, in which a number of contributions, constituting separate and independent works in themselves, are assembled into a collective whole." 17 U.S.C. §101. Newspapers, magazines, encyclopedias, and collections of literary works are often collective works. A CD with various songs could be a collective work, with the author of each separate contribution retaining copyright in that individual work. The author of the collective work acquires only "the privilege of reproducing and distributing the contribution as part of that particular collective work, any revision of that collective work, and any later collective work in the same series." 17 U.S.C. §201(c).

Suppose Editor puts together a book of poems for children with the permission of the various copyright holders. The parties could arrange ownership interests between them. For example, Editor could acquire all the copyrights or acquire exclusive rights to publish all the poems. If the parties do not specify, then each copyright holder retains the copyright in his or her poem, while Editor has the copyright in the collective work. Editor has the right to make and distribute copies (sell, give away, rent, and so on) of the collective work.

Editor also has the right to make and distribute copies of a revision of the work or of a "later collective work in the same series." In *New York Times v. Tasini*, 533 U.S. 483 (2001), the Supreme Court rejected the argument that a newspaper's right to use contributions (written by freelancers) in "revisions" of the newspaper extended to putting the articles on Lexis, an online periodical database. In deciding whether a work was a revision of a collective work, the Court focused on how the work is presented to and perceptible by a user. Online databases "present articles to users clear of the context provided either by the original periodical editions or by any revision of those editions." *Id.* at 516. A user searches thousands of files for articles from thousands of collective works, then receives separate items as search results. Articles appear "without the graphics, formatting, or other articles with which the article was initially published" or without the other pages in the original work. *Id.* at 500. Such presentation was quite different than the presentation in a newspaper, so the online database did not qualify as a revision of the newspaper.

Examples

1. *Collective work or derivative work?* Jarvis provides a group of photographic images that K2 uses in advertising. After the parties fall out, K2 continues to use the images in making a collage. The collage shrinks, expands, and overlays the images in creative ways. K2 argues that it has the right to do so as the holder of the copyright in the collective work, the group of images (even if Jarvis has the copyright in the individual images). Does K2 have that right?

2. *Shorties.* Here's a round-up of all the rules. Who owns the copyright?
   a. Jada, a freelance writer, writes a history of Gown Town, using the computer and historical records in the town library.
   b. Same, except Jada is a historian employed by Gown Town, assigned to write the book.
   c. Same, except Jada is a freelance historian, commissioned by Gown Town to write its history for a lump sum, with free rein on how, when, and where to proceed (and no health or pension benefits). To everyone's surprise, Edur Studio offers millions for the movie rights to the book.
   d. Same, except Jada and Gown Town sign a contract providing that the copyright will belong to Gown Town.
   e. Davion, a freelance composer working in Hawaii, writes the score for the movie. His contract with Edur Studio provides that the score will be a work made for hire, but Davion is his own boss, not an employee of Edur Studio.
   f. Edi compiles *Best Short Stories of 2006*, with the permission of the copyright holders in the various stories.
   g. Bim and Bam, independent researchers, work closely together as equals in writing a study of the U.S. National Park system.
   h. Same, except Bim and Bam are employees of Gorp Incorporated.
   i. Same, except Bim and Bam do the work as employees of the U.S. Park Service, a federal agency.

Explanations

1. The collage is a derivative work, rather than a collective work, so the collective work right to make a revision of the work does not apply. *See Jarvis v. K2*, 486 F.3d 526 (9th Cir. 2007). A work is only a collective work if the individual works remain "unintegrated and disparate," and here they were combined into a new work. The author of a collective work does not have the right to prepare derivative works based on the individual works.

2. a. Jada, as the author, would own the copyright. Whether she used facilities of others to create the work is irrelevant.

   b. Gown Town is deemed the author and owns the copyright, where Jada created the work as an employee within the scope of her employment. Note that Jada would own the copyright if the work was outside the scope of her employment, such as if she was a judge employed by the town and did the project on her own time and initiative.

   c. Jada would be the author. She is not an employee of Gown Town, so it is not a work made for hire, even though Gown Town commissioned it and paid for it. Gown Town would presumably get an implied license to make contemplated uses of the work, such as printing up copies for local distribution, but Jada would own the copyright, including the ability to sell the movie rights.

   d. The copyright would initially belong to the author, Jada, but it would transfer as agreed to Gown Town. This illustrates the practical point that parties are well advised to expressly address copyright ownership in the contract.

   e. It will be a work made for hire, so Edur Studio is the author and owns the copyright. This illustrates the second category of works made for hire: specially commissioned works that fall into specified categories (one of which is "a part of a motion picture or other audiovisual work," applicable here), where the parties sign an agreement designating it to be a work made for hire, as they did here. There need be no employee relationship for this category to apply.

   f. Edi holds the copyright in *Best Short Stories of 2006*, even though Edi did not write any of the stories. It is a collective work: "a work, such as a periodical issue, anthology, or encyclopedia, in which a number of contributions, constituting separate and independent works in themselves, are assembled into a collective whole." 17 U.S.C. §101. But that does not give Edi the copyright in the various stories. Rather, Edi's copyright in the collective work comprises "the privilege of reproducing and distributing the contribution as part of that particular collective work, any revision of that collective work, and any later collective work in the same series." 17 U.S.C. §201(c).

g. Bim and Bam are joint authors. Each may license the work independently, but must account to the other for profits. Bim could authorize the sale of the book. Bim would have to pay a share of the profits (if any) to Bam.

h. If they created the work as employees working within the scope of their employment, the author and copyright owner would be the employer, Gorp Incorporated.

i. Thrown in for review: No one would own the copyright. There is no copyright in a work created by an employee of the U.S. government working within the scope of employment.

OWNERSHIP OF COPYRIGHT DISTINGUISHED FROM OWNERSHIP OF MATERIAL OBJECT

Collector purchases a painting. A year later, she is disturbed to see that a local gift shop is selling posters of the painting. But she owns the painting—doesn't the shop owner need her permission to make copies? If not, can she at least set up in competition and sell her own posters? No and no:

> Ownership of a copyright, or of any of the exclusive rights under a copyright, is distinct from ownership of any material object in which the work is embodied. Transfer of ownership of any material object, including the copy or phonorecord in which the work is first fixed, does not of itself convey any rights in the copyrighted work embodied in the object; nor, in the absence of an agreement, does transfer of ownership of a copyright or of any exclusive rights under a copyright convey property rights in any material object.

17 U.S.C. §202. Painter created the painting, so Painter owned the painting (under property law) and the copyright (under copyright law). Collector bought the painting. A sale of the painting does not implicitly include the copyright. Likewise, if Painter had sold Collector the copyright, that transaction would not have automatically included the painting. Indeed, if Collector bought the copyright without buying a copy of the work, she would have the exclusive right to make copies but not be able to exercise it since she owned no copy to work from.

Examples

1. *Scarlet's letter.* Scarlet writes a letter in longhand to Red, musing at length about philosophy and relating a number of amusing incidents, using her considerable wit and wisdom. Red then offers to sell the letter to Ashy. Ashy is aware that sale of an object does not convey the copyright in a

work. Ashy decides to make sure that the contract clearly conveys the copyright. Ashy and Red sign a sales contract, agreeing that Red conveys ownership of both the letter and the copyright in the letter. Ashy pays the agreed price. Who owns the copyright in the letter?

2. *Services rendered.* Sculptor, a self-employed artist, agrees to create a sculpture for Mogul's garden. Mogul supplies a large block of stone. Sculptor, over several days, uses various tools to fashion various abstract geometric forms in the stone. Mogul is delighted with the result and hands over the agreed fee. Sculptor then prepares to load the sculpture into a truck, much to Mogul's dismay. Sculptor claims ownership of the sculpture, on the grounds that the sculpture was not a work made for hire, and they did not agree that the copyright would belong to Mogul. Who owns the copyright? Who owns the sculpture?

3. *My music.* Boutique Owner purchases a CD of songs written and performed by the group Dansel. Boutique Owner likes the CD so much she plays it several times a day in her boutique. She then hears from the owner of the copyright in the songs, who claims that Boutique Owner is infringing the copyright owner's exclusive right to perform the songs in public. Boutique Owner is dumbfounded. Does she need permission to play a CD she owns?

4. *Your tape, my music.* Forward, a music enthusiast, hears The Destroyers play at a blues bar. Impressed, he invites them to record a demo tape of their songs at a studio, all expenses paid. The demo helps the Destroyers get a record deal, and they agree to let Forward keep the tape for his own enjoyment. Years later, when the Destroyers are famous, Forward decides to reproduce his tape and sell copies to the public. May he?

5. *Ambiguous question.* If the Pink Panther stole the demo tape and sold it, would the Pink Panther be liable to Forward or to the Destroyers?

Explanations

1. Scarlet owns the copyright in the letter. Scarlet gave Red the letter but did not give Red the copyright in the letter. Transfer of ownership of a copy of a work (even when the copy is the original form of the work) does not convey the copyright in the work. Scarlet did not convey the copyright to Red, so Scarlet retains the copyright. The fact that Red agreed to convey the copyright to Ashy does not help Ashy; Red cannot convey something Red does not own or have power to transfer. So Scarlet owns the copyright, and Ashy is left with a breach of contract action against Red for failing to convey the copyright Red promised to Ashy.

Scarlet owns the copyright, but Red owns the physical letter. So although Scarlet has the exclusive right to make copies, she would need Red's permission to make copies (unless she has a terrific memory).

2. The sculpture belongs to Mogul. The copyright belongs to Sculptor because the work was not a work made for hire, and the parties did not agree to a transfer of the copyright. But ownership of the sculpture, a physical object, is entirely separate. Since Sculptor agreed to make it, using materials supplied by Mogul, property and contract law likely would deem the sculpture to belong to Mogul. So Sculptor does not have the right to take the sculpture away.

3. This problem contains some preview of the next chapter. Boutique Owner does need authorization from the copyright holder (or from some provision of the Copyright Act, as the next chapter discusses) to play the CD publicly. Boutique Owner bought the CD; she did not buy the copyright or receive a license of any of the exclusive rights. The copyright owner in the musical works has the exclusive right to perform the work publicly, which includes playing the songs publicly on a CD player. Boutique Owner can, however, play the songs privately without permission. So ownership of a copy of the work does not give the owner unlimited rights to use that copy (as the next chapter discusses in more detail), in particular under the first sale and fair use provisions.

4. Forward owns the tape. But the Destroyers own the copyright to their music and, assuming the controlled the session, to the sound recording. If Forward makes copies and distributes them, he would infringe both copyrights. *See Forward v. Thorogood*, 985 F.2d 604 (1st Cir. 1993).

5. Both. Pink Panther would be liable to Forward, for stealing his physical property and selling it (conversion) and to the Destroyers for distributing a copy (that he does not own, so first sale does not apply, as discussed later in the book) of their copyrighted work to the public (copyright infringement).

COPYRIGHT AS PROPERTY: LICENSING, RECORDATION, TERMINATION, AND COMMON LAW

Licensing

Author writes her brilliant novel. She owns the copyright, with its basket of exclusive rights. So she has the exclusive rights to make copies, sell them, make a movie out of her book, distribute and exhibit the movie, translate the book into Swedish, and so on. She may wish to do those things for various reasons—to make money, to deliver her work to audiences, to gain the esteem of the public and her peers. But she need not do those things personally. Rather, she could enter into contracts with publishers, movie studios, translators—or, to make it simpler for her, she could simply sell the entire copyright and leave it to the buyer to exploit the rights. She can even use the copyright as collateral to get a loan. Universities are increasingly involved in intellectual property licensing, both licensing their own works and getting licenses to use material. Hence such tech transfer offices as the "INVO Innovation and New Ventures Office" (Northwestern University), "Center for Technology Transfer and Enterprise Creation" (Carnegie Mellon), "Office of Licensing and Ventures" (Duke), and "Office of Industry Engagement" (Georgia Tech). There are many mechanisms by which copyright owners can grant some or all of their rights to others. Such agreements allow her to do various things: get licensing fees, control how the work is distributed, adapted, and disseminated. So copyright transactions serve both the incentive purpose of copyright (by providing an avenue to receive income, which is an incentive to create in the first place) and the author's rights purpose (by allowing authors a measure of control over how the work appears to the public: how it is distributed, adapted, performed).

Selling the Copyright

The author can simply sell the copyright outright. She may sell it for cash, for a promissory note, for a percentage of the buyer's revenue. She might sell it along with other assets in the sale of a business, or she might sell it along with a promise to perform services for the buyer (such as promoting, adapting, or updating the work). Authors can sell their copyrights before the work is even created. Employee and independent contractors, for example, often sign contracts providing that copyright in works they create will belong to the hiring party. Copyrights may also be conveyed for noncommercial reasons, such as donating to a museum or foundation the copyright in a work.

Exclusive Licenses

Other transactions allow the copyright owner to retain some rights, while granting some rights to others. An *exclusive license* allows author to grant a chunk of her rights to another. For example, Author might sell publication rights to Publisher: She might sell to Publisher an exclusive license to make copies and distribute copies of the work in book form. She would retain all other rights, such as the right to make a movie out of the book and to write a sequel. Through a contract, Author can define the rights conveyed quite specifically. Publisher might get the exclusive right to publish the book in hardcover form in English in the United States for a limited number of years.

Nonexclusive Licenses

Copyright owners also grant *nonexclusive licenses*, both for commercial and noncommercial purposes. Software companies that "sell" software typically grant nonexclusive licenses. Someone who purchases the software may use it (because they get a license), but cannot exclude others from using it (because the license is nonexclusive). Two competitors might settle a copyright infringement suit by granting each other nonexclusive licenses (thereby freeing each other of their respective infringement claims). An author might give permission for an anthology to include large portions of the novel, or a filmmaker might agree to let her footage be used in another's documentary. The permissions would likely take the form of a nonexclusive license.

The author may also wish to allow others to use her work freely. Copyright licensing is used to make works available to the public for free. Software, for example, may be distributed subject to a free or open source license. The license may provide that anyone may freely use, copy, adapt, improve, or do anything they like with the software — provided that they do not impose any legal restrictions on use of the software or on the changes they make. The practice is being followed by some writers, musicians, and other creators. An author may use a "Creative Commons" license, which permits others to use her work, subject to conditions of the author's choosing (such as giving proper attribution or use for nonprofit purposes). In short, licensing has become a substantial practice area among copyright lawyers.

Examples

1. *Abandoned?* Model railroad enthusiasts use Jacobsen's copyrighted software to control model trains. One can visit Jacobsen's Web site and download the code by agreeing to the terms of the Artistic License, which allows most uses but conditions that permission on proper attribution. A company downloads the code and incorporates it into a commercial product without giving any credit to Jacobsen. The company argues that Jacobsen cannot sue for copyright infringement, because he has agreed that anyone can make copies and otherwise use the software. They may have failed to give attribution, but that would merely be a breach of the licensing contract, not copyright infringement. Has Jacobsen given up his right to sue for copyright infringement by allowing the world to freely use the code?

2. *Commercial Use?* Timor writes a play satirizing the political events of the year and releases it under a Creative Commons Noncommercial license. Nonprofit loves the play and decides to distribute hundreds of copies across the nation's capital. Nonprofit has a commercial copyshop make

500 copies of the play, for which the copyshop makes a nice profit. Is the copyshop liable for breaching the "noncommercial" condition of the license?

Explanations

1. Jacobsen can sue for copyright infringement because the permission to use the code is conditioned on compliance with the license. *Jacobsen v. Katzer*, 535 F.3d 1373 (Fed. Cir. 2008). The copyright holder can sue for copyright infringement (on the theory that unauthorized use beyond the conditions in the license took the licensee beyond the scope of the non-exclusive license) and is not limited to an action for breach of license. Open source licenses are enforceable contracts, not gifts. They can be a tool to encourage the use of the subject matter but control the manner in which it is used.

2. One court has held that a party making a nonprofit use may use the services of profit-making entity, such as a for-profit copyshop, to achieve its permitted noncommercial use.[1]

Is There a Contract?

A key contract law issue for nonexclusive licenses: under contract law, what does it take to get binding consent to the conditions in a copyright license? The formalities of a signature and a signed writing may not be necessary, but some agreement (express or implied) is necessary before a court will enforce the terms against the purported licensee. This can be especially important where the licensor uses the license not just to convey rights, but also to condition use of the material on various restrictions, which may well go beyond what copyright alone gives the rights holder. Copyrighted content is increasingly provided online, with click-through licenses that seek to protect the copyright holder and to limit the use of information. The limited case law has generally proved favorable for licensors. *Register.com, Inc. v. Verio, Inc.*, 356 F.3d 393 (2d Cir. 2004), for example, held a license binding, even where the user would not encounter it before using the material. The defendant was a repeat visitor to a database. The contractual restrictions would not appear until sent with a response to each request for information. Such restrictions may not have bound a one-time visitor. But since the defendant used the database numerous times, it was well aware of the practice of providing information subject to restrictions. By continuing to use the database, it was deemed to manifest assent.

---

1. Great Minds v. FedEx Office & Print Servs., 2017 U.S. Dist. LEXIS 26332, *12-13 (E.D.N.Y. Feb. 24, 2017).

Formalities

For many grants to be effective, there must be a writing signed by the copyright owner. Copyright vests initially in the author, but he can authorize others to take advantage of these exclusive rights. Copyright law distinguishes between a transfer of copyright ownership and a nonexclusive license. A "transfer of copyright ownership" is broadly defined as

> assignment, mortgage, exclusive license, or any other conveyance, alienation, or hypothecation of a copyright or of any of the exclusive rights comprised in a copyright, whether or not it is limited in time or place of effect, but not including a nonexclusive license.

17 U.S.C. §101. Any such agreement is not valid unless reflected in "an instrument of conveyance, or a note or memorandum of the transfer" signed by the owner. 17 U.S.C. §204(a). Many transactions involving a copyright must be reflected by a writing signed by the transferor. Validity requires a signed writing if the author sells his copyright, grants a studio an exclusive right to make a movie, uses the copyright as collateral for a loan ("hypothecation," as the statute quaintly puts it), gives a bookstore the exclusive right to sell the book in Boston, or gives another author exclusive rights to write a sequel to the book. Judge Kozinski has nicely summarized the rationale:

> Common sense tells us that agreements should routinely be put in writing. This simple practice prevents misunderstandings by spelling out the terms of a deal in black and white, forces parties to clarify their thinking and consider problems that could potentially arise, and encourages them to take their promises seriously because it's harder to backtrack on a written contract than on an oral one. *Effects Associates v. Cohen*, 908 F.2d 555, 557 (9th Cir. 1990).

No special form is required by the statute. But not every writing meets the statutory requirement of "an instrument of conveyance, or a note or memorandum of the transfer" signed by the transferor. A fax that simply references a deal, without specifying even the general terms of the deal, is insufficient. See *Radio Television Espanola v. New World Entertainment*, 183 F.3d 922 (9th Cir. 1999). Likewise, a writing that refers to contracts that are not yet finalized is insufficient. Id.

A nonexclusive license, however, need not be reflected by a writing. One must therefore distinguish between exclusive and nonexclusive licenses. A license is exclusive if the author cannot then grant the same rights to someone else. So an exclusive license could be broad (the exclusive right to make copies of author's book) or narrow (the exclusive right to sell copies of the book in Dubuque, Iowa). An exclusive license effectively conveys parts of copyright holder's rights to the licensee, so it is treated as a transfer of ownership. By contrast, a nonexclusive license effectively says, "I authorize you to do the following, but I can turn around and authorize someone else to do it as well." So if an author gives a nonexclusive license to Publisher 1 to print and sell the book, the author could authorize Publisher 2 to do it as well. Some examples of nonexclusive licenses are a playwright who authorizes a theater troupe to perform her play publicly; an author who gives permission to publisher to reprint excerpts of his novel in a book on creative writing; a software developer who allows others to freely use, copy, and adapt her computer program, provided they abide by certain conditions; a software company that allows users to use its software, for a fee. Provided each copyright owner retains the ability to grant similar licenses to others, all would be nonexclusive licenses.

No signed writing is required for a nonexclusive license. Oral permission is sufficient. The grant of permission need not even be explicit. A nonexclusive license may be implied from the conduct of the parties. If an author and an investor form a partnership to publish a book on how to restore Ford F-100 pickup trucks, the investor supplies the capital, and the author hands over a manuscript, there is an implied license from the author to the partnership to use the manuscript. *See Oddo v. Ries,* 743 F.2d 630 (9th Cir. 1984).

Examples

1. *Change of heart.* Gray phones Leonardo, a gifted artist. Gray requests permission to include Leonardo's drawings of human figures in Gray's anatomy text. Leonardo tells her to go right ahead. After Gray's book becomes a fixture on every medical student's bookshelf, Leonardo demands royalties and threatens to sue. Leonardo does not deny that he gave permission. Oral permission, he contends, is insufficient. Since there is no signed writing, the permission is invalid. Is Leonardo correct?

2. *Not worth the paper it's not written on.* Palette shows her latest painting to Baron, who immediately is enthralled. The two orally agree that Palette will sell both the painting and its copyright to Baron for an agreed sum, immediately paid by Baron. Baron's art collection is included in a show that tours the country. Palette's painting becomes renowned. Baron decides to market posters with reproductions of the painting. Palette's lawyer contacts Baron, contending that the copyright was not validly conveyed to Baron. Was there a valid transfer of copyright ownership?

   Suppose instead that Baron purchased the painting and Palette orally gave him permission to make and distribute posters that reproduced the painting. Is such oral permission valid?

3. *Transfer of copyright ownership?* As the statute states, a "transfer of copyright ownership, other than by operation of law, is not valid unless an instrument of conveyance, or a note or memorandum of the transfer, is in

writing and signed by the owner of the rights conveyed." Which of the following would require a signed writing?

a. Jot sells Print the copyright to Jot's new novel.

b. Print sells Press the copyright to Jot's novel.

c. Press sells Mag the exclusive right to reprint a chapter from the novel, with such right limited to publication in a magazine during December of that year.

d. Editor phones Potaster and receives permission to include one of Potaster's sonnets in a collection of poetry.

e. Jute sells Museum the manuscript to Jute's new novel.

f. Jape gets a loan from Bank, putting up the copyright in a software package as collateral.

4. *Sign-off.* Newfie Museum purchases a painting from Artist. Newfie writes a check payable to Artist. On the back of the check, it states "By signing this, you acknowledge that rights to the painting belong to Newfie." Artist signs the back of the check and deposits it in his account. Does Newfie now hold the copyright in the painting (including, for example, the exclusive right to publish a copy of the painting in a magazine)?

5. *Invitation withdrawn.* The copyright page of *Fitz's Guide to Linux* states: "To help spread the word about Linux, the author hereby grants permission to anyone to republish the contents of this book." Fitz had orally instructed the publisher to include that statement, but never put anything in writing. Thusi takes Fitz at his word and prints and sells thousands of copies of the book. Fitz, enraged that Thusi is profiting from his generosity, sues Thusi for copyright infringement. The permission is not valid, Fitz contends, because it was not signed by Fitz.

6. *Policy.* Foraste works as a photographer for Brown University, taking photos which are used in various Brown publications. Brown has adopted a copyright policy:

Ownership: It is the University's position that, as a general premise, ownership of copyrightable property which results from performance of one's University duties and activities will belong to the author or originator. This applies to books, art works, software, etc.

After Foraste leaves his job at Brown, he claims copyright in all the photos he took. Is the university policy sufficient to transfer copyright to him?

7. *Implied exclusive license?* Freelancer orally agrees to shoot some wildlife footage for Auteur's feature film. Freelancer spends a couple of weeks camping and shooting digital video in Alaska, returning with some great grizzly footage. In exchange for $100,000, Freelancer hands several storage disks with the best footage, which Auteur incorporates into the film. Auteur is then enraged several months later when she sees the same

footage used in a competing film, with permission of Freelancer. Auteur argues that the generous fee gave her an implied transfer of the exclusive right to use the footage in a film. Was there an implied exclusive license?

8. *Or not to tweet.* Twitter's terms of service, which grant Twitter a nonexclusive license to photographs uploaded by users. Would that authorize Twitter's users to reproduce the photos, such as other media outlets using them for news reporting?

Explanations

1. No writing was necessary, because Gray is not claiming that there was a transfer of copyright ownership. If she claimed to have exclusive rights to use the drawings, that would be a transfer of copyright ownership (as an exclusive license), requiring a signed license. But Gray claims only that Leonardo gave her permission to use the drawings. That would be a nonexclusive writing, which may be oral (or even implied). So oral permission is sufficient. The court must also determine, as a matter of state contract law, whether the agreement is valid.

2. No valid transfer of copyright ownership occurred. A transfer of copyright ownership is not valid without a writing signed by the transferor. Here the parties had only an oral agreement, so the necessary writing is absent. Palette still owns the copyright, and Baron would potentially infringe if he started making and selling copies of the painting.

   The result would be different if Palette had given Baron oral permission to make and sell copies. If she did not give him the exclusive right to do so, such permission would be a nonexclusive license. A nonexclusive license need not be in writing to be valid.

3. a. A conveyance of the copyright is a transfer of copyright ownership and requires a signed writing for validity.
   b. This is also a conveyance of the copyright and likewise requires a signed writing. The rule is not limited to a conveyance by the initial author but applies to any transfer of copyright ownership.
   c. The exclusive license is a transfer of copyright ownership and requires a signed writing for validity. The definition of "transfer of copyright ownership" explicitly includes the transfer of an exclusive right, even if there are limits as to time and place (such as the limits to publication in a magazine during December).
   d. Permission to reprint the sonnet in a collection of poetry is not a transfer of copyright ownership; rather, it is a nonexclusive license, which does not require a writing for validity. The permission is nonexclusive because Potaster could give permission to someone else to likewise

include the sonnet in a collection of poetry. It would be exclusive only if Potaster granted permission to publish and agreed that Potaster could not authorize others to do the same thing. In other words, the license is exclusive if it excludes others from the rights at issue.

e. Sale of the manuscript is not a transfer of copyright ownership. Sale of the manuscript is not a transaction involving the copyright at all but simply the sale of an object. Contract law governs whether a signed writing is required (and, under the UCC, if the price is paid, no writing is required for enforcement of the contract).

f. Putting a copyright up as collateral falls within the definition of "transfer of copyright ownership" as a "hypothecation" of a copyright. Accordingly, a signed writing is required for validity.

4. Newfie probably does not hold the copyright on the grounds that there was not a sufficient signed writing. This case is really a matter of contract law and of interpreting the parties' writing. A note or memorandum of transfer of copyright need be in no special form. If the check had read, "By signing this, you acknowledge that the copyright in the painting is transferred to Newfie," and the author signed it, it would have been sufficient. But the note or memorandum must show the parties' intent to transfer the copyright. "Rights to the painting" does not clearly do so. Rather, it seems to refer to ownership of the painting itself. So a court likely would not hold it to be a note or memorandum of transfer of ownership. *Compare Playboy Enterprises v. Dumas*, 53 F.3d 549 (2d Cir. 1995).

5. The permission did not need to be signed. Fitz granted "permission to anyone to republish the contents of this book." He did not grant exclusive rights to anyone, so it was a nonexclusive license, which does not require a signed writing. It was therefore effective.

6. The court held that the policy was insufficient to convey the copyright to Foraste. It held that the policy was not sufficiently clear to show specifically which rights had been conveyed, because it spoke only of a general policy, and the specific works referred to were books, art works, and software, quite different from the catalog photographs taken by Foraste. *See Foraste v. Brown Univ.*, 290 F. Supp. 2d 234, 236 (D.R.I. 2003). It lacked the requisite specificity to meet the requirements of §204.

With respect to university copyright policies generally, another problem for employees may be the requirement of a signature. If, for example, the policy is adopted by vote of the faculty or by inclusion in an employee handbook, there may be no actual signature by the university. Rather, the employee may need to find a writing signed by the university (such as an employment contract that incorporates the employee handbook by reference). A careful employee may have it spelled out in writing in the employment contract.

7. Auteur cannot get an implied exclusive license. A transfer of copyright ownership (which includes an exclusive license) must be evidenced by a signed writing to be valid. So such a transfer cannot be implied from the conduct of the parties. A nonexclusive license need not be in writing, so courts can infer a nonexclusive license from conduct. If Auteur used the footage, a court likely would hold that Auteur did not infringe because, under the circumstances, Auteur received implied permission to use it. But such implied permission would not be exclusive.

8. Permission to Twitter does not give permission to Twitter's users. So if others make use of the photos, they could be liable for infringement. *See Agence France Presse v. Morel*, 769 F. Supp. 2d 295 (S.D.N.Y. 2011).

Open Source Licenses and Free Software ("Think Free Speech, Not Free Beer")

Someone that writes software can give the world permission to use it for free, subject to certain restrictions, by using an open source license (also known as a free software license). Open source software is not in the public domain. The software is kept under copyright, but freely licensed under one of various open source licenses, such as the General Public License ("GPL," used as verb, noun, adjective, and every other part of speech); the certification mark, "OSI Certified"; or the Artistic License. *See* Stephen McJohn, *The Paradoxes of Free Software*, 9 Geo. Mason L. Rev. 25 (2000).

Ariel develops a computer program that translates text from Swedish to Finnish. She could make it freely available to others under an open source license. Such licenses state that anyone who gets a copy of the software can use it, change it, make and distribute more copies, and even sell copies or adaptations, without paying royalties to the original author. The open source license requires little, but it does not abandon the copyright. It may restrict uses, such as not permitting commercial applications or certain adaptations. It may require attribution, meaning that the author must be given credit. Most open source licenses seek to ensure the software remains free, by providing that anyone who incorporates it into software must make that software available under an open source license.

The idea spread from software to other creative fields. Creative Commons licenses are often used with works (literary works, music, film, and beyond). A CC license allows others to use this work, subject the author's choice of restrictions:

Noncommercial. You let others copy, distribute, display, and perform your work—and derivative works based upon it—but for noncommercial purposes only.

No Derivative Works. You let others copy, distribute, display, and perform only verbatim copies of your work, not derivative works based upon it.

Share Alike. You allow others to distribute derivative works only under a license identical to the license that governs your work.

CC used to provide an option as to attribution, but no one ever chose to make their work available without requiring attribution. Even people who give their work away feel credit should be given, suggesting that attribution is a core value of intellectual property generally.

Example

Abandoned? Jacobsen's copyrighted software is used by model railroad enthusiasts to control model trains. One can visit Jacobsen's Web site and download the code, by agreeing to the terms of the Artistic License, which allows most uses but conditions that permission on proper attribution. A company downloads the code and incorporates it into a commercial product without giving any credit to Jacobsen. The company argues that Jacobsen cannot sue for copyright infringement, because he has agreed that anyone can make copies and otherwise use the software. They may have failed to give attribution, but that would merely be a breach of the licensing contract, not copyright infringement. Has Jacobsen given up his right to sue for copyright infringement, by allowing the world to freely use the code?

Explanation

Jacobsen can sue for copyright infringement, because the permission to use the code is conditioned on compliance with the license. *Jacobsen v. Katzer,* 535 F.3d 1373 (2008). The copyright holder can sue for copyright infringement (on the theory that unauthorized use beyond the conditions in the license took the licensee beyond the scope of the nonexclusive license) and is not limited to an action for breach of license. Open source licenses are enforceable contracts, not gifts. So they can be a tool to encourage the use of the subject matter but control the manner in which it is used.

Recordation

Transfers of copyright ownership and other documents pertaining to a copyright may (not must) be recorded in the U.S. Copyright Office. Recordation gives other persons constructive notice of the facts within, provided the work has been registered, and the document so identifies the relevant copyright that a reasonable search of the records would disclose it. As between two conflicting transfers, the first to be *executed* has priority if it is recorded within a month (two months if executed abroad). Otherwise, the first to be *recorded* takes priority if the transferee took it in good faith, for consideration, and without notice. 17 U.S.C. §301(d). So if an author sells his copyright twice, the second buyer may take priority if she records first.

One important question remains open. If a creditor agrees to take an interest in a copyright as collateral, she will wish to perfect her security interest. An unperfected security interest is likely to be nullified if the debtor goes into bankruptcy or if other creditors perfect first. It is unsettled whether a security interest in a copyright is perfected by filing in the state UCC office (as for many types of personal property) or in the U.S. Copyright Office. But a careful creditor can simply file in both offices.

Examples

1. *Stake your claim.* Author writes her brilliant novel and registers her copyright. She signs a contract with Publisher, transferring the copyright for a payment of $1 million. A year later, Author signs a contract with Studio, granting Studio the exclusive right to make a movie from the book. Studio knows nothing of Author's agreement with Publisher. Studio records the contract with the U.S. Copyright Office. Publisher did not record. Studio makes the film and begins showing it nationwide. Publisher claims copyright infringement. Studio claims that it owns the copyright, having bought it from Author. Publisher responds that Author had no copyright to sell, having already sold it to Publisher. Who has priority?

2. *File under "bogus claims."* Entrepreneur holds the copyright to Soft Granite, a new computer game. Entrepreneur signs a sales contract with Bolly, selling the copyright for $200,000. Bolly does not record the sales contract with the U.S. Copyright Office. A year later, Soft Granite has become wildly popular. Entrepreneur delivers a check to Bolly for $200,000 and states that the copyright still belongs to Entrepreneur, due to Bolly's failure to record the transfer. Who owns the copyright?

Explanations

1. Because Studio recorded before Publisher, Studio takes priority. This is true even though Publisher's agreement came first in time. Publisher should have recorded its agreement, thereby putting others on constructive notice of the transfer of copyright. Publisher has a cause of action against Author but not against Studio.

2. The copyright belongs to Bolly, pursuant to the agreement between the parties. Recordation is not necessary to have a valid transfer of copyright ownership. Rather, recordation provides protection against the claims of a subsequent good-faith purchaser. Here, there is no subsequent good-

faith purchaser. The dispute is between the seller and the buyer—and the seller is bound by their valid agreement.

Termination of Transfers and Licenses Granted by Author

In 1938, the creators of Superman sold their rights in the comic for $130—rights which later proved to be worth millions. In 1997, however, the heirs of one author were entitled to terminate the transfer and get the rights back.

The 1976 Copyright Act created two statutory rights to terminate grants of transfers or license of copyright. The two termination rights, in §304(c) and §203, have different rationales. Section 304(c), which applies to pre-1978 grants, deals with this issue: Suppose in 1966, Author transferred her copyright to Publisher. The potential term of copyright at that time was 56 years. The copyright was due to expire in 1980. But in 1976, Congress extended the copyright term by 19 years and by another 20 years in 1998. Now the copyright has a potential term of 95 years (until 2019). Should Publisher get the extra 39 years or should Author get them? Section 304(c) gives the option to Author to get the extra time. Provided that Author (or Author's heirs) give timely notice, Author may terminate the grant at either the 56-year point or the 75-year point.

The other termination right under §203 applies to post-1977 grants. It allows authors to terminate grants after 35 years. Section 203 is somewhat paternalistic. It limits the ability of authors to sell their copyrights. Rather, it effectively limits a conveyance of rights to 35 years. A starving artist or struggling novelist who sells his or her work will be able to get rights back in 35 years. In other words, after 1977, Author cannot sell her copyright; she can only sell the next 35 years of her copyright.

Termageddon is nigh. Grants made after 1977 may be terminated after 35 years. The first terminations will take effect in 2013, which is soon upon us. So copyright holders in works from 1978 and on will soon face a possible wave of terminations each year. Music companies in particular must address the issue, because many works from around 1978 are commercially significant.

Termination rights do not apply to works made for hire. In addition, if the grant was made by joint authors, a majority of the grantors must join in the termination. So an issue in many cases will be whether the work was an individual work (where termination applies), joint work (multiple grantors must join), or work made for hire (termination not applicable). This may require resolving questions of fact based on works created decades ago. A work made for hire is one made by an employee, as opposed to a free-lancer. Courts may be asked, for example, to determine the precise working arrangement of rock bands working in the 1970s, where the memories of key witnesses are likely to be affected by narcissism, narcotics, or necromancy (especially with drummers, as noted in the film *Spinal Tap*).

Several rules apply to both types of termination. The right of termination does not apply to works made for hire. This means that if the employer sells or licenses the copyright (whether to the employee that created the work or to a third party), the employer will not be able to terminate that transfer. Employers were not thought to need protections intended for starving artists and struggling novelists.

Termination is not automatic. Rather, Author must give notice within the specified time or the grant will not be terminated. The right to terminate is inalienable, meaning a waiver of termination rights is not effective. Finally, termination has an exception: The grantee may continue to utilize derivative works prepared pursuant to the grant but does not have the right to prepare new derivative works.

To take a §203(c) termination by way of example: suppose that Author writes her children's novel in 2001 and assigns the copyright to Megacorp on January 1, 2002. The book becomes an enduring commercial success. Over the next decades Megacorp sells thousands of copies every year. Megacorp also makes a successful movie, which is a long-running success. Author (or her heirs or estate) may terminate the transfer of the copyright, effective anytime from January 1, 2037 (35 years from the grant, not from the beginning of the copyright) for the next five years. The same would be true if she had made a lesser grant, such as a license of the publication rights. She must give at least two years' prior notice and record a copy for termination to be effective. The copyright would revert to Author, who could now sell the book or make another movie. She would not get the copyright to the movie made by Megacorp, which could continue to utilize the movie. Megacorp could not make another movie that was a derivative work of the book. If Author did not terminate the transfer, then Megacorp would continue to own the copyright for its entire term (Author's life plus 70 years).

Note that if Author had written the book as an employee of Megacorp, there would be no right of termination. The termination right does not apply to works made for hire. As a work made for hire, the copyright would belong to the employer, Megacorp. Neither Megacorp nor Author would have termination rights. Author would have no right to get it "back" after 35 years. If Megacorp sold the copyright (or granted a license), Megacorp would have no statutory right of termination.

Copyright as Personal Property

Beyond the Copyright Act, copyrights are governed by common law property and contract principles (provided that such state law rules are not preempted by specific provisions or by general policies of the Copyright Act). So in determining the enforceability and effect of copyright agreements, courts must consider both the rules of the statute and any applicable rules of contract or property law. For example, property law would likely govern the effectiveness of transfers if no specific statutory rule applied.

Contract law often comes into play. Whether an implied license is given depends on common law principles. Explicit licenses, like other agreements, often must be interpreted to determine the parties' respective rights and duties. For example, a copyright owner might grant permission to make use of a work without making clear whether the permission was limited in time. Courts must also determine how broad the rights granted are. Such issues have included whether a circa 1900 grant to utilize a work in dramatic works applied to making films, whether permission to distribute a film applied to distribution of videotapes, and whether the right to publish a work included the right to post it on a Web page. Courts would determine the likely intent of the parties, based on the words of the agreement and other relevant evidence.

Examples

1. *Home is where the art is.* Starving Artist sells a painting, painted post-1978, entitled *Goth with the Twin* and the copyright in the painting to Investor. Their contract provides that the transfers of ownership of the painting and the copyright "shall be permanent, irrevocable, and apply to all rights under personal property law and under copyright law that Artist has now, or shall have in the future, in the works." Investor pays the agreed contract price.

   Investor hangs the paintings in a local museum. Over the succeeding years, Investor makes quite a lot of money by licensing the copyright for various uses: the image appears on posters, coffee cups, and window shades. Investor also has an employee paint an adaptation of the work, *Goth Triplets.* Investor has plans for several more paintings, starting with *Goth Quadruplets.*

   Some 35 years later, Starving Artist sends written notice to Investor that Starving Artist is exercising his right of termination under §203(c). The notice demands that Investor do the following:
   - cease exercising any of the exclusive rights of the copyright holder,
   - return the painting to Starving Artist,
   - hand over all revenues earned from licensing the copyright,
   - cease utilizing *Goth Triplets* and hand it over, and
   - cease the planned preparation of *Goth Quadruplets.*

   Which of Artist's demands are legally his right to make? Would it be any different if Starving Artist had made the painting as an employee of ArtsyFacts, who then sold the painting and the copyright to Investor?

2. *A book by any other name.* In 1974, the successful author Monarch signed a contract with a publisher, Hidebound. The contract provided that Hidebound would receive the "exclusive right to publish the novel *Scarrie*, in book form." The contract further stated that "Monarch retains all other rights, including without limitation the right to publish the novel in magazine or any other form other than books." By 2001, Hidebound had entered a new form of distributing fiction, the "e-book." For a set price, consumers could download text files containing various works sold by Hidebound. Does Hidebound have the right to sell *Scarrie* as an e-book?

3. *Yo-yo.* In 1946, Hermana wrote a love song, "Hesse." She published with the required notice in 1946. She sold the copyright to Robert Records in 1950 (along with renewal rights, which Robert subsequently secured). In 2006, "Hesse" still generates a nice income. Robert Records gets royalties from past recordings of the song. They also get royalties from sales of sheet music containing Hermana's original arrangement of the music and lyrics. Herman wonders whether she can somehow get the copyright back, along with the rights to royalties. Can she?

4. *Lassie, come home.* In 1938, Eric Knight sells to Lassie Television the motion picture and television rights in his story introducing Lassie. In 1978 (after the copyright has been duly renewed and the 1978 statute extends its term by 19 years), Knight's heirs sign over all motion picture and television rights in the Lassie story to Lassie Television. In 1996, the heirs seek to terminate the original grant of rights. Lassie Television contends that the 1978 agreement prevents them from doing so. Can the heirs get Lassie back?

Explanations

1. Even though Starving Artist agreed that the copyright would pass permanently to Investor, Starving Artist may still terminate the transfer after 35 years. Termination rights may not be effectively waived.

   The question then becomes what the effect of termination is. Termination causes all rights to revert to the author. One exception is that the licensee may continue to utilize derivative rights prepared pursuant to the grant, but may not prepare new derivative works. Accordingly, only some of the demands are supported by the termination right. Investor must cease exercising the rights of the copyright holder because those rights revert to Author. The exception for derivative works applies, however, to *Goth Triplets*. Investor is entitled to continue utilizing that derivative work but is not authorized to prepare *Goth Quadruplets*, a new derivative work. The termination rights only cause copyright rights to revert. They do not apply to ownership of physical copies or retroactively apply to pretermination exploitation of the work. So Investor is not required to return the painting to Artist or to hand over revenues earned from licensing the copyright.

2. Hidebound does not have the right to sell *Scarrie* as an e-book. Although this case involves a copyright, it is really a contract law issue: Did the agreement convey the right at issue? The court would try to determine the intent of the parties, looking primarily to the words of the contract, but also considering other relevant factors. The narrow issue, then, is whether an e-book is a book, as the parties used the word. The rights were narrowly limited to publication in the form of a "book," and all other rights carefully reserved to Monarch. The court would likely hold that distributing the text using a computer network falls into the category of "all other rights." Cf. *Random House v. Rosetta LLC*, 283 F.3d 490 (2d Cir. 2002).

3. The grant was made pre-1978, so §304(c) governs. Hermana may terminate within the five years after the 56 year total term. Note that the starting date is the beginning of the copyright, not the date of the grant. 1946 plus 56 is 2002, so the five-year period will end in 2007. It is 2006, so Herman can terminate the grant.

   Termination will give her back the copyright, but Robert Records may still utilize derivative works under the terms of the grant. They will continue to receive royalties for the sound recordings. Unlike Mills Music, the agreement does not require them to pay a percentage to Hermana. The sheet music is Hermana's original arrangement, not a derivative work, so they have no rights to that.

4. They can. *Classic Media Inc. v. Mewborn*, No. 06-55385 (9th Cir. 2008). Even if the 1978 agreement were a waiver or transfer of the termination right, it would not be effective. Termination "may be effected notwithstanding any agreement to the contrary." 17 U.S.C. §304(c)(5). *See also Siegel v. Warner Bros. Ent.*, 542 F. Supp. 2d 1098 (C.D. Cal. 2008) (upholding 1997 termination of 1938 grant of rights in Superman comics, despite grants of rights subsequent to the 1938 grant).

   Another author's heirs were less successful in seeking return of rights to famous works. *Penguin Group v. Steinbeck*, No. 06-3226 (2d Cir. 2008). John Steinbeck's widow, during the time when she could exercise termination rights, signed a contract with Penguin continuing and expanding the original publishing contract. In that case, the court held that the second agreement was an effective waiver of termination rights. The difference between the two cases was that the Lassie's heirs agreed to a second contract year before they could terminate the first, so they never had a right of termination. That sort of agreement cannot overcome the right to terminate. By contrast, Steinbeck's heirs could have terminated the original grant, but chose not to, and indeed signed an expanded contract. In that case, they had a present option to terminate and agreed to a new contract (as opposed to waiving a future option to terminate). So the new contract was an effective grant of rights. *Accord Milne v. Stephen Slesinger, Inc.,* 430 F.3d 1036 (9th Cir. 2005).

FORMALITIES: COPYRIGHT NOTICE, DEPOSIT, AND REGISTRATION

Until 1989: No "©," no copyright. Until 1992: no renewal, bye-bye copyright. This chapter tells how Picasso lost his copyrights—and got them back, decades later.

Nowadays, copyright arises automatically. To have her copyright, an author need not register the work, publish with a copyright notice, or deposit a copy with the Library of Congress. Registration is very useful, however. The biggest advantage—especially for works of low commercial value—is that infringement of a registered copyright gives a right to statutory damages. Even if there are no actual damages, statutory damages are $750 to $150,000 per work infringed.

Until 1989, authors, especially foreign authors and publishers less familiar with U.S. copyright law, often lost their U.S. copyright by failing to publish with a copyright notice or failing to file a renewal application for the second 28-year term. Such has been the fate of works by, among others, George Orwell, Igor Stravinsky, J.R.R. Tolkien, and Virginia Woolf.

At one time, formalities represented a great risk to authors. The greatest hazard was the requirement of a copyright notice ("© 1936 Zora Neale Hurston") on published copies. If a work was published without a copyright notice, the work lost copyright protection in the United States. Suppose Allie Author published her novel in 1966 and omitted to put a copyright notice on it. A simple "© 1966 Allie Author" on the copyright page would have been sufficient, but Allie simply did not know of the legal requirement of a copyright notice. Because she published without the notice, Allie's book would go into the public domain. She would have no copyright in her book under the federal copyright statute or state common law. She would not have the basket of exclusive rights (to make copies, adapt the work, distribute copies to the public, publicly perform the work, and publicly display the work). Anyone would be free to make and sell copies, copy elements of her novel into their works, or make a movie from her novel.

Another hazard was the need to file for the renewal term. Registration of copyright with the U.S. Copyright Office was not a condition to copyright. But, until 1978, copyright lasted 28 years, with an additional 28 years of protection only if the copyright owner filed for the renewal term. Even until 1992, it was necessary to register and file for renewal for pre-1976 works to receive the entire term of copyright. So failure to file for renewal also caused many works to go into the public domain.

Such formalities are no longer a condition of copyright. The old rules are still important, because they often control whether works published between 1923 and 1989 are under copyright or not. In particular, from 1909 to 1989, publication of the work without a copyright notice could mean loss of copyright (although from 1978 to 1989, the statute provided a means to cure such deficiencies in many cases). Until 1992, renewal of registration was also required to secure the full term of copyright. Many works went into the public domain for failure to comply with such formalities, especially works by foreign authors or by authors without timely legal advice.

Today, an author no longer risks losing her copyright for failure to include a copyright notice or register and renew the work. However, many practical advantages remain for notice, registration, and deposit.

Copyright Notice

A copyright notice is simple: "© 1926 Fitzgerald." For works published before March 1, 1989, however, it was essential to copyright protection.

In considering copyright notice, three time periods are key:

1909 to December 31, 1977. Under the 1909 Act, federal copyright generally began on publication with proper notice (or for some works, upon registration). State common law generally gave copyright in unpublished works. Copyright (federal and state) was generally forfeited for works first published without proper notice, although there were narrow savings provisions.

January 1, 1978, to February 28, 1989. Under the 1976 Act, federal copyright began upon fixation of the work in tangible form, so federal copyright law governed both published and unpublished works. Copyright could be lost by first publication without effective notice, but there were generous savings provisions.

March 1, 1989, and after. The 1976 Act is still in effect but amended to conform to international treaties. Formalities are no longer required for copyright. No "©," no problem.

Works Published Between 1909 and Dec. 31, 1977

Before 1978, when the 1909 Act was in effect, federal copyright applied primarily to published works. State copyright could potentially apply to unpublished works. Federal copyright protection was generally secured by placing a proper copyright notice on copies of the work when it was first published (some unpublished works could also receive copyright by registration). So Allie Author could get a federal copyright simply by including "© 1966 Allie Author" on the copyright page (the back of the title page) of the first published copies of her book. But if she published without that simple notice or included a defective notice, it was a divestive publication—meaning her book was not under copyright, and she lost the ability to claim copyright. An unsettled question is whether publication without proper notice outside the United States would divest U.S. copyright.

Several reasons have been offered for the notice requirement. *See, e.g.,* House Report 94-1476 (legislative history to 1976 Act). The rule put works into the public domain unless the copyright holder took a relatively easy step to preserve her rights. Copyright would not apply to works that were unclaimed, meaning that others could use works where the copyright owner had not reserved her rights. Notice of a claim of copyright also put others on notice that a work was copyrighted, like a No Trespassing sign. The notice also identified the copyright holder, so potential users could seek permission to use the work, where permission was required. It provided the date of publication, from which one could determine the duration of copyright. So the notice requirement provided an incentive for authors to claim copyright if they wished. But it also created a harsh forfeiture for authors who failed to meet the requirement.

The 1909 Act excused some failures to comply with the notice requirement. Section 21. Where the copyright owner sought to comply, "the omission by accident or mistake of the prescribed notice from a particular copy or copies" did not invalidate the copyright. Section 21. In order to come within the provision, the proprietor must have attempted to comply; it would not excuse one who did not know of the requirement or its dire consequences. It also excused only a relatively small failure ("a particular copy or copies"). In addition, the copyright owner could not recover damages from an innocent infringer who relied on the lack of notice.

A common issue was whether the work had been published or not. Because publication without notice resulted in such a harsh forfeiture, courts sometimes seemed to reach to find that no publication occurred. Some courts even applied different standards for publication, reasoning that to get copyright (an investive publication with notice) a lower standard applied; to lose copyright (a divestive publication without notice), a higher standard applied.

Courts held forfeiture required a "general publication," meaning that the work be made available to members of the public "without regard to their identity or what they intended to do with the work." By contrast, there was no forfeit by a "limited publication," where the work was made available to only selected persons for limited purposes, such as circulation of an academic paper for comments from chosen colleagues. In deciding whether a publication was general, courts looked at such factors as the number of recipients, how they were chosen, what restrictions were placed on the work, and whether the work became disseminated further. If an author sold copies of her short story to the public without affixing a copyright notice, the book would go into the public domain. If an author merely distributed some copies to members of a writing class for criticism, with instructions not to show the story to anyone else, then there would be no publication and no forfeit. She would not have a federal copyright yet, but could still obtain copyright by publishing with the proper notice of copyright.

The leading case on publication under the 1909 Act is *Estate of Martin Luther King, Jr. v. CBS*, 194 F.3d 1211 (11th Cir. 1999). The result at first seems counterintuitive: Dr. King's famous speech using the phrase "I have a dream," was held not to be published, even though it was delivered before some 200,000 people and a nationwide television and radio audience, and copies of the speech were distributed to journalists. But the case invoked two of the long-standing rules on publication. First, a limited distribution for limited purposes is not a distribution. So distributing copies of the text to journalists was not publication (as opposed to distributing copies of the text to the public). Second, Dr. King delivering the speech was a performance of the work and a performance (as opposed to a distribution or a display) has been consistently held not to be publication.

Works Published Between Jan. 1, 1978, and Feb. 28, 1989

In 1978 (upon the effective date of the 1976 Copyright Act), several things changed. First, the subject matter of copyright was expanded to include both published and unpublished material. Federal copyright no longer began upon publication or registration. Rather, copyright began as soon as the work was fixed in tangible form. So if Abby Author wrote a book in 1981, she had copyright as soon as she wrote it.

The 1976 Act did continue the rule requiring copyright notice on publication, but made it much less harsh. If Abby published her book without including a copyright notice ("© 1981 Abby Author"), she could still lose her copyright, but omission of the copyright notice did not invalidate the copyright if:

1. Notice was omitted "from no more than a relatively small number of copies or phonorecords distributed to the public"; or
2. The works was registered no later than five years after publication without notice, and "a reasonable effort is made to add notice to all copies or phonorecords that are distributed to the public in the United States after the omission has been discovered"; or
3. Notice was omitted by a licensee in violation of an express written requirement in a licensing agreement.

If Author's story was published without the required notice, she would not lose her copyright if only a few copies were published without notice, she registered within five years (while attempting to add notice to existing copies), or the publisher had omitted the notice despite a clause in the publishing contract. Although Author would not lose copyright, she would not be able to collect damages from an innocent infringer who relied on a copy with no copyright notice. 17 U.S.C. §405(b).

Works Published After March 1, 1989

Effective March 1, 1989, Congress did away with the requirement of notice as a condition for copyright. The United States removed the requirements of formalities because they were inconsistent with the leading international copyright treaty, the Berne Convention. Berne provides that "the enjoyment and the exercise" of copyright "shall not be subject to any formality." Berne Convention for the Protection of Literary and Artistic Works 5(2). One can see the difference between Berne (no formalities allowed) and the pre-1989 U.S. law (must publish with notice to keep copyright) as rooted in two different views of copyright. U.S. copyright is often seen as providing an incentive for authors. In order to encourage authors to produce works, they are entitled to claim exclusive rights in their works. If copyright is an incentive to produce, then requiring authors to meet formalities helps limit copyright to those authors who really had copyright in mind when creating the work. By contrast, Berne is often seen as representing the view that copyright is a moral right. An author, as the creator of the work, has a natural entitlement to control uses of the work. Such natural rights should not be conditioned on complying with legal formalities.

The actual change in the U.S. copyright statute dealing with copyright notice was small. Where pre-1989 law provided that a copyright holder *shall* use a copyright notice (at the risk of forfeiting copyright), the statute now provides that the copyright holder *may* use a copyright notice. The Copyright Act no longer requires copyright holders to use copyright notices, but it continues to authorize the practice. Although notice is not required, copyright owners continue to use copyright notices as a matter of course. The cost of including a notice is small, and there are considerable legal and practical advantages. If a defendant has access to a copy or phonorecord with a proper copyright notice, she cannot generally raise the "innocent infringement" defense, which may reduce damages. The copyright notice both identifies the owner (or purports to) and makes clear that the person claims those rights. The notice both serves as a warning to potential infringers, but also as a guide to potential licensees: "This is the person to contact if you wish to make a use of this work within the rights of the copyright owner."

The Limited Information in a Copyright Notice

A copyright notice provides little information: a named person claims copyright in the work, along with a publication date. There may be much in the work that is not protected by copyright. Ideas, facts, preexisting material, functional matter, and other elements are not protected by the copyright. So someone who wishes to copy from the work does not receive direct information about which particular elements are subject to the copyright claim. One exception is that where a work consists predominantly of works of the U.S. government (which are noncopyrightable), the copyright notice must identify the portions that embody protected material. Section 403.

Copyright notices may be wrongly used to claim protection in works that are in the public domain. It is common to find a copyright notice on an edition of a noncopyrighted work, such as a symphony by Beethoven or a play by Shakespeare. *See* Paul J. Heald, *Payment Demands for Spurious Copyrights: Four Causes of Action*, 1 J. Intell. Prop. L. 259 (1994). If the claimant added new material, the copyright claim may have some basis to it. But if the claimant simply copied existing public domain material and put a copyright notice on it, the claim would be spurious. Federal copyright law does not provide a civil cause of action for such spurious claims. But, where the claim lacks any basis, there could be liability under various state law theories, such as fraud, unjust enrichment, consumer protection, or breach of warranty. *Id.*

Form of Notice

The Copyright Act no longer requires copyright holders to use copyright notices, but it continues to authorize the practice. A copyright owner may place a copyright notice on visually perceptible copies or on phonorecords. 17 U.S.C. §401(a). The statute provides that the notice shall have three elements:

1. for copies: the familiar "©," or "Copyright," or "Copr."; for phonorecords: ℗;
2. the date of the work's publication (with rules for compilations and derivative works), which may be omitted for certain works; and
3. the name of the copyright owner (or abbreviation or alternative designation).

The notice must be placed in a manner and location that gives reasonable notice of the claim of copyright. 17 U.S.C. §§401(c), 402(c).

Although notice is not required, copyright owners continue to use copyright notices as a matter of course. The cost of including a notice is small, and there are considerable legal and practical advantages. If defendant had access to a copy or phonorecord with a proper copyright notice, she cannot generally raise the "innocent infringement" defense, which may reduce damages. The copyright notice both identifies the owner (or purports to) and makes clear that the person claims those rights. The notice both serves as a warning to potential infringers, but also as a guide to potential licensees: "This is the person to contact if you wish to make a use of this work within the rights of the copyright owner."

Registration

Copyright protection does not require registration. A work is copyrighted when it is fixed in tangible form. But registration is permitted and has a number of advantages. The United States is unique in having a Copyright Office for registration of copyrights, for deposit of copies of works, for recording various documents relating to copyrights, and for maintaining records and permitting public searches of the records. Some other countries have copyright offices, but none with such a range of services. The copyright owner (or owner of any of the exclusive rights) may register the work at any time during the copyright term. 17 U.S.C. §408. Both published and unpublished works may be registered.

Registration requires filling out the appropriate form, paying a modest fee, and depositing a copy or two of the work. Forms and clear directions are available at the U.S. Copyright Office Web site: *http://www.loc.gov/copyright/*. An examiner makes a limited examination and allows registration unless it is clear that the material is not copyrightable or other requirements (including ownership) are not met.

Copyright registration has several advantages. 17 U.S.C. §411. This requirement is limited to "United States works," that is, works first published in the United States or unpublished works by U.S. residents. *See* 17 U.S.C. §101.

Registration is also a prerequisite for certain remedies for infringement. Statutory damages and attorneys' fees are generally available only for infringement of registered works (unless the work is unpublished or is registered no later than three months after publication). 17 U.S.C. §412. Note a distinction here. Copyright registration is a condition for filing an infringement action, but it need not precede the infringement, only the filing of the subsequent lawsuit. But registration must precede the infringement (or registration must occur no later than three months after publication) for statutory damages or attorneys' fees to be awarded. In practical terms, infringement of an unregistered work may lead to a lawsuit, but not to an award of statutory damages or attorneys' fees. This is an important consideration.

The certificate of registration is prima facie evidence of the validity of the copyright, provided the work is registered no later than five years after first publication. 17 U.S.C. §410(c). The court, however, has discretion as to the weight to give that evidence, and courts readily hold registered works to be noncopyrightable if other evidence shows lack of originality or other requirements. Registration also has the practical advantage of making a public record of the copyright ownership, one that is readily available to anyone who searches the U.S. Copyright Office records. In addition to registering the copyright, one may record transfers of copyright ownership or other documents relating to a copyright. *See* 17 U.S.C. §205. Such recordation provides constructive notice of the documents to others, but only if the copyright has been recorded. 17 U.S.C. §205(c).

The advantages of copyright registration (statutory damages and attorney's fees in case of infringement, presumption of validity, and ownership of copyright; constructive notice of recorded documents) are dependent on a valid copyright registration. Errors such as mistakenly identifying a work as a work made for hire or failing to identify preexisting works from which the work was adapted can invalidate the registration. But not every mistake will void registration. Some courts have held that inadvertent mistakes do not invalidate the registration, but intentional fraud by the claimant will. *Urantia Found. v. Maaherra*, 114 F.3d 955, 963 (9th Cir. 1997). Other courts are less forgiving, holding that substantial mistakes are sufficient to invalidate the registration, even if made innocently.

Deposit

There are technically two separate deposit requirements. Copyright owners that register works must make a deposit (of one or two copies or phonorecords, depending on the type of work) with the U.S. Copyright Office. Copyright owners of published works are required to deposit two copies or phonorecords with the Library of Congress. Within three months of publication, a copyright owner must deposit two copies or phonorecords with the U.S. Copyright Office, "for the use or disposition of the Library of Congress." §407(a). But a copyright owner is permitted to use the Library of Congress deposit to also fulfill the registration deposit requirement. Copyright owners that neither register nor publish have no deposit requirement to meet.

All copies and phonorecords that are deposited become the property of the United States Government. 17 U.S.C. §704(a). The deposited material is available to the Library of Congress for its collections (subject to narrow exceptions for some unpublished works). 17 U.S.C. §704(b). The deposit requirement has helped give Library of Congress a huge collection of works. The Library of Congress chooses which works to retain and which to discard.

The regulations of the U.S. Copyright Office exempt many works from the deposit requirements, in whole or in part. For example, for computer programs, it is necessary only to deposit the first 25 and last 25 pages of the source code. In addition, if the program contains trade secrets, the copyright owner may omit portions of the code and thereby avoid disclosing the code to competitors or others. For secure tests (like the LSAT), the Copyright Office returns the copy after examination. Compendium II: Copyright Office Practices 315. The rules are expanding to accommodate the increase in number of works and the changing nature of works. For example, Copyright Office interim regulation limits the need to deposit electronic works (if they are published in the United States and available online) and provides that any electronic deposits shall not be made generally available to the public.[2]

The penalties for failing to deposit are modest and do not affect the validity of the copyright. If deposit is not made for a published work within three months of publication, then the Register of Copyrights may demand that it be made. If deposit still is not made, fines of up to $2,500 may be imposed, together with paying for the Register to buy copies. 17 U.S.C. §407.

There can be greater risks in connection with deposit. Deposit is required as part of registration. If deposit is done incorrectly, that may invalidate the registration. In addition, if the copy deposited does not match the copy allegedly infringed, that could likewise invalidate registration. This could mean that there is no claim for statutory damages. So copyright owners in works that are frequently revised, like computer programs, must be careful to register succeeding versions of the work. In addition, the copyright holder should be careful to maintain its own copies of each version registered, in order to prove any alleged infringement. She cannot rely on retrieving copies from the Copyright Office if necessary. As noted above, the copies deposited with the Copyright Office may not be complete copies, and the Copyright Office may discard those copies.

Restoration of Lost Copyrights for Foreign Authors

Many foreign copyright holders lost their U.S. copyrights due to failure to comply with requirements of formalities. If Zondag published in the United States without "© 1945 Zondag," she would lose her U.S. copyright. Copyright could be lost by publication without a copyright notice, during the years that U.S. law had such a requirement. Even if the work was published with a copyright notice, the owner could lose part of the copyright term by failing to file for renewal of the copyright. So if Zondag published with "© 1945 Zondag," but did not file a renewal, her U.S. copyright would expire in 1974, instead of 2001 (and loss of the benefit of the extension to 2040, under the extension in 1976 and 1998). U.S. authors rarely suffered such losses in other countries, because few countries required such formalities as a condition to copyright. Indeed, the leading international copyright treaty, Berne, forbade imposing such requirements on foreign authors.

---

2. *See Mandatory Deposit of Published Electronic Works Available Only Online*, 75 Fed. Reg. 3863 (2010).

The United States, like Ireland before it, had once been a haven of copyright "piracy." In the twentieth century, the U.S. became a major exporter of music, movies, software and other copyrighted products, and so more solicitous of intellectual property rights. U.S. cultural exports, often mixed with foreign artists, pervade the world. A pub in Galway advertising traditional Irish music may, for locals, switch to a medley of Bob Dylan, the Bee Gees, and Van Morisson. As intellectual property became part of international trade negotiations, the United States agreed to restore some of the foreign copyrights due to failure to comply with U.S. formalities requirements. Under legislation implementing U.S. adherence to TRIPS (Trade-Related Aspects of Intellectual Property Agreement) 1994, certain copyrights of foreign authors were restored, effective January 1, 1996. *See* 17 U.S.C. §104A—meaning Zondag could get her copyright restored. Restoration applies if several conditions are met:

- the work was first published in an eligible country (a country other than the United States that adheres to Berne, the WIPO Copyright, the WIPO Performances and Phonograms Treaty; is a member of the World Trade Organization; or is subject to a special presidential proclamation), at least 30 days before U.S. publication;
- the work has not passed into the public domain in its source country due to expiration of the period of protection;
- the work is in the public domain in the United States due to failure to comply with formalities (such as publication without a copyright notice or failure to file for the renewal term), due to lack of protection before 1972 in the United States for sound recordings, or due to lack of national eligibility; and
- the author was a national of an eligible country.

The foreign copyright holder is entitled to the remainder of the term that the copyright would have had, but for the loss of protection. The copyright holder need not file any form to have the copyright restored. Restoration is automatic. But the copyright holder may file a Notice of Intent to Enforce (NIE) a restored copyright with the Copyright Office. In addition, the copyright holder may serve notice of intent to enforce upon "reliance parties," persons that used the work while it was in the public domain.

The owner of a restored copyright generally has the right to enforce the copyright like other copyrights against infringement that occurs after the date of restoration. But reliance parties have limited protection. They are not liable for acts that occur before the claimant files with the Copyright Office or serves notice on the reliance party. The reliance party then gets a grace period (about one year) after filing or service. The reliance party may not make new copies during the grace period, but may sell existing copies and exploit derivative works. After the grace period, a reliance party may continue to exploit a derivative work prepared outside the United States, provided it pays reasonable compensation to the owner of the restored copyright.

The Supreme Court has held that the restoration provisions are constitutional. *Golan v. Holder*, 565 U.S. 202 (2012). The lower court had held that the restoration provisions of §104A were subject to First Amendment scrutiny, because §104A takes works that were in the public domain and puts them under copyright protection. *Golan* interpreted the Court's earlier decision in *Eldred* to hold that copyright laws that stay within copyright's "traditional contours," meaning fair use and the nonprotection of ideas, are generally insulated from First Amendment scrutiny, because those "built-in" First Amendment safeguards are sufficient to protect freedom of expression. So as long as fair use and the nonprotection of ideas are continued (and restored works are subject to those limitations), the First Amendment is not implicated. The *Golan* Court also reject the argument that Congress's powers to pass copyright laws is limited to enactments that give incentive to create works, as opposed to provisions that extend copyright protection to works that are already created (as with restoration).

Examples

1. In 1966, Gertrude self-published a thriller, *The Confounded*. She had 100 copies printed and sold them through a bookstore in Denver. Because Gertrude knew nothing of copyright law, she did not include a copyright notice on any copies. The issue was never raised until 2006. That year, the movie *Confabulated* was released. Gertrude saw it and immediately realized that the script was taken practically verbatim from her book. The producers admit the copying, but claim the book was not under copyright. Gertrude now has several arguments. Gertrude argues that she did not intend to put the book into the public domain and also that the requirement of formalities was abolished in 1989. Finally, at the least, she can use restoration to get her copyright back. Will these arguments work?

2. In 1986, Gertrude self-published her second thriller, *Children of the Confounded*. Again, she published a mere 100 copies without a copyright notice and sold them through a Denver bookstore. Now it is 2006. Given the success of *Confabulated*, publishers and producers are quite interested in the rights to *Children of the Confounded*. Does Gertrude have a copyright?

3. In 1996, Gertrude self-published *Grandchildren of the Confounded*. One hundred copies, no copyright notice, sold in Denver. Does it matter?

4. *And the copyright goes to* . . . Each year, the Academy of Motion Picture Arts and Sciences awards various Academy Awards (Best Picture, Best Director, etc.). The awards are given at a public ceremony, and each winner gets an Oscar statuette. The winners frequently hold them up

to be viewed by photographers, the admiring public, and their envious colleagues. From the 1929 to 1941, the Oscars were handed out without a copyright notice. After that, a notice was put on every statuette. The happy recipients generally kept their Oscars. The estate of one winner sold his, but it was eventually bought by the Academy.

Creative Choices has the clever idea to make Oscar statuettes for companies to give to Best Salesman and Best In-House Attorney in a Supporting Role. When the Academy sues, Creative contends that Oscar went into the public domain, by publication without notice. He's been on TV, in many newspaper photos, and was handed out year after year from 1929 to 1941. What result?

5. *Type A sees typo?* The perfectionist Boss of Squarer Records personally examines a CD from his company's most popular singer, Rhoda Rooner. Rooner wrote all the music and supervised the recordings. The CD case has the CD embodying the recording, along with a booklet with artwork, the lyrics to the music, and various information about Rooner. Under Rooner's contract, the copyrights in all her work transfer to Squarer Records. The copyright notice on the CD and on the booklet reads: "©,℗ 2002 Squarer Records." First, Boss wonders, shouldn't Rooner's name be included? Second, why does the notice have both © and ℗?

6. *Keeping a lid on it.* Spakester writes a humorous five-act play. He distributes copies to a number of local writers. They all agree the play will be a huge hit. One friend suggests that Spakester register the copyright in the play. Spakester responds that he will wait until the play is published. Spakester believes that he has no copyright until the play is published and that registering before then would not give him any benefits. Moreover, he figures, until the play is published or produced on stage, no one could possibly infringe. Would Spakester get any benefit from registering the copyright?

7. *Smitten with code.* Alga registers the copyright in her computer program, a useful piece of software for doing architecture. Over the next few years, she continues to test and adapt the program. A copy of the latest version is somehow purloined from her laptop and passed on to Smite Architects, who makes more copies and permits several of its to make use of the software. Alga is pleased that she took the step of registering the program. Because it was registered at the time of the infringement, she may get attorney's fees and statutory damages. In addition, she need not wait to register before filing her infringement action. Any problem?

8. *Restoration.* Gen's dissertation was published in Japan in 1965, and in the United States in 1968, both without a copyright notice. Gen's dissertation is still under copyright in Japan. Is there anything Gen can do to recover his U.S. copyright? What if the dissertation had been first published in

the United States without the requisite notice? Or what if it had been published without notice in 1920?

Explanations

1. Gertrude's book is not under copyright, because she published without copyright notice, during the time the harsh provisions of the 1909 Act were in effect. Her intent is irrelevant. No intent to put the work in the public domain is required. The fact that she published only 100 copies will not save her. Under the 1909 Act, where the proprietor sought to comply, "the omission by accident or mistake of the prescribed notice from a particular copy or copies" did not invalidate the copyright. But she had made no attempt to comply, so the provision does not apply to her case. Even if she had, omission of the notice from 100 copies may be too much to qualify as "particular copy or copies."

   The abolition of the formality requirement in 1989 does not affect her, because it did not apply retroactively to works published before that time. Nor does restoration help her, because it applies only to copyrights owned by foreign authors.

2. This time, Gertrude published without notice, during the decennial period governed by the 1976 Act's initial notice provisions. Under the 1976 Act, there is no loss of copyright if notice was omitted "from no more than a relatively small number of copies or phonorecords distributed to the public." The question here is whether the 100 copies were a relatively small number. As compared to books generally, 100 copies is not too many, so a court might hold that it was "relatively small." On the other hand, it was *all* the copies she had printed, so a court might hold that it was not *relatively* small.

   The other saving provisions would not help her. She did not register and try to fix the missing notices. Nor was the notice omitted by a licensee, in violation of instructions from her.

3. This time, Gertrude published without notice, during the time governed by the post March 1, 1989, rules. Copyright notice on published copies is no longer a condition for copyright protection, so she has her copyright. She may be subject to the innocent infringer defense, but her rights generally are not affected.

4. The court held that there was no divesting publication. *See Academy of Motion Picture Arts & Sciences v. Creative House Promotions*, 944 F.2d 1446 (9th Cir. 1991). The Oscars were distributed to the winners and shown to news photographers without a copyright notice. But the distribution was a limited distribution, not to the general public. They were given to winners of the Academy Awards. When one went on auction, the

Academy managed to eventually buy it. The display was also somewhat limited. Unlike public display of a sculpture, with no limits on copying, the three-dimensional statuettes were made available to photographers, who made two-dimensional photos. The court held that did not permit unrestricted copying (although one wonders how the defendant could then have made the allegedly infringing statuettes).

5. The compact disc is a phonorecord, embodying both the musical work and the sound recording. The booklet is a copy of the musical work (at least the lyrics of the music), as well as the art work, and perhaps a literary work (the other info). So use of both symbols is appropriate, © for copy, ℗ for phonorecord.

6. Spakester would benefit from registering the copyright. Works may be registered whether published or not. His copyright could certainly be infringed before publication or production. Several copies are already circulating among writers, who may pass them on to others. The benefit of registration would be that if the copyright is infringed, the remedies available may be greater. Statutory damages and attorneys' fees may be awarded only for infringement of registered copyrights. Spakester would have much greater leverage in litigation if the copyright is registered. In addition, registration and deposit provide some evidence that he wrote the work by the date of registration, which would compare favorably against an infringing author who denies copying the work.

7. Alga may have a problem. She registered and deposited one version of the computer program. She then continued to test and adapt the program. It may well be that the version that was infringed was sufficiently different that it was a separate derivative work, not registered by Alga.

8. The restoration provisions would give Gen his copyright back. To maximize his ability to enforce the copyright, Gen could file a Notice of Intent to Enforce with the Copyright Office, which would limit the ability of reliance parties to continue acts that would infringe Gen's copyright.

PERIOD OF PROTECTION

Mark Twain argued that copyright should last forever, like most property rights. Some argue that copyright should last just a few years, which would be sufficient to provide an incentive to authors but would also put works into the public domain quickly. Copyright law takes a position closer to Twain's. Copyright lasts a long time. *The Great Gatsby* (published 1925) and *Finnegans Wake* (1939) are still under copyright (although *Gatsby*'s copyright will finally expire in 2021). The period of protection depends on when a work is created.

For works created on or after January 1, 1978, the following rules apply. The general rule is "life plus 70": copyright endures from creation of the work and terminates 70 years after the author's death. 17 U.S.C. §302(a). For joint works, the 70 years runs from the death of the last surviving author. 17 U.S.C. §302(b). The term is not keyed to the length of the author's life for a work made for hire (where the employer is the author), an anonymous work (one that does not identify the author), or a pseudonymous work (one that identifies the author under a fictitious name). Such a work has a term of "95 years from the date of its first publication, or a term of 120 years from the year of its creation, whichever expires first." 17 U.S.C. §302(c).

For works published before January 1, 1978, the general rule is that the work has an effective term of 95 years from publication (or, in some cases, from registration). 17 U.S.C. §304. For works created but unpublished and unregistered on January 1, 1978, the term is at least until 2047. 17 U.S.C. §303. This applies only if the work is published before 2003; otherwise, some such unpublished works could go into the public domain in 2003. All of the foregoing is subject to some particular exceptions. In particular, for works created before 1990, one must check to make sure that the work did not go into the public domain for failure to comply with formalities such as the notice requirement or the renewal requirement.

January 1, 1978 is the dividing line because that was the effective date of the last wholesale revision of the Copyright Act. The original term of copyright was 28 years (two 14-year terms). Congress has several times increased the term. Effective 1978, Congress extended the 56-year term under the 1909 Act by 19 years to 75 years. Works published before 1923 had expired copyrights (1978 − 1923 > 56), but works published 1923 or later remained under copyright. Congress again extended the term of most copyrights by 20 years in 1998. The term for pre-1978 works increased from 75 to 95 years. Works from the 1920s (1923 and later) and 1930s that were soon to go into the public domain now remained under copyright for another 20 years.

Under the 1909 Act, it was necessary to file a renewal certificate during the last year of the initial 28-year term to secure the 28-year renewal term. Fred Fisher Music Co. v. M. Witmark & Sons, 318 U.S. 643 (1943), held that assignments of renewal rights are assignable. However, Miller Music Corp. v. Charles N. Daniels, Inc., 362 U.S. 373 (1960), held that if the author dies before renewal, the assignment would be ineffective. In order to file a renewal certificate, it was necessary to register the work. If no valid renewal certificate was filed, the work went into the public domain after the initial 28-year period. The 1976 Act did not change that requirement. For works copyrighted (i.e., published with notice or registered) before 1978, it remained necessary to file for renewal in the 28th year to get the renewal term. In 1992, Congress made renewal automatic. So for works copyrighted from 1964 to 1977, renewal is automatic.

To sum that up:

- Works published before 1923: in public domain
- Works published 1923-1977: 95 years from publication (if published before 1964, must have filed for renewal after initial 28 years)
- Works created 1978 or later: generally protected from creation, duration life +70 years; for works-made-for-hire, anonymous, or pseudonymous works, shorter of 95 years from publication or 120 years from creation.

The statute also has special rules for works created before 1978 and published 1978 or later.

Eldred v. Ashcroft, 537 U.S. 186 (2003), rejected two challenges to the constitutionality of the extending the terms of existing copyrights. Under the Copyright Clause, Congress has the power "To promote the Progress of Science and useful Arts, by securing for limited Times to Authors and Inventors the exclusive Right to their respective Writings and Discoveries." One can read the power as limited to granting copyrights as an incentive to create works. Nothing Congress did in 1998 could give an incentive for authors in the 1920s to write more books. But *Eldred* held that Congress had the power to choose the intellectual property regimes that would serve the ends of the clause. The Court also rejected the First Amendment argument, that Congress could not keep copyrighted expression out of the public domain without a countervailing benefit. The Court held that First Amendment scrutiny would generally not apply to copyright. Rather, freedom of expression is sufficiently protected by traditional copyright law's safeguards, such as fair use and the exclusion of ideas from protection. Future cases, however, may consider the appropriate analysis where Congress has gone beyond the traditional forms of copyright protection (such as the anticircumvention provisions discussed in the next chapter, which are quite different from the usual exclusive rights, are not limited to protection of expression, and are not explicitly subject to fair use). *See* Stephen M. McJohn, *Eldred's Aftermath: Tradition, the Copyright Clause, and the Constitutionalization of Fair Use,* 10 Mich. Telecomm. & Tech. L. Rev. 95 (2003).

Dastar Corp. v. Twentieth Century Fox Film Corp., 123 S. Ct. 2041, 2047-2049 (2003) rejected the use of trademark law to effectively extend copyright protection. Twentieth Century Fox had held copyrights in videos about World War II, but the copyrights had expired due to failure to renew. Dastar subsequently republished the videos, after removing credits to the original producers. Fox could not sue for copyright infringement. But Fox contended that by failing to properly attribute authorship, Dastar had made a "false designation of origin" of the goods, in violation of trademark law. But "origin of goods," the Court held, "refers to the producer of the tangible goods that are offered for sale, and not to the author of any idea, concept, or communication embodied in those goods." Trademark law would not provide a cause of action for failing to attribute authorship. In so holding, the Court sought to maintain the distinction between the proper domains of copyright and trademark: "To hold otherwise would be akin to finding that §43(a) created a species of perpetual patent and copyright, which Congress may not do." Under *Dastar*, once a work falls into the public domain, the former copyright holder may not use trademark law to prevent its use by others.

If copyright subsists automatically on fixation of a work and requires no formalities, can the author affirmatively put her work into the public domain? Copyright cases on abandonment are scarce. Abandonment can occur if (1) the copyright owner has intent to surrender rights in the work, and (2) she makes an overt act evidencing that intent. Melville B. Nimmer & David Nimmer, "The Defense of Abandonment of Copyright," in *Nimmer on Copyright* 13.06. Failure to exploit the work or failure to enforce the copyright against infringers does not constitute abandonment.

Examples

1. *No starter.* Azure wrote *False Start*, a novel, in 1960. She quickly published, not even pausing to put "© 1960 Azure" on published copies. When does her copyright begin and end?

2. *A little more careful.* Azra wrote *Twenty-Eight Years of Solitude*, an epic poem, in 1960. He meticulously put "© 1960 Azra" on every published copy. Then he went into advertising and forgot about the work. When does his copyright begin and end? What result if he had published the work in 1970?

3. *Belt and suspenders.* Nevaeh wrote "Four Score and Fifteen Years Ago," a ballad, in 1960. She made sure copyright notices appeared where required. She registered the work and duly filed a renewal certificate in 1988. When does her copyright term begin and end?

4. *Portrait of the artist as a young man.* In 1960, Ellis published a superhero comic book, *Invisible Man*. He included a copyright notice, thereby securing federal copyright in the work. He then sold the copyright to Chilton Publishing, along with an assignment of the renewal rights. During the last year of the initial 28-year term, Chilton is about to file a renewal certificate when Ellis objects. The assignment of renewal rights is not enforceable, he argues, because the whole purpose of renewal is to give the author his copyright back—and prevent struggling young artists from irrevocably signing away their rights.
   a. Who owns the rights to the renewal term?
   b. What if Ellis had died and his heirs were seeking the rights? If Chilton had made a movie based on the book, would it retain the right to keep showing the movie?

5. *Life is short; copyright is long.* In 2000, Miranda wrote down the choreography of her dance, *Trailer*. She published the work without including a

notice of copyright. She never registered the copyright or filed a renewal certificate.

a. When would her copyright begin and end? Would it make a difference if the work was never published? Would it make a difference if the author was not identified, making it an anonymous or pseudonymous work?

b. Suppose the dance was a work made for hire, so that the author and copyright owner was her employer, Hurricane Dance Co. When would the copyright expire?

6. *Alternate universe.* Suppose that, rather than life plus 70, the basic term of copyright was life of the author. How would that change things?

7. *The dog that did not bark.* Arthur Conan Doyle's stories featuring Sherlock Holmes were variously published from 1887 to 1927. The last ten were published after 1922 and are therefore still under copyright. The earlier stories are no longer under copyright. Would someone need permission from the copyright owner to create new works with the character of Sherlock Holmes? Would it matter if the character changed somewhat in the final ten stories?

8. *Yes we have no more copyright.* The immortal song "Yes! We Have No Bananas" was published with a proper copyright notice in 1923 and properly renewed. How long did its copyright last?

Explanations

1. Under the 1909 Act in effect in 1960, when she created the work, she had state law copyright protection. When she published without notice, however, she put the work into the public domain, meaning she had neither state nor copyright protection. This example shows how the subject of this chapter, duration of copyright, often depends on the formalities rules discussed earlier.

2. Under the 1909 Act in effect in 1960, Azra secured the initial 28-year term by publishing with notice. But he did not file for a renewal certificate, which was necessary to get the renewal term, so his copyright term began in 1960 and ended in 1988.

   Had he published in 1970, the result would be different. As a result of the 1992 amendments, filing for renewal is not necessary for works copyrighted after 1963. So he would get an effective term of 95 years (28-year initial term plus 67-year renewal term, comprised of 28 years under the 1909 Act, extended by 19 years in 1976, and another 20 years in 1998). 1970 + 95 = 2065.

3. Neveah got her copyright in 1960 by publishing with notice and duly renewed, so she would get an effective term of 95 years (28-year initial term plus 67-year extended renewal term). 1960 + 95 = 2055.

4. a. Ellis cannot get the renewal term back. Notwithstanding the policy underlying renewal, *Fred Fisher Music* held that assignments of renewal rights are enforceable.

   But all is not lost. As discussed later in the book, Ellis would have rights under §304 to terminate the transfer and get his copyright back, effective 56 years into the term of the copyright. 1960 + 56 = 2016. He would then get the last 39 years of the extended renewal term. (If he missed in 2016, he could terminate effective 2035.)

   b. Had Ellis died, the result would be different. Under *Miller Music*, if the author dies before the renewal term vests, an assignment of rights is not effective and the heirs have the right to the renewal term. All rights under the copyright would belong to Ellis's heirs. Had Chilton made a movie based on the book, it would no longer be able to show the movie (which would infringe the public performance right) or make copies of it (which would infringe the reproduction right) or do anything else that would infringe the copyright.

5. a. The §302 rules for post-1977 works would apply. Miranda's copyright term begins when the work is fixed in tangible form and would last for her life plus 70 years. If she died in 2040, for example, the copyright would endure until 2130. Whether the work was published or not makes no difference. Were it an anonymous or pseudonymous work, the term would be 95 years, lasting until 2095.

   b. If it were a work made for hire, her employer would own the copyright, with a term of 95 years.

6. Under existing rules, works published after 1922 are likely to remain under copyright. Works later than 1950, for example, may be under copyright until 2045. Under the copyright-for-life rule, works would frequently pass into the public domain. Authors, unlike copyright, reach the end of their term with regularity. Such a rule would also yield quite dramatic results. Each time a noted author passed away, her works would become free for all, sort of an impromptu copyright amnesty—but it would also introduce considerable uncertainty. It would add risk to making films, for example, because the author of an underlying work might die during production, opening the door to other filmmakers.

7. Because the earlier stories are no longer under copyright, anyone is free to copy them or adapt them, such as using Sherlock Holmes or his sidekick, Dr. Watson. There might be infringement if someone copied creative expression from the stories that are still under copyright. In those stories, Holmes has grown to like dogs, and Watson has been

twice married. Copying such later-added elements could be infringement, provided they qualified as protected creative expression. But there is no longer copyright protection in elements from the earlier stories, such as the characters or plots. *See Klinger v. Conan Doyle Estate, Ltd.*, 755 F.3d 496 (7th Cir. 2014).

8. 1923 + 28 + 28 + 19 + 20 = 2018. The copyright expired at the end of 2018. After the extensions in 1976 and 1998, Congress did not add 20 more years in 2018 (as of writing this in summer 2018). So finally works from 1923 and after are starting to enter the public domain as their copyrights will expire.

BRING BACK FORMALITY REQUIREMENTS?

Recent years have seen several proposals to reinstitute requirements of formalities. As of 1989, formalities no longer were a condition for copyright in the United States. But other trends in copyright law, as commentators have noted, actually strengthened the argument for some formality requirements. The 1976 Act broadened the scope of copyright to include unpublished works. Computer software has become an increasingly important category of copyrighted material, although its functional nature makes it something of an awkward fit into copyright. The term of copyright has been repeatedly extended. The notice requirements did have the advantage of putting works into the public domain, unless the copyright claimant took affirmative steps to claim copyright (by using a copyright notice or registering the work).

One suggestion has been to condition copyright protection on registration, with periodic renewal. *See* Lawrence Lessig, *The Future of Ideas* 249 (2001) (proposing five-year copyright term, renewable 14 times); William M. Landes & Richard A. Posner, *Indefinitely Renewable Copyright*, 70 U. Chi. L. Rev. 471 (2003) (proposing 20-year terms, renewable indefinitely). Landes and Posner propose a trade-off: permitting indefinitely renewable copyright in exchange for requiring renewal. Their empirical analysis showed that, when renewal was required for the second 28-year term, fewer than 11 percent of copyrights were renewed. In addition, most copyrighted works have a relatively short economic life expectancy. Moreover, copyright owners are sensitive to fees, meaning renewals would not be numerous if even modest fees were required. Therefore, few works would remain under copyright beyond the initial term. Owners of valuable copyrights would renew as long as permitted, but Landes and Posner see that as beneficial, because keeping copyrights as private property provides incentives for efficiently exploiting them (though others might differ on that). Landes and Posner even suggest an interesting side benefit of permitting indefinitely renewable copyright:

around 2015, when the 20-year-term extension in 1998 would otherwise be soon to run out, there would be fewer resources wasted in attempting to convince Congress to once again extend the term.

One could have a formality regime that was less harsh than the old version. Until 1989, an author could lose copyright by failing to publish with a copyright notice. A kinder rule would provide that a work would not be copyrighted until publication with notice or perhaps filing of a registration, but failure to carry out such formalities would not forfeit copyright completely; rather the author would not have copyright until she eventually complied.

The greatest legal obstacle to bringing back formalities as a condition to copyright would be that it might violate U.S. treaty obligations, unless the rule applied only to U.S. authors. But one proposal avoids that problem. The DMCA (discussed in subsequent chapters) gives legal protection for anti-copying and anti-access technology used on copyrighted works. But those protections are distinct from copyright itself. So it may be permissible to require formalities as a prerequisite for such legal protection. *See* Pamela Samuelson & Jason Schultz, *Should Copyright Owners Have to Give Notice About Their Use of Technical Protection Measures?*, 6 J. Telecomm. & High Tech. L. 41 (2007) (conference agenda). If a copyright owner wished to have legal protection for anti-copying or anti-access technology (such as scrambling cable TV signals or putting anti-copying code on music files), she might be required to put some kind of notice on the work.

Exclusive Rights: Their Enforcement and Limitations

To establish infringement, two elements must be proven: (1) ownership of a valid copyright, and (2) copying of constituent elements of the work that are original.

Feist Publns., Inc. v. Rural Tel. Serv. Co., 499 U.S. 340, 361 (1991).

The previous chapters discussed what it takes to have rights in a valid copyright. This chapter discusses the exclusive rights that copyright confers and how these rights are enforced. "Copyright law" might be called "Copyadaptdistributeperformdisplayrights law." Under 17 U.S.C. §106, the copyright owner has the exclusive rights to do or authorize the following:

1. reproduce the work in copies or phonorecords (often called the reproduction right or the right to make copies);
2. prepare derivative works based on the work (adaptation right);
3. distribute copies or phonorecords of the work to the public by sale or other transfer of ownership, or by rental, sale, or lending (public distribution right);
4. perform the work publicly (public performance right); and
5. display the work publicly (public display right).

17 U.S.C. §106.

These exclusive rights are not absolute: all are subject to a number of limitations discussed here and in subsequent chapters (such as the fair use doctrine, the first sale doctrine, and more specific limitations). People can do all sorts of things with a work that the copyright holder may not like, but there is no copyright infringement unless their actions trespass on one of her exclusive rights. To see whether copyright infringement has occurred, ask the following questions:

1. *"Actual copying"*: Has defendant potentially infringed (that is, copied from the copyrighted work, made a derivative work based on the work, distributed a copy of the work to the public, performed the work publicly, or displayed a copy of the work publicly)? As part of this, does one of the limitations protect defendant's activity?
2. *Misappropriation*: Did defendant copy (or adapt, distribute, perform, or display) copyright-protected material, or did defendant only use nonprotected material (such as nonoriginal expression, facts, ideas, or functional elements)?
3. *Substantial similarity*: Is defendant's work substantially similar?

Note that copyright infringement need not be for commercial purposes, result in financial gain, be deceptive, involve improper acts, or even be knowing or intentional. Defendant is liable even if he did not know he was using copyrighted material.

A key limitation is that intellectual property is territorial. If infringing conduct occurs outside the United States, then the mere fact that it was supported by some conduct within the United States will not trigger liability under the U.S. copyright statute (although it may be infringement under the laws of that country).[1] However, unauthorized streaming of copyrighted televisions programs into the United States was held to infringe under U.S. law, on the theory that it caused performance of the programs to occur on users' computers in the United States.[2]

It may be that simply authorizing someone else to perform one of the protected rights is infringement. *Banco Popular de Puerto Rico v. Asociacion de Compositores y Editores de Musica Latinoamericana*, 678 F.3d 102 (1st Cir. 2012), held, without much discussion, that a party that licenses copyrights that it does not own is liable for copyright infringement. In any case, that would probably give rise to secondary liability (discussed in a later chapter).

This chapter also discusses other types of protections available under the copyright statute. Certain authors (not necessarily the copyright holder) of "works of visual arts" receive protection under 17 U.S.C. §106A against distortion or destruction of their artworks or misattribution of authorship. The statute provides certain legal protections to technological measures used to prevent people from accessing or copying works, as well as legal protection to "copyright management information" provided in connection with copies of works. 17 U.S.C. §§1201, 1202.

---

1. Geophysical Service, Inc. v. TGS-NOPEC Geophysical Co., 850 F.3d 785 (5th Cir. 2017).
2. Spanski Enters. v. Telewizja Polska, S.A., 883 F.3d 904, 915 (D.C. Cir. 2018).

EXCLUSIVE RIGHTS OF THE COPYRIGHT OWNER

Reproduction Right

Copyright takes its name from the exclusive right to make copies of the copyrighted work. The owner of the copyright has the exclusive right "to reproduce the copyrighted work in copies or phonorecords." 17 U.S.C. §106(1). Copies are "material objects, other than phonorecords, in which a work is fixed by any method now known or later developed, and from which the work can be perceived, reproduced, or otherwise communicated, either directly or with the aid of a machine or device." 17 U.S.C. §101. Phonorecords are defined in similar terms to include material objects in which sounds (other than those accompanying a motion picture or other audiovisual work) are fixed. These broad definitions give the copyright owner exclusive rights to make copies in a variety of forms. For example, the owner of a copyright in a song has the exclusive right to make copies in sheet music or make phonorecords on tape or compact discs. Likewise, the copyright owner in a computer program has the right to make copies in source code (the form in which a developer writes the program), in object code (the set of binary instructions and data in which the program runs on a computer), or embedded in permanent form on a chip.

The reproduction right, unlike the performance, distribution, and display rights, is not limited to public acts. A defendant can infringe by making a copy alone in her office.

Volition or Causation

The copyright owner has the exclusive right to make copies of the work. Someone who makes copies potentially infringes. The statute does not require additional elements such as knowledge of the copyright, intent to infringe, or motive of commercial gain. Courts have even held that subconscious copying is infringement. Copyright is often described as a type of strict liability. But courts have required a minimal showing of "volition or causation" by the defendant.

Suppose Business allows a customer to use one of Business's photocopy machines. Unbeknownst to Business, the customer uses the machine to make unauthorized copies of various poems. Courts agree that, although Business owns and controls the copy machine, Business has not made copies and therefore is not an infringer. Likewise, courts have held, where customers of an Internet service provider (ISP) use their access to post copyrighted photos, the Internet service provider has not made copies. Provided that the Internet service provider did not play an active role, the fact that its network was used did not mean that it made copies. "[W]e hold that ISPs, when passively storing material at the direction of users in order to make that material available to other users upon their request, do not 'copy' the material in direct violation of §106 of the Copyright Act." *CoStar Group v. LoopNet*, 373 F.3d 544, 555 (4th Cir. 2004). If the ISP went beyond merely providing the use of a network, however, it could be held to make copies (or be liable as a secondary infringer, discussed later in the book).

Example

Volition, volition. Giganews allows users to download a browser app, Mimo. Using Mimo, users can view material that they access through USENET, a network of users that share messages and content. Is Giganews liable for infringement of the display right if the browser app it provided is used to view copyrighted images?

Explanation

The court reasoned that although users may use Giganews's reader to display infringing images, that does not constitute volitional conduct by Giganews. "'Mimo is just a reader, a piece of software that allows a user to view an image,' and therefore, '[t]o the extent that Mimo is used to view infringing images, this is done by the user.'" *Perfect 10, Inc. v. Giganews, Inc.*, 847 F.3d 657, 668 (9th Cir. 2017) (quoting trial court with approval).

Actual Copying

The copyright owner has the right to make copies of the work. Someone else potentially infringes if they copy the work, even if they do not copy the entire work and even if they make a copy that is similar but not identical. But independent creation is not infringement. So if someone makes a similar work without copying from the copyrighted work, there is no infringement—no matter how similar the works are. If Composer writes "Ode to Glee," she holds the copyright. If Composer hears a subsequent composition by someone else that sounds extremely similar, she may claim copyright infringement. But the second comer is liable only if she copied from Composer's work (directly or indirectly, such as by copying from a work that copied from the copyrighted work). If she simply happened to come up with a similar work, or copied elements in the public domain from another work, she is not liable.

To show potential infringement of the exclusive right to make copies, plaintiff must show that defendant actually copied from the copyrighted work, that defendant took protected material, and that defendant's work was substantially similar to the copyrighted work. Liability requires copying; independent creation is not infringement. To determine whether actual copying took place, the fact finder looks to the degree of similarity between the works and the amount of access defendant had to the work. The more similar the works and the more access defendant had to plaintiff's work, the more likely it is that defendant copied rather than created her work independently. The fact finder also considers evidence of independent creation by defendant, such as notes or drafts.

Examples

1. *"You're the One for Me."* Plaintiff alleges that his song "You're the One (for Me)" was copied by defendant record company to make a song entitled "You're the One." Both songs, like many others, use "You're the One for Me" in the lyrics. The melodies are vaguely similar: "their relationship is something more akin to that of second cousins, twice removed," but those similarities are shared by many songs already in the public domain. They both use harmonic progression, a common composing technique. They both repeat the same note three times (as do many other songs). There is little evidence that defendants had access to plaintiff's song, beyond the fact that plaintiff delivered one copy of it to a sometime coworker. By the same token, Defendant has little evidence of independent creation, such as tapes from the recording session. Is there sufficient evidence to get to a jury?

2. *"How Deep Is Your Love?"* Ronald Selle composed the song, "Let It End," and performed it with his band a few times in the Chicago area. Selle sent a tape and sheet music to a number of music companies, but received no response other than getting his material returned. Selle applied for and received a copyright registration. A couple of years later, Selle heard another song, "How Deep Is Your Love?" by the group, the Bee Gees. That song was a huge seller and featured in a Hollywood hit, *Saturday Night Fever*. Selle sued for copyright infringement.

    The two songs were similar in many ways. Many notes were "identical in pitch and symmetrical position." Many of the "rhythmic impulses" were also the same. But there is no evidence that the Bee Gees ever had access to Selle's song, with its very limited distribution. There is also considerable evidence of independent creation, from witnesses and from tapes, capturing some of the evolution of the Bee Gees' composition of their song. Is there sufficient evidence to support a finding of actual copying?

Explanations

1. The evidence would not be sufficient to support a finding of actual copying. *See Johnson v. Gordon,* 409 F.3d 12, 24 (1st Cir. 2005). The court will consider similarity between the works, defendant's access to plaintiff's works, and evidence of independent creation. Here, the slight similarities are no more than would occur by coincidence: use of a hackneyed phrase, vaguely similar melodies, common compositional techniques, and using a note three times. Nor was there substantial evidence of access to the work. So plaintiff would not meet the burden of showing actual copying.

2. The court held there was insufficient evidence to show actual copying. *See Selle v. Gibb,* 741 F.2d 896, 900 (7th Cir. 1984). There was a high showing of similarity, but no showing of access and considerable evidence of independent creation. For a plaintiff to succeed by showing similarity alone, the similarity would have to be so great that it could be explained only by copying. If two lengthy symphonies were absolutely identical, one must have been copied from the other. But striking similarity between two songs could be caused by things other than copying from the Selle's song.

Misappropriation

Actual copying alone does not establish infringement. As discussed above, many aspects of copyrighted works are not protected by copyright: ideas, facts, functional aspects, and nonoriginal elements, for example. Someone may copy such elements from a copyrighted work without infringing (although, as discussed in earlier chapters, distinguishing protected expressive elements from the unprotected elements can be difficult). An author who copies unprotected elements from another author's novel is not liable for copyright infringement. A software developer may copy the unprotected method of operation of a software package. A filmmaker may copy the unprotected facts set forth in a history book. In addition to proving copying, the plaintiff must show that defendant copied protected expression.

Substantial Similarity

Finally, there is no infringement unless the works are substantially similar. The defendant need not produce an identical copy. Copying need not be literal to give rise to liability. As previous chapters discuss, protected elements of a work go well beyond the exact form of the copyrighted work. A writer who paraphrases another novel or a photographer who closely models her photo on another is liable. The issue is whether the defendant takes protected expression or unprotected elements (such as ideas, functional aspects, and nonoriginal elements).

Cases differ considerably, to put it mildly, on the test for "substantial similarity." Some of the most important issues are these:

1. Should one consider the works as a whole or only the protectable elements in deciding whether there is substantial similarity between the works?
2. Should expert testimony be used to guide the decision?
3. From whose point of view must the works be substantially similar? To a reasonable person? To an expert? To the intended audience or an ordinary observer, such as the average consumer of such works? One court held that whether a defendant's dinosaur Halloween costume was substantially similar to a copyrighted work featuring Barney (the famous purple dinosaur) should be determined from the viewpoint of the young children to whom such works are targeted. *See Lyons Partnership v. Morris Costumes*, 243 F.3d 789 (4th Cir. 2001).

Sound recordings are an exception to this rule. The reproduction right in a sound recording is infringed only by a literal copy, one that recaptures the actual sounds fixed in the sound recording. 17 U.S.C. §114(b).

The DRAM Issue: Is a Temporary Copy Inside a Computer a Potentially Infringing Copy?

Creative works now often come in digital form, as strings of 0s and 1s. Texts were once typewritten or manually typeset; now they are likely to be created and stored using word processing programs. VHS is joining Betamax in the format graveyard. Tapes and records generally have been supplanted by CDs and MP3 files. Digital cameras are eclipsing film cameras.

The increasing use of digital technologies broadens the potential applicability of the right to make copies. First, digital copies can be easy to duplicate and are the same as the original (as opposed copies of other products, which are often inferior in quality to the original). Second, the process of exploiting digital works often involves making additional copies. Suppose someone has access to a digital copy of a copyrighted work, such as a computer program, an image, or the text of a short story. He could have the copy on a floppy disk or on a hard drive, or be able to download it from a Web site. For his computer to run the program (or view the image or text), it must copy part of the program into its DRAM (the temporary, high-speed memory that constitutes the computer's working memory). The statute does not clearly state whether such a temporary copy is a copy, and good policy arguments have been made against the application of the exclusive rights to such fleeting copies. The trend among the few courts to consider the issue is to hold that making a DRAM copy is indeed making a copy for the purposes of copyright law. *See, e.g., MAI Systems v. Peak Computer*, 991 F.2d 511 (9th Cir. 1993). Moreover, some recent amendments to the copyright statute appear to assume that a DRAM copy is a copy for the purposes of copyright law. If a DRAM copy counts as a copy, then someone could potentially infringe copyright by using the program (or viewing the image or text on a computer) without authorization of the copyright owner. This is quite different from works such as books or paintings. Reading a book (or using processes described in it) or viewing a painting does not touch on the exclusive rights of the copyright owner. For electronic digital works, the copyright comes closer to giving an exclusive right to "use" the work. Some courts, however, have held that copies that last for only a second or less would not constitute copies, for the purpose of infringement.

Example

Makin' copies? Cablevision's customers can use its "Remote Service DVR System" to record cable television shows. The computer files with the recorded programs are saved not on consumer's machine (as occurs with TIVO or a home recorder), but recorded first in a temporary buffer (for about one second), then saved on central hard drives housed and maintained by Cablevision, in an undisclosed location. Has Cablevision made copies of the copyrighted programs (either by making copies in the temporary buffer or by saving copies on the hard drives)?

Explanation

The Second Circuit held that Cablevision did not make copies, and therefore did not infringe the copyrights in the recorded programs. *The Cartoon Network LP v. CSC Holdings, Inc.*, 536 F.3d 121 (2d Cir. 2008) ("*Cablevision*"). The court first held that the buffer copies were not copies for the purpose of infringement, because they were not "for a period of more than transitory duration." If other courts follow this reasoning, this could limit the otherwise gigantic scope of copyright in the online age. Temporary copies of works are made constantly on devices ranging from handhelds to laptops to the various computers linked by the Internet and other networks.

The court also held that the permanent copies were not made by Cablevision. The customer, not Cablevision, entered the instructions that caused the copies to be made. Cablevision merely supplied access to the equipment used. That could make Cablevision liable as a secondary infringer (such as inducement liability), but that issue was not raised in the case.

Adaptation Right

The copyright owner has the exclusive right "to prepare derivative works based upon the copyrighted work." 17 U.S.C. §106(2). A derivative work is "a work based upon one or more preexisting works, such as a translation, musical arrangement, dramatization, fictionalization, motion picture version, sound recording, art reproduction, abridgment, condensation, or any other form in which a work may be recast, transformed, or adapted. A work consisting of editorial revisions, annotations, elaborations, or other modifications which, as a whole, represent an original work of scholarship, is a 'derivative work.' " 17 U.S.C. §101.

If an author owns the copyright on a novel, potential derivative works include a translation into French, a movie based on the novel, a sequel, and an annotated version for scholars. A derivative work need not be "fixed," unlike a copy. So it could infringe the derivative right to orally translate a copyrighted song into Swedish, but would not infringe the reproduction right (because no fixed copy was made).

Read too broadly, the derivative right gives the copyright owner control over almost any use of the work. Two rules limit the scope of the right. First, the better view is that no derivative work is made unless a new copyrightable work is made. Gluing reproductions of artworks on ceramic tiles is not making derivative works of the artworks. *Contra Mirage Editions v. Albuquerque A.R.T.*, 856 F.2d 1341 (9th Cir. 1988). *See also Lee v. A.R.T.*, 125 F.3d 580 (7th Cir. 1997) (rejecting *Mirage Editions* on narrower grounds). Simply speeding up the play of a video game does not create a derivative work. *Contra Midway Mfg. v. Artic Intl.*, 704 F.2d 1009 (7th Cir. 1983). Note that gluing a reproduction on a plate or changing the speed of a video game might constitute a derivative work even under the "new copyrightable work" requirement if done in such a creative way that the new version was a parody of the original or was otherwise a new work. The derivative right is also limited by the rule that no infringement occurs unless the alleged derivative work is substantially similar to the copyrighted work. A movie not substantially similar to a screenplay does not infringe, even if the movie is made with the screenplay in mind. *See Litchfield v. Spielberg*, 736 F.2d 1352 (9th Cir. 1984).

Copyright in the derivative work applies only to material contributed by the author of the derivative work. 17 U.S.C. §103(b). Material taken from the original work is protected by the copyright in the original work (if any). Accordingly, use of the derivative work could potentially infringe both copyrights. For example, publicly showing a film based on a short story could be performing both the story and the film. *Cf. Stewart v. Abend*, 495 U.S. 207 (1990) (holding that performance of public domain film constituted performance of underlying short story). Note also that copyright does not apply to any portion of a derivative work in which material is used unlawfully. 17 U.S.C. §103(a). So the author of an infringing derivative work may have no copyright protection.

The adaptation right does not extend infinitely. Copyrighted works may create value beyond adapting the work. Many American films have created commercial value from added tourism to their locations (such as *The Quiet Man* in Galway, the *Sound of Music* near Salzburg, *The Lord of the Rings* in New Zealand, *The Last Jedi* and Skellig Michael). But those locales are not adaptations of the films, so copyright does not capture that value (nor does trademark, as long as tour operators avoid claiming authorization or sponsorship).

Examples

1. *If it ain't fixed.* Martha licenses F Troupe to perform her copyrighted choreographic work, *Febrile Convulsions.* The agreement provides that F Troupe may perform the work, but may not make copies or create derivative works. F Troupe stages its production. Martha watches from the balcony and is horrified that F Troupe's performance has altered the work in many ways. By changing the composition and arrangement of bodily movements, F Troupe produces an entirely different dance. Martha sues for unauthorized preparation of a derivative work. F Troupe responds that they are not liable, because there is no new physical work. They did not write anything down, or videorecord it. Did they prepare a derivative work?

2. *Stick-ons.* Dragoon sells stick-on tattoos, intended for use by kids. They get a big order from Sporty Goods and send out several hundred boxes. They then learn that Sporty Goods sticks the tattoos onto the basketballs it sells, making them appealing to kids. Sporty Goods sells the basketballs at a nice premium. The idea to stick the tattoos on the balls was not Sporty's; rather, it learned of it from kids. Dragoon, perturbed that it has missed this marketing opportunity, sues Sporty Goods for copyright infringement. Is Sporty Goods liable?

3. *Stolen idea.* "Qualia," an original story written by Rico, tells the story of the doomed civilization of Vroom, who unknowingly used up all their mineral resources. The plot line is adopted by a filmmaker in a general way, to make a film about the collapse of a myopic civilization. The resulting film does not copy any of the expressive elements of "Qualia." Rico sues for unauthorized preparation of a derivative work, arguing that the film would not have been made without "Qualia." Infringement?

4. *Underlying rights.* Broadway loves musicals adapted from films, like *The Producers, Lion King,* and *Spamalot.* Suppose a Broadway producer decides to stage a musical, 2001. The production will be based on the movie. None of the people involved have even heard of the underlying science fiction story, let alone read it. But many original, creative elements of the story were used in the film, and will be used again in the musical. The musical's producer will need permission from the holder of the film

copyright. Will she need permission from the holder of the copyright in the science fiction story the movie was made from?

Explanations

1. F Troupe did prepare a derivative work. The better view is that there is no fixation requirement for derivative works. They transformed the work into a new creative work, thereby creating a derivative work, without authority of the copyright owner.

2. Dragoon's argument is that sticking the tattoos on the basketballs constitutes preparation of a derivative work, because they are "recast, transformed, or adapted" into another form. This raises a split between courts. Some courts have held that mounting a picture on a ceramic tile would be preparation of a derivative work. Others (probably the better view) hold it does not, because preparation of a derivative work requires sufficient creativity to qualify for copyright protection. Sporty did not meet the creativity requirement, rather simply mounted stickers in an unoriginal manner.
   The better view is no infringement.

3. No infringement. As with all the exclusive rights, there is no infringement unless the defendant has used protected creative elements from the copyrighted work. Copying of ideas is not infringement of any of the exclusive rights.

4. She will need permission from the story's copyright owner. Copying from a derivative work can potentially infringe the copyright in the underlying work. The film was a derivative work based on the story. The film's copyright applied only to creative elements that originated with the authors of the film. Any creative elements that were copied from the story are subject to the copyright in the story. So if elements from the story are copied into the musical (via the movie), that could potentially infringe the copyright in the story. To avoid infringement, she needs permission from the story's copyright owner. Practical note: that requires identifying the copyright owner. The original author may well have transferred the relevant rights.

To Distribute Copies or Phonorecords of the Work to the Public

The copyright owner has the exclusive right "to distribute copies or phonorecords of the copyrighted work to the public by sale or other transfer of ownership, or by rental, lease, or lending." 17 U.S.C. §106(3). If a bookseller sells unauthorized copies of a copyrighted novel, the bookseller potentially infringes the distribution right. This is true even if bookseller had not made the copies. The distribution right is a separate right.

At least one court has held that making copies available to the public may be distribution, even without a showing that a member of the public received a copy:

> When a public library adds a work to its collection, lists the work in its index or catalog system, and makes the work available to the borrowing or browsing public, it has completed all the steps necessary for distribution to the public. At that point, members of the public can visit the library and use the work. Were this not to be considered distribution within the meaning of §106(3), a copyright holder would be prejudiced by a library that does not keep records of public use, and the library would unjustly profit by its own omission.

Hotaling v. Church of Jesus Christ of Latter-Day Saints, 118 F.3d 199, 203 (4th Cir. 1997). Other courts, however, are likely to hold that infringement requires distribution of copies. Unlike the patent statute, the copyright statute does not provide that offering for sale constitutes infringement. Rather, *Hotaling* may be narrowly read as a case about the burden of proof in showing that distribution to the public has actually occurred.

As with the other rights, digital technologies also raise questions about the extent of the exclusive rights. If a Web site allows browsers to download works (such as pictures or songs), does that constitute distribution of copies? How about peer-to-peer file sharing? One could hold it is distribution, on the theory that copies of the work have been given to the public. Others might hold that one did not "distribute copies or phonorecords" by such electronic dissemination of the work. When a Web user downloads a work from a Web site or gets it from a file-sharing network, one could argue that the defendant does not distribute a copy to her. Rather, her computer receives an electronic signal which causes it to make a copy. Some would limit the distribution right to distribution of discrete copies, like books or CDs, which are themselves delivered to the public.

The statute also brings importation within the distribution right, providing that importation of a copy acquired outside the United States, without the authorization of the copyright owner, is infringement of the distribution right. 17 U.S.C. §602(a). So if Importer buys 500 copies of author's book abroad and ships them back into the United States, she potentially infringes the distribution right (although she may be protected by the first sale doctrine, discussed below). Section 602(a) exempts copies brought in as personal baggage, single copies imported for personal use, and certain governmental or nonprofit entities.

Examples

1. *Pass it around.* Em, a typesetter at Oldstyle Publishing, steals a prepublication copy of a forthcoming book, the autobiography of a former president. After offering the book for sale on eBay, Em sends the copy to the highest bidder, a magazine called *Imagination*, which prints selected excerpts. Is Em liable for copyright infringement without even making a copy?

2. *Making available.* Suppose that Em had given the copy to a local library, which shelved it in the biography section and listed the book in its index. There is no record of anyone checking the book out, because this particular library simply does not keep records of user activity. Is the library liable for copyright infringement?

3. *No sale.* In addition to selling its own goods, Amazon provides third-party sellers the use of Amazon's logistical network. Amazon stores the goods for the seller, then ships them off when sold on the Amazon site. Does Amazon infringe the distribution right, if goods are bootlegs?

Explanations

1. Em is potentially liable for copyright infringement. Em did not make a copy, but she did distribute a copy to the public. Note that it was not a private transaction but a distribution to the highest bidding member of the public. Em might argue fair use but would have a tough time.

2. The library has not made a copy, adapted the work, performed it publicly, or displayed the work publicly (putting a book on a shelf does not display its contents). There is no record that the library actually distributed a copy to the public. Under *Hotaling* (discussed above), there would be distribution: "When a public library adds a work to its collection, lists the work in its index or catalog system, and makes the work available to the borrowing or browsing public, it has completed all the steps necessary for distribution to the public." But *Hotaling* really stretched to find distribution. A more literal reading would require the plaintiff to show actual distribution.

3. Amazon did not distribute the goods by "sale or other transfer of ownership, or by rental, lease, or lending." Title to the goods did not pass from Amazon to the buyer. The court rejected arguments that Amazon was akin to a consignee and so should be treated as selling the goods. *Milo & Gabby LLC v. Amazon.com, Inc.*, 693 F. App'x 879 (Fed. Cir. 2017). Note that there could be possible liability for contributory or vicarious infringement, discussed later in the book.

To Perform the Work Publicly

The copyright owner has the exclusive right to perform the work publicly. 17 U.S.C. §106(4).[3] Note that the right only applies to *public* performances. A fan can sing a copyrighted song at home with his family without infringing copyright. How many people must be present to have a public performance? A performance is public if the location is open to the public, if there are more people present than family and social acquaintances, or if the work is transmitted to the public. 17 U.S.C. §101.

The copyright statute defines "perform" much more broadly than the word's everyday meaning: "to recite, render, play, dance, or act it, either directly or by means of any device or process or, in the case of a motion picture, or other audiovisual work, to show its images in any sequence or to make the sounds accompanying it audible." 17 U.S.C. §101. To play a CD of music, to watch television, or to have the radio on is "performing" the music or show. Moreover, the performance right applies to most categories of works, not just to works in the performing arts. For example, reading a letter aloud publicly constitutes a public performance, although we do not usually speak of "performing" such texts.

The performance right in sound recordings is limited to the right to "perform the copyrighted work publicly by means of a digital audio transmission." 17 U.S.C. §106(6). Recall, for example, that when a song is recorded, there are potential copyrights in the musical work and the sound recording. A performance of a sound recording that involves no transmission or that uses analog format does not infringe. A business playing a CD of music on a stereo or a radio station playing music over an analog radio transmission does not infringe the sound recording copyright. The former is not a transmission, and the latter is not in digital format. But both are publicly performing the musical works in question.

The second paragraph of the definition of public performance (called the "transmission clause") was added to the statute to cover rebroadcasting by cable companies. In early days, cable companies would capture broadcast television shows on antennas and rebroadcast the shows over their cable network. Courts had held that this was not a public performance and so the cable company did not need permission from the television show copyright holder. Those copyright holders promptly convinced Congress to include such rebroadcasting in their exclusive rights. In 2008, the Second Circuit interpreted the clause narrowly in *Cablevision* (discussed above). The Second Circuit[4] held that there was no public performance, where custom-

---

3. The performance right does not apply to architectural, pictorial, graphic, or sculptural works and for sound recordings is limited to performances via digital audio transmissions. 17 U.S.C. §106(4)(6).

4. *Cartoon Network LP, LLLP v. CSC Holdings, Inc.*, 536 F.3d 121 (CA2, 2008).

ers of Cablevision used remote storage provided by Cablevision to record programs and watch them at their leisure. The court noted the broad scope of the transmission clause, applying where members of the public receive the transmission "in the same place or in separate places and at the same time or at different times." But the clause applies only to members of the public "capable of receiving the performance." Because the performance is the single copy transmitted, the court reasoned, only the single customer was capable of receiving it, meaning that it was not a public performance. Rather, many Cablevision customers could make private performances of the same program from their individual remote storage devices provided by Cablevision.

American Broadcasting Cos. v. Aereo, Inc., 134 S. Ct. 2498 (2014), involved a convoluted rebroadcasting system designed specifically to piggyback on the *Cablevision* decision. Aereo's system had thousands of tiny antennas, each coupled with a small storage device. An Aereo customer could control their antenna and storage to record programs or rebroadcast them to the customer. The Second Circuit again held that meant that each customer had a private performance, even if thousands of customers were watching the same broadcast show. The Supreme Court reversed, looking both to the broader language ("in the same place or in separate places and at the same time or at different times") and to the purpose of the statute. In the Court's view, Aereo was doing the same sort of rebroadcasting that the definition was designed to target:

> Aereo sells a service that allows subscribers to watch television programs, many of which are copyrighted, almost as they are being broadcast. In providing this service, Aereo uses its own equipment, housed in a centralized warehouse, outside of its users' homes. By means of its technology (antennas, transcoders, and servers), Aereo's system "receive[s] programs that have been released to the public and carr[ies] them by private channels to additional viewers."

Fortnightly Corp. v. United Artists, 392 U.S. at 400, 88 S. Ct. 2084, 20 L. Ed. 2d 1176.

The question after *Aereo* is how broadly it would apply. The Court took care not to cast a cloud on technological development, stating that it was not ruling on issues of cloud computing, remote storage DVRs, and other novel issues to arise in other cases.

Collective Rights Organizations

Suppose Little Music Company holds the copyright in the musical work "Just Another Song." Little Music released a recording of the song in 1995, and it is still often played on the radio. Various bands perform the song live. Bars and other businesses often play the recording over their sound systems. All those public performances are subject to Little Music's copyright. But enforcing that copyright would be quite difficult for Little Music, operating alone. To locate every potential use and reach a licensing agreement would be more trouble than it is worth.

Over decades, collective rights organizations like ASCAP (American Society of Composers, Authors and Publishers) and BMI (Broadcast Music, Inc.) have made the enforcement of musical copyrights more efficient. Rather than every copyright owner trying to go around locating users (and infringers) and negotiating license agreements, ASCAP, BMI, and the like do much of the work. ASCAP and BMI represent the owners of millions of copyrighted musical works. They offer a range of licenses to potential users. A bar that plays recorded music as well as hosting bands performing music could find a single license that would get the necessary permissions. They also enforce the copyrights. Representatives of ASCAP and BMI regularly visit public establishments, monitor broadcasts, and browse the Internet to find unauthorized users. Software searches the Internet (especially sites like YouTube) and sends automated take-down notices, cease-and-desist letters, and demands for payment.

When many sellers in a market band together, there is a risk of anticompetitive behavior. Both ASCAP and BMI have been subject to antitrust suits and operate under consent decrees that limit the sort of licenses and terms they can offer.

Example

Public performance? Cablevision, at the request of customers, records cable programs for them and replays them on demand. Has Cablevision infringed the public performance right of the copyrights in the programs?

Explanation

Cablevision has infringed, courts would likely hold. The *Cablevision* court rejected the theory of infringement of the public performance right. Each program is performed for a different subscriber at a different time, in their private home. Such performances, the court reasoned, are not public performances, even though the service is one that Cablevision offers to the public. But that reasoning was subsequently rejected by the Supreme Court in *Aereo* (discussed above). *Aereo* held there were infringing public performances, where Aereo, using a separate antenna for each customer, recorded and transmitted programs to the customers on request.

To Display the Work Publicly

The copyright owner has the exclusive right "to display the copyrighted work publicly." 17 U.S.C. §106(5).[5] Copyright law also has a broad definition of "display": "to show a copy of it, either directly or by means of a film, slide, television image, or any other device or process or, in the case of a motion picture or other audiovisual work, to show individual images non-sequentially." 17 U.S.C. §101. Like the performance right, the display right is limited to public displays. But the broad definition of the right goes well beyond putting a copy of the work on exhibit. Wearing a T-shirt bearing a copy of a copyrighted work could constitute a public display — as could posting a copy of the work on a Web site.

Example

Framed and displayed. When returning results of image searches, Google arguably displays thumbnail images to the public, but that likely qualifies as fair use. Google also allows the user to see the full-size image, indirectly, under the legend: "Below is the image in its **original context** on the page." To do so, Google's computers send HTML code to the user's computer, which then sends a request to the page with the image. By so "framing" the image, is Google displaying a copy of the work to the public?

Explanation

The Ninth Circuit held that Google was not displaying a copy of the work to the public. *Perfect 10 v. Amazon*, 508 F.3d 1146 (9th Cir. 2007). Google did not send a copy, rather sent the address of the original page. The user's computer could request a copy from the original page, and display that copy if sent. So Google would not be liable for infringing the public display right. Google might be liable on other theories (such as contributory infringement, discussed later in the book), but those would require showing other elements, such as knowledge of the infringing activity.

The Southern District of New York, however, reached the opposite result in a *somewhat* similar case. Someone tweeted a copyrighted photo of quarterback Tom Brady. Many news organizations embedded the tweet on their own pages in reporting, meaning that they did not reproduce the photo, but had code that would make the photo appear on a user's browser in the midst of the news article. The court held that this did constitute a public display of the photo by the news organization. It first held that physical possession of a copy is not necessary to infringe the display right. It

---

5. The display right does not apply to architectural works and for motion pictures and other audiovisual works is limited to individual images. 17 U.S.C. §106(5).

then distinguished *Perfect Ten*: "In Perfect 10, Google's search engine provided a service whereby the user navigated from webpage to webpage, with Google's assistance. This is manifestly not the same as opening up a favorite blog or Web site to find a full color image awaiting the user, whether he or she asked for it, looked for it, clicked on it, or not. Both the nature of Google Search Engine, as compared to the defendant Web sites, and the volitional act taken by users of the services, provide a sharp contrast to the facts at hand." *Goldman v. Breitbart News Network, LLC*, 2018 U.S. Dist. LEXIS 25215, at *29-30 (S.D.N.Y. Feb. 15, 2018).

The bounds of the display right online are under construction.

Section 106A: Moral Rights in Works of Visual Art

Franz sells the copyright in his novel to MegaPub. By publication, editors have metamorphized Franz's tender tale of a struggling writer into a scary story of a hunger artist. Copyright law would not give Franz grounds to object. He sold the copyright, including the right to adapt the work. It would be different if Franz had sold a painting. In the United States, copyright gives works of visual art special protection against modification, distortion, misattribution, and destruction.

Moral rights present a considerable difference between copyright law in the United States and in other jurisdictions. Many countries explicitly recognize several types of moral rights, including such things as rights of attribution (others must acknowledge the author, and cannot wrongfully claim to be the author), rights of integrity (protecting against destruction or distortion of the work), and rights of disclosure (the right to decide whether and when a work will be published). *See* Robert Merges, Peter Menell, & Mark Lemley, *Intellectual Property in the New Technological Age* 443 (2003). Some give such rights as the right of withdrawal (to take a work such as a book off the market), the right to reply to criticism, and right to resale royalties (a.k.a. "following rights," such as the right of a painter to receive a percentage if her work is sold, even long after she has sold the work). By contrast, copyright statutes in the United States have given little explicit recognition to moral rights, as such.

The different approach to moral rights is often cited as showing a fundamental difference in approach between U.S. copyright law and copyright law in other jurisdictions, especially Europe. Other jurisdictions may see copyright as a type of natural right. Because an author creates a work (a novel, a painting, some music), she should be able to control what happens to the work. The work is an expression of the author's personality. The author's reputation is tied to the work. Someone that injures the work injures the author. In the United States, by contrast, copyright is thought to be less a matter of philosophy than of economics. In order to provide an incentive for authors to create works, copyright law provides a basket of exclusive rights.

The difference in approaches to moral rights was long considered a stumbling block to U.S. adherence to the Berne treaty, the leading international copyright law treaty. Berne requires its members to grant a measure of moral rights:

> Independently of the author's economic rights, and even after the transfer of the said rights, the author shall have the right to claim authorship of the work and to object to any distortion, mutilation or other modification of, or other derogatory action in relation to, the said work, which would be prejudicial to his honor or reputation.

Berne Convention for the Protection of Literary and Artistic Works, Art. 6bis. So Berne requires members to recognize an author's rights of attribution and integrity.

Effective 1989, the United States adhered to the Berne treaty. In doing so, Congress took what has been called a "minimalist" approach to moral rights. Congress could have broadly provided that all authors have rights of attribution and integrity with respect to their works. The general U.S. position, however, was that U.S. law already provided the protections required by Berne. Although the U.S. copyright statute did not explicitly grant rights of integrity and attribution, authors receive equivalent protections from various provisions of the copyright statute and other laws. If a work is distorted, for example, that could infringe copyright by creating a "derivative work." Distortion of the work could violate the license under which the work was used, giving rise to a claim under contract law. Misattribution of authorship could violate trademark law, as trademark infringement, as false designation of origin, or simply as false advertising. Misattribution or distortion that harmed the author's reputation could amount to defamation or unfair competition. In short, the United States did not amend its copyright statute to explicitly provide moral rights to copyright holders, but instead relied on protections in existing law. But, not long after joining Berne, Congress did provide such rights to "works of visual art," a narrow set of works, in the Visual Artists Rights Act of 1990 (VARA), now set forth in §106A of the Copyright Act.

In addition to the exclusive rights under 17 U.S.C. §106, the author of a "work of visual art" enjoys rights of attribution and integrity under 17 U.S.C. §106A, commonly called "moral rights." If Pamela paints a portrait, she has the rights to (1) claim authorship of the work and prevent misattribution of her name as author to any work of visual art she did not create; (2) prevent use of her name as the author in a manner that would be prejudicial to her honor or reputation if the work has been distorted, mutilated, or otherwise modified; (3) prevent intentional distortion, mutilation, or other modification of the work that would be prejudicial to her honor or reputation; and (4) if it is a work of recognized stature, to prevent destruction of the work. In short, authors of works of visual art are entitled to proper attribution of authorship and to protection of the physical work itself.

Section 106A imposes many limitations on these rights of attribution and integrity. They apply only to works falling within the definition of "work of visual art": single works; signed and numbered limited editions of no more than 200 copies; or photographic prints produced for exhibition, paintings, drawings, prints, and sculptures. 17 U.S.C. §101. So novels, poems, movies, songs, and many other creative works are not protected by §106A. Many visual works of a commercial or functional nature, such as maps, technical drawings, and advertisements, are also excluded from coverage. "Merchandising," "advertising," and "promotional" material is excluded. The fact that the work reflects artistic expertise will not necessarily qualify it for protection. For example, where an artist made a banner for a political advocacy group for the purposes of drawing attention to a lobbying desk, which used conspicuous text crafted by the group, the banner did not qualify as a "work of visual art." *Pollara v. Seymour*, 344 F.3d 265 (2d Cir. 2003). Accordingly, the artist was not entitled to the rights under §106A, so a building manager was not liable for removing and destroying the work.

In addition, §106A is inapplicable if the work is a work for hire, so employees that create works of visual art are likewise outside §106A. The protection against distortion applies only to the physical work itself, so someone can make a distorted copy without infringing §106A. Finally, the rights are not transferable, but they may be waived.

Section 106A provides protection for only a narrow category of works. But authors may also use other provisions of intellectual property laws to protect rights of integrity and attribution. Modification of a work, for example, could constitute preparation of a derivative work. Wrongly attributed works might also be infringing copies and could violate the new provision governing copyright management information, discussed briefly below. The right of termination (discussed below) prevents many authors from permanently giving up all rights in their work. More generally, trademark law and other areas of the law provide protections against some misattribution of works of authorship.

Examples

1. *VARA protected?* Which of the following works would be protected by §106A (a.k.a. VARA)?
   a. The song "Pretty Woman."
   b. A Pulitzer Prize–winning photograph of a marathon winner, taken by a news photographer for publication.
   c. An oil painting of the CEO of Megacorp, painted by a Megacorp employee as part of her job.
   d. A lithographic print of a leaping lizard, by Gratho. She made only 50 of the prints.
   e. A mural depicting the workers of the world, made by the employees of a human rights organization for their headquarters. After the lease

ran out, the property has been leased to a bank, which plans to paint over the mural.

f. A 1966 painting by Picasso, which he sold in 1968.

g. A 1966 painting by Picasso, which he never sold. It is out of copyright in the United States, due to publication without a copyright notice in 1967.

h. A creative painted banner depicting marathon runners, made by an artist commissioned by Alligator Fuel Sport Drink. The banner was used as advertising at the Hendersonville Marathon.

i. A 1990 painting by Ashley, which she sold in 1992 to a collector. Ashley also sold the copyright to the painting in 1993 to Alligator Fuel.

j. "Falling Weather," a still photograph by Geoff. He made only one print, for exhibition at his gallery.

2. *Unfinished.* Buchel, an artist, works on an installation in the Massachusetts Museum of Contemporary Art. In "Training Ground for Democracy," visitors would play such roles as immigrants, activists, looters, and judges, working their way through installations ranging from a movie theater to an aircraft fuselage. The artist and museum, however, did not manage to finish the project together. When the museum proposed showing the unfinished work, the artist sued, claiming that would violate his rights under VARA. Is an unfinished work protected?

3. *Burning question. La Contessa* is "a mobile replica of a 16th-century Spanish galleon for use at the Burning Man Festival." Extensively adorned, the bus still functioned as a bus, at least until the festival organizers banned the drivers for unsafe driving. Does VARA protect *La Contessa*?

4. *Don't move.* A landscape artist created an integrated set of sculptures for a park. The owner of the park decided to remove the sculptures to make way for a new overall design of the park. The first artist argues that this would violate his right to the integrity of the work. Even if the sculptures were not physically modified or distorted in removing them, it would modify and distort the work as a whole, because it was an integrated, site-specific work of art. Removing it from its site, along with the backdrop of the nearby oceanside, would be like painting over the background landscape in the *Mona Lisa.* Does the VARA prohibit moving the sculptures?

5. *Better to seek permission than forgiveness?* 5Pointz was group of dilapidated warehouses. Artists created large graffiti paintings with the permission of the buildings' owners. A leader selected works to preserve, and the 5Pointz appeared "in films, television, newspaper articles, blogs, and online videos, in addition to social media buzz." In time, the owners made plans to raze the buildings and develop the real estate. The artists asserted rights against destruction of their work. In response, the owners whitewashed the walls, destroying the 45 paintings. VARA liability?

Explanations

1. a. The VARA protects only "works of visual art," which must be a painting, drawing, print, sculpture, or photographic image. The song would not be protected.

   b. Photographs may be protected, but only if they are taken for exhibition purposes only. News photos would not qualify, so the VARA does not protect this prize-winning photo.

   c. A work made for hire is not protected, even if it is a painting, drawing, print, sculpture, or photographic image.

   d. A limited edition work may be protected, but only if the individual prints are consecutively numbered and signed by the author. That was not done here, so no VARA protection.

   e. A work made for hire is not protected, so not protected. *See Carter v. Helmsley-Spear*, 71 F.3d 77 (2d Cir. 1995).

   f. A work created before June 1, 1991, is protected only if the artist had not transferred title before that date. Picasso had sold it, so no protection.

   g. Works are not protected by the VARA if they are out of copyright, so no protection.

   h. The VARA does not protect "any merchandising item or advertising." So the banner would not be protected. *Cf. Pollara v. Seymour*, 344 F.3d 265 (2d Cir. 2003).

   i. The painting would be protected by the VARA. The fact that the author no longer owns the work or the copyright does not affect VARA rights (in post-1991 works).

   j. This photograph would be protected, as a still photograph produced for exhibition purposes only.

2. The definition of "work of visual art" does not require a work to be finished. Not protecting unfinished works would leave a considerable gap. The court held that moral rights do apply to unfinished works, and so the artist had the right to protect his rights of integrity and attribution. *See Massachusetts Museum of Contemporary Art Found., Inc. v. Büchel*, 593 F.3d 38 (1st Cir. 2010). An earlier case, reasoned that VARA rights to not apply until a work is finished. .

3. Protected works include "painting, drawing, print, or sculpture," but not "applied art." The statute does not defined "applied art." The Second Circuit reasoned that an object is applied art if it serves a useful function. A functional, adorned school bus was deemed applied art. *Cheffins v. Stewart*, 825 F.3d 588, 592 (9th Cir. 2016).

4. *Phillips v. Pembroke Real Estate, Inc.*, 459 F.3d 128, 137 (1st Cir. 2006), addressed this difficult conceptual issue about the scope of the right to prevent modification and distortion of the work. The court held that the

case was addressed by the public presentation provision, which permits modification of "public presentation, including lighting and placement." The VARA does not give absolute protection to artistic integrity. Rather, with its various limitations and exceptions, the VARA represents a compromise between protecting the moral rights of artists and protecting the freedoms of others whose actions may affect the art. As the court put it, protecting outdoor art against any change in its lighting and placement could, in theory, put limits not just on the property owner but also on any neighbors whose use of their property could come within the scope of the artwork.

Such a reading does not leave artists without legal protection. The VARA provides a gap-filling rule where the parties have not reached their own specific agreement. An artist may seek greater protection by agreement with the commissioning party. Such provisions could be made binding on future owners of the land through easements or covenants running with the land.

5. *The works qualified as works of visual art.* They also had attained "recognized stature," as evidenced by the curation and media attention. A building owner may destroy a work incorporated into a building, but only after giving 90 days' written notice — which was not done here. Rather, the owner deliberately destroyed the works before the dispute was settled. The court awarded the maximum statutory damages of $150,000 per work, for a total of $6,750,000.

Walter's Grand Slam: A Quick Review of the Exclusive Rights

The Internet provides a good example for application of the various exclusive rights because it can be seen as a global machine for making, transforming, distributing, performing, and displaying copies of works.[6] Suppose that Walter runs a Web site devoted to a pop star. Visitors to the Web site can view pictures of the singer, listen to her songs over streaming audio, and download Walter's own recordings of her songs, which he has rewritten from sappy ballads into political satire. Suppose also that Walter is using copyrighted pictures and music without authorization. He could potentially infringe all the exclusive rights in 17 U.S.C. §106 (but not the moral rights in 17 U.S.C. §106A), although the application of the exclusive rights in the Internet context is still being hashed out in the courts. Here is a quick review of exclusive rights as they pertain to Walter's situation:

---

6. For a comprehensive analysis of the application of the exclusive rights to online communications, *see* Mark A. Lemley, *Copyright Owners' Rights and Users' Privileges on the Internet: Dealing with Overlapping Copyrights on the Internet*, 22 Dayton L. Rev. 547 (1997).

1. *Reproduction right:* He made copies by loading copies of the works onto his server.
2. *Adaptation right:* He prepared derivative works by rewriting the songs.
3. *Distribution right:* He distributes copies and phonorecords to the public by sending copies to visitors who download material.
4. *Performance right:* He publicly performs the musical works by enabling visitors to listen to streaming audio versions of the music. He also violates the narrow performance right in the sound recordings because the streaming audio qualifies as a "digital audio transmission."
5. *Display right:* He displays copies to the public by causing the images to be viewed on the visitors' screens. *See Kelly v. Arriba Soft Corp.,* 280 F.3d 934 (9th Cir. 2002).
6. *Section 106A moral rights:* Even if Walter grossly distorts the songs with his revisions, he does not violate the rights of integrity and attribution afforded by 17 U.S.C. §106A because §106A protects only the narrow category of works of visual art.

Examples

1. *Practice with §106.* After years of painstaking research, Arthur Author writes a book of history. The work describes the lives of several generations of Illinois farmers. Arthur draws most of the details from his personal research, which ranges from village records to estate sales to long interviews with various Illinoisans. But Arthur contributes a great deal of original expression to the work through his selection and arrangement of facts, his graceful and concise prose, and his vivid descriptions. The book sells very well. Two years after the book is published, Arthur visits his attorney. Arthur has learned of various activities related to his work and wonders if any fall within his exclusive rights. Of the following, which fall within the exclusive rights of the copyright holder?[7]

   a. Knockoff copies large parts of Arthur's book verbatim into Knockoff's own book about Midwestern life. Knockoff proudly shows the manuscript to several friends. Knockoff has not yet offered the manuscript to a publisher or made any commercial use of the manuscript.

   b. Fan borrows a copy of the book, digitizes the text with a scanner, and saves the text in a file on the hard drive of her computer. Fan returns the book and reads the book at her leisure from the computer.

   c. Nemesis purchases and promptly sets fire to a copy of the book.

   d. Critic writes a scathing review of the book. Critic does not copy any of Arthur's original expression. Critic makes several factual statements

---

7. Note that acts that fall within the exclusive rights might not be infringement, if they are protected by one of the limitations discussed below, such as fair use.

about the work that he knows are false and that are very likely to harm sales of the book.

e. Plago publishes a historical novel, set in the time and place covered in Arthur's book. Plago copies a number of facts and ideas from Arthur's book but does not copy any original expression.

f. Scribbler buys a copy of the book and writes a screenplay based on the novel. The screenplay follows the book very closely, copying not just facts and ideas but also much original creative expression. Producer, with Scribbler's permission, makes a movie based on the screenplay. The movie, like the screenplay, uses much original creative expression from the book. Cinepeps, a local movie house, shows the movie to the public for several weeks.

g. Every week, Fan holds Arthur Appreciation Night at a local bar. Fan and other adherents of Arthur take turns reading portions of the novel aloud to the crowd.

h. Fan holds Arthur Appreciation Night in her home instead and reads the book aloud to her family and friends.

i. Baton runs an advertisement and offers copies of Arthur's book at a huge discount. Baton receives payment from hundreds of buyers but never ships them any copies. Indeed, Baton had never acquired even a single copy.

j. Veb borrows Fan's scanned copy of the book. Veb then sets up a Web site, which permits viewers to read the book one page at a time.

2. *Artist's rights.* Vincent paints a portrait of himself wearing a straw hat. George buys the painting from Vincent and makes a poster featuring reproductions of the painting. George sells many copies of the poster to the public. When Vincent objects, George crudely draws horns onto the portrait, purely out of spite toward Vincent. Do George's action fall within any of Vincent's exclusive rights?

3. *What goes around.* Songs writes a hit song called "Edsel Medley." Songs sells the copyright in the song to Music Co. Songs continues to perform "Edsel Medley" in concert. Songs also records a follow-up song, which copies much of the original creative expression from "Edsel Medley." Music Co. writes to Songs, demanding that she cease and desist from performing "Edsel Medley" and from making any copies of the follow-up. Songs laughs at the idea that she could be accused of stealing her own work. Has she done anything within the exclusive rights of the copyright holder?

4. *Souvenir.* Lines, a software developer, works for Microfuzzy. Lines has worked for several years on Dindles, a strong-selling video graphics program. Because Lines is a key developer, Microfuzzy provides her with a laptop loaded with the source code version of Dindles. Dindles is sold to the public in object code, and only a very limited number of people are

given access to the source code version, which Microfuzzy considers to be a key competitive asset. Lines decides to give up the software business and become a songwriter. She resigns from Microfuzzy and moves to the mountains of Montana, taking the laptop with her. She has never so much as turned the laptop on. By leaving with a valuable copy of an unpublished version of a copyrighted work has Lines done anything within the exclusive rights of the copyright holder? What if, on arriving in Montana, she prints out the source code so she could read it in the great outdoors?

5. *Matinee.* Bones operates a used clothing store. Bones enjoys listening to the music of Texas, a country singer. Early one afternoon, several customers are browsing in the store. Bones is playing Texas's most recent CD. A woman walks in with a clipboard, listens for a few minutes, and then asks to speak to the manager. She informs Bones that he is infringing the copyright in the musical works on the CD. Bones protests that he has not sold any copies of the CD or charged anyone for admission to the store. She informs Bones that he has nonetheless publicly performed the music. Has he?

6. *Thinner copyright.* Skins is devoted to classical music and pursues her interest with new technology. She obtains the music to Smaller's *Third Symphony.* She knows that the music is not under copyright because it was published in 1818. Skins records her audio synthesizer performing the symphony. In making the recording, Skins makes a number of creative decisions, so she has a copyright in the sound recording. She sells several copies of the recording on CDs. Among the buyers are Bones and Akimbo. Skins then learns that Bones has taken to playing the recording in his used-clothing store. She also learns that Akimbo has made a recording of the same symphony. Akimbo does not copy any of the actual sounds of Skins's recording but does imitate her recording in a number of ways. Have Bones or Akimbo come within Skins's exclusive rights in the sound recording?

Explanations

1. a. Knockoff potentially infringes the reproduction right by copying protected expression from Arthur's book. Knockoff has not yet commercially exploited the book. Commercial exploitation, however, is not required for infringement. Knockoff's showing his manuscript to several friends does not infringe the display right because that exclusive right extends only to public displays.

   b. When Fan scans and saves a digitized version of the novel, she is making a copy. By doing so she potentially infringes the reproduction right.

   Every time she reads the book on her computer, a portion is copied from the computer's permanent memory (the hard drive) into its fast, temporary memory (the DRAM). This DRAM copying probably constitutes making an infringing copy as well. As noted in the text, whether making a copy in DRAM infringes the reproduction right is not definitively addressed in the statute, but such a reading is supported by most of the few cases on point, read together with recent statutory amendments.

c. By burning the novel, Nemesis might offend Arthur but does not infringe copyright. Section 106 grants five exclusive rights: to make copies, to distribute copies to the public, to prepare derivative works, to perform the work in public, and to display the work in public. None of those is triggered by burning a copy of the work—even if it is the only copy. Copyright does not grant a general property right in the protected work; it grants only the specific rights in the statute. Author might think Nemesis's actions are an infringement of his rights of integrity and attribution under 17 U.S.C. §106A. But §106A applies only to works of visual art (paintings, sculpture, and the like), not to novels.

d. Simply writing a scathing, even an untrue, review is not copyright infringement because it does not implicate any of the exclusive rights.

Critic does not copy any protected expression and therefore does not infringe. A sophistic argument for Arthur might be that Critic's false calumny reduced the sales of Arthur's book and therefore impinged on Arthur's exclusive right to distribute copies to the public. But copyright is infringed by those who wrongfully exercise one of the copyright owner's exclusive rights. There is not a secondary layer of rights protecting the copyright owner's ability to ply his trade.

e. Plago does not infringe any of the exclusive rights. Copying from a copyrighted work is not infringement as long as protected expression is not copied. Plago copies, but only copies unprotectable facts and ideas.

Arthur might argue that Plago infringes the adaptation right (the right to prepare derivative works) by adapting Arthur's book of history into a historical novel. But none of the exclusive rights is infringed unless protected expression is used.

f. By writing the screenplay that copies much protected expression, Scribbler infringes both the reproduction right and the adaptation right. By making the movie that likewise copies much of Arthur's protected expression, Producer likewise infringes those rights. By showing the movie to the public, Cinepeps infringes the right of public performance. Note that this is true even if Producer and Cinepeps are unaware of the fact that the screenplay is copied from Arthur's book. The plaintiff need make no showing of negligence or knowledge. Plaintiff need simply show that defendant did something that fell within plaintiff's exclusive rights.

g. By reading the book aloud to the crowd, Fan and the others potentially infringe the right of public performance. Infringement does not require a showing that the infringer acts for commercial purposes or gains money from the acts. Note also how broad the performance right is — simply reading a book aloud probably would not be thought of as a performance in the everyday use of the word.

h. If Fan simply reads the book aloud to her family and friends, there is no infringement. The copyright owner's exclusive rights extend only to public performance.

i. Baton does not infringe. Offering to sell the copyrighted work does not fall within the exclusive rights. Baton has not distributed or made copies. She would not be liable for copyright infringement, although presumably other legal theories such as fraud would apply.

j. Veb potentially infringes the right of public display. Veb does not infringe copyright by acquiring the copy that Fan made. Acquisition and possession of a copy do not fall within the exclusive rights of the copyright holder, even if the copy is made through infringement. But by showing the book page by page to visitors to the Web site, Veb is displaying the work publicly. A public display includes a transmission to the public. If the members of the public are enabled to view the work on the Web site, that constitutes a transmission, even if the people view it at separate times in different locations.

2. George has infringed Vincent's reproduction right (by making copies of the painting) and distribution right (by distributing copies to the public). George bought the painting, not the copyright on the painting. George may have also infringed Vincent's adaptation right by preparing a derivative work. That depends on whether drawing the horns on the painting had the requisite originality to create a new work, based on Vincent's painting. Some courts do not require that a derivative work be separately copyrightable, rather that any adaptation is potentially infringing. Under that approach, drawing the horns would presumably suffice to create a derivative work. But the better view is that no derivative work is created unless the work meets the standards for being an original work of authorship. Beyond the §106 rights, George may have infringed Vincent's right of integrity under §106A. Liability requires a showing that the modification is prejudicial to Vincent's honor or reputation. The offensive change to the portrait appears to meet that standard.

3. Songs may be liable for infringing the copyright in her own work. The copyright owner has the exclusive rights of 17 U.S.C. §106. Songs owned those rights but sold them to Music Co. So Songs is infringing Music Co.'s exclusive right to perform "Edsel Medley" in public. By making the follow-up, which copies her own original creative expression, she potentially infringes both the reproduction and adaptation rights.

4. Lines is not infringing the copyright in Dindles (though she may be in possession of a copy without authority). Ownership of particular copies of works is largely governed not by copyright but by property law. Lines

has not done anything that falls within the copyright owner's exclusive rights. She did not make a copy, adapt the work, distribute a copy to the public, perform the work publicly, or display it publicly.

If Lines prints out the source code from the laptop, she potentially is infringing the reproduction right. Printing out the code constitutes making a copy. Although the copy of the program is not one that could be run on a computer, the reproduction right can encompass making a copy in any medium.

5. Bones has made a public performance of the work, potentially infringing the copyright in the work. Bones might reasonably think that performing a song means singing it yourself. He might also wonder whether one performs "publicly" in a store with only a few customers present, their attention on the merchandise they are browsing. But the right to public performance is very broad. "Performance" includes playing the work using a device. "Publicly" encompasses a place open to the public. Beyond the requirement that the performance be public, the statute does not require that it be before a paying audience or serve any commercial purpose. So Bones has made a public performance of the musical works.

6. Neither Bones nor Akimbo has infringed Skins's copyright in the sound recording. The reproduction right and the right of public performance are both limited for sound recordings. The performance right in a sound recording extends only to a performance via a "digital audio transmission." Bones did not transmit the recording; he only played it aloud in his store. The reproduction right is infringed only by making a duplication that captures the actual sounds in the sound recording. Akimbo imitated Skins's recording but did not capture the actual sounds. Akimbo did not mechanically duplicate Skins's actual recording but only imitated the recording.

Both results would be different if the work at issue were a musical work, as opposed to a sound recording. Bones could potentially infringe by a public performance. Akimbo would infringe by making a duplication that was substantially similar and copied protected expression.

Digital Rights Management: Protection for Anti-Copying Technology, Anti-Access Technology, and Copyright Management Information

Copyright holders have long resorted to technical means to prevent or detect copying, from watermarked paper to digital watermarks. Early computer game programmers relied on "obfuscation and slight format alterations," writing code such that copied games would not work correctly. To discourage circulation of unauthorized copies, some games required users to answer questions like "What is the first word on page 17 of the manual?" so one would need a copy of the manual to play the game. *See Copy Protection,* Wikipedia, http://en.wikipedia.org/wiki/Copy_protection. A user might need to register software, have a special serial number, or plug in a dongle (a piece of encoded hardware). Videotapes, audio CDs, CD-ROMs, DVDs, and other media have likewise seen various attempts to control copying. The various devices and techniques prevented some copying. But just as they might frustrate some potential infringers, they also sometimes prevented use by authorized users. Historians, hobbyists, and archivists now sometimes struggle to circumvent copy protection devices on old software in order to study the old works.

More recently, digital rights management (DRM) technologies seek to both prevent unauthorized use and to facilitate licensing systems. Ideally (from the point of the copyright holder), DRM would permit products to be efficiently licensed on different terms to different classes of users (one fee for individuals, one fee for companies), while preventing any use not authorized by the copyright owner. DRM could control how many times a work could be used and what levels of the work could be accessed, and allow the copyright holder to remotely monitor or control use of the work. Users could benefit from these controls. By allowing copyright holders to tailor the products they offer, works could be made more widely available and consumers would have more choices.

Commentators raise many potential problems: DRM schemes — "crippleware" to critics — may prevent legitimate uses, such as fair use. DRM may lock up noncopyrightable elements of work, by controlling access to them. DRM monitoring raises issues of privacy. Price discrimination between users may be unfair. The promises of DRM makers have not always withstood scrutiny by technologists. Various DRM systems have failed to work as promised, prevented users from getting promised content, or even introduced potential bugs or security flaws into the users' systems. DRM systems may also discourage innovation, by discouraging adaptations and development of products that work together with existing products (although they may encourage innovation by hackers, both good and bad). *See* Jonathan Zittrain, *The Future of the Internet — And How to Stop It* (2008).

New types of protection for copyright owners were added to the Copyright Act in 1998. The statute now provides legal protection for two types of technological measures that copyright owners might use: anti-copying technology and anti-access technology. *See* 17 U.S.C. §1201. A copyright owner might use a technological measure to prevent copying of the work. For example, sometimes software disks or videotapes have devices intended to prevent them from being copied. Someone in possession of the original disk or tape can use it but cannot make another copy (to the extent the anti-copying device works as intended). Anti-access technology is intended to prevent someone who has possession (or can otherwise access) copy of a work from being able to *effectively* access the work. For example, pay-per-view movies are transmitted in scrambled form, and some products in digital form are encrypted. Someone might have a copy of an encrypted e-book but be unable to read it, without circumventing the anti-access technology (that is, decrypting the copy).

Section 1201 is a complex provision. Broadly stated, §1201 has two types of prohibitions:

1. it prohibits the circumvention of anti-access technology; and
2. it prohibits the making and selling of devices or services to circumvent either anti-access or anti-copying technology. *See* Digital Millenium Copyright Act of 1998, Copyright Office Summary.

Circumventing an anti-access measure violates the statute, but circumventing an anti-copying measure does not. The distinction was made on the theory that making unauthorized copies is often permitted by fair use, but (here some might well differ) fair use does not authorize unauthorized access. By contrast, making or selling devices or services to circumvent either type of technology is prohibited. So if Reader circumvents technology to make a copy of an e-book, he does not violate §1201. But if Reader circumvents technology to read the e-book, then he violates §1201. If Entrepreneur sells goods or services to others for either purpose, she violates §1201 (even, apparently, if she sells her services to help users exercise their fair use rights). Section 1201 gives copyright owners a powerful set of protections. Such legal protection was thought necessary (in addition to the practical protection provided by the technology itself) because electronic digital works are so easily copied and distributed. The section also contains various exemptions for certain nonprofit institutions, for certain governmental activities, for reverse engineering, for encryption research, and others. But the rights are not explicitly made subject to fair use.

Courts are presently struggling with the question of how broadly to construe the protections. For example, the provision protects technological measures that control access to a copyrighted work. "Access" can be read narrowly (to apply only to forms of access related to copyright protection, such as access to copy or perform the work) or broadly (to cover any form of access, including using noncopyrightable elements of the work). *Chamberlain Group v. Skylink Technologies*, 381 F.3d 1178, 1182 (Fed. Cir. 2004) considered whether there was a §1201 violation, where a competitor sold a device that provided a "rolling code" necessary to activate a computer controlled garage door opener. The plaintiff, a garage door maker, argued that the code was protected anti-access technology, because it was necessary to use the code in order to use the copyrighted program that operated the garage door. To use the program, under this view, constituted making "access" to the copyrighted work.

Chamberlain, however, held that there was no "connection between Skylink's accused circumvention device and the protections that the copyright laws afford." The court reasoned that copyright does not protect the functional aspect of works, rather only their creative aspects. The device in question served only to activate the garage door opener, thereby triggering the function of the program, without copying any of its expressive aspects. Because the device did not serve to access the protected aspects of the work, it did not trigger the anti-access provisions of §1201. Hence, there was no liability for circumventing the code.

A related question is how broadly to construe "circumvent." *Lexmark Intl. v. Static Control Components*, 387 F.3d 522 (6th Cir. 2004) considered whether a code sequence necessary to use a copyrighted program on a printer qualified as a protected access control device. Someone in possession of a *Lexmark* printer could easily print out a copy of the computer program, so the code sequence did not control access in the sense that it was an obstacle to getting a copy of the program. Rather, the code sequence was necessary to use the program, one of a number of programs that ran the printer. The court concluded that the code was not a protected access technology, because the code was not necessary to *access* the program; rather, it was necessary to *use* the program: "No security device, in other words, protects access to the Printer Engine Program Code, and no security device accordingly must be circumvented to obtain access to that program code."

Courts are split on how broadly to read the anticircumvention rules. Some courts have held that here is a violation of the anticircumvention or antitrafficking rules only if the activity has a nexus to copyright infringement. *See, e.g., Chamberlain Group v. Skylink Technologies*, 381 F.3d 1178, 1182 (Fed. Cir. 2004). In this view, it would not be a violation to market software that unlocked a garage door opener or a video game, if the party in possession of the work had authority to use it.

By contrast, some courts have directly rejected that interpretation. *See MDY Industries, LLC v. Blizzard. Entertainment, Inc.* 629 F.3d 928 (9th Cir. 2010). Copyright gives a set of exclusive rights (to make copies of the work, and to adapt, distribute, perform, or display the work). In addition, in this view, the DMCA created a new right to control access to the work. So circumvention to permit use beyond the scope of a license may violate the protections for access controls (because it permits unauthorized access), even if it does not cause infringement of copyright (because the users had a license, even though the circumvention allows them to use the software beyond the scope of the license). Under this approach, MDY was liable for selling Glider, software that allowed players of the online game World of Warcraft to use bots to play the game and progress more rapidly through levels. Glider circumvented certain technological controls that limited the uses of the World of Warcraft software. MDY did not infringe copyright but did violate the separate right to control access to the work.

Ford Motor held that Autel did not violate the DMCA, by circumventing anti-access measures in order to access diagnostic data in the vehicles. Autel copied data, but was not alleged to copy the aspects of a database that would be protected by copyright, which would be its selection, coordination, and arrangement of data.[8] Ford Motor's reading of the DMCA would narrow its scope, because the provisions would be violated only where a party was likely infringing copyright anyway. But the contrary reading would give copyright-like protection that would go well beyond copyright.

Another open question is whether §1201 is subject to fair use. Section 1201 does not contain an explicit fair use provision. *Universal City Studios v. Corley*, 273 F.3d 429 (2d Cir. 2002) declined either to read fair use into §1201 or to analyze whether the lack of fair use would be an unconstitutional limitation on free speech. By contrast, *Chamberlain* considered the potential effect on fair use in interpreting the scope of §1201, rejecting a reading that "allow any copyright owner, through a combination of contractual terms and technological measures, to repeal the fair use doctrine with respect to an individual copyrighted work—or even selected copies of that copyrighted work."

There are a number of safe harbors, for specifically authorized activity. The list sounds like the sort of activities that are protected by fair use. One exemption applies to nonprofit libraries, archives, and educational institutions. Other exemptions apply to reverse engineering and encryption research. But the exemptions are so narrowly drafted that they are far from playing the broad role of fair use. In addition, the Librarian of Congress is authorized to grant exemptions to the anticircumvention provision (but not the antitrafficking provision, so the exemption may not authorize selling services that rely on the exemption). The 2011 exemptions (which last three years) allow parties to:

- circumvent the Content Scrambling System DVD's educational uses, documentary filmmaking, and Noncommercial videos
- enable wireless phones to execute software applications or connect to a wireless network, (also known as "jailbreaking")
- circumvent controls in order to test security measures on video games
- circumvent obsolete dongles on software
- circumvent controls on e-books to enable read-aloud function or put text into special format, such as for visually impaired readers

The statute also prohibits the unauthorized removal or alteration of "copyright management information," which is defined to include information identifying the work, the author, the copyright owner, and others, as well as terms and conditions for use of the work. 17 U.S.C. §1202. Section

---

8. Ford Motor Co. v. Autel US, Inc., 2015 U.S. Dist. LEXIS 133201 (E.D. Mich. Sept. 30, 2015).

1202 also prohibits the distribution or provision of false copyright information when done with intent to facilitate infringement.

Examples

1. *The poet didn't know it.* Delving through the archives, Researcher finds a long-lost 200-year-old poem, published only once in a local newspaper. Researcher wishes to strictly control circulation of the text. She encrypts a file containing the text of the poem and sends copies of the encrypted file to other researchers in the field. She separately sends them directions for decrypting the text. Interloper acquires a copy of the encrypted text by tricking one of the recipients. Interloper manages to decipher the encryption and gets a copy of the text. Has Interloper violated §1201?

2. *Shell-fishing expedition.* Consulting Information has compiled a large database with information about the lobster industry. Consulting used considerable creativity in selecting and arranging the information. Consulting considers the database to be a valuable trade secret. It takes several measures to keep the information secure. Access is limited by encryption and password protection. Nevertheless, a competitor circumvents these technological measures and copies the entire database. Has the competitor violated §1201? What if the competitor had selectively copied only a small number of the entries in the database?

3. *It's not just TV.* For a modest fee, Sharpie customizes cable service for homeowners (with permission from the cable company). By making a few choice adjustments to the homeowner's cable box, Sharpie allows the homeowner to access premium cable channels without paying the premium fee. Sharpie is sued for, among other things, violating §1201. Sharpie argues that §1201 is inapplicable. Section 1201 applies only if a technological measure effectively controls access to work. But, Sharpie argues, the cable scrambling does not effectively control access to the works. The scrambling is obviously ineffective, because Sharpie is so easily able to circumvent it. Would his argument succeed?

4. *Patients isn't a virtue.* Yonda the Yodeler operates a Web site that allows members to listen to her music online. For a small monthly fee, each member receives a password that allows unlimited access to Yonda's oeuvre. Patients, a thrifty and diligent fan, visits the Web site and tries several hundred times to guess a password. Finally, using a combination of Yonda's children's names, Patients guesses a valid password and is able to access the music. Has Patients violated §1201?

5. *McBoxed into a corner.* McPix sells McBoxes, handheld electronic video game players, for a nominal price. McPix makes most of its money from selling game cartridges to use on the handheld players. Each handheld player is

run by an operating system computer program. Only game cartridges sold by McPix will work with the computer program because of special coding in the program. A competitor cleverly builds game cartridges that, when inserted in a McBox, load another operating system computer program that runs the McBox and works well with any game cartridge. Has the competitor violated §1201?

6. *Not my bad.* Angry Burglars is a popular, copy-protected video game. Jeremy hacks a copy and modifies the game to comic effect. Maddie uses the game to draw traffic to her Web site. Maddie has a license to use the game on her site, and the license does not prohibit using adapted versions. But is she liable for violating the anticircumvention provisions?

7. *Sin of omission.* Clara pulls a photo offline and puts it on her personal Web site, to illustrate a joke to her family. That would be fair use. But if, in the process of posting the photo, she unknowingly stripped away the copyright notice, would she be liable for removing copyright management information?

Explanations

1. Interloper has not violated §1201, which prohibits circumvention of a technological measure that "controls access to a work protected under this title." The encryption did control access to the text of the poem. But the poem was not "a work protected under this title." A poem that had been published 200 years ago could not be under copyright. Section 1201 only applies to technological measures that protect works protected by the copyright statute.

2. The competitor has violated §1201 by circumventing an anti-access measure. The database is protected by copyright. Even though it consists mainly of noncopyrightable facts, it also includes copyrightable expression in the creative selection and arrangement of data. The competitor circumvented a measure controlling access to a copyrighted work, violating the anticircumvention rule.

   The result might be different if the competitor, after gaining access, had only copied a few facts (which are not protected by copyright), rather than the entire database. The copyright holder would argue that §1201 prohibits circumvention without limiting it to circumvention that results in copyright infringement. But, under *Lexmark* and *Chamberlain*, a court might hold that §1201 does not prohibit circumvention intended only to exploit nonprotected elements of a work.

3. Sharpie's argument would not succeed. The anticircumvention prohibition indeed applies only to a measure that "effectively controls access to

a work." But that phrase is defined to mean a measure that ordinarily requires the application of information, a process, or a treatment to get access. To "effectively control" does not mean that the measure is impossible or even difficult to get around. Awkwardly drafted, but it makes sense. There would not be a point to the statute if it protected only measures that were completely effective—because they would not need legal protection.

4. The question here is whether Patients has *circumvented* an anti-access measure. Yonda would argue that Patients has circumvented the password-protection technology. Circumvention is defined to mean "to descramble a scrambled work, to decrypt an encrypted work, or otherwise to avoid, bypass, remove, deactivate, or impair a technological measure, without the authority of the copyright owner." 17 U.S.C. §1201(a)(3)(A). Yonda would argue that Patients avoided or bypassed the requirement of an authorized password by guessing a password. Patients would argue that she did not "circumvent" it (in the sense of getting around it); rather, she used the technology. She submitted a password, it was accepted, and she was granted access—exactly the way the technology is supposed to work. One court has held in accord with Patients. *I.M.S. Inquiry Mgt. Sys. v. Berkshire Info. Sys.*, 307 F. Supp. 2d 521, 532-533 (D.N.Y. 2004) ("Defendant did not surmount or puncture or evade any technological measure to do so; instead, it used a password intentionally issued by plaintiff to another entity."). Unauthorized use does not violate §1201 if there is no circumvention. Other courts, however, have held that unauthorized use of a password is circumvention, especially is done through guessing the password or using repeated attempts (which may be done by software).

5. The question again is whether the competitor has circumvented an anti-access measure. It has removed the program containing the anti-access measure and replaced it with another program. So a court reading §1201 narrowly would hold that, rather than circumvent the measure, it has simply removed it. In addition, the competitor did not try to access the computer program, rather simply deleted it. So the better result would be that the competitor has not circumvented an anti-access measure. Note that this assumes that the code qualified as an anti-access measure to begin with. A court might hold that, if it simply controlled the *use* of the program, then it would not be protected under §1201 because it did not control access in a way linked to the copyright holder's bundle of exclusive rights.

6. Where Maddie used the software only after the measures had been removed, she is not liable for circumvention. *MGE UPS Sys. v. GE Consumer & Indus. Inc.*, 612 F.3d 760 (5th Cir. 2010) (holding that there is anticircumvention liability only where there is a showing that party engaged in circumvention, as opposed to used work after circumvention).

7. No. There is only a violation for removal or alteration with the intent to cause copyright infringement. Clara did not intentionally remove the information, nor did she intend to cause copyright infringement.

LIMITATIONS ON THE EXCLUSIVE RIGHTS

Fair Use

Fair use lies at the heart of copyright law. A small amount of copying from a song into a musical: fair use.[9] Copying and editing a YouTube video to critique it: fair use.[10] Incorporating an old newspaper article in the video of a news report: not necessarily fair use.[11] Fair use is a flexible doctrine allowing use of copyrighted works without permission or payment. Under 17 U.S.C. §107, fair use of a copyrighted work is not infringement of the rights granted under §106 or §106A. The statute does not define "fair use." Rather, the court must first consider whether the use at issue falls into one of the specified favored uses: "criticism, comment, news reporting, teaching (including multiple copies for classroom use), scholarship, or research." 17 U.S.C. §107. If it does, then fair use is more likely, but the categorization is not determinative either way. A favored use may not qualify as fair use, and a use outside those categories may nevertheless be fair use. Section 107, then, requires the court to consider four factors:

1. the purpose and character of the use, including whether such use is of a commercial nature or is for nonprofit educational purposes;
2. the nature of the copyrighted work;
3. the amount and substantiality of the portion used in relation to the copyrighted work as a whole; and
4. the effect of the use upon the potential market for or value of the copyrighted work.

The effect on the market for the work may be the factor that sways courts most. *See* Barton Beebe, *An Empirical Study of U.S. Copyright Fair Use Opinions, 1978-2005*, 156 U. Pa. L. Rev. 549 (2008).

Fair use was first made part of the copyright statute as part of the Copyright Act of 1976. As part of the long process leading up to the

---

9. Corbello v. DeVito, 2017 U.S. Dist. LEXIS 91164, *57-58 (D. Nev. June 13, 2017).
10. Hosseinzadeh v. Klein, No. 16-cv-3081 (KBF), 2017 U.S. Dist. LEXIS 134910, at *19-20 (S.D.N.Y. Aug. 23, 2017).
11. Hirsch v. CBS Broad. Inc., 2017 U.S. Dist. LEXIS 123468 (S.D.N.Y. Aug. 4, 2017).

enactment of the statute, in 1961 the Copyright Office provided several examples of cases held fair use:

> quotation of excerpts in a review or criticism for purposes of illustration or comment; quotation of short passages in a scholarly or technical work, for illustration or clarification of the author's observations; use in a parody of some of the content of the work parodied; summary of an address or article, with brief quotations, in a news report; reproduction by a library of a portion of a work to replace part of a damaged copy; reproduction by a teacher or student of a small part of a work to illustrate a lesson; reproduction of a work in legislative or judicial proceedings or reports; incidental and fortuitous reproduction, in a newsreel or broadcast, of a work located in the scene of an event being reported. . . .

Copyright Office Circular FL 102.

The Supreme Court has rested the constitutional place of copyright on fair use. In *Eldred v. Ashcroft*, one issue was whether Congress had violated the First Amendment's freedom of speech, by extending the terms of existing copyrights by 20 years. *Eldred v. Ashcroft*, 123 S. Ct. 769 (2003). *Eldred* held that copyright protection is generally not subject to First Amendment scrutiny, largely because copyright law has "built-in First Amendment accommodations," such as the nonprotection of ideas and the right to make fair use of works for such purposes as education, criticism, news reporting, or research.

Fair use is a notoriously troublesome doctrine because the rule provides little guidance about what weight to give the various factors. Accordingly, the voluminous case law is key in application of the fair use, especially the Supreme Court cases. The leading cases, discussed here, show how fact-specific the analysis is. In *Sony Corp. v. Universal City Studios*, 464 U.S. 417 (1984), the Court held fair use applicable to unauthorized home recording of television programs, which were made to watch the programs at a later time. The nature of the use was a noncommercial and nonprofit activity (private recording for personal use), not a commercial use. The nature of the works varied, because many programs were copied, but some were highly protected creative works. The amount copied was the entire work, which normally weighs against fair use. But that was undercut by the fact that the material copied had been broadcast for free viewing. With respect to the final factor, the plaintiffs made no concrete showing of specific market harm or loss of value from the practice of time-shifting.

In *Harper & Row, Publishers v. Nation Enterprises*, 471 U.S. 539 (1985), the *Nation* magazine managed to get a copy of President Gerald Ford's autobiography shortly before its publication. The *Nation* article included verbatim quotations amounting to some 300 words (from a manuscript of some 200,000 words), including portions of Ford's description of his thoughts at the time he pardoned former President Richard Nixon. As a result, *Time* magazine canceled its agreement to print prepublication excerpts from the book. The

Court held fair use inapplicable. The nature of the use was news reporting (a favored use), but was also commercial (less likely to qualify). Moreover, the *Nation* could have freely copied the unprotected facts and ideas in the work. So it could have accomplished the favored use of news reporting without taking any protected expression. The *Nation* had also "knowingly exploited a purloined manuscript." The nature of the work was a factual work. Because facts are not protected by copyright, such works are more subject to fair use than works of fiction or fantasy. But the *Nation* copied not only facts but freely took expressive elements of the work. Moreover, the work was unpublished, which is a key factor against fair use. The amount used was small, only a few pages of a lengthy book. But the portion taken was the heart of the book, the section most interesting to potential readers. Finally, a specific market harm was shown—the loss of prepublication licensing revenue from *Time*. So the factors taken together weighed against fair use.

In *Campbell v. Acuff-Rose Music*, 510 U.S. 569 (1994), the Court addressed parody as fair use. 2 Live Crew made a rap parody version of Roy Orbison's song, "Pretty Woman." By changing the lyrics and music somewhat, they inverted the viewpoint of the song. Their version was a cutting commentary on both the music and worldview of Orbison's original. The lower court had rejected fair use, relying on the commercial nature of the use and the fact that the parody had used substantial amounts of the original. The Supreme Court reversed and remanded for a more nuanced analysis. A parody must borrow some from the original to make its point. The parody at issue was a criticism and commentary on the original "Pretty Woman," so was more likely to be fair use than a parody that simply took material to free-ride on the efforts of others. In addition, parody is a transformative use, meaning that defendants added independent creative material to the work. The nature of the work was a highly protected creative work, but such would normally be the case where parody is at issue. The amount taken was no more than necessary for the favored use of commentary, especially as the parody version departed from the original in both words and music. The Court held on remand that a key factual issue was whether there was a showing of market harm, that is, whether the rap parody version had decreased any potential licensing revenue for other versions that plaintiff would have authorized.

In *Stewart v. Abend*, 495 U.S. 207, 238 (1990), the Supreme Court held that it was not fair use for the producers of Alfred Hitchcock's film *Rear Window* to continue showing the film, after their rights were terminated in the underlying story, *It Had To Be Murder*. *Stewart* was decided between *Sony* and *Harper & Row*. Although cited much less frequently than the three cases above, *Stewart* casts considerable light on fair use.[12] As in the other cases, loss of potential licensing revenue was the determinative factor. In

---

12. See Stephen McJohn & Lorie Graham, *Thirty-Two Short Stories About Intellectual Property*, 3 Hastings Sci. & Tech. L.J. 1 (2011).

Stewart, the two parties to the case had been parties to a licensing transaction. The author agreed to sell the movie rights to Hitchcock for the entire effective copyright term. Hitchcock, however, had lost the movie rights back to the author's estate, due to a quirky series of copyright cases. In effect, Hitchcock sought to use fair use to gain greater rights than had been gained in the transaction. There was an argument that continuing to allow Hitchcock to exploit the movie would be fair. The parties had agreed that Hitchcock would have the movie rights to the story permanently. Only because of the author's death and because of some complex decisions involving renewal of copyright did Hitchcock lose the bargained-for rights back to the heirs. Allowing Hitchcock to continue showing *Rear Window* would not have prevented the heirs from making their own movie based on the story. Nevertheless, fair use was held inapplicable, on the theory that a party to a transaction is entitled to what the law grants from that transaction. If Hitchcock continued to show his film, then that would have a negative impact on the potential market for other films based on the same short story. The context of the market discussion, however is quite different than the other cases. In the other three Supreme Court cases, the fair use issue arose between strangers, not parties who were disputing a previous transaction. Under *Stewart*, fair use will rarely allow a party to gain rights greater than the party gained by agreement.

Because fair use is so fact-specific, it can be difficult for parties to decide whether a potential use is fair use. A teacher including material in a coursepack, a writer quoting lengthy passages from a letter, a documentary filmmaker who captures other's images or music in her footage, a student group that would like to show a film, the maker of a mash-up—such users often seek guidance about fair use. That raises the hazard that people will err on the side of caution, effectively adding to the scope of copyright—not to mention the dead weight loss of uses that do not occur. *See* James Gibson, *Risk Aversion and Rights Accretion in Intellectual Property Law*, 116 Yale L.J. 882 (2007). Some have responded by drafting advice tailored to specific creators that frequently rely on use of other works. *See Documentary Filmmakers' Statement of Best Practices in Fair Use*, and the *Code of Best Practices in Fair Use for Online Video*. Another possibility would be to have a Fair Use Board in the U.S. Copyright Office, with authority to declare a proposed use to qualify as fair use. *See* Michael W. Carroll, *Fixing Fair Use*, 85 N.C. L. Rev. 1087 (2007).

Summing up Fair Use

Fair use is always a fact-based determination. But a number of general principles can be drawn from the cases. Note how the factors are interdependent.

Purpose and Character of the Use, Including Whether Such Use Is of a Commercial Nature or for Nonprofit Educational Purposes

Commercial uses are less likely to qualify, because there is likely to be market harm and because a commercial user is apt to bear the cost. Private, nonprofit uses are more likely to qualify, but certainly do not have categorical immunity. Moreover, there is really a spectrum, because private uses may have a commercial quality if they substitute for purchases or if they are used for barter.

Uses specifically mentioned by the statute are favored: "criticism, comment, news reporting, teaching (including multiple copies for classroom use), scholarship, or research." But other uses may be favored. Productive uses, where works are used as part of another activity, are more likely to be fair use than reproductive uses, where the defendant simply uses the work. Transformative uses, where the work is used to make another creative work, or the work is put to a different use are highly favored.

Another favored type of use is one that attempts to exploit unprotected aspects of the copyrighted work. Reverse engineering may entail making copies of a computer program in order to study its nonprotected functional aspects or to create another program that will operate together with it. A work might be copied to disseminate the unprotected ideas or facts in the work, as opposed to its protected creative expression of those elements. Such a use is more likely to qualify for fair use where the copyright owner is attempting to censor others, as opposed to protect a market for the work.

Courts may also consider the good faith of defendant's actions. Where defendant made a good faith attempt to get permission to use a work, the court may weigh that in favor of fair use. If defendant obtained a copy of the work through breach of contract, theft, or other bad faith actions, that will weigh against fair use. The copyright owner's motivations may also be relevant. A blogger was protected by fair use in posting an "unflattering" photo of a business person, where the subject had purchased the copyright to get the photo taken down.[13] Fair use defeated a city's assertion of copyright in its videos of city council meetings from recovering from a critic who posted portions, with subtitles and commentary.[14]

Nature of the Copyrighted Work

The more creative expression in a work, the more protection it has against fair use. Fair use applies more to thinly protected functional works (like computer programs or useful articles), factual works (like databases) and

---

13. Katz v. Google Inc., 802 F.3d 1178 (11th Cir. 2015); *see also* http://blog.ericgoldman.org/archives/2015/10/another-censorious-copyright-case-results-in-a-big-fee-shift-inglewood-v-teixeira.htm.
14. City of Inglewood v. Teixeira, 2015 U.S. Dist. LEXIS 143380 (C.D. Cal. Oct. 8, 2015).

nonoriginal works (like judicial reports or works that reproduce public domain works).

Unpublished works, under *Harper & Row*, are less subject to fair use. If a copy of an unpublished work has been obtained wrongfully, then this factor weighs even more strongly against fair use.

Amount and Substantiality of the Portion Used in Relation to the Copyrighted Work as a Whole

Copying (or distributing or adapting or performing or displaying) the entire work is less likely to qualify for fair use than using only a portion. But fair use often protects use of the entire work, as in *Sony*. This is especially true if the work is thinly protected, where copying the entire work still copies only a little protected expression (as may occur with a computer program or database). The particular portion copied is important. There was no fair use in *Harper & Row* for copying less than 1 percent of a book, where the copier chose the "heart" of the book. Whether the portion chosen is itself highly protected, creative expression is also relevant.

The key is whether the amount taken is appropriate to the favored use. There are several aspects to this. The first issue is whether the copier took an amount that fit the proposed use, for example, whether the reviewer quoted only sections relevant to her analysis of a book. The second issue is whether there was an alternative to taking the portion copied. *Harper & Row* again is key, with its argument that the magazine could largely have accomplished the favored purpose of news reporting by copying unprotected facts, ideas, and nonoriginal material. The third issue is whether the amount taken was likely to diminish a potential market for the copyright owner.

Effect of the Use upon the Potential Market for or Value of the Copyrighted Work

The effect on the market for the work may be the factor that sways courts most. *See* Barton Beebe, *An Empirical Study of U.S. Copyright Fair Use Opinions, 1978-2005*, 156 U. Pa. L, Rev. 549 (2008). There are several ways to show market harm. Lost sales of the copyrighted work (or sales of copies of the work by the defendant) may be the most direct way, but other markets will count. The statute speaks of "potential market," so it is enough to show harm in a market that the copyright owner was likely to enter. In addition, under *Sony*, it may be sufficient to show that, if defendant's use became a widespread practice, the copyright owner would suffer market harm. But there must generally be a concrete showing. There is a presumption of market harm for "verbatim copying of the original in its entirety for commercial purposes." But for other uses, mere speculative theories will not suffice. Rather, the copyright owner should make a concrete showing, such as by market surveys or other evidence.

Some types of market harm are not cognizable. Uses like criticism may decrease sales, but that does not weigh against fair use. Rather, it serves the underlying purpose of copyright to foster exchange of ideas. Likewise, uses like reverse engineering may permit copying of unprotected elements of the work. If use of unprotected elements leads to a product that buyers prefer, there is no cognizable market harm.

Finally, as commentators and courts have stressed, there is a tension between permitting fair use and permitting market mechanisms to develop. If photocopying was generally considered to be fair use, there would be no incentive to seek permission. If it is not considered fair use, then market mechanisms will develop to facilitate licensing, such as the Copyright Clearance Center. Music downloading is another area where some see conflict between free use and the development of permitted use. Courts are likely to struggle to find a balance.

Examples

1. *Sweet charity.* "Touchdown!" is a famous, beloved photo by Snapz. It captures three toddlers deliriously raising their arms in delight at some unshown performer. Snapz has earned considerable revenue from licensing various uses of the photo. He is surprised to find the photo being used on the front of Footie chocolate cookie boxes. When Snapz's agent contacts the seller of Footie cookies, she is informed that no permission was sought because the use is considered a fair use. Footie is a nonprofit company that sells cookies to fund various charitable activities. Millions of dollars are earned by selling Footies (with "Touchdown!" on the front), and all the money (other than expenses, which are rigorously minimized) goes to support a number of highly praiseworthy efforts, such as fighting infectious disease and aiding those harmed by earthquakes. Does the use of "Touchdown!" qualify as fair use?

2. *Kopy Kop Kop.* Photoshoppe, a commercial copy shop, makes coursepacks for students at a local university using reading lists provided by university instructors. Each coursepack contains several hundred pages of text from up to ten different sources. The sources range from textbooks to scholarly articles to newspaper articles. Most of the sources are under copyright, but Photoshoppe does not seek permission or offer to pay licensing fees. Photoshoppe refuses to seek licenses even when directly contacted by the various copyright owners. Other copy shops in the area do seek permission and pay fees when making such coursepacks. Photoshoppe, however, takes the position that making and distributing the coursepacks is protected as fair use, as a noncommercial educational activity. Does fair use protect Photoshoppe?

3. *Reverse engineering.* SoMak sells a popular word processing program, Word Prefect. Word Prefect is sold to the public in its object code version,

meaning it is sold in the form on which it is run on a computer and not the source code form that a software developer could easily read and modify. Strive, an engineer, purchases a copy of Word Prefect at a local office supply store. Strive then prints the object code version on several hundred sheets of paper. Strive spends several months studying the object code quite closely to see how the program functions. Strive then writes her own word processing program, Sendense. Strive is very careful only to copy unprotected, functional aspects of Word Prefect into Sendense. Her avowed purpose is to win over market leadership from Word Prefect.

SoMak sues Strive, alleging infringement of the copyright in Word Prefect. Strive contends that she cannot have infringed because she only copied nonprotected elements. She then realizes that she did make a copy—she printed out the program on paper—but she decides that fair use protects her. Does fair use apply?

4. *Trouble in parodies.* "Evermore," a ballad written and sung by Wangelis, is often heard on the radio. The song tells the tale of a modern Romeo and Juliet, set to soothing electronic sounds. Smiling Al, a popular comedian, uses the words and melody of the song for his recording, "Mevermore." Al rewrites the words into an amusing tale of a trip to the Mount Mevermore, a mound in the Everglades. "Mevermore" uses the melody from "Evermore" but does not explicitly or implicitly comment on or criticize "Evermore." Rather, the use of the familiar tune from "Evermore" makes "Mevermore" more marketable. Because listeners know and like the tune, they are more likely to stay tuned and listen to the new version. When Wangelis claims infringement, Smiling Al claims that "Mevermore" is a parody and therefore protected under fair use. Does fair use protect this use?

5. *Thumbnails.* An Internet search engine helps users find images on the Web. The search engine automatically browses the Web, collecting as many images as it can. Using both humans and software, it compiles an index of keywords associated with the images. If a user types "Panda" into the search page, it will return all the pictures it has associated with the word "Panda." It does not show the original pictures but rather "thumbnail" versions. Thumbnails are small, low resolution versions of the pictures. To view the original, the user can click on the link and be sent to the page where the original is found. A photographer, who posts original photos on his site, sues for infringement. Fair use?

6. *Panned.* Critic writes a review of *Slidder*, a new detective novel from best-selling author Austen. Critic makes ten verbatim quotations from the book, of one to four sentences each. The review convincingly argues that Austen is simply recycling plot lines and characters from her previous books. The quotations are carefully selected to support Critic's argument. Critic's review is printed in newspapers across the land. *Slidder* becomes

Austen's first book in years not to make the top of the best-seller charts. Austen blames Critic, and sues for copyright infringement. She contends that fair use will not apply, where Critic's use of her very own words destroyed the market value of the work. Was demolition fair use?

7. *Extraction by copying.* Data Gatherer compiles property information for municipalities. The municipalities send out forms to their residents, with various questions about their real property (including such things as ownership, lenders, residents, use, renovations, and additions). When the forms come back, Data Gatherer's employees input them into a database, which is stored on computers in the municipal offices and may be accessed by the public and by municipal employees. Data Gatherer has made several creative choices about how to organize the information. The municipalities pay a fee to Data Gatherer.

   A rival compiler sends in workers, who download the entire database and take the copy to their home office. There, they extract all the information into their own database. Their database does not copy Data Gatherer's creative arrangement of information, rather only the unprotected facts. But Data Gatherer claims infringement for the first copying, which was done in order to extract the information. Infringement or fair use?

8. *Checksheets.* The book *Big League Sales* describes techniques and cases histories for salespeople to overcome their prospective customers' "brick overcoat" of fear. The Church of Scientology develops "checksheets" and "drill sheets," which it sells to be used with the book. Students (paired as "twins") can use the sheets to track completion of reading assignments and practical exercises. The holder of the copyright in *Big League Sales* claims that the checksheets and drill sheets are infringing derivative works. Are they?

9. *Flipendo Lexicon.* RDR Books seeks to publish the *Harry Potter Lexicon,* an encyclopedia listing terms, events, characters, and various other aspects of the Harry Potter books and movies. The encyclopedia sticks close to the text of the books, with its entries quoting many passages largely verbatim. The Harry Potter copyright holders seek an injunction. Among other reasons, Harry Potter's author plans her own reference work. The *Lexicon's* publishers argue fair use on the theory that the work is a reference work, useful for research and scholarship; that the purpose of the work is transformative, like the protected parody in the "Pretty Woman" case; that the amount taken is appropriate, and that the material taken was largely nonprotected factual material, relating what happened to who in the books; and that the Lexicon would not hurt the huge market for Harry Potter.

10. *Google Print.* Google undertakes a library digitization project. Google's plans are flexible, but suppose it takes the following approach: with the cooperation of several libraries, Google will scan their collections, book

by book. Google will include the material in a huge database. Google users will be able to search the database using Google Print. A user will not be able to download the book's text, rather will get back only a few lines of text with each search result. The user may get links to places to buy the book (like Amazon.com) and advertisements keyed to the search and its results. To do this, Google will have to do a lot of copying (scanning, saving into the database, giving snippets to users, and more) of copyrighted works (as well as a lot of noncopyrighted works). Publishers object and suggest Google negotiate licensing fees. Fair use?

That question sparked a lot of online discussion. A Google search for "google print" and "fair use" yielded about 11,300 results (along with one sponsored link to "Search Books With Google on Google Print"). Opinions were all over the spectrum. What do you think?

11. *All's fair?* The United States commissioned a sculpture for the Korean War Veterans Memorial. In the agreement, the sculptor adamantly retained the copyright. The U.S. Postal Service subsequently put a photo of the sculpture on a postage stamp and sold millions of copies. The photographer had made the image of the snow-bedecked sculpture as a present for his father, a Korean War veteran. The Postal Service signed a license agreement getting permission only from the photographer. The sculptor was not consulted. Fair use?

12. *Sample.* Public Announcement's song, "D.O.G. in Me," makes repeated use of a sample from George Clinton's "Atomic Dog." The sampled elements are "the use of the word 'dog' in a low voice as 'musical punctuation,' the rhythmic panting," and the refrain: "Bow wow wow, yippie yo, yippie yea." Many others paid to sample from "Atomic Dog," but Public Announcement did not. Fair use?

13. *Enlargement.* The Los Angeles County Sheriff's Department buys 3,663 licenses to use Wall Data's software, but installs the software onto 6,007 computers, configuring its network so no more than 3,663 copies will be in use at any one time. Fair use?

14. *Fair use,* Rasta. Prince, a successful appropriation artist, tore prints of photos from a book, *Yes Rasta,* and alters them dramatically with paint, printing, and pasted elements. After the altered prints are sold for gigantic sums, the photographer sues for infringement. Fair use?

15. Meltwater's "Global Media Monitoring" service enabled "users to monitor the news based on the presence of certain words or phrases in news articles appearing on the Internet and to receive excerpts of those news articles. Meltwater uses automated computer programs or algorithms to copy or 'scrape' an article from an online news source, index the article, and deliver verbatim excerpts of the article to its customers in response to search queries." Fair use?

16. *Posting bills*. Would it be fair use for a nonprofit to copy and post online "private sector codes and standards [drafted] in order to advance public safety, ensure compatibility across products and services, facilitate training, and spur innovation," where such code have been given legal effect by adoption by governmental agencies?[15]

17. *Sony?* VidAngel markets itself as a one dollar movie streaming service VidAngel purchased movies on DVDs, circumvented access controls, and copied the movie to permit streaming to customers. It characterized its transactions with customers as selling the disc to the user for $20, streaming the movie, and then repurchasing it for $19, all the while maintaining physical possession of the disc, so the user was streaming their own copy. Fair use?

18. *Oracle again*. Recall from earlier in the book that the APIs for the Java programming language were held to be protected by copyright. Google copies the Java APIs to write its own code to run Java, so that developers could use Java to write apps for the Android operating system distributed by Google. In plain English, APIs are snippets of software code that programmers use to tell software to do things. Was it fair use for Google to copy the Java APIs in order to write software that would run Java, a common practice in the software industry?

Explanations

1. The use does not qualify as fair use. Indeed, although the ultimate purpose is to fund highly praiseworthy activities, every factor in the fair use analysis weighs against finding fair use here. It does not fall into one of the favored uses: "criticism, commentary news reporting, teaching, scholarship, or research." The purpose is arguably charitable (indirectly), but the direct use is simply commercial. Moreover, the use simply reproduces the work without adding any creative expression, so that factor is at best neutral — and more likely weighs against fair use. The nature of the work is a highly protected creative work, which weighs against fair use. The amount copied is the entire work, again a strong factor against fair use. Finally, Snapz earns licensing revenue from various uses of the photo. The failure to pay him licensing while widely exploiting the work make the fourth factor also weigh against fair use.

2. Recent decisions have denied fair use to systematic photocopying for commercial uses, even when associated with education or research. *See Princeton Univ. Press v. Michigan Document Services*, 99 F.3d 1813 (6th Cir. 1996) (*en banc*);

American Geophysical Union v. Texaco, 60 F.3d 913 (2d Cir. 1994). The nature of the work depends on the materials chosen for copying, but expressive texts are likely to be highly protected literary works. The purpose of the copy shop is commercial, and courts are not likely to consider the purpose of the students, who buy the coursepacks for educational purposes. The amount taken would often not be the whole work, but presumably the instructor would choose what she deemed to be important sections. Remember that *Harper & Row* denied fair use to a few hundred words copied from a book and deemed especially significant (although that was unpublished work, which is much less subject to fair use). The last factor weighs strongly in favor of the copyright owners. Other copy shops do pay licensing fees, so the practice would cause the copyright holders market harm.

We need to know more, such as the length of the excerpts and whether there is a practical way for the university to get a license. All the fair use factors must be considered with the particulars of each use. *Cambridge Univ. Press v. Patton*, 769 F.3d 1232 (11th Cir. 2014). The court looked to whether practicable licensing agreements were available to universities. Where the works were not available to be licensed, such "electronic reserves" were more likely to be fair use. Where licenses were available, such as through the Copyright Clearance Center, fair use still might permit use of smaller portions. Under this case, by making copyrighted works available for licensing, a rights holder makes it less likely that unauthorized use would be fair use. One could see that as shrinking fair use because a publisher can inoculate its book against broad fair use by signing up with a licensing service. But one could also see it as benefitting users by encouraging publishers to make works available, which avoids the troublesome issue of figuring out how much use is fair—a little like buying copyright infringement insurance.

3. Strive has a strong argument that making a copy for purposes of reverse engineering is fair use. *See, e.g., Sony Computer Ent. v. Connectix*, 203 F.3d 596 (9th Cir. 2000); *Atari Games v. Nintendo of Am.*, 975 F.2d 832 (Fed. Cir. 1992); *Sega Enterprises v. Accolade, Inc.*, 977 F.2d 1510 (9th Cir. 1992). The purpose of the use is commercial, but it is also research. Moreover, making a copy may sometimes be the only way to gain access to the unprotected functional aspects of works. The nature of the copyrighted work is a computer program, a functional work rather than a highly expressive work whose nature lies at the core of copyright. The amount copied was the entire work, but such intermediate copying was necessary to study the functional aspects, and none of the expressive aspects were copied into the final product. Finally, SoMak may lose sales, not because Strive is selling infringing copies, but because Strive is selling noninfringing copies in legitimate competition. Such market harm does not weigh against fair use, in the same way the loss of sales from the criticism in a book review or a parody does not weigh against fair use.

If, to gain access to the work, Strive had circumvented some protective technology (such as encryption), the case would present some interesting issues on the new anticircumvention provisions in 17 U.S.C. §1201 (which this chapter only briefly touches on) — in particular, the interplay between fair use and the new provision.

4. Smiling Al is about to lose his smile. He is not protected by fair use. Parody can be protected by fair use, as in *Campbell*. But there is a key distinction in this case. The purpose of the parody in *Campbell*, in part, was commentary. The parody version was an effective critique of the very worldview of the copyrighted work. Here, the parody does not comment on or criticize the original work. Rather, the parody borrows the tune of the original to profit from its popularity, which verges on the very free-riding that copyright exists to reduce. The parody does add creative expression and somewhat transform the original work. But such elements would appear in almost any derivative work.

5. Probably fair use. *See Kelly v. Arriba Soft Corp.*, 336 F.3d 811 (9th Cir. 2003). The use is commercial, especially if the search engine uses the service to sell advertising. The works are highly protected creative works. But the use is a productive use. The search engine made at least two copies (downloading a copy and making a thumbnail version). But the downloading was permitted by the Web site, and the thumbnail was no more than necessary for the favored productive use. Nor would there likely be harm to the potential market. The use did not serve as a substitute for the copyrighted works (because the thumbnails had greatly diminished resolution). Nor is there a market for licensing works to search engines.

6. Fair use. Critic did use protected expression without permission, but the factors would favor fair use. Critic made a favored use, criticism. The work was a highly protected creative work, but such works are certainly subject to criticism, so the factor would not weigh heavily. The amount used was not large and was also appropriate for the favored use. There was market harm, but not a cognizable harm. The author lost sales not because Critic sold copies of the work, but because Critic convinced people not to buy the work.

7. Fair use. Intermediate copying, done for the purpose of accessing noncopyrightable facts, may qualify as fair use. The rationale is similar to that permitting copying of software in order to reverse engineer its unprotected functional aspects. *See Assessment Technologies of WI, LLC, v. Wiredata, Inc.*, 350 F.3d 640 (7th Cir. 2003).

8. The court soundly rejected the infringement claim. *Peter Letterese & Associates v. World Inst. of Scientology Enterprises*, 533 F.3d 1287 (11th Cir. 2008). The sheets do not copy creative expression from the book; rather at most, they copy only functional elements. Not every work that is based on a copyrighted work is a derivative work. It must copy protected expression.

9. The federal court in New York rejected fair use. *Warner Bros. Ent. Inc. v. RDR Books*, No. 07 Civ. 9667 (S.D.N.Y. 2008). Harry Potter's author cannot prevent others from writing reference books about the young magician's tales. Nor can she prevent copying of ideas and nonoriginal material (such as preexisting witchcraft lore she used). Others may make fair use even of her original creative expression. But the *Lexicon* exceeded the bounds of fair use. The key factor was that the *Lexicon* used much more of her expression than necessary to provide a reference work. There was also a showing of potential market harm, by her concrete plans to write an authorized Harry Potter reference.

10. There's a lot of room for argument on this one, because the general topic of fair use and the Internet is still very unsettled. Two sides of the argument might run this way:

    a. "Of course it is fair use. The nature of the use is helping people to identify books that they are interested in. This is far from a merely reproductive use; rather it is a productive, if not transformative, use. It assists the free flow of ideas — a prime policy of copyright — without distributing more than a tiny amount of creative expression, because users only get a few lines of text with each search result. Two factors might weigh against fair use. Many of the works are highly protected creative works, and they are being copied in their entirety. But those are both undercut. The creative aspects, like the works as a whole, are copied only as part of facilitating research and the dissemination of ideas. Those creative aspects are not distributed. Google adjusted its plans, announcing that it would suspend scanning for three months and honor requests by publishers to opt out of the project. Willingness to omit books on request weighs in favor of good faith use and fair use, but that is only part of one of the factors. Finally, there is no showing of an adverse effect on the market. The snippets in no way serve as a substitute for the books, or even as a substitute for excerpts from the books — just like reverse engineering, where you make an intermediate copy of the whole work in order to get at its unprotected aspects."

    b. "Of course it is not fair use. This is systematic copying of entire libraries, well beyond the scope of anything that ever qualified as fair use. No market harm?! Google makes e-books by scanning the paper books. Google uses those e-books to compile indexes. Well, publishers already sell e-books and indexes to the contents of books. If Google wants electronic copies of the books or searchable indexes, it should buy them from the publishers or get permission to scan them. The use is commercial, just like the photocopying cases. The users may use Google Print for research or education, but Google is doing this as a commercial entity to sell advertising, to accumulate useful marketing data, and to establish itself as a key source of information — other people's copyrighted information! Finally, there is a clear showing of market harm. As Google's actions show, there is a demand for the use of copyrighted books in databases. We stand willing to negotiate a price."

In a related case, the Second Circuit held that fair use protected unauthorized scanning and compiling of books into a searchable database. *See Authors Guild, Inc. v. HathiTrust,* 755 F.3d 87 (2d Cir. 2014). Google did the scanning of books from the collection of member libraries, such as universities. The database allowed three types of uses. Anyone could search the database and receive results showing only books containing the search terms, along with page numbers (no snippets of text, unlike Google Books). Member libraries could use the database to enable readers with disabilities (such as blindness or inability to turn pages) to use adaptive technologies, such as software that magnified the text or read it aloud. Member libraries could also use electronic copies to replace lost originals.

Next, the Second Circuit held that fair use protected copying by the Google Book project broadly, which involved scanning libraries of books, putting the files in a database, and permitting online text searches that returned snippets of the books. Although the database might conceivably cost some book sales, where such a snippet made buying the book unnecessary, that factor was outweighed by the valuable uses. "The search engine also makes possible new forms of research, known as 'text mining' and 'data mining.' Google's 'ngrams' research tool draws on the Google Library Project corpus to furnish statistical information to Internet users about the frequency of word and phrase usage over centuries. . . . It also allows researchers to comb over the tens of millions of books Google has scanned in order to examine 'word frequencies, syntactic patterns, and thematic markers' and to derive information on how nomenclature, linguistic usage, and literary style have changed over time." *Authors Guild v. Google, Inc.,* 804 F.3d 202, 209 (2d Cir. 2015).

The digital age will continue to raise many issues of fair use. *See, e.g.,* Matthew Sag, *Copyright and Copy-Reliant Technology,* 103 Nw. U. L. Rev. (2009) (discussing technologies that rely on copying for nonexpressive uses, such as "search engines, plagiarism detection software, reverse engineering and Google's nascent library cataloging effort").

11. Most photos of national monuments would qualify for fair use. But this use did not qualify, for several reasons. The use by the Postal Service was commercial (selling millions of stamps). The photographer's image was not held transformative, rather simply a beautiful image of the sculpture in snow. Moreover, any transformative use was by the photographer, not by the Postal Service. In addition, the parties here were not strangers. The negotiated agreement did not grant the United States the copyright or a license to make derivative works. Fair use is not way to transform the agreement itself. *See Gaylord v. United States,* 595 F.3d 1364 (Fed. Cir. 2010).

12. Infringement. The use was commercial. It was also transformative, but did not criticize or comment on the original. Although the elements copied were small, they were among the most distinctive elements of the song. Market harm was shown by the many others that paid to license samples of the song. *See Bridgeport Music, Inc. v. UMG Recordings, Inc.*, 585 F.3d 267, 277-279 (6th Cir. 2009).

13. Infringement. "The Sheriff's Department could have bargained for the flexibility it desired, but it did not. Whenever a user puts copyrighted software to uses beyond the uses it bargained for, it affects the legitimate market for the product." *See* 447 F.3d 769 (9th Cir. 2006).

14. The Second Circuit held the adaptations were fair use, emphasizing that the use was "transformative" because it altered the original with "new expression, meaning, or message . . . These twenty-five of Prince's artworks manifest an entirely different aesthetic from Cariou's photographs. Where Cariou's serene and deliberately composed portraits and landscape photographs depict the natural beauty of Rastafarians and their surrounding environs, Prince's crude and jarring works, on the other hand, are hectic and provocative." *Cariou v. Prince*, 714 F.3d 694 (2d Cir. 2013).

15. The court rejected fair use, looking primarily to the effect on the market for the copyrighted works: "By refusing to pay a licensing fee to AP, Meltwater not only deprives AP of a licensing fee in an established market for AP's work, but also cheapens the value of AP's work by competing with companies that pay a licensing fee to use AP content in the way that Meltwater does." *AP v. Meltwater U.S. Holdings, Inc.*, 931 F. Supp. 2d 537 (S.D.N.Y. 2013). Unlike typical search engines that return thumbnail versions of photographs or snippets of text, Meltwater provided the very information sought and so replaced the original works. Likewise, fair use did not protect a news clipping service, which charged clients for access to a searchable database of news clippings from others' copyrighted newscasts. *Fox News Network, LLC v. TVEyes, Inc.*, 883 F.3d 169 (2d Cir. 2018)

16. Well, the court held it was not fair use, because it would eat into the licensing control of those who expended efforts to create those useful works. Others would differ, on the theory that material drafted with the intent that it have legal effect should be free for republication.

17. The Ninth Circuit held that fair use did not apply. *Disney Enters. v. VidAngel, Inc.*, 869 F.3d 848, 862 (9th Cir. 2017). First, VidAngel did not stream an authorized copy of the movie, rather circumvented access controls and copying controls in order to make a digital copy from the DVD for streaming. Whether the customer owned the movie was not decisive. First sale authorizes one to distribute that copy, not to make

more copies—otherwise one could buy one copy of a movie and make thousands of copies. Nor was the use transformative, because editing out content did not transform the work—and in any case users typically requested little or no editing, rather simply watched the movie. Nor did it qualify for time-shifting as under *Sony*, which involved a consumer copying a movie on a VCR for the consumer's later use.

18. In a surprise to many in the software industry, the Federal Circuit held that it was not fair use for Google to copy the Java APIs. First factor: the use was commercial. Google gives Android away, but Android plays an important role in Google's commercial plans. The court deemed the use not transformative, because it simply allowed Google to develop software that had similar functionality to Oracle's software. Second factor: the work copied was largely functional and so had only thin copyright. But the court gave the factor little weight. The third factor, amount of copying, was deemed to weigh against Google, because it copied more code than necessary to implement Java. The last factor, market harm, was deemed to weigh heavily against fair use, because Google's copying enabled Android to take over the smartphone market, leaving any possible competition from Oracle in the dust. *Oracle Am., Inc. v. Google LLC*, 2018 U.S. App. LEXIS 7794 (Fed. Cir. Mar. 27, 2018).

Others might have held fair use applicable, where the copying was geared toward allowing Google to copy the functional aspects of Java and the market harm likewise flowed from Android's functional aspects, not any consumer interest in the creative aspects of Java. Such a result would be consistent with cases holding fair use applicable to copying done to exploit functional aspects of works, such as copying done to reverse engineer software or to extract nonprotected facts from a database.

First Sale

Someone who purchases an authorized copy of a book may resell it. Used book stores sell copyrighted books. Video rental services rent copyrighted movies. Museums display copyrighted works to the public. Resellers recirculate copies of copyrighted software. Libraries lend copyrighted books. None need permission from the copyright owner, as long as they own a copy that was made lawfully, such as a copy that was made by or licensed by the copyright owner. A copyright owner's exclusive right to distribute copies and display copies to the public is subject to the first sale doctrine. Once the copyright owner sells a copy, her rights with respect to that particular copy are limited. The owner may distribute it or display it (but not copy, adapt, or publicly perform it, unless protected by fair use, permission, or something else).

The first sale doctrine is an important limit on a copyright holder's exclusive rights of public distribution and display. As discussed earlier, copyright law distinguishes between ownership of a physical copy of the work and ownership of the copyright. Sale of the physical object does not include transfer of the copyright. If Painter sells her latest landscape to Collector, Collector owns the painting, but Painter still owns the copyright. So if Collector makes copies of the work or makes derivative works, Collector potentially infringes the copyright. But 17 U.S.C. §109, often called "the first sale doctrine," does give the transferee some rights. Under §109(a), the owner of a lawfully made copy or phonorecord may sell or otherwise dispose of that copy or phonorecord. Under §109(c), the owner of a lawfully made copy may display the copy to the public. So Collector may sell, rent, or donate the painting (even though that is distributing a copy to the public) or put the painting on display (even if that means displaying the painting publicly). In short, the owner of a book or painting or video game or sculpture may sell it, rent it, give it away, or otherwise dispose of it (unless that copy was a bootleg, knockoff, or otherwise infringing copy).

The first sale doctrine has distinct limits. The fair use doctrine, discussed above, can apply to any of the five exclusive rights. But the first sale doctrine only limits the distribution right and the display right. So if the owner of a copy makes copies, makes derivative works, or performs the work in public, first sale cannot protect her (although fair use or some other limitation might apply). In addition, the first sale right to display the work is limited to display "directly or by the projection of no more than one image at a time, to viewers present at the place where the copy is located." 17 U.S.C. §109(c). Moreover, the first sale doctrine applies only to the owner of a lawfully made copy or phonorecord. Had Collector stolen the painting, he would not be the owner and therefore would not have first sale rights.

The Supreme Court has applied first sale broadly in the patent context. *See Quanta Computer, Inc. v. LG Electronics, Inc.,* 128 S. Ct. 2109 (2008). Where the holder of several chipset patents licensed the patents to a chipset manufacturer, the patent holder was barred by patent exhaustion from pursuing infringement claims against the licensee's customers. The sale of authorized products embodying the patents terminated the patent rights in those products, meaning that the purchasers were free to incorporate them into otherwise infringing products. *Quanta* is a patent case, but its broad application of first sale may affect the first sale analysis is copyright, which shares underlying policy considerations. This suggests that some contract provisions that purport to override first sale will be ineffective.

The first sale protections apply only to the particular copy owned. It would not authorize the distribution of other copies. So if Collector makes and sells a copy of the painting, Collector would potentially infringe both the right to make copies and the distribution right.

First sale also only applies to a lawfully made copy. Had the painting itself been an infringing copy, Collector would have no rights under first sale. First sale does not authorize the owner to make more copies, rather only to distribute or display that copy. Note that the statute does not require that the copyright owner authorized the making of the copy, rather that the copy was "lawfully made." As the legislative history puts it:

> To come within the scope of section 109(a), a copy or phonorecord must have been "lawfully made under this title," though not necessarily with the copyright owner's authorization. For example, any resale of an illegally "pirated" phonorecord would be an infringement, but the disposition of a phonorecord legally made under the compulsory licensing provisions of section 115 would not.

House Report No. 94-1476. A copy that was made under fair use or some other provision could qualify.

Examples

1. *First sale.* Imagick sells 700 copies of her copyrighted illustration, Bikealot. Imagick assures the buyers that the work is a limited edition, so they are buying a relatively scarce commodity. The illustration, in Imagick's distinctive hand, shows what the Knights of the Round Table might have looked like had they been members of the Hell's Angels. The purchasers of several copies do things that seem to fall within Imagick's exclusive rights as a copyright owner. State which of the following are protected by the first sale doctrine:
   a. Sleepy advertises his copy for sale and sells it to a collector for a premium price, three times what Sleepy paid to Imagick.
   b. Grumpy decides he does not like the illustration. Grumpy skillfully uses charcoal to change the expressions of the riders depicted by Imagick, changing them from fierce bikers to snooty tourists.
   c. Sneezy puts his copy on display in his gallery, admitting members of the public for a fee.
   d. Doc makes several copies of his copy and sells them outside Sneezy's gallery.
   e. Arb buys a copy from Doc and then sells it online to a buyer for a nice profit.
   f. Dopey sets up a Web cam that allows visitors to Dopey's Web site to view Dopey's copy.
   g. Imagick gives one copy to Ingrate as a birthday present. Ingrate promptly turns around and sells the copy for a nice price.

2. *Clips.* Snippy runs a clipping service. Snippy reads several papers a day, and clips out stories that may be of interest to one client or another. A story may mention a client, a competitor of a client, or a topic of special interest to a client. She pops the stories in the mail. The stories are all copyrighted. Is Snippy infringing? Would it be different if she read

the stories online and then copied and pasted them into e-mails to her clients?

3. *Owner?* Ada purchased a copy of some music software, *Mister Moon.* She agreed to the standard purchase contract, which provided she would get permanent possession of a copy of the software, but the software company would retain ownership of the copy. After using the software for a year, she decided to sell her copy on eBay. Would she violate the copyright owner's exclusive right to distribute copies?

4. *Wet Blanket.* Becky purchases a CD of tunes by her favorite singer, DeeVeeDee. Becky brings the CD to her job at the university library reference desk. Becky proceeds to play the CD over the public address system, to the surprise of the patrons and staff. The library director suggests that Becky has violated not just library rules but copyright law by publicly performing the copyrighted musical works. Becky contends that she is protected by first sale because the sale of the CD to her eliminated the copyright owner's interest in that particular copy. Does first sale protect Becky? Would it make a difference if Becky had bought an authorized copy of sheet music and sung it over the PA system?

5. *ReDigi or not.* ReDigi allowed users to sell their authorized music files. The user would upload the file to ReDigi, who would sell it. Does first sale apply to such digital resales?

Explanations

1. a. Sleepy is protected by first sale. He owns the copy, so 17 U.S.C. §109 authorizes him to sell the copy.
   b. Grumpy is not protected by the first sale doctrine. He has potentially infringed the adaptation right by transforming the work into a new creative work. He owns the copy, but ownership is not a general defense to copyright infringement. Rather, first sale protects the owner from infringement of the distribution or display rights. It is not a limitation on the copyright owner's exclusive rights of reproduction, adaptation, and performance.
   c. Sneezy is protected by first sale. As the owner of a lawfully made copy, Sneezy may display it.
   d. Doc is not protected by first sale. Doc made copies of the work without permission. First sale does not apply to infringement of the reproduction right. Nor does it protect Doc's distribution of the copies he made because it authorizes distribution only of lawfully made copies.
   e. Arb is likewise not protected by first sale. He is the owner of a copy but not a lawfully made copy. So Arb had no first sale protection at all.

He infringes the distribution right by selling the copy to a member of the public.

f. Dopey is not protected by first sale. He has made a potentially infringing public display. First sale authorizes the owner to display the copy only at the place where the copy is located. It is narrower than the display right, which encompasses display via a transmission to other places.

g. Ingrate is protected by first sale. The owner of a lawfully made copy is protected by the first sale doctrine, and Ingrate received a lawfully made copy from Imagick as a gift. The owner need not have purchased the copy to acquire first sale rights.

2. Snippy is not infringing. She owns the copies of the copyrighted stories and may distribute them as she wishes.

It would be different if she made copies of the stories. It would also be different if she read the stories online, made copies, and e-mailed them to her clients. First sale does not authorize the making of copies, only distribution (and display). By making copies, she would potentially infringe. (She might argue fair use, but such reproductive, commercial use would probably not qualify, as discussed in later chapters. Better that she simply e-mails links to her clients).

3. The software company might argue that Ada has no first sale rights, because she is not the owner of a copy. Rather, she has possession of a copy that belongs to the software company. Courts may accept such formalism, but are increasingly likely to hold that where Ada has paid the price and is entitled to keep the copy forever, she owns it, and is therefore protected by first sale.

4. Becky is not protected by first sale. First sale limits only the distribution and display rights. Becky has potentially infringed the performance right. She performed the musical works publicly by playing them over the PA system. The same would be true if she had bought the sheet music and performed it herself.

5. The court held first sale inapplicable. *Capitol Records, LLC v. ReDigi Inc.*, 934 F. Supp. 2d 640 (S.D.N.Y. 2013). First sale, as the statute says, applies only to a "particular copy or phonorecord lawfully made under this title." ReDigi's service might offer the functional equivalent of resale, but the customer was not selling their copy, rather sending another copy. The court declined to judicially rewrite the statute to extend first sale to fit the digital age, reasoning that "the first sale doctrine was enacted in a world where the ease and speed of data transfer could not have been imagined." The court also declined to apply fair use to protect the service.

Limits on First Sale Rights in Sound Recordings and Computer Programs

Under first sale, the owner of a copy of a work may lease out the copy without infringing the copyright holder's distribution right. For some works, this could lead to infringement. Someone could open up a music or computer program rental store in which customers rented musical recordings or computer programs for an hour or two to make copies, avoiding having to buy authorized copies. At the urging of affected copyright holders, special protections for music and software copyrights limit the scope of first sale.

> Notwithstanding the provisions of subsection (a), unless authorized by the owners of copyright in the sound recording or the owner of copyright in a computer program (including any tape, disk, or other medium embodying such program), and in the case of a sound recording in the musical works embodied therein, neither the owner of a particular phonorecord nor any person in possession of a particular copy of a computer program (including any tape, disk, or other medium embodying such program), may, for the purposes of direct or indirect commercial advantage, dispose of, or authorize the disposal of, the possession of that phonorecord or computer program (including any tape, disk, or other medium embodying such program) by rental, lease, or lending, or by any other act or practice in the nature of rental, lease, or lending. Nothing in the preceding sentence shall apply to the rental, lease, or lending of a phonorecord for nonprofit purposes by a nonprofit library or nonprofit educational institution.

17 U.S.C. §109(b)(1)(A). In short, no rentals of software or music.

Section 109 does not authorize the owner of a phonorecord or a person in possession of a copy of a computer program to rent or lend the phonorecord or computer program for commercial advantage. In short, first sale does not protect rental of sound recordings or of software. This restriction only applies to rental or lending for commercial advantage, so people may still loan out their music or software gratis. The provision also specifically excludes nonprofit schools and libraries. Public libraries can loan out music and software.

Note that first sale still protects other types of rental, such as video rentals. Presumably Congress did not consider the danger of unauthorized copying of rented movies to be as risky to copyright owners as with music or software. Movies are often watched just once, as opposed to music or software, which may be used many times. Copying and distributing copies of movies was also more cumbersome than with music and software, although that is rapidly changing.

There is also an exception to the exception. It does not apply to computer programs embodied in machines (where the program cannot be copied in ordinary operation) or in computers specially designed for playing video games. Many products, from cars to microwave ovens, have embedded computer programs. Video game players likewise contain software that runs them. This provision means that such products may be rented, without infringing the copyright in the software they carry.

Examples

1. *Tunes to let.* Becky is looking for new employment. She decides to take advantage of the first sale doctrine. She buys dozens of popular CDs and goes into business from her apartment, renting the CDs by the day. Does first sale authorize Becky's activity?

2. *Audiobook—a book or a record?* The Local Bookie rents movies and audio-books, such as a recording of Stephen Fry reading a Harry Potter book. First sale authorizes the rental of movie. But, with respect to audiobooks, is the Local Bookie covered by first sale, which does not authorize rental of phonorecords or computer program?

Explanations

1. First sale does not authorize Becky to rent the CDs. First sale generally does authorize the owner of a lawfully made copy to dispose of it by sale or otherwise, which includes rental. But there is an exception for sound recordings, computer programs, and musical works: rental is not authorized. Otherwise, customers could simply rent the works briefly, take them home, and make copies without buying the author's work.

2. The Sixth Circuit held that the record rental exception does not apply to audio books. *See Brilliance Audio, Inc. v. Haights Cross Communications, Inc.,* 474 F.3d 365 (6th Cir. 2007). The court viewed the question as whether the exception to first sale "applies to all sound recordings, or only sound recordings of musical works." From a policy point of view, one could argue that the same exception should apply because audio books are subject to the same risk of unauthorized copying as audio recordings of music. On the other hand, one could argue that consumers are less likely to compile and trade copies of stories than music, because stories are more likely to be listened to just once (but children's books are a different story). In addition, applying the exception to all sound record-ings would take it beyond the commercial arena. Rather than trying to resolve such policy matters, the court relied on the language of the stat-ute, which refers to "the musical works embodied therein." The court held that the first sale doctrine applies without triggering the excep-tion for sound recordings, so businesses may rent audio books without infringing.

Copyright Holders May Seek to Limit First Sale Rights

Because first sale protects only the "owner" of a copy (or someone authorized by the owner), some copyright owners seek to avoid first sale by characterizing transactions in such a way that ownership of the copy does not pass to the recipient. Computer software, for example, is often "sold" pursuant to a license. If User downloads some software, or purchases it at a store and walks out with it, she may often find that the seller has characterized the transaction as a licensing transaction. The terms will provide that User does not own the copy that she possesses. Rather, ownership of that copy remains with the software company. Rather, the company simply grants User a license to use the software, subject to various restrictions set forth in seller's forms.

If User claims the protections of the first sale doctrine, the software company may contend that first sale does not apply, because User does not own the copy. Several issues may arise. The first would be, as a matter of contract law, whether User agreed to the terms in the form. One party may not unilaterally characterize the transaction. Rather, the restriction would only apply if the other party did something to become bound by the restriction. Usually this would be by agreeing to the license agreement. In some cases, agreement might be inferred from the conduct of the parties.

The next question would be whether the contract terms control, or whether courts will look to the substance of the transaction. Section 109 expressly limits first sale rights to one who owns a lawfully made copy: first sale does not apply "to any person who has acquired possession of the copy or phonorecord from the copyright owner, by rental, lease, loan, or otherwise, without acquiring ownership of it." 17 U.S.C. §109(d). A number of decisions have held that where the parties agree that the recipient does not own the copy, that agreement will control. *See, e.g.*, *Vernor v. Autodesk, Inc.*, 621 F.3d 1102 (9th Cir. 2010); Stephen McJohn, *Top Tens in 2010: Copyright and Trade Secret Cases*, 9 Nw. J. Tech. & Intell. Prop. 325 (2011). This approach allows the parties to allocate rights and risks between them. If User pays the agreed price in exchange, in part, for giving up first sale rights, then it might be unfair to override the agreed terms to give User first sale rights. In the leading case, Vernor bought copies of AutoCAD, sophisticated computer-aided design software, and sold them on eBay. Autodesk objected on the grounds that such sales infringed its exclusive right to distribute copies of the software to the public The court looked at three factors in deciding whether a software user should be classified as a licensee, rather than the owner of a copy:

- whether the copyright owner specifies that a user is granted a license.
- whether the copyright owner significantly restricts the user's ability to transfer the software.
- whether the copyright owner imposes notable use restrictions.

All three factors, in the court's view, indicated a license rather than a sale. Autodesk's license stated that the transaction was a license, not a sale of the software, and that Autodesk retained title to the software. There were transfer restrictions: the license was nontransferable without Autodesk's written consent, and could not be transferred outside the Western Hemisphere. There were use restrictions: it prohibited use outside the Western Hemisphere; prohibited modifying, translating, or reverse-engineering the software; and prohibited removing trademarks or copy protection devices. In short, *Vernor* appears to hold that a software transaction characterized as a license will be treated only as a license, if the seller so chooses and provides significant restrictive clauses.

By contrast, some courts will hold that User owns the copy, where User has paid the price, received transfer of the copy, and is entitled to retain that copy forever. This is consistent with commercial law, where economic reality, rather than the parties' description, control whether a transaction is treated as a sale, a lease, or a secured loan. This approach could get some support from patent law. The Supreme Court has applied first sale broadly in the patent context. *See Quanta Computer, Inc. v. LG Electronics, Inc.*, 128 S. Ct. 2109 (2008). Where the holder of several chipset patents licensed the patents to a chipset manufacturer, the patent holder was barred by patent exhaustion from pursuing infringement claims against the licensee's customers. The sale of authorized products embodying the patents terminated the patent rights in those products, meaning that the purchasers were free to incorporate them into otherwise infringing products. *Quanta* is a patent case, but its broad application of first sale may affect the first sale analysis in copyright, which shares underlying policy considerations. This suggests that some contract provisions that purport to override first sale will be ineffective.

First Sale and Digital Works

The owner of a lawfully made copy of a work (a book, a song, a picture . . .) may distribute or display *that* copy. But with digital works, distributing a copy (such as sending the copy to a friend) or displaying a copy (putting it online) involves making more copies. First sale authorized display and distribution of the lawfully owned copy. It does not authorize making copies or distributing or displaying additional copies. The owner of a digital copy can utilize first sale — by hand-delivering that particular copy (or mailing it, . . .). But first sale fits awkwardly with the usual means of distributing or displaying digital works.

Examples

1. *Owner?* Ada purchased a copy of some music software, *Mister Moon*. She clicked to agree to the standard purchase contract, which provided she would get permanent possession of a copy of the software, but the software company would retain ownership of the copy. After using the software for a year, she decided to sell her copy on eBay. Would a sale violate the copyright owner's exclusive right to distribute copies?

2. *Restricted gift.* UMG Recordings mails promotional CDs of copyrighted music. Each CD bears this legend: "This CD is the property of the record company and is licensed to the intended recipient for personal use only. Acceptance of this CD shall constitute an agreement to comply with the terms of the license. Resale or transfer of possession is not allowed and may be punishable under federal and state laws." There was no provision for response by the recipient, such as clicking to agree to the terms of use. If a recipient sells the CD, is that copyright infringement?

3. *Peasgood's Nonsuch.* Psystar buys a copy of the Mac operating system, Mac OS X Snow Leopard, adapts it to run on non-Apple computers, then loads copies on the computers built and sold by Psystar. With each computer, Psystar included an unopened copy of Snow Leopard, purchased from Apple. The Snow Leopard license provides:

   This License allows you to install, use and run one
   (1) copy of the Apple Software on a single-Apple labeled
   computer at a time. You agree not to install,
   use or run the Apple Software on any non-Apple
   labeled computer, or to enable others to do so.

Does first sale protect Psystar from copyright infringement?

Explanations

1. Under the first sale doctrine, the owner of a lawfully made copy may sell that copy, without infringing the copyright holder's exclusive right to distribute copies. The software company, however, might argue that Ada has no first sale rights, because she is not the owner of a copy. Rather, she has possession of a copy that belongs to the software company, delivered along with a license to use it. A number of courts have accepted this argument, allowing parties to limit first sale rights by agreement. Some other courts regard it as a formalism and would hold that because Ada has paid the price and is entitled to keep the copy forever, she owns it and is therefore protected by first sale.

2. In this case, the attempt to limit first sale rights would not succeed. The recipients did not agree to the terms and so were not bound by them.

The CD was simply a gift, and the owner, under first sale, could sell it. *See UMG Recordings Inc. v. Augusto*, 628 F.3d 1175 (9th Cir. 2011).

3. First sale did not protect Psystar. The transaction was not deemed a sale but rather a license. So Psystar did not have an unrestricted right to redistribute the copies that it had acquired. In addition, Psystar made copies and arguably adapted the work, neither of which would be authorized by first sale.

FIRST SALE AND IMPORTATION

Recall that §602 provides that unauthorized importation of copies or phonorecords infringes the public distribution right. If first sale permits the owner of a copy to distribute the copy, does that mean she may import it? The Supreme Court has held that, because first sale limits the right to distribute copies, first sale authorizes the owner of a lawfully made copy to import that copy. *See Quality King Distrib. v. L'Anza Research Intl.*, 523 U.S. 135 (1998). But because first sale applies only to a copy or phonorecord "lawfully made under this title," the holding was limited to reimportation of copies lawfully made in the United States. Whether first sale protects importation of an authorized copy made outside the United States remains an open question.

Some courts had held that first sale does not apply to a copy made outside the United States. *See, e.g., Omega S.A. v. Costco Wholesale Corp.*, 541 F.3d 982 (9th Cir. 2008). If an author authorized a book to be printed in Canada, then copies of the book shipped to the United States would not be subject to first sale. So it would be potential infringement to import the copies or to sell them in the United States. The rationale in such cases is to respect the territorial limits of U.S. copyright law. If U.S. copyright law applies only within the borders of the United States, the reasoning is, then copies made abroad are not made "lawfully under this title." The policy argument is that the copyright holder should have the right to control the sales in different markets. A counterargument is that such a holding suggests that such copies are made unlawfully, even if they are authorized by the copyright holder. Moreover, it seems to open up a potential loophole in first sale, because a copyright holder could have all copies manufactured abroad, then imported free of first sale protections.

The Supreme Court rejected that line of cases. Supap Kirtsaeng came from Thailand to study in the United States. Observing that the same textbook was much more expensive in the United States, he started a nice business in arbitrage, having relatives purchase books at low price in Thailand and ship them to him to resell at a higher price in the United States. *Kirtsaeng v. John Wiley & Sons, Inc.*, 133 S. Ct. 1351 (2013). *Kirtsaeng* held that "lawfully made under this title" meant simply that making the book was not unlawful under U.S. copyright law. So Kirtsaeng can purchase authorized books abroad and import them into the United States. *Kirtsaeng* put great weight on the fact that "reliance upon the 'first sale' doctrine is deeply embedded in the practices of those, such as booksellers, libraries, museums, and retailers." If first sale were limited to works sold in the United States, then it could be infringement to resell an imported book, for a library to lend an imported book, or for a museum to exhibit a Picasso.

Example

Neither lawfully nor unlawfully made? Murky Glurky's heroic adventures amuse children everywhere. Murky Glurky appears in best-selling books, movies on DVD, and music CDs. Children love them and so parents buy them. If anyone tries to distribute a used copy of any Murky Glurky product (selling on eBay, Craigslist, or a used-book store—or even renting from a video store), the copyright holder in Murky Glurky products claims infringement. If the defendant argues fair use (I bought this copy, so first sale allows me to sell this copy, rent it, or give it away), plaintiff responds that first sale does not apply, because all Murky Glurky products are made overseas and shipped to the United States. Is Murky Glurky clear of first sale?

Explanation

Some courts had held that first sale does not apply to copies made overseas, because they are not "lawfully made under this title"—that is, are not lawfully made under U.S. copyright law, which has no applicability overseas. Such courts viewed such copies as neither lawfully nor unlawfully made under U.S. copyright law, rather made beyond the reach of U.S. copyright law. This also permits the copyright holder to control the work in various markets. But the Supreme Court took the opposite view in *Kirtsaeng*. Under that view, where a copyright owner has authorized the making of copies, even though abroad, they are lawfully made and subject to first sale. Otherwise, as with Murky Glurky, copyright holders could circumvent first sale's protection. Moreover, museums, libraries, and used-book sellers would face massive potential liability.

Compulsory License for Nondramatic Musical Works

We hear many cover versions of songs. Dozens of musicians have released covers of "Dust My Broom." But dozens of authors do not release their own versions of *Harry Potter*—and there are not dozens of competing versions of movies. A special provision allows musical works to be recorded and distributed without permission of the copyright owner, as long as statutory procedures are followed and statutory royalties paid. Nondramatic musical works are subject to the compulsory license of 17 U.S.C. §115. Once authorized phonorecords of the work have been distributed in the United States, anyone else may obtain a compulsory license to make and distribute phonorecords of the work. One must promptly serve notice of intention to obtain the license on the copyright owner. The copyright owner is entitled to royalties, set by statute. The rationale for the compulsory license is to keep musical compositions available to the public, while assuring the copyright holder of licensing fees.

The compulsory license is subject to several limitations. It is available only if the primary purpose is to make and distribute copies for private use. It authorizes the making of a new recording, not simply duplication of the publicly released recording. It authorizes making a musical arrangement of the work to adapt it to another performance, but the arrangement may not change the "basic melody or fundamental character of the work." The license authorizes making and distributing phonorecords but not publicly performing the work. So a musician may record and sell a cover version of a copyrighted song, but could infringe if he radically alters the song or performs it in concert.

Limitations on Exclusive Rights in Computer Programs

Suppose Writer buys an authorized copy of a word processing program, which she gets on floppy disk. To use the program, she must put the floppy disk into her computer. Her computer will copy all or part of the program into its temporary memory to run the program. Writer may also wish to copy the program onto her computer's hard drive or to make another floppy disk copy as a backup. She might also need to make some changes to the program to run it on her particular system. Section 117, sometimes called "computer fair use," authorizes her to make copies or adapt the program when the "new copy or adaptation is created as an essential step in the utilization of the computer program" or "such new copy or adaptation is for archival purposes only." 17 U.S.C. §117(a). Without the authorization of §117, Writer arguably would be liable for infringing by making copies and by preparing a derivative work (adapting the program). But Writer must also stay within §117's narrow scope. If a copy is made to use the program, it must be used in no other manner. If Writer's right to possess the copy ends, all archival copies or adaptations must be destroyed.

The two rights above apply only to the owner of an authorized copy of a computer program. Software copyright owners often seek to avoid application of §117 by characterizing the transaction as delivery of possession of a copy of the program, with the copyright owner retaining ownership of the copy. Under this view, the recipient has whatever rights are provided for in the license but does not have any rights under §117. Congress has now added a narrow right—for computer maintenance and repair—that does not require ownership of the program. Under §117(c), the owner or lessee of a computer may make or authorize the making of a copy of a program that the computer lawfully contains, when such copy is made by activation of the computer to maintain or repair the computer. In plain words, the owner of a computer may authorize a technician to turn the computer on to service it, even if that causes the computer to make a copy of a program that is lawfully contained in the computer. The copy must be used for nothing beyond maintenance and repair and must be destroyed after the maintenance and repair. The Federal Circuit has read the provision broadly, by construing "maintenance" to cover a broad range of activities to support use of a program. *See Storage Tech. Corp. v. Custom Hardware Engr. & Consulting, Inc.*, 421 F.3d 1307 (Fed. Cir. 2005). The court held that relatively long-term copies were authorized under §117, as copying done for the purpose of "maintenance" of the computers. In so doing, the court rejected a narrow reading of maintenance that would restrict it to replacement or tending of machine parts. Rather, "maintenance" could also include service for the software, to keep it running. The court found statutory support in the reference to both "maintenance" and "repair," which suggests something more than basic parts repair was intended. This reading jibed with the purpose of the provision, which was to prevent software copyright owners from using their copyright to control ancillary markets for services. *See* Stephen McJohn, *Fair Use of Copyrighted Software*, 28 Rutgers L.J. 593 (1997).

Other Limitations on the Exclusive Rights

Title 17 of the U.S. Code provides a number of other limitations on the copyright owner's exclusive rights. The following lists some of these:

- Section 108 grants libraries and archives limited rights, subject to a number of conditions, to make copies of some works for users and for preservation purposes.
- Section 110 authorizes certain public performances or displays by educational and nonprofit groups. Section 110(5) also authorizes certain public receptions of broadcasts. For example, a corner store can play a homestyle radio, even though that constitutes a public performance of the copyrighted songs.
- Section 120 limits the rights in architectural works. One can make a photograph or other picture of a building visible to the public, even though that constitutes making a copy of the work. The owners of a building may alter or destroy the building, even though that could constitute preparing a derivative work.
- Section 1008 protects consumers against infringement actions arising out of specified noncommercial recording of musical recordings, authorizing certain "home recording" uses (but not online swapping of music).

Under section 111, if material is broadcast, cable companies may receive it and retransmit it to their customers, by using a compulsory license. Internet streaming services were unsuccessful in convincing courts to extend to them the compulsory license for retransmission by cable systems.[16]

Example

Building? Frank designs and builds a sculpture of a convoy of soldiers, which is displayed in a public park. Is the sculpture a building—meaning anyone can make and distribute images of the sculpture?

Explanation

The legislative history indicates that "buildings" include places that people enter (such as houses, temples, or schools), but not structures, such as bridges and highways. People do not enter the sculpture the way they enter a house. A person that took a picture of the sculpture would likely be protected by fair use (discussed in the next chapter). But someone who made commercial use of an image of the sculpture might be infringing. Buildings are an exception to the general rule: publicly displayed works retain the full protection of copyright. *See Gaylord v. United States*, 595 F.3d 1364 (Fed. Cir. 2010).

Examples

1. *New wine in old bottles.* Lofty composes *My New Minuet* and records a version with her string quintet. The recording succeeds with critics and fans alike and becomes a best seller in its genre. Lofty then receives notices from several people, each stating that the sender intends to use the compulsory license under 17 U.S.C. §115 to utilize the work. State which of the following people could use the compulsory license (subject to compliance with the notice and fee requirements):

    a. Producer intends to assemble her own quintet and then to record and sell a version of *My New Minuet*.
    b. Low Budget intends to record directly from Lofty's recording and sell low-priced copies in supermarkets.
    c. Spieler intends to record another version with another quintet and use the music as the background music to a new movie.
    d. Smiling Al intends to record and sell a parody version that uses tin cans rather than violins, to great comic effect.
    e. Viola intends to perform the work at Carnegie Hall.

---

16. Fox TV Stations, Inc. v. AereoKiller, LLC, 851 F.3d 1002 (9th Cir. 2017).

2. *Section 109 plus* §117. Chops purchases a copy of a computer program from Bender. Bender bought the copy directly from its copyright owner, Abble. The program runs accounting services for a small business, and Chops intends to use it in his restaurant. Chops learns that the program needs to be adapted somewhat to run on his computer. Fortunately, the necessary documentation is supplied with the copy. Chops hires a grad student, who makes the necessary changes. Abble claims Bender infringed Abble's copyright by selling the copy to Chops because that infringed Abble's exclusive right to distribute copies to the public. Abble also contends that adapting the work infringes Abble's copyright because it constitutes the unauthorized preparation of a derivative work. In addition, Abble states that using the program also violates the copyright because loading it on the computer and running it necessarily makes copies of large portions of the copyrighted code. Does Chops own a copy of a program he cannot use?

3. *Framed.* When returning results of image searches, Google shows the user "Below is the image in its original context on the page." To do so, Google's computers send HTML code to the user's computer, which then sends a request to the page with the image. By so "framing" the image, is Google creating a derivative work based on the image?

Explanations

1. a. Producer could use the compulsory license. This is the typical example—making a new version of a previously released, copyrighted musical work. Provided Producer complies with the statutory procedures, Producer does not infringe by making and distributing the recording, even without Lofty's permission (or even if Lofty specifically objected).

   b. Low Budget could not use the compulsory license. The compulsory license does not authorize duplicating the sound recording itself, as Low Budget plans. Record companies cannot use compulsory licenses to copy and sell each other's recordings. Rather, the license authorizes the making of a new recording.

   c. Spieler could not use the compulsory license. The compulsory license authorizes only the making of recordings to distribute to the public for private use—such as making CDs to sell in music stores. It does not authorize other uses, such as using the song in a movie soundtrack, in commercials, and so on.

   d. Smiling Al could not use the compulsory license. The compulsory license does not authorize an arrangement that changes the fundamental character of the work. Smiling Al's parody version with tin cans probably would exceed that limit.

    e. Viola could not use the compulsory license. The compulsory license does not authorize public performances, but only making and distributing recordings.

2. Bender is the owner of a lawfully made copy, so first sale authorizes Bender to sell it. Chops is now the owner of a lawfully made copy of a computer program, which gives Chops the rights under §117 to adapt it or make a copy, provided such steps are necessary to utilize the program on a computer. Here, such actions are necessary to utilize the program on Chops's computer, so Chops did not infringe.

3. No derivative work is created here. Note that Google did not infringe by making a copy, because a copy was send from the original image page to the user's page — Google just supplied the address. Framing the image on the user's computer would be no more a derivative work than putting a frame on a printed photograph. The better view is that such mounting of a work is not creating a new derivative work.

CONTRIBUTORY INFRINGEMENT AND VICARIOUS LIABILITY

Suppose Boss has Employee make and sell 1,000 unauthorized copies of a popular computer program and give the proceeds to Boss. Could Boss avoid liability on the grounds that she herself did not make or distribute copies? In addition to direct infringement, courts recognize liability for two types of indirect infringement: contributory infringement and vicarious liability.

    For both contributory infringement and vicarious liability, there must be a direct infringer. Contributory infringement applies when "one who, with knowledge of the infringing activity, induces, or materially contributes to the infringing conduct of another." *Gershwin Publg. v. Columbia Artists Mgt.*, 443 F.2d 1159 (2d Cir. 1971). Vicarious liability applies when "the right and ability to supervise coalesce with an obvious and direct financial interest in the exploitation of the copyrighted materials — even in the absence of actual knowledge that the copyright monopoly is being impaired." *Shapiro, Bernstein & Co. v. H. L. Green Co.*, 316 F.2d 304 (2d Cir. 1963). In our hypothetical, Boss is liable under both contributory infringement and vicarious liability theories. She controlled Employee and profited directly from the infringement, and she induced Employee to act. Only vicarious liability would apply if Employee had done the acts on her own initiative as part of her job with Boss and sold the infringing copies for Boss's profit. Only contributory infringement would apply if Boss had talked a friend into making and selling the copies. In short, contributory infringement requires a higher showing of knowledge, while vicarious liability requires a higher showing of control.

A special case of contributory infringement arises when the defendant sells goods used by the direct infringer. Is Xerox liable if people use its copiers to make infringing copies? In *Sony Corp. v. Universal City Studios*, 464 U.S. 417 (1984), the Court adopted the same standard as in patent law: simply selling a "staple article or commodity of commerce suitable for substantial noninfringing purposes" is not contributory infringement. Sony was not liable for selling videocassette recorders, which (as discussed above in the fair use section) have a substantial noninfringing purpose. Likewise, Xerox is not liable because there are many noninfringing uses of photocopy machines.[17]

The Court next addressed contributory liability some 20 years later in *MGM v. Grokster*. Grokster, like Napster, distributed software used by consumers to swap music files. Grokster worked differently. With Napster, users searched for music on directories on Napster's servers, and downloaded from other users only by sending requests to Napster, who then would link the two users. In short, everything went through Napster. Grokster, by contrast, simply distributed software, which users could then use to share music without going through Grokster. Grokster argued that it was protected by the *Sony* safe harbor rule. It could not be contributorily liable for distributing software, because the software had substantial noninfringing uses (sharing of music where the copyright holder did not object, noncopyrighted music, or other works).

The *Grokster* Court held that *Sony* was inapplicable. In its view, *Sony* held that a defendant could not be liable *merely* for distributing a device that had substantial noninfringing uses. But Grokster did not merely distribute its software; it promoted its use for infringing purposes. The *Grokster* Court focused on the element of intent in contributory infringement: "*Sony's* rule limits imputing culpable intent as a matter of law from the characteristics or uses of a distributed product. But nothing in *Sony* requires courts to ignore evidence of intent if there is such evidence, and the case was never meant to foreclose rules of fault-based liability derived from the common law." 125 S. Ct. at 2779. The Court formulated a standard for addressing cases that went beyond distribution of a device: "We hold that one who distributes a device with the object of promoting its use to infringe copyright, as shown by clear expression or other affirmative steps taken to foster infringement, is liable for the resulting acts of infringement by third parties." 125 S. Ct. at 2770. The Court emphasized that "mere knowledge of infringing potential or of actual infringing uses would not be enough here to subject a distributor to liability. Nor would ordinary acts incident to product distribution,

---

17. Whether and how the *Sony* rule applies to provision of services raises interesting issues. *See A&M Records v. Napster*, 239 F.3d 1004 (9th Cir. 2001).

such as offering customers technical support or product updates, support liability in themselves. The inducement rule, instead, premises liability on purposeful, culpable expression and conduct, and does nothing to compromise legitimate commerce or discourage innovation having a lawful promise." 125 S. Ct. at 2780.

The Court saw a number of factors that would support a conclusion that Grokster had not just knowledge of infringement, but that it acted with the object of promoting infringement with its software. First, Grokster offered itself to consumers as a successor to the shut-down "notorious file-sharing service, Napster." It offered software designed to be similar to Napster, sought to divert requests to Napster to its own site, and derived its name from Napster. Second, it did not attempt "to develop filtering tools or other mechanisms to diminish the infringing activity using their software." Third, its advertising sales were dependent on high-volume use, which was in turn dependent on the availability of downloads of copyrighted music.

Grokster should not be read too broadly. A party may finance to an infringing transaction without being liable for contributory infringement. Credit card companies were not liable for processing credit card payments to infringing Web sites despite having knowledge of the existence of ongoing infringement. *See Perfect 10, Inc. v. Visa Intl. Serv. Assn.*, 494 F.3d 788, 796 (9th Cir. 2007). Providing credit card payment services was not a material contribution, because it did not have a direct connection to the infringing activity. Providing financing made it easier for the businesses to continue its operation, but did not directly cause the infringing activity. There is a distinction between parties like credit card companies, which provide services that generally facilitate commercial transactions, and entities like search engines or user-created content sites, which actually make copies of copyrighted material and direct consumers to Web sites. If one of the latter continues to host infringing material after notice, it is more likely to be held liable. An advertising supported Web site that urged user to download movies using BitTorrent and provided technical support was liable for inducement of copyright infringement. *Columbia Pictures Indus. v. Gary Fung*, 710 F.3d 1020 (9th Cir. 2013).

IMMUNITY FOR INTERNET SERVICE PROVIDERS

A frequent sight on YouTube: "This video is no longer available because of a copyright claim by" a music company, news source, or other copyright claimant. Users of Internet services often infringe: posting copyrighted material to YouTube, sharing copyrighted music, cut-and-pasting stories, . . . (as always, fair use might apply in some cases). Congress has provided immunity for infringement to internet service providers, on the condition that they act to take down material they know is infringing and respond to take-down notices sent by copyright holders. That is why, when looking for a video on YouTube, we often see a screen simply stating that the work has been taken down by request of the copyright holder. If an online service provider were held responsible for all copyright infringement by its customers, the liability could be large. Copies of music, video, text, and images are all made in the course of transmitting, hosting, and providing other services for customers. Section 512 offers online service providers protection at a certain cost. An online service provider receives limits on liability for certain types of copying, if it takes certain actions designed to reduce the amount of infringement and facilitates suits against customers that infringe.

Section 512 limits the liability of online service providers for several categories of copying that are frequently made in the operation and use of computer networks (such as copies made in transmission, routing, or providing connections; caching; copies made by users; and copies made in the use of search tools). To gain the protection of the safe harbors, an online service provider must adopt and implement certain policies. It must have a procedure to receive notification of alleged infringement by users and take specified actions to remove infringing materials and terminate accounts of repeat infringers. *See Ellison v. Robertson*, 357 F.3d 1072 (9th Cir. 2004) (America Online not entitled to rely on safe harbors, where it "allowed notices of potential copyright infringement to fall into a vacuum and to go unheeded," by failing to update e-mail address for notification of alleged infringement); *EMI Christian Music Group v. MP3tunes, LLC*, 840 F.3d 69 (2d Cir. 2016) (no immunity for online service provider who was not scrupulous in cancelling accounts of repeat infringers). It must accommodate technical measures used to protect works. Some providers must respond to certain subpoenas intended to identify infringing customers.

To take advantage of the safe harbors, a service provider must act if it is "aware of facts or circumstances from which infringing activity is apparent." 17 U.S.C. §512(c)(1)(A)(ii). This duty is not triggered if the notification of alleged infringement does not meet the requirements of the statute, because such notices cannot be deemed to impart such awareness. The statute only requires a service provider to act when it knows or should know about copyright infringement. The service provider is not required to monitor its customers' activity or to actively police for potential copyright infringement. *See Perfect 10, Inc. v. CCBill, LLC*, 488 F.3d 1102, 1112 (9th Cir. 2007). There must be knowledge of specific infringing material. Just general knowledge that infringing material is on the site will not give rise to liability, unless there are simple measures available to identify and remove infringing material. Giganews was not liable for infringement by its users, where the only means to identify and remove the material were "onerous and unreasonably complicated." *Perfect 10, Inc. v. Giganews, Inc.*, 847 F.3d 657, 671 (9th Cir. 2017). *Viacom Intl. Inc. v. YouTube Inc.*, 676 F.3d 19 (2d Cir. 2012) likewise held that YouTube was responsible only if it knew of specific infringements or deliberately insulated itself from knowledge of such infringement by its users. Awareness that much of the material on the site infringed did not trigger a general duty to police postings by users. To be protected for secondary copyright infringement liability, an internet service provider must have a reasonably implemented notice and take-down policy. The standard is quite malleable, with that classic word for legal standards, "reasonable." Courts have held such a policy to require the ISP to have a working notification system, to have a procedure for dealing with DMCA-compliant notifications, and not to actively prevent copyright owners from collecting information needed to issue such notifications.

A party that sends a take-down notice in bad faith may be liable. Bad faith could include sending a notice for works not under copyright (such as very old books or government records) or already known to be removed could rise to liability. A party could be liable if it issued a notice where it did not hold the copyright, where it had authorized the use, or where the use was clearly fair use. *See Lenz v. Universal Music Corp., 801 F.3d 1126 (9th Cir. 2015).* Universal Music sent such a take-down notice to YouTube, where Lenz had posted a video of her toddler dancing, with Prince's "Let's Go Crazy" playing in the background. *Lenz* held that a sender of a take-down notice may be liable for bad faith, if they send it without considering whether fair use authorized the posting. Many of the millions of take-down notices are generated by software, meaning that copyright owners may need to adjust their software to avoid possible liability.

Examples

1. *Blind eye?* A number of television and movie companies sued YouTube for secondary copyright infringement. YouTube responded to take-down notices. YouTube also took down specific material it knew was infringing, even without receiving a take-down notice. But YouTube did not police the site to find and take down infringing material. Is YouTube immune?

2. *Take that.* Iago is jealous of his competitor Othello's successful parody video business. Othello makes short animated parodies of famous movies and posts them on YouTube, along with craftily placed advertisements. Iago sends take-down notices, falsely claiming power to act for the movies' copyright holders. Iago also knows the videos are protected by fair use (as parodies that directly comment on the relevant movies). Does Othello have any recourse?

3. *Volunteer trouble.* Users send photographs to the LiveJournal Web site. Volunteer moderators, controlled by LiveJournal, review posts and delete posts, depending on whether they deem them to comply with the sites' standards. Most of the photographs posted infringe. Is LiveJournal shielded from liability?

Explanations

1. YouTube does have immunity. *See Viacom International, Inc. v. YouTube Inc.*, 676 F.3d 19 (2d Cir. 2012). The court rejected the argument that awareness that infringement was common on the site gave YouTube actual knowledge of infringement. Rather, the court held it sufficient that an online service provider responds to "knowledge of specific and identifiable infringements of particular individual items," not just general knowledge of infringement. *Viacom* has considerable impact because it does not require service providers to actively seek out and take down infringing material. It simply requires them to respond when they gain knowledge of the infringement. Other courts have followed this interpretation. *See Capitol Records, Inc. v. MP3tunes LLC*, No. 1:07-cv-09931-WHP-FM (S.D.N.Y. 2011).

2. Iago is doubly liable. He falsely represented to act on behalf of the copyright owner. He also falsely stated that use of the material was not permitted by the copyright owners or *by law* — but fair use permits the use. The statute explicitly provides liability for false representations about whether the material is infringing. It would likely to be read to apply liability for the other misrepresentation.

3. The court held that LiveJournal could be liable. *Mavrix Photographs, LLC v. LiveJournal, Inc.*, 853 F.3d 1020 (9th Cir. 2017). It remanded for the trial court to determine whether the photos were posted by users or by moderators. Immunity only applies for posts by users. If by users, immunity would not apply if LiveJournal was aware of the infringing posts, which in turn could depend on whether the moderators were agents of LiveJournal. So online service provider immunity can involve tricky balances.

STANDING AND REMEDIES

Federal courts have exclusive jurisdiction over copyright infringement cases. 28 U.S.C. §1338.[18] The legal or beneficial owner of any of the exclusive rights has standing to bring an action for infringement. An author who sells his copyright but retains a right to a share of any revenue is an example of a beneficial owner. A mere assignee of rights to collect would not be an owner of the copyright, and would lack standing.

---

18. Whether the action "arises under" the copyright statute is sometimes unclear: If the issue is ownership of the copyright or whether a license agreement has been breached, the case might be characterized as state law (property or contract), rather than copyright.

"Happy Birthday to You" is a staple of copyright lore. It illustrates how long copyright lasts, because the song was still subject to a registered copyright, despite being written in the 1920s (and using music from before then). Enforcement of the copyright illustrates the scope of the exclusive rights. It could be copyright infringement for restaurant staff to publicly perform "Happy Birthday to You" to a customer or for a scene in a movie to have a family sing the song at dinner over a cake. To avoid licensing fees, restaurants trained their staff to sing other songs and screenwriters avoided birthday song scenes. The song also illustrates possible murkiness of copyright ownership. In 2015, a court held that the Warner/Chappell, which had collected millions in royalties for more than eight decades for "Happy Birthday to You," could not prove that it had been transferred the copyright, a long-standing registration notwithstanding.[19]

As noted previously, 17 U.S.C. §411 requires registration of U.S. works, as defined in the statute, to bring an infringement action. That requirement is not jurisdictional, so may be waived in a rare case (such as, perhaps, a class action). See Reed Elsevier, Inc. v. Muchnick, 559 U.S. ___, 130 S. Ct. 1237, 176 L. Ed. 2d 18, 26-28 (2010). The federal courts of appeals have split on the issue, "whether registration occurs when an owner files an application to register the copyright or when the Register of Copyrights registers the copyright."[20] Registration may occur upon filing, or may occur only when the Copyright Office acts. It can take weeks or months for a registration to issue, so the issue has practical importance (especially if the statute of limitations is running out).

As some put it, remedies are what you get when you win a lawsuit. The Copyright Act provides several remedies for infringement. Note that under 17 U.S.C. §412, statutory damages and attorneys' fees are generally unavailable for infringement of unregistered works, except for infringement of a published work registered within three months of its first publication. So a plaintiff has much more leverage if her copyright was registered at the time of infringement.

Injunction: The court may "grant temporary and final injunctions on such terms as it may deem reasonable to prevent or restrain infringement of a copyright." 17 U.S.C. §502. Injunctions are a powerful remedy. If defendant's film infringes the copyright in a movie, book, or song, that means the court may order defendant to cease showing the film. But injunctions are not automatic, but rather require showing harm that damages could not remedy. See Salinger v. Colting, 607 F.3d 68 (2d Cir. 2010) (permitting possible continuing publication of infringing sequel to Catcher in the Rye, subject to payment of damages).

---

19. Marya v. Warner/Chappell Music, Inc., 131 F. Supp. 3d 975 (C.D. Cal. 2015).

20. Fourth Estate Public Benefit Corp. v. Wall-Street.com, LLC, 2017 U.S. App. LEXIS 8766, *1 (11th Cir. Fla. May 18, 2017); Cosmetic Ideas, Inc. v. IAC/Interactivecorp, 606 F.3d 612, 619 (9th Cir. 2010) (registration occurs on filing); La Resolana Architects, PA v. Clay Realtors Angel Fire, 416 F.3d 1195, 1197 (10th Cir. 2005) (registration occurs upon approval of application).

Damages and profits: The successful plaintiff may choose to recover either her actual damages, together with any additional profits of the infringer attributable to the infringement, or statutory damages. 17 U.S.C. §504. Courts may also measure damages by the license fee that would have been negotiated. Such a "hypothetical transaction test" is often used in patent cases, and can apply in copyright as well. There must be a basis for the amount, based on such factors as market conditions or previous licensing transactions by the copyright owner. *Oracle Corp. v. SAP AG*, 2014 U.S. App. LEXIS 16840 (9th Cir. Aug. 29, 2014) (affirming trial court's decision to overturn verdict). A court applied the hypothetical transaction test and looked at previous license agreements in holding the United States Postal Service liable for $684,844.94, for using an image of the Korean War Memorial without the authorization of its sculptor. *Gaylord v. United States*, 112 Fed. Cl. 539 (Fed. Cl. 2013).

Statutory damages: Statutory damages are to be set in the range of $750 to $30,000 per work infringed. For willful infringement, the amount may be increased to no more than $150,000. If the infringer proves that she was reasonably unaware that her acts constituted infringement, the amount may be reduced to no less than $200 per work, or to zero for certain specified infringers (such as employees of libraries) who reasonably believed they were protected by fair use. The lower level of $200 applies to an "innocent infringer," one who "was not aware and had no reason to believe that his or her acts constituted an infringement of copyright." But the innocent infringer defense is not available where a copyright notice appeared "on the published phonorecord or phonorecords to which a defendant in a copyright infringement suit had access." At up to $150,000 per work, the threat of statutory damages can be a big incentive to settle (think of a university student with a few hundred downloaded songs on her computer).

Courts are struggling to determine the limits on statutory damages. In two noted cases involving music downloading, juries awarded hefty statutory damages: $1.92 million for 24 songs and $675,000 for 30 songs, respectively. *See Capitol Records, Inc. v. Thomas-Rasset*, 692 F.3d 899 (8th Cir. 2012) (affirming award); *Sony BMG Music Ent. v. Tenenbaum*, 719 F.3d 67 (1st Cir. 2013) (remanding for reconsideration; award repeated below).

Impounding and disposition of infringing articles: The court at any time may order impounding of copies or phonorecords produced or used in infringement and of articles used to produce them, such as film negatives or master recordings. 17 U.S.C. §503. At final judgment, the court may order destruction or other disposition of such articles.

Attorneys' fees and costs: The court may award costs to the prevailing party, which may include reasonable attorneys' fees. 17 U.S.C. §505. This is a big strategic consideration in litigation.

Criminal offenses: Criminal sanctions apply to specified willful infringement done for commercial advantage or private financial gain, or done by making or distributing, within a 180-day period, copies or phonorecords with a commercial value of more than $1,000. 17 U.S.C. §506. Some courts hold that criminal copyright liability requires that the defendant knew of the illegal nature of the activity. *See United States v. Liu*, 731 F.3d 982 (9th Cir. 2013).

Declaratory judgment: Where someone has been threatened with a copyright infringement claim, they can resolve the uncertainty by bringing action themselves, seeking a declaratory judgment of no infringement.

Examples

1. *Notwithstanding.* Web sites, bloggers, and commenters often post stories cut and pasted from media Web sites. That may be infringement, or it may be fair use. Righthaven purchased rights to sue for many alleged infringements and filed hundreds of actions, but Righthaven did not purchase any of the exclusive rights. Copyright holders might be willing to sell their rights to sue for infringements (past and future) for either a specified payment or a percentage of the proceeds. That would allow the copyright holder to have income without playing the role of enforcer, which could be costly not just financially but also to its reputation. But the copyright holder may be reluctant to transfer the entire copyright, or even the exclusive rights most likely to be infringed. That would take away its control over the exploitation of the work and also bar certain forms of exploitation of the work. Did Righthaven have standing to sue for the alleged infringement?

2. *Actual or not?* Writer sues Studio, alleging that Studio's blockbuster movie infringed Writer's short story. Would Writer probably be more interested in actual or statutory damages? If Student sued Yearbook Co., alleging that the latter used 50 photos created by Student and posted on her blog, would Student be more interested in actual or statutory damages? Would it matter if the copyrights were registered or not at the time of infringement?

Explanations

1. A number of defendants settled, but once defendants started to resist, several courts held that Righthaven had not received transfer of sufficient rights to sue. *Righthaven L.L.C. v. Hoehn*, 716 F.3d 1166 (9th Cir. 2013). An assignment of rights to sue for copyright infringement without conveyance of actual exclusive rights does not give standing to sue for infringement. The narrow rule for standing in copyright cases makes it difficult to structure an entity that is solely in the business of enforcing copyright infringement. Some courts awarded attorney's fees against Righthaven. At last report, one of Righthaven's major partners had terminated their agreement, stating on reflection, "It was a dumb idea."

2. Then range of statutory damages runs from a minimum of $750 to $30,000 per work infringed, extended for willful infringement up to $150,000. So Writer could get a maximum of $150,000 for infringement of one work (the story). Actual damages from blockbuster movie might be considerably a great deal more than that. By contrast, Student's actual damages look pretty modest, whereas minimum statutory damages would be 50 times $750 = $37,500 — and the maximum, if willful infringement is shown, is 50 times $150,000 = $7,500,000 (!). Statutory damages are more important in low commercial value cases.

If the copyright was not registered at the time of infringement (or within three months of publication), then statutory damages — and attorney's fees — are not available. This is a good reason to register the copyright in a work. It makes the copyright much stronger to enforce.

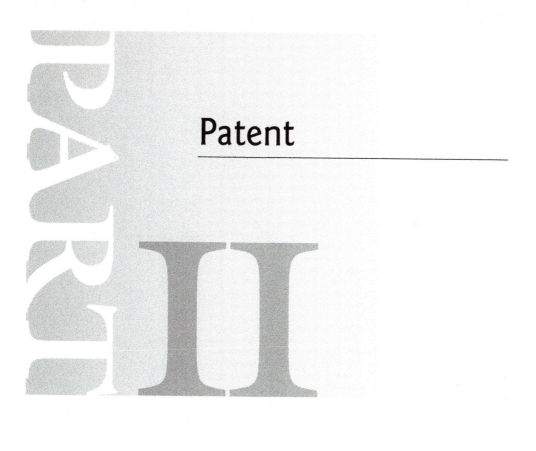

Patent

6

CHAPTER

Patentable Subject Matter: Products and Processes

Patent law is a completely different animal than copyright law. An author has a copyright in her work simply by fixing it in tangible form. The author need not register the work, use a copyright notice, or even know copyright law exists. The copyright is infringed by someone that copies creative expression from the work, but copyright protection does not apply to any useful elements of the work. But it is not necessary to identify copyrightable elements to obtain a copyright. Rather, that is often first addressed in court.

Patent law reverses all the above. An inventor who puts her invention in tangible form has no patent until she submits a patent application and the U.S. Patent and Trademark Office (USPTO) allows her claims. She must distinctly identify what is new and useful about invention in her patent claims. She must file in timely fashion, or lose her rights to a patent. The patent is infringed by anyone who makes, uses, or sells the invention (whether they copied from the inventor or developed the product or process independently). Patent protection applies only to useful inventions. Patent differs from copyright in subject matter (it covers only useful elements) and procedurally (the burden is on the inventor to claim her rights with a detailed patent application).

A key practical difference is that patent infringement does not require copying. Patent infringement is often done unknowingly (as opposed to copyright infringement, which requires copying from the copyrighted work). See Anthony Cotropia & Mark Lemley, *Copying in Patent Law* (2008). A patent may read on a product or process that was developed independently. Software Corp. may spend years developing its new software package for managing a supply chain. Upon going to market, it may face a claim that its software infringes a patent on an invention that Software Corp. never knew

249

of, much less copied from. The risks and rewards of patent law are much different than copyright.

Why do people seek patents?

1. *Market power:* A patent excludes others from making and selling the patented product or process. As one patent lawyer wisely put it, no one sues himself. It is nice to have a patent on your own product, but nicer to have a patent that also covers your competitors' products. The scope of patent protection is important, meaning that drafting the patent claims is key. Patents can give market power in several ways. The invention may be in a market by itself, as in a patented drug with no equivalent. Other patents may discourage others from entering a market (a barrier to entry) or require competitors to expend resources to avoid infringing (as in designing around a patent).

2. *Licensing:* A patent holder need not make and sell the invention herself. She can seek licensing fees from others who make and sell products or processes that fall within the patent claims. Some parties hold patents not to make and sell the invention, rather to seek license fees. The term for someone like that may depend on the speaker's point of view: "non-practicing entity" (a neutral term), "troll" (comparing such licensing requests to extortion by the troll under a bridge), or "small inventor," even "university" (many universities actively use tech transfer offices to seek patents and licensing revenue, not to mention spreading knowledge).

3. *Investors:* Start-up companies find it easier to get the ear of venture capitalists if they have patents on their technology. Larger companies likewise tout their patent portfolio, as an indicator of their technological prowess.

4. *Reputation:* An inventor often lists her patents along with her degrees and other accomplishments. Articles in *Scientific American* frequently mention the patents related to the scientific discoveries discussed. Universities plug professors' patents.

5. *Marketing:* Patents are often touted in the marketing of products, from cars to sport drinks, on the theory that potential buyers see that as a mark of superiority. Note: A patent means USPTO has deemed the invention new and nonobvious, not necessarily effective, safe, or better than other technology (although it may be).

6. *Defense:* If a party has a patent portfolio, she may use that to fend off patent claims by her competitors. Businesses often seek patents as a form of insurance. Note that this is less effective against a non-practicing entity (a.k.a. troll, small inventor, or university), that does not itself sell products.

7. *Peacock's tail:* Companies may seek patents not just to protect their technology, but to signal that they are robust beasts. *See* Clarissa Long, *Patent Signals,* 69 U. Chi. L. Rev. 625 (2002).

8. *Attribution (a.k.a. right of paternity)*: Legally, patents simply grant a set of exclusive rights to an applicant—a set that does not include a right of attribution. Culturally, patents do play that role. Patents are often treated as authoritative determination of inventorship. The USPTO sometimes plays Solomon. Alexander Graham Bell is considered the inventor of the telephone. He got the patent, although Elisha Gray filed the same day, February 14, 1876. Bell's lawyers won the dispute over priority (using underhanded means, according to some). An Italian immigrant, Antonio Meucci, reportedly filed several years before, but could not afford the fees to proceed through the patent process. Credit for innovation and discovery is disputed not just for legal rights, but for status in fields from science to art to engineering. Many a patent applicant seeks not just basket of rights, but the equivalent of a diploma to hang on the wall (along with the right to control the baby's fate).

So what can be patented?

CATEGORIES OF PATENTABLE SUBJECT MATTER

Section 101 sets out the categories of patentable subject matter:

> Whoever invents or discovers any new and useful process, machine, manufacture, or composition of matter, or any new and useful improvement thereof, may obtain a patent therefor, subject to the conditions and requirements of this title.

35 U.S.C. §101. "Invention" is simply defined as "invention or discovery," 35 U.S.C. §100(a), which makes clear that the invention may include discovering new processes or products, as opposed to creating them. What constitutes the "invention," as we will see in later chapters, depends on the drafting of the patent claims. If an inventor patents a new digital camera, her patented invention is not defined by the machine she has built, but rather by the invention set forth in her patent claims.[1]

Section 101 provides for four categories of inventions (process, machine, manufacture, or composition of matter), which are conventionally divided between processes and products (machine, manufacture, composition of matter). An inventor can also patent an improvement on a process or product. The improvement itself is a process or product.

---

1. "Patents" in this book generally refers to "utility patents," meaning patents on inventions. The patent statute also provides for plant patents and design patents. The word "patent" generally means a "grant of some privilege, property, or authority, made by the government or sovereign of a country to one or more individuals." *Black's Law Dictionary*. For example, grants of land made to homesteaders by the government were sometimes referred to as patents.

Processes

"Process" means "process, art or method, and includes a new use of a known process, machine, manufacture, composition of matter, or material." 35 U.S.C. §100(b). A process could be a method for "*making* something," such as "a method for making high-strength polymer fabric"; a "method for *using* something," such as "a method for controlling weeds near rice plants by applying a specific chemical compound"; or a method for *doing* something, such as administering a mutual fund or creating an antigravity illusion. Donald S. Chisum & Michael A. Jacobs, *Understanding Intellectual Property Law* 2-19 (1992). Patented inventions include such diverse processes as a method for producing a chemical, a method of putting in golf, and a method of calculating information to store in a database.

An inventor may invent a process, a product, or both. For example, an inventor may develop a new manufacturing process that he uses to build a new type of chair. He might then seek both a process patent on the manufacturing process and a product patent on the chair. If others use his process to build couches or tables, they potentially infringe the process patent. Had the inventor simply patented the chair, others would have been free to use the process as long as they did not produce a product that infringed the chair patent. Conversely, if someone devises a different process for producing the chair, she would not infringe the process patent — but she would infringe the product patent. Inventor can cover both the process and product in a single patent application, but must have separate claims.

Not every inventor can seek both process and product claims. Many processes do not produce a product. Other processes may produce a nonpatentable product. For example, imagine an inventor devises a new process for producing a common type of chair. His chair would not be patentable (it is not novel), but the process might be. Likewise, processes for such things as purifying water or isolating chemicals might produce products (cleaner water, purer chemicals) that are not new. But the process itself may be patentable. Or the inventor may not be able to sufficiently describe the product. For example, the process could produce a useful chemical, but the inventor cannot quite determine the nature of the chemical. Here, the inventor may not be able to specifically describe the product, so she cannot apply for a patent on it; but she may be able to describe the process sufficiently.[2]

Conversely, an inventor might use a nonpatentable process to produce a patentable product. To use the chair example again, an inventor might invent a new chair. But she makes it using tried and true manufacturing techniques or a new technique that is nonpatentable (because, for example,

---

2. Chapter 8 shows that sometimes an inventor uses product-by-process claims to claim a product made by a specified process.

it is obvious or she did not patent it in time). But although she could not patent the process, she can patent the chair itself.

A common type of process patent is a "use" patent—a new use for an existing product. For example, suppose a drug is known to be useful for treating high blood pressure in humans. A pharmaceutical company then discovers that the drug is useful in treating cold symptoms. Even if the product itself is not new—and even if it had been invented by someone else—a pharmaceutical company could patent the new use as a new process.

An inventor may often have stronger enforcement rights if she can patent her invention using both process and product claims.

Products

The other three §101 categories—machines, articles of manufacture, and compositions of matter—are conventionally called "products." The categories are not mutually exclusive. A genetically altered organism, for example, is both a manufacture and a composition of matter. *See Diamond v. Chakrabarty*, 447 U.S. 303 (1980). It generally makes little difference which category a product falls into, as opposed to the question of whether a claim covers a process or a product. A patent may claim an invention as a product and as a process, but it must do so in separate claims.

Machine

A "machine" does something. "The term machine includes every mechanical device or combination of mechanical powers and devices to perform some function and produce a certain effect or result." *Corning v. Burden*, 56 U.S. 252, 267 (1853). Machines would include a piano, a hammer, a compact disc player, and a merry-go-round.

> A machine is a device or combination of devices by means of which energy can be utilized or a useful operation can be performed. It is adapted to rendering a mechanical service or to the fabrication of material so as to change its form or produce a desired product.

Nestle-Le Mur Co. v. Eugene, 55 F.2d 854, 857 (6th Cir. 1932). Some of the best-known inventions were patented machines, such as the pioneer inventions listed in *Chakrabarty*: the "telegraph (Morse, No. 1,647); telephone (Bell, No. 174,465); electric lamp (Edison, No. 223,898); airplane (the Wrights, No. 821,393); neutronic reactor (Fermi & Szilard, No. 2,708,656); laser (Schawlow & Townes, No. 2,929,922)." 447 U.S. at 316 n.10.

The broad understanding of machine goes well beyond such familiar machines. A cell in an organism is a machine: It performs various intracellular processes such as producing hormones. *See Amgen v. Chugai Pharmaceutical*, 902 F.2d 1532, 1537 (9th Cir. 1990). A computer is a machine. Loading a new computer program onto a general-purpose computer can create a new, patentable machine. *See In re Alappat*, 33 F.3d 1526 (Fed. Cir. 1994). Accordingly, software inventions are often claimed both as a product and a process, which gives the patentees broader rights.

Note that a patent on a machine does not automatically apply to the processes that the machine carries out. Rather, the machine itself is the subject of the patent. A different machine that carries out the same process does not necessarily infringe the patent.

Manufacture

The Supreme Court has read "manufacture" as "the production of articles for use from raw or prepared materials by giving to these materials new forms, qualities, properties, or combinations, whether by hand-labor or by machinery." *Chakrabarty*, 447 U.S. at 306. This is a very broad category. Clothing, furniture, toys, food, and anything else made by man could potentially fall within the category of "article of manufacture."

To get the broadest protection possible, a patent applicant may find a way to characterize her invention with both process and product claims. Because "article of manufacture" is so broadly understood, the category lends itself to such inventive drafting. A computer program, for example, is a set of instructions. A software patent application is likely to have claims for the invention as a process. But other claims will use the program as part of a product. As noted above, the applicant can claim a new machine that consists of a general-purpose computer loaded with the new program. An even broader claim is to claim a computer program on a floppy disk as an article of manufacture. *See In re Beauregard*, 53 F.3d 1583 (Fed. Cir. 1995).

The article of manufacture is within patentable subject matter only if the invented elements are functional. Descriptive or aesthetic elements lack the requisite functionality. A writer cannot patent a book with the text of her new novel because the new aspect is only her text, and the book itself is simply a standard product of a printing press. If a publishing engineer invents a new form of book (say, one constructed in a novel fashion that both made page turning easier and made the book last longer), the invention does fall within patentable subject matter.

Composition of Matter

A "composition of matter" includes "all compositions of two or more substances and . . . all composite articles, whether they be the results of chemical union, or of mechanical mixture, or whether they be gases, fluids, powders or solids." *Chakrabarty*, 447 U.S. at 308. Like the other categories, "composition of matter" is very broad. It reaches from human genes to toothpaste.

Improvements (Herein of Blocking Patents)

Curie devises a new eraser for pencils. The eraser has a spinaltapical shape (an 11-sided form that makes it especially effective) and is made from plubundum (an especially durable material). One could not patent a pencil with an eraser attached. That is not new technology. But Curie could patent "a pencil with an eraser attached, where such eraser is shaped in a spinaltapical form and is composed of plubundum." Even if the ironing board is not new, one could patent an improvement, such as an ironing board designed to keep the electrical cord safely out the way. *See* U.S. Patent No. 1693615, granted to Raymond McJohn (1928).

An inventor may patent a product or process, or an "improvement thereof." Suppose Inventor One invents and patents a new and useful rocket launcher. Inventor Two then comes up with a new and useful improvement on the invention. Inventor Two is entitled to a patent on the improvement (assuming, as always, that she meets the other requirements of patentability).

Inventor One owns the patent on the rocket launcher, and Inventor Two owns the patent on the improvement. Who could make, use, sell, offer to sell, and import the improved version of the rocket launcher, without infringing either patent? Without permission from both inventors, no one. Suppose Rocket Company makes and sells the improved rocket launcher. By doing so, it infringes both patents. If Inventor One makes the improved rocket launcher, she infringes Inventor Two's patent. If Inventor Two makes the improved rocket launcher, he infringes Inventor One's patent. Such patents are called "blocking patents." Only if Inventors One and Two enter into some kind of agreement, such as a cross-license, could either practice the second invention (or license it to others) free of infringement claims.

The existence of blocking patents illustrates the technical legal nature of a patent holder's right. Strictly speaking, a patent holder does not have the exclusive right to make, use, sell, offer, and import the invention. Rather, she has the right *to exclude* others from doing those things, not necessarily the right to do them herself.

An improvement patent need not result in a blocking patent. Inventor could improve a product or process that was not patented. She would have the patent on the process. Others could still practice the product or process, but if they practice her improved version they potentially infringe her patent.

Examples

1. *Doing wheelies.* For each of the following, state whether it qualifies as a process, a product (machine, manufacture, or composition of matter), or neither.[3]
   a. bicycle
   b. a technique for riding a bicycle
   c. glue used to fix flat bicycle tires
   d. TRONDASTIC, a brand name used to sell bicycles
   e. newly discovered information about the history of the bicycle
   f. a special tire shaped to maximize speed, as determined by applying the laws of aerodynamics
   g. a manufacturing procedure, used to make the special bicycle tires
   h. an oven used for curing rubber, essential for the manufacturing procedure
   i. the rules of Tread, a new card game, which are modeled after the rules used in the Tour de France

2. *A better mousetrap.* Tinker's barn is plagued with mice. Tinker has tried every mousetrap on the market, but none of them puts a dent in the problem. Tinker begins experimenting on her own. She makes a number of changes to mousetraps she has bought, trying to increase their effectiveness. Tinker removes the part of one trap that usually fixes the mouse in place and uses a small bell in its place. She finds that although the trap does not kill the mice, the ringing of the bells drives them away in hordes. She wonders whether she can patent her creation. A friend scoffs at her: "You can't patent the mousetrap. That machine has already been patented." Does Tinker's invention fall into the categories of patentable subject matter?

3. *A new trick.* Meuse purchases some motor oil for his model train set. He notices from a patent marking on the container that the oil is patented. Some time later while working in his woodshop, Meuse realizes he has run out of the liquid he usually uses to condition the wood. Meuse rubs the motor oil in the wood, and finds it works far better than the liquids usually sold for such purposes. Meuse wants to seek a patent, but wonders how he can patent something that is already patented. Does Meuse's new application of the motor oil fall into the categories of patentable subject matter?

---

3. Note that to be entitled to a patent, the invention must not just fall within patentable subject matter (discussed in this chapter) but also meet the other terms and conditions for patentability (discussed in the following chapters).

4. *Brief interlube.* Gearhead devises a new way of lubricating automobile engines. Her engines use normal motor oil, together with some common additives. By adjusting the engine in a particular way, the oil and additives form a particularly viscous combination, resulting in more efficient engine operation. Gearhead understands that she can patent the process for creating this especially low-friction combination. She is concerned that others could design around that patent by designing processes that achieve the same result in a different way. Would the combination of oil and additives itself fall into the categories of patentable subject matter?

5. *The birds.* Poing, a jet manufacturer, is troubled by several mysterious crashes of its products. After expending enormous resources, Poing discovers the source of the problem. Certain snow geese, unknown to biologists, manage to fly up to extreme altitudes while migrating to take advantage of the jet stream. Poing realizes that this new information is important to a number of industries, from passenger jets to satellites. Poing wishes to patent its findings. Does this new information fall into any of the categories of patentable subject matter?

6. *Iced.* Dude invents the Iceboard, which he sees as the next step in the evolution from the surfboard to the skateboard to the snowboard. Dude's invention is a snowboard adapted for use on an ice rink. He hopes that one day Iceboards will be used for hockey, figure skating, and recreation. His prototype admittedly does not work very well, permitting him only to plod slowly across the rink. But Dude reasons that the key thing is to be first. Any subsequent iceboard inventor will only have improved Dude's invention. Accordingly, by virtue of their blocking patents, Dude will share in the royalties of any improvements in the field. If Dude patents his Iceboard, will any subsequent board made for use on ice necessarily be an improvement of Dude's?

7. *New sounds.* Movie Maker develops a novel process for synchronizing a character's lip movements with dubbed dialog. If an Italian film is given an English soundtrack, the actor's lips will seem to match the new English soundtrack. Movie Maker can patent the new process. But can she also patent the newly dubbed films?

8. *Combo combo combo.* Errors by pharmacies in filling prescriptions can have serious consequences. Packaging Company develops a color-coding system for prescription packages. The combination of colors on a package discloses such information as the normal prescribed amount, the expiration date, special categories of patients that may not receive the drug, and possible effects from combination with other drugs. The colors on the packaging are designed to alert a pharmacist to a number of possible problems. Packaging Company seeks a patent on its packages. The USPTO

rejects the claims as outside the scope of patentable subject matter, on the grounds that combinations of color are nonpatentable aesthetic elements. Are the packages outside patentable subject matter?

9. *Patented propagated signal?* Nuitjen invents a new process for sending a new type of signal—a new type of signal with a "watermark" that carries information about the data being transmitted. Nuitjen can patent the process. Can he patent the signal itself?

Explanations

1. Remember that if an invention is a product, whether it is a machine, article of manufacture, or composition of matter makes no real substantive difference.

   a. A bicycle is a product: a machine and also an article of manufacture.

   b. A technique for riding a bicycle is a process. Even if the technique consists only of a way of sitting on the bicycle, it could be described as a series of steps.

   c. Glue used to fix flat bicycle tires is a product, a composition of matter.

   d. A brand name such as TRONDASTIC is neither a process nor a product. The name alone is not a process, although one could devise a marketing process that involved use of a name. One might argue that if TRONDASTIC was a coined word, that it is an article of manufacture, being something made by man. But articles of manufacture must have some physical presence. Moreover, the word lacks the necessary functional aspect, having only a descriptive or aesthetic aspect.

   e. Newly discovered information about the history of the bicycle is neither a process nor product. Such information could be used to develop a process or product, but by itself does not fall into the categories of patentable subject matter.

   f. The special tire, designed with the laws of aerodynamics in mind, is a product (an article of manufacture, and arguably a machine).

   g. The manufacturing procedure used to make the tire is a process.

   h. The oven used in the manufacturing procedure is a product (a machine).

   i. The rules of a game (in distinction to laws of nature) are a process—they constitute the instructions for playing the game.

2. Tinker's invention does fall into patentable subject matter. Her new contraption is a machine, an improvement of an existing machine. Although a mousetrap has been patented, that does not remove a category of available subject matter. Improvements of existing processes or products fall within patentable subject matter.

3. Meuse does have an invention within patentable subject matter. He cannot patent the oil itself, because evidently someone else invented it. But Meuse has invented a new use for the oil. Such use patents are a common type of process patent. So Meuse's patented invention is something along the lines of "Method of Conditioning Wood Using Motor Oil."

4. Gearhead's combination of oil and additives does fall into patentable subject matter. As a specified mixture of ingredients, it is a composition of matter, a product. *See In re Breslow*, 616 F.2d 516 (C.C.P.A. 1980). The statute contains no requirements that products be durable, fixed in any medium, stable, visible, and so on. Indeed, as the text notes, patents have been issued for such fleeting articles of manufacture as a propagated electric signal.

5. Poing has discovered some distinctly useful information. But the information is neither a product nor a process. He could patent an application of the information, such as a goose catcher for jets.

6. A subsequent board developed for use on ice would not necessarily be an improvement on Dude's. Accordingly, Dude's patent would not necessarily cover all subsequent iceboards. An invention is only an improvement of a prior patented product if it incorporates all the claimed elements of the prior product. Another inventor might invent an iceboard that was better than Dude's iceboard and did not contain all the elements of Dude's board. So the first inventor in a field does not get a patent that encompasses all subsequent products in the field, rather only those that are improvements on his specific claimed invention.

7. The newly dubbed films are not patentable subject matter. Movie Maker might argue that they are articles of manufacture, the products of her new process. But the content of the films is not functionally related to her invention. Put another way, a new process for producing an old product does not permit a patent on the old product. A new process for filtering water does not let the inventor patent purified water. The result would be different if the film itself were technologically new, for example, by using different materials or being made according to new specifications. Cf. *Bloomstein v. Paramount Pictures*, No. 99-1051 (Fed. Cir. Sept. 3, 1999).

8. Packaging Company does have an invention within the scope of patentable subject matter. The arrangement of colors is not simply aesthetic in nature. Rather, it plays a functional role. The system as a whole passes information to pharmacists, as a means for preventing various categories of mistakes. The packages themselves play a functional role in displaying that information. Cf. *In re Levin*, No. 96-1180 (Fed. Cir. 1997).

9. The Federal Circuit held that a "transitory, propagating signal" did not fall into any of the four categories, and so was not within the scope of

patentable subject matter. *In re Nuijten*, 500 F.3d 1346, 1354 (Fed. Cir. 2007). In the court's view, the four listed categories are not simply illustrative, but rather "describe the exclusive reach of patentable subject matter." The claimed invention was not a *process*, because it was not "an act or series of acts." It was not a *machine*, because it did not contain "concrete structure." It was not a *manufacture*, because it was not a tangible article or commodity. Nor did it qualify as a composition of matter: "A signal comprising a fluctuation in electric potential or in electromagnetic fields is not a 'chemical union,' nor a gas, fluid, powder, or solid." The four categories are very broad but do not cover all types of technology, and as technology becomes more advanced, more inventions will likely fall outside the scope of the statute.

EXCLUDED SUBJECT MATTER

One could argue on policy grounds that certain categories of inventions should not be patentable: new types of weapons, because that encourages invention of destructive devices; human cells, because that grants a type of ownership over the human organism; methods of cloning humans, because that gives proprietary rights to hotly disputed uses of science; computer programs and ways of doing business, because such inventions are not the sort of invention contemplated by the original patent scheme; genetically altered foods, because that encourages hazardous tinkering with nature; materials discovered through studying indigenous people, because that appropriates traditional medicines and native cultures; and so on.

Early cases applied a number of doctrines, not found in the patent statute, to bar patentability to particular categories of subject matter. Courts have held that immoral inventions, business methods, algorithms, livings things, human beings, processes including "mental steps," printed matter, processes with no "physical result," processes that "depended on the reaction of a human," and other subject matter are outside the scope of patents. However, more recent cases leave most of the exceptions in question.

The present patent statute applies to broad categories of subject matter: machines, manufacture, and compositions of matter. In *Diamond v. Chakrabarty*, the Supreme Court reasoned that Congress intended (by choosing such broad categories, prefaced by the comprehensive word *any*) for patent law to apply to "include anything under the sun that is made by man." The Court reaffirmed, however, that "the laws of nature, physical phenomena, and abstract ideas" are not patentable. 447 U.S. 303, 309 (1980).

In 2014, the Supreme Court stated that the core reason for each of the three exceptions is to avoid preemption of the "building blocks of human ingenuity." Drawing from earlier opinions, the Court stated (citations and quotation marks omitted, for readability):

> Laws of nature, natural phenomena, and abstract ideas are the basic tools of scientific and technological work. Monopolization of those tools through the grant of a patent might tend to impede innovation more than it would tend to promote it, thereby thwarting the primary object of the patent laws. . . .
>
> At the same time, we tread carefully in construing this exclusionary principle lest it swallow all of patent law. At some level, all inventions embody, use, reflect, rest upon, or apply laws of nature, natural phenomena, or abstract ideas. Thus, an invention is not rendered ineligible for patent simply because it involves an abstract concept. Applications of such concepts to a new and useful end remain eligible for patent protection.

Alice Corp. Pty. Ltd. v. CLS Bank Intl., 134 S. Ct. 2347 (2014).

The Court distilled a test from earlier cases: first, the court should determine whether the claims at issue are directed to one of the three patent-ineligible concepts. If so, the court asks whether the additional elements "transform the nature of the claim" into a patent-eligible application. The Court described step two as a search for an "inventive concept, an element or combination of elements that is sufficient to ensure that the patent in practice amounts to significantly more than a patent upon the ineligible concept itself" (citations and quotation marks again omitted).

Laws of Nature

Laws of nature cannot be patented. Einstein could not have patented his theories of relativity. But the useful application of a law of nature may be patented. If Rocket Scientist uses Einstein's theories to design a gravity-wave-powered spacecraft, that invention does fall within patentable subject matter.

The exclusion applies to less grand laws of nature as well. Suppose Inventor discovers that color television sets can emit an unsafe level of radiation. He investigates whether color television sets currently on the market are dangerous. He finds that some televisions (which use alkali earth metals in their screens) are safe, while the rest (which use other materials in their screens) allow dangerous levels of radiation to pass through to the viewer. He then files a patent application for "A Safer Television Set," claiming any television set with an alkali earth metal screen is safe. His application also includes a process claim, encompassing watching such a television.

Inventor is not entitled to a patent. He has not invented a new product or process, nor has he invented a new use or improvement of an existing product or process. Cf. *Nippon Electric Glass Co. v. Sheldon*, 539 F. Supp. 542 (S.D.N.Y. 1982). He has made a new (and valuable) scientific discovery but has not applied it to making a new invention. If he had invented a new type of television screen, he would have patentable subject matter. If he had invented a new method of watching television, he would have a potentially patentable process ("A Method of Safely Watching Television from Behind a Lead Screen"). But he is simply claiming existing television sets and existing methods of watching television. His application has the effect of claiming his scientific discovery and, accordingly, falls outside the subject matter of patents.

The Supreme Court addressed the exclusion for laws of nature in *Mayo Collaborative Services v. Prometheus Laboratories, Inc.*, 132 S. Ct. 1289 (2012). The claimed invention was a diagnostic method: administering a drug, testing the levels of metabolites in the blood associated with the drug, and adjusting the dosage levels according. The Court held the claim beyond patentable subject matter: "The question before us is whether the claims do significantly more than simply describe these natural relations. To put the matter more precisely, do the patent claims add enough to their statements of the correlations to allow the processes they describe to qualify as patent-eligible processes that apply natural laws? We believe that the answer to this question is no." The Court reasoned that the claim included only a law of nature, combined with "well-understood, routine, conventional activity previously engaged in by scientists who work in the field." Under Prometheus, what constitutes an unpatentable "law of nature" is unclear. The "law" in Prometheus was rather pragmatic, the finding that certain patients seemed to respond best to certain dosages of a type of drug. Understood broadly, that would raise many questions with respect any process patent that sought improved results.

CellzDirect, 827 F.3d 1042 (Fed. Cir. 2016), upheld a patent on preserving a type of liver cell, in the face of the argument that it was directed at an unpatentable law of nature. The inventors had discovered, contrary to belief in the field, that some fraction of the cells would survive being frozen and thawed multiple times. They patented the process of "(A) subjecting previously frozen and thawed cells to density gradient fractionation to separate viable cells from non-viable ones; (B) recovering the viable cells; and (C) refreezing the viable cells."[4] The court held that the claim was not directed at the discovery, but was rather was "directed to a new and useful laboratory technique for preserving hepatocytes."[5]

Physical Phenomena (and Biotechnology Patents)

Biotechnology patents have been contentious both in the courts and in society at large. *Diamond v. Chakrabarty* addressed the issue "whether a live, human-made micro-organism is patentable subject matter under 35 U.S.C. §101." 447 U.S. 303, 305 (1980). *Chakrabarty* held that a genetically

---

4. Id. at 1047.
5. Id. at 1048.

engineered oil-eating microorganism was patentable, which set the stage not only for the widespread patenting of biotech inventions and discoveries, but also for elimination of a number of judicial exceptions from patentability in other areas. Chakrabarty, a microbiologist, set out to find a way to make protein from crude oil. *See* Ananda M. Chakrabarty, Diamond v. Chakrabarty: *A Historical Perspective,* in *Principles of Patent Law* 758 (2d ed. 2001). In places where oil was cheap and protein expensive, animal feed could be made from oil. Chakrabarty was able to add genetic material to a particular bacterium to make it do the job. In the meantime, oil became expensive. Chakrabarty realized there was another use for his oil-eating microbe—the clean-up of oil spills. He filed for a patent on the process for making the microorganism (which consisted of adding genetic material to a naturally occurring bacterium) and for the product—the oil-eating microorganism. The patent examiner allowed the process claims but denied the claims for the microorganism itself, on two grounds: "(1) that microorganisms are 'products of nature,' and (2) that as living things they are not patentable subject matter under 35 U.S.C. §101." 447 U.S. at 306. The first ground was contrary to well-established law. That particular microorganism was not a "product of nature" because it did not occur naturally in that form. Rather, genetic material had been added to a naturally occurring microorganism. The second ground raised a broad question: Is a life-form patentable? The Supreme Court declined to read an exception for living things into the Patent Act, leaving it to Congress to amend the patent statute if it saw fit.

After *Chakrabarty,* biotech inventions are within the scope of patent law generally. Following *Chakrabarty,* other inventions have been upheld, such as the "Harvard mouse," a genetically engineered mouse useful in cancer research. The courts had also upheld patents on genes. Such a patent does not raise the issue of patenting a living thing (a gene by itself is not alive), but what of the exception for "products of nature"? If a researcher manages to identify a human gene, hasn't she simply discovered a nonpatentable natural phenomenon? As the *Chakrabarty* Court stated, "a new mineral discovered in the earth or a new plant found in the wild is not patentable subject matter." 447 U.S. at 309. The gene as it occurs in nature is not patentable. But courts had held that an isolated or purified form of the gene is not a product of nature. Courts reasoned that substances that occur in nature (genes, hormones, and other chemicals) nonetheless may be patentable subject matter if they are purified, isolated, or concentrated (or otherwise changed to a different form). Such processing of the substance renders it a new product for practical purposes. For example, purified adrenaline extracted from animal tissue qualifies as a new product. Even if the adrenaline occurs in nature, the purified form is for "every practical purpose a new thing commercially and therapeutically." *Parke-Davis & Co. v. H. K. Mulford Co.,* 189 F. 95 (C.C.D.N.Y. 1911).

The distinction between products of nature and patentable products remained unclear, under *Funk Bros. Seed Co. v. Kala Innoculant Co.*, 333 U.S. 127 (1948). In *Funk Brothers*, the product was a combination of bacteria. Several species of bacteria were known to be useful for nitrogen fixation (extracting nitrogen from the air, enriching the soil). Mixing the various species generally resulted in inhibiting this useful activity, so they were generally sold to farmers separately. This was somewhat inconvenient because farmers had to buy several different species for use on different crops. The inventor discovered that some strains did not have this mutually inhibitive effect and could be isolated and sold in combination. The Court held, however, that the combination of nonmutually inhibiting strains of bacteria was not patentable. Because that combination occurred in nature, the applicant was simply claiming a newly discovered natural principle.

Broadly read, *Funk Brothers* could stand for the proposition that a new combination of natural products is still a product of nature and hence nonpatentable. But the case has not been applied so broadly. In particular, the Court relied on the fact that "their use in combination does not improve in any way their natural functioning." *Id.* at 131. So if the combination of natural products causes them to function in a way that they would not achieve separately, then the combination would be beyond *Funk Brothers*. Note also that *Funk Brothers* did not involve a process patent. Had the inventor managed to patent the process of isolating and/or combining the bacteria, that claim could have survived the invalidity of the product patent.

Assn. for Molecular Pathology v. Myriad Genetics, Inc., 133 S. Ct. 2107 (2013) addressed whether human genes are patentable. The exception for natural phenomena bars a patent on a human gene as that gene appears in the body. The *Myriad* Court rejected the theory that isolating a gene resulted in a patentable invention. DNA identical to that in the body is not patentable, although its shape is different, and it is no longer entangled with other materials. The Court held, however, that one could patent complementary DNA ("cDNA"), a synthetic molecule which consisted only of the DNA which matched the sequence in humans that codes for genes. So the Court invalidated Myriad's patent claim on DNA sequences matching those in the body, but left as valid those claims on DNA sequences created by discarding DNA that did not code for genes. Under *Myriad*, something even slightly different from a naturally occurring material may be patentable.

Example

As the court described it: "In 1996, Drs. Dennis Lo and James Wainscoat discovered cell-free fetal DNA ("cffDNA") in maternal plasma and serum, the portion of maternal blood samples that other researchers had previously discarded as medical waste. cffDNA is non-cellular fetal DNA that circulates freely in the blood stream of a pregnant woman. Applying a combination of known laboratory techniques to their discovery, Drs. Lo and Wainscoat implemented a method for detecting the small fraction of paternally inherited cffDNA in maternal plasma or serum to determine fetal characteristics, such as gender. The invention, commercialized by Sequenom as its MaterniT21 test, created an alternative for prenatal diagnosis of fetal DNA that avoids the risks of widely-used techniques that took samples from the fetus or placenta. In 2001, Drs. Lo and Wainscoat obtained the '540 patent, which relates to this discovery."[6] After *Myriad*, within patentable subject matter?

Explanation

The Federal Circuit held the patent invalid, as preempting a natural phenomenon: "The dependent claims are broad examples of how to detect cffDNA in maternal plasma. The dependent claims are focused on the use of the natural phenomenon in combination with well-understood, routine, and conventional activity. . . . The concern is that 'patent law not inhibit further discovery by improperly tying up the future use of these building blocks of human ingenuity.' [quoting *Alice*] In other words, patent claims should not prevent the use of the basic building blocks of technology—abstract ideas, naturally occurring phenomena, and natural laws."

In short, in the court's view, Sequenom discovered that certain free floating chemicals in pregnant women's blood could be tested to determine the gender of the fetus. They could not broadly claim the use of such tests, as opposed to particular tests that applied that knowledge.

Abstract Ideas (Herein of Mathematics, Computer Software, and Business Methods)

An abstract idea cannot be patented. Pure mathematics cannot be patented. That rule is most relevant to inventions that are abstract (like software or business methods), meaning that the invention may be applied in many different areas of endeavor. A business method or software package might be usable in many industries, in quite different settings. A series of cases have tried to apply those rules to computer software. The early cases had broad language that seemed to make software generally nonpatentable. Later cases turned the tide decisively toward patentability. It remains unsettled how much exclusionary force the early cases have. By looking at the key cases in sequence, we can see what issues face those interested in software and business method patents.

The Supreme Court first took up the issue of the patentability of software in *Gottschalk v. Benson*, 409 U.S. 63 (1972). The invention was a method

---

6. Ariosa Diagnostics, Inc. v. Sequenom, Inc., 788 F.3d 1371 (Fed. Cir. 2015).

of programming a digital computer to convert signals from binary-coded decimal form into pure binary form. Computers process everything as binary numbers. The number 53 (in decimal form, as numbers are usually expressed) is 110101 in binary form. To make reading computer materials easier, numbers are sometimes put in binary-coded decimal form. In this form, 53 is 0101 0011 (5 is 0101 and 3 is 0011, so 53 becomes 0101 0011 in binary-coded decimal). Sometimes it is necessary to convert from binary-coded decimal form to binary form: for example, convert 0101 0011 to 110101. The patented invention was a method of programming a computer to perform that sort of conversion. The Court characterized the invention as an algorithm, "a procedure for solving a given type of mathematical problem." Id. at 65.

The Court held that the algorithm fell on the side of the unpatentable (scientific truths, abstract principles, fundamental truths, mental processes, abstract intellectual concepts, hitherto unknown phenomenon of nature) as opposed to their patentable applications (a useful structure created with the aid of knowledge of scientific truth, or an application of the law of nature to a new and useful end). The algorithm was an abstract principle, not a useful application of mathematics, because it was not tied to any particular application. Any future computer programmer, working in any area, would need permission if he wished to use that method of conversion. Patent should not apply to such "basic tools of scientific and technological work." Id. at 67.

Benson seemed to stand for the proposition that an algorithm (a procedure for solving a type of mathematical problem) is not patentable. If algorithms were not patentable, the exclusion would be very broad, depending on how broadly "algorithm" were interpreted. Every process performed by a computer program could potentially embody a nonpatentable algorithm. Every computer program takes numbers as input and produces numbers as output (even if from the user's point of view the program is a word processor, a video game, or a tool for analyzing genetic databases).

Parker v. Flook, 437 U.S. 584 (1978), seemed to affirm the bar against patenting software. The invention was a method for calculating updated alarm limits. During a catalytic conversion process, problems often develop if a variable (such as the temperature, pressure rate, or flow rate) exceeds its alarm limit. The alarm limits change during the process; for example, the alarm limit for the temperature at the start-up of the process could be 150 degrees, but later in the process that alarm limit would change to 200 degrees. The only novel feature of the Flook calculation method was a mathematical formula. Like Benson, the case involved a process for calculating a number from other numbers. The scope was somewhat more narrow since the method applied only for use in catalytic conversion; Benson was unlimited in its potential applications. Nevertheless, Flook held that "a claim for an improved method of calculation, even when tied to a specific end use, is unpatentable subject matter under §101." Id. at 595.

Both *Benson* and *Flook* were careful to state that the mere use of a computer or an algorithm would not necessarily make an invention unpatentable. In *Diamond v. Diehr*, 450 U.S. 175 (1981), the Court upheld patent claims that included use of a computer. The invention at issue in *Diehr* was a process for curing rubber. The process consisted of constantly measuring certain temperatures, then feeding that information into a computer, which would calculate the time to terminate the curing process. The Court held that the process was within the subject matter of 35 U.S.C. §101, even though it included use of an algorithm. The Court distinguished *Flook*, on the grounds that the patent would not preempt use of the equation. Rather, the applicant claimed only the use of the equation together with all the other steps of the process. As in *Flook*, the only novel element of the process was a method of calculating a number (the alarm limit in *Flook*, the cure time in *Diehr*). Accordingly, the majority opinion arguably permitted the patenting of an algorithm.

The Supreme Court, after several decades, returned to the issue in 2010. *Bilski v. Kappos*,[7] rejected specific rules or categorical exclusions with respect to patent subject matter, emphasizing instead the ultimate issue, preventing patents on abstract concepts that would preempt entire areas of endeavor. The specific issue in *Bilski* was whether a general process for using commodity exchange transactions to hedge risks fell within patentable subject matter. The Court held that business methods were not excluded from patent protection. *Bilski* rejected a rigid test formulated by the Federal Circuit, under which a process was only patentable if it was tied to a particular machine or transformed an article. That test, if narrowly applied would have barred many patents on business methods, software, and biotech processes (such as diagnostic methods). *Bilski* also rejected earlier tests that courts had formulated, such as the *State Street*[8] useful-concrete-tangible test, the rule against patenting "mental steps,"[9] or the applied-algorithm test.[10] *Bilski* did not, however, formulate a new test for patentable subject matter, rather leaving standing only the long-standing rule that bars patents for laws of laws of nature, physical phenomena, or abstract ideas. The Court set out the key policy issue that patent subject matter limitations should seek to address, especially with respect to new technologies: "With ever more people trying to innovate and thus seeking patent protections for their inventions, the patent law faces a great challenge in striking the balance between protecting inventors and not granting monopolies over procedures that others would discover by independent, creative application of general principles."

---

7. 561 U.S. 593, 130 S. Ct. 3218, 177 L. Ed. 2d 792 (2010).

8. *See State Street Bank & Trust Co. v. Signature Financial Group, Inc.*, 149 F.3d 1368, 1373 (1998).

9. *See In re Comiskey*, 499 F.3d 1365, *1377 (Fed. Cir. Jan. 13, 2009) (pure mental process not patentable).

10. *See In re Freeman*, 573 F.2d 1237, 1245 (C.C.P.A. 1978) (formulating test known as the Freeman-Walter-Abele test used primarily in software).

Turning to the claim at issue in the case, the Court held it beyond the scope of patent subject matter, in language that emphasized the broad, policy-based approach to the subject matter question: "The concept of hedging, described in claim 1 and reduced to a mathematical formula in claim 4, is an unpatentable abstract idea, just like the algorithms at issue in *Benson* and *Flook*. Allowing petitioners to patent risk hedging would pre-empt use of this approach in all fields, and would effectively grant a monopoly over an abstract idea." So the Court emphasized that patent subject matter would not be determined by proxies, by specific rules that attempt to implement the underlying policies, such as rules against patenting business methods, requiring a useful-concrete-tangible result, barring mental steps, or the most recent attempt, the machine-or-transformation test. Rather, patent subject matter would be directly measured by applying the underlying policy itself: whether allowing the patent claim in question would preempt the use of an abstract idea. As in copyright law, a broad rule directly looking to the fundamental policy against granting rights in ideas would serve as the border of protectable subject matter. Given the many unsuccessful attempts by the Federal Circuit to implement that policy in more specific rules, it seems likely that the broad approach of *Bilski* will be more successful and no less predictable.

In 2014, the Supreme Court addressed a business method implemented on a computer. *Alice Corp. Pty. Ltd. v. CLS Bank Intl.*, 134 S. Ct. 2347 (2014): "Petitioner's claims involve a method of exchanging financial obligations between two parties using a third-party intermediary to mitigate settlement risk. The intermediary creates and updates 'shadow' records to reflect the value of each party's actual accounts held at 'exchange institutions,' thereby permitting only those transactions for which the parties have sufficient resources. At the end of each day, the intermediary issues irrevocable instructions to the exchange institutions to carry out the permitted transactions."

The *Alice* Court applied the test cited above: (1) Is the patent claim directed to an ineligible category (a law of nature, a natural phenomenon, or abstract idea)? (2) If so, is there an "inventive concept, an element or combination of elements that is sufficient to ensure that the patent in practice amounts to significantly more than a patent upon the ineligible concept itself"?

First step: the claim was directed to an abstract idea. The "concept of intermediated settlement, i.e., the use of a third party to mitigate settlement risk" was like the risk hedging in *Bilski*, "a fundamental economic practice long prevalent in our system of commerce." Second step: the claim did not have additional elements that sufficiently applied the idea. In particular, merely implementing the idea on a computer was not specific enough to avoid the danger of preempting the abstract idea. The Court did supply possible guidance as to what software patents would be valid, those that "purport to improve the functioning of the computer itself" or "effect an improvement in any other technology or technical field." After *Alice*, putting an old idea on a computer does not merit a patent. Putting a new idea on a computer may, provided the inventor also applies the idea to achieve a technological improvement.

The Federal Circuit provides examples of applying the test. The Chicago Transit Authority's patent on a method of using bank cards for fares was invalid as abstract, as simply "directed to the collection, storage, and recognition of data."[11] The Federal Circuit reversed a jury verdict of over $500 million for infringement on a payment system patent, because "the asserted claims are directed to the abstract idea of conditioning and controlling access to data based on payment."[12] The United States Postal Services patented system for using codes to identify and route packages during mailing was abstract and nonpatentable.[13] Claims on "multicasting" (which might apply broadly on the Internet) were held abstract and nonpatentable.[14] By contrast, the court upheld claims "directed to an improved computer memory system, not to the abstract idea of categorical data storage,"[15] on the grounds that the specification (if not the claims themselves) identified specific technological improvements in the operation of the computer itself.[16]

To summarize:

Supreme Court:

- *Benson* (1972) held unpatentable: method of programming a digital computer to convert signals from binary-coded decimal form into pure binary form.
- *Flook* (1978) held unpatentable: method for calculating updated alarm limits during a catalytic conversion process.

---

11. Smart Sys. Innovations, LLC v. Chicago Transit Auth., 873 F.3d 1364 (Fed. Cir. 2017).

12. Smartflash LLC v. Apple Inc., 2017 U.S. App. LEXIS 3833, *11 (Fed. Cir. Mar. 1, 2017).

13. The claims of the three sets of patents are not limited by rules or steps that establish how the focus of the methods is achieved. Instead, the claims embrace the abstract idea of using a marking affixed to the outside of a mail object to communicate information about the mail object, i.e., the sender, recipient, and contents of the mail object. Because the claims are directed to an abstract idea, we turn to the second step of the *Alice* inquiry. Secured Mail Solutions, LLC v. Universal Wilde, Inc., 873 F.3d 905 (Fed. Cir. 2017).

14. Two-Way Media asserts that the claim solves various technical problems, including excessive loads on a source server, network congestion, unwelcome variations in delivery times, scalability of networks, and lack of precise recordkeeping. But claim 1 here only uses generic functional language to achieve these purported solutions. Two-Way Media Ltd. v. Comcast Cable Commc'ns, LLC, Nos. 2017 U.S. App. LEXIS 21706, at *15 (Fed. Cir. Nov. 1, 2017).

15. Visual Memory LLC v. NVIDIA Corp., 867 F.3d 1253, 1259 (Fed. Cir. 2017).

16. As with *Enfish*'s self-referential table and the motion tracking system in *Thales*, the claims here are directed to a technological improvement:

> an enhanced computer memory system. The '740 patent's claims focus on a "specific asserted improvement in computer capabilities" — the use of programmable operational characteristics that are configurable based on the type of processor — instead of "on a process that qualifies as an 'abstract idea' for which computers are invoked merely as a tool." *Enfish*, 822 F.3d at 1336.

Visual Memory LLC v. NVIDIA Corp., 867 F.3d 1253, 1259-1260 (Fed. Cir. 2017).

- *Diehr* (1978) held patentable: method for curing rubber, by constantly measuring certain temperatures, then feeding that information into a computer, which would calculate the time to terminate the curing process.
- *Bilski* (2010) held unpatentable: method of hedging risks in the commodities field by using derivative securities.
- *Alice* (2014) held unpatentable: computer-implemented method of intermediated settlement.

Immoral Inventions, Human Beings, Tax Strategies, Atomic Weapons, and Medical Procedures

Formerly, courts denied patents to gambling devices or other inventions deemed contrary to public morals. But now regulation is generally left to other areas of the law. Several specific subject matter areas, however, are specifically regulated.

The 2011 Patent Act provided a specific limitation on patentable subject matter in the area of life sciences: "Notwithstanding any other provision of law, no patent may issue on a claim directed to or encompassing a human organism."[17] The provision would bar patents on genetically altered humans and cloned humans, and very likely, chimeras combining humans and other species. Interpreting the rather brief provision could require answering questions of both biology and philosophy: at what point does a genetic alteration take one away from the status of human? Would a latter-day Frankenstein monster be a human organism? At what point does the status of human apply? Read broadly, the provision could apply to human cells, such as stem cells. "Directed to" and "encompassing" are not defined terms, so it could be read, at least in theory, to apply to methods of medical treatment, fitness programs, or weight-loss methods. "Encompassing a human organism," in literal terms, could encompass a game of Ring A Ring A Rosy. Given the rapid change of techniques in the life sciences and the undefined language of the provision, together with the highly charged issues in the area, knotty questions of interpretation could arise. The USPTO stated its view that the provision simply codifies existing USPTO policy against issuing a patent that "embraces" a human being. Although that policy is likewise vague (would it bar a method of administering a hug or the Heimlich maneuver?), the USPTO has issued many patents on genes, human cells, animals with human genes, and other human biotech inventions, so presumably those remain patentable subject matter until the courts read the statute otherwise.

---

17. Leahy-Smith America Invents Act, Public L. No 112-29, 112th Cong., 1st Sess., 125 Stat. 284-341 (Sept. 16, 2011), Sec. 33. This provision, counterparts of which had been including in previous budget legislation, was not codified into the Patent Act. It applies to applications pending on, or filed after, Sept. 16, 2011.

The 2011 Act also effectively barred patents on "any strategy for reducing, avoiding, or deferring tax liability, whether known or unknown at the time of the invention or application for patent." This very specific limitation was a reaction to some tax strategy patents that had issued in recent years. The statute provided that it did not bar patents on tax software or financial management methods that did not claim rights in tax strategies.

National security takes priority over patent law. A statutory provision from outside the Patent Act bars patents on atomic weaponry. Under 42 U.S.C. §2181(a), no patent may issue for an invention that is useful only in atomic weaponry. In addition, a patent relevant to "state secrets" may be effectively unenforceable. Under the judicially created Military and State Secrets privilege, the United States may prevent discovery in a lawsuit of any information that, if disclosed, would adversely affect national security. *Crater Corp. v. Lucent Technologies, Inc.*, 2005 U.S. App. LEXIS 19258 (Fed. Cir. 2005).

Medical procedures, such as surgical procedures, are patentable. But Congress has limited the enforceability of some such patents. Under 35 U.S.C. §287(c), no remedy is available if a "medical practitioner" infringes a patent on a "medical activity." "Medical practitioner" includes "any natural person who is licensed by a State to provide the medical activity [] or who is acting under the direction of such person in the performance of the medical activity."

"Medical activity" is defined as

> the performance of a medical or surgical procedure on a body, but shall not include (i) the use of a patented machine, manufacture, or composition of matter in violation of such patent, (ii) the practice of a patented use of a composition of matter in violation of such patent, or (iii) the practice of a process in violation of a biotechnology patent. 35 U.S.C. §287(c)(2)(A).

So a licensed health care professional is not liable for infringing a patent on a medical or surgical procedure as such, but has no insulation against patents on things like surgical tools, chemicals, or biotech patents.

Examples

1. *Subject matter?* To fall within the subject matter of patents, an invention must be a process or product, and not be excluded as an unpatentable law of nature, physical phenomenon, or abstract idea. Which of the following fall within the subject matter of patents?[18]
   a. Astronomer, after studying reams of data from satellites, determines that there is a large, hitherto unknown deposit of oil under Syracuse, New York.

---

18. For the inventor to be entitled to a patent, the invention must fall within patentable subject matter and meet the requirements of patentability discussed in the following chapters (be new, useful, and nonobvious).

    b. Driller devises a new method of extracting oil from under a city without disturbing the residents.

    c. In developing her new method, Driller finds that drill bits she makes out of titanium are the most effective. Titanium is a naturally occurring substance but has never been used for drill bits before.

    d. Biologist, trekking in the Rocky Mountains, encounters the Yodo bird, a species of bird never before recorded.

    e. Miner, while digging for gold in the Rockies, comes across a large deposit of a new mineral, kabloondium.

    f. Driller experiments and finds that kabloondium is even better for use in drill bits than titanium.

    g. Driller experiments in the chemistry lab and creates a new alloy, a specified mixture of titanium and kabloondium, the combination creating many useful properties.

    h. Lawyer invents "a method and system for mandatory arbitration involving legal documents, such as wills or contracts."

2. *Oil bug.* Astronomer decides to go into the oil exploration business. He invents a new method of searching through geological data to find oil. His method is to go through specified categories of information about an area, considering 17 factors that affect the likelihood of finding oil. The initial results are used to focus the search on more likely places, which in turn are considered using a larger range of information and other factors. The results of the process are to select the most likely places to have oil from the initial list of candidates and then to assign a probability to each. Astronomer wonders if patent law can offer him any protection. Skeptic advises him that, when all is said and done, he has simply claimed unpatentable facts of nature — the likelihood that certain areas will yield oil. Does Astronomer have an invention within patentable subject matter?

3. *Space.* Stats, a psychologist, researches the effect on humans of lack of personal space in workplaces. She determines that, unless a worker is afforded a minimum of ten square feet of free space during the average workday, the person is much more likely to enter into conflicts with coworkers. Stats then files a patent application on "Workspace That Reduces Workplace Conflict," which covers any workspace of ten square feet or more. Would Stats's invention fall within patentable subject matter?

4. *A nice warm shower.* Swan, a biologist, studies the effect of ultraviolet rays on humans. Although Swan initially focuses his research on skin, he finds that UV rays have much deeper effects. Increased exposure to UV rays, he determines, results in a subtle form of memory impairment. People who spend a lot of time exposed to the sun are slightly less adept at remembering the names of places. The condition, however, is reversible. By shining an infrared light on the head for a few minutes a day, the memory is quickly restored. Swan devises a method to put the data to

practical use, which consists of searching for people who might have suffered from UV memory loss, testing them, and then treating those who show impairment. Swan intends to seek a patent. Skeptic advises Swan that he has made an admirable scientific discovery, but patent law does not offer protection for it. Does Swan have an invention within patentable subject matter?

5. *Rust bug.* Prospector digs a mine in California. Rather than gold, he discovers a rich vein of bacteria. More accurately, the bacteria find him. Their favorite food is rust, and Prospector has rickety, rusty equipment. The bacteria eat rust voraciously but are otherwise rather benign. Prospector realizes that they would be very useful as a nontoxic means to combat rust in buildings and machines. Prospector would like to help the world fight rust, but he would also like to share in the benefits of his discovery. Is the bacterium within patentable subject matter?

6. *Nature loves a vacuum.* Hoover, a geologist, surveys the Alaskan tundra for mineral deposits. Hoover encounters a family of friendly little mammals with long noses, which she dubs "wacks." Hoover observes the wacks for hours, fascinated by their feeding habits. The wacks are filter feeders. They poke their noses all over the ground, sucking up dirt, pebbles, but also edible vegetation and insects. The wacks manage to filter out the nutritious bits and spit out the other stuff in a big tidy pile. Hoover brings several home. Hoover knows that natural phenomena are not patentable. But machines are, and living things are — so she files a patent, claiming the wack as "A Totally Organic Vacuum Cleaner." Does Hoover have an invention within patentable subject matter?

7. *Drinket.* Marathoners suffer much for their sport. Loafer, a sports doctor, studies the physiological effects of long-distance running. Loafer devises a drink that he considers to be the perfect drink for a marathoner. The drink is mainly water, but with a special mixture of naturally occurring sugars. His formula requires very exact amounts of the several sugars in each quart of the drink, which he calls "Zoop." He determines the various levels by considering the numerous effects of running on the body's consumption of its energy deposits. Zoop, he believes, offers the most effective form of replenishing those supplies during the typical course of a marathon. Does Zoop fall within patentable subject matter?

8. *Solved.* Farley's Last Problem has perplexed mathematicians for decades. Before she retired from mathematics and disappeared, Farley wrote on the back of an envelope a challenge to prove a long-standing conjecture, together with some enigmatic hints. Although thousands tried, no one else proved the truth of the conjecture, before or after that time. Finally, after years of work in her attic, Trig sets forth an iron-clad proof of the conjecture. Can Trig patent her proof?

9. *Opening up a one-way street.* Suppose *A* and *B* are two really big prime numbers. Using a computer, it is a snap to multiply them to get their product, the really, really big number C. On the other hand, if we start with the number C, it is much slower to figure out what two really big numbers it is divisible by. There are well-known, reliable methods to do so, but even using a computer, they can take years (for really, really big numbers). This mathematical one-way street has been put to practical use. Many methods of encrypting information rely on it. Svenmail, an e-mail program, uses such an encryption system to allow its users to communicate securely. Svenmail's encryption method is quite different than most other programs, although it relies on the same general principles.

    Baylis devises a new, efficient method for finding the prime factors of even really, really big numbers, which would make it much easier to decode data that was encrypted using the methods described above. Does Baylis have an invention within patentable subject matter? Suppose Baylis wrote a computer program that performed the task: Now would he have an invention within patentable subject matter? What if Baylis specifically developed a method for decoding messages encrypted by the Svenmail program?

10. *Penrose tiling.* Penrose tiling is a mathematical formula for producing nonrepeating tiling patterns, conceived by Sir Roger Penrose. A Penrose tiling is likely to be a pleasing geometric pattern that at first glance seems to be simply a typical pattern such as one would see on a tiled floor. On a closer look, however, one sees that the pattern never repeats itself, no matter how far in any direction the tiling formula is applied. Such nonrepeating patterns are of immense interest to mathematicians. Does the formula for Penrose tiling fall within patentable subject matter ("A Method for Producing Nonrepeating Patterns")? If Sir Roger uses it to produce patterns on rolls of paper (nonrepeating patterns function better because the paper is less likely to stick to the roll and takes up less space), does he have patentable subject matter?

11. *Permitted procedures.* Which of the following are protected by 35 U.S.C. §287(c)? (The rule governing medical procedures is really just one nook of the subject matter of patents, but §287(c) makes for good practice in applying the patent statute.)
    a. Heart Surgeon performs a triple bypass, using the patented "Method of Performing Heart Surgery with Eyes Closed."
    b. Heart Surgeon reads about a new, patented "Combination Artificial Heart and FM Radio" in the *New England Journal of Medicine*. She builds her own and uses it the next day to save the life of a corporate executive.
    c. Naturopath uses a patented "Method of Massage to Reduce Blockage in Arteries," invented by Heart Surgeon.
    d. Mr. Type A has a heart attack in a remote Alaskan village. Local Teenager performs lifesaving surgery on him, following directions over the

phone from Heart Surgeon and reading from a faxed copy of the patent on "Method of Performing Heart Surgery with Eyes Closed."

12. *Fountain of youth.* Ponce, a gerontologist, figures out how to genetically engineer humans to produce a human whose altered immune system adds years to the average lifespan. Ponce files his patent application on a "Longer Living Human Being." Is his invention within patentable subject matter? What if it were instead a longer-living guinea pig?

13. *Human cells.* Suppose instead Ponce had specifically made genetically engineered human kidney cells which would likely extend the lifespan of their carrier, by squelching various diseases in the bud?

14. *Patent medicine.* Suppose instead that Ponce developed a novel diet and exercise plan. By following its steps carefully, a person extends his or her life expectation by ten years. Would that fall within patentable subject matter?

Explanations

1. a. The information that there is oil under Syracuse is not patentable subject matter. Rather, it is an unpatentable physical phenomenon or product of nature.
   b. The new method of extracting oil is within patentable subject matter. It is not simply an abstract idea (let's get the oil out without displacing the residents) but rather a specific process for attaining that goal.
   c. The new titanium drill bits are within patentable subject matter. Titanium itself is an unpatentable product of nature. But a specific application that takes advantage of titanium's properties does not amount to a patent on titanium. The result would be different if Driller had discovered that titanium was especially durable and attempted to patent all uses of titanium that exploited that quality.
   d. The Yodo bird is an unpatentable product of nature. The result would be different if Biologist had created the Yodo bird by introducing new genes into an existing species of bird.
   e. Kabloondium is an unpatentable product of nature. Even if kabloondium is a composition of matter never known to man before, it is produced by nature, not man. The result would be different if Miner had created kabloondium by treating existing minerals under extreme heat and pressure.
   f. Kabloondium drill bits are within patentable subject matter as an application of the unpatentable product of nature.
   g. The alloy would be a new composition of matter, not an unpatentable product of nature.
   h. This would probably be unpatentable, like the method of hedging risk in *Bilski*, unless the method claimed a quite specific application that did not preempt the abstract idea.

275

2. Astronomer does have an invention within patentable subject matter—his process for determining the likelihood of finding oil. The probability that oil exists in a particular location is a physical phenomenon. But that is not what Astronomer's application would claim. He would claim his process for determining that likelihood. He would also not run afoul of the abstract idea exception. His process is not simply an abstract mathematical process, one not tied to any specific application. Rather, the application is quite specific, limited not only to geology but to a particular problem within geology.

3. Stats's invention does not fall within patentable subject matter. She has discovered a new scientific fact—the deleterious effect on workers of having less than ten square feet of space. Her broadly characterized invention amounts to a patent on any application of that idea. In essence, she has said, "Science shows that workers need ten square feet of space. So give your workers ten square feet of space—and send me a licensing fee for letting you know that fact." Stats has done essentially the same thing as Inventor, in the text, who discovered that some color television sets on the market (those made with alkali earth metal) emitted lower levels of radiation. Inventor was not entitled to patent existing television sets, despite having made the valuable discovery that such sets were safer to watch. Likewise, many people already have more than ten square feet in their work area. Stats cannot patent that practice simply because she has determined that it is beneficial to workers' mental states and workplace harmony. If an individual had discovered that smoking caused lung cancer, she would not have been able to patent a "Method of Reducing Lung Cancer Risk," which was to not smoke. Many people already do not smoke, so such a claim would amount to a claim on the scientific discovery itself, not a new product or process.

   If Stats applied that fact to a specific product or process, the invention would fall within patentable subject matter. For example, she could patent a new type of office cubicle or an office chair with long spikes. Such inventions would put the discovery to work without monopolizing its use. Others, however, would be free to utilize her discovery by means that did not use her specific applications.

4. Swan probably has an invention within patentable subject matter. Swan has discovered a hitherto unknown cause of a health problem. Swan has also discovered the physical phenomenon that infrared light can remedy the problem. Neither discovery is within patentable subject matter. But Swan also has invented a specific process that puts the discoveries to a specific application. Although the process takes advantage of the discoveries, the process goes beyond the discoveries themselves. The process consists of searching for people who might have suffered from UV memory loss, testing them, and then using a specific treatment for those who show

impairment. Provided that Swan claimed it the method narrowly enough not to preempt other applications, Swan should be entitled to a patent.

5. The bacterium is not within patentable subject matter. Chakrabarty's oil-eating bacterium was patentable, but Prospector's rust-eating bacterium is not. The difference is that Chakrabarty made his (by using genetic engineering), whereas Prospector found the rust bug. The rust bug is a product of nature.

   The result would be different if Prospector had isolated, purified, or concentrated the bacterium in such a way that it was "something new." But Prospector simply scooped up the bacteria as they appear in nature.

6. Hoover does not have an invention within patentable subject matter. The wack is indeed a machine and is indeed a living thing. But it is a product of nature.

7. Zoop does fall within patentable subject matter. Zoop is a combination of naturally occurring sugars. The sugars are not patentable because they are products of nature. Nor, under *Funk Brothers*, would a combination of the sugars be patentable if it did not affect their natural functioning. If Zoop simply combined the sugars in a way that did not affect the way that they functioned separately, Zoop would fall outside patentable subject matter. For example, if all the sugars were known to be good for runners, and Zoop simply provided a way for a runner to drink them all at once, it probably would not escape the exclusion for products of nature. But the particular combination of sugars in Zoop does affect the natural functioning of the sugars in the human metabolism. The sugars have a different (and improved) effect in that particular combination. And unlike the combination in *Funk Brothers*, the combination in Zoop does not occur naturally. Rather than discovering the beneficial effects of a naturally occurring combination, Loafer has invented a combination.

   A possible counterargument: If Zoop were really the perfect sports drink, then it might not be patentable, because such a patent would monopolize a scientific principle.

8. Trig's proof falls outside of patentable subject matter. It is excluded as an abstract idea, not tied to any specific application. Pure mathematics is considered to be an excluded area.

9. *Alice* provides the applicable test: first, the court should determine whether the claims at issue are directed to one of the three patent-ineligible concepts. If so, the court asks whether the additional elements "transform the nature of the claim" into a patent-eligible application. As the Court put it, step two looks for an "inventive concept, an element or combination of elements that is sufficient to ensure that the patent in practice amounts to significantly more than a patent upon the ineligible concept itself" (citations and quotation marks again omitted).

Baylis's method for factoring large numbers is not patentable subject matter. The method consists of taking one number and finding the other numbers that, multiplied together, give the first number. The method is not tied to any specific application. It is excluded as pure mathematics. Indeed, it is a grander version of the conversion algorithm in *Benson*, which simply converted one type of number to another type of number. Remember that a process that takes a number and yields other numbers as a result may be patentable, but only if those numbers stand for something (that is, the process has been put to a specific application). If Baylis wrote a computer program that accomplished the same task, the program would likewise be nonpatentable. Although embodying the algorithm in a computer program is a step toward putting it to a specific application, this program serves nothing but a purely mathematical task.

If Baylis developed a method for decoding messages encrypted by Svenmail, that process *might* be within patentable subject matter. Baylis would have taken the unpatentable factoring algorithm and put it to a very specific application. That could provide the "inventive concept" that transforms the claim into a patent-eligible application of the abstract idea.

10. The formula for producing Penrose tiling is a process that falls outside patentable subject matter. For a process to be patentable, it must still be tied to some application outside pure mathematics.

But even under *Alice*, a method for producing nonsticking toilet paper is an application that falls within patentable subject matter. The application transforms the toilet paper. Nor would a patent on such a process hazard granting exclusive rights to the algorithm itself. There are plenty of other uses, in mathematics, décor, and elsewhere.

11. a. Heart Surgeon is protected by §287(c) (assuming she is a licensed surgeon). She infringes the patent but is not subject to any remedy.
    b. Heart Surgeon is liable for patent infringement, for making and for using a patented machine. She falls into one of the exceptions in the definition of medical activity.
    c. It would depend on whether Naturopath is subject to licensing in his state and is licensed to perform such procedures.
    d. Local Teenager is working under the direction of a licensed practitioner and so is insulated.

12. Ponce's invention would not be within patentable subject matter. The USPTO has taken the position that an "invention embracing a human being is not within patentable subject matter." This has not been definitively tested in court, but represents the apparent trend of authority.

    If it were a guinea pig, then it would be patentable. The guinea pig would have to be different from guinea pigs as they occur in nature. But a number of genetically modified organisms have been patented, from Chakrabarty's oil-eating microbe to the Harvard mouse and beyond.

13. Human cells, as opposed to human beings, are within patentable subject matter.

14. A method for extending life would be patentable (as long as it was not effectively a patent on a natural law). Indeed, many products (such as pharmaceuticals) and processes (from exercise plans to medical treatments) that have the effect of extending life have been patented. Enforcement of the patent might be difficult. Obtaining a patent requires that Ponce file an application describing his invention and how to practice it. The patent, including that information, becomes open to the public. If his method were in fact effective, there would be little he could do to stop people from using it. Note also that if someone did invent a miracle drug or diet that acted as a fountain of youth, the political pressure to allow legal access to the invention would be enormous. But questions like that about the scope of patentable subject matter remain for some future brave new world.

    Should a miracle drug be patentable? One can think of some pretty good arguments against giving one person the right to exclude others from making, selling, or using something with such enormous value. But one can also argue that the carrot of patent protection provides a great incentive for putting resources into searching for the fountain of youth.

CHAPTER 7

Substantive Standards for Protection: New, Useful, and Nonobvious Inventions

As we learned in Chapter 6, Curie has invented a pencil with a spinaltapical-shaped eraser attached. "Spinaltapical" refers to the 11-sided shape of the eraser, which Curie finds makes it especially effective in erasing. Curie is entitled to a patent if and only if her invention meets the requirements that the invention be new (spelled out in detail in 35 U.S.C. §102), be useful (§101), and be nonobvious (§103).

What it means for an invention to be "new" depends on when the patent application was filed. In 2011, Congress passed legislation moving the United States from a first-to-invent system to a first-to-file system. Under the 1952 Act (governing patent applications filed up to March 16, 2013), Curie's invention would not be new if, on Curie's date of invention, she was subject to:

- anticipation: a pencil with a spinaltapical eraser was already in public use or had been published;
- priority: someone else had already invented the same invention and was diligently proceeding toward patenting it; or
- derivation: Curie had learned of the invention from someone else.

The invention must also be new in a different sense. Curie must not have waited too long to file her patent application. She would have lost her right to a patent, if she filed more than one year after the invention was made public (by a public use, a publication, or an offer to sell) by her or anyone else.

Under the 2011 Act (governing patent applications filed after March 16, 2013), the critical date is the filing date, not the date of invention. Curie's invention would not be new if, before she filed her application, another inventor had filed a patent application on the same invention, or the invention had been published, in public use, or otherwise available to the public. The new regime encourages prompt filing, hence it's often called first-to-file (or first-inventor-to-file, to be more accurate). There is still a one-year grace period for disclosures stemming from Curie herself. If she publishes her invention, she still has a year to file her patent application in the U.nited States (other countries are stricter).

In coming years, many patents will be governed by the 1952 Act, many by the 2011 Act, so lawyers will deal with both sets of rules.

In addition to "new," the invention must also be "useful." This requirement is simple for inventions like an eraser. As long as it works, that is sufficient utility. Utility is trickier in areas closer to scientific research, where researcher may have a promising new molecule, genetically modified organism, or nanotech modulator, but not have a practical application for it yet.

The invention must also be nonobvious. If the invention would be obvious to someone in the pencil eraser field (in light of previous relevant technology), Curie is not entitled to a patent. Suppose that spinaltapical erasers were already on the market. No one had attached one to a pencil yet, but that would be obvious in light of the many pencils with erasers. Curie would not be entitled to patent that obvious invention. Suppose to the contrary that although mathematicians had discovered the spinaltapical shape, no one had reason to apply it to erasers. Curie's innovation was a technological step forward. In that case, she would be entitled to a patent.

Note: Whether an invention is new and nonobvious may depend on how it is claimed in the application. A pencil with a spinaltapical eraser may not be new or nonobvious. But Curie might have other novel elements to her invention, such as making the eraser from plubundum, which is especially durable and has never been used in the eraser field. A pencil with a spinaltapical eraser made from plubundum might be new and nonobvious. More of that in the next chapter, which deals with the patent claims.

"NEW": NOVELTY AND LOSS OF RIGHT

An invention must be "new" to be patentable. If an invention is already known to the public, there is little reason to grant a patent, which gives its holder the right to foreclose others from making, using, offering, selling, and importing the invention.

1952 Act Rules Apply to Patent Applications Filed up to March 16, 2013

The 1952 statute has several sets of conditions that go to this requirement. These are divided into rules governing novelty, loss of right (also known as statutory bars), and priority.

Under 35 U.S.C. §102, the invention must be new in several senses. It must be new (as in unprecedented in publicly accessible knowledge) at the time of invention:

1. Anticipation (§102(a),(e)): It was not already known to the public or in public use (in the United States) and had not been published (anywhere) or described in a pending U.S. patent application (which led subsequently to an issued patent).
2. Priority (§102(g)): It was not already invented by someone else who was diligently proceeding toward making the invention and patenting it.
3. Derivation (§102(f)): The patent applicant must be the inventor, not one who has learned of an invention from someone else.

It also must be new in the sense that inventor may lose her right to a patent if she does not file her application in time:

1. Statutory bars, also known as loss of right: She must file no later than a year after the invention is put in public use, or is published, or is put on sale (§102(b)).[1]

Novelty

Anticipation (§102(a), (e))

Anticipation bars a patent for an invention that was already publicly known (in specifically defined ways) on the applicant's date of invention. The applicant is not entitled to patent an invention that, on the inventor's date of invention, was known to the public or in public use in the United States, or had been patented or published anywhere. 35 U.S.C. §102(a).

---

1. In addition, two other statutory bars exist, but rarely come into play. Under §102(c), an inventor loses a right to patent by abandoning the invention (abandonment issues generally arise in priority disputes). Under §102(d), an inventor loses her right to a U.S. patent if she obtains a foreign patent before filing her U.S. application and if the foreign application was made more than one year before the date of her U.S. filing. For most applicants, this provision presents few practical problems because it requires considerable delay. Moreover, the United States is party to a number of treaties that facilitate international filings, so an applicant can use readily available procedures to preserve the applicant's U.S. rights.

In patent law terminology, an invention is not patentable if it is in a *reference* (a publication or product or other evidence of public knowledge) in the *prior art* (the various sources that contain potential references) that *anticipates* the invention (contains all of the elements of the claimed invention) on the *critical date* (for anticipation, the date of invention). Suppose a chemist develops a useful chemical compound. This invention is not novel if anywhere in the prior art (all things that had been published or publicly known on the date of invention) there is a reference (such as an article published in a journal of chemistry) that anticipates the invention (describes a composition of matter with all the elements of chemist's claimed invention). Even if the inventor is unaware of the publication or public use, his invention is unpatentable.

Absolute novelty is not required under this provision. Rather, whether an invention is novel is judged only against the references found in the specified categories of prior art: references that have been published (anywhere) or were in public use or public knowledge in the United States. If someone else has made a nonpublic use, used the invention in another country, or written about it without publishing the writing, none of those would bar a patent under §102(a).

A publication would encompass any medium that makes the reference publicly accessible. It need not be widespread. A chemical invention was published when it was described in a doctoral thesis that was placed in the stacks and listed in the catalog of a university library in Freiburg, Germany. *See In re Hall*, 781 F.2d 897 (Fed. Cir. 1986). There was publication where a cell culture scientist orally presented a paper at a conference to an audience of some 50 to 500 cell culturists and afterward handed out copies without restrictions to some six people. *Massachusetts Inst. of Tech. v. AB Fortia*, 774 F.2d 1104 (Fed. Cir. 1985). An invention was deemed published by display in a printed slide presentation on poster boards during two academic meetings, totaling about three days, where the display permitted the information to be freely copied. *In re Klopfenstein*, 380 F.3d 1345 (Fed. Cir. 2004). By contrast, a paper would not be published if it were stored or distributed in a way that kept the paper from being accessible to others.

An invention can also be anticipated by a product or process that is in public use by someone other than the inventor in the United States. Secret use by a third party not controlled by the inventor, even if commercial, does not count as public use against an inventor. But public use by a third party may be an invalidating public use. A use need not be obvious or even accessible to the public to qualify as public. An ordinary commercial use of the invention qualifies as a public use.

In addition to publications and public use under 35 U.S.C. §102(a), §102(e) provides that an invention can be anticipated by "secret prior art": a disclosure in a patent application pending before the U.S. Patents and Trademarks Office (USPTO), if that application later leads to an issued patent. Suppose Inventor One files a patent application claiming a "Blue Laser" (which is subsequently allowed). As part of her application, she describes a "Tangerine AC/DC Adapter" but does not seek a patent on it. While the application is pending (and not available to the public), Inventor Two invents a "Tangerine AC/DC Adapter" (every element of which was described in Inventor One's application). Inventor Two is barred from a patent. The theory behind the rule is that, but for the time taken by the USPTO to examine the application, the information would have been public knowledge.

Novelty is judged as of the date of invention. Exactly when invention occurs may be difficult to determine. The earlier the date of invention, the more likely it is that the invention will be novel. If the applicant can prove the date of conception (when he had fully conceived the invention in its operable form), that is the date of invention (as long as he then proceeded diligently to make the invention or file a patent application). He may not be able to prove the date of conception. Indeed, some inventions are so complex that having a complete mental conception would be impossible. Absent a date of conception, invention occurs on "reduction to practice": when the inventor made the invention and performed any necessary testing. If he cannot prove a time of reduction to practice, the date of invention is simply the date of filing his patent application. *See Amgen v. Chugai Pharmaceutical*, 927 F.2d 1200 (Fed. Cir. 1991).

The single reference must describe and "enable" the invention. In other words, it must both disclose all the elements[2] of the invention and provide the information necessary to make and use the invention. An invention is not barred unless there is "identity of invention," meaning every element of the claimed invention is found in a single prior art reference. A claim to an invention comprising elements A, B, and C is not anticipated by a reference that comprises only elements A and B. The analysis cannot combine references: There is no anticipation even if one reference comprises elements A and B and another reference comprises elements B and C, so the two together disclose A, B, and C.

The reference may disclose elements either expressly or inherently. Under the inherency doctrine, references include elements that, although not expressly stated, are necessarily present in the product or process described in the reference. For example, an article in the journal *Russian Metallurgy* disclosed a particular alloy. Some years later, an inventor discovered several useful properties of the alloy, such as its corrosion resistance. The inventor could not patent the alloy, however, because the alloy was disclosed in the prior art, even though its subsequently discovered useful properties were not. *See Titanium Metals v. Banner*, 778 F.2d 775 (Fed. Cir. 1985). The properties were inherent in the alloy—even if not known at the time. The inherency doctrine has been limited somewhat. A process will not be anticipated when it occurred

---

2. Neither the statute nor the case law defines specifically what constitutes an "element" of a claim.

only as an accidental and unwitting byproduct in some previous process. *See Tilghman v. Proctor*, 102 U.S. 707 (1880); Robin Weatherhead, *Investigating Inherency: Inception to AIA*, 97 J. Pat. & Trademark Off. Soc'y (forthcoming).

The inherency doctrine can guard against double patenting. A substance produced by using a patented pharmaceutical would be inherently disclosed by the prior patent. That means that the patent holder could not effectively extend the term of the first patent by discovering previously unknown byproducts and attempting to patent them. *See Schering Corp. v. Geneva Pharm.*, 339 F.3d 1373 (Fed. Cir. 2003). The inherency doctrine also makes products of known processes to be prior art in determining obviousness (discussed below).

A new process to make an old product is sufficiently novel for patentability. If a pharmaceutical company finds a new way to make a well-known drug, the process itself is novel. The pharmaceutical company is not entitled to a patent on the drug (because it is not new), but may be able to patent the new process.

Examples

1. *Anticipation?* Inventor's patent application claims a "Single-Hand Digital Calculator," comprising elements *A*, *B*, and *C*. Which of the following anticipate the invention (thereby rendering the claim nonallowable for lack of novelty)?

   a. A single-hand digital calculator with elements *A*, *B*, and *C* had been in public use in Illinois before Inventor's date of invention. Would the result be different if it were in public use in Iceland?

   b. A single-hand digital calculator with elements *A*, *B*, and *C* had been patented in Iceland before Inventor's date of invention.

   c. A single-hand digital calculator had been patented in Iceland before Inventor's date of invention. It did not have elements *A*, *B*, and *C*, but was far superior to Inventor's invention, in terms of efficiency, accuracy, and several other properties.

   d. Two single-hand digital calculators, one with elements *A* and *C* and one with elements *B* and *C*, had been patented in the United States before Inventor's date of invention.

   e. A single-hand digital calculator with elements *A*, *B*, and *C* had been in public use in Kentucky and had been described in a publication before Inventor filed her patent application (but after Inventor's date of invention).

   f. An article in *Calculator Weekly*, published one week before Inventor's date of invention, described a single-hand digital calculator. The article described a device with elements *A*, *B*, and *C*. But the description was so sketchy that it did not provide sufficient information for a calculator engineer to make and operate such a device. In other words, it proved such an invention had been conceived but did not enable one to make it.

    g. Hobbyist publishes a weekly *Oddity Newsletter*, which he sends to several hundred subscribers. The newsletter is also advertised in several well-known magazines. An article in the newsletter, published six months before Inventor's date of invention, describes a single-hand digital calculator with elements *A*, *B*, and *C* and how to make it.

    h. Leonarda, a brilliant inventor, builds a single-hand digital calculator with elements *A*, *B*, and *C*. She describes it and how to build it in her inventing diary, which has never been published. She then abandons the invention to pursue her many other interests. No more is heard of her calculator. Ten years later, Inventor invents his single-hand digital calculator.

2. *Unknown properties.* Little Powder Company has made and sold a special baking powder for many years. Unknown to Little Powder Company, the baking powder is highly resistant to radiation, which would make it useful in various applications such as construction of nuclear power plants. Zeus Chemical Company, after years of experimenting, develops a special construction powder that is identical to the baking powder. Zeus seeks to patent the powder. Can Zeus patent the powder?

3. *Beam me up.* Inventor, a genius scientist and engineer, makes a number of breakthroughs and builds a transporter just like the one on *Star Trek* that transports people instantly from place to place. It even looks just like the transporter on *Star Trek*. So is it novel?

4. *Printed publication?* Suppose an invention is described in an article in an obscure medical journal—so obscure that although 1,000 copies of the relevant edition of the journal are printed, they are never shipped and remain sitting in the journal's warehouse. After the articles are printed and then stored, Bottle invents a process identical to one described in one of the articles. Is Bottle's invention unpatentable due to anticipation? Suppose that the article is indeed sent out and accessible to the public. This occurs after Bottle's date of invention, but before one month goes by Bottle files his patent application, claiming an invention that was described in the published article. Is the claimed invention anticipated?

Explanations

Although the 2011 is discussed below, the answers here will also discuss where the result would be different under the 2011 Act rules, which apply to patent applications filed after March 16, 2013.

1. a. The public use of a product in the United States with all the elements of the invention does anticipate the claim, meaning Inventor is not entitled to a patent for the invention so claimed. If the public use had been in Iceland, the result would be different. Public use outside the

United States is not anticipation. The result would be the same under the 2011 Act, which looks to novelty at the time of filing the application. A public use before the date of invention must have also been before the date of the subsequent patent application.

b. The publication of a patent in Iceland does make the claim nonallowable because it anticipates the claimed invention. A publication, unlike a public use, need not be in the United States to count as prior art for anticipation. Same result under the 2011 Act.

c. This does not destroy novelty because the reference does not disclose the identical invention. Even though the earlier calculator is far better, it is not identical. Rather, it does not have elements A, B, and C. Anticipation requires identity of invention: Every element of the claimed invention must be found in the anticipating reference. Same result under the 2011 Act.

d. These references do not destroy novelty because there is not a single reference that discloses an identical invention. Anticipation requires that all the elements are disclosed in a single reference. If all the elements appear separately in different references, there is no anticipation. This is true even if most of the elements appear in a single reference. Indeed, it is quite common to find a combination of references that, taken together, disclose all the elements of a claimed invention. Same result under the 2011 Act. Note the references, taken together, may render the invention obvious and so nonpatentable, as discussed later in the chapter.

e. There is no anticipation here because the product was not in public use before Inventor's date of invention. If Inventor invents before the other reference is in public use or is published, then Inventor invented something not already in the public knowledge. The later public use does not anticipate. Under the 2011 Act, however, a public use before Inventor's filing date will bar a patent for Inventor. The shift to using the filing date as the critical date can make a considerable difference.

f. There is no anticipation. The reference must disclose not only all the elements of the invention, it must enable one to make and use the invention. Again, it could possibly make the invention obvious and so nonpatentable.

g. There is anticipation here. Even though the invention was published in an obscure journal outside of Inventor's field of work, that does not prevent anticipation. References are not limited to publications that Inventor has read or even is likely to read. Same result under the 2011 Act.

h. Leonarda did not publish the invention or put it into public use, so there is no anticipation under §102(a). She has abandoned the invention, so there would not be a priority dispute under §102(g) either. Inventor did not learn of the invention from her, so it is not barred by derivation under §102(f). Rather, Inventor has invented something that is not in the public store of knowledge and, therefore, is entitled to a patent. Same result under the 2011 Act.

2. The construction powder is anticipated by the identical baking powder. A product with all the elements of Zeus' powder was already in public use on Zeus' date of invention. In other words, Zeus has not invented a new composition of matter but discovered a property of a known composition of matter. But the discovery of a new property is simply an unpatentable natural phenomenon. Note that Zeus could still seek a process patent on a new use of the powder.

3. The transporter is novel. A reference (here, the television show *Star Trek*) anticipates an invention only if the reference describes and enables the invention — that is, provides disclosure that enables someone skilled in the art to make and use the invention. The transporter used in *Star Trek* was just a box with lights. *Star Trek* did not provide information that would enable someone to make and use the transporter.

4. The invention is not anticipated by the product disclosed in the article. The effective date of a publication is when it becomes accessible to the public. On Bottle's invention date, the article had not been published. Even though it was published before Bottle filed his patent application, it does not anticipate his invention. The critical date for anticipation is the date of invention, not the date of filing the application. Under the 2011 Act, however, the critical date is Inventor's filing date. The invention would not be novel.

Derivation (§102(f))

Only the inventor is entitled to patent an invention. Someone who merely learns of an invention is not entitled to patent the invention — even if the inventor freely discloses it and has no plans to patent it herself. *See* 35 U.S.C. §102(f). Even if the inventor assigns her rights to someone else, that person must correctly identify the inventor in the patent application. Not every suggestion or proffered idea constitutes invalidating derivation. Rather, the applicant is not entitled to a patent if a fully operable conception of the invention is communicated to the applicant. A famous example of derivation concerns ENIAC, the first general-purpose digital computer. The developers of ENIAC were held to have derived the invention from another, so their patent was invalid. Meanwhile, it was too late for the original inventor to file a valid application, so he could not hold the patent either. Hence, no one was entitled to claim a patent on that rather useful invention.

Examples

1. *Derivative.* Engineer reads the latest issue of *Scientific American*, which discloses a newly created chemical compound with special superconducting properties. Engineer realizes that the compound might be useful in building a superefficient refrigerator. After much research and experimentation, Engineer builds such a superefficient refrigerator. Her project involves making several innovations in the refrigeration arts. Is she barred from a patent on the grounds of derivation under §102(f) because she learned of the superconducting material from another source?

2. *Folk medicine.* Anthropologist spends a year living with indigenous people in Central America. They show him how they use the leaf of the Candlestick tree (never before known to others) to treat rashes, after Anthropologist spends one day hiking through Poison Dartbush thickets (also never before known to others). When he returns to the United States, he seeks a patent, claiming the method of treating rashes with the Candlestick tree leaf as a process. Can he patent the process?

Explanations

1. Engineer is not barred on the grounds of derivation. Derivation requires that a fully operable conception of the invention be communicated to the inventor. That did not occur here. Engineer learned about the new chemical and its properties from the *Scientific American* article. But Engineer's invention is an application of that knowledge and therefore required considerable additional inventive contribution from Engineer. Same result under the 2011 Act.

2. Anthropologist is barred from a patent on the ground of derivation. He did not invent the subject matter to be patented. Derivation does not require that the information be published or be public knowledge. Rather, the question is whether the invention was original to the inventor. Here, it was not. A fully operable conception of the invention was communicated to Anthropologist. Same result under the 2011 Act.

   Note that the public use of the method does not bar the patent, under the 1952 Act, because only public use in the United States acts as a bar, both for novelty under §102(a) and statutory bars under §102(b). So a researcher in the United States who had independently developed the method would not have been barred from patenting it (assuming it had not been published, which need not be in the United States). Under the 2011 Act, public use outside the US counts. In any case, Anthropologist did not invent the method; he learned of it from someone else.

Priority (§102(g))

Under the 1952 Act, in the United States, if two inventors (or two groups of inventors) claim the same invention, the patent generally belongs to the first to invent. 35 U.S.C. §102(g).[3] The U.S. rule (first to invent takes priority) differs from almost all other jurisdictions, which grant the patent to the first to file her patent application. A first-to-file rule has the advantage of clarity. If a first-to-file patent office discovers it has two pending applications for the same invention, it simply gives priority to the first to file. The USPTO must follow the first-to-invent rule, which requires a much more complicated factual determination. In those cases, the USPTO declares an "interference" proceeding (even if a patent has already issued to one inventor) to determine which inventor is entitled to priority.

The 1952 Act rules for priority can be summarized as follows. The first inventor to reduce his invention to practice (either actually—by making and testing the invention—or constructively—by filing a patent application) has priority, unless: (1) that inventor "abandoned, suppressed, or concealed" the invention, either affirmatively or by simply delaying for an unreasonable period of time; or (2) the other inventor conceived the invention (and proceeded with reasonable diligence toward making and patenting it) before the competing inventor had conceived the invention. A much-watched interference proceeding involves the patent rights to CRISPR-Cas9 "gene editing" techniques. The USPTO determined that neither party had priority, rather, that the applications were on separate inventions. Although the Berkeley group might have invented the use of CRISPR in the DNA of cells, that did not make obvious the invention of the MIT group, how to use CRISPR in eukaryotic cells (such as plant, animal and fungi).[4] Appeals in the United States and Europe were pending in 2018.

Loss of Right (§102(b))

Suppose inventor's invention does not run afoul of the novelty requirements. It was new when she invented it. The statutory bars in 35 U.S.C. §102(b) are another kind of time limit, linked not to the date of invention but the date of filing the patent application. In effect, §102(b) of the 1952 Act says that once the invention becomes public knowledge, an inventor has one year to file her application. So there must first be a triggering event

---

3. Note that the U.S. patent statute formerly disregarded foreign inventive activity for the purposes of determining priority. If Inventor A conceived the invention and reduced to practice abroad, she could only use the date of filing her U.S. patent application to establish priority, while her competitor in the priority contest could rely on his conception and reduction to practice dates in the United States. The statute now largely recognizes foreign inventive activity.
4. Broad Inst. Inc. v. Regents of the Bd. of the Univ. of Cal., No. 106,048 (PTAB Feb. 15, 2017).

("the invention was patented or described in a printed publication in this or a foreign country or in public use or on sale in this country"). This may be done by others or by the inventor herself. If the inventor does not file before a year passes from the effective date of that reference, she loses the right to patent the invention (even if she was unaware of the public use, knowledge, or publication). There are several reasons behind the statutory bars. The bars give inventors a strong incentive to file patent applications promptly, thereby disclosing to the public useful inventions once a patent issues. Once an invention has been in unrestricted public use and knowledge, others may have a reliance interest. The rule also prevents an inventor from delaying an application with the hopes of effectively gaining a longer period of protection.

Inventor invents her new supersticky glue. She publishes an article in *Glue Research Journal* that describes the glue and how to make it. That publication starts the one-year period. The clock also starts running if the inventor starts selling the glue to the public. Someone else could start the clock running against her as well, even if she did not know about it. If someone else starts selling or publicly using an identical glue in the United States or publishes an article describing the identical glue (even if the article appears in a foreign country), the one-year period begins.

Note that the one-year period is more forgiving than the patent law of many countries. Many foreign patent laws provide that an invention is not patentable if it is disclosed to the public (by use, sale, patent, or other publication) before the date of the patent application. The U.S. law, by contrast, has the effect of a one-year grace period for inventors. But that will only apply to U.S. patent rights. A U.S. inventor interested in patent rights abroad (and many are interested in international markets) must abide by the rules of the relevant jurisdiction.

Section 102(b) does not require the same "identity of invention" as §102(a). For anticipation under §102(a), the reference must be identical: It must disclose every element of the claimed invention. Under §102(b), however, courts hold it sufficient if the reference discloses the identical invention or if the invention is obvious in light of the reference.[5]

The one-year period begins if the invention is patented or otherwise published anywhere. As with novelty, this is not limited to patents or publications that our inventor would be expected to read. A foreign patent, not published in the United States, or a publication in an esoteric journal may

---

5. This rule is called 102(b)/103 anticipation. Technically, it is more accurate to call it a finding that the invention is obvious under §103, using the prior art identified by §102(b). But courts frequently discuss it as anticipation under §102(b). Note that most of the cases involve products similar to the invention. One might reach a different result if it were a publication (rather than a product) from an unrelated field (rather than a similar product). See the discussion of prior art under §103, below.

start the clock ticking as long as the reference is accessible to one skilled in the relevant art.

The one-year period may also be triggered by a public use of the invention in the United States, whether by the inventor or by others. Whether the inventor's use is "public" depends more on policy than on whether the use is actually known to the public. (Some would read the 2011 Act to only apply to public uses that were available to the public, as discussed below). Secret use by the inventor for commercial purposes is deemed a public use. The inventor cannot commercialize his invention and subsequently seek a patent on a "new" invention. Otherwise, an inventor could gain a patent after utilizing an invention for years, extending the effective period of the patent. He would also have failed to disclose his invention in timely fashion, as the statutory bars encourage. By contrast, an experimental use by the inventor is not public use, even if it has public aspects. For example, an inventor used his new and improved wooden pavement on a public toll road for some six years. But the purpose of the use to test the pavement's usefulness and durability was experimental. See City of Elizabeth v. Am. Nicholson Pavement Co., 97 U.S. 126, 137 (1877). But it was public use to allow a close friend to wear an invented corset, under her clothing, for some years. See Egbert v. Lippmann, 104 U.S. 333 (1881). The use was barely public, but it was not undertaken for purposes of experiment.

Inventor also loses her right to patent if the invention is on sale in the United States more than one year before the inventor files her patent application. Two conditions are necessary for the invention to qualify as "on sale." First, the invention must be the subject of a commercial offer for sale. Second, the invention must be ready for patenting, meaning that the inventor had reduced it to practice or sufficiently described it to do so. See Pfaff v. Wells Electronics, 525 U.S. 55 (1998). The on-sale bar applies to processes as well as products. A process can be on sale if products of the process are sold, products embodying the process are sold, or if the inventor offers to use the process for compensation. An offer to lease a computer program that performs a process triggers the on-sale bar. But the process itself must be offered: The sale of information about a process (such as a transfer of trade secrets or know-how), or performance of related services, is not a sale of the process.

Any commercial sale triggers the bar, even if the invention is far from available to the public. The sale could be by the inventor, by a competitor that developed the invention independently, or by a supplier to the inventor (using specifications given by the inventor). Courts have applied the bar even when the inventor had not commercialized the invention but offers were triggered by someone who had wrongfully taken the invention from the inventor.

The invention may become public in some senses without starting the one-year clock. Suppose that Black Hole displays its new vacuum cleaner at a trade show. But Black Hole does not demonstrate it (which would be a public use), take orders (which would trigger the on-sale bar) or publish details (a publication). The one-year clock would not start ticking, so even if Black Hole filed for a patent more than one year after the trade show, it would not have lost its patent rights.

Examples

1. *Loss of right to patent?* For each of the following, has the inventor lost the right to a patent, due to the statutory bars of §102(b) (Inventor must file patent application no later than one year after public use, patented abroad, publication, or offered for sale ("on-sale bar")):

   a. Ian invents a skunk scarer. He publishes an article in *Mephitis Mechanics* describing the device and how to make it. He then realizes he forgot to file his patent application before publishing.

   b. Ivanna invents a hockey skate. She starts selling the skates. Sales are slow during the summer, but pick up in January. Finally, eighteen months after her first sale, she files a patent application.

   c. Ivan invents a safer seesaw. He keeps his invention to himself. Over the next 18 months, he works on improving it. Then he finally files a patent application on his first version.

   d. Inez invents a new and useful bike helmet. She puts an ad in the paper, announcing that she has developed a better helmet and that it is coming soon to the market. She gets inquiries, but does not make or take offers for some 18 months. Shortly after that, she files her patent application.

2. *She who hesitates.* Delia, a stone mason, spends great effort trying to devise a better granite chisel. After many attempts, she comes up with a great innovation, the Splay-Spackling Chisel. Delia quickly realizes the large market that likely exists for such a chisel. Seven months later, she reads an article in *Mason Magazine* that describes a chisel just like hers that had been invented a week before the article was published (several months after Delia's date of invention). A year and a half passes, and Delia finally files her patent application. The USPTO examiner informs her that she is not entitled to a patent, even if she did invent first. Is the examiner correct? What if Delia had written the article herself? What if Delia had filed her application six months after the article was published?

3. *Public use?* Grandma invents a new form of baby blanket. Over many years, she gives several dozen as gifts for her grandchildren and others. The blankets go with the tots in their strollers to local parks and malls. After several years, Grandma files a patent application on her baby blanket. Has she lost her right to patent?

4. *Waiting game.* Bide, a financial advisor, develops an integrated process for efficiently keeping track of various financial data, implementing

strategies, and determining when to communicate with clients. He decides not to file a patent application, reasoning that the value of the patent does not justify the expenses, disclosure, and other costs. Bide does not tell anyone about the process. To the contrary, he takes considerable measures to keep the process a secret. He programs the computer himself and uses password protection on all the relevant software implementing the program. He uses the process in his work. He does not market the process or its results to clients, but uses it strictly to run his business more efficiently. After three years, Bide decides to get a patent after all and files a patent application. Has his delay cost him the right to a patent?

Suppose instead that Bide abandons the use of the process, as well as completely rejecting any interest in filing a patent application. Another financial advisor, Clyde, independently develops the same process. Is Clyde barred from a patent by (a) the fact that Bide invented first, or (b) the fact that Bide had used the process for three years?

5. *Getting it right.* Velo is a bicycle equipment designer. He is trying to develop a bicycle pedal that doubles as a running shoe for use by triathletes. After several attempts, Velo makes prototype #6. After using it in his own training for a week, Velo is encouraged. He then makes 50 more models of the prototype and ships a dozen each to four leading triathletes. Using Velo's shoes, the triathletes enjoy considerable success. Velo has them carefully document the performance of the shoes. Velo also has the triathletes sport VELO in huge letters on the shoes to start building up brand-name recognition. But he also has them sign nondisclosure agreements in which they promise to keep the new elements of the shoe confidential. Over the next 18 months, Velo carefully keeps track of how the shoes are working. In response to the data, he makes several fine adjustments in his preferred version of the shoe. At the end of the 18 months, he files a patent application, claiming the shoe (broadly enough to encompass prototype #6 and its subsequent improvements). A USPTO examiner, who had seen the shoe on a televised race over a year ago, advises him that Velo has lost his right to patent. Has he?

6. *Trust.* Lisle Corp. invents an inner rod tie tool, for use by auto mechanics. To improve the tool, Lisle delivers the tool, without charge, to a select pool of auto mechanics, with whom it has long-standing relationships. The mechanics do not sign confidentiality agreements, but understand the use is experimental. There are no restrictions on the use of the tools. Lisle seeks periodic feedback from the mechanics, and uses it to adjust the design of the tools. Lisle files its patent application more than a year after the mechanics use the tool. Is it barred from a patent by public use?

7. *Experimental use?* Noyzy develops a new, tiny stereo speaker. The speaker functions extremely well. Noyzy sells several from her store but does

not expend resources on a large marketing campaign. Noyzy is not sure whether there is a market for her device. Its components are very expensive. Other tiny speakers are on the market. Their performance is not as good, but their price is well under Noyzy's. Noyzy is not sure if the marginal improvement in the quality of her product will be sufficient to lure buyers to a considerably higher price. She is also concerned that competitors may come out with a superior product. Before expending resources on seeking a patent, Noyzy spends two years doing market research. She shows the speakers to potential buyers, who fill out surveys. Noyzy also demonstrates the speakers to some potential investors, who could share the risks of marketing. The results convince her that the speaker will be a huge hit, so she quickly files a patent application. Has she lost the right to patent, or is she protected by the experimental use exception?

8. *Cash bar.* Machine Maker develops a fully operational prototype of its new roulette machine. It enters into a contract with Casino to sell 100 machines but holds off producing any of its commercial models yet. Two years later, Machine Maker files its patent application, claiming the new roulette machine. Is Machine Maker's claim valid?

9. *Vaporware.* DotKom, a software producer, sends a brochure to several animation studios, offering to sell copies of its image extractor. The proffered machine is described in considerable detail, heralding its ability to take a typical movie, scan the images of the principal actors in action, and transform the actors' images into dazzling animated characters. Several studios pay considerable amounts to purchase the machines. This greatly disappoints Pickles, a software developer, who had recently invented a similar machine.

After about a year, it turns out that DotKom sold more than it could deliver. Its machine actually is unable to perform any of the claimed functions. DotKom's engineers, in fact, were unable to devise a working model or even plans of the machine. Pickles now decides to patent her image extractor. But DotKom's image extractor was offered for sale more than a year before Pickles files her patent application. Does the on-sale bar prevent Pickles from obtaining a patent?

10. *Sale to inventor.* Inventor conceives her "Flushable Vehicle Spittoon." She then enters into a contract with Spittoon Builders, under which Spittoon Builders would produce the spittoons and sell them to the public. Spittoon Builders makes 100 spittoons as directed by Inventor, but the parties then part ways. Spittoon Builders sells the 100 spittoons to Inventor. Two years later, she files her patent application. Has she lost her right to a patent?

11. *Sold out?* Sparta Engineering signs a contract to sell Athens Corp. a release plate for digital pianos. The contract describes the performance

requirements, such as size, durability, touch sensitivity, and so on, but leaves it to Sparta to design and build the device. Sparta's engineers subsequently address a number of thorny engineering issues, and manage to design a release plate that meets all the requirements. About two years after signing the contract, Sparta files for a patent on the release plate. Does the on-sale bar apply, where more than a year has gone by after Sparta signed contract to sell the device?

Explanations

1. a. Ian is not barred. In the United States, the critical date for the statutory bars is one year before filing the patent application. In effect, U.S. law gives a one-year grace period. So as long as he files no later than one year after publishing, he retains patent rights. The 2011 Act also gives a one-year grace period before the filing date for disclosures by the Inventor, although disclosures by others count if they are before the filing date. Note that many other jurisdictions have no grace period, so an inventor loses patent rights by publishing before filing. U.S. inventors interested in retaining rights abroad must therefore be careful.

   b. Ivanna has lost the right to patent. Her skates were on sale more than one year before she filed her patent application. Once the invention has been in public use, published, or on sale, the inventor must file within one year or lose her right to a patent. Same result under the 2011 Act.

   c. Ivan is not barred by §102(b). None of the triggering events (publication, on sale, public use, or foreign patent) have occurred yet, so the one-year period has not yet begun. Note that if someone else files an application claiming the same invention, Ivan's delay could hurt him in a priority dispute.

   d. No bar. No triggering event has occurred. Inez did not publish the invention, because she did not publish an enabling disclosure (one that would allow others to make the invention). Rather, she simply announced that she had made a better helmet. Nor was it in public use. Nor was it on sale. The on-sale bar is triggered only by an offer to sell that amounts to a commercial offer (an offer for the purposes of contract law). She did not make an offer that would create a binding contract, rather simply announced that the helmet would soon be on sale. Same result under the 2011 Act.

2. This is an example of the application of the statutory bars in §102(b) (the loss of the right to a patent, if the application is not filed less than a year after the invention is made public, even if that is done by someone other than the applicant). The invention is novel (and survives §102(a)) because it was not published before the date of invention. Delia invented before the identical device was described in a publication. But she then lost her right

to patent by waiting too long to file her application. The application must be filed no less than a year after the invention is published, put into public use or knowledge, or placed on sale. Same result under the 2011 Act.

Would it make a difference if Delia had written the article herself? No. Section 102(b) can be triggered by the actions of Inventor or by third parties.

If Delia had filed her application six months after the article was published, she would have escaped the statutory bar (under the 1952 Act, but not under the 2011 Act). The critical date for the statutory bars is one year before the application date. The effective date of the publication was after that (six months before Delia's application date), so the statutory bar would not apply. Many countries bar patents for inventions that were public knowledge before the patent application was filed. The United States gives the inventor a one-year leeway. (Note how confusing the rule can be to apply.)

3. Grandma has lost her right to patent. The invention is barred if it was in public use for more than one year before the date of the patent application. The use of the blanket here constitutes public use. Cf. *Comfort Silkie v. Seifert*, No. 98-1476 (Fed. Cir. July 16, 1999). Several dozen blankets were used by various relatives of Grandma. Grandma did not place any restrictions on the use or disclosure of her invention. The use was not commercial in nature, and the blankets were not generally available to the public. But those two factors would not overcome the showing that Grandma had permitted public use of the blanket for more than a year before filing her application. In *Egbert v. Lippmann*, an inventor permitted a single individual to wear a corset for several years, which the Court ruled constituted public use, where there was no requirement of secrecy and no reason for delaying the patent application. The use here is even more public. Same result under the 2011 Act, unless possibly courts read that Act only to apply to references available to the public (many would argue that for policy reasons, that may not be the best reading).

4. The patent would be barred on the grounds that the invention was in public use for more than one year before the application was filed. A secret use by the inventor for commercial purposes constitutes a public use. Otherwise, some inventors could effectively prolong patent protection by having a period of secret use and then having a full patent term. If this had been an experimental use, it might not be deemed public use. But Bide's use was not experimental. Same result under the 2011 Act, if it counts as a public use.

If the issue were whether Bide's use barred another inventor, it would be a closer question. Secret use by third parties usually does not constitute public use. A use in the ordinary course of business by a third party can constitute public use, even if the use is not made known to the public. But when, as here, the third party deliberately keeps knowledge of the use secret, then the use is less likely to be deemed public.

5. Velo probably would not be barred. Section 102(b) bars a patent if the invention is in public use for more than one year before the date the patent application is filed. The use here probably would be deemed experimental rather than public. Velo carefully tested the performance of the shoes and made design changes as a result of the test results. The use was not very widespread (four athletes) and no wider than necessary for the purposes of experimentation. The use did have some public aspects. The use in the races is not a strong factor against experimental use because that probably represented a reasonable method to test such shoes (rather than, for example, requiring people to run triathlons in private). Velo did put VELO on the side of the shoes. But that would not amount to the sort of commercial exploitation that would refute experimental use. He did not directly seek to commercially exploit the invention as such during the testing period. So Velo's use very likely would be deemed experimental, which would not start the one-year clock running. Same result under the 2011 Act, (if "public use" is construed the same way).

6. There was no public use, so the one year period did not begin to run. Rather, the use was held to be experimental use, which is not public use. *Lisle Corp. v. A.J. Mfg. Co.*, 398 F.3d 1306, 1315 (Fed. Cir. 2005). Experimental use need not be secret use. There were no explicit confidentiality agreements. But there was an understanding that the use was experimental, and there was no charge for the tools. The inventor used the mechanic's feedback to improve the tools. This would be experimental use, under *City of Elizabeth*. Same result under the 2011 Act.

7. Noyzy would be barred from a patent because the invention was in public use for more than a year before the application was filed. Noyzy might argue that this was experimental use. But all the experimentation was directed to the marketing, rather than refining or testing the functioning of the invention. The amount of public use was considerable. Noyzy did not make any attempts to restrict the flow of information about the invention. Same result under the 2011 Act.

8. The claim would be barred by the on-sale bar in §102(b). The invention was ready for patenting (as evidenced by the fully operational prototype) and a commercial sale had been made. Same result under the 2011 Act.

9. Pickle's claims would not be subject to the on-sale bar. There had been a commercial sale, but the invention was not yet ready for patenting. An operable embodiment had not been built, nor had sufficient plans been made to implement it. Same result under the 2011 Act.

10. She would lose her right to patent due to the on-sale bar in §102(b). A commercial sale of the invention starts the one-year period. If the patent application is not filed within that time, the right to patent is lost. Even a commercial sale to Inventor will count. If Spittoon Builder had breached

the contract and sold the spittoons to a third party, the on-sale bar would still apply. Same result under the 2011 Act.

11. Sparta would not be subject to the on-sale bar. The on-sale bar requires that there be a commercial offer to sell the invention. Here, the invention had not been invented at the time of the offer. Therefore, the one-year time period did not begin to run. This is consistent with the purpose of the on-sale bars (and the statutory bars generally). Once the invention has been put into the public knowledge, by putting it on sale (or by publication or by public use), the inventor must file within a year or lose her right to a patent. This gives an incentive to file quickly, restricts patenting inventions that have been made public, and prevents an inventor from effectively extending the patent term by waiting to file despite use of the invention. It would be illogical to start the one year clock ticking before the invention has even been conceived. The offer to sell could hardly have put the as-yet nonexistent invention into the public knowledge, and the inventor likewise could not use the nonexistent invention. *See Sparton Corp. v. United States*, 399 F.3d 1321, 1324 (Fed. Cir. 2005). Same result under the 2011 Act.

2011 Act Rules Apply to Patent Applications Filed After March 16, 2013

Rather than looking to the date of invention (which can be tricky to determine) and the date one year before the application was filed, the 2011 Act shifted to a simpler, first-to-file system, harmonizing the United States with the patent systems of its many trading partners. An applicant is not entitled to a patent if, on her filing date, another inventor had already filed an application claiming the same invention or the invention had been made public. In the words of the now-streamlined §102, an applicant is not entitled to a patent if "the claimed invention was patented, described in a printed publication, or in public use, on sale, or otherwise available to the public before the effective filing date of the claimed invention" or if a valid application claiming the same invention had already been filed by another inventor.

If two patent applications claim the same invention under the 1952 Act, the dispute must be resolved in a complicated interference proceeding in the USPTO, asking such questions as when each inventor conceived and made the invention and whether they proceeded diligently to file a patent application. Under the 2011 Act, the question is simply who filed first?

The 2011 Act, however, retains a narrower one-year grace period. The applicant is still entitled to a patent if the applicant files no later than one year after the applicant herself (or a joint inventor or someone who got the information from her or a joint inventor) makes the invention public knowledge. So an inventor can establish priority by publicly disclosing the invention, as long as she files her application within a year. Her public disclosure will invalidate applications by other inventors but will not bar hers. So, as some have put it, the 2011 establishes a first-to-file-or-disclose system. So the system gives strong incentives to disclose (to establish priority) and to file early (to avoid anticipation by other's disclosure or applications).

It will take years of experience with the 2011 Act to settle the question, whether it benefited or burdened the classic small inventor as opposed to the corporate research and development sector. First-to-file was, for decades, opposed by inventors and their representatives, keeping the United States as the only major industrial nation to hew to such a policy, on the theory that small inventors would be robbed of the rightful patents by the deeper pockets and more sophisticated legal representatives of corporations, who would lose the race to innovate but win the race to the patent office. Others questioned that theory, reasoning that priority disputes were settled in expensive legal disputes (interference proceedings) before the USPTO or more expensive litigation in the federal courts, both of which favored parties with greater resources. So small inventors, even if theoretically entitled to priority, would be hard-pressed to demonstrate their legal rights. Under the 2011 first-to-file system, a first-in-time inventor can safeguard her rights by quickly filing a patent application. That requires resources, as well as legal representation or acumen, but is a race that does not tilt so heavily toward the side with greater weight in lawyers. So both first-to-file and first-to-invent have characteristics that may benefit or hurt the classic small inventor with a lack of legal and financial resources, as compared to the corporate inventor. It must also be noted that many small inventors have more acumen with respect to patents and patent law than some corporate interests, especially in sectors where patents play a smaller role in the shared knowledge base of an industry. In addition, today's small inventor may be part of larger social, business, or academic networks in which the practicalities of patenting are the subject of discussion and in which sources of information and representation are more readily available, as with the increased interest among universities in establishing technology transfer offices to both facilitate their academic inventors and to create a potential source of revenue and reputational benefits.

The definition of prior art under the 2011 Act is a little different, encompassing inventions "described in a printed publication, or in public use, on sale, or otherwise available to the public before the effective filing date of the claimed invention." That keeps the categories of publications, public use, and on-sale—but adds the general category of "otherwise available to the public." That could broaden the scope of prior art in some respects, by adding information available to the public that did not fall into the other categories. It could also be read to narrow it—if an invention had been published in a very obscure journal, perhaps it would not be deemed "available to the public," if that phrase were read to limit all categories of prior art. Likewise, one could argue that a secret commercial use is not a "public use." Courts, however, may continue to apply underlying policies to encourage both disclosure of commercialized inventions and improvement through experiments on inventions. They may read "public use" to apply to secret, commercial use by the inventor. Likewise, courts may read "public use" not to apply to experimental use. Indeed, the Federal Circuit, in *Helsinn Healthcare S.A. v. Teva Pharm. USA, Inc.*[6] stated that the new clause would be construed with the same meaning as the old clause, on the theory that if Congress intended such a sweeping change in the law, it would have done so more clearly.

The 2011 Act also no longer limits prior art to references within the United States, where the 1952 Act does not encompass public uses or sales outside the United States.

Example

Shorties. On March 29, 2012, Ian invents a method of automatically installing software programs. He files his U.S. patent application on March 20, 2013. Which of the following would be prior art under the 2011 Act in deciding whether the invention was new (and, later in the chapter, whether it was obvious)?

a. An article in Linux Forum, published March 19, 2013.
b. A patent application filed by Squishy on March 19, 2013. She invented her method on March 18, 2013.
c. A patent application filed by Homer on March 21, 2013. He invented his method on March 11, 2011.
d. A post on Ada's well-known blog on March 1, 2013.
e. A blog post by Ian on March 1, 2013.

Explanation

a. The article would be prior art. It was published long after Ian's date of invention, and only the day before his patent application. But under the first-to-file system, that disclosure would count against a subsequent application.
b. Squishy filed first, so would have priority over Ian, even though her date of invention was almost a year after Ian's.
c. The patent application was filed after Ian's, so would not be prior art. Nor would Homer have priority, even though he invented first, because he did not file first. If he had publicly disclosed the invention, that disclosure would have counted against Ian.

---

6. Helsinn Healthcare S.A. v. Teva Pharm. USA, Inc., 855 F.3d 1356 (Fed. Cir. 2017).

  d. A blog post may or may not be a publication, but that does not matter under the 2011 Act, which also includes any other information "otherwise available to the public before the effective filing date of the claimed invention." So Ada's blog post would count.
  e. Ian's blog post would not count against him. Disclosures by the inventor (or by a joint inventor or coming indirectly from the inventor) do not count against the inventor, if made less than a year before the filing date. They count against other inventors, so public disclosure can be used to establish priority.

"USEFUL": THE REQUIREMENT OF UTILITY

To be patentable, an invention must be "useful." 35 U.S.C. §101. This requirement echoes the constitutional provision that Congress may extend patents to promote the "useful Arts." The utility requirement is modest, met if the invention is capable of providing some identifiable benefit. The benefit need not be socially beneficial. An invention whose purpose is to deceive consumers may nonetheless meet the utility requirement. *See Juicy Whip v. Orange Bang*, 185 F.3d 1364 (Fed. Cir. 1999). But the benefit must be functional in nature. Utility is not met if the invention has only aesthetic or descriptive qualities.

To have utility, an invention must work. This does not mean that the invention works efficiently, or better than other products on the market, or even safely. Rather, the invention must be operable: capable of fulfilling its described function. Accordingly, this requirement is not difficult for many applicants to meet. It bars a patent for something that does not work. It also bars patents for things that cannot work, such as perpetual motion machines, the process of cold fusion, or devices that purportedly produce more energy that they consume. The requirement of specific and substantial utility also prevents inventors evading the utility requirement by thinking up some use for an invention. Otherwise, someone seeking a patent on a nonfunctioning time machine could meet the utility requirement by stating that the machine could be used as landfill. PTO Final Examiner Guidelines on Utility Requirement, 66 Fed. Reg. 1092.

The benefit must be specific, substantial, and practical. In *Brenner v. Manson*, 383 U.S. 519 (1966), the applicant claimed a process to produce a chemical compound, a steroid. Similar steroids had proven effective in inhibiting tumors in mice, and the inventor hoped that this steroid would also have that effect. But no testing had been done to determine whether the steroid in question had that effect. Moreover, with that class of steroids, effects were unpredictable; similar compounds were not necessarily likely

303

to have similar effects. The utility requirement was not met by showing that the steroid might inhibit tumors; substantial likelihood would be necessary. It was not sufficient that the compound was worthy of further scientific investigation. Nor was the process to produce the steroid useful since it produced a product without utility.

Allowing patents on inventions without a showing of specific utility represents a hazard. A patent grants a broad array of exclusive rights. To give one inventor rights in a product without showing a specific benefit could prevent others from discovering such specific benefits.

Specific utility is more likely to be an issue in fields like biotechnology and chemistry. Recall that the statutory definition of "invention" includes "invention or discovery." 35 U.S.C. §100(a). Researchers in biotechnology and chemistry often identify something before they can show a specific beneficial use for it. Courts do not require, for example, that the inventor show a product can treat disease in humans; it is enough to show that it has some pharmacological activity in the laboratory. But simply identifying a potentially useful product or process, as in *Brenner*, is insufficient.

For researchers, there can be real conflict between the requirements that the invention be new and that it have specific utility. Suppose Scientist develops a nano-scale modulator, which can convert light into signals for computing purposes. The modulator has no commercial application, nor can it yet be put to use in a circuit (other technical obstacles remain). It may not yet meet the utility requirement—or maybe it does, because it does act as a modulator, albeit one with no use other than demonstrating that it can be done. If Scientist files a patent application, it may be denied (or if a patent issues, the patent held invalid) for failure to meet the utility requirement. But if Scientist waits a few years until the modulator is ready for commercial application, she may have lost the right to patent if more than one year has passed since the invention was published or put into public use. So the tension between patentable applications and nonpatentable scientific discoveries shows up again, in the conflict between utility (wait until it is ready for filing) and novelty/loss of right (file before it's too late).

Examples

1. *Go outside and play.* Maya develops a video game, Frugger. The gamer guides Frugger through a garden, over streams, up stairs, all to find little frogs, eat butterflies, and amass points. Maya suspects that the game helps develop hand-eye coordination, timing, and logical thinking, but she has no evidence of that. All she knows is that some kids like to play the game. Does her invention meet the utility requirement?

2. *Worse mousetrap.* Orbur, in his spare time at the bike shop, invents a new mousetrap. His invention is an ingenious combination of sprockets,

chains, mirrors, and wire. He tests the mousetrap over a period of months. It works—just not very well. The typical mousetrap from Home Depot is far cheaper and more effective. Does Orbur's invention meet the utility requirement?

3. *Untitled.* Artist builds a beautiful sculpture. It serves no functional purpose, but its beauty inspires all who see it. Artist seeks to patent the sculpture. Does it have the requisite utility?

4. *Untitled Part II.* Bristles makes a painting depicting the landscape around Mt. Shasta. Bristles consults an attorney because she wishes to patent her painting. The attorney informs her that the painting lacks the necessary utility because its inventive aspects are not functional. Bristles argues that the painting provides several benefits. It provides geological and botanical information about the region. As psychologists have documented, viewing pleasing images of nature causes pleasant feelings in those who view them, resulting in lower blood pressure and less stress. Does the painting meet the utility requirement?

5. *Untitled Part III.* Coombs finishes his latest sculpture, an abstract form chipped out of anthracite. Coombs seeks to patent his sculpture but meets rejection for lack of utility. Coombs proceeds to demonstrate that the sculpture has uses beyond its artistic aspect. The hand-sized piece of rock works very well indeed for such mundane functions as a paperweight, a nutcracker, or a doorstop. Does the sculpture have the requisite utility?

6. *First Step.* Vaab seeks a patent for an automobile engine that uses only water as fuel and emits no pollution. The prospect of a world freed from dependence on oil and from auto pollution drives her more than desire for money or fame. But she would like a patent to ensure that the benefits from her invention are not diverted to corporate profits. Vaab has spent years designing, building, and modifying the engine, constantly experimenting along the way. She freely admits that, as yet, the engine does not work. But the potential benefits to humankind easily meet the requirement of utility, she argues. Does her invention have the requisite utility?

7. *Lab work.* Instrument Company invents an Electrospectrobulator, an instrument very useful in investigating the properties of steroid compounds. Does such an invention lack practical utility under *Brenner* because its sole use is for research?

8. *Snookered?* Labster discovers a new steroid compound. Labster hopes that it will have therapeutic properties, in common with other similar compounds. Under *Brenner*, such potential utility does not suffice for patentability, so Labster does not file a patent. But she publishes her results in a

scientific journal while pursuing her research. As she guessed, years later the compound proves to be a highly effective drug. Has she lost her right to a patent?

9. *Gene fragments.* Many researchers are hunting for genes, in organisms from humans to roundworms. Rather than looking for entire genes, Athena isolates and identifies the composition of expressed sequence tags (ESTs), which are essentially portions of genes. When Athena identifies an EST, she knows it can identify some DNA that codes a portion of a gene, although she does not know what function the gene itself serves. Athena applies for patents on several ESTs. ESTs might be used for a number of purposes in research. ESTs could be markers used in mapping the entire genome or in locating other genes; they could be used to measure the amount of genetic activity in a cell; or they could be used to help identify which genes are active in a cell. Athena has not yet used them for any of those purposes. Are the ESTs patentable?

10. Inventor files a patent application on a method of treatment (by administering a drug) for Alzheimer's disease. The method is promising, but at the time of filing the patent application, the applicant cannot show efficacy of the drug, through either in vitro test results or animal test results. Inventor can make a good argument, however, that it is likely the drug works. Does Inventor meet the utility requirement?

Explanations

1. Maya's invention does meet the utility requirement. The invention need not be socially beneficial or praiseworthy. It need only provide some identifiable benefit. The game works as a game, and that is sufficient. Many patented inventions provide dubious social benefits.

2. Orbur's mousetrap meets the utility requirement. It provides an identifiable benefit—it works to catch mice. An invention need not be an improvement on previous technology; to be patentable, it need only be new and useful. By the same token, Orbur's patent likely does not have much commercial value.

3. The sculpture does not have the requisite utility. Aesthetic appeal alone does not meet the requirement of utility. By contrast, a process for making sculptures would have the requisite utility because it would have a functional aspect.

4. The painting lacks the requisite utility. It may provide geological and botanical information, in addition to its purely aesthetic appeal. But purely descriptive material likewise lacks the necessary functionality

for utility. Likewise, the utility requirement is not met by showing that pleasing paintings in general have beneficial effects on their viewers. Bristles has not invented the painting, rather only made a new painting. Accordingly, the utility of her invention is purely aesthetic. And aesthetic appeal does not meet the utility requirement (even if aesthetic qualities serve functional roles in general).

5. Coombs's sculpture also fails to meet the utility requirement. The piece of rock can indeed be used as a paperweight, a nutcracker, or a doorstop, but Coombs is not claiming a paperweight, nutcracker, or doorstop as his invention. The invention must have specific utility, meaning that the utility is related to the claimed inventive aspects. His sculpture's novelty lies in its function as a sculpture, not as a weight or tool.

6. Vaab's invention does not have the requisite utility. One aspect of utility is that the invention must be operable, and her engine does not work.

7. The Electrospectrobulator does meet the utility requirement, even if its only use is in research laboratories. The compound in *Brenner* was useful only as a *subject* of research, whereas the device here is used to conduct research.

8. Labster has lost her right to a patent. When the invention had been published more than a year before the patent application was filed, §102(b) provides that the applicant is not entitled to a patent. This example illustrates a tension between the utility requirement and the statutory bars. In some areas of scientific research, there is likely to be a significant time period between a scientific advance and the practical application of the advance. A researcher may be forced to choose between publishing her results (and thereby contributing to the public store of scientific knowledge) and keeping them under wraps (to preserve patent rights).

9. Athena has not shown the necessary "specific and substantial" utility. *See* In re Fisher, 421 F.3d 1365 (Fed. Cir. 2005). She has identified a number of potential uses of the ESTs. But she has not identified any specific use with a substantial utility. Like the process claimed in *Brenner*, the ESTs are "worthy of further scientific investigation" but do not yet have any specifically identified benefit. As the *Fisher* court put it, granting a patent for the claimed ESTs "would amount to a hunting license because the claimed ESTs can be used only to gain further information about the underlying genes and the proteins encoded for by those genes. The claimed ESTs themselves are not an end of Fisher's research effort, but only tools to be used along the way in the search for a practical utility."

10. No. Utility requires a specific showing, not just analytic reasoning. *Janssen Pharmaceutica v. Teva*, 583 F.3d 1317 (Fed. Cir. 2009).

NONOBVIOUSNESS

The patent statute bars patents for obvious inventions:

> A patent may not be obtained though the invention is not identically disclosed or described as set forth in section 102 of this title, if the differences between the subject matter sought to be patented and the prior art are such that the subject matter as a whole would have been obvious at the time the invention was made to a person having ordinary skill in the art to which said subject matter pertains.

35 U.S.C. §103(a). The requirement of nonobviousness reflects the strong set of exclusive rights that patent law grants. The patent holder has the right to exclude others from making, using, offering to sell, selling, or importing her invention. To get such strong protection, a patent applicant has to meet high procedural and substantive standards. The nonobviousness requirement is often considered the core requirement of patentability—it has been called the "ultimate condition of patentability." An inventor is not entitled to a patent if her invention would have been obvious to someone working in the field, if that person took into account all the "prior art" (everything in relevant fields that had been published, in public use, and so on).

Obviousness is an issue that frequently arises in patent litigation. Sued for infringement of Curie's patent on a pencil with a spinaltapical eraser, defendant will argue that the Curie's patent is invalid as obvious. Most often, defendant will produce an element of prior art that the patent office had not considered in granting the patent. Defendant will produce an article from Pencil Technology (dated before Curie's date of invention) disclosing an eraser with ten sides, and argue that an 11-sided eraser would have been obvious. Or defendant will produce an 11-sided sander, and argue that it would be obvious to use the same shape on an eraser.

The Supreme Court case of *Graham v. John Deere Co.*, 383 U.S. 1 (1966), sets forth the nonobviousness analysis:

1. The scope and content of the prior art are to be determined.
2. Differences between the prior art and the claims at issue are to be ascertained.
3. The level of ordinary skill in the pertinent is determined.
4. The obviousness or nonobviousness of the subject matter is determined by looking to those three determinations, and also to such secondary considerations as commercial success, long-felt but unsolved needs, failure of others, and so on.

The Scope and Content of the Prior Art

An invention is not patentable if it is obvious in light of the "prior art" (relevant material that has been published or in public use, and so on). Section 103 does not identify the "prior art" that courts should consider in deciding whether an invention is obvious. Courts look to the categories of prior art identified in 35 U.S.C. §102. Here there will be a difference between the 1952 Act cases (governing applications filed before March 17, 2013) and the 2011 Act (governing subsequent applications). Under the 1952 Act's first-to-invent system, one could argue that not all §102 prior art should be used for obviousness analysis. Section 103(a) of the 1952 Act asks whether the invention would have been obvious "*at the time the invention was made* to a person having ordinary skill in the art" (italics added). Several categories of §102 prior art would not have been available to such a person at that time. But courts have consistently held that all §102 prior art potentially qualifies as §103 prior art. So an article published after the date of invention but more than one year before the application would qualify as prior art. Under the 2011 Act's first to file system, prior art is simpler (and broader) because it includes all references before the date of filing (except disclosures stemming from the inventor, less than one year before filing).

Prior art may be harder to find in some areas. The work in a particular area of chemistry or civil engineering may be well-documented and accessible to those in the field. A practical problem of software patents and business methods, compared to more traditional categories, springs from their abstract nature. A new algorithm is likely to have applications in many fields. A method of sorting data may be useful in genetics, in business applications, and in astronomy. In addition, innovations are often not published, even if they are put into public use. The new sorting algorithm may be used in software without ever publishing the software to others in the field. This means that prior art in software is often difficult to locate, because it is spread across a diverse field of endeavor and buried in program code.

But to qualify as prior art for §103, the reference must not fall only within the §102 categories, it must also be "reasonably pertinent" to the invention. The scope of prior art for obviousness under §103 is restricted in a way that §102 prior art is not. Obviousness is to be judged from the point of view of "a person having ordinary skill in the art." 35 U.S.C. §103(a). Accordingly, only prior art that is "reasonably pertinent" to the invention is considered under §103. To determine whether references fall within the relevant prior art, an examiner first looks at the nature of the problem facing the inventor. Then, he asks whether the reference falls "within the field of the inventor's endeavor." *See, e.g., In re Paulsen*, 30 F.3d 1475, 1481 (Fed. Cir. 1994). If not, the examiner asks whether the reference is "*reasonably pertinent* to the particular problem with which the inventor is involved." *Id.* For example, the claimed invention in *Paulsen*, was a "clam shell" case for a portable computer. Obviousness was judged not just on the basis of previous work on computers, but looking to references in such areas as housings, hinges, latches, and springs, such as design of cabinets and washing machines. The problems facing the computer designer were similar to those faced by designers of cabinets and washing machines: connecting and securing the housing while meeting specified size and functionality constraints. Likewise, toothbrush technology is relevant to a hairbrush invention, because the two are within the same broad field of endeavor. *See In re Bigio*, 381 F.3d 1320, 1325 (Fed. Cir. 2004).

Differences Between the Prior Art and the Claims at Issue

The next step in the nonobviousness analysis is to identify the differences between the prior art and the inventor's claimed invention. Some differences must exist, or the invention would not even be novel, let alone nonobvious. The differences could be of two types. First, the invention may contain elements that do not appear anywhere in the prior art. In this case, the obviousness question becomes whether adding the missing elements would have been obvious to a person skilled in the relevant art. Second, all of the elements of the claimed invention may already exist in the prior art. But they may not all appear in a single reference. So the obviousness question is whether it was obvious to combine the references to solve the particular problem the inventor was working on. Most obviousness issues fall into this second category. As courts have noted, almost every invention is a combination of existing elements.

The Level of Ordinary Skill in the Pertinent Art

An invention is not patentable if it would have been obvious—but obvious to whom? Albert Einstein worked as a patent examiner for several years early in his career. Should a modern Einstein working in the USPTO reject every application he sees on the grounds it would have been obvious to him?

Obviousness is judged from the point of view of "a person having ordinary skill in the art to which the subject matter pertains." 35 U.S.C. §103(a). Several factors are relevant to determining the ordinary level of skill in the art:

1. the types of problems encountered in the art;
2. the prior art solutions to those problems;
3. the rapidity with which innovations are made;
4. the sophistication of the technology; and
5. the educational level of active workers in the field.

See Ruiz v. A. B. Chance Co., 234 F.3d 654 (Fed. Cir. 2000). The skill of the *actual* inventor is not relevant to the obviousness analysis. The question is whether the invention would have been obvious to a person having ordinary skill in the art. So an invention may have been obvious to the actual inventor (because she was superintelligent or had much more knowledge than the typical worker in that field) but would not be obvious for purposes of patent law. Likewise, the actual inventor may have a lower level of skill than the hypothetical person with ordinary skill. She may have been new to the subject area or been very young. So while the invention might have taken tremendous insight on her part, it would have been obvious to one with ordinary skill in the art.

Obvious or Not?

After determining the scope and content of the prior art, how it differs from the claims at issue, and the relevant level of skill, the question whether the invention was prima facie obvious can be initially decided. But how does one decide whether something is obvious? Even if the invention is quite different from the prior art, it may be obvious. If one took an existing business method and simply translated it to online commerce, that could be obvious. Likewise, an incremental difference from the prior art may not be obvious.

In *KSR Intl. Co. v. Teleflex Inc.*, 550 U.S. 398 (2007) the Supreme Court emphasized that the "diversity of inventive pursuits and of modern technology" required a flexible approach to nonobviousness. Courts may consider not just the specific disclosures in the prior art, but also the effects of market demand, and the likely inferences that someone skilled in the art might make. An invention is obvious if all the elements of the invention and a reason to combine them are known. It may also be obvious if the innovation was likely to occur in the ordinary course of events, given not just technical considerations but also market demand and the responsiveness of innovators to such incentives: As the Court put it, "A person of ordinary skill is also a person of ordinary creativity, not an automaton." Under this approach, the expansion of patent subject matter into software and business methods receives some degree of safeguard. The prior art in such areas may not be as readily cataloged and published as in established and bounded disciplines, but the courts and the USPTO no longer are as dependent on identifying suggestions in the prior art. Rather, *KSR* gives leeway for courts (with guidance, where appropriate, for expert witnesses or even court-appointed specialists) to consider the nonobviousness issue in a broader context. *KSR* held that it was obvious to use an electronic sensor on a gas pedal (in the place of existing mechanical devices), where "there existed a marketplace that created a strong incentive to convert mechanical pedals to electronic pedals, and the prior art taught a number of methods for achieving this advance." In considering obviousness, however, a court must avoid the hazard of hindsight. Many insights appear obvious in hindsight.

After considering the technical aspects of the invention, *Graham* counsels consideration of "economic and motivational" issues. They can rebut a prima facie finding of obviousness based on the technical factors discussed above. Courts look to such factors as the following:

1. *Commercial success*: If buyers choose one product over others, the reason may be that the seller invented something that ordinary sellers would not have invented.
2. *Long-felt but unsolved need*: If an opportunity presented itself but was not taken, the inference is that the solution was not obvious.
3. *Failure of others*: If many have tried and failed, it is likely that the solution was not obvious.
4. *Copying (the sincerest form of flattery)*: This is especially probative when others failed to solve the same problem and finally resorted to copying.
5. *Unexpected results or properties of claimed invention*: If the results were unexpected, the invention likely was not obvious.
6. *Skepticism of experts*: When experts in the field did not see a solution, the solution likely was not obvious.
7. *Licensing and acquiescence by others*: If competitors licensed the patent rather than attempting to solve the problem themselves or denying the validity of the patent, it suggests that the solution was not obvious to them.
8. *Adoption by the industry*: If the industry as a whole adopted the invention as the industry standard, maybe it was better than others.

Even though an invention may seem obvious after considering the technical issues, a strong showing of secondary considerations may show the invention was nonobvious. However, obviousness may be so clearly established by the prior art analysis that the secondary considerations cannot change the result.

To be evidence of nonobviousness, such evidence must have a connection (a "nexus") to the claimed inventive aspects of a product. A new sports drink may sell well because a great basketball player endorses it, not because of its particular composition. If the market leader introduces a new pen, it may sell well because of the seller's trademark. Simply showing strong sales does not show commercial success arising out of the claimed inventive features of the new pen. *See Pentec Inc. v. Graphic Controls Corp.*, 776 F.2d 309 (Fed. Cir. 1985). The same is true of the other types of secondary considerations. Other competitors might agree to licenses for other reasons than access to the patented technology. *See In re GPAC*, 57 F.3d 1573 (Fed.

Cir. 1995). An expert might have shown skepticism due to doubts about the inventor's ability, rather than an appraisal of the particular problem.

Even a very low-tech invention may still be held nonobvious, and so patentable. The use of foam straps for sandals was held to be a patentable invention, largely because previous work in the field "taught away" from foam straps. *Crocs, Inc. v. U.S. Intl. Trade Commn.*, 598 F.3d 1294 (Fed. Cir. 2010) Straps had been used on shoes, and foam had been used in shoes, but the inelastic nature of foam made it seem unsuitable as a strap material. By contrast, taking old technology and putting it online is obvious. *See Western Union Co. v. MoneyGram Payment Sys. Inc.*, 626 F.3d 1361 (Fed. Cir. 2011) (holding it obvious to simply adapt funds transfer system using telephones and faxes to an internet implementation).

Examples

1. *Prior art under §103?* Inventor files a patent application on her "Ambulatory Sleeping Bag." Which of the following items are prior art under the 1952 Act? Under the 2011 Act?
   a. A patent on a "Sleeping Bag with Leg Holes for Escaping Bears," issued prior to Inventor's date of invention.
   b. An application filed before Inventor's date of invention (but still pending and confidential on Inventor's date of invention) for a patent subsequently issued on "A Combination Sleeping Bag and Three-Leg Race Sack."
   c. A patent on a "Method of Growing Rice in Arctic Climates" issued prior to Inventor's date of invention.
   d. Before Inventor's date of invention, a friend told Inventor that an "Ambulatory Sleeping Bag" would be a great idea and suggested some general ways to address the various design problems, without communicating the invention as later conceived by Inventor.
   e. After Inventor's date of invention, but more than a year before Inventor filed her patent application, camping stores in the United States sold an "Upright Sleeping Bag."

2. *Made public?* Wei develops a nice piece of software, the Web browser Viola. Wei demonstrates Viola to two employees of Sun Microsystems. Wei freely offers the information, without placing any obligation of secrecy or limits on use. More than one year after that date, Eolas files a patent application on a hypermedia method which allows use of a Web browser in a fully interactive environment. Eolas subsequently files an infringement action, alleging that Microsoft's Internet Explorer infringes Eolas's hypermedia patent. Microsoft argues that the patent is invalid, because the invention was obvious. In deciding whether the invention was obvious, will the Viola browser count as prior art?

3. *I never would have thought of that.* Inventor seeks to patent his "Device for Restraining Geese," which is an improvement on a prior goose restrainer. Ample evidence shows that the invention would have been obvious to a typical worker in the field. But both Inventor and the inventor of the previous device testify credibly that the improvement was not obvious to Inventor. He did not normally work in the field but had taken on the problem as part of a volunteer program. He was not familiar with either the practical aspects of goose control or with the technology in the field. Accordingly, the problem was a very difficult one for him. But he stepped up and designed a solution. Does the fact that the invention was in fact far from obvious to Inventor meet the nonobviousness requirement?

   To reverse the facts: Suppose Inventor was the foremost expert in goose control and related technology. He admits that the solution was instantly obvious to him. But the evidence establishes that it would not have been obvious to one skilled in the relevant art. Would that establish that the invention was obvious?

4. *Rocket scientists.* Inventor patents a new type of satellite. When Inventor sues Competitor for building an identical satellite, Competitor argues the patent is invalid for obviousness. The claimed invention is a combination of elements that already appear in various references in the relevant prior art. Nothing in the prior art suggests combining the references. But there is a very high level of skill in the relevant art of satellite engineering. Competitor argues that such a high skill level means that one skilled in the art would find any combination of references to be obvious. Should the court accept that argument?

5. *Home run?* Pitchers in baseball throw several types of pitches: fastballs, curveballs, change-ups, knuckleballs, split-finger fastballs, and more. For each type of pitch, a pitcher uses a different grip on the baseball. In 2002, Lobo, an experienced pitching coach, devises and makes instructional baseballs for teaching young pitchers the appropriate grips for the various types of pitch. On the surface of each ball is drawn finger shaped outlines. By placing her finger on the outline, a pitcher can learn the correct grip for the pitch that is illustrated. Lobo quickly markets sets of instructional baseballs. The product is an instant success. Coaches and players all over the country buy up the balls as fast as they are produced. A maker of instructional sports equipment signs a contract, getting licensing rights in exchange for a nice fee to Lobo.

   In the same year, 2002, Lobo files a patent application, claiming his instructional baseball. A patent is issued. Shortly thereafter, Cobb, a major sports equipment maker, begins making and selling balls that fall within Lobo's patent claim. Others also copy the invention. When Lobo sues for infringement, Cobb argues that the patent is invalid because the invention was obvious. There are four references cited as prior art (none of which Lobo had known about):

a. A dummy used for training students in CPR. The dummy had outlines of fingers drawn in various places to show students where to place their hands when performing the different tasks in CPR. There were finger outlines drawn over the heart, over the carotid artery, on the chin, on the nose, and on the stomach. The dummy was in public use by 1987.

b. An instructional football. The football had outlines of fingers drawn on it to show players the correct way to grip the football for various purposes: running, throwing, snapping. The football was first in public use in 2003.

c. An instructional baseball. The baseball had markings on it for use in teaching students to throw knuckleballs. The knuckleball is different than most pitches because the pitcher grips the ball with just his fingertips, rather than his entire fingers. Five circles were drawn on the ball to indicate where the pitcher's fingertips should be when he gripped the ball to throw it. The ball has been sold publicly since 1992.

d. An instructional book entitled *Fundamental Baseball Techniques*. The book explains how to perform all the common acts in baseball, including pitching. The book has text describing all the commonly known pitches, with photographs for each showing a pitcher's hand gripping the ball correctly. The book also has drawings showing the correct grips. Each drawing shows a pitcher's hand with the fingers slightly above the surface of the baseball and with dotted lines leading to outlines drawn on the baseball showing the correct placement of the fingers for each grip. The book was published in 1998.

e. relevant art is instructional sports material. The relevant level of skill is that of someone with years of experience playing and coaching sports. This level of ordinary skill reflects little formal academic instruction on the subject, but many years of learning from other coaches and players, in various setting such as games, practices, and clinics.

Was the instructional baseball obvious under the *Graham* analysis?

6. *Joint effort.* Nick and Tony, plumbing engineers, have both signed agreements assigning patent rights in their work to their employer, Super Plumbing. Nick spends considerable effort trying to develop a soaperator. Although Nick makes great progress, he does not quite develop the desired invention. Tony, however, continues the quest, relying in part on Nick's work. Tony finally develops a soaperator, "A Device for Aerating Water and Providing Soap for Hand Washing." In deciding whether Tony's invention was nonobvious, does Nick's work count as prior art?

7. In deciding if a board game invention is obvious, should a court consider electronic versions of similar games?

8. *Doing the impossible?* Can an invention be deemed obvious, where it combines features from two devices that could not themselves be combined?

Explanations

1. a. Yes, under both Acts. This is classic §103 prior art. It qualifies under §102 (both §102(a) and §102(b)) and is clearly relevant to the problem at hand.
   b. Yes, under the 1952 Act. Inventor might argue that such prior art should not be considered. If the issue is whether Inventor's invention was obvious at the time of invention, it seems unfair to consider prior art that was not accessible to the public (and to Inventor). But courts have held that all §102 prior art is potentially available (provided it is relevant). This would qualify under §102(e) ("secret prior art") and is clearly relevant. Note that there would be a different result if the disclosure was in a patent application that did not result in an issued patent.

   Under the 2011 Act (assuming it did not claim the same invention), it could be deemed not available to the public if it had not been published *at the time of Inventor's filing date*.
   c. No, under both Acts. It qualifies under §102 as a previous patent but it is not relevant. Note the difference here. Such a reference could be used under §102 to destroy novelty or act as a statutory bar or any other §102 purpose, even if it was not relevant to the problem at hand. But to qualify as §103 prior art, it must be §102 prior art that is also pertinent to the problem facing the inventor.
   d. Yes, under the 1952 Act, this is prior art under §102(f) ("derivation"). The friend did not conceive the invention, so §102(f) does not bar a patent. But the communication itself does qualify as prior art under §102(f), so Inventor would be entitled to a patent only if her invention were nonobvious, even taking friend's information into consideration. Same result under the 2011 Act (unless that were read not to apply to disclosures not available to the public).
   e. Yes, under both Acts. This is prior art, for the 1952 Act, under §102(b) (also known as 102(b)/103 prior art). Inventor might again find it unfair. If the question is whether the invention was obvious at the time she invented it, shouldn't later coming technology be excluded? Again, courts consider all §102 prior art on the theory that the ultimate question is to bar patents for incremental, obvious improvements in technology.

   For the 2011 Act, the question is simpler. Public uses and sales before the date of filing are prior art.

2. The Viola browser did count as prior art. *See Eolas Technologies, Inc. v. Microsoft Corp.*, 399 F.3d 1325, 1334 (Fed. Cir. 2005). A reference will be used as prior art if it fits any of the §102 categories, and this one is public use under §102(b). A disclosing public use need not be widely public (again, some might read the 2011 Act not to apply to disclosures not available to the public). Rather, a demonstration of software without any limitation, restriction, or obligation of secrecy constitutes public use. So note that the Viola browser will be included, without any requirement that Eolas actually knew of the Viola browser when Eolas conceived its own invention.

3. The invention would have been obvious to one skilled in the art, so it is not patentable. The inventors' testimony would be insufficient to show that the invention was not obvious. The question is whether the invention would have been obvious to one skilled in the relevant art, not whether it was actually obvious to the inventor or anyone else. Inventor was not skilled in the relevant art. To the contrary, she was a novice in the field. So even if the invention was quite an achievement for the actual inventor, it may not be patentable.

   In the reverse situation, an invention may be patentable even if it was actually obvious to the inventor. If it would not have been obvious to one skilled in the art, it satisfies §103. The fact that it actually was obvious will not render it unpatentable.

4. The court should not accept that argument. The case law provides that there must be something in the prior art to suggest combining the references, or at least something such as market forces that would make the invention likely. For such a sophisticated combination invention to be obvious, there must be a teaching, suggestion, or motivation in the prior art. This remains true even if the level of skill in the art is very high. Otherwise, almost any invention in the field would be deemed obvious because almost all inventions are combination inventions.

5. The invention probably would not be held obvious. *Cf. McGinley v. Franklin Sports*, 262 F.3d 1339 (Fed. Cir. 2001).

   Of the four references, only *c* and *d* would qualify as pertinent prior art and therefore be considered in the obviousness determination. Reference *a* falls well outside the relevant art (instructional sports material). Nor would it qualify as analogous art because CPR dummy design deals with a quite different set of problems than instructional sports material. Reference *b* does not qualify as prior art. It was not in public use at the date of invention or by a date a year before the filing of the application, so does not qualify under the 1952 Act. Nor (if the dates were different) would it qualify for 2011 Act purposes (if we added, say, 10 years to all dates). It was in public use only after the application was filed, so would not be considered. Only references that would qualify as prior art under one of the §102 categories may qualify as prior art for §103 obviousness determinations. Generally, they would be references with effective dates either before the date of invention (because such references would be prior art for novelty determinations) or before a date one year prior to the filing of the patent application (because these would be prior art for statutory bar determinations). A reference with an effective date after the date the application was filed would not be prior art.

The differences between the prior art and the invention are (1) that the baseballs used finger outlines, rather than just circles showing the fingertip placement; (2) that the baseballs showed the grips for all the pitches, not just for one pitch that was unusual in that it involved holding the ball by the fingertips; and (3) that the finger placements were actually drawn on the ball to be used by the pitcher's hand, as opposed to outlines depicted on a drawing of a ball in the book to be viewed by the reader.

The obviousness determination then depends on whether those differences were obvious. The invention can be viewed as a combination invention, combining the depiction of the grip on the ball itself (in the knuckleball instructional ball) with the depiction of the finger outlines (from the drawings in the instructional book). For this combination to be obvious, there must be a suggestion in the prior art to combine those elements. Nothing in the prior art seems to contain such a suggestion.

The secondary considerations also favor a determination that the invention was not obvious. The balls were immediately adopted by numerous coaches. This commercial success suggests that the invention was not obvious. The defendant and others copied the balls, which also suggests that the invention was not obvious. A major manufacturer agreed to license the invention, which also weighs against obviousness. None of the other secondary considerations appears relevant, but those weigh strongly in favor of nonobviousness.

Note the importance of defining the prior art. If reference b, the instructional football, had been in public use earlier and so counted as prior art, the result would likely be different.

6. Nick's work would not count as prior art, in deciding if Tony's invention was nonobvious (and hence patentable). Under §103, obviousness will not bar a patent based on such prior art subject matter developed by persons working as fellow employees or on a joint research project, provided appropriate invention assignments have been executed.

7. Yes, they would be analogous technology, included within the obviousness analysis. *See Innovention Toys LLC v. MGA Entertainment Inc.*, 637 F.3d 1314 (Fed. Cir. 2011).

8. The court reasoned that the impossibility argument was a red herring. It could be obvious to combine *features* from the two devices to make the invention.[7]

---

7. Allied Erecting & Dismantling Co. v. Genesis Attachments, LLC, 825 F.3d 1373, 1381 (Fed. Cir. 2016).

CHAPTER 8

Obtaining Protection, Ownership, and Licensing: Of Hoops and Pitfalls

Copyright is automatic. As soon as Roth puts his novel on paper or in his computer, he has a copyright. Patent, by contrast, requires a conscious choice to apply (and disclose the invention to the world), along with considerable fees and effort. To patent or not to patent, that is the question. An inventor must file an application to receive a patent on an invention. The advantage is that the inventor will have certain exclusive rights to make, use, and sell the invention (if she gets the patent). The inventor (or whoever owns the patent rights, such as her employer or investors) may be able to get commercial advantages, along with the reputation benefits. Competitors or joint venturers may cross-license technology. Beyond market concerns, patents are flaunted on resumes, tenure applications and as evidence of a product's qualities (the Galmont spa advertised its treatments with "patented bio-degradable heat technology." On the other hand, applying for a patent is costly (from thousands to tens of thousands of dollars), requires publicly disclosing how to make and use the invention (some inventors prefer to keep their work secret from competitors — rivals in commerce, science, or otherwise), is uncertain (the application may not be allowed), and takes time (it can take several years for the patent to issue).

Some inventors and companies forgo patent protection and use the invention as a trade secret. If Manufacturing Co. develops a new method of making microchips or potato chips, it may simply use the process as a trade secret. That keeps it away from the knowledge of competitors (if Manufacturing Co. can keep its employees from disclosing it and competitors cannot figure out the process by reverse engineering the chips). SpaceX reportedly does not patent its rocketry inventions, thinking such patents impossible to enforce against foreign competition, while giving them the blueprints to its technology. It saves the fees of the U.S. Patent and Trademark Office (USPTO) and lawyers. It may last longer (as long as it is useful and secret, as opposed to approximately 17 years for a patent). Likewise, if Software Co. develops a new process for handling supply chain logistics, it may simply keep the software in-house and not seek patent protection. The scope of patent protection for software is particularly uncertain. Whether the process is new and nonobvious may be difficult to assess because who knows what has already been done by others in the software field. Much of the prior art is not easy to obtain.

Other inventors cannot rely on trade secret protection. If Curie sells her pencil with a spinaltapical eraser attached, potential competitors will have the information they need to copy it. A process for making a pencil could be kept confidential, but a product on the market is public. Even inventions that could be trade secrets may be patented. If Manufacturing Co. patents its process, it no longer need worry that employees or industrial spies will make it public. Manufacturing Co. will also be free to tout the process to investors, analysts, and the world.

If Curie seeks a patent, she must submit an application that describes the invention and how to make it. She must also claim the invention. Claim drafting involves key choices. Curie might prefer a broad claim: "I claim a pencil with a spinaltapical eraser." Anyone that made, used, or sold such an eraser would be potentially infringing her patent. But she might also prefer a slightly narrower claim: "I claim a pencil with a spinaltapical eraser made of plubundum." That is more likely to be patentable. If someone has already sold a pencil with a spinaltapical eraser, the first claim is not novel but the second one is. The second claim, however, would only be infringed by pencils with spinaltapical, plubundum erasers. A broader claim gives more patent protection, but a narrower claim is more likely to be patentable. But Curie need not choose between the two. Rather, she can (and most applicants do) submit an application with multiple claims, each narrower than the last.

THE PATENT APPLICATION AND EXAMINATION

Patent prosecution (the process of seeking a patent from the USPTO) looms large in patent law. First, an inventor has no exclusive rights until the USPTO issues a patent. One gets a copyright by creating a work and trademark by using the mark; registration is optional for copyrights and trademarks. A patent requires an application to the USPTO and an argument persuading it to issue a patent. Second, the scope of rights depends on the inventor's application and the course of prosecution. How the applicant drafts and amends the application (especially the claims) will determine whether she is entitled to a patent and (if a patent issues) how broad her rights to enforce the patent will be.

Inventor perfects her new organic sports drink, Zoop. Zoop is a combination of various natural nutrients, which Inventor believes is the optimum drink for marathoners. Cf. U.S. Patent No. 5,780,094 (issued July 14, 1998), for a "Sports Drink." Now Inventor wonders if she could patent Zoop and if so, what benefits that would bring her.

Someone who invents or discovers a new and useful process or product is entitled to a patent, subject to the conditions and requirements of the patent statute. 35 U.S.C. §101. Inventor may prosecute the patent application herself or be represented by someone licensed to practice before the USPTO, a patent lawyer or patent agent. Inventor may seek to patent a process (such as the method for making Zoop or the method of using Zoop to treat a human) or a product (such as Zoop itself or some ingredient of Zoop) or both. The inventor must file a patent application with the USPTO. The USPTO examines the application to determine whether a patent should issue. The examination is performed by an examiner who works in the subject matter area of the invention.

The requirements for the patent application are much more demanding than those for copyright or trademark registration, reflecting the higher requirements for patentability. The patent application must contain a "specification" (including a written description of the invention and claims), 35 U.S.C. §112;[1] drawings, if necessary to understand the invention (and frequently used even when not necessary), 35 U.S.C. §112; and an oath by the applicant, together with the fee, 35 U.S.C. §113. The USPTO may require the applicant to submit a model or, for compositions of matter, specimens of ingredients for inspection or experiment. 35 U.S.C. §114.[2] The regulations of the USPTO further prescribe a preferred format for the application.

The invention must be within the subject of patents. As discussed in previous chapters, some subject matter is not patentable, such as laws of nature, physical phenomena, and abstract ideas. The invention must also be novel, useful, and nonobvious in light of the prior art (the publicly accessible sources of knowledge pertinent to the invention, such as patents,

---

1. The statute permits a "provisional application" that does not require patent claims and has a lower fee. The provisional application may subsequently be converted into a nonprovisional application with claims. The benefit of a provisional application is that it allows the applicant to use the provisional filing date as its filing date for some purposes. But there are also some hazards. For example, the subsequent claims must be supported by the written description of the invention in the provisional application. *See New Railhead Mfg. v. Vermeer Mfg.*, No. 02-1028 (Fed. Cir. July 30, 2002).

2. It is a rare case where the USPTO performs testing of the invention rather than relying on results of testing submitted by the applicant or on other sources of information.

publications, other products, and processes). Before filing, the applicant should search the prior art. A search attempts to gather the applicable prior art and determine whether the invention is new and nonobvious. A search does not just tell inventor whether to file. The results of a search may be used in drafting the application to meet the requirements of patentability. The application must disclose all material items of prior art known to the inventor. The examiner also makes an independent search of the prior art.

The patent application must describe the invention and set forth claims "particularly pointing out and distinctly claiming the subject matter which the applicant regards as his invention." 35 U.S.C. §112. The claims are the most important part of the application. They ultimately determine whether the invention is patentable. Moreover, if the application issues as a patent, the patent claims will also determine the scope of the inventor's right. So an applicant will need to draft claims with a mind toward both patentability (narrower claims are more likely to be patentable) and enforcement (the broader, the better).

The application filed by the inventor of Zoop might include a product claim such as this:

I claim:

1. A sports drink for marathoners comprising an aqueous solution including Juptose (with a concentration of 0.5 to 5.0% w/v), Merctose (with a concentration of 2.0 to 3.0% w/v), Neptose (with a concentration of 0.7 to 1.4% w/v).

The examination process is ex parte, meaning that persons who might oppose Inventor's application are not made parties to the process or given an opportunity to participate (unlike trademark law, and patent law in some other jurisdictions, which provide for "oppositions"). One check on the lack of an adversary is a duty of candor and good faith. Inventor must disclose to the USPTO all material information that she learns through the search or otherwise. Intentional failure to disclose material references or other "inequitable conduct" can render a patent unenforceable. The inventor is not required to search the prior art, but she must disclose what she knows. Ironically, some lawyers counsel applicants not to read about work in the field, so that they are not required to disclose it to the patent office.

The examination process is also partly confidential. Inventor must disclose her invention to the USPTO but need not disclose it to the public while the application is pending. The USPTO will then publish it if a patent issues. If the application is still pending after 18 months (most are), the USPTO will publish the application, unless one of several exceptions apply. Inventor can prevent publication by simply certifying that she is not seeking a patent in any other country that publishes patent applications. Or she can choose to abandon the application and avoid publication.

The prosecution of an application usually entails several communications between the applicant and the USPTO. The examiner will issue an office action, giving the applicant a preliminary notification of whether the claims will be allowed. If the examiner rejects claims, he must give reasons for the rejections, citing specific prior art references where relevant. There are often several office actions and opportunities to amend the application to overcome the reasons for rejections. In some instances, the examiner must suggest how to amend the claims. If Inventor prosecutes the application herself (rather than being represented by a professional), she may even choose in some cases to have the examiner draft claims on her behalf. The applicant may also meet with the examiner or be permitted to submit other material, such as the results of testing. If the USPTO determines that another applicant or issued patent claims the same invention, an interference proceeding may be declared to determine priority.

A final action will ultimately reject the application or allow a patent issuance (that is, allow some or all of the applicant's claims and issue a patent on payment of the issue fee). If there is a final rejection, the applicant may appeal to the Patent Trial and Appeal Board. If the board upholds the rejection, the applicant may appeal for *de novo* review by the federal district court in the District of Columbia. The applicant is not limited to material considered by the USPTO but may introduce any competent evidence. *Kappos v. Hyatt*, 132 S. Ct. 1690 (2012). The applicant may also choose to appeal directly to the U.S. Court of Appeals for the Federal Circuit (the Federal Circuit), which will consider the appeal on the existing record.

If a patent issues, the amended application, with some small additions and changes, becomes a patent. Inventor (now a "patentee") gains the right to exclude others from making, using, selling, offering to sell, or importing the invention, as defined by the claims of the patent.[3] The patent term is 20 years from the date of filing the application (not from the date the patent issues).

How long does it take? This depends in part on the area of technology. To take some examples from a study, it took about 3.7 years until the first office action (and issuing the patent can take several office actions) in the Fuel Cell and Battery Technology unit of the patent office, 3.6 years for Pharmaceutical Formulations, 3.5 years for Business Methods, down to 1.7 years in Manufacturing Devices. Dennis Crouch, *How Long Do I Wait for a First Office Action?*, Patently-O, http://patentlyo.com (November 8, 2008). The effect of such delays is different in various industries. For a pharmaceutical maker, it may not matter, because going through testing and getting FDA approval may take even longer. For someone in a fast-moving area, like software or communications devices, the patent may come out after the invention has become passé.

---

3. If the application had been published, the patentee has "provisional rights" to receive a reasonable royalty from anyone, even before the patent issued, had actual notice of the application and practiced the identical invention. *See* 35 U.S.C. §154(d)(1).

There are possible post-issuance proceedings. If a defect is found in the patent, the patentee may file an amended application seeking reissue of the patent. Likewise, the statute provides for correction in some cases in which a person was named as inventor or in which an inventor, without deception on her part, was omitted from the application.

The 2011 America Invents Act introduced procedures to challenge the validity of a patent in post-grant proceedings before the USPTO's Patent Trials and Appeals Board. Post-grant challenges in various forms had existed before, but seen relatively little use. The new procedures are subject to a tighter timeline (of some 18 months); have much more limited preclusive effect, which encourages challenges; may look more broadly to prior art; permit more active participation by the challenger; and have more extensive appellate review available.[4] Thousands of such proceedings have been brought, and patent claims invalidated in a substantial number of proceedings. Some argued that only the federal courts, not the USPTO, could invalidate a patent, but the Supreme Court upheld the constitutionality of post-grant challenges. *Oil States Energy Servs., LLC v. Greene's Energy Group, LLC*, 200 L. Ed. 2d 671 (U.S. 2018).

WRITTEN DESCRIPTION REQUIREMENTS

Written Description

The patent application must "contain a written description of the invention" in "clear, concise, and exact terms." 35 U.S.C. §112.[5] The inventor must disclose her invention to the public in definite terms. By describing the invention in the requisite detail, the inventor shows she has in fact succeeded in inventing her claimed invention.

The test of the written description is whether it shows one skilled in the relevant art that the applicant was in possession of the invention at the time the application was filed. The description requires the inventor to mark her trail with "blaze marks" for others to follow. *Purdue Pharma L.P. v. Faulding Inc.*, 230 F.3d 1320 (Fed. Cir. 2000). A description of a genus that could include over 500,000 chemical compounds was not sufficiently definite to support

---

4. *See* Robert P. Merges, Peter S. Menell & Mark A. Lemley, *Intellectual Property in the New Technological Age*, 317-324 (2017 edition) (comparing new post-grant procedures to their forebears).

5. *See also* USPTO, *Guidelines for Examination of Patent Applications Under the 35 U.S.C. Sec. 112, Par. 1 "Written Description" Requirement*, 66 C.F.R. 1099 (2001). The Patent Office regulations provide that the description should describe the background of the invention, summarize the invention, and give a detailed description of the invention.

a claim to one of those compounds. *See In re Ruschig*, 379 F.2d 990 (C.C.P.A. 1967). The inventor must clearly describe the invention, but it does not mean she has to explain how it works or how she developed it. *See Newman v. Quigg*, 877 F.2d 1575 (Fed. Cir. 1989). Indeed, even if the inventor did not know how it works, that would not bar her from a patent.

The written description requirement can be met in several ways. The applicant can describe an actual reduction to practice; if she had made the invention and can describe it, she must be in possession of what she claims. Even if the inventor has not actually made the invention, she can show she was in possession of the claimed invention with words, drawings, sufficiently detailed formulas, or other ways to convey information. The written description requirement is most difficult to meet in areas like biotech and chemistry, where an inventor may be able to make a useful invention before she has determined just how to describe what it is. Such symbolic means may be impracticable to describe some inventions, especially biological material. Accordingly, the Federal Circuit has held that when a written description of biological material is not practical, applicants may meet the written description requirement by depositing a sample in a publicly accessible repository. *See Enzo Biochem v. Gen-Probe*, 296 F.3d 1316 (Fed. Cir. 2002).

The written description requirement also serves to balance the timing issues of patent prosecution. A patent applicant must provide a written description of the invention, as well as claims that define the invention. The applicant may amend the claims during the process of patent prosecution. That way, if the USPTO denies the application because the claims are too broad or otherwise defective, the applicant may amend the claims in order to receive a patent. Otherwise, deserving inventors might be denied patents simply because they did not draft claims that were deemed acceptable. But the ability to amend claims raises some hazards. An applicant may amend claims in order to cover the processes or products of others that became public after the application was filed. At its extreme, submarine patenting involved amending patent applications decades after they were filed, to cover after-developed technology. But less dramatic cases also show the hazards of amending claims.

Centocor filed a patent application on a pharmaceutical, a mouse antibody targeted at treating arthritis. Abbott, a competitor, subsequently marketed a pharmaceutical for treating arthritis, based on a similar human antibody. Centocor amended its patent claims in the pending application to cover human antibodies, obtained a patent, and sued for infringement. A jury awarded $1.67 billion in damages.

The Federal Circuit overturned the award, reasoning that the claims were invalid, as not supported by the written description. *See Centocor Ortho Biotech, Inc. v. Abbott Laboratories*, 636 F.3d 1341 (Fed. Cir. 2011). The written description requirement applies to the application as of the date of application. It therefore acts as a limitation on an applicant's ability to amend the claims during the application. Centocor did not meet the written description requirement for a human antibody by identifying the properties of a mouse antibody in the application, even if it did disclose that the method might subsequently be developed to produce a human antibody. Accordingly, the description did not support the subsequent amendment to the claims in the patent application.

Enablement

"Enablement" requires that the applicant disclose to the public how to make and use the invention, as of the date of the application.

> The application must describe the manner and process of making and using it, in such full, clear, concise, and exact terms as to enable any person skilled in the art to which it pertains, or with which it is most nearly connected, to make and use the same.

35 U.S.C. §112.

The enablement requirement serves three general purposes. First, like the utility requirement, it bars inoperable inventions from patent protection. An inventor might be able to describe her time machine in intricate detail, but if she cannot get it to work, then she won't be able to tell others how to make and use it. For example, a patent application for a cure for baldness did not meet the enablement requirement because it failed to disclose any observations concerning the operation of the active ingredient. In re Cortright, 165 F.3d 1353 (Fed. Cir. 1999). Even if an application discloses a solution to a problem, that may be insufficient. In a case in which an applicant disclosed a mathematically ideal solution to a sorting problem, but only a theoretical way to implement the solution, the claims were not enabled. See National Recovery Technologies v. Magnetic Separation Systems, 166 F.3d 1190 (Fed. Cir. 1999).

Second, the enablement requirement guards against overly broad claims. The classic case for this rule is O'Reilly v. Morse, 56 U.S. 62 (1854). The Supreme Court upheld most of the claims in Morse's patent application for telegraphy inventions (including Morse code and various machines and processes used in telegraphy). Such claims all specifically claimed inventions described in the patent specification. But the Court invalidated a claim for every use of electricity to print symbols at a distance. Such a claim would encompass not just Morse's invention, but any future device that transmitted symbols. In modern terminology, the claim was not "enabled": It did not enable one skilled in the art to make the inventions that fall within its scope. The enablement requirement is key to limiting patent rights to the actual invention, especially for abstract technologies like software and business methods. *See* Stephen McJohn, *Scary Patents*, 7 Nw. J. Tech. & Intell. Prop. 343 (2009).

Third, the enablement requirement serves the disclosure role of patent law. An inventor must not show only that she is "in possession" of the invention, she must also disclose the information necessary for others to make and use the invention. It could be insufficient to disclose steps of a process that require calculations without disclosing information necessary to write software to implement those steps.

Applicants frequently meet the enablement requirement by providing examples that describe how they have practiced the invention. Enablement does not require the applicant to provide every possible piece of information necessary for a person to make and use the invention. A patent application for a rocket need not explain rocket science to explain to the general reader how to make and use the claimed rocketry invention. Rather, the description must enable one skilled in the art to make and use the invention "without undue experimentation." The inventor need not enable the invention as embodied in subsequent commercial applications, even though such applications may fall within the claims of the patent. Indeed, many inventors do not put the invention into its subsequent standard commercial form.

For applications on biological subject matter, the applicant may satisfy the enablement requirement (like the written description requirement) by placing a sample on deposit. Providing public access to the sample enables others to make the invention. Note that access must be given to the USPTO on filing, but access to the public is not necessary until after the patent issues.

Example

Not supported. ALZA files a broad patent claim on a method for using a drug to treat attention deficit and hyperactivity disorder. The patent application does not disclose the method of ascertaining dosage for the full range claimed but does show how to ascertain some dosages. Is ALZA entitled to a patent on the broad claim?

Explanation

No. The enablement requirement requires the applicant to disclose how to make and use the full scope of the claimed invention. In short, the enablement requirement guards against parties claiming more broadly than the invention they have disclosed. It likewise guards against patenting ideas because it requires a broad claim to be supported by description of how to fully make and use the invention.

Best Mode

Not only must the application enable others to practice the invention, it must disclose the inventor's best mode of doing so. Section 112 requires the applicant, in addition to describing the invention and how to use and make it, to "set forth the best mode contemplated by the inventor of carrying out his invention." 35 U.S.C. §112. The purpose of the best mode requirement is to ensure that the inventor fully discloses the practical use of her invention. If she has developed special devices or methods that she considers to be the best way of practicing the invention, she must disclose them, even though they are not claimed as part of the invention. Before 2011, failure to disclose best mode could invalidate a patent. The 2011 Act, however, provided that "the failure to disclose the best mode shall not be a basis on which any claim of a patent may be canceled or held invalid or otherwise unenforceable." So the requirement remains but with little teeth (except for litigation commenced before September 17, 2011).

Examples

1. *Gift horse.* Purple algae are often a problem in swimming pools. They grow in unsightly colonies and, when dead, cause toxic waste. Cabana experiments with various chemicals, seeking one that eliminates purple algae without disturbing the delicate balance of the other additives used to keep pools clean. Cabana tries quartzic, a chemical compound. Quartzic, used at certain levels, works very well indeed. It causes the purple algae to shrivel up and dissolve without leaving any waste. Quartzic is also completely safe for humans and does not interfere with any of the other pool maintenance material. Cabana files a patent application for her "Method of Safely Ridding Pools of Purple Algae." The specification contains an exact description of her method, including the amounts of quartzic to use and how often. Cabana receives a patent. Arch soon begins using Cabana's patented method in his pool maintenance service. Sued for infringement, Arch argues that Cabana's patent is invalid because she failed to explain how her method works. Cabana admits that she actually has no idea how quartzic kills purple algae or why it leaves their remains in such a benign state. All she knows is what she detailed in her application: what her method is and the fact that it works. Did she fail to give an adequate written description?

2. *Pig in a poke.* Harrow, using genetic engineering, removes a gene from the cocoa plant and introduces it into a yeast. The genetically engineered yeast proves especially useful in producing thick, rich stout beer. Harrow files a patent application claiming his new yeast. His application describes as much as a reasonably skilled scientist in that field can about the structure of the yeast, which is somewhat incomplete. Harrow

describes his data in somewhat general terms because he cannot determine exactly which gene he pulled out, where exactly it went among the yeast's genes, or what protein the gene codes for. Harrow does deposit a sample of his invention in a depository. Using the sample, it is quite easy to produce more of the yeast, exactly like Harrow's. Harrow's patent application also details information about the deposit and authorizes access to others wishing to make the yeast. Has Harrow provided a sufficient written description?

3. *Road map.* Gnome researches bluenosis, a rare blood disease. After studying families affected by bluenosis, Gnome establishes that bluenosis is caused genetically, not by diet, infection, or environmental factors. Gnome further establishes that a single gene is probably responsible and that the gene is on the Y chromosome. Although Gnome has not yet located the gene, Gnome's research agenda for the next several years is set. Using conventional methods, Gnome is likely to be able to locate the gene and determine its exact sequence. She is reluctant to wait any longer to file her patent application, worried that someone else will beat her to the punch. Gnome files a patent application claiming the gene. She describes the discoveries she has made, details exactly how her planned research will proceed, and demonstrates that it is quite likely that she will exactly identify the gene. Has she provided a sufficient written description?

4. *Pick one.* The poolah plant converts a common sugar molecule into choohahgum, a delicious substance. Chemical Company seeks to find the enzyme that the poolah plant uses to produce choohahgum. After considerable research, engineers at Chemical Company establish that the enzyme must be one of 1,000 chemicals, but they cannot determine which one it is. Chemical Company files a patent application that describes the structure of each one of the 1,000 candidates, details the best way to make them, and claims them all as potential choohahgum-producing enzymes. Has Chemical Company met the written description requirement?

5. *Spell it out?* Inventors apply for a patent on genes designed to enhance the immune response, specifically "Chimeric Receptor Genes and Cells Transformed Therewith." Inventors do not provide the DNA sequences of the genes, but they do provide information for making the genes, by which someone in the field would readily know the DNA sequences (which are a combination of known DNA sequences). Must an applicant for a gene patent always spell out the sequence?

6. *Proprietary information.* Hemlock Hall develops a special glue for use in wooden boats. The glue is made by combining specified ingredients in a pressure cooker. The process of using the pressure cooker requires calculating very precisely the temperatures, pressures, and time periods of use. Hemlock has used the process for years in making many types of glue,

including the new glue. Hemlock considers this process a closely guarded trade secret. Hemlock files a patent application, claiming the new glue as his invention. Hemlock's application describes very exactly the ingredients and chemical structure and properties of the glue. It further states that the glue is made using a pressure cooker. Rather than disclose his secret process, Hemlock only generally describes how to use the pressure cooker. Without a more exact description, others in the field cannot make the glue themselves. But by reading his application, they can definitely see exactly what his claimed invention is and that he has indeed made it. Does the patent application contain a sufficient description?

7. *Breakthrough.* Gilt files a patent application for a new type of automobile engine. The Gilt engine uses gasoline much more efficiently than any other automobile engine on the market. It is the only one that can achieve an efficiency rating of 125 KABC (a standard industry testing scale). Her application meticulously describes the engine and how to make and operate it. Her single patent claim reads in its entirety: "Claim 1. I claim any automobile engine that achieves an efficiency rating of 125 KABC." Has she provided a sufficient description of the invention?

Explanations

1. Cabana did provide a sufficient written description. The applicant must describe the invention and how to make and use it. Cabana did that. The description need not explain why or how the invention works. Indeed, it is relatively common for inventions such as drugs to be proven to work, although the precise action of the drug is unknown.

2. Harrow has satisfied the written description requirement. The actual writing he has supplied, standing alone, would be insufficient. The applicant must describe the invention in full, clear, concise, and exact terms. Harrow can do no more than approximately describe his invention in writing. But patent law also permits the written description requirement be met by use of a deposit, under appropriate circumstances. As with many biological inventions, the state of knowledge in Harrow's field does not permit precise information about the structure of the invention. But the deposit rule allows an inventor to meet the policies behind the written description requirement: prove he is in possession of the invention and enable others to practice the invention.

3. Gnome has not satisfied the written description requirement, which requires that the applicant demonstrate that she is in possession of the

claimed subject matter. Gnome instead has described a plan that is likely to lead to her being in possession of the invention she seeks, an isolated form of the bluenosis gene.

4. This is a classic failure to meet the written description requirement. Chemical Company is not in possession of the claimed invention in the sense courts require. Rather, it has identified a forest. But courts require it first place a blaze mark on the relevant tree in its patent application. *See, e.g., Purdue Pharma L.P. v. Faulding Inc.*, 230 F.3d 1320 (Fed. Cir. 2000) (application disclosed "a multitude of pharmacokinetic parameters" without identifying which one to use in claimed method). An alternate ground of invalidity is that it has failed to prove specific, practical, and substantial utility for each of the 1,000 compounds it claims.

5. The Federal Circuit rejected a bright line rule that always required disclosure of the DNA sequence. Rather, the applicant must only provide sufficient information to disclose the technology to the public and to prove that the inventor was in possession of the invention. "The descriptive text needed to meet these requirements varies with the nature and scope of the invention at issue, and with the scientific and technological knowledge already in existence. The law must be applied to each invention that enters the patent process, for each patented advance is novel in relation to the state of the science. Since the law is applied to each invention in view of the state of relevant knowledge, its application will vary with differences in the state of knowledge in the field and differences in the predictability of the science." *Capon v. Eshhar*, 2005 U.S. App. LEXIS 16865 (Fed. Cir. 2005).

6. Hemlock's application does not contain a sufficient description because it does not meet the enablement requirement. Hemlock does describe the invention in sufficient detail to show that Hemlock is indeed in possession of the claimed subject matter. But the applicant must also describe how to make and use the invention. Hemlock has not done that because he has not disclosed a necessary piece of information, the details of the pressure cooking process necessary to make the glue.

7. Gilt has not provided a sufficient description of the invention. She has not met the enablement requirement. She has claimed *any* engine that would achieve an efficiency rating of 125 KABC but has described only one such engine. She has not enabled others in the field to build every engine that could meet such a standard. The enablement requirement means the inventor must limit her claims to what she has invented. Otherwise, an inventor could monopolize an entire field, well beyond her actual invention.

THE CLAIMS

In patents, "the name of the game is the claim." *See* Janice Mueller, *An Introduction to Patent Law* (Aspen 2012) (quoting Judge Giles Rich). The inventor must submit an application that "particularly" and "distinctly" claims the invention. Poorly drafted claims make it much more likely that the application will be rejected—or that if the patent is granted, the patent will be held invalid. Patent rights depend not on what the inventor has invented but rather on how she claims her invention. Plain language of a claim may govern, even where it apparently contradicts the written description of the invention in the application.[6]

The claim plays several roles. Whether the invention is new and useful (meaning inventor is entitled to a patent) is evaluated by comparing the claims against previous work in the field. If inventor gets a patent, then whether others infringe the patent is evaluated by comparing their products or processes against the claims. Narrow patent claims get a patent more easily because the more narrowly the invention is claimed, the more likely it is to be new and useful, compared to previous work in the field. But broader patent claims are more valuable because the broader the claim is, the more products or processes it will cover, and the more rights it gives the patent holder. So narrower claims are more likely to be valid, and broader claims give greater rights against infringers. The patent applicant need not choose one over the other. Rather, the typical application includes both broad claims and narrow claims covering the same invention.

The claims are the heart of the patent application and, if the application issues as a patent, become the heart of the patent. The statute provides in part, "The specification shall conclude with one or more claims particularly pointing out and distinctly claiming the subject matter which the applicant regards as his invention." 35 U.S.C. §112. The written description describes the invention and tells others how to practice the invention, but ultimately everything depends on the claims: The claims "measure the invention." The claims determine whether the applicant's invention is patentable and determine the patentee's exclusive rights. If a claim "reads on" a product or process, that determines whether the product or process infringes the claim (or, if the product or process is in the prior art, whether it anticipates the claim).[7]

Below are the four claims (an independent claim and three dependent claims) from U.S. Patent No. 5,443,036 ("Method of Exercising a Cat").

---

6. *See Arlington Industries Inc. v. Bridgeport Fittings Inc.*, 632 F.3d 1246 (Fed. Cir. 2011).

7. As some have put it, "That which will literally infringe, if later, will anticipate, if earlier." *Beckson Marine v. NFM*, 292 F.3d 718, 726 (Fed. Cir. 2002). Of course, this is subject to expansion by obviousness (if earlier) and doctrine of equivalents (if later, in infringement).

1. A method of inducing aerobic exercise in an unrestrained cat comprising the steps of:
   (a) directing an intense coherent beam of invisible light produced by a hand-held laser apparatus to produce a bright, highly focused pattern of light at the intersection of the beam and an opaque surface, said pattern being of visual interest to a cat; and
   (b) selectively redirecting said beam out of the cat's immediate reach to induce said cat to run and chase said beam and pattern of light around an exercise area.
2. The method of Claim 1 wherein said bright pattern of light is small in area relative to a paw of the cat.
3. The method of Claim 1 wherein said beam remains invisible between said laser and said opaque surface until impinging on said opaque surface.
4. The method of Claim 1 wherein step (b) includes sweeping said beam at an angular speed to cause said pattern to move along said opaque surface at a speed in the range of five to twenty-five feet per second.

The statute does not prescribe any particular format for patent claims (other than how dependent claims relate to independent claims). A claim conventionally consists of one sentence with three parts: a preamble, a transition phrase, and a body.

The preamble generally identifies the invention or puts it in context (often by referring to the parts of the product or process that are not novel). The preamble states whether the claim goes to a process or a product (it must be one or the other) and can continue on to state broadly what sort of product or process is claimed. The preamble to Claim 1 identifies it as a particular type of process: "A method of inducing aerobic exercise in an unrestrained cat." Preambles may be broad, such as "an apparatus" or "a compound," or quite specific, such as "elongated balloon dilatation catheter." The preamble does not necessarily act as an element of the claim (a limitation on the invention). *Kropa v. Robie*, 187 F.2d 150, 152 (C.C.P.A. 1951) (preamble is limiting when it is "necessary to give life, meaning and vitality to the claims or counts"). For example, if a claim read, "I claim a sports drink for marathoners comprising elements A, B, C, and D," a court might have to decide whether the claim applied only to drinks for marathoners or to all drinks with those elements.

The transition phrase sets the stage for the body of the claim. In particular, the transition phrase may be open or closed. An open transition phrase, such as "comprising the steps of" in Claim 1 above, means that the claim encompasses a device (or process) with additional elements not listed in the body. *See AFG Indus. v. Cardinal IG Co.*, 239 F.3d 1239 (Fed. Cir. 2001). A closed transition phrase, such as "consisting of," means that the claim describes a device (or process) that does not have additional elements. A device with elements A, B, and C could infringe a claim reading "comprising A and B" but not a claim reading "consisting of A and B." For that reason, applicants much prefer to use open transition phrases. They may have to use closed transition phrases, however, to meet the various requirements of patentability. A claim may also use a partially closed phrase, such as "consisting essentially of," that would describe a device or process containing insubstantial elements in addition to the listed elements.

The body lists the elements (or "limitations") of the claim. In Claim 1, the elements are everything after the preamble and transition. The claims must list the invention's structural elements (for a product claim) or steps (for a process claim). The elements of the claim must do the brunt of the work in "particularly pointing out and distinctly claiming the subject matter which the applicant regards as his invention." 35 U.S.C. §112. The gist of Claim 1 is "wiggling a light in front of a cat"; but note how much more limited the elements are. To take just part of the claim—"directing an intense coherent beam of invisible light produced by a hand-held laser apparatus to produce a bright highly-focused pattern of light"—note the many limitations in that language. The claim does not read on a method that does not "direct" the beam (for example, one left to go by itself), does not use "an intense coherent beam" (for example, one using a flashlight, rather than a laser), or that is not a beam of light (for example, one using a spray of water or gas).

The claims play a central role in determining both whether the applicant is entitled to a patent and later whether the actions of others infringe that patent. These dual roles present certain conflicts for the claim drafter. The narrower the claims are, the more likely the application is to meet the requirements for a patent: The narrowly claimed invention is more likely to be novel (because it is less likely that an identical product or process appears in the prior art), more likely to escape the various statutory bars (because it is less likely that a sufficiently similar device or process was published, known to the public, or on sale on the critical date), less likely to be obvious, more likely to match (or not exceed) the written description, and be easier to enable (because a narrower claim is less likely to be overbroad). On the other hand, the more narrow the claims are, the less rights the patent will give—it will read on fewer devices or processes and it will be easier for others to design around the patent. So the drafter faces a tension between getting a valid patent and getting a patent that is valuable.

To some extent, the drafter can address that by using multiple claims and by using dependent claims that narrow previous claims. For example, in the cat exercise patent, the drafter includes an independent claim (Claim 1) followed by increasingly narrower dependent claims (Claims 2-4). If Claim 1 is rejected or later held invalid, the narrower Claim 2 still survives. Although Claim 2 might survive because it is narrower, it is also less powerful to enforce exactly because it is narrower. Someone who exercises a cat with a method that does not contain the limitation in Claim 2 ("said bright pattern of light is small in area relative to a paw of the cat") does not infringe Claim 2. The Patent Office regulations place some limit on using dependent claims to hedge against claim invalidity.

Patent law permits two special forms of claim drafting: product-by-process claims and means-function claims. A product-by-process claim covers a product but claims the product by describing the process for making it. Such a claim may be used when the applicant otherwise is unable to sufficiently describe the product. For example, Chemist may isolate a new drug that proves effective in treating a disease. But although Chemist has isolated and used the drug in tests, she is not able to describe its structure. She can use a product-by-process claim. Cases differ on whether such a claim reads only on products made using the described process. The statute also allows a means-function claim. Such a claim expresses an element as a means for performing a function, rather than reciting specific "structure material, or acts." 35 U.S.C. §112. The written description, however, must describe something that can act as such a means.

Section 112 requires that patent claims be definite ("particularly pointing out and distinctly claiming the subject matter which the applicant regards as his invention"). The test is whether the claim will "reasonably apprise those skilled in the art of the scope of the invention." *Solomon v. Kimberly-Clark Corp.*, 216 F.3d 1372, 1378 (Fed. Cir. 2000) (quoting standard language from cases). For example, claims that simply describe the function of the invention are invalid as indefinite because they do not specify the product or process that performs that function.

Likewise, claims are not valid if they are too ambiguous. Vague claims are not valid. Section 112 imposes a definiteness requirement, which is met if "a patent's claims, viewed in light of the specification and prosecution history, inform those skilled in the art about the scope of the invention with reasonable certainty." *Nautilus, Inc. v. Biosig Instruments, Inc.*, 134 S. Ct. 2120 (2014).

Whether claims are sufficiently definite depends not just on the language of the claims. The claims need not be clear standing alone. An apparently indefinite claim may be sufficiently clear to one versed in the relevant art. A claim for a purified protein with a "specific activity" of "at least about 160,000" units was held to be indefinite. *See Amgen v. Chugai*, 927 F.2d 1200, 1218 (Fed. Cir. 1991). But the court carefully noted that the words "at least about" could be sufficiently definite in another context. A claim is sufficiently definite if it can be construed to give a sufficiently definite meaning. *See Exxon Research & Engineering v. United States*, 60 U.S.P.Q.2d 1272 (Fed. Cir. 2001).

The claims are indefinite if they do not make sense, such as a claim that, applied to the real world, would be nonsensical: "the claims describe the step of extracting machine code instructions from something that does not have machine code instructions. . . . The claims are nonsensical in the way a claim to extracting orange juice from apples would be, and are thus indefinite."[8]

Examples

1. *Draft day.* Curie has invented a new eraser, especially handy for pencils. Curie's patent agent drafts the following claims for her:
   1. I claim a writing implement, comprising of a pencil with a spinaltapi-cal-shaped eraser attached.
   2. The writing implement of Claim 1, wherein such eraser is composed of plubundum.

   Identify: the independent claim, the dependent claim. For Claim 1, iden-tify: the preamble, the transition phrase, and the body.

   Why use two claims? What other claim drafting strategies might Curie consider?

2. *Mostly friendly.* Brock files a patent application for a new organic pesti-cide. The pesticide is a combination of various natural ingredients. It is very safe for plants, humans, and all other animals, except that it wipes out a common pest, the burrowing cucumber mite. Brock's application contains this claim: "I claim an organic pesticide that kills the burrowing cucumber mite and is safe for everything else." Is the claim valid?

3. *Hedging.* Winger drafts a patent application for her method of admin-istering an online sports betting parlor. Winger's draft application has a single claim, which lists the steps of the method as she practices it, which we can call steps *A* through T. Winger then becomes concerned that someone else will use her patent to come up with a system that does not infringe but uses her basic method. So she adds a phrase to the end of her patent claim, which now reads: "I claim a method of administer-ing a sports betting parlor, comprising steps *A* though T, or any method similar to this method." Is the claim valid?

4. *Less is more.* Zoop is Inventor's new sports drink, a mixture with elements *A, B, C,* and *D*. Inventor wishes to file a patent application. He searches the prior art and discovers that Spring Forward, a drink long on the market, is a mixture with elements *A, B, C, D,* and *E*. Inventor fears that if he seeks to patent Zoop, the claimed invention will lack novelty because it was anticipated by Spring Forward, which contained everything in Zoop and more. Inventor considers changing Zoop to avoid anticipation. But his research shows that any change in Zoop will make it work less

---

8. Trs. of Columbia Univ. v. Symantec Corp., 811 F.3d 1359, 1366-1367 (Fed. Cir. 2016) (citations and quotation omitted).

effectively. The reason Zoop is effective is that it is an optimum combination for marathon runners. Adding or subtracting ingredients will make it work less well because it will affect a runner's metabolism differently. Can Inventor draft a patent claim for Zoop that is not anticipated by Spring Forward?

5. *Matter of taste.* Datamize holds a method patent on an "Electronic Kiosk Authoring System." The claimed invention is a series of steps to create user interfaces for electronic kiosks. One step of the claimed invention is "providing interface screen elements with aesthetically pleasing look and feel." Is the patent claim valid?

Explanations

1. Claim 1 is the independent claim. Claim 2 depends on Claim 1, by limiting the claimed invention to erasers made of plubundum.

   Claim 1: Preamble: "a writing implement"
   Transition phrase: comprising
   Body: "of a pencil with a spinaltapical-shaped eraser attached."

   Why use two claims? Claim 1 is broader, so would give greater protection if granted. Anyone that made, used, sold, offered, or imported a pencil with a spinaltapical-shaped eraser attached would potentially infringe. But Claim 1 (and we do not know what prior art is out there) might be anticipated (if such a pencil was in the prior art, for example, if it was already published or in public use, either before Curie's date of invention or more than one year before she filed her application) or obvious (if the pencil would be obvious in light of the prior art). Claim 2 is narrower, limited to plubundum erasers, so it is less likely to be anticipated or obvious. It is not as broad but is a fallback. Patent law allows the applicant to submit a number of claims, and applicants typically submit a set of increasingly narrower claims.

   What other strategies? The two big things again are (1) avoiding prior art for patentability and (2) keeping the claim broad to increase the scope of protection. Here are some strategies for broader claims that still hew to the invention.

   • Drafting a broader claim to the eraser (not just the eraser attached to the pencil): "I claim a spinaltapical-shaped eraser." If her innovation is making an eraser with a spinaltapical shape, this gives her broader protection. Someone that made and sold the eraser by itself would not infringe a claim to a pencil with a spinaltapical eraser attached.

- Deleting the preamble, "a writing implement"; otherwise, a court might consider her claim not to cover a pencil used for drawing (as opposed to writing).
- Making Claim 2 a little broader. It is limited to an eraser composed of plubundum, practically inviting someone to design around the patent by using an eraser composed partially of plubundum. So it could be drafted to read on an eraser composed, say, 75 percent or more of plubundum.

Curie might even consider whether her claims should encompass other uses of the spinaltapical shape: sandpaper? Sanding machines? But of course she could not claim all uses. That claim would be too broad (and probably anticipated, anyway).

2. Brock's claim is not valid. The claim must point out and distinctly claim the subject matter of the invention. Brock's claim simply describes the function of the invention. But the claims must list the invention's structural elements (for a product claim) or steps (for a process claim). Brock's claim is also invalid as indefinite (indeed, wildly overbroad). If another inventor invented a completely different product that safely killed cucumber mites, it would fall within such a claim.

3. The revised claim including the phrase "or any method similar to this method" is not a valid claim. The claims must be definite ("particularly pointing out and distinctly claiming the subject matter which the applicant regards as his invention"). The test is whether the claims reasonably apprise one in the field what the scope of the invention is. Winger's claim does not do this. Rather, the claim is indefinite, vaguely claiming any method "similar" to the specified method. Such a claim could hardly fulfill the two main purposes of claims: determining whether the invention meets the requirements of patentability and, if a patent issues, giving notice to the world of what the patentee's rights are.

4. Inventor can draft a claim that would not be anticipated by Spring Forward: "I claim a drink consisting of elements A, B, C, and D." That claim uses the closed transition phrase, "consisting of." It would be anticipated only by a sports drink that had elements A, B, C, and D and no other elements. Spring Forward had elements A, B, C, D—and element E. So Spring Forward did not anticipate the invention claimed. In common-sense terms, Spring Forward does not anticipate the narrowly written claim for Zoop. Any addition of elements would change the functioning of Zoop, and Spring Forward had an additional element. By narrowing his claim so that it only covers his particular mixture, Inventor can have a novel invention (but his exclusive rights will also be limited to that narrowly claimed invention).

5. The patent claim is not valid because it is indefinite. *See Datamize, LLC v. Plumtree Software, Inc.*, 417 F.3d 1342 (Fed. Cir. 2005). A patent claim must "reasonably apprise those skilled in the art of the scope of the invention." The claim includes the step of providing interface screen elements with an "aesthetically pleasing look and feel." "Aesthetically pleasing" is not definite. To the contrary, it could vary widely according to taste. Accordingly, it is impossible for someone reading the claim to know what elements the claim covers.

OWNERSHIP AND LICENSING

Inventorship (and Misjoinder)

The actual inventor or inventors must apply for the patent.[9] Two common issues arise. First, when an employee invents, who owns the rights to patent the invention? Second, if more than one person is involved in the process, when are they deemed joint inventors?

An employee, not his employer, generally owns the rights to an invention he conceives or reduces to practice. The parties can expressly agree to assignment of patent rights. If the rights have been assigned, the owner may file the application even if the inventor does not cooperate. *See* 35 U.S.C. §118. Even absent express agreement, there may be an implied assignment that the employer owns the patent rights if the employee was hired to invent such products or processes or to solve such problems. Even when the employee retains the right to the patent, the employer may have a limited "shop right": the right to use the invention without consent from or payment to the employee. But the employee remains free to commercialize it himself, such as licensing the patent to competitors.

There may be more than one inventor. Joint inventors need not work together, make the same sort of contribution, or contribute to every claim of the patent. 35 U.S.C. §116. Rather, a joint inventor must contribute in a significant manner to the conception or reduction to practice of the full invention. Such contribution must be inventive. It is not sufficient to explain existing concepts or simply supply resources to the real inventors. Joint owners of a patent may each exercise any of the patent rights, without the consent of other joint owners, and with no obligation to share revenue. 35 U.S.C. §262.

---

9. If the inventor has assigned his right to the patent and refuses to participate in the application, the statute provides that the assignee may still pursue the application. But all inventors must still be accurately identified.

If the correct inventor is not named as the applicant, or one of the inventors is not named, or a noninventor is named as one of the inventors, the patent may be invalidated by such nonjoinder or misjoinder. But an error may be corrected by the USPTO or court (with notice to all parties), provided there was no deceptive intent on the part of the true inventor (as opposed to deceptive invent by others, such as noninventors listed as inventors). *See Stark v. Advanced Magnetics*, 119 F.3d 1551 (Fed. Cir. 1997).

The federal Bayh-Dole Act of 1980 has led to considerable commercial development of university research. The Act sets up a framework under which universities may elect to patent inventions made through federally funded research or may allow the researchers to seek patents on the inventions. The narrow issue in *Board of Trustees of the Leland Stanford Junior University v. Roche Molecular Systems*. 131 S. Ct. 2188 (2011), was whether the patent rights vest automatically in the university or only after the researcher makes the required assignment of patent rights. The Supreme Court held that the general rule in patent law applies: the inventor initially has the right to patent, which passes only after an effective assignment has been made (even if, as in Bayh-Dole, the inventor is required to make that assignment).

Patents as Property: Assignment and Licensing

Patents are personal property. 35 U.S.C. §261. As such, patent owners may license their patents to others for various purposes. An inventor might simply sell her patent or sell the exclusive rights to make and sell the invention in a particular market or for particular purposes. Parties in a joint research venture may cross-license their patents (as may competitors with dueling patents that settle cross-claims of infringement). A software seller, beyond delivering copies of the software, may license the buyer to use the software free of patent claims. A patent owner may freely license others to use the invention, in order to encourage its wider adoption (such as an industry standard). Universities license patents not just for revenue but to encourage innovation and research.

Patent rights are freely assignable, but such assignments must be in writing. Assignments may also be recorded with the USPTO. Unless an assignment is recorded, it is void against a subsequent purchaser or secured creditor. Whether this provision preempts state law recording of security interests in patent rights under the Uniform Commercial Code (UCC) has not been definitively determined. A careful creditor files both in the state office for UCC filings and the USPTO.

Courts limit the ability of patentees to protect themselves from challenges to the validity of the patent. In *Lear v. Adkins*, 395 U.S. 653 (1969), the Supreme Court declined to apply the doctrine of licensee estoppel. Under licensee estoppel, a licensee who has benefited from a patent is estopped from denying the validity of the patent. But a more important policy is that of encouraging challenges to invalid patents. Licensees (who are familiar with patent and the invention in question and are under obligation to pay royalties if the patents are not invalidated) are the ones most likely to challenge patents. Under *Lear*, even if the licensee has benefited from the patent, the licensee may raise invalidity as a defense.

But the *Lear* rule has been limited to its rationale in subsequent decisions. The Federal Circuit enforced a promise not to challenge validity when the licensee did not notify the licensor that it was questioning the validity of the patent until after a lawsuit was filed seeking royalties. *See Studiengesellschaft Kohle m.b.H. v. Shell Oil*, 112 F.3d 1561 (Fed. Cir. 1997). The policy of encouraging challenges did not weigh heavily when the licensee in fact simply stopped paying royalties without challenging validity. By contrast, the Federal Circuit held that a pre-litigation agreement not to contest patent validity was not enforceable. *Rates Technology Inc. v. Speakeasy Inc.*, 685 F.3d 163 (2d Cir. 2012). Requiring a lawsuit will enable the parties to use discovery of evidence as to whether the patent is actually valid. In addition, enforcing pre-litigation agreements not to contest validity would result in to patent holders simply calling license agreement settlement agreements, especially if there had been a cease-and-desist letter. Likewise, when another important policy is implicated, an assignee may be bound by a promise not to challenge validity. Courts have applied *assignor estoppel:* If an inventor assigns her rights to a patent and is subsequently sued for infringement of the patent, she may be barred from challenging the validity of the patent. When an inventor has applied for a patent and then sells the rights, she may be barred from contending that those rights were worthless. *See Diamond Scientific Co. v. Ambico*, 848 F.2d 1220 (Fed. Cir. 1988).

On the other side, courts apply assignor estoppel in patent cases. "Assignor estoppel is an equitable doctrine that prevents one who has assigned the rights to a patent (or patent application) from later contending that what was assigned is a nullity."[10] Courts reason that "an assignor should not be permitted to sell something and later to assert that what was sold is worthless."[11] A patent applicant also signs an oath, affirming their belief that the patent is valid. But whether the doctrine applied broadly makes sense today is a live question, when patent rights are often assigned but not really sold. Employees typically sign over future patent rights when taking a job and the doctrine may protect the employer, who controlled the application. An applicant may have no reason to doubt their invention is not patentable, but may learn later of work in the field that made their invention obvious (or may simply have not understood the legal effect of the claims in the application, and their relation to the employee's work). The

---

10. Diamond Sci. Co. v. Ambico, Inc., 848 F.2d 1220, 1224 (Fed. Cir. 1988).
11. Diamond Sci. Co. v. Ambico, Inc., at 1224.

doctrine creates an implied promise not to contest the patent, which would be nonenforceable (even if in an explicit clause by a licensee, under *Lear)*. Extending the rationale to licensors would not be a large step.

Duration

The patent grant is effective for a term "beginning on the date on which the patent issues and ending 20 years from the date on which the application for the patent was filed." 35 U.S.C. §154(a)(2). The inventor cannot exclude others from using his invention until he files and prosecutes the application and the USPTO issues a patent—usually more than 18 months from the application date. Until 1995, the term was 17 years from the date the patent issued.[12] Because the term is now measured from the date of filing the application, the term is effectively 20 years minus the time taken for the examination process. The term may be extended in certain cases, such as some types of delay by the USPTO or regulatory authorities. 35 U.S.C. §154.

For applications filed before June 8, 1995, the former patent term of 17 years from the date of issuance remains effective. In determining patent term, then, the date of application is key.

A quirky, much-criticized patent licensing rule remains. In 1964, *Brulotte v. Thys Co.*[13] held that a patent holder cannot continue to charge royalties based on use of the invention after the patent expired. The rule has long been criticized on the theory that an agreement made *during* the patent term for royalties payable after the term does not leverage the patent beyond its term, rather gets a promise payable in the future. After the patent expires, the patent holder has no leverage. But the Supreme Court declined to overrule the case, reasoning that the rule may be dubious, but it was harmless. *Kimble v. Marvel Entertainment*[14] made clear that *Brulotte* is little more than a formality. As long as parties to a licensing transaction are aware of the rule, they can structure their transaction to implement their deal, with compliance with *Brulotte* presenting only drafting issues.

Examples

1. *Whose patent?* Duosys hires Bonk to work on Image Camera Project. Bonk's assignment is to test the camera's optical properties and to pass the information on to other engineers who are designing the camera. Bonk is also strongly encouraged to suggest any improvements to the camera design that occur to him. Duosys requests that he sign a form transferring patent rights to Duosys in any inventions he makes while an employee.

---

12. The statute has transition provisions addressing the change in term.
13. Brulotte v. Thys Co., 379 U.S. 29, 85 S. Ct. 176, 13 L. Ed. 2d 99 (1964).
14. Kimble v. Marvel Entertainment, 135 S. Ct. 2401 (2015).

Bonk refuses to sign the form and clearly states that he should own the patents to any such inventions. Bonk, on his own initiative and on his own time, tests the camera to confirm some problems he had detected and redesigns the camera's optic system. He files a patent application on his improvement. Duosys claims that the patent rights belong to it. Who owns the patent rights?

2. *Drafting partner.* Peoria, a gifted mechanical engineer, invents a Barber Chair with Mew and Yaw Controls. Peoria attempts to draft her own patent application but quickly learns that she has neither the necessary knowledge nor inclination. Her first attempt is a rambling account of her development of the chair, together with some photos. Peoria can describe the chair quite well but has great difficulty in drafting claims that point out precisely what about the chair distinguishes it from other work in the field. Peoria hires Dekalb, an experienced patent attorney. Dekalb interrogates Peoria extensively, researches the prior art in the area, and drafts a patent application. Dekalb determines that the claims must be drafted very carefully because the barber chair field is thick with patents and other prior art. Claims that are too broad fail for lack of novelty because there are so many pieces of prior art. Claims that are too narrow are not valuable because they leave too much leeway for competitors to copy from Peoria's work. Dekalb meets the challenge and drafts a strong set of claims. Dekalb then informs Peoria that they must both be listed as inventors on the application because Dekalb has made such a substantial contribution to the enterprise. Is Dekalb a joint inventor?

3. *Rematch?* Feet sues Deffen for infringement of Four Feet's patent for a "Modular Composite Brace." The parties settle the lawsuit. Deffen agrees to cease and desist from producing its accused product and to pay a stipulated sum. Deffen also agrees not to challenge the validity of the patent in the future. Although Deffen ceases, it does not desist. Six months later, Deffen resumes production of the accused device, and Four Feet files a patent infringement action. Deffen raises invalidity of the patent as a defense, despite its earlier agreement never to challenge the validity of the patent. Is Deffen bound by the agreement not to challenge validity of the patent?

4. BDA licenses its network technology patents to a number of manufacturers. In each license agreement, BDA includes the following clauses.
   a. Licensee stipulates that BDA's patents are valid.
   b. Licensee promises not to challenge the validity of BDA's patents in court.
   c. Licensee agrees to continue paying licensing fees during any such patent challenge.

    d. Licensee agrees not to bring any such challenge in the Eastern District of Texas.

    e. To resolve any dispute between the parties, and to facilitate an agreement, Licensee agrees not to challenge the validity of BDA's patents.

    f. Licensee stipulates that, absent a license, Licensee would be infringing BDA's patents.

      Why include such duplicative clauses?

5. a. Inventor filed an application on June 1, 1990, and the patent issued on June 1, 1994. What is the patent term?

    b. Inventor filed an application on June 1, 2000, and the patent issued on June 1, 2004. There are no grounds, such as USPTO delay, for extending the patent term. What is the patent term?

Explanations

1. The right to the patent belongs to Bonk. An employee generally has the right to patent subject matter that he invents. Duosys would argue that an exception to that rule is applicable here, that Bonk was employed to invent such improvements and accordingly the patents belong to the employer. But the employed-to-invent theory is an implied contract theory and requires a tacit understanding between the parties. Bonk's clear refusal to assign patent rights makes the doctrine inapplicable. Cf. *Banks v. Unisys Corp.*, 228 F.3d 1357 (Fed. Cir. 2000).

2. Dekalb does not qualify as a joint inventor. A joint inventor must make a significant inventive contribution to the conception or reduction to practice of the full invention. Dekalb provided legal advice and expertise and also researched and explained the prior art. But Dekalb did not contribute to conceiving or making the invention.

3. Deffen is bound by the no-contest clause. For public policy reasons, courts may not enforce a clause in a patent license agreeing not to challenge the validity of the patent. But, as noted in the text, this rule is subject to other policies. There is also a strong public policy in favor of resolving lawsuits through settlements, rather than litigation. Accordingly, courts will enforce a no-contest clause in a bona fide settlement agreement or consent decree. Otherwise, it would be rather difficult to reach a lasting settlement in many disputes.

4. *Lear* held that licensee estoppel would not bar a challenge to patent validity. But *Lear* left open the enforceability of such clauses as stipulations to validity, agreements not to challenge, and agreements to continue paying licensing fees. Where it is unclear which ones will be enforceable, BDA has decided to throw them all in and see which ones stick.

5. a. The application was filed before June 8, 1995, so the term is 17 years from the date of *issuance*. The patent will expire in 2011.

    b. The application was filed after June 8, 1995, so the term is 20 years from the date of *application*. The patent will expire in 2020. Note that the patent term in this case is 16 years because prosecution of the patent took four years. The new rule gives applicants an incentive to avoid delay during patent prosecution.

CHAPTER 9

Rights and Infringement: "The Benefit of His Invention"

Some call patent litigation the Sport of Kings, for its expense and high stakes. If Curie has a patent on her pencil with a spinaltapical-shaped eraser, she has the exclusive right in the United States to make, use, offer to sell, or import such a device. So her patent could be infringed by a factory operator that made and sold it, by the wholesaler who sells it, by the stationery store that sells it, and even by the consumer or business that uses it (patent holders rarely sue end users—not good to antagonize the users of your invention; better to sue your competitors or potential licensees).

A fairly typical patent infringement case: Unknowing Pencils has successfully sold Dyno Writer pencils with an 11-sided eraser for a couple of years. Unknowing receives a letter, which claims that Dyno Writer infringes a patent recently issued to Curie on her pencil with a spinaltapical-shaped eraser, and Curie demands royalties. Unknowing refuses and Curie sues for patent infringement.

It is no defense that Unknowing developed its pencil independently. Patent infringement does not require copying. But several issues would likely be addressed. The two most common are:

- *claim interpretation*: whether the Dyno Writer falls within the claims of Curie's patent, and
- *validity*: whether Curie's patent is valid (it would not be if Unknowing can produce evidence that Curie's invention was not new or nonobvious—such as evidence that similar pencils had been in public use before Curie's invention date—or evidence that Curie waited more than a year after she had sold or publicly used the pencil to file her patent application).

Other issues in some cases include defenses such as inequitable conduct (Curie misled the patent office), first sale (I sold a pencil that Curie had sold), repair (I did not make the pencil, I simply repaired one), and antitrust (Curie is threatening patent litigation in order to control the market for all pencils with erasers, not just with her patented eraser).

If Curie wins, she may be entitled to damages (money) and an injunction (an order that Unknowing stop selling its pencil, unless it gets permission from Curie, which would no doubt involve more money).

Patent litigation comes in many other forms. Some alleged infringers do copy, such as generic pharmaceutical makers that make patented drugs, where they contend the patents are invalid. When joint ventures go awry, the former partners may sue over the patent rights. When patent licenses go sour, the licensee may continue making the product, prompting a lawsuit (or the licensee may sue, seeking a declaration that the patent is invalid). In each case, the key issues are often claim interpretation (just what does the patent cover) and validity (is this patent valid).

How can a party be assured that they are not infringing anyone's patent? The only sure way is to make, sell, or use nothing—not a viable business or life plan. In some industries, persons in the field may be able to do good patent searches. A drug company with a new molecule should be able to figure out if that molecule is patented. In other areas, particularly software and business methods, it is much more difficult to find out if one of the millions of patents out there applies. Software and business method patents are often quite abstract, meaning that they are difficult to locate. An accounting firm could easily infringe a patent filed by a glue manufacturer, where it covers an inventory control system. Some companies try to keep track of patents in the field and avoid infringement. Other companies rely on luck—the risk of patent infringement, after all, may pale next to their other risks, such as getting funding.

INFRINGEMENT ANALYSIS

Scope of the Rights to Exclude

The patentee does not own the patented invention in a general sense. Rather, the statute gives the patentee the right to exclude others from certain activities involving the invention:

> Whoever without authority makes, uses, offers to sell, or sells any patented invention, within the United States or imports into the United States any patented invention during the term of the patent therefore, infringes the patent.

35 U.S.C. §271.

The patent rights are limited in several ways:

1. *Specified rights to exclude:* The patentee has a set of specific rights to exclude, not general ownership of the invention.
2. *Geographic limits:* Infringement is defined as activity within the United States.
3. *Time limits:* The patentee's rights are limited to the term of the patent.
4. *Limited to claims and equivalents:* Infringement must involve the patented invention, so the inventor's rights are limited to the invention as claimed (including equivalents to the claims) in the patent.

There is no infringement unless one of the specified rights is infringed. The patentee has the right to exclude others from making, using, offering to sell, selling, or importing the patented invention. If an inventor patents a new type of television, it is infringement to use, make, sell, offer, or import the new TV. It is not infringement to possess an infringing TV set, to give one away, to burn one, or to take it apart to see how it works.

On the other hand, infringement requires only acts that infringe one of the specified rights. There are no additional requirements with respect to mental state, commercial gain, or quantum of harm. Infringement need not be intentional, knowing, reckless, or negligent. The activity need not be public, commercial, or benefit the infringer at all. The activity need not harm the patent holder; no evidence of damages or lost sale is required. Even a good-faith belief of noninfringement is not a defense to infringement. Nor does patent infringement require copying. Even if a second inventor comes up with the same invention on her own without any knowledge of the first inventor's patent, she still infringes by making the patented invention.

The rights to exclude are limited to the invention as claimed in the patent (including equivalents). It is not infringement to make, use, sell, offer to sell, or import a product or process that does not fall with any of the patent claims. Indeed, the disclosure in the patent may enable others to "design around" the patent. A competitor may be able to build and sell a very similar type of TV as long as his does not infringe the claims of the patent. This is true even if he works from the patent itself.

Infringement is not limited to the utility disclosed in the patent. If our inventor patented a new chemical useful for cleaning clothes, the patent could be infringed by anyone who makes, uses, sells, or imports it, even if for some other purpose. So if the new chemical was also useful for making computer chips, anyone who made or sold it for that purpose nevertheless would infringe the patent.

Defendant infringes if she "makes, uses, offers to sell, or sells any patented invention, within the United States or imports into the United States any patented invention." 35 U.S.C. §271. If inventor has a U.S. patent on her new pharmaceutical, someone who makes or sells the chemical in South Africa does not infringe the U.S. patent (although it might infringe a patent issued by South Africa).

Whether the activity occurs in the United States may be disputed—and may depend on whether the patent claim covers a product or a process. When a Blackberry wireless communication device is used within the United States, it triggers operation of network equipment in the United States but also triggers a relay at the Blackberry maker's center in Canada. The Federal Circuit held that such use infringed the U.S. patent on "[t]he use of a claimed system under section 271(a) is the place at which the system as a whole is put into service." *NTP, Inc. v. Research in Motion, Ltd.*, 75 U.S.P.Q.2d (BNA) 1763 (Fed. Cir. 2005). The court held, however, that the process claims in the patent were not infringed, because not all the steps of patented process were done within the United States.

The patent statute does have provisions intended to prevent parties from using foreign activity to effectively circumvent a U.S. patent. It is infringement to export all or a substantial portion of the components of a patented invention to have the invention made outside the United States. 35 U.S.C. §272(f)(1). But there is no liability if components are made outside the United States and shipped to foreign buyers outside the United States. *See Pellegrini v. Analog Devices*, 375 F.3d 1113 (Fed. Cir. 2004).

Likewise, it can be infringement to import the product of a patented process. 35 U.S.C. §272(g).[1] Here, a "product" refers to a product of a manufacturing process. Information produced by using a patented process (or products identified by using a patented process) are not products of the process for the purpose of infringement. There was no infringement, where a patented process was used to identify substances as potential pharmaceuticals, where that research data, along with the substances, were then sent into the United States. *See Bayer AG v. Housey Pharmaceuticals*, 340 F.3d 1367 (Fed. Cir. 2003). In addition, the provision does not apply if the product has been materially changed by subsequent processes or is a trivial component of another product. Remedies are also limited in the case of noncommercial use or retail sales.

Determination of Infringement

In patent litigation, there is frequently no dispute that the alleged infringer made (or used, sold, offered to sell, or imported) a product or process. The issue is more often whether that product or process was the patented invention, which depends on whether the accused product or process infringed

---

1. Liability is limited in the case of noncommercial use or retail sales. 35 U.S.C. §271(g).

the patent claims. Determination of infringement has two steps. The patent claim at issue must be construed to determine its scope and meaning. Then one determines whether the accused device or process infringes the properly construed claim, either literally or under the doctrine of equivalents.[2]

Claim Interpretation

Lawyers and judges often have to interpret sentences to apply to particular cases—in statutes, contracts, rules, or other writings. To take a famous example, "no vehicles in the park" seems like a nice, clear rule. It would apply to cars and trucks but probably not bicycles. But what about pedicabs? Or a parade float? Or a walking house?

Curie sues someone for allegedly infringing this patent claim: "I claim a writing implement, comprised of a pencil with an eraser attached, where such eraser is spinaltapical in form and composed of plubundum." Depending on the product the defendant made (or used, or offered, or sold, or imported), there could be questions of interpreting the claim:

- Is Curie's claim limited to "a writing implement"? Would a pencil used for drawing infringe?
- What does "spinaltapical" mean? Curie's eraser has 11 straight sides—would her claim be infringed by an eraser with 11 slightly curved sides?
- What does "attached" mean? Would the claim be infringed by a pencil with an eraser loosely held on by friction? What does "composed of plubundum" mean? Would the claim be infringed by an eraser composed 95 percent of plubundum and 5 percent of granvillium?
- Would it read on a pencil with two erasers attached?

Because language is never perfectly precise, a court often must interpret the claims. Claim interpretation may be required as part of infringement analysis or any other issues involving the scope of the claims, such as determining whether prior art anticipated the invention. The interpretation of claims is a job for the court, not the jury. *Markman v. Westview Instruments*, 517 U.S. 370 (1996). Courts face such issues of claim interpretation as:

- whether the word "window" in a patent held by Apple Computer was broad enough to include devices called "palettes" in earlier computer patents;
- whether "feeding" in a claim is broad enough to cover ingesting a substance not for nutrition but for medical purposes;
- what "anion" means, in a pharmaceutical patent;

---

2. There are special issues with respect to means-plus-function claims and product-by-process claims that are not addressed here.

- whether "adjacent" means touching or merely near to;
- whether a patent claim's transition phrase "composed of" was open (like "comprising") or closed (like "consisting of"); and
- whether "a" means "one," or "one or more."

This means that a patent claim is not interpreted definitively until the inventor has applied for and received a patent, there has been a trial court determination of the patent's meaning, and the case has been appealed and resolved. That introduces quite a bit of uncertainty into patent practice. Just what a patent covers is often unclear—and often remains unclear. Oftentimes, neither patent holders nor potential infringers know how broad a patent is (or even if it is valid, of course).

The meaning of the claims depends primarily on the language of the claims. Because of the important role the claims play in determining patentability and in providing notice of the invention to the public, courts are reluctant to consider an interpretation that is at odds with the literal meaning of the claims. But the claims may be unclear on their face. Moreover, apparently literal language often becomes vague and ambiguous in light of other facts.

The court next looks to the written description, the drawings, and anything else in the patent. Because the claims define the invention, courts try to avoid redefining them by using the rest of the patent. In particular, there is a widely noted tension between interpreting the claims by using the written description (allowed) and reading limitations from the description into the claims (not allowed). If a claim clearly has a broad meaning, it should not be construed more narrowly just because the invention is described more narrowly in the rest of the specification. When the patent application defines a term, the court generally uses that term in interpreting the claims, even if the applicant uses the word in an unusual way. The definition need not be explicit. A consistent use of a term can give a definition by implication.

Courts should be careful not to limit the scope of the claim to the specific embodiments of the invention described in the application. That could discourage applicants from providing useful disclosure and encourage broad generic disclosure. Rather, courts can protect against broad claims by interpreting claims to cover only the invention to the extent the application describes it and enables others to make and use it. That approach encourages disclosure, a key purpose of the patent system. *See* Stephen M. McJohn, *Patents: Hiding from History*, 24 Santa Clara Computer & High Tech. L.J. 961 (2008).

After the patent itself, the court can look to the entire file wrapper (the record of the application process before the U.S. Patent and Trademark Office (USPTO)). The prosecution history of the patent may give meaning to the claims that ultimately are issued. If the patent applicant and the USPTO had exchanges involving the meaning of a claim, those can guide subsequent claim interpretation. In particular, if an applicant disclaims certain subject matter during the prosecution process, she will not be permitted to argue that the claims in the issued patent should cover that subject matter.

Beyond the file wrapper, the court can look to any other competent evidence ("extrinsic" or "extraneous" evidence) to give meaning to the claims. Courts try to maintain the primacy of the patent and use extrinsic evidence only to interpret, not to contradict or supplement the patent claim. Extrinsic evidence can include testimony of the parties, expert testimony, prior art, and dictionaries.

In addition to where to look, courts also have guidance in how to look. Patent law has a number of canons of interpretation. Some of the most frequently invoked canons are the following:

- Claims should be given the same meaning both validity and for infringement.
- The language of a claim will be given its ordinary and accustomed meaning.
- Claims should be construed as broadly as possible.
- If claims are ambiguous, they will be construed to preserve validity. But a court will not read a limitation into a claim simply to preserve validity.
- The same term will not be given different meanings in different claims.

Such canons do not provide a mechanical means for construing claims. Rather, they guide the court and implement patent law policy.

Literal Infringement

Once the claim has been construed, the accused device or process can be compared to the claim, as construed. The question of literal infringement is closely linked to the interpretation of the claims. When the court interprets the claims, it does not address every possible interpretation. Rather, it focuses on alternative readings of the claims relevant to the case at hand. Once interpretation determines the meaning and scope of the claims, the fact finder decides whether the claims read on the accused device or process. If there are no factual issues about the accused device or process, then the question of literal infringement may be straightforward. Indeed, the question of literal infringement may be controlled by the claim interpretation. But even if claim interpretation makes clear the meaning and scope of the claim, there may be factual issues about the nature of the accused device or process.

Infringement Under the Doctrine of Equivalents

Infringement by Equivalent Device or Process

If the accused device or process does not fall within the literal terms of the claim, there may still be infringement under the doctrine of equivalents. The doctrine of equivalents is a judicially created doctrine under which a device or process that does not fall within the literal terms of the patent claims may nevertheless infringe if it is "equivalent" to the claimed invention.

One reason for the doctrine is to prevent "fraud on the patent" by an "unscrupulous copyist." If claims were applied only literally, a competitor could search the claims and make a device or process with an insubstantial difference that fell just outside the literal claims. But the doctrine of equivalents is not limited to cases in which the defendant has copied from plaintiff's work. An independently developed but equivalent device or process can infringe. Nor is the doctrine limited to applications that were disclosed by the patent specification itself, to equivalents that were known at the time the patent was issued, or to cases in which applying the doctrine is deemed equitable. See Warner-Jenkinson Co. v. Hilton Davis Chemical Co., 520 U.S. 17 (1997).

For infringement, every element of the patent claim must have its literal or equivalent counterpart in the accused device or process. An element is equivalent if the difference would be insubstantial to one with ordinary skill in the relevant art. In addition to element-by-element equivalence, case law requires overall equivalence: that the accused device or process overall perform the same function in the same way to achieve the same result. But overall equivalence alone is not sufficient for infringement. Every element of the claim must have its literal or equivalent counterpart. Notably, the courts have not clearly defined what constitutes an "element" of a claim. Nor is equivalence an easy determination. Courts must give the claims their fair breadth, without effectively broadening the claim beyond the substance of the claimed invention. In particular, courts seek to avoid giving the patentee broader claims than she sought, especially if such broader claims would have been unpatentable (as obvious, non-novel, or not supported by the written description of the invention). Rather, the courts seek to give equitable effect to the claims that the applicant submitted and the USPTO allowed.

Prosecution History Estoppel

Prosecution history estoppel is an important limitation on the doctrine of equivalents. During the prosecution process, an applicant may amend the claims in her patent application. Prosecution history estoppel applies when an applicant makes an amendment that narrows a claim and makes that amendment to satisfy any requirement of patentability. Such an amendment might narrow a claim to avoid prior art or so that the claim agrees with the written description of the invention. When such a narrowing amendment is made, the patentee is estopped from using the doctrine of equivalents for that claim.

The rationale for estoppel is that the patentee narrowed the claim to obtain the patent and therefore should not be allowed to use the doctrine of equivalents to effectively broaden the scope of the claim. The patentee may rebut the estoppel if the equivalent device or process was not reasonably foreseeable. The patentee must make the difficult showing that one skilled in the art could not have been reasonably expected to draft a claim that literally encompassed the alleged equivalent device or process. See *Festo Corp. v. Shoketsu Kinzoku Kogyo Kabushiki Co.*, 122 S. Ct. 1831 (2002).

The estoppel applies to narrowing amendments (on the theory that the applicant has surrendered potential equivalents), not amendments that broaden the claim or that have no effect on its scope. A narrowing amendment could specifically narrow existing claim limitations or add new claim limitations. Rewriting a dependent claim into independent form could have the effect of narrowing the claim. See *Honeywell Intl. v. Hamilton Sundstrand Corp.*, 370 F.3d 1131 (en banc) (Fed Cir. 2004).

Reverse Doctrine of Equivalents

Under the doctrine of equivalents, patent claims are given scope beyond their literal language to give effect to the equitable scope of the invention. Under the "reverse doctrine of equivalents" (much less frequently invoked), the scope of a patent claim may be narrowed to less than its literal language to avoid the claim reaching beyond the equitable scope of the invention. An accused device that falls within the literal language of the claim may nevertheless perform the function in a substantially different way. To apply the doctrine, the court must first determine the equitable scope of the invention, looking at the application, prosecution history, and the prior art. It then must determine whether the accused device is so different that it falls outside the equitable scope of the invention. See *Scripps Clinic & Research Found. v. Genentech*, 927 F.2d 1565 (Fed. Cir. 1991).

Indirect Infringement

One who does not directly infringe nevertheless may be liable for indirect infringement, provided there is a direct infringer. There are two categories of indirect infringement: active inducement and contributory infringement. Anyone who actively induces infringement of a patent is liable as an infringer. 35 U.S.C. §271(b). Contributory infringement lies where one offers, sells, or imports material she knows is a component of a patented invention or is used in practicing a patented process. 35 U.S.C. §271(b). Importing a single component cannot constitute the "substantial portion" of an infringing device required for secondary liability.[3] And there remains a need to show importation of components sufficient to contribute to infringement.[4] The material must be specially made or adapted for such infringing use. There is no liability for providing a "staple article of commerce" that is "suitable for substantial noninfringing uses."

When should one be liable for infringement by another? The patent statute requires knowledge of the infringement for secondary liability. In *Global-Tech Appliances Inc. v. SEB S.A.*, 131 S. Ct. 2060 (2011), the Supreme Court held that "willful blindness" to infringement is sufficient to meet the knowledge requirement. Pentalpha hired an attorney to advise whether Pentalpha's deep fryer infringed any patents (without disclosing that Pentalpha had copied the deep fryer made by SEB). Pentalpha did not know that its fryer infringed the SEB fryer. Indeed, its attorney had not discovered any patents that that the Pentalpha fryer infringed. But had the attorney been advised that the fryer was copied from SEB, it's much more likely the attorney would have looked at the SEB patent and advised otherwise. After deliberately insulating itself from knowledge of patent infringement, Pentalpha could now not argue that lack of knowledge protected it from infringement liability.

Liability for indirect infringement requires a direct infringer. It is not sufficient that someone induced separate parties to commit acts that, added together, would add up to infringing. The Supreme Court rejected that theory of "divided infringement" in *Limelight Networks, Inc. v. Akamai Technologies, Inc.*, 134 S. Ct. 2111 (2014). But the Court left open the possibility that there could be infringement under such facts, if the parties were working together and jointly infringed. The Federal Circuit followed that broad hint and abandoned its prior requirement that joint infringement requires agency or contract, not simply two parties working together. "We conclude, on the facts of this case, that liability under §271(a) can also be found when an alleged infringer conditions participation in an activity or receipt of a benefit upon performance of a step or steps of a patented method and establishes the manner or timing of that performance. . . . Alternatively, where two or more actors form a joint enterprise, all can be charged with the acts of the other, rendering each liable for the steps performed by the other as if each is a single actor."[5]

---

3. Life Techs. Corp. v. Promega Corp., 137 S. Ct. 734, 743 (2017) ("We hold that the phrase 'substantial portion' in 35 U.S.C. §271(f)(1) has a quantitative, not a qualitative, meaning. We hold further that §271(f)(1) does not cover the supply of a single component of a multicomponent invention.").

4. Cisco Sys., Inc. v. ITC, 873 F.3d 1354 (Fed. Cir. 2017).

5. Akamai Techs., Inc. v. Limelight Networks, Inc., 797 F.3d 1020, 1023 (Fed. Cir. 2015) (en banc).

Examples

1. *Illicit offer.* Jack obtains a U.S. patent on his invention, holographic game cards. Not long afterwards, Jill gets a copy of the patent. Jill runs advertisements in several hobbyist magazines and offers holographic game cards for sale. In the ads, Jill uses Jack's written description from the patent. The holographic game cards that Jill offers to sell quite clearly fall within the claims of Jack's patent. Jill receives hundreds of orders for the cards. She simply puts the money in the bank. Not only does she not ship any cards, she doesn't even make any.

   Jack sues Jill for patent infringement. She responds that she may be liable to her customers for breach of contract, but she has not infringed Jack's patent. Even though she offered the invention for sale, she never used, made, or sold the invention. Rather, she simply ran an advertisement and banked the incoming money. Has Jill infringed the patent?

2. *Useful information.* Goldi also gets a copy of Jack's patent for his holographic game cards. Goldi studies the written description very carefully. Goldi realizes that Jack's mode for making holographic game cards also could be used to make holographic greeting cards. Goldi then goes into the greeting card business, making and selling thousands of greeting cards. The cards that Goldi makes do not fall within the claims of Jack's patent (either literally or under the doctrine of equivalents). But Goldi does not deny that the information she gleaned from the patent was essential to her in making the greeting cards. Jack sues for infringement. Jack acknowledges that Goldi has not made, sold, offered, or imported the invention. But, Jack contends, Goldi used Jack's patent in making her greeting cards and therefore is liable for infringement. Is Goldi liable for patent infringement?

3. *Design around.* Jack's cards draw the attention of Magellan, a toy manufacturer. Magellan's consumer surveys indicate that holographic game cards could be a growing market. Magellan has its engineering department go to work on developing a product. Magellan's engineers buy several dozen boxes of Jack's cards and also get copies of Jack's patent. After closely studying the cards and the patent, Magellan's engineers design a new type of holographic game card. Magellan's card does not fall within the terms of Jack's patent claims (either literally or under the doctrine of equivalents). Magellan's cards, however, are very similar to Jack's from the viewpoint of the typical consumer. A typical buyer seeking holographic game cards would be equally satisfied with Jack's or with Magellan's. Likewise, for all the typical uses that consumers have found for Jack's cards, Magellan's cards would be good substitutes. Has Magellan infringed Jack's patent?

359

4. *Innocent abroad.* Nam, a tourist from South Korea, purchases a set of Jack's holographic game cards in a San Francisco toy store. Nam is so taken with the cards that he uses the patent marking on the box to look up Jack's U.S. patent. Nam takes a copy of the patent with him to Seoul, where he begins to make and sell holographic game cards. Nam makes and sells the cards only in South Korea. Nam's cards are quite different than Jack's, but Nam's cards clearly fall within the claims of Jack's patent. Has Nam infringed Jack's U.S. patent?

5. *Unknowing infringer.* Tesla is a self-employed inventor. Some time after Jack's patent is issued, Tesla sets out to develop holographic game cards. Tesla is completely unaware of Jack's cards. After months of experimenting and testing, Tesla manages to independently arrive at the same invention as Jack. Tesla begins to make and sell holographic game cards that fall within the terms of Jack's patent claims. Tesla, however, is able to supply ample evidence that she developed the invention independently, without copying from Jack's cards or Jack's patent, directly or indirectly. Jack nonetheless sues Tesla for infringement, seeking an injunction to shut down Tesla's holographic game card business. Has Tesla infringed Jack's patent?

6. *Biding time.* Jack's patent term is due to expire July 26, 2004. Clover intends to be ready at that time to begin selling holographic game cards. Clover is very careful not to sell any of the cards during the patent term. Rather, Clover makes several offers and signs contracts, each of which stipulate that the sales shall occur on July 27, 2004, and that the cards will be shipped on that date. Clover notes that the patent statute clearly states that an offer to sell only infringes if the sale occurs before the expiration of the term of the patent. To be ready, Clover also manufactures thousands of sets of holographic game cards, which fall within the terms of Jack's patent claims. Has Clover infringed Jack's patent?

7. *Foreign competition.* Drugs has a U.S. patent on its "Process for Screening Chemical Compounds for Potential Use as Pharmaceuticals." Users of the patented process can determine which chemical compounds out of thousands are likely to be useful in treating certain viral diseases. Once the biological action of the virus is known, the process helps to find chemical compounds that would act in a similar way. If the chemical compound is introduced into the body, it may block the virus. The process also shows which compounds cannot be used because of such hazards as toxicity. Using the process is much more efficient than simply testing the compounds one by one in the laboratory to see whether they have the desired effect. Manchester, a pharmaceutical company in the United Kingdom, learns of the patented process through trade publications. Manchester then uses the process in its London laboratory. Manchester screens thousands of chemical compounds, thereby selecting one compound as a potential treatment for Charlton's Syndrome. After further testing, the

compound proves to be an effective treatment. Manchester manufactures a pharmaceutical containing the compound, ships it to the United States, and sells it in drugstores. Has Manchester infringed Drugs's U.S. patent?

8. *Component comportment.* Microsoft makes software in the United States. Microsoft exports the software on a golden master disk to computer makers abroad, who make copies and load the software onto the computers they make. The computers allegedly infringe certain computer program patents, largely because they include the Microsoft software. Could Microsoft be liable for infringement, even where the computers are assembled outside the United States?

9. *New use of old stuff.* Wicket holds a U.S. patent on a composition of matter. In Wicket's patent application, Wicket stated that the utility of the invention was its use as a waterproof glue. Wicket sells the invention as Zooper Sticky glue, used to glue plumbing fixtures. Zooper Sticky is not very successful and sells only a few hundred bottles a year. Fez, a veterinarian, discovers that Zooper Sticky is very useful as an ointment for ridding lizards of parasites. Fez starts to manufacture an identical composition of matter and sells it as Wizard of Liz. When Wicket sues Fez for patent infringement, Fez contends that he is not infringing because he is using the invention for a completely different purpose than the utility set forth in the patent. Is Fez infringing?

10. *Alternatives?* Krazy Devices invents and patents a handheld radar gun, which determines the speed of objects. The device is designed for use by police officers in detecting speeders. The patent's only claim includes the element "an electronic display showing the speed of the fastest or the strongest target detected." The written description in the patent describes several embodiments of the invention. Each one includes a display, which the user could set to show either the fastest target or the strongest target. The user could decide whether to show the speed of the fastest vehicle on the road (which might give a weak signal because it was a small car or because it was partly behind another vehicle) or the speed of the target returning the strongest signal (which the user could choose by pointing the device directly at a vehicle). The record shows that Krazy chose this configuration because it would be difficult for a device to calculate the speeds of both the strongest and fastest targets quickly enough to display both at once.

Speedy Machines begins to make and sell its own radar gun. Speedy's gun is identical to the devices described in Kustom's patent, save for one difference. Speedy's gun displays the speeds of both the fastest target and the strongest target. Krazy sues Speedy for patent infringement. Speedy argues that its device does not contain the element in Krazy's claim of "an LCD display showing the speed of the fastest or the strongest target detected." Speedy contends its device does not show the speed of the fastest or the strongest target; rather its device shows the speed of the fastest *and* the strongest target. Has Speedy infringed?

11. *Baffled by dictionaries.* The scope of a patent on modular, steel-shell panels (especially useful in building prison walls) depends on how broadly one reads the term "baffle." Dictionaries give it a broad reading, such as "something for deflecting, checking, or otherwise regulating flow." In the written description of the invention in the relevant patent, however, the term is used much more narrowly, to refer only to structures that regulate flow and that do not stick out beyond a certain angle. The patent holder argues that, notwithstanding its use of the term in the written description, the meaning of the term is its dictionary meaning. "Baffles" should be read broadly in the patent claims (meaning the claims will be broader, giving greater rights). Which meaning should the court use in interpreting the claims, the dictionary meaning or the meaning implicit in the written description of the patent application?

12. *Infringing equivalent?* Backpackers buy thousands of Warm Blanket's patented thermal camping blanket. The blanket uses both special insulating material and an intricate self-erecting structure to create a thin layer of air around the sleeping camper, conserving body warmth. A competitor, Comfy Products, sees the popularity of the product and begins to make and sell a similar blanket. Comfy uses somewhat different material and uses an erecting structure that requires some work by the camper, rather than the automatic operation of Warm Blanket's product. Both achieve essentially the same result. Warm Blanket sues Comfy, contending that Comfy has infringed one of the claims in Warm Blanket's patent. Warm Blanket acknowledges that Comfy's device does not literally infringe the claim. Warm Blanket further acknowledges that Comfy's device does not have elements that are equivalent to some of the elements of the claim. But Warm Blanket contends that the device nevertheless infringes the claim under the doctrine of equivalents because Comfy deliberately copied the product, and Comfy's device performs the same function in the same way to achieve the same result. Has Comfy infringed?

13. *Amend claim, lose equivalents.* Potato applies for a patent on a reclining chair. The examiner disallows Claim 1 of the application, on the grounds that it was anticipated by a chair described in an article in *Recline and Fall*, an industry periodical. Potato amends the claim, narrowing the claim so that the other chair no longer fits the claim. The examiner allows the claim, and soon the patent issues. Potato later sues the seller of a rival reclining chair, alleging infringement of Claim 1. The accused chair does not literally infringe the claim, but Potato alleges that it is equivalent to the invention claimed in Claim 1. Can Potato use the doctrine of equivalents?

14. *Edit.* Lorikeet applies for a patent on her "Disposable Container for Drinking Water." During the course of prosecuting the patent, Lorikeet amends Claim 7 of the application. The amendment broadens the claim by changing it from reading on only cardboard containers to reading on

362

containers made of any material. Lorikeet is issued a patent. Two years later, she learns that Albatross is selling beverage containers that are very similar to hers. Lorikeet sues Albatross for patent infringement, specifically alleging infringement of Claim 7 of the patent. Albatross's containers do not literally infringe Claim 7, but Lorikeet alleges infringement under the doctrine of equivalents. Albatross responds that Lorikeet cannot use the doctrine of equivalents with respect to Claim 7. When an applicant amends a claim, he argues, the applicant implicitly surrenders the right to argue that the claim covers equivalents. Does prosecution history estoppel prevent Lorikeet from relying on the doctrine of equivalents here?

15. *Indirect infringer.* Dipsy holds a patent on a "Pedal-Powered Custard Maker." Dipsy sells thousands of the custard makers to restaurants across the country. Po decides to acquire some for export. Rather than buy from Dipsy, Po contacts Spec Manufacturing. Po asks Spec to make 200 units of the machine and supplies Spec with a copy of Dipsy's patent, which describes how to make the custard maker. Po agrees to pay a specified price for 200 of the machines. Spec makes the machines, delivers them to Po, and receives the payment from Po. Shortly thereafter, Spec goes into bankruptcy.

    Dipsy sues Po for patent infringement. Po freely agrees that Spec infringed the patent by making and by selling the patented invention. But Po contends that she has not infringed. The patentee has the right to exclude others from making, using, selling, offering to sell, or importing the patented invention—and Po has done none of those things. Rather, she bought, possessed, and exported the patented invention, none of which constitute infringement. Has Po infringed Dipsy's patent?

16. *Many hands.* Akamai holds a patent on a method of delivering electronic data using a content delivery network. Limelight provides similar services to Limelight's customers. Limelight performs some of the steps of the patented process and its customers perform the other steps of the patented process. Is Limelight liable for inducement of infringement?

Explanations

1. Jill has infringed the patent. The patentee has the right to exclude others from making, using, offering to sell, selling, or importing the patented invention. Jill did not make, use, or import the invention. But she did offer it for sale (even though she did not actually have any to sell). So Jill is liable for infringement.

2. Goldi is not liable for patent infringement. Jack has the right to exclude others from using the patented invention. But Goldi did not use the patented invention (the holographic game cards, as claimed in the patent).

Rather, Goldi used the information in Jack's patent. Nor did Goldi make, offer to sell, sell, or import the invention. She made and sold an article that did not fall within the terms of Jack's patent claims. So Goldi did not infringe Jack's patent. Indeed, Goldi's activity is the sort of thing that patent law encourages. To gain a patent, Jack must permit certain information to be disclosed to the world in the issued patent. The information is free for others to exploit, provided they do not infringe the patent claims.

3. Magellan has not infringed Jack's patent. Magellan's product does not fall within the claims of Jack's patent (either literally or under the doctrine of equivalents). So Magellan has made holographic game cards, but it has not made Jack's patented invention. Magellan does not infringe if it makes, uses, offers to sell, sells, or imports a product that does not fall within Jack's patent claims. Note that this conclusion depends on Magellan's product falling outside Jack's patent claims.

4. Nam has not infringed Jack's U.S. patent. The patentee has the right to exclude others from making, using, offering to sell, or selling the invention in the United States or importing the patented invention into the United States. Nam purchased the cards in the United States and exported them to South Korea, neither of which acts (buying and exporting) infringe the exclusive rights (using, making, selling, offering to sell, importing). Nam then made and sold the cards, but in South Korea, not in the United States. So Nam did not infringe Jack's U.S. patent. Nor did Nam import the cards into the United States, which would constitute infringement. Rather, Nam sold them only in South Korea.

5. Tesla has infringed Jack's patent. Patent infringement does not require that the infringer copied the invention from the inventor in any way. Someone who independently develops a product or process is still liable for infringement if they make, use, sell, offer to sell, or import a product or process that falls within the patent claims. Good faith and independent work are not defenses to patent infringement. Accordingly, even someone who develops (or seeks to develop) his own product or process may be well advised to do a patent search to avoid infringement (and also to avoid duplicating work that has already been done).

6. Clover has infringed Jack's patent. Clover is correct in asserting that she has not infringed by offering the invention for sale. The statute does provide that an offer for sale infringes only if the sale occurs within the patent term. But Clover has also manufactured thousands of sets of infringing game cards. So Clover is liable for making the patented invention during the term of the patent (even though she has not sold or offered to sell the invention within the patent term).

7. Manchester probably has not infringed Drugs's U.S. patent. The patentee has the right to exclude others from making, using, offering to sell,

selling, or importing the patented invention. Manchester used the process outside the United States, so Manchester did not infringe by using the patented process. But the statute also imposes liability for importing a product made by a patented process. So the issue here is whether the pharmaceutical imported by Manchester was made by Drugs's patented process.

Manchester did not directly use the process to make the pharmaceutical. The process is not a process for making a pharmaceutical. Rather, the process is used to select a preexisting chemical that may be used as a drug. The chemical presumably is made by some other process. So although Manchester used the process to decide what pharmaceutical to make, it did not use the process to actually make the pharmaceutical.

The counterargument would be that Manchester "used" the process to make the pharmaceutical, in the sense that without using the process it would not have been able to make the pharmaceutical. But that would give a very broad meaning to the phrase "a product which is made" by a patented process. Put another way, the pharmaceutical in a sense is an indirect product of using the patented process, but the process is not actually used to make the pharmaceutical. Rather, the provision is more aptly applied only to products of manufacturing processes. *See Bayer AG v. Housey Pharmaceuticals*, 340 F.3d 1367 (Fed. Cir. 2003).

8. Microsoft was not liable for exporting a component that was incorporated into a patented invention. *See Microsoft Corp. v. AT&T Corp.*, 550 U.S. 437 (2007). Software can be a component of an invention. "Inventions" can be both products and processes, and a process can be a "component" of an invention. While the term "component" might seem to signify a physical piece of a product, like a machine part, a "component" can also be a process. Here, software, which encodes a process, not a product, is a component of the larger process that constitutes the invention.

But the component was not incorporated into the invention. Rather, Microsoft shipped a master disk containing a copy of Windows. The Court reasoned that one copy shipped from the United States could not be the same component installed into thousands of computers. A copy was made from the master disk and installed into each computer. The Court reasoned that the various copies were the components of the computers, and those copies were made abroad, not shipped from the United States. Interpreting the statute with a presumption against extraterritorial application, the Court held there was no infringement.

9. Fez is infringing Wicket's patent. Infringement depends only on whether the alleged infringer makes, uses, offers to sell, sells, or imports the patented invention. The patented invention is defined by the patent claims. The invention must have utility to be patentable, but, unless that utility were included as an element of the patent claims, the scope of the patent

is not limited to the utility that supported the granting of the patent. Fez has made and sold the patented invention and therefore has infringed the patent.

10. Speedy probably has not infringed Krazy's patent. The result would depend on how the court construed the claim language, "an LCD display showing the speed of the fastest or the strongest target detected." Specifically, it would depend on whether the court construed the word "or" as used in the claim to be an exclusive "or" (as in "either *A* or *B*") or to be an inclusive "or" (as in "*A* or *B* or both *A* and *B*"). If the court interprets the "or" to be an exclusive "or," Speedy has not infringed because Speedy's device displays both the strongest and fastest targets, not just one or the other. If the court interprets the "or" to be an inclusive "or," Speedy has infringed.

    Claim interpretation is very fact-specific, so there is no general rule governing whether an "or" used in a claim will be interpreted as exclusive or inclusive. The same word is frequently interpreted to carry different meaning in the claims of different patents. In this case, it is likely the court would interpret it as an exclusive "or." Krazy's application contained descriptions only of guns that displayed the fastest or the strongest target, not both targets. It would have been difficult for Krazy to make a gun that displayed both targets, so Krazy's written description may not have met the enablement requirement. In common usage, the word "or" is most often understood in the exclusive sense, although the inclusive sense is also quite often used. All those factors would probably lead the court to interpret the claim to apply to guns that displayed the fastest or strongest target, but not both. Cf. *Kustom Signals v. Applied Concepts*, 264 F.3d 1326 (Fed. Cir. 2001).

11. The Federal Circuit has strongly indicated that the primary source to find the meaning of terms used in a patent claim is the patent. *See Phillips v. AWH Corp.*, 415 F.3d 1303, 1310 (Fed. Cir. 2005). In construing patent terms, the court should look first to the patent itself, then to the prosecution history of the patent, and only then to extrinsic evidence, such as expert and inventor testimony, dictionaries, and learned treatises.

12. Comfy Products has not infringed Warm Blanket's patent. For infringement, the accused device or process must contain a literal or equivalent counterpart to every element of the patent claim in question. Even copying a product is not infringement if the copy does not fall within the claims of the patent. Here, Warm Blanket acknowledges that there are elements of its patent claim that do not appear (either literally or as equivalents) in Comfy's product. Warm Blanket argues that there is overall equivalence between the two products, but that is insufficient. In addition, the fact that the two products are substitutes from the consumer's point of view is insufficient to support infringement under the doctrine of equivalents.

13. Potato cannot use the doctrine of equivalents for Claim 1. Under prosecution history estoppel, if an applicant narrows a claim for a reason related to patentability, the applicant may no longer use the doctrine of equivalents for that claim. The rational is that the applicant conceded that the claim should be narrower and should not be able to use the doctrine of equivalents to effectively broaden it.

14. Prosecution history estoppel does not prevent Lorikeet from relying on the doctrine of equivalents with respect to Claim 7 of her patent. Prosecution history estoppel applies when the applicant makes an amendment to a patent claim that narrows the claim, for reasons related to patentability. The theory is that by narrowing the claim, the applicant effectively surrenders the right to argue that the claim should be interpreted more broadly to cover not only its literal scope but also equivalents. But Lorikeet did not make an amendment that narrowed the scope of the claim; her amendment broadened the scope of the claim. Prosecution history estoppel applies only to narrowing amendments, so it does not apply in this case.

15. Po is liable as an infringer. Po did not directly infringe the patent because Po did not make, use, offer to sell, sell, or import the patented invention. But one that actively induces infringement of a patent is liable as an infringer. Po actively induced Spec's infringement by asking Spec to make and sell the patented invention to Po, providing the specifications for the process, accepting delivery of the machines, and paying Spec for them.

16. Limelight is not liable for inducement because there is no infringement. Limelight performs some of the steps, its customers perform some of the steps. But no one infringes by performing all the steps of the patented process. Note: this result could change if the Federal Circuit relaxes the strict rule that infringement requires that a single party perform all steps, as opposed to recognizing infringement through the actions of joint parties working together. Cf. *Muniauction, Inc. v. Thomson Corp.*, 532 F.3d 1318 (Fed. Cir. 2008) (rejecting joint infringement theory).

Jurisdiction and Venue

A foreign entity that licensed and enforced intellectual property rights in the United States was subject to personal jurisdiction in the United States.[6]

---

6. *Xilinx, Inc. v. Papst Licensing GmbH & Co. KG*, 848 F.3d 1346, 1357 (Fed. Cir. 2017). Moreover, there are other facts that, under the *Burger King* analysis, confirm the view that the burden on the defendant is not undue. For instance, the burden on Papst is mitigated by Papst's status as a nonpracticing patent holder residing outside the United States. This is not a case like *RedWing*, where the defendant conducts its affairs in one state and is called to litigate

Until 2017, a substantial portion of all U.S. patent cases were filed in the Eastern District of Texas. The patent venue statute requires that a defendant can be sued where it does business or resides. In *TC Heartland*, the Supreme Court rejected the Federal Circuit's permissive reading of the patent venue statute.[7] When Congress amended related statutes to broaden the definition of a defendant's "residence," it did not intend to amend the patent jurisdiction statute to have such a broad sweep. Delaware is now the most likely court for patent infringement cases. As to "doing business" to support venue, the Federal Circuit rejected tenuous link to a district.[8] The court rejected the holding of the Eastern District of Texas that a defendant was doing business there, where a single employee had his home office there, but he "was not listed in any business directories or websites, he did not maintain product literature or products at his home, and he was the only employee within the district."[9]

DEFENSES

Invalidity

An issued patent is presumed valid, but an alleged infringer may challenge validity, contending that the applicant failed to meet any of the requirements for patentability. 35 U.S.C. §282. In deciding the validity of the patent, the court is not limited to reviewing the material considered by the USPTO. Rather, the defendants may produce prior art or other evidence to attack validity and raise arguments not raised before the USPTO. Studies have found that somewhere between one-third and one-half of litigated patents are held invalid. An alleged infringer has considerable incentive to uncover invalidating prior art that neither the applicant nor the USPTO found, to formulate better arguments against validity than the USPTO considered, and to discover other evidence that undermines validity. Likewise, federal litigation of a patent devotes much more resources to scrutinizing its validity than does the work of an examiner at the USPTO. *See* Mark A. Lemley, *Rational Ignorance at the Patent Office*, 96 Nw. U. L. Rev. 1495 (2001).

---

in a distant state rather than its own residence. *See* 848 F.3d at 1357. By the very nature of its business, Papst must litigate its patents in the United States in fora far from its home office. In this context the burden on Papst to litigate in California appears not undue.

The lack of significant burden on Papst is also evidenced by Papst's prior litigations in California itself. Papst has repeatedly availed itself of the California federal court system—at least seven times—by filing patent infringement lawsuits there.

7. TC Heartland LLC v. Kraft Foods Group Brands LLC, No. 16–341 (U.S. 2017). The Supreme Court also held laches inapplicable in patent cases, as in copyright law. SCA Hygiene Prods. Aktiebolag v. First Quality Baby Prods., LLC, 137 S. Ct. 954 (2017).

8. In re Cray Inc., 871 F.3d 1355 (Fed. Cir. 2017).

9. In re Cray Inc., 871 F.3d 1355, 1364 (Fed. Cir. 2017).

A patent should not issue if the claimed invention is not new. But showing that something had been done before is not always easy. With software patents especially, it may be difficult to find code (which is often not widely available) that prefigures a subsequent patent. Something that complicates the issue is that once the patent is issued, it is presumed valid and can only be invalidated with "clear and convincing" evidence. That gives a lot of leverage to patent holders. When an inventor applies for a patent, the examiner must decide if the invention has already been sold or commercially used (in the United States) or published (anywhere in the world). The examiner, however, has limited resources to look for all those possible references.

Where a party presented evidence that had not been considered by the patent examiner, a court could use the general "preponderance" standard: if it was more likely than not that the patent was wrongly issued, it would be held invalid. In patent litigation, parties often uncover relevant references not considered during the application process. Compared to a single examiner, a patent defendant has much greater incentives (many millions may be at stake) and resources to research whether the invention was truly new. The Supreme Court, however, declined to depart from the existing standard (clear and convincing evidence required to establish invalidity), leaving it to Congress to change the patent statute if it so chose. *Microsoft Corp. v. i4i Ltd. Partnership*, 131 S. Ct. 2238 (2011).

A party may also challenge the validity of a patent before the USPTO, by filing a post-grant challenge. Someone sued for infringement may, in addition to defending in court, challenge the validity of the patent in the USPTO. Within nine months after a patent issue, a party may file a Post Grant Review, challenging the validity of the patent on any grounds. Beyond that time window, a patent may be challenged in an Inter Partes Review. The grounds for challenge in IPR are limited to novelty and nonobviousness. Even if no litigation is pending, anyone can file challenges in the USPTO to patents they claim are invalid. So now competitors are challenging each others' patents in the USPTO, nonprofits are challenging patents (such as the EFF's challenge to a patent claimed to cover podcasting or challenges to some pharmaceutical patents), and even investors are filing patent challenges to drive down a company's stock price (so called "PTAB trolls").

Patent holders have become very aware of the risks of the PTAB post-grant challenges. Allergan, an Irish pharmaceutical company, avoided the PTAB by transferring the rights to its lucrative patents on the drug Restasis to the Saint Regis Mohawk Tribe, agreeing to pay a fee and royalties for an exclusive license to the patents.[10] The court in a related infringement action expressed skepticism: "The Court has serious concerns about the legitimacy of the tactic that Allergan and the Tribe have employed. The essence of the

---

10. *Allergan, Inc. v. Teva Pharm. USA, Inc.*, No. 2:15-cv-1455-WCB, 2017 U.S. Dist. LEXIS 170825, at *6 (E.D. Tex. Oct. 16, 2017).

matter is this: Allergan purports to have sold the patents to the Tribe, but in reality it has paid the Tribe to allow Allergan to purchase — or perhaps more precisely, to rent — the Tribe's sovereign immunity in order to defeat the pending IPR proceedings in the PTO."[11]

Inequitable Conduct

Until 2010, a common ground for attacking the enforceability of a patent is inequitable conduct by the applicant during prosecution of the patent application. Inequitable conduct may be affirmative misrepresentations, failure to disclose information, submission of false information, or other misleading conduct. The defense became much more difficult to establish after the decision in *Therasense, Inc.* (*Now Known As Abbott Diabetes Care, Inc.*) *v. Becton, Dickinson & Co.*, 649 F.3d 1276 (Fed. Cir. 2011) (en banc). *Therasense* held that "the accused infringer must prove that the patentee acted with the specific intent to deceive the PTO" and that the "PTO would not have allowed a claim had it been aware of the undisclosed prior art." Since such evidence would invalidate the patent anyway, inequitable conduct has become much less useful as a defense.

Implied License and First Sale

An authorized sale of a patented article includes an implied license to use it. If inventor sells her patented umbrellas, she implicitly grants buyers a license to use them. The parties to a transaction may decide to govern such matters explicitly, in which case there is no place for an implied license. But the implied license doctrine makes it unnecessary for parties to expressly provide for licenses. Umbrella buyers and sellers need not waste resources on making sure that the necessary patent licenses have been granted.

The first sale doctrine (also known as "exhaustion") authorizes the buyer to use and to sell the article. The theory is that the patentee, by selling the patented article, has surrendered his right to control use and sale of that particular article. The buyer may use the article and may sell it to another buyer, who likewise may use and sell the article without infringement. Without the first sale doctrine, both would be liable for infringement (the first for selling a patented invention, the second for using it). Like implied license, first sale rights rest on implied agreement and may be altered by express agreement or other circumstances.

The Supreme Court has applied first sale broadly. *See Quanta Computer, Inc. v. LG Electronics, Inc.*, 128 S. Ct. 2109 (2008). In *Quanta*, the patent holder, LG Electronics

---

11. Allergan, Inc. v. Teva Pharm. USA, Inc., No. 2:15-cv-1455-WCB, 2017 U.S. Dist. LEXIS 170825, at *10 (E.D. Tex. Oct. 16, 2017).

(LGE) licensed a number of patents to Intel. The patents covered processes used in microprocessor and chipset technology. LGE brought infringement against some Intel customers. The Supreme Court held that first sale did apply to process patents. The Court also held that first sale applied, even though the Intel products did not embody all the patent claims. The Court also held that the sale by Intel constituted an authorized sale of the invention, even though it was not specifically authorized by LGE. The Court formulated a broad statement of first sale: "The authorized sale of an article that substantially embodies a patent exhausts the patent holder's rights and prevents the patent holder from invoking patent law to control postsale use of the article."

For decades, courts had permitted patent holders to limit first sale by contract. If a product was sold under a contract that prohibited resale, then it would be infringement to resell the product or for the buyer to use it. That ended in 2017. The Supreme Court in *Impression Products v. Lexmark International*[12] held that a first sale exhausts the patent rights of the seller in that particular item sold. Resale or use of the item would not be patent infringement. Contractual restrictions to the contrary will not make it infringement (although they may still be effective against parties to the sale). "We conclude that Lexmark exhausted its patent rights in these cartridges the moment it sold them. The single-use/no-resale restrictions in Lexmark's contracts with customers may have been clear and enforceable under contract law, but they do not entitle Lexmark to retain patent rights in an item that it has elected to sell."[13] The decision rested on the policy of preventing restraints on alienation: "More is at stake when it comes to patents than simply the dealings between the parties, which can be addressed through contract law. Instead, exhaustion occurs because, in a sale, the patentee elects to give up title to an item in exchange for payment. Allowing patent rights to stick remora-like to that item as it flows through the market would violate the principle against restraints on alienation."[14]

In addition, the decision applies to reimportation or importation of authorized goods (sometimes called "gray market goods"). If a U.S. patent holder sells a patented device overseas, it may be imported and used in the United States without infringement.

Both implied license and first sale apply to the actual article sold. They do not authorize the buyer to make or use additional embodiments of the patented invention. If buyer buys a patented digital camera, she may use

---

12. Impression Prods. v. Lexmark Int'l, 2017 U.S. LEXIS 3397, *11-12 (2017). This case presents two questions about the scope of the patent exhaustion doctrine: First, whether a patentee that sells an item under an express restriction on the purchaser's right to reuse or resell the product may enforce that restriction through an infringement lawsuit. And second, whether a patentee exhausts its patent rights by selling its product outside the United States, where American patent laws do not apply. We conclude that a patentee's decision to sell a product exhausts all of its patent rights in that item, regardless of any restrictions the patentee purports to impose or the location of the sale.
13. Impression Prods. v. Lexmark Int'l, 2017 U.S. LEXIS 3397, *17 (2017).
14. Impression Prods. v. Lexmark Int'l, 2017 U.S. LEXIS 3397, *36 (2017).

and sell that physical article. She does not gain the right to make, use, or sell additional cameras.

Bowman v. Monsanto Co., 133 S. Ct. 1761 (2013) addressed a fine line. Monsanto's patented Ready Roundup seeds have "a genetic modification that enables soybean plants to survive exposure to glyphosate, the active ingredient in many herbicides." When Monsanto sells those seeds to farmers, it cannot sue them for using the seeds. But the issue in *Bowman* was whether patent exhaustion applies when the authorized seeds grow into corn and produce seeds of their own. The Supreme Court held that the second-generation seeds were "additional copies," not subject to the patent exhaustion doctrine. Otherwise, farmers would "need only buy the seed once, whether from Monsanto, a competitor, or (as here) a grain elevator. The grower could multiply his initial purchase, and then multiply that new creation, ad infinitum—each time profiting from the patented seed without compensating its inventor." The Court, however, left open application of the rule to developments in biotechnology, computer science, and other fields: "Our holding today is limited—addressing the situation before us, rather than every one involving a self-replicating product. We recognize that such inventions are becoming ever more prevalent, complex, and diverse. In another case, the article's self-replication might occur outside the purchaser's control. Or it might be a necessary but incidental step in using the item for another purpose."

Repair and Reconstruction

The repair defense follows from the implied license to use. The owner of a patented article has a broad right to repair it. For example, it was not infringement to replace the fabric on a patented automobile convertible top. *See Aro Manufacturing Co. v. Convertible Top Replacement Co.*, 365 U.S. 336 (1961). The owner of the patented article likewise may replace each of the unpatented components of the article as they wear out. But she may not go beyond repair and reconstruct it after the entity, viewed as a whole, has become spent. The difference between extensive repair (permissible) and reconstruction (prohibited) is very fact-specific.

Experimental Use: A "Truly Narrow" Exception

Courts have recognized an experimental use defense to patent infringement but have construed it rather narrowly.[15] The Federal Circuit held that experimental use protects only actions performed "for amusement, to satisfy idle curiosity, or for strictly philosophical inquiry." A use will not be protected

---

15. *See* Janice M. Mueller, *No "Dilettante Affair": Rethinking the Experimental Use Exception to Patent Infringement for Biomedical Research Tools*, 76 Wash. L. Rev. 1, 17 (2001).

if it has "definite, cognizable, and not insubstantial commercial purposes." The experimental defense will not protect pharmaceutical research or even basic scientific research if the research could lead even indirectly to commercial results. Now that most major research universities have partnerships with industry and run technology transfer offices to patent research results, the defense will rarely apply. *See Madey v. Duke Univ.*, 307 F.3d 1351 (Fed. Cir. 2002). So patent law does not have a counterpart to fair use in copyright. There is a good argument for a broader experimental use defense because users often increase the value of an invention by coming up with better ways to exploit it. *See* Katherine Strandburg, *Users as Innovators: Implications for Patent Doctrine*, 79 U. Colo. L. Rev. 467 (2008); Maureen O'Rourke, *Toward a Doctrine of Fair Use in Patent Law*, 100 Colum. L. Rev. 1177 (2000).

Congress has enacted a specific safe harbor for some testing with respect to seeking FDA approval of such products as generic versions of patented pharmaceuticals. It is not infringement to make, use, sell, or import a patented invention "solely for uses reasonably related to the development and submission of information under a Federal law which regulates the manufacture, use, or sale of drugs." 35 U.S.C. §271(e)(1). The Supreme Court rejected a narrow reading of the provision, which would have limited protection to clinical testing to supply information when seeking FDA approval of a drug. Rather, the Court read the provision to be broad enough to encompass research uses, provided the research might lead to development of a drug that would be submitted for FDA approval. *See Merck KGaA v. Integra Lifesciences I, Ltd.*, 125 S. Ct. 2372 (2005).

Laches

The equitable defense of laches may apply in patent litigation. A defendant may establish laches by showing (1) the patentee unreasonably and inexcusably delayed bringing an infringement action and (2) the delay caused material prejudice to the defendant. The Supreme Court has held, however, that laches does not apply in copyright cases because the statute of limitations is intended to govern the time limits on bringing suit. *Petrella v. MGM*, 134 S. Ct. 1962 (2014). Future cases may extend that reasoning to patent cases, which are subject to a six-year statute of limitations. 35 U.S.C. §286.

The Federal Circuit has also recognized the doctrine of prosecution laches, under which unreasonable and unexplained delay in prosecuting the patent application may bar enforcement of the patent. *See Symbol Technologies, Inc. v. Lemelson Med., Educ. & Research Found., LP*, 277 F.3d 1361 (Fed. Cir. 2002).[16]

---

16. Section 273, under the 1952 Act as amended, also provides a prior use defense, applicable only to patents that claim "a method of doing or conducting business" (a rather vague category). The defendant has a defense if she is "acting in good faith, actually reduced the subject matter to practice at least 1 year before the effective filing date of such patent, and

This would bar the enforceability of "submarine patents," where the inventor delays the issuance of a patent to wait until the technology becomes adopted.

The defense is of little practical importance for applications filed after June 8, 1995 because the patent term is now 20 years from date of application, meaning that delay in prosecution reduces the patent term.

Antitrust and Patent Misuse

A patent grants a broad right to exclude others from certain market activities. The patentee may be the single seller of the invention but generally is not a monopolist in the economic sense, with the power to set prices in a given market. Rather, for most patented inventions, there are competitive products or processes not covered by the patent (if indeed there is a market for the patented invention at all). But some patent holders may hold market power or be able to use cross-licensing agreements with competitors to control a market. Section 271(d) provides a safe harbor for certain practices but does not provide patentees general immunity from antitrust laws. Courts have held the antitrust laws violated by such practices as "tying" (requiring licensees to purchase separate goods or services), bad-faith claims of infringement, and fraud in obtaining patent rights. Courts also apply the defense of patent misuse, which renders the patent unenforceable when the patentee uses restrictive practices to effectively broaden the scope of the patent grant, with anticompetitive effect (such as by requiring royalty payments beyond the patent term). As is true in antitrust law generally, courts struggle to distinguish anticompetitive practices from bona fide commercial licensing. Possession of a patent does not give rise to a presumption of market power, so restrictive practices may not violate the antitrust laws. See *Illinois Tool Works Inc. v. Independent Ink, Inc.*, 547 U.S. 28 (2006). In addition, patent misuse is a separate doctrine, which does not require showing an antitrust violation.

Federal Trade Commn. v. Actavis, Inc., 133 S. Ct. 2223 (2013) addressed whether "reverse payment" settlements could violate antitrust laws. When a pharmaceutical patent holder sues the maker of a generic version of the drug, the parties sometimes settled with the generic maker agreeing to stay out of the market for a period of time in return for a payment from the patent holder. That is the reverse of the usual settlement, where the alleged infringer pays the patent holder. Courts had upheld such "reverse settlements" as

---

commercially used the subject matter before the effective filing date of such patent." For patents issued after September 16, 2011, the defense was broadened: a party is entitled to a defense, if they, more than one year before the patent was issued, used the subject matter "either in connection with an internal commercial use or an actual arm's length sale or other arm's length commercial transfer of a useful end result of such commercial use."

reflecting the exclusionary rights of the patent holder. But the *Actavis* court held such agreements subject to scrutiny under the antitrust rule of reason, as to whether their restrictive effects were outweighed by positive effect on competition. That encourages generic makers to litigate the validity of pharmaceutical patents. How broadly *Actavis* may affect the validity of patent settlements generally remains to be seen.

Examples

1. *Needle in a haystack.* Mimmy, a tireless inventor, spends years of experimentation in developing quick-drying underwater paint for use on bridges and submarines. She finds a perfect combination of ingredients that enables the paint to be applied in cold saltwater while retaining the desired color and remaining in place. Mimmy decides to seek a U.S. patent after a thorough search of the prior art discloses no reference that would render her invention nonpatentable. The USPTO also searches the prior art and determines that Mimmy is entitled to a patent. After Mimmy's patent issues, Smoky reads about it in a trade publication. Smoky, using the disclosure in Mimmy's patent, manufactures and sells an identical product.

   Mimmy sues Smoky for patent infringement. Smoky's attorney hires a consultant, Buster, to search for prior art. Buster, after months of research and discussions with various experts, manages to find a reference that anticipates the invention. Many years before Mimmy's invention date, an article in an obscure (now defunct) engineering journal described an identical product, including instructions enabling one to make it. Smoky accordingly claims that Mimmy's patent is invalid because her invention was not novel. Mimmy responds that Smoky cannot rely on the newly found prior art for several reasons. Mimmy developed the paint herself rather than deriving it in any way from the prior publication. Both Mimmy and the USPTO did thorough searches of the prior art and found nothing. Finally, Smoky copied the invention from Mimmy, not from the newly found prior art. Can Smoky rely on the newly discovered reference to raise a defense of invalidity?

2. *Hiding the ball.* Christo decides to apply for a patent on his new tear-resistant wrapping paper. Christo's attorney searches the prior art and comes across a Japanese patent on a rather similar product. The inventions are not identical, but the disclosure in the Japanese patent might render Christo's invention obvious (and nonpatentable). The rules of the USPTO do not require applicants to submit translations of foreign patents. Christo decides to submit a copy of the Japanese patent with his application. He also submits a short English-language summary of the patent. He intentionally drafts the summary in a way that ignores the sections of the patent that could be used to deny Christo's application. Rather, the summary discusses only elements that are not relevant to

Christo's invention. Christo also falsely states that no product similar to his had ever been made, whereas such a product was described in the Japanese patent (although it was different in several respects). Christo receives a U.S. patent and subsequently files an infringement suit against Hughes Paint.

Hughes contends that Christo's invention was obvious and non-patentable. Hughes submits several items of prior art, including a full translation of the Japanese patent. Hughes also contends that the patent is unenforceable on the grounds that Christo engaged in inequitable conduct in prosecuting the application. The court determines that, although it is a close call, the invention was nonobvious over the prior art (including the Japanese patent). The court holds that the Japanese patent raised a prima facie case of unpatentability, but that would have been rebutted by other evidence submitted by Christo. The other evidence included references that "teach away" from the invention (that is, would make a worker in the field less likely to try to make the invention) and secondary considerations (evidence that tended to show the invention had not been obvious, such as that the invention sold very well, was licensed by others in the field, and solved a problem that had long baffled others). Christo argues that there is not a sufficient showing of inequitable conduct to deny enforceability. First, Christo submitted the Japanese patent rather than trying to conceal it from the USPTO, and the rules did not require submitting a translation. Second, even with disclosure of the full translated patent, the invention was patentable, so Christo's alleged conduct would not have made any difference. Is the patent enforceable?

3. First sale. Pinky holds a patent on an insulated grape-crushing chamber used in making particular varieties of wine. Pinky learns that Noma has made and sold one of the chambers to Winery. Noma falsely told Winery that Pinky had authorized the manufacture and sale. Winery has been using the chamber in making its wine and intends to continue using it. Pinky delivers a cease-and-desist letter to Winery. Winery responds that the first sale doctrine authorizes Winery to use the chamber because Winery bought the chamber in good faith for full value. Does first sale insulate Winery from patent infringement?

4. R and R? Kamera Ko. makes and sells a patented single-use camera. A consumer typically buys the camera (which comes with film already loaded), takes a roll of photos, sends the entire camera off for processing, and receives her photos back from the processor. If she wants to take more photos, she buys another single-use camera. Processor is in the business of processing such pictures. When it receives a single-use camera from a consumer, it carefully opens the camera, removes and processes the film, and returns the finished photos. But it does not then dispose of the single-use camera. Rather, Processor inserts a new roll of film, resets the film

counter, repairs the damage it did in opening the camera, cleans the camera off, and sells the used single-use camera to unfinicky consumers. Kamera Ko. sues Processor for infringement, arguing that Processor is making and selling the patented device without authority. Is Processor infringing?

5. *Experimental use?* The Nanometrics Lab of Grout Corporation is engaged in cutting-edge research in microchip technology. Scientists at the Lab are attempting to develop the smallest possible components to use on microchips (which are used in various types of electronics). The Lab does not have any specific products as goals but rather seeks to develop technology that other departments of the corporation may commercialize. To foster creativity at the Lab, Grout encourages the scientists to pursue scientific and engineering progress on the theory that commercial products will arise as a by-product.

   The Lab seeks to purchase a multifunk spectrometer, an invention patented by Greep Corporation, a competitor of Grout. When Greep refuses to sell one to Grout, the Lab scientists make their own (using descriptions of the machine from scientific journals and other sources). The Lab scientists use the machine in testing a new form of chip technology, which someday might be used to make faster video games. Greep sues for patent infringement. Does Grout qualify for the experimental use defense?

6. *Carve-up.* Between them, Tweedle Co. and Twiddle Co. sell almost all of the garage doors bought by home builders. Both Tweedle and Twiddle hold a number of patents on garage door technology. Tweedle and Twiddle enter into an agreement under which they grant each other cost-free licenses to all their patents and agree to keep prices set at a level that is profitable to both.

   Humpty notes the high prices of garage doors and decides he could profitably make and sell garage doors at a lower price. He enters into discussions with several home builders and quickly learns that home builders would vastly prefer to buy doors built to the same specifications as Tweedle and Twiddle's doors to comply with standard building practices. Humpty knows that such doors will fall within the claims of various patents held by Tweedle or Twiddle. He seeks licenses from Tweedle and Twiddle. They agree to offer licenses on the condition that Humpty will sell doors only at the prices they set. Humpty refuses those terms. He advertises in trade journals, offering to sell garage doors and describing doors that clearly fall within the Tweedle and Tweedle patent claims. Sued by Tweedle and Twiddle for patent infringement, Humpty raises the defenses of antitrust violations and patent misuse. Twiddle and Twiddle argue that they simply have exercised the right of any patent owner, which is to license the patent on terms agreeable to them. Have Tweedle and Twiddle violated the antitrust laws or misused the patents?

7. *Lost and found.* Rip receives a patent on her "Elbow-Operated Television Remote Control Device." Rip then sticks the patent up in the attic and forgets about it. She makes no effort to commercialize the product. Ten years later, an engineer at Telly Products runs across Rip's patent while researching another matter. The engineer shows it to his colleagues. A few weeks later, Telly ships several thousand units to electronics stores around the country. Rip happens to see one in a store and recognizes her invention. She soon files an infringement action. Can Telly raise the defense of laches against Rip?

8. *Better never than late.* Starting in 1954, Jerome Lemelson filed a series of related patent applications on automatic identification bar code technology. The USPTO allowed some of the patent claims. But before the patents could issue, the applicant refiled applications with identical claims, in order to delay issuance of the patents. Due in part to such delays, the patents eventually issued after a delay of some 18 to 39 years. This meant the patents would have a term of 17 years from issuance, extending into the twenty-first century. (The filings were governed by the old patent term rule of 17 years from date of issuance, rather than the present rule, 20 years from date of filing the application). In the 1990s, the patent owner sought to enforce its patent rights in bar code technology invented in the 1950s and 1960s. Now that bar codes are so widely used, are the patents gold mines?

Explanations

1. Smoky can rely on the newly discovered reference to challenge the validity of the patent. An issued patent has a presumption of validity. But in litigation over infringement of the patent, the alleged infringer may claim that the application did not meet the requirements for patentability. In reviewing validity, the court is not limited at all to the documents and other materials that were before the USPTO when it decided to allow the claims. So it is irrelevant that the journal article was not reviewed by the USPTO, that the applicant and the USPTO made thorough searches and did not find the article, and that the applicant did not derive her invention from the article. Rather, when validity is raised in litigation, the patent frequently receives much greater scrutiny than the examiner was able to give it at the USPTO.

2. The patent is not enforceable. By attempting to mislead the USPTO with respect to material information, Christo engaged in inequitable conduct. An applicant is required to submit with the application all material prior art references of which he is aware. If Christo had not known about the Japanese patent, failure to submit it would not have been inequitable conduct. The rules do not require submitting translations of foreign

patents, so if Christo had innocently submitted the Japanese patent without a translation, that would not have been inequitable conduct. But here, Christo submitted an English-language summary, which was drafted and submitted solely to mislead the examiner about the relevance of the Japanese patent. Christo engaged in behavior intended to mislead the USPTO and thereby engaged in inequitable conduct.

The information also met the requirement of materiality, even though it would not have prevented Christo from receiving a patent. The court determined that the Japanese patent did not in fact render Christo's invention unpatentable. But the information was material for two reasons. The Japanese patent raised a prima facie case of unpatentability. It was also inconsistent with statements that Christo had made to the examiner. For those reasons, the misleading summary of the Japanese patent would have been material to the USPTO.

The court would also likely determine that the conduct was sufficiently culpable to deny enforceability. Christo drafted and submitted a document solely for the purpose of misleading the USPTO about the nature of a prior art reference. That is a classic case of inequitable conduct, and the appropriate remedy would be to deny enforceability, to deter other applicants from such conduct. Cf. *Semiconductor Energy Lab. v. Samsung Elecs.*, 204 F.3d 1368 (Fed. Cir. 2000).

3. Neither first sale nor implied license protects Winery here. Both of those doctrines apply only when the patentee has authorized sale of a patented article. Under both doctrines, the patentee implicitly authorizes the buyer to use the article. But in this case, the patentee did not authorize the sale of the article in question. Rather, Noma made and sold the chamber without authorization. Winery bought the chamber from Noma and would get only whatever rights (explicit or implied) that Noma had to give. But Noma could not authorize Winery to use the chamber. Pinky did not sell the chamber to Winery and so did not give any authority (express or implied) to Winery to use the invention. Accordingly, Winery infringed Pinky's patent by using the chamber, and if Winery continues to use the chamber or sells it, Winery will infringe Pinky's patent. The facts that Winery acted in good faith and paid full value are insufficient because it did not deal with someone who could give it authority to use the patented invention.

4. Processor probably is not infringing. A court likely would hold that it did not infringe by making the invention (by reconstructing the patented single-use case camera) but rather that it engaged in permissible repair. It therefore also would not infringe by selling the invention because the first sale doctrine authorizes it to resell a patented article that had been subject to an authorized sale.

The issue is whether putting the cameras back together and replacing the film constitutes repair (permitted) or reconstruction (infringement).

The owner of a patented article has a broad right to repair it. But she may not go beyond repair and reconstruct it after the entity, viewed as a whole, has become spent. The patentee would argue that a single-use camera, by definition, is spent when it has been used once. But although the cameras in question were sold as single-use cameras, they apparently were capable of multiple uses. Processor opened the camera, replaced the film, reset the counter, repaired the damage it had itself made in opening the film, and cleaned the camera. All those acts would seem to fall within the normal scope of repairing a product that has been used. Cf. *Jazz Photo v. International Trade Commn.*, 264 F.3d 1094 (Fed. Cir. 2001).

5. Grout probably does not qualify for the experimental use defense. The courts have applied the defense very narrowly. It is not sufficient that the purpose of the alleged infringer's activity is experimental. The defense does not apply if there is any substantial commercial motivation for the use. In this case, there is a substantial commercial motivation. Grout funds and supports experimental research, but the underlying purpose is commercial. Grout believes that although no specific commercial goals have been set, research in the area will yield developments that can be commercialized by Grout. This commercial purpose probably would make the experimental use exception inapplicable.

6. Tweedle and Twiddle cannot enforce their patents against Humpty. Humpty would be able to establish the defenses of patent misuse and of antitrust violation. Tweedle and Twiddle have entered into an agreement to set prices in given market. Although antitrust is beyond the scope of this book, a price-fixing agreement between competitors (with no other purpose than to keep prices up) is an obvious violation of the antitrust laws. The patent statute grants some safe harbors for licensing activity, but price-fixing is not one of them. Likewise, the use of patent rights to give effect to the price-fixing agreement is patent misuse, a clear example of attempting to impermissibly expand the scope of the patent rights.

7. Telly cannot establish laches here. Laches requires showing (1) the patentee unreasonably and inexcusably delayed bringing an infringement action and (2) the delay caused material prejudice to the defendant. Rip's conduct did not meet either requirement. Rip may have delayed commercializing the product, but that is not the basis for laches. Rather, delay in enforcing the patent may give rise to laches. With respect to the second requirement, Telly cannot show material prejudice here. Rip's delay did not harm Telly. This example shows that long lapses do not automatically give rise to laches.

8. The patents were not enforceable. *See Symbol Technologies, Inc. v. Lemelson Med., Educ. & Research Found., LP,* 2005 U.S. App. LEXIS 19439 (Fed. Cir. 2005). Under prosecution laches, unreasonable and unexplained delay in

prosecuting the patent application may bar enforcement of the patent. A delay of between 18 and 39 years is not reasonable, and there no reasonable explanation was offered. In particular, it is not reasonable to delay issuance in order to wait for the relevant technology to become widespread.

Prosecution would not bar enforcement where there was a reason for the delay. Gordon Gould, an inventor of laser technology, fought with the USPTO and rival inventors for decades to get a patent. He invented a form of the laser in 1957 but did not get a patent until 1977. The delay helped him, because in the meantime the laser had found many commercial applications, from scanners at grocery stores to CD players. Because he had ample reason for delay, prosecution laches would not have barred his claims.

PATENT LITIGATION

Jurisdiction

Federal courts have exclusive jurisdiction over cases arising under the patent laws (or where a party has asserted a compulsory counterclaim arising under the patent statute). 28 U.S.C. §1338. A case arises under the patent laws if review of the plaintiff's complaint establishes that the patent law creates the cause of action or the right to relief depends on resolution of a substantial question of patent law. An action may be brought in any U.S. district court (subject to venue requirements).

Not every case involving a patent raises the necessary substantial question of patent law. *Gunn v. Minton*, 133 S. Ct. 1059 (2013) held that a state law malpractice claim based on alleged faulty patent prosecution involved not a real question of patent law but rather only questions of fact involving hypothetical patents:

> Because of the backward-looking nature of a legal malpractice claim, the question is posed in a merely hypothetical sense: If Minton's lawyers had raised a timely experimental-use argument, would the result in the patent infringement proceeding have been different? No matter how the state courts resolve that hypothetical "case with a case," it will not change the real-world result of the prior federal patent litigation. Minton's patent will remain invalid.

The state court's interpretation would not be binding authority on federal courts, so it would not set binding patent law precedent.

In addition to patentees suing for infringement of patents, patent litigation frequently involves declaratory judgments brought by alleged infringers. Suppose Pharmaceutical Company is developing a new drug. Competitor

381

takes the position that the making, using, or selling the new drug infringes a patent held by Competitor. Rather than waiting for Competitor to sue for infringement, Pharmaceutical Company may seek a declaratory judgment that its drug did not infringe the patent or that the patent was invalid. There are a number of reasons why a potential defendant may, in effect, start a suit against itself. It may choose the initial forum for the action. It resolves the uncertainty before expending too much investment. Its potential investors or customers may be deterred by a possible infringement action. Even though the alleged infringer initiates the case, the burden of showing infringement rests on the patent holder. *Medtronic, Inc. v. Mirowski Family Ventures, LLC*, 134 S. Ct. 843 (2014).

But jurisdiction requires an "actual controversy" between the parties. 28 U.S.C. §2201. The test is "whether the facts alleged, under all the circumstances, show that there is a substantial controversy, between parties having adverse legal interests, of sufficient immediacy and reality to warrant the issuance of a declaratory judgment." *See MedImmune, Inc. v. Genentech, Inc.*, 549 U.S. 118 (2007). Under this test, there was jurisdiction to hear a declaratory judgment action brought by a licensee in good standing who had paid all licensing fees but disputed the validity of the patent. The Supreme Court held, in a trademark case, that the rights holder can destroy jurisdiction by committing not to sue for infringement, and so making the dispute moot. *Already, LLC, dba Yums v. Nike, Inc.*, 133 S. Ct. 721 (2013).

Appeals in patent cases do not go to the court of appeals that normally takes appeals from the district court in question. Rather, the Federal Circuit has exclusive jurisdiction of appeals in patent cases. So the Federal Circuit hears both appeals from the USPTO and from federal district courts in patent cases. Congress created the Federal Circuit in 1982 to have a single court hearing appeals in patent cases (as well as some other specified types of cases) and to encourage expertise in the judges and uniformity in patent law. The Federal Circuit case law, then, is an authoritative source of authority in patent law, although subject to Supreme Court review.

Standing

To bring an action for infringement, the plaintiff must have had legal title to the patent at the time of the infringement—which could be ownership of the entire patent or of any of the rights to exclude, or the rights in a geographic region. A nonexclusive licensee would lack standing to bring an infringement action.

Remedies

The patent statute offers several remedies for infringement.

Injunctions

The patent statute authorizes courts to grant injunctions "in accordance with the principles of equity to prevent the violation of any right secured by patent, on such terms as the court deems reasonable." 35 U.S.C. §283. Injunctions against infringers are not automatic. The Supreme Court has held that

> a plaintiff seeking a permanent injunction must satisfy a four-factor test before a court may grant such relief. A plaintiff must demonstrate: (1) that it has suffered an irreparable injury; (2) that remedies available at law, such as monetary damages, are inadequate to compensate for that injury; (3) that, considering the balance of hardships between the plaintiff and defendant, a remedy in equity is warranted; and (4) that the public interest would not be disserved by a permanent injunction.

eBay Inc. v. MercExchange, L.L.C., 547 U.S. 388, 391 (2006).

Damages

> Upon finding for the claimant the court shall award the claimant damages adequate to compensate for the infringement, but in no event less than a reasonable royalty for the use made of the invention by the infringer, together with interest and costs as fixed by the court.

35 U.S.C. §284. Damages may include lost profits (arising out of lost sales, reduced prices to compete with the infringer, or increased expenses). *See Rite-Hite v. Kelley Co.*, 56 F.3d 1538 (Fed. Cir. 1995) (en banc). The Panduit test is the standard for a patentee's showing of lost profits:

1. demand for the patented product;
2. absence of acceptable noninfringing substitutes;
3. manufacturing and marketing capability to exploit the demand; and
4. the amount of the profit it would have made.

Panduit Corp. v. Stahlin Bros. FibreWorks, 575 F.2d 1152 (6th Cir. 1978). Even if such a showing is made, the infringer may rebut it. The amount of a reasonable royalty may be set by the hypothetical royalty that would have likely been paid, had the parties entered into a license.[17]

---

17. An amendment to the patent statute has a special provision for reasonable royalty with respect to published applications, before a patent issues. If someone with actual notice of a published application makes, uses, offers, sells, or imports a substantially identical device or process as the claimed invention, such person is liable for a reasonable royalty. 35 U.S.C. §154(d).

For design patents specifically, after *Apple v. Samsung*, 137 S. Ct. 429 (2016), where a product has multiple components, damages will be the portion of profits allocable to the component with the infringed design. So when Samsung infringed the design patent of the Apple iPhone shape, profits would be reckoned by the component (the phone's case), not the entire phone. A patentee is not limited to lost profits (or a reasonable royalty) with respect to the patented invention. Rather, plaintiff is entitled to "full compensation for any damages suffered as a result of the infringement." *General Motors Corp. v. Devex Corp.*, 461 U.S. 648 (1983). The court is also authorized to "increase the damages up to three times the amount found or assessed," 35 U.S.C. §284. The Supreme Court has held that treble damages should be granted only in egregious cases, but that the determination of whether a case was egregious should be left to the discretion of the trial court, guided by all relevant factors identified in the case law, not the strict determination of objective recklessness.[18]

Patent law has a specific limitation on the availability of damages. Persons selling patented articles may give notice of the patent, such as by putting "U.S. Patent 6,123,456" on the article itself if practicable or on the packaging or label. A patent holder cannot recover damages for infringement of unmarked patented articles unless the defendant had actual notice of the infringement, such as by a letter from the patentee. 35 U.S.C. §287.

Attorneys' Fees

Patent litigation is such a costly endeavor that some practitioners refer to it as "the sport of kings." In some cases, one party may have her fees paid by the opponent. In exceptional cases the court may award reasonable attorneys' fees to the prevailing party. 35 U.S.C. §285. The Supreme Court has held that "an 'exceptional' case is simply one that stands out from others with respect to the substantive strength of a party's litigating position (considering both the governing law and the facts of the case) or the unreasonable manner in which the case was litigated." *Octane Fitness, LLC v. ICON Health & Fitness, Inc.*, 134 S. Ct. 1749 (2014). The *Octane* court further held that the decision on whether to award fees is within the discretion of the trial court, not subject to exacting review. As in other areas, parties may be liable for bringing baseless suits or for misconduct in litigation. *See, e.g., Eon-Net LP v. Flagstar Bancorp*, 653 F.3d 1314 (Fed. Cir. 2011) (attorneys' fees awarded where party filed a baseless case, failed to make a reasonable pre-suit investigation, destroyed evidence before filing the suit, and engaged in obstructive conduct during the case.).

---

18. Halo Elecs., Inc. v. Pulse Elecs., Inc., 136 S. Ct. at 1932-1935 (2015).

Remedies Against the United States

Infringement by the United States gives the patent holder a right to damages but not an injunction. 28 U.S.C. §1498.[19] The statute further deems infringement by a contractor or other entity with authorization or consent of the government to be "use of manufacture for the United States." Accordingly, the statute would appear to enable the federal government to effect a "taking" of a patent—such as authorizing a contractor to make a patented pharmaceutical with compensation to the patent holder.

The patent statute expressly subjects states to liability for patent infringement. But the Supreme Court has held that Congress lacks the power under the intellectual property clause to subject states to liability for damages (as opposed to an injunction against a state official) for patent infringement (although Congress may seek to reenact such liability under the due process clause). *Florida Prepaid Postsecondary Educ. Expense Board v. College Savings Bank*, 527 U.S. 627 (1999).

Examples

1. *Seeking an advisory opinion?* Moptop makes disposable mops. Moptop receives a letter from Popmop, which states that Moptop's mops infringe Popmop's patent and that unless Moptop immediately ceases making and selling the mops, Popmop will file a patent infringement action. Moptop's patent attorney looks into the matter and sends Popmop a letter explaining why there is no infringement. Popmop responds with a letter graciously stating for the record that it was in the wrong and promising not to sue. Moptop nevertheless files a declaratory judgment that its mops are noninfringing to reassure investors. Does the court have jurisdiction of the action?

2. *Notice?* Vroom for many years has made and sold high-speed escalators for shopping malls and offices, featuring a double-block sprocket gearing assembly. One day Vroom receives a cease-and-desist letter from Chunkachunka Toys. Chunkachunka holds a patent on a double-block sprocket gearing assembly. Chunkachunka has used the assembly in mechanical trains sold as children's toys. Each train bore the legend, "U.S. Patent No. 5,007,007." Chunkachunka demands that Vroom pay fees to license the patent and for Vroom's past use of the technology. Vroom agrees to license the patent in the future. Vroom refuses to pay fees retroactively. Vroom argues that it should not be held liable for damages because it had no notice of the patent, and no reasonable party in its position would have known of a patent on toy technology that covered escalator technology. Would Vroom's reasonable lack of notice spare it from liability from damages?

---

19. Jurisdiction of the action is in the U.S. Court of Federal Claims.

Explanations

1. The court does not have subject matter jurisdiction over the declaratory judgment action. Jurisdiction requires an "actual controversy" between the parties. The plaintiff must practice, or be prepared to practice, an allegedly infringing device or process. The plaintiff must also have a reasonable apprehension of suit if its activity continues, based on the conduct of the patentee. Here, Popmop had initially alleged that Moptop was infringing its patent. But Popmop subsequently stated in writing that there was no infringement and that it promised not to pursue an infringement action. Under these facts, Moptop would not have the necessary reasonable apprehension of suit.

2. Vroom is liable for damages. The issue is not whether a reasonable party would have known of the patent. Rather, the relevant rule states that if a patented article is sold without a patent marking, an infringer is not liable for damages unless she had actual notice of the infringement. But here Chunkachunka did not sell a patented article without a patent marking. Rather, it put "U.S. Patent No. 5,007,007" on each of the toy trains it sold.

Trademark

Subject Matter of Trademark Law

CHAPTER 10

A trademark is a symbol used by a person in commerce to indicate the source of the goods and to distinguish them from the goods sold or made by others. 15 U.S.C. §1127. The symbol can be a word, a phrase, a design, an image, a sound, a color, or even a fragrance. Some well-known trademarks are APPLE for computers, NIKE for shoes, COCA-COLA for beverages, and the NEW YORK TIMES for newspapers. A service mark serves a similar role to identify the source of services. Well-known service marks include EBAY for online auction and trading services, the rivals LEXIS and WESTLAW for computer-aided legal research services, and MTV for television broadcasting. But beyond such well-known marks, trademarks and service marks are practically everywhere in modern society.

Trademark law serves to keep lines of communication clear between sellers and buyers. In a world without trademarks, buying would be more difficult. If a buyer wanted to buy a phone but could not rely on the reputation of the seller, she would have to test the phone (or car or mango or database software or . . .) herself. Consumers deal with far too many products to assess each one individually. Rather, consumers (and business buyers) rely on the reputation of sellers: their experience with the seller's product or service, what others have told them about the seller, what *Consumer Reports* has to say, what's been said online or on the playground.

If there were trademarks but no trademark law, there would be great temptation to free-ride on the success of others by selling goods or services under the names of attractive sellers. This in turn would make it difficult for potential buyers to distinguish between the seller they seek and impostors. Trademark law responds by forbidding uses of a trademark by others that

389

are *likely to cause confusion or deception*. Note how that standard differs from copyright and patent, where the rights owner has a basket of exclusive rights. Trademark serves to distinguish one seller in the market from others. To preserve that distinction, the standard is tailored to preventing confusion or deception among the relevant consumer.

What good is a trademark? It allows a seller to build goodwill, a valuable reputation among consumers. The seller can establish a brand, which allows her to capture the value from positive associations (created by marketing, consumer experience with the product, etc.). That can allow her to compete, both against others in the market and against potential entrants. A trademark can be a very valuable asset. So trademark law provides incentives for sellers to build goodwill.

The Lanham Act, the federal trademark statute, provides several related causes of action:

1. *Trademark infringement*: Someone who uses a mark or similar symbol in a way that is likely to cause confusion about the source of goods or services may be liable to the mark's owner for infringement.
2. *Dilution*: The owner of a famous mark may be able to obtain an injunction against the use of a mark that decreases the distinctiveness of the mark.
3. *False designations of origin*: The Lanham Act goes beyond protection of registered marks to impose liability for infringement of unregistered marks and for false designations of origin.
4. *False advertising*: False advertising that causes competitive injury can also give rise to liability under the Lanham Act, which goes well beyond protection of marks to govern other deceptive practices.
5. *Anti-Cybersquatting Act*: The Lanham Act also provides remedies for bad-faith registration of Internet domain names that are similar to trademarks.

This book discusses trademark law mainly in the context of the federal statute. Trademark law developed as state law. The federal statute does not preempt the field. Rather, state statutes and common law provide similar protection.

Trademark protection benefits both trademark owners and their customers. The rights of the mark owner allow her to invest resources in developing goodwill in the mark. Enforcement of trademarks reduces deceptive practices. Trademarks also can reduce the consumer's costs of searching for, testing, and purchasing products by allowing the consumer to rely on the reputation of the mark, based on the consumer's experience with the mark and any other information he might acquire. Trademark protection also has costs, from administering and adjudicating trademark rights to more diffuse costs, such as limitations on speech.

CATEGORIES OF MARKS

Trademarks

A trademark is a symbol used by a person to identify and distinguish her goods from those manufactured or sold by others and to indicate the source of the goods. 15 U.S.C. §1127. "Goods" are any type of product. They include typical consumer goods such as soft drinks (Coca-Cola, Seven-Up), food (Campbell's Soup, Domino's Pizza), clothing (Gap, Nike), electronics (Canon, Dell, Nikon), and toys (Fisher-Price, Tonka). But trademarks are not limited to consumer goods. Boeing 747 and Caterpillar Tractors are marks used to identify sources of airliners and huge tractors. Goods include products with intangible aspects. Trademarks are used on e-books, software, music, or video, even when sold through Internet downloads.

Service Marks

A trademark identifies a source of goods, and a service mark identifies a source of services. Generally, the same rules apply to both. 15 U.S.C. §1053. Indeed, this book often uses "trademark" to refer to both trademarks and service marks.

"Services" is not defined in the statute but has been broadly read to cover the multitude of services that people can conceive. Some notable examples are Federal Express, for air transport of cargo; Google, for providing information from searchable indexes and databases of information; Massachusetts General Hospital, for hospital services; The Simpsons, for entertainment services in the form of television programs; and Harvard University, for educational services (and as a trademark for such items as coffee mugs).

Not every symbol used by a business in marketing qualifies as a service mark. Rather, the symbol must be used to identify specific services. At the minimum, a service is a distinct activity, not merely ancillary to a larger business, that the mark owner does for the benefit of others. A symbol that merely identifies someone engaged in some activity for his own benefit is not a service mark. If Hammerhead Investments is a business that researches companies and buys their stock on a public exchange, then Hammerhead Investments does not constitute a service mark because Hammerhead is not providing services to anyone other than itself. If Hammerhead Investments, by contrast, sells investment advising services to clients, then Hammerhead Investments might be used as a service mark.

The services need not be the principal business of the mark owner. A service mark could be used by a manufacturing company in connection with its offering of pension services to its employees. A vendor (such as an automobile dealership) could use trademarks to sell goods and a service mark to sell related services, such as repairs or driving lessons. But services that are expected or routine in connection with the sale of goods are not "services" within the meaning of service mark. Designing and manufacturing goods or providing basic warranties on the goods are not likely to qualify as separate services.

Trade Dress

Trade dress is a particular type of trademark or service mark. Rather than a symbol placed on the goods or packaging or used in selling the services, trade dress is the total image of the product and its overall appearance: "the design and appearance of a product together with the elements making up the overall image that serves to identify the product presented to the consumer." *Chrysler Corp. v. Silva*, 118 F.3d 56, 58 (1st Cir. 1997). The original meaning of "trade dress" was much narrower, referring to the "dress" of the product: "the overall appearance of labels, wrappers, and containers used in packaging a product." J. Thomas McCarthy, *Trademarks and Unfair Competition*, §8:1 (3d ed. 1992). But the concept of trade dress (like trademarks generally) has expanded. Trade dress can be the design of the product itself or the design of the packaging of the product. Trade dress can include "features such as size, shape, color or color combinations, texture, graphics, or even particular sales techniques." *Two Pesos v. Taco Cabana*, 505 U.S. 763, 764 n.1 (1992) (citing case law and the Restatement (Third) of Unfair Competition).

Trade dress is not limited to goods; the product can be services or a combination of goods and services. For example, the trade dress for a fast-food restaurant was

> the total image of the business. Taco Cabana's trade dress may include the shape and general appearance of the exterior of the restaurant, the identifying sign, the interior kitchen floor plan, the decor, the menu, the equipment used to serve food, the servers' uniforms and other features reflecting on the total image of the restaurant.

Id. at 764 n.1. Courts and commentators have recognized trade dress in a broad range of symbols, leaving the present limits of the doctrine unsettled. Trade dress may be the design of a piece of furniture, the appearance of a video game, or the look and feel of a Web site, "generated by the color, graphics, animations, designs, layout, text, or combination of web sites' features." Xuan-Thao N. Nguyen, *Should It Be a Free for All? The Challenge of Extending Trade Dress Protection to the Look and Feel of Web Sites in the Evolving Internet*, 49 Am. U.

L. Rev. 1233 (2000). Courts have held that trade dress may apply to a line of products, provided that there is a consistent overall look. *See Rose Art Industries Inc. v. Swanson*, 235 F.3d 165 (3d Cir. 2000).

Because trade dress is so vaguely defined, its enforcement risks permitting trademark law to give the sort of protection against copying of goods and services that is more appropriately governed by patent or copyright. One guard against this risk is to require the trade dress claimant to very specifically detail the elements that constitute the trade dress. In addition, the substantive limits on trademark (discussed in the following chapters), such as requirements of distinctiveness and bars to protection for functional matter, play a key role in trade dress analysis.

Collective Marks

The Lanham Act defines "collective mark" as a trademark or service mark used by the members of a group or organization. 15 U.S.C. §1127. For collective marks, the requirement that the mark be associated with specific goods or services is somewhat relaxed. The term includes marks indicating membership in a union, an association, or other organization. *Id.* The mark may be used to distinguish the goods and services of members of the group from nonmembers. The mark ILGWU can be used for garments, to show the garments were made by members of the International Ladies' Garment Workers' Union. A collective mark can also be used by the members to indicate that they are members. Members of the AFL-CIO can use that mark simply as indicia of membership of the organization. Jaycees indicates membership in an association that promotes community improvement, civic pride, and cooperation between the business community and the public.

Certification Marks

A certification mark is a symbol used by a person *other than its owner* "to certify regional or other origin, material, mode of manufacture, quality, accuracy, or other characteristics of such person's goods or services or that the work or labor on the goods or services was performed by members of a union or other organization." 15 U.S.C. §1127.

A certification mark is not used by the owner of the mark. Rather, persons other than the owner use the mark to certify to potential purchasers that their goods or services meet the standards set by the mark's owner. For example, Underwriter's Laboratory is an independent, nonprofit organization that establishes product standards and tests products against those standards. Products that pass the tests may be marketed using such certification marks as "Underwriter's Laboratory Approved," which carry considerable weight with informed consumers. A toaster sold with a mark of Underwriter's Laboratory is not made or sponsored by Underwriter's Laboratory but is represented to meet the Underwriter's Laboratory standards. Very likely, the toaster will also carry the trademark of the manufacturer or seller.

A certification mark allows the potential purchaser to rely on a third party — the owner of the certification mark — for information about a seller's goods or services. A certification mark could certify the regional origin of goods (such as wool from the Shetland Islands), the materials (such as the grade of wool), the mode of manufacture (whether garments were made in accordance with certain labor standards, such as child labor prohibitions), or other characteristics of the goods or services. Certification marks are used in diverse ways, such as certifying compliance with environmental protection standards, with religious rules governing food preparation, with professional qualification standards, with free software licensing practices, and with authenticity standards for goods made by indigenous peoples.

Because consumers rely on the owner's approval of the mark's use, the Lanham Act imposes certain requirements on the owner for the mark to remain valid (even though the owner is not the one using the mark). The owner of the certification mark may not use the mark herself in marketing or producing the relevant goods or services, although she may engage in activities to promote use of the mark. *See* 15 U.S.C. §1064. The owner must be able to control use of the mark, must not allow use of the mark for purposes other than to certify, and may not refuse certification to those that meet the relevant criteria set by the mark holder. Otherwise, the mark may lose its status as a certification mark.

Examples

1. *Quick picks.* What type of marks are the following:
   a. SALOMON used on skis
   b. SALOMON BROTHERS used for investment advising services
   c. FRASER RIVER SALMON COOP, used to indicate that fish were farmed by a member of that cooperative
   d. SUPERIOR QUALITY SHETLAND SALMON, which may be used by any salmon farm that meets specified quality standards and conditions
   e. The Cannery Row image of a seafood restaurant chain, with décor and menu that evokes the flophouses and sardine canneries of long-ago Monterey, California

2. *Soft goods.* Softie sells copies of its popular Woop software package, both on floppy disks and through Internet downloads. The mark WOOP is prominently displayed on boxes containing the disks and displayed

whenever the software is downloaded or used. Softie's main expenses in producing Woop are the salaries of the software engineers that design, code, and test the software. Softie does not provide any technical support or other direct services. A smaller percentage of the cost comes from paying for the physical delivery of copies. Is WOOP a trademark or a service mark?

3. *Lifetime guaranty.* A snowboard manufacturer sells a line of snowboards bearing the trademark TEMPORIZE. The key selling point for the boards is durability. The manufacturer certifies that every TEMPORIZE board will last for ten years under normal use, and the company offers full refunds for any boards that do not. Is TEMPORIZE a trademark or a certification mark?

4. *Self-promotion.* Cola Maker begins a new marketing campaign that seeks to increase the sales of its Stoop cola beverage. The marketing campaign is a parody of a political campaign. Cola Maker sends brochures and runs ads that extol the virtues of Stoop and make campaign promises about how Stoop drinking will improve society. The slogan for the campaign is the nonsense word Pootsstoop, which appears prominently to distinguish the promotional material and provide a unifying element to the campaign. Members of the public do indeed become aware of the campaign and of the role that Pootsstoop plays to identify information of a political campaign. Cola Maker sends brochures and runs magazine ads that extol the service mark. Is Pootsstoop used to identify services?

5. *Better living through cola.* Stooper Daze is Cola Maker's name for its next promotion for Stoop cola. Stooper Daze is a promotional contest. Stoop drinkers send in 25-word essays on the virtues of Stoop. If the essay is approved by the contest administrators, the author is entered in a lottery. The essays are used in the many advertisements run in connection with the contest. Numerous prizes are awarded to randomly chosen winners. Consumer surveys show that entrants enjoy both composing the essay and having a chance to win prizes. Cola Maker uses Stooper Daze in advertising and displays to distinguish the material. Is Stooper Daze used to identify services?

6. *Old wine in new bottles.* Newfane University, a small liberal arts college, teeters on the edge of bankruptcy. In an effort to raise funds, Newfane University Press issues a new line of classic literature. The editors scour through the classics to identify works that are both edifying and entertaining. The university sells the books with thoroughly modern covers, all of which conform to a beach vacation design theme. The books are big sellers. The editors are fearful that another publisher will start selling knockoffs. Due to their beach vacation theme, the books are readily

identifiable in the literature section of any bookstore. The editors can specifically list a number of design elements in the book covers that, taken together, serve to distinguish the line of books from the books sold by others. But there is no single image or word that is common to all the covers. Can the total image of the line of books be a trademark?

7. *Rubber stamp.* TechnoTesters is a small, respected testing laboratory. It tests electronics products to see if they conform to TechnoTesters' criteria for safety and efficiency. The products that conform are permitted to be sold under the "TechnoTesters Certified" certification mark. TechnoTesters is bought by Crave Conglomerate. Crave fires all the scientists at TechnoTesters and sells the laboratory building and equipment. The only asset it keeps is the "TechnoTesters Certified" mark. Crave no longer tests whether products actually meet the published criteria for certification. Rather, Crave simply raises the licensing fee and allows any company that pays the fee to use the certification mark. Many companies take up the offer, pay the fee, and start using the mark on all kinds of goods of various quality. Gidgetal Cameras simply starts using the "TechnoTesters Certified" mark on its cameras without permission from Crave or even offering to pay. Can Crave enforce its rights in the "TechnoTesters Certified" mark?

8. *The in-crowd.* The Chamber of Commerce for Manilla County seeks to promote the local grape industry. The Chamber registers the certification mark, "CCMC Certified" to certify that grapes were grown in Manilla County. After Manilla grapes receive favorable press in various trade publications, sales skyrocket. The "CCMC Certified" mark is widely recognized, and grapes bearing the mark command a hefty premium. After a countywide election, the Chamber of Commerce becomes controlled by cronies of the Snopes family, a local grape-producing dynasty. The Chamber thereafter refuses to license use of the mark to anyone other than the Snopes family and their numerous associates, who are careful to use the mark only on grapes that were indeed grown in Manilla County. The Chamber refuses permission even to potential users who clearly meet the qualifications for certification and offer to pay the fee. Does the Chamber have a valid certification mark?

9. *Fine line.* The Broccoli Coop is the name for a loose-knit group of broccoli growers. The growers decide to get a mark to distinguish their products. Acting together, they begin to use the "BrikABrok Certified" mark. Use of the mark on broccoli certifies that the broccoli was grown by a member of the Broccoli Coop. Is the "BrikABrok Certified" mark a collective mark or a certification mark?

10. *Born and raised.* Jasper LaGrange was the founder of the town of LaGrange in 1818. Some present residents of LaGrange, who take great pride in

tracing their ancestry to him, form the Descendants of Jasper Society. The society does not engage in any activities. Rather, its only purpose is to mark its members as descendants of Jasper. Such members take to using "Member, DJS" after their names. Is MEMBER, DJS a collective mark?

11. *Tribute or trademark?* Artist sells his paintings of Tiger Woods playing golf. The paintings' biggest appeal to buyers is that they show Tiger Woods, as opposed to the pure artistic merit of the works. Tiger Woods has licensed his likeness to be used for a number of golf-related products. Is his likeness a trademark, potentially infringed by its unauthorized use in the paintings?

12. *Infamy.* I.M. Pei, a world-famous architect, designs a unique building for The Rock and Roll Hall of Fame and Museum in Cleveland, Ohio. Can the Museum enforce the image of the building as a trademark (and so prevent others from selling pictures of the building, which copyright does not prohibit)?

Explanations

1. a. Trade mark, a mark used to identify the source of goods
   b. Service mark, a mark used to identify the source of services
   c. Collective mark, a mark used by members of a group, associated with goods or services
   d. Certification mark, a mark not used by the owner of the mark, rather used by others (with the owner's permission, often subject to a fee) to show compliance with certain standards
   e. Trade dress, the total image of the product, when used as an indicator of source

2. WOOP is a trademark, not a service mark. When people buy Woop software, they are paying primarily for the services that went into producing the goods. But in differentiating between goods and services, trademark law takes the much simpler approach of simply distinguishing between things (goods) and things done (services). Software is treated as a thing. It may not be as tangible as goods such as furniture or automobiles, but it is nevertheless treated as goods for the purposes of trademark law. Having said that, in general it makes little difference whether a mark is a service mark or a trademark. Trademark law treats them the same, with only a few minor differences (such as how to use the mark to acquire rights).

3. TEMPORIZE is a trademark, not a certification mark. A certification mark is used by persons other than the owner of the mark, as a certification according to standards set by the owner of the mark. If the owner uses a

mark on goods, it is a trademark—even if the owner provides warranties, certifications, or other undertakings along with the goods.

4. Pootsstoop is not used to identify services and therefore is not a service mark. Services, for the purpose of service mark protection, are an activity carried out for the benefit of others and are not merely ancillary to the larger activity of a business. Neither condition is met here. The promotional activity identified by Pootsstoop is done for the benefit of Cola Maker itself, to promote the main business of selling Stoop cola. One could argue that consumers benefit from the promotional campaign because it provides them with information about Stoop cola—and the fact that consumers buy Stoop means that it, in the buyer's estimation, provides a benefit. But if services were understood that broadly, any activity would qualify as a service provided that it had some plausible indirect benefit to someone. Cf. In re Dr. Pepper Co., 836 F.2d 508 (Fed. Cir. 1987).

5. Whether Stooper Daze is used to identify services is a close question. There are strong arguments that the promotion fails to qualify as services for two reasons: It benefits the mark owner, not others; and it is merely ancillary to the main business of Cola Maker. But it could be seen as a separate activity that does directly benefit others. Stoop drinkers choose to participate in the contest, and numerous entrants receive prizes. So the entrants receive the services of participation in a game as well as the chance of winning prizes.

6. The total image of a line of books could qualify as a trademark as trade dress. If the beach vacation design theme has identifiable elements that serve to identify the books and distinguish them from those made or sold by others, the design is performing the same task as a brand name. As subsequent chapters discuss, the application of trademark law to trade dress raises many issues. Trade dress is difficult to define and raises special issues with respect to such matters as distinctiveness and functionality.

7. "TechnoTesters Certified" is no longer a valid certification mark. If the owner of a certification mark fails to control use of the mark or allows it to be used for purposes other than to certify, the mark is invalid and subject to cancellation. Here, Crave controls use only to the extent that it requires fees; it no longer attempts to ensure that the mark is not used on goods that fail to meet the relevant standards. The wholesale use by others also goes beyond use for certification. This mark is simply being used as an endorsement by the holder of the "TechnoTesters Certified" mark, especially since use is not limited to those goods for which the standards are relevant. The owner of a certification mark is held to a high standard for the mark to remain valid.

8. The "CCMC Certified" mark is no longer a valid certification mark because the owner has discriminately refused use to those who meet the relevant criteria. The use of the mark is limited to goods that meet the relevant criteria, but it is further limited to the Snopes family and their cronies. In addition to limiting use to conforming goods, the owner must also permit use by conforming goods and not discriminately refuse use of the mark. When other grape producers meet the standard and are ready to pay the relevant fee but are refused permission to benefit one group, the owner has placed impermissible limits on the use of the mark.

9. The "BrikABrok Certified" mark is a collective mark. There is some overlap between certification marks and collective marks. Both can be used to certify that goods were produced or services rendered by members of a certain group. But a certification mark may not be used by the owner of the mark. Here, the owners of the mark are using the mark. One might argue that the owner of the mark is the Broccoli Coop, which is not itself using the mark; rather the individual members are each using the mark on their respective goods. But the Broccoli Coop does not appear to be a legal entity but simply a name used for the loose-knit group. The rationale for the limitation on use by the owner also applies here. To make the owner somewhat impartial as to users of the mark, the owner may use the mark or discriminately refuse use by others. That rationale militates against characterizing the use by the group of a mark owned by the group as a certification mark. So the better answer is that the mark is a collective mark.

10. A collective mark is a trademark or service mark used by members of a group or organization. To be a trademark or service mark, it must identify goods or services. The MEMBER, DJS symbol is used to identify descendants of Jasper LaGrange, not to identify the source of goods or services. A sufficient link to services may be met with members of a union or another group that perform services. The definition of "services" has not been applied as stringently with collective marks as with other areas such as promotions. But here, there do not appear to be any plausible services linked to the mark. The Descendants of Jasper Society does not engage in any activities whatsoever. So the symbol does not qualify as a service mark and, accordingly, not as a federal collective mark. Note that the society could meet the requirement if it simply rendered some services such as community enrichment.

11. An image of a famous person could be a mark. But not every image of that person would be a mark:

> ETW asks us, in effect, to constitute Woods himself as a walking, talking trademark. Images and likenesses of Woods are not protectable as a trademark because they do not perform the trademark function of designation. They do

not distinguish and identify the source of goods. They cannot function as a trademark because there are undoubtedly thousands of images and likenesses of Woods taken by countless photographers, and drawn, sketched, or painted by numerous artists, which have been published in many forms of media, and sold and distributed throughout the world.

ETW Corp. v. Jireh Publishing, Inc., 332 F.3d 915, 922 (6th Cir. 2003).

12. A building, like a person, cannot be a trademark, because it does much more than serve as a source indicator. *See Rock and Roll Hall of Fame and Museum, Inc. v. Gentile Productions,* 134 F.3d 749 (6th Cir. 1998).

SYMBOL

A mark must be a "word, name, symbol, or device, or any combination thereof." 15 U.S.C. §1127. That definition could be read as limiting the categories of potential marks. In particular, "symbol or device" could be read as terms of art that refer only to an emblem or artistic figure. *See* Glynn S. Lunney, Jr., *Trademark Monopolies,* 48 Emory L.J. 367 (1999). But in *Qualitex v. Jacobson Products,* 514 U.S. 159 (1995), the Supreme Court interpreted the definition broadly: "Since human beings might use as a 'symbol' or 'device' almost anything at all that is capable of carrying meaning, this language, read literally, is not restrictive." *Id.* at 1302-1303.

Accordingly, a trademark may consist of anything used as a source-identifying symbol (provided it meets the substantive requirements discussed in following chapters). Most marks consist of words or names. A mark may use existing words (such as APPLE COMPUTER, TOMB RAIDER, or ROUNDER RECORDS) or invented words (such as PROZAC, PIXAR, or MYST). But a mark can be a number, a drawing, a shape, even a sound, a fragrance, or a color. The mark can also be a combination of such elements, such as a word written in a stylized fashion or a picture with the name of the mark owner embedded within.

Examples

1. *What's your sign?* Snowboard Manufacturer, a start-up, has finished the design and testing of her line of snowboards. She is now considering what to use as a trademark. She knows that a trademark must be a "word, name, symbol, or device, or any combination thereof." Which of the following meet that requirement?
   a. a word she coined: Zzzzzamplidude
   b. an image she copied from a painting by Vincent Van Gogh

   c. The Reapers: a phrase she copied from the title of a painting by Van Gogh
   d. a phrase from the U.S. Constitution: Promote the progress of science and useful arts
   e. a recording of a nightingale singing
   f. the smell from a spouting whale
   g. the melody from Beethoven's Ninth Symphony, played on a tuba

2. *Cat.* Sally is a freelance copyeditor. Word-of-mouth from happy authors leads to a considerable number of calls from prospective clients. Sally decides to start a copyediting service, subcontracting some jobs to reliable colleagues. For marketing purposes, she decides to use a trademark. Sally figures that her amiable cat Anastasia would be a cordial and memorable symbol for the business. Can a cat be a symbol that could be used as a trademark?

Explanations

1. The answer is all of the above. Humans can learn to attach meaning to almost anything, and therefore almost anything can be a symbol. The requirement that the mark be a "word, name, symbol, or device, or any combination thereof" is not a limitation. But not every symbol used in association with goods or services is a mark. There are requirements and limitations with real bite, discussed in the rest of this chapter and those that follow.

2. Almost anything can be a symbol, so Sally can take something about Anastasia and adopt it as her service mark. A photo of Anastasia, a drawing of Anastasia, the word ANASTASIA, even a recording of Anastasia's meow could all qualify as a symbol. In order for the chosen symbol to qualify as a service mark, it would take more, as the next chapter and a half describe. Sally would have to use the symbol to distinguish her services from those of others, and the symbol would have to steer clear of the various exclusions (such as likelihood of confusion with existing cat-based trademarks).

SOURCE-IDENTIFYING FUNCTION

Almost anything capable of carrying meaning may be a symbol. But to be a trademark, a symbol must be used as a source identifier: used "to identify and distinguish his or her goods, including a unique product, from those manufactured or sold by others and to indicate the source of the goods." 15 U.S.C. §1127.

There are many ways in which the mark owner may be the "source" of the goods. The mark owner could actually manufacture or process the goods. The mark owner could buy the goods from others and sell them under his mark, such as a retail store that sells a house brand of appliances. The mark owner could distribute goods that were manufactured by subcontractors. Conversely, the mark owner could license others to make and sell the goods using the mark, under specifications provided by the mark owner. Or the mark owner could simply allow the mark to be used as an endorsement of the goods. The mark owner could also supply one component of the goods and allow the mark to be used on the goods. Because goods can have more than one source, goods may bear more than one trademark. A product's packaging might bear the marks of the manufacturer, a distributor, and an endorser.

The mark must indicate the source only in the sense that it distinguishes the goods from the goods of others. The mark need not identify the mark owner. It is sufficient that consumers identify the mark with a single source, even if the source is unknown. HUGGIES can be a mark for diapers without consumers knowing that the Kimberly-Clark Corporation makes the diapers. Nor must the meaning of the symbol relate to the nature of the goods or services.

To decide whether a symbol acts as a source identifier, courts employ a test drawn from the Restatement (Third) of Unfair Competition: The symbol must create a separate and distinct commercial impression that identifies the source of the merchandise to consumers. This determination is made by looking at the use of the symbol in the context of the marketplace, considering its size and placement, use of trademark notices or disclaimers, visual design elements, use of other marks, industry practices, and any other factors that affect the impression made by the mark. There are several ways in which a symbol may fail to function as a source identifier. First, a symbol may be perceived as fulfilling some other function. The words "Innocent Beige" on hair color were deemed simply to indicate the color of the product, rather than indicate the source of the goods. *See Clairol v. Gillette*, 389 F.2d 264 (2d Cir. 1968). The phrase "Damn I'm Good" on jewelry was held to be the message of the product rather than a source identifier and so not to serve as a mark. *See Damn I'm Good v. Sakowitz*, 514 F. Supp. 1357 (S.D.N.Y. 1981). Symbols may also be deemed to fulfill an aesthetic function, rather than act as a source identifier. Consumers might see a geometric design or a pretty drawing on a product's package as primarily decorative, rather than as serving to signify source.

If use of the symbol does not differentiate the product from others in the market, it cannot serve as a source identifier. For example, The Self-Realization Fellowship Church used the name of a prominent yoga guru frequently and prominently in their materials, identifying him as the founder of the tradition and attesting to the church's fidelity to his teachings.

But other yoga groups also associated themselves with his teachings. So his name did not function as a service mark for one group. *See Self-Realization Fellowship Church v. Ananda Church of Self-Realization*, 59 F.3d 902 (9th Cir. 1995).

The context of the use is key (as in trademark law generally). An image of a person can be used to indicate the source of goods. But the fact that one image of a person is used as a mark does not mean that every use of the person's likeness is use of the mark. For example, even though some images of Elvis Presley have been used as a mark indicating a source of goods or services, not every image could be said to serve that function. *See Estate of Presley v. Russen*, 513 F. Supp. 1339 (D.N.J. 1981).

A symbol might also fail to qualify as a mark because the symbol does not create an independent impression. Suppose that a fruitcake seller marks the boxes of her products with the legend Turtle Park Cakes, together with a rainbow design in the background. A competitor begins to sell cakes, not using the Turtle Park Cakes phrase but with a rainbow design in the background. Fruitcake seller claims a trademark in the rainbow design. To determine whether the design by itself functions as a mark (as opposed to being part of a composite mark composed of the words Turtle Park Cakes with a rainbow background design), a court will ask whether the rainbow design creates a "distinct commercial impression." If the design creates a separate and distinct impression on consumers, it could be an indicator of source. If the design does not make a separate impression but is perceived only as one component of the overall mark, the design is not protectable as a separate mark.

A common basic shape or letter, such as a square or the letter "b," would not be deemed to serve as a source identifier. Such a common symbol would not be perceived by consumers as associated with one particular seller. But a basic shape or letter could be made distinctive, as with a special design or by making it part of a composite mark.

The symbol must also indicate a source of the goods or services, as opposed to simply identifying the goods or services themselves. The text of a famous book cannot serve as its own trademark. A random clip from a familiar television show would not be a trademark for the show. Only if the text or the clip were used as a mark for some other goods or services would they serve as trademarks. For example, "Sweet Georgia Brown" functions as a service mark for the Harlem Globetrotters basketball team.

Examples

1. *No logic required.* Dough Co. sells a popular brand of pizza using the trademark Bungee Pizza. The pizza boxes have Bungee Pizza plastered across them and come in delivery trucks with Bungee in huge letters. A typical pizza buyer seeing a box of Bungee pizza instantly distinguishes it from the pizza of other companies. A competitor seeks to siphon off business

by using the word "Bungee" with her own pizza in a way likely to confuse pizza buyers. She receives a cease-and-desist letter from the owner of the BUNGEE mark. She wonders whether BUNGEE could possibly be a trademark for pizza. A trademark must identify the source of the goods, she reasons, and the word "Bungee" could not possibly do that. The pizzas do not come from a bungee, are not made by a bungee, are not made out of bungee, or in any way emanate from a bungee. Dough Co. sells the pizza; there is no such entity as Bungee Co. Does BUNGEE act as a source identifier?

2. *An open secret.* Paul Figman makes a delicious salad dressing, which he sells by the bottle. The dressing is widely sold in retail supermarkets. Each bottle of the dressing contains a detailed list of the ingredients. Consumers disregard the list. A comparison of Paul's ingredients with the ingredients in other salad dressings shows that his recipe is unique, which may account for the dressing's great popularity. A competitor prepares a new salad dressing, working from the list of ingredients on a bottle of Paul's dressing. Paul claims that copying the list is trademark infringement. The list of ingredients is a trademark, he argues, because it distinguishes Paul's dressing from dressings made or sold by others. Is the list of ingredients a source-identifying symbol?

3. *Fictional source.* Uncle Casper's ice cream occupies frozen shelf space in many cities. Each carton has the words "Uncle Casper's Ice Cream" in big letters, together with a blurry depiction of a farmer turning the handle of an ice cream maker. The drawing has a faintly comical aspect. Consumers would not likely think that there actually is an Uncle Casper or that the mass-produced ice cream is made by hand. Can such a fictional source act as a source-identifying symbol?

4. *Background check.* A rival ice cream seller decides to borrow from the packaging of Uncle Casper's. The rival does not copy the words "Uncle Casper's" but does copy the blurry picture of the farmer and places it on her ice cream cartons. Consumers are familiar with the words "Uncle Casper's" and frequently ask for the ice cream by name. But consumers rarely notice the picture of the farmer and would not recognize it when not accompanied by the words "Uncle Casper's." Nevertheless, before now the picture had never appeared on any ice cream other than Uncle Casper's. Is the picture a source-identifying symbol?

5. *Password.* Zembla is a secret sign of authenticity. Beer Maker produces and sells several brands of beer, using various trademarks. To detect fraudulent versions of its beer, Beer Maker puts the word "Zembla" on each bottle in an inconspicuous place. Usually Zembla appears among the small print listing ingredients or nutritional information. Beer Maker wonders whether Zembla is a trademark. The word functions solely to distinguish

genuine Beer Maker products from the products of others. Is Zembla a source-identifying symbol?

6. *Multiple sources.* Pat purchases a juice box for his young child. He notices that the box carries several purported trademarks. The symbol & appears next to the name of the company that makes the juice, a picture of a popular cartoon monster named Olmo, the name of a movie studio that makes Olmo's animated films, and name of the company that makes the boxes. Can so many symbols be source identifiers for one juice box?

7. *Designs.* Zep sugar comes in paper sacks. The ZEP mark is prominently and unmistakably used as a trademark on the sacks. The sacks also carry a beautiful geometric design, quite different from any other sugar bag on the market. The design is quite subtle, however, and sugar buyers pay it little attention. To the extent consumers notice the design at all, they regard it as ornamental and do not associate it with any particular brand of sugar. A rival of Zep begins to use the design on its own bags of sugar. Zep argues that the design is a trademark because it appears only on Zep sugar. Is the design a source-identifying symbol?

8. *Guarding angel.* Doll Maker sells a popular angel doll. Doll Maker claims trade dress protection in the image of the doll. Specifically, Doll Maker claims that the following elements compose the trade dress of the product: a round head, a triangular body, white clothing, a halo, and an overall angelic appearance. Many angel dolls made and sold by others share those elements. Indeed, any doll designed to represent an angel likely would share the same elements. Can Doll Maker claim a trademark in the claimed trade dress?

9. *Picture prefect.* Art Images is the best-known vendor of digital images of Old Master paintings. Because such paintings are so old, no one holds a copyright in them. But although anyone may make and sell copies, they need access to the paintings (or copies of them) to do so. Art Images pays several museums handsome fees in exchange for exclusive access to the paintings to make digital reproductions. Art Images sells CD-ROMs with the digital images. Buyers must promise not to make copies of the images.

Picture Company obtains copies of the images from a noncompliant buyer. Picture Company promptly makes and sells multiple copies. Art Images claims trademark infringement. Art Images argues that because purchasers in the field know only Art Images has access to the paintings, the digital images are trademarks belonging to Art Images. Are the digital images source-identifying symbols?

10. *AAA minus.* Grumpy is a well-known investment analysis service. Grumpy compiles great amounts of information about publicly traded companies and their relevant industries. Grumpy's analysts, using their own expertise

and Grumpy's sophisticated software, rate the stocks and bonds of the companies, using a scale running from AAA down to FFF. The ratings are widely respected among professional investors, who pay considerable sums to receive Grumpy's newsletter with the most recent ratings.

Grumpy is irked by the fact that many newsletter subscribers use Grumpy's ratings in their own communications with clients and investors. A typical subscriber is a stockbroker who advises his clients to purchase a particular bond, stating that it was rated AAA. Grumpy considers the ratings to be service marks belonging to Grumpy on the theory that investors widely recognize that the ratings stem from Grumpy's analysis. Are the ratings source-identifying symbols?

11. *Georgi-O.* After some consumers order "Stoli O" for Stolichyna orange-flavored vodka, Georgi Vodka decides to spice up its label. Georgi adds a large, elliptical letter O under Georgi on the label, hoping to teach consumers to order "Georgi O" when they are looking for orange-flavored vodka. Competitors start tacking O's on their orange-flavored products. On Georgi's packaging, the O is too separate from Georgi for Georgi-O to be a mark. Rather, consumers notice the stylized O and interpret it as denoting a brand of orange vodka. Can a stylized O be a mark by itself?

Explanations

1. Bungee does act as a source identifier and could be a trademark for the pizza. To be a source identifier, the symbol must create a separate and distinct commercial impression that identifies the source of the goods to consumers. The symbol need not name the source, describe it, or refer to it in any way. Rather, the symbol can identify the goods and distinguish them from others simply by being a prominent symbol that is different from the identifiers for the other goods on the market. The trademark for Tide detergent does not tell the consumer anything about the detergent but does distinguish the product from the other detergents on the shelf. Likewise, pizza buyers can distinguish Bungee pizza from the pizza sold by others.

2. The list of ingredients is not a source-identifying symbol. To be a source identifier, the symbol must create a separate and distinct commercial impression that identifies the source of the goods to consumers. The list of ingredients does not create a distinct commercial impression; rather, it is largely unnoticed by consumers. To the extent that consumers pay it attention, they do not regard it as serving a source-identifying function. Rather, they see it as serving a different function: stating what the salad dressing is made out of. So not everything that could distinguish the goods from the goods of others can qualify as a trademark. Rather, it

must be something that in fact does distinguish the goods from those of others in the eyes of the relevant public.

3. The fictional symbol for Uncle Casper's ice cream can act as a source-identifying symbol. The symbol need not identify the source in the sense of naming the maker or telling where the product actually came from. Rather, it must simply act to set the goods apart from other goods on the market. The UNCLE CASPER mark does perform that function, differentiating the ice cream from other ice cream on the market.

4. The blurry picture of the farmer is not a source-identifying symbol and accordingly does not independently qualify as a trademark. To be a trademark, the symbol must create a separate and distinct commercial impression. The picture fails to do that because consumers rarely notice the picture and would not recognize it when not accompanied by the words Uncle Casper's. So it does not create a separate impression and would not be entitled to a separate trademark. Note that the test turns on the impression made on the consuming public in the context of the mark's use, not just on the quality of the mark itself.

5. Zembla is not a source-identifying symbol in the sense required to qualify as a trademark. To be a mark, the symbol must create a separate and distinct commercial impression that identifies the source of the goods to consumers. The Zembla symbol does identify the source of goods to those who know about it, such as the beer maker. But it is placed so inconspicuously that it does not make any impression at all on consumers, let alone an impression as a source identifier.

   If Beer Maker wanted to make Zembla a source identifier, it could do so two ways. First, it could put Zembla in huge letters on each bottle. Second, it could still hide it away but use advertising to educate consumers about where to look for the Zembla mark. But this would defeat its antiknockoff role because makers of fraudulent beer would also be alerted to the proper placement of Zembla.

6. Goods can and often do bear multiple source identifiers. The source of goods can mean a number of things: the manufacturer, the shipper, an endorser, the maker of an ingredient, the parent company of the manufacturer, and more. There need not be a single source.

7. The design is not a source-identifying symbol. The design appears only on sacks of Zep sugar. Someone who knows that could use it to identify sacks of Zep sugar. But to be a source identifier for trademark purposes, the symbol must make a separate and distinct commercial impression as an indicator of source. Sugar buyers rarely pay any attention to the design, so it apparently does not make a separate and distinct impression. Even if it did, those who see it regard it as fulfilling a different function—not as a source indicator but rather as ornamental. So the

design does not qualify for a separate trademark. Even if the design is distinctive, it must serve as a source identifier to be a trademark.

8. Doll Maker does not have a protectable trademark in the claimed trade dress. Trade dress can be the overall image of the product. But to qualify for protection, trade dress, like other trademarks, must act as a source identifier. Here, the claimed elements do not differentiate the goods from other goods on the market. To the contrary, angel dolls made and sold by others share the same elements. So the claimed elements do not distinguish Doll Maker's products from those of others. Indeed, granting trademark protection would have the effect of giving one seller control over the market by giving it exclusive rights in common elements of the product. Cf. *Kaufman & Fisher Wish Co. v. F.A.O. Schwartz*, 184 F. Supp. 2d 311 (S.D.N.Y. 2001).

9. The digital images are not source-identifying symbols. They do not act as symbols that distinguish the source of the goods; rather, they are the goods themselves. Because buyers know that Art Images is likely the only one with the necessary access to make the images, buyers can infer that the images originate with Art Images. But that is different from using the images as source identifiers. The images do not create a commercial impression as a source identifier. Rather, they primarily serve another purpose, that of representing reproductions of Old Master paintings. Cf. *Bridgeman Art Library v. Corel Corp.*, 25 F. Supp. 2d 421 (S.D.N.Y. 1998).

10. The ratings are not source-identifying symbols. Rather, they are more like the goods themselves. Grumpy does not use the symbols to identify its services and distinguish them from others. Grumpy uses the symbols to rate stocks and bonds. The ratings do not make a commercial impression as an identifier of source. Rather, they make an impression as ratings for stocks and bonds — issued by a respected source. Cf. *In re Moody's Investors Serv.*, 13 U.S.P.Q. 2d 2043 (T.T.A.B. 1989).

11. A stylized letter O can be a mark by itself. *See Star Indus. v. Bacardi & Co.*, 412 F.3d 373 (2d Cir. 2005). It must act as a source identifier, which means that it must make a separate and distinct commercial impression as an indicator of source. In this case, the stylized letter O does make such an impression on consumers, because they interpret it as marking a brand of orange vodka. The result would be different if it were simply a common basic shape or letter, which would probably not be interpreted as a source-identifying symbol. But because the letter was specially shaped, and unique in the industry, it could act as a source identifier. By the same token, giving trademark protection to one particular stylized letter O would still allow other vodka sellers to use the letter O, as long as they did not use the same stylized design.

Substantive Standards for Protection: "The Source-Distinguishing Ability of a Mark"

11

A mark must be distinctive. This requirement often maddens marketing people. If a business is about to put a new strep diagnosis kit on the market, the marketers would like to call it Fast Efficient Strep Diagnosis Kit. Their lawyer (if they consult one) would have to say, "You can use that name, but it will not be protected as a trademark. It is descriptive." What would be protected? A symbol that is not descriptive—like Meercat or Borogrove. But marketers want descriptive names for their products—and isn't trademark law supposed to facilitate communication between buyers and sellers? It is, but one seller should not be able to communicate with consumers at the cost of shutting out other sellers. If Fast Efficient Strep Diagnosis Kit was a trademark for one seller in that market, the other strep kit sellers would risk infringement if they used words like "fast," "efficient," and "strep diagnosis kit." So trademark protection is limited to distinctive symbols, not symbols that are merely descriptive. All is not lost for the marketing department. They can use both: Meercat Fast Efficient Strep Diagnosis Kit, although only the "Meercat" component will have trademark protection.

The previous chapter discussed the basic requirements for trademark protection: that a mark be a symbol used as a source identifier for goods or services. This chapter discusses the substantive standards for protection, many of which are refinements of those basic requirements. The substantive requirements fall into two categories. First, the mark must be distinctive: If it is not distinctive, it cannot distinguish the relevant goods or services. A mark can be inherently distinctive or it can acquire distinctiveness (by becoming known to the public as an indicator of source). Second, there are a number of categorical exclusions: A symbol cannot be protected as a

409

mark if it is likely to cause confusion with an existing mark, is deceptive, is functional, or falls into other excluded categories.[1]

DISTINCTIVENESS

To qualify as a mark, a symbol must be distinctive—it must "identify and distinguish" the goods or services. *See also* 15 U.S.C. §1052. If a symbol is not distinctive, its use by others does not cause customer confusion as to source, so protecting it does not serve the purposes of trademark law. 15 U.S.C. §1127. *See Wal-Mart Stores v. Samara Bros.*, 529 U.S. 205 (2000). Claimed marks fall into three categories of distinctiveness:

1. *Inherently distinctive marks:* Arbitrary, fanciful, or suggestive marks that stand alone are sufficiently distinctive to qualify for protection.
2. *Marks that are capable of acquired distinctiveness:* A symbol that is merely descriptive does not signify source, so it is unprotected. But a descriptive symbol may acquire "secondary meaning" (when the mark's primary significance to the public is to indicate source). Other nondistinctive symbols are likewise protectable only if they acquire secondary meaning: misdescriptive terms, colors used as marks, product design trade dress, surnames, and geographic marks.
3. *Generic terms:* Marks that designate the category of product, rather than one specific provider of such products, are not distinctive and are unprotectable as marks.

The rationale for limiting protection of generic and descriptive terms goes beyond considerations of whether the symbol acts as a source identifier. Equally important are considerations of competition. In deciding whether a mark is distinctive (and hence protectable), a court ultimately decides an issue of competition, not semantics: Is this symbol one that a single seller should have exclusive right to use as a mark or one that all sellers should be able to use? If one competitor in a market could trademark the generic term for the product, other competitors would be at a great disadvantage. If one scooter seller could trademark SCOOTER, other scooter sellers would be hamstrung in communicating with potential customers. Not every use of

---

1. In the federal statute, many of the substantive standards are stated as bars to registration of marks. Unregistered marks are also enforceable under the Lanham Act. But unregistrable marks, as discussed in the infringement chapter, are rarely enforced as marks, although deceptive use of a registered mark could give rise to false advertising liability. Some state law also provides protection to a mark that is barred from federal registration, but state law is generally consistent with the federal standards.

the word "Scooter" would infringe the mark, but they could use the word only with great care. Allowing trademark protection of descriptive terms also limits competitors. If one scooter seller has the trademark CRIMSON Scooters, then others must search for different ways to describe the color of their scooters. But unlike generic terms (where there may be only one commonly used generic term for a product, such as "scooter"), descriptive terms leave alternatives for others to use. Another scooter seller may use "red," "vermilion," "bloody," or "scarlet," not to mention "blue." In addition, consumers may have become so accustomed to the first seller's use of CRIMSON that they associate the phrase with her scooters and think that scooters bearing that language come from her. The primary meaning of the term is to indicate a particular source, and the descriptive sense becomes secondary. Accordingly, descriptive terms are protectable, provided that such a "secondary meaning" exists (although competitors remain free to use the descriptive word "crimson" in its descriptive sense, as opposed to its mark use). Finally, if the symbol is inherently distinctive, then it is clearly a source indicator: PLUNKADUNK Scooters. Making PLUNKADUNK unavailable as a mark to competitors still leaves them an infinite number of alternative marks. So inherently distinctive marks are protectable, even without a showing of secondary meaning.

The distinctiveness of the mark depends on its use in the marketplace context, not only on an examination of the mark itself. The distinctiveness depends on the nature of the goods or services. "Safari" is a generic term when used for travel services to view wildlife, but it might be a descriptive mark for camping equipment or an inherently distinctive mark for yo-yos. In addition, whether a mark is distinctive is judged on the mark as a whole, not simply by summing its parts. A mark may be distinctive even if it is made up of generic or descriptive terms. "Scooter" is generic for scooters, but "Green Ball Goof Scooters" is inherently distinctive. The distinctiveness of a mark can also change over time. A descriptive mark can acquire secondary meaning, which makes it protectable. In the other direction, an inherently distinctive mark can become so closely associated with a product that it becomes generic (and hence nonprotectable).

I. Inherently Distinctive Marks

A mark is inherently distinctive if its "intrinsic nature serves to identify a particular source." *Two Pesos v. Taco Cabana*, 505 U.S. 763, 768 (1992). Such a mark inherently signals to the potential buyer that it designates the source of the product rather than some other type of information. They "almost *automatically* tell a customer that they refer to a brand." *Qualitex v. Jacobson Products*, 514 U.S. 159, 162-163 (1995). Because the mark is inherently distinctive, it is protectable without showing that it has acquired distinctiveness in the public mind. Inherently distinctive marks conventionally are grouped into three categories: arbitrary, fanciful, and suggestive.

Arbitrary and Fanciful Marks

Marks are arbitrary or fanciful if they do not describe or suggest any characteristic of the product. A canonical example is APPLE for computers. If a consumer is shopping for computers and sees one prominently designated with the brand name APPLE, she should know that "Apple" does not mean "computer" or describe computers. She is shopping for a computer, not an apple. Nor is she looking for a computer made from apples, weighing the same as an apple, or apple-sized. So she is likely to infer that APPLE refers to the source of the goods. APPLE is an inherently distinctive mark for computers.

An arbitrary mark is an existing symbol chosen to serve as mark that has no logical relation to the goods. A fanciful mark is one devised to serve as a mark that likewise does not name or describe the product. So APPLE is an arbitrary mark for computers, whereas KHLOZUBIDUB is a fanciful mark for computers. If an archaic, obsolete, or rare word (such as "Uberty" or "Esperable") is chosen as a mark, it is often deemed fanciful as well. Whether the mark is deemed arbitrary or fanciful is not important as to distinctiveness. The key is that because the symbol's meaning is not related to the goods, it therefore is likely to be interpreted as a source indicator.

Suggestive Marks

Suggestive marks suggest, but do not describe, the nature or characteristics of the product. Suggestive marks are slightly less distinctive than arbitrary or fanciful marks but nevertheless are inherently distinctive. If there is a link between the product and the symbol, the mark is not arbitrary or fanciful. But if the link is sufficiently tenuous, a potential buyer might understand that the symbol suggests the product but nevertheless serves to indicate the source. Suggestive marks fall between arbitrary and fanciful marks on the one hand and descriptive marks on the other hand. TRAP for cameras, BASE CAMP for refrigerators, REEF for legal services, and NOAH for a zoological garden are suggestive marks. Because the symbol merely suggests what the goods are, a potential purchaser is likely to regard the symbol as a source indicator.

By choosing a suggestive mark, a marketer can strike a balance between legal and business considerations. Because the mark is suggestive, it is protectable without secondary meaning. That means the mark is protected as soon as the seller uses it as a mark. With a descriptive mark, the mark is not protected until it acquires secondary meaning (and most descriptive terms never acquire secondary meaning). A suggestive mark serves not only as a protected trademark, it can serve (by its very suggestiveness) to win over the public by suggesting the product qualities a buyer may be seeking.

In differentiating between a suggestive mark and a descriptive mark, courts look at several factors. If the symbol literally describes the goods or some characteristic of them, the symbol is likely descriptive. On the other hand, if a prospective customer must use imagination to infer something about the goods, the symbol may be deemed suggestive. But courts look beyond the literal meaning. Courts also consider whether competitors are likely to need the terms used in the trademark in describing their products and consider the extent to which a term actually has been used by others marketing a similar service or product. A picture of a Labrador retriever was held descriptive for Internet search engine services. The image of the dog does not literally describe using a database to help users find relevant Web pages, but the retriever is a common industry metaphor for such information retrieval services. *See Labrador Software v. Lycos*, 32 F. Supp. 2d 31 (D. Mass. 1999).

2. Marks That Are Protectable Only with Acquired Distinctiveness

A merely descriptive term is not inherently distinctive. The consuming public would likely interpret the term to describe the product, not to denote the source of the product. But a descriptive mark can acquire distinctiveness if it acquires "secondary meaning." A mark acquires secondary meaning when, "in the minds of the public, the primary significance of [the mark] is to identify the source of the product rather than the product itself." *Inwood Laboratories v. Ives Laboratories*, 456 U.S. 844, 851, n.11 (1982). A familiar example is Coca-Cola. At one time, the term was descriptive: a cola drink including ingredients derived from the coca plant. But COCA-COLA has become so well known *as a mark* that the primary significance of COCA-COLA is now as an identifier of source—to distinguish Coca-Cola from the beverages of Pepsi and other cola sellers. COCA-COLA is now distinctive because it has acquired distinctiveness.

Descriptive marks can be protected if they acquire secondary meaning. As discussed below, several other categories of marks are protectable only if they acquire secondary meaning. But the requirement of secondary meaning is a difficult one, usually fatal to a would-be mark. The "primary significance" to the public must be to indicate source. But most marks never have any significance to the public. Moreover, not only must the mark attain significance to the public, its primary significance must be to indicate source, as opposed to describing the product or serving some other function. So showing secondary meaning presents a formidable hurdle. A business contemplating what symbol to adopt as a mark is well advised to steer clear of marks that might be deemed descriptive (or other marks, as discussed below, that require secondary meaning for protection). But businesses often wish to use a mark precisely because the mark is descriptive—a common source of friction between trademark lawyers and their clients. Suppose that a manufacturer develops a cheap and reliable testing kit for detecting byzium enzymes. It wants to market the product as "Low-Cost Reliable Byzium Enzyme Testing Kit," but such a descriptive term is not protected as a mark unless it acquires secondary meaning. An arbitrary term, such as "Afflatus," is protectable without a need for secondary meaning (though it might well not catch the eye of the intended buyer).

In determining whether a mark has acquired secondary meaning, courts look to several factors, such as extent of sales and advertising leading to buyer association, length of use, exclusivity of use, the fact of copying, customer surveys, customer testimony, the use of the mark in trade journals, the size of the company, the number of sales, the number of customers, and actual confusion. *Ford Motor Co. v. Summit Motor Products,* 930 F.2d 277, 292 (3d Cir. 1991). The factors are not applied according to any formula. Rather, they simply guide the court in determining the primary significance (if any) of the mark to the public.

Several categories of marks are protectable only if they acquire such secondary meaning.

Merely Descriptive Marks

A descriptive term identifies a characteristic or quality of the goods or services. Whether a mark is descriptive is judged by its meaning to the likely purchaser of the relevant goods or services in the context of the relevant market. It need not fully describe the goods or services. Rather, the term may be deemed to be merely descriptive if it identifies anything about the product: its purpose, size, color, ingredients, intended users, origin, or anything else. A descriptive term need not be an adjective—it could be a noun, a verb, or any other part of speech. Descriptive terms need not be words. Drawings or other symbols can be descriptive. Nor need the description go to the basic nature of the product—it can describe a characteristic that is related only tangentially to the overall product. Even a "laudatory" term may be held merely descriptive on the theory that the term is likely to be interpreted as praising the goods, as opposed to indicating the source. The following are examples of terms held to be descriptive:

> Beer Nuts for nuts with salt, 5 Minute for fast-setting glue, Intelligent Modem for modems, Rich'n Chips for chocolate chip cookies, Shear Pleasure for a beauty salon, Tender Vittles for cat food, Trim for nail clippers, Vision Center for optician services, World Book for an encyclopedia.

J. Thomas McCarthy, *Trademarks and Unfair Competition* §11.24 (3d ed. 1992).

A descriptive symbol (protectable only if it has acquired secondary meaning) falls between a suggestive mark (protectable without even showing secondary meaning) and a generic term (never protectable as a mark). So the question of descriptiveness arises most often in two contexts: (1) Is the term suggestive or "merely descriptive" (where the mark holder is arguing that the mark is not descriptive)? Or (2) is the term descriptive and not merely generic (where the mark holder is arguing that the mark is descriptive)?

Note that a marketer might well want to use a descriptive term as a trademark. Someone marketing goods or services may wish to use a mark that tells potential buyers about the product. An apple seller might want to use the mark VERMILION to describe the color of the apples. But such a descriptive term would be protected only if it acquired secondary meaning. An inherently distinctive symbol (arbitrary (PARALLEL), fanciful (LARARARA), or suggestive (INSIDER)) would be protectable but would tell a potential buyer little about the product. So in choosing the mark (among many other considerations), there is a trade-off between increasing the descriptiveness and decreasing the distinctiveness (and the legal strength) of the mark.

Even where a descriptive term becomes a trademark right, others retain considerable rights to use the term.

> The common law's tolerance of a certain degree of confusion on the part of consumers followed from the very fact that in cases like this one an originally descriptive term was selected to be used as a mark, not to mention the undesirability of allowing anyone to obtain a complete monopoly on use of a descriptive term simply by grabbing it first. The Lanham Act adopts a similar leniency, there being no indication that the statute was meant to deprive commercial speakers of the ordinary utility of descriptive words.

KP Permanent Make-Up, Inc. v. Lasting Impression I, Inc., 125 S. Ct. 542, 550 (2004) (citation omitted). The trademark owner retains the benefits of describing the product for a cost in lower trademark protection.

Primarily Geographically Descriptive Marks

"Primarily geographically descriptive" marks also require secondary meaning to be distinctive.[2] Not every geographic term is primarily geographically descriptive. The question is whether the consuming public is likely to assume that the named location is where the product originated. Suppose ALASKAN is used as a designation for water and that consumers are likely to

---

2. The statute provides that one type of geographic mark does not require secondary meaning: indications of regional origin, which are collective or certification marks used to certify the geographical provenance of the product.

interpret it to mean that the water comes from Alaska. The term is primarily geographically descriptive, and therefore protected, only if it acquires secondary meaning. But if the water is sold using the mark PLANET JUPITER, the mark is not geographically descriptive. The public would not think the water came from the planet Jupiter. Rather, the choice of such a symbol is arbitrary and hence inherently distinctive. ANTARCTICA used on soft drinks would not be taken to denote that they were made there. RODEO DRIVE on perfume would connote luxury rather than the address of the perfume factory. See In re Jacques Bernier, Inc., 894 F.2d 389 (Fed. Cir. 1990).

Primarily a Surname

A mark that is primarily a surname likewise requires secondary meaning before it is protectable. If a fast-food restaurant opens up using FARLEY'S on its goods and services, it does not have protected trademarks or service marks in "Farley's," a surname. But if the mark acquires secondary meaning, then trademark and service mark protection does attach. Such marks as MCDONALDS and SEARS are surnames but are nonetheless distinctive because they have acquired distinctiveness.

As with geographic marks, the rule applies only if the consuming public is likely to consider the primary significance of the term to be a surname. "Peregrine" is a surname for some people. But if an optics maker sold PEREGRINE binoculars, clearly using the word as a brand name, consumers probably would not interpret "Peregrine" as a surname. Rather, they likely would interpret "Peregrine" as a suggestive mark and an indication of source. So the mark would be protected, even if it had not acquired secondary meaning.

Deceptively Misdescriptive Marks

Under the Lanham Act, "deceptive" marks are not protectable, but "deceptively misdescriptive" marks are protectable if they acquire secondary meaning. 15 U.S.C. §1052(f).

A mark may be misdescriptive but not deceptively so. If a farmer sells SOLID GOLD apples, the consuming public would not think that the apples are made of solid gold. Likewise, AUTOMATIC RADIO may be misdescriptive when used for air conditioners, ignition systems, and antennas but not deceptively misdescriptive because buyers can readily determine that such products do not function as automatic radios. See In re Automatic Radio Mfg. Co., 404 F.2d 1391, 1396 (C.C.P.A. 1969). Such misdescriptive terms are protectable provided they meet the other requirements for protection.

The next step up the ladder is "deceptively misdescriptive." Farmer's CRIMSON apples may in fact be a color other than crimson. Unlike SOLID GOLD, a buyer might reasonably believe they were crimson. But such a designation nevertheless may not rise to the level of "deceptive" if the description does not affect whether a buyer decides to buy the apples. Courts distinguish between "deceptive" and "deceptively misdescriptive" marks on the basis of materiality. *See* J. Thomas McCarthy, *Trademarks and Unfair Competition* §11:58 (3d ed. 1992). If the misdescription is not *material* to potential buyers, the mark is, like a descriptive mark, protectable if it acquires secondary meaning. So if buyers come to regard CRIMSON primarily as a source indicator rather than a description of the apples, the seller can protect it as a mark. But if the misdescription is material to potential buyers, the mark is deceptive and hence nonprotectable.

Color

A color may be protected as a trademark. But the Supreme Court has ruled that color cannot be inherently distinctive. *See Wal-Mart Stores v. Samara Brothers*, 529 U.S. 205 (2000) (interpreting the earlier *Qualitex* opinion). A color, by itself, does not indicate to the buyer that it denotes one particular source of goods or services. However, a color might acquire distinctiveness. If it is used consistently over time, the consuming public might come to associate that color with one source.

Product Design

Companies hate for their products to be copied. For some, copyright or patent provides protection. But some products, such as clothing or other functional products that are not patented, have little protection under copyright or patent. Trademark's protection for product design is limited. The Supreme Court has also held that product design trade dress can be distinctive, and therefore protectable, only if the trade dress acquires secondary meaning. *Id.* The plaintiff claimed trade dress protection in the design of a line of children's clothing, "spring/summer one-piece seersucker outfits decorated with appliques of hearts, flowers, fruits, and the like." The plaintiff argued that the trade dress was inherently distinctive, and therefore protectable, without showing secondary meaning. In rejecting such a theory, the Court differentiated between trade dress that is product packaging and trade dress that is the design of the product itself. The primary purpose of product packaging is to market the product. Consumers are likely to view distinctive product packaging as indicating the source of the product. But the primary purpose of product design is generally to make the product more appealing or more useful. A consumer is not as likely to regard a distinctive design as an indicator of source. Accordingly, product design can be protected as trade dress only on a showing of secondary meaning. But whether claimed trade dress is product design or product packaging (or some third category that the Court suggested might include such things as the trade dress of a restaurant) is not always clear. If a line of bicycles is painted with a distinctive checkerboard pattern that has nothing to do with the function of the bicycle, one could argue that the pattern is product packaging, although it appears on the product itself.

3. Generic Terms Are Not Protectable as Trademarks

If potential buyers understand a term to refer to a category of goods or services, as opposed to the source of the product, the term is generic. Generic terms are not protectable as marks. The term refers to the product, regardless of the source, so it does not distinguish one seller of the product from other sellers. Moreover, granting one seller trademark rights in the generic term would cause considerable problems in communication between other buyers and sellers.

One seller in a market cannot own the very term her competitors need to denote their product. This applies even where the product is not highly commercial. The term "Universal" has been held generic for the mark of a church.[3] One court held that it remained a question of fact whether "Comic-Con" is generic for comic book conventions.[4]

The term's use by consumers governs whether it is generic. A term can be generic even if it does not appear in the dictionary. The term need not be the only name for a product. Some products go by more than one generic term: car and automobile; pop and soda; candy and sweets. Generic terms need not be as broad as "bar" or "restaurant"; rather, more narrow categories of goods or services still have their own generic terms, such as "ale house" and "crab house." See *Ale House Management v. Raleigh Ale House*, 205 F.3d 137 (4th Cir. 2000). "Duck Tour" has been held to be a generic term for amphibious-vehicle sightseeing tours. See *Boston Duck Tours, LP v. Super Duck Tours, LLC*, 531 F.3d 1 (1st Cir. 2008).

Generic terms fall into two categories. In the first, the claimant to a mark seeks to take a word that is already generic and use it as a mark. In the second, a distinctive trademark becomes generic through widespread use

---

3. Here, finding that "universal church" is generic would grant plaintiff a monopoly over the word "universal" as used in church names, a monopoly which plaintiff has already indicated that it would enforce aggressively. We are persuaded that the trademark law is simply not intended to allow the mark to be weaponized by plaintiff in this way.

Universal Church, Inc. v. Universal Life Church/ULC Monastery, 2017 U.S. Dist. LEXIS 127362, at *22 (S.D.N.Y. Aug. 8, 2017).

4. David Kravets, "Comic-Con" trademark may have to activate superpowers to survive attack — Epic intellectual property battle: San Diego Comic-Con versus Salt Lake Comic Con, Ars Technica (Sept. 21, 2017), https://arstechnica.com/tech-policy/2017/09/comic-con-trademark-may-have-to-activate-superpowers-to-survive-attack/, discussing San Diego Comic Convention v. Dan Farr Prods., No. 14-1865 (S.D. Cal. Sept. 22, 2017).

and loses trademark protection. Such was the fate of such well-known terms as trampoline, aspirin, cellophane, thermos, and shredded wheat.

Sometimes a term from a language other than English is generic in a market outside the United States. If the product is sold in the United States, is the foreign language term generic in the United States? Under the doctrine of foreign equivalents, some courts hold that a generic term is a generic term, irrespective of language. *See Enrique Bernat F., S.A. v. Guadalajara, 210 F.3d 439 (5th Cir. 2000).* The rule applies to foreign terms used in the United States, such as the term "Magnesita" for refractory products using magnesite.[5] Similarly, a foreign term often treated as generic in the United States may be proved nongeneric in fact, as was the case with the term "tequila" for spirits.[6] Another view is that the term may be merely descriptive when sed in the United States if ready alternatives exist. Note that a mark with generic components may, as a combination, be distinctive. To take an example from Fethard, Tipperary: "McCarthy's Publican, Restaurant, Undertaker" is inherently distinctive, although its components are a surname and three generic terms.

If a seller introduces a new type of product to the market, then seller's brand name may be the only well-known term for the product. But as long as consumers understand the term to designate source, it is not generic. 15 U.S.C. §1064(3).

Examples

1. *Quick picks.* A potential mark may be inherently distinctive, which means it is protected as soon as it is used as a mark; protectable if it acquires distinctiveness, meaning that it is protected if it becomes so well known that consumers associate it with a particular seller; or unprotectable if it is generic. Where do the following fall along the range of distinctiveness:
   a. MOUSE for mice, sold as pets
   b. MOUSE sold for small devices moved on a surface to point to objects on a computer screen
   c. WIRELESS OPTICAL MOUSE to describe a computer mouse that does not need a cord or friction
   d. SQUEAKY for mice sold as pets
   e. MOUSE used for personal training services

2. *Free for all.* The only law firm in the town of Springfield calls itself Legal Services. It has a huge sign outside the office proclaiming "Legal Services." Its letterhead bears the name "Legal Services," and members of the firm

---

5. *See* The TTAB Blog, CAFC *Affirms TTAB: MAGNESITA is Generic for . . . . Guess What?* (Nov. 28, 2017), http://thettablog.blogspot.com/2017/11/cafc-affirms-ttab-magnesita-is-generic.html (discussing *In re Magnesita Refractories Co.*, No. 16-2345 (Fed. Cir. Nov. 27, 2017).

6. Luxco, Inc. v. Consejo Regulador del Tequila, A.C., No. 91190827 (TTAB Jan. 23 2017).

consistently identify themselves as lawyers from "Legal Services." The use of the name is so well known among the populace of Springfield that people frequently refer to the firm as "Legal Services." The primary meaning of the phrase "legal services," however, retains its everyday meaning to refer to the services rendered by lawyers. Springfieldians regularly refer to "legal services" rendered by lawyers in other towns. Is Legal Services a distinctive service mark for the firm that uses that name?

3. Blitz. The leading messenger service in Springfield identifies its services with the term "Lightning Messengers." The term appears on its envelopes, on the clothing and bikes of its messengers, and on its advertising and stationery. Springfieldians are well acquainted with the firm and regularly advise anyone in need of quick delivery services to contact "Lightning." Is LIGHTNING MESSENGERS a distinctive service mark for the messenger firm?

4. Zapped. Sigmunda recently completed her training as a psychologist. She founds a small firm to offer counseling services. She uses the symbol CARING & INSIGHTFUL to identify her services. The phrase aptly describes her counseling style. Is CARING & INSIGHTFUL a distinctive service mark for her counseling services?

5. Round one. Sigmunda's brother Dom recently completed his doctorate in medieval literature. Unable to land a job right away, Dom opens a pizza delivery store. Dom adopts the symbol QJAAB (by using the next letter after each letter in "pizza") to identify his store as the source of pizza. He uses QJAAB on the pizza boxes, on the delivery uniforms, and in a few modest ads. As of yet, the QJAAB name remains virtually unknown to the relevant public. No other pizza businesses use the term. Is QJAAB a distinctive trademark for Dom's pizza?

6. Trouble in paradise. Massage Salon provides various forms of massage, from therapeutic massage to sports massage to massage techniques associated with countries in Europe and Asia. Massage Salon uses the term "Bliss Massage" in advertising, displays, and elsewhere to identify its services. Many other operators in the salon business use the word "bliss" in connection with their goods and services, but none use the word as part of their title or to identify their services. Massage clients do not achieve literal bliss in the dictionary sense of perfect joy or felicity. But the word suggests the sort of ultimate relaxation that a perfect massage might enable. Few other words would serve as well to promote massage services. Massage Salon is just one salon of many, and consumers do not associate "bliss" with any particular salon. Massage Salon seeks an injunction against a new salon that opened up just down the street, calling itself Bliss World. Is BLISS MASSAGE a distinctive mark for Massage Salon?

7. *Let's go to the tape.* A consumer products manufacturer begins to market a new duct tape. It adopts the mark BLISS to sell the duct tape. Each roll has BLISS DUCT TAPE prominently displayed on the label. Because the tape is new, consumers are not familiar with the use of "Bliss" to identify the duct tape. When consumers encounter Bliss duct tape, none interpret "Bliss" as referring to any quality of the tape or to the effect it will have on the user. Rather, consumers find the name "Bliss" used on tape to be comical. Although the mark has been in use for several months, there is very little awareness of Bliss tape among consumers as a whole. Is BLISS a distinctive trademark for the duct tape?

8. *Place name.* Grape Grower sells raisins, using the brand name Sonoma County. Grape Grower is indeed located in Sonoma County, California, and sells only Sonoma-grown grapes. Consumers typically surmise that Sonoma County brand raisins come from Sonoma County. But consumers do not associate the term "Sonoma Grapes" with Grape Grower. Is SONOMA COUNTY a distinctive trademark for Grape Grower's raisins?

9. *Hyperbole.* Detergent Maker sells Pumpkin brand laundry detergent. Every box of Pumpkin detergent bears a prominent slogan, "Cleans Faster Than Light!" Consumers do not interpret the phrase literally. Rather, consumers typically take it as praise of Pumpkin detergent. Pumpkin is a relatively minor brand on the market, and consumers do not associate the "Cleans Faster Than Light!" slogan with Pumpkin. Indeed, consumers have little awareness of Pumpkin. Is CLEANS FASTER THAN LIGHT! a distinctive mark for the detergent?

10. *Cold potatoes.* Potato Farmer raises her crop in Idaho and sells them under the brand name North Pole. When consumers see a bag of North Pole potatoes, they do not take the name to mean that the potatoes were grown in the Arctic. They do interpret it to distinguish those potatoes from the products of others. Consumers do not associate the North Pole name with Potato Farmer, who is merely one of many potato sellers on the market. Is NORTH POLE a distinctive mark for the potatoes?

11. *Namesake.* A shoemaker uses the name McGuire's to identify his shoes. Consumers do not associate the shoes with any real person named McGuire, nor are they aware of McGuire's as indicating the source of shoes. Rather, consumers typically regard McGuire as a name. Is MCGUIRE's a distinctive mark for the shoemaker's shoes? Would the result be different if consumers know that McGuire is a common surname, but the shoes were so well known that the primary significance of McGuire's in the context of shoes was an indication of source?

12. *Sweets.* A delicious line of sugar candy is sold under the trademark HOLIDAY. The candy is good but obscure and little known among consumers. Consumers are aware that "Holiday" often serves as a surname. But consumers that encounter the candy interpret "Holiday" as simply referring to festive days of the year and, in the context of a box of candy, to be the product's brand name. Is HOLIDAY a distinctive mark for the candy?

13. *Evolution.* Cane Men is a very popular brand of candy whose sickly sweet figures come in various colors. The CANE MEN mark is well known among consumers. Consumers interpret the term to mean the candy is made with cane sugar, although the sugar in the candy comes strictly from sugar beets. But consumers would buy the candy just as happily if they knew that it was made from sugar beets. The primary significance of CANE MEN to consumers is an indicator of source, as a sign that the candy comes from the reliable source of that favored candy. Is CANE MEN a distinctive mark?

14. *Purple revolution.* Cigars usually are sold in somber-toned boxes. Cigar Seller begins to market her cigars in bright purple boxes, a color very different from any of the other packages in the cigar market. The few prospective cigar buyers to see the boxes react with great surprise. Some love the packaging; some dislike the departure from tradition. But the purple boxes are as yet just a drop in the ocean. Cigar buyers generally are completely unaware of the new purple-packaged brand. Is the color purple a distinctive mark for Cigar Seller's cigars?

15. *Color code.* A start-up software company adopts the word "purple" as a trademark for its software. The company has sold quite a few boxes of software with the mark PURPLE prominently featured but, as yet, has made little dent on the market as a whole. Other software sellers make little if any use of the word "purple" or the color purple in their marketing. Is PURPLE a distinctive mark for this software company's software?

16. *New form.* Inventor starts selling his new hands-free scooter. The scooter has an unprecedented, bizarre shape. The shape does not affect the way the scooter works in any way. Inventor chose the shape not for engineering reasons but only from Inventor's whimsy. The shape of the scooter is quite different from any other on the market and stands out among other scooters. Few consumers have seen it yet, but those who have really like the scooter's unusual shape. The shape features prominently in efforts to sell the scooter. Inventor claims trade dress protection in the design of the scooter. Is the scooter design a distinctive mark for Inventor's scooter?

17. *Too successful.* Smartel designs, builds, and sells a very popular line of microprocessor chips, sold under the trademarks that include the 286,

the 386, and the 486. Smartel works hard to convince computer makers to use its chips and to adopt its technical standards. Indeed, Smartel is so successful that its technical standards become the industry standard. Almost all personal computer makers use Smartel's standards, but they may buy the chips from other chipmakers. Because Smartel's chips set the standards, such terms as 386 and 486 come to refer not only to chips made by Smartel but to any chips that are made following Smartel's standards. Does Smartel have distinctive trademarks in 386 and 486?

18. *Fine line.* In-line skates were rare until they were sold under the mark ROGERBLADES. For some time, Rogerblade was the only substantial seller of in-line skates. Indeed, "Rogerblades" and "Rogerblading" were often used by consumers to denote in-line skating. Soon, other manufacturers began to make and sell in-line skates. Suppose that now consumers sometimes talk about "going Rogerblading," but do regard "Rogerblades" as referring to only one brand of in-line skates. Is the word "Rogerblades" a distinctive mark for the in-line skates?

19. *Moving to Montana soon (a.k.a. Joe Montana).* MBNA seeks to register MONTANA as a mark for credit card services. The term is used on "regional affinity" credit cards depicting scenes of Montanan life and scenery. The target market is anyone with an affinity for the state of Montana, such as a corporate lawyer who'd rather wrangle horses than clients. The mark is barely known among consumers. MBNA argues that the mark is not merely descriptive (because it does not describe credit card services) or geographically descriptive (because consumers won't think the cards come from Montana). Is MONTANA inherently distinctive for credit card services (i.e., protectable without showing secondary meaning)?

20. *Generic Freebies Magazine.* Freebies Magazine gives information about free mail-order offerings. Freebies.com is a new Web site with information about getting free stuff for doing business with merchants. When Freebies Magazine sues, Freebies.com argues that "Freebie" is a generic term for free stuff and therefore not protected as a trademark. Freebies Magazine responds that a generic term is the term for the seller's product or service. It sells magazines, not freebies. Is "Freebie" generic here?

21. *Bing me.* People refer to "googling" for information, whether the search engine used is Google, Bing, Baidu, or something else. Has GOOGLE become generic, meaning it is no longer a valid mark?

22. Could Hasbro register as a trademark the scent of Play-Doh: "sweet, slightly musky, vanilla fragrance, with slight overtones of cherry, combined with the smell of a salted, wheat-based dough"?

Explanations

1. a. MOUSE for mice is generic (the word for the very product consumers seek), so nonprotectable.

   b. MOUSE for a computer mouse is likewise generic, the very word for what a consumer wants to buy.

   c. WIRELESS OPTICAL MOUSE is generic, the name for a more specialized product.

   d. SQUEAKY for mice sold as pets is descriptive — so it could be protected as a mark in the unlikely event that SQUEAKY mice become so well known that consumers associate the mark with a particular seller.

   e. MOUSE for personal training services is inherently distinctive (in this case, an arbitrary term or perhaps a suggestive one). It would be protectable as soon as it was used as a mark.

2. LEGAL SERVICES is not a distinctive service mark for the firm. Rather, it is a nonprotectable generic term. The term has acquired a high level of recognition associated with the firm. It probably has acquired secondary meaning when used in the context of the law firm. Used in that context, the relevant public understands it as a source identifier, identifying a source of legal services. But a generic term is not protectable as a mark, even if it has acquired secondary meaning. The result would be different if the term were merely descriptive, such as "reliable." A descriptive term that acquires secondary meaning is sufficiently descriptive. The result also would be different if the term "Legal Services" became so closely associated with the firm that it lost its primary significance as a generic term (a rare occurrence). In other words, the term would no longer be generic if people stopped using "legal services" to refer to the services rendered by lawyers but used the phrase to refer only to the firm.

3. LIGHTNING MESSENGERS is a distinctive service mark for the messenger firm's services. The MESSENGERS component of the symbol is clearly a nonprotectable generic term, but the issue turns on the symbol as a whole. It is not clear whether "Lightning Messengers" is a suggestive term (which is inherently distinctive) or a merely descriptive term (which may acquire distinctiveness by acquiring secondary meaning). "Lightning" is not literally descriptive but is an obvious metaphor for speed that requires little thought. But whether the mark is suggestive or descriptive does not matter in this case because it clearly has attained secondary meaning. The primary significance of the term to Springfieldians is as an indicator of source. So it is a distinctive mark, either inherently distinctive or through acquired distinctiveness.

4. CARING & INSIGHTFUL is not a distinctive service mark for Sigmunda's counseling services. It may be an apt description, but the question is not how accurate the description is. A merely descriptive term is not inherently

distinctive; it may acquire distinctiveness if it acquires secondary meaning. Secondary meaning requires that the primary significance to the relevant public be as an indicator of source. But Sigmunda has just opened a small firm, and consequently her term has no meaning to the public as an indicator of source, let alone a primary meaning as an indicator of source.

5. QJAAB is a distinctive mark for Dom's pizza. It is an inherently distinctive mark. It is not descriptive. QJAAB does not tell the consumer anything about the pizza. It could be characterized as suggestive, although the link between QJAAB and "pizza" would likely escape most consumers. Because QJAAB is inherently distinctive, it is a distinctive mark, even though it has no recognition among consumers. This is an example of the advantage of using an inherently distinctive mark. It becomes protected on use, whereas a descriptive mark becomes protected only if it acquires secondary meaning (a difficult task, which most descriptive product names never attain).

6. BLISS MASSAGE likely would be held to be a nondistinctive mark because it is a descriptive term that has not achieved secondary meaning. It is clear that the term has not acquired secondary meaning. The salon is just one of many, and consumers do not associate "bliss" with any particular salon. BLISS MASSAGE nevertheless would be a distinctive mark if "bliss" were inherently distinctive. So the issue is whether "bliss" is suggestive (inherently distinctive) or descriptive (requires secondary meaning to acquire distinctiveness).

   In differentiating the suggestive from the descriptive, courts look to such factors as the literal meaning of the term, whether competitors need to use the term, and whether competitors actually use the term. "Bliss" is not quite literally descriptive because even a great massage does not transport the client into such perfect felicity. But it comes quite close to being literally descriptive. Competitors do not absolutely need to use the term, as there are a number of other words that can describe the pleasant effects of a massage. Consumers do not necessarily prefer massage salons that use the word. But competitors do frequently make actual use of the word, which indicates that there is considerable desire to use the word for its descriptive effect. On balance, the term likely would be deemed descriptive. Because it has not acquired secondary meaning for Massage Salon, it therefore is nondistinctive. Cf. *Bliss Salon Day Spa v. Bliss World*, 60 U.S.P.Q.2d 1443 (7th Cir. 2001).

7. BLISS is a distinctive mark for the duct tape. "Bliss," in this case, is not a descriptive term. Consumers do not regard it as descriptive of the tape or any of its qualities or characteristics, whether literally or metaphorically. Rather, consumers regard the use of "Bliss" on duct tape as a comical indicator of source. Accordingly, BLISS is an inherently distinctive mark

425

(in this case, an arbitrary symbol). So it is distinctive without any need to show acquired distinctiveness. The fact that there is little awareness of the mark among consumers does not prevent it from being distinctive.

8. SONOMA COUNTY is not a distinctive mark for Grape Grower's raisins. The term is a primarily geographically descriptive term because the primary significance of the term to consumers is to indicate the geographic origin of the goods. Geographically descriptive terms (like merely descriptive terms) are not inherently descriptive, although they can acquire distinctiveness. SONOMA COUNTY has not acquired distinctiveness as a mark for Grape Grower's raisins. Far from acquiring secondary meaning, the term is not associated by consumers with Grape Grower.

9. CLEANS FASTER THAN LIGHT! is not a distinctive mark for the detergent. Rather, it is merely a descriptive term that has not acquired distinctiveness. It would not be barred as a deceptive term, even though it is not literally true. Consumers do not interpret it as literally making the implausible suggestion that it acts faster than the speed of light. Rather, consumers simply interpret it as praising the product. Such "laudatory" terms are treated as descriptive ones because they describe the product as a good product in a broad sense. Accordingly, laudatory terms must acquire secondary meaning to be distinctive. The slogan has not acquired much recognition among consumers, let alone the primary meaning as an indicator of source. So it is not a distinctive mark for the detergent. In short, consumers regard the slogan as fulfilling the function of praising the product, not identifying its source.

10. NORTH POLE is a distinctive mark for the potatoes. If it were a primarily geographically descriptive mark, it would not be distinctive because it has not acquired secondary meaning. But although it names a geographic location, consumers do not interpret it as indicating the place where the potatoes come from. So it is not primarily geographically descriptive (or misdescriptive). In addition, consumers do regard it as an indication of source, distinguishing the potatoes from other brands. So it is an arbitrary mark, a symbol with no logical link to the product. Accordingly, it is inherently distinctive, requiring no secondary meaning to become distinctive.

11. McGUIRE's is not a distinctive mark for the shoes. A mark that is primarily a surname is, like a descriptive mark, protectable only if it has acquired secondary meaning. The primary significance to consumers of McGuire is as a surname, so it is subject to the requirement of secondary meaning. The result would be different if consumers knew the term was a name but, in context, regarded the primary significance as an indicator of that particular source. Such secondary meaning is sufficient for the mark to be distinctive because it would have acquired distinctiveness.

12. HOLIDAY is a distinctive term for the candy. "Holiday" is used as a surname. The term is treated as a surname for trademark purposes if the primary significance to consumers is as a surname. Consumers are aware that "Holiday" can be a surname but, in the context of the candy, do not regard it as such. Rather, consumers interpret it to refer to "Holiday" in the sense of festive days of the year. For candy, the mark is arbitrary or perhaps suggestive but, in any event, an inherently distinctive mark. So it is distinctive without having acquired secondary meaning.

13. CANE MEN is not a distinctive mark for the candy. Consumers interpret it as describing the ingredients of the candy. The description is inaccurate, so the term is misdescriptive. The information is not material to consumers, so the term is not deceptive. But consumers do interpret it as describing the candy, so it falls into the category of deceptively misdescriptive, which requires secondary meaning to be distinctive. CANE MEN has not acquired secondary meaning, so it is a nondistinctive mark.

14. The color purple is not a distinctive mark for the cigar boxes. Even though the use of a color may be distinctive in a design sense, color alone is not deemed inherently distinctive as an indicator of source. Accordingly, color alone used as a mark requires secondary meaning to be distinctive. Secondary meaning is not shown here, so the color purple is not a distinctive mark for the cigar boxes.

15. PURPLE is a distinctive mark for the software company's software. Color alone used as a mark is distinctive only if it has acquired distinctiveness. But the mark here is a word mark (the word "purple"), not color used as a mark. The word mark PURPLE in this context is inherently distinctive. It does not describe the software or any of its characteristics, there is no need for competitors to use the word, and there is no use of the word in marketing in the industry. PURPLE for the software is an arbitrary, and hence inherently distinctive, mark. The result would be different if, rather than using the word mark PURPLE, the software company used a different word mark and sought to use the color purple as a separate trademark (by using only purple boxes and using purple prominently in its other packaging and advertising). Color alone used as a mark requires secondary meaning to be distinctive. If the software has made little impact on the market, the necessary link in the public mind between the color purple and one particular source of goods is not met.

16. The unprecedented, bizarre shape of the scooter is probably not a distinctive mark for Inventor's scooter. Product design trade dress is distinctive only if it has acquired distinctiveness by acquiring secondary

meaning. The theory is that consumers regard product design as serving other functions, such as usefulness or aesthetics. Even a bizarre product design is not inherently distinctive as a source indicator.

The initial question is whether the bizarre shape of the scooter is product packaging or product design. The shape was used from whimsy, not for any engineering reasons. It does not affect the functionality of the product. The strange shape affects the marketing of the scooter. Inventor might argue that an element that affects only marketing and not functionality is product packaging, not product design. But the very shape of the scooter seems to necessarily be part of the design of the product because it is the shape of what is sold.

Assuming the scooter shape falls into the category of product design, it is not distinctive because it has not acquired secondary meaning.

17. Smartel does not have distinctive trademarks in 386 and 486. Rather, the terms have become generic terms in the industry, unprotectable as trademarks. The terms 386 and 486 are no longer used to refer to chips made by Smartel, but rather to chips from any source that are made according to those standards. Accordingly, the terms do not refer to a particular source but represent generic terms for referring to a category of product. They no longer serve to distinguish Smartel's goods from others and hence are not distinctive trademarks. Cf. *Intel Corp. v. Advanced Micro Devices*, 756 F. Supp. 1292 (N.D. Cal. 1991).

18. ROGERBLADES is a distinctive mark for the in-line skates. The ROGER component of the mark probably qualifies it as inherently distinctive. Even if the mark is not deemed inherently distinctive, it has acquired distinctiveness because consumers regard it primarily as an indication of a single source of in-line skates. The term is not generic (which would be unprotectable). Although consumers frequently use the term to refer to in-line skating, the primary significance has remained as a source identifier rather than a name for the type of product (in-line skates). Consumers understand "Rogerblades" to refer to one source of in-line skates, not to refer to all in-line skates. The widespread use may qualify the term as descriptive, but the mark would nevertheless be distinctive because it has secondary meaning. The example shows the fine line between a very strong trademark and a nonprotectable generic term.

19. MONTANA is not inherently descriptive for credit card services, where it was used on cards depicting images related to Montana. *See In re MBNA Am. Bank, N.A.*, 340 F.3d 1328, 1332 (Fed. Cir. 2003). Consumers know the card is not from Montana, so MONTANA is not geographically descriptive. But a mark is descriptive if it conveys information

concerning a quality or characteristic of the product or service. The MONTANA term may not describe aspects of credit card services generally (such as fees, availability of credit); the services associated with this card are broader than those general services. At issue here are "'regional affinity' credit card services—a financial service in conjunction with satisfying a social or lifestyle association with a particular city or state." Rather than acting as a source indicator, MONTANA indicated an affinity with Montana, a quality that the consumer sought in the services provided. It was descriptive, and not protectable without a showing of secondary meaning.

20. "Freebie" is generic here. A generic term can be broader than a particular good or service. "Freebie" could refer to providing any good or service for free, but it could also be generic for publishing information about such free material. Consumers have great interest in freebies. Granting exclusive rights to one seller would put others at a considerable disadvantage in marketing their free goods or services. *See Retail Services Inc. v. Freebies Publishing,* 364 F.3d 535 (4th Cir. 2004).

21. No. "As one scholar has stated, 'top-of-mind use of a trademark in its verb form, far from indicating the mark's generic status, may well indicate the enduring fame of the brand.' Laura A. Heymann, *The Grammar of Trademarks,* 14 Lewis & Clark L. Rev. 1313, 1348 (2010)." *Elliot v. Google Inc.,* No. 2:12-cv-01072-SMM (D. Ariz., Sept. 10, 2014). Affirming, the Ninth Circuit emphasized that the key is whether the word was understood to refer to Internet search services generally or to that particular provider of Internet search services.

> [V]erb use does not automatically constitute generic use. For instance, Elliott purports to offer an example of generic use by T-Pain, a popular rap music artist. But we will not assume that T-Pain is using the word "google" in a generic sense simply because he tells listeners to "google [his] name." T-Pain, *Bottlez,* on rEVOLVEr (RCA Records 2011). Without further evidence regarding T-Pain's inner thought process, we cannot tell whether he is using "google" in a discriminate or indiscriminate sense.

Elliott v. Google, Inc., 856 F.3d 1225, 1235 (9th Cir. 2017).

22. The USPTO registered the mark. As long as the scent is distinctive, it could act as a source-identifying symbol. Note that many distinctive scents would not be protectable because they are functional (see below), such as the bouquet of wine or the scent of a perfume.

UNPROTECTABLE SYMBOLS

Several classes of symbols are nonprotectable as marks.

Likely to Cause Confusion with an Existing Mark

The very purpose of a mark is to distinguish the source of goods and services. A mark is not protectable if it is likely to cause confusion with a prior mark. 15 U.S.C. §1052(d).[7] The rule does not necessarily bar protection to a mark that is identical or similar to an existing mark. If the mark APPLE is used for computers, the use of the mark APPLE for piano-tuning services is not likely to cause confusion. Indeed, identical or similar marks are often used in various markets.

Likelihood of confusion is determined by considering a number of factors, such as the strength of the plaintiff's mark, the degree of similarity between the marks, the proximity of the products in the marketplace, actual confusion, defendant's good faith in adopting its own mark, the quality of defendant's product, and the care and sophistication of the relevant consumers. Similar factors govern the determination of likelihood of confusion in infringement and are discussed in more detail in the infringement chapter. The application of the factors is similar, although infringement analysis considers actual uses, whereas the analysis here considers prospective uses.

Functional Matter

As with copyright law (and unlike patent and trade secrets), trademarks do not protect functional matter. There are three ways that a feature can be deemed functional:

1. it is essential to the use or purpose of the device; or
2. it affects the cost or quality of the device; or
3. its exclusive use by one seller would put competitors at a significant nonreputation-related disadvantage.

TrafFix Devices v. Marketing Displays, 532 U.S. 23 (2001).

A dual-spring design for temporary road signs is not protectable trade dress because it serves to keep the signs standing in the wind. Even if the sign's design acquires secondary meaning (in other words, the public tends to think that dual-spring signs are made by one particular source), the

---

7. The next chapter discusses determination of priority between confusingly similar marks. Note also that a mark may not be protectable if it causes dilution of a prior famous mark.

design is not protected as a trademark. Color also can be functional (and nonprotected). The green color of farm machinery is functional because farmers prefer the color green. The black color of outboard boat motors serves both to reduce the apparent size of the motor and to be compatible with other colors. The design of a wind turbine was likewise not protectable as trade dress, due to its many functional advantages, such as "generates electricity regardless of wind direction."[8]

Examples

1. *What goes around.* Can the round design of a beach towel be a trademark?

2. *Paper profits.* Georgia-Pacific's toilet paper has a "quilted diamond design," which improves its perceived softness and bulk and reduces "nesting and ridging." After the patent on the distinctive design expires, Kimberly-Clark copies it on its toilet paper. Trademark infringement?

3. *The angels want to wear my red shoes.* Designer Louboutin's shoes are well known for featuring red soles. Louboutin sues Yves St. Laurent, who sells all-red shoes. Can red soles be a trademark for shoes?

4. *Color scheme.* Can John Deere protect its well-known trade dress of green and yellow for farm machinery?

5. Is the iconic shape of the London taxi protectable as a mark (assuming U.K. law is similar to U.S. law)?

6. *Phone?* Is the recognizable design of the iPhone protectable as trade dress?

Explanations

1. No. The circular shape is functional, because a round towel will work differently than a towel of a different shape. *Jay Franco & Sons Inc. v. Franek,* 615 F.3d 855 (7th Cir. 2010).

2. No. The design may be distinctive, but it is functional, so may not be protected by trademark. *Georgia-Pacific Consumer Products L.P. v. Kimberly-Clark Corp.,* 647 F.3d 723 (7th Cir. 2011).

3. Yves St. Laurent argued that the color of a fashion item is functional and so is not protected. The court did not reach the question because it held there would be no infringement anyway: Consumers would not be confused between shoes with red soles and all-red shoes. *Christian Louboutin S.A. v. Yves Saint Laurent Am. Holding, Inc.,* 696 F.3d 206 (2d Cir. 2012). Whether color can be a mark for fashion items or is functional remains

---

8. In re Change Wind Corp., No. 86046590 (TTAB July 20, 2017).

an open question. Some courts would apply what has been called "aesthetic functionality" to decide.

4. John Deere & Co.'s "green and yellow color scheme as it is used on John Deere tractors is a 'strong trademark.'"[9] Green alone may not be protected as functional. But the combination of green and yellow is not needed as broadly.

5. The shape of a vehicle, although distinctive, is functional , due to aerodynamics and mechanical engineering considerations.[10]

6. *Apple v. Samsung Elecs. Co.* held the product configuration of the iPhone to be functional, and so not protected as trade dress, meaning competitors that copied would not be liable for trademark infringement.

> For example, rounded corners improve "pocketability" and "durability" and rectangular shape maximizes the display that can be accommodated. A flat clear surface on the front of the phone facilitates touch operation by fingers over a large display. The bezel protects the glass from impact when the phone is dropped. The borders around the display are sized to accommodate other components while minimizing the overall product dimensions. The row of dots in the user interface indicates multiple pages of application screens that are available. The icons allow users to differentiate the applications available to the users and the bottom dock of unchanging icons allows for quick access to the most commonly used applications.

> Apple Inc. v. Samsung Elecs. Co., 786 F.3d 983, 993 (Fed. Cir. 2015) (citations to record omitted).

> Note that the decision does not mean that product design cannot be protected as intellectual property. Foresighted manufacturers can still use design patents to protect design, as Apple in fact had.[11]

Deceptive Matter

As discussed above, a "deceptively misdescriptive" mark is protectable provided it has acquired secondary meaning. But "deceptive matter" is not protectable. 15 U.S.C. §1052(a). These seemingly inconsistent rules turn

---

9. Deere & Co. v. Fimco Inc., No. 5:15-CV-105-TBR, 2017 U.S. Dist. LEXIS 169711, at *90 (W.D. Ky. Oct. 13, 2017).
10. Annsley Merelle Ward, *Arnold J's latest judgment flags down the iconic (but not distinctive) London black cab* (Feb. 9, 2016), http://ipkitten.blogspot.com/2016/02/arnold-js-latest-judgment-flags-down.html.
11. *See Apple, Inc.* at 996-1003 (holding that Samsung breached Apple's valid design patents).

on the higher threshold for "deceptive matter." To qualify as deceptive, the matter must be material to a potential buyer's decision. If the misrepresentation makes no difference to consumers, protection of the mark does not harm them. But if the misrepresentation is material, such a deceptive mark is not protectable.

Example

Was CANINE CAVIAR a mark registrable for dog food, which contained no caviar (fish roe?)?

Explanation

The USPTO registered the mark. The term was misdescriptive. But the USPTO had confidence in consumers to recognize the metaphorical use of CAVIAR, as connoting high-quality food, as opposed to its literal meaning of fish eggs.

Primarily Geographically Deceptively Misdescriptive Marks

A "geographically deceptively misdescriptive mark" (quite a mouthful) is not protected, even if it does not rise to level of deceptive. 15 U.S.C. §1052(e)(2). In other words, even if consumers do not deem the geographic term to be material, the mark is not protected. So WISCONSIN used on cheese from Illinois is unprotectable, even if consumers do not consider the origin of the cheese in deciding to buy it. The same would be true of knitwear with ARAN ISLANDS in the mark, if not knitted or shorn in the Aran Islands. The rule serves to protect producers in certain geographic locations from deceptive practices, even when the deception does not matter to the relevant consumers.

This finishes out the deceptive/misdescriptive categories. To keep things straight:

1. *Deceptive*: nonprotectable
2. *Deceptively misdescriptive*: (misdescribes the goods but not in a way material to consumers)
   a. If primarily geographic, not protectable

433

  b. If some other category, protectable if it has acquired secondary meaning

3. *Nondeceptively misdescriptive:* (although literally descriptive, not understood that way and likely to be inherently distinctive); protectable without need for secondary meaning

To further complicate things, the Federal Circuit has held that a mark is only a "geographically deceptively misdescriptive mark" if the geographic part is material to consumers. *See In re California Innovations,* 329 F.3d 1334, 1341 (Fed. Cir. 2003). Like a deceptive mark, a "geographically deceptively misdescriptive mark" is not protectable. That means, the court reasoned, that materiality should be required, as with deceptive marks. As Professor Lunney has pointed out, that holding seems to defeat the purpose of treating geographic marks differently, which was to reduce trademark protection for misleading geographic terms. Rather, a misleading (but non-material) geographic mark would be protected even without secondary meaning—whereas a primarily geographically descriptive term requires secondary meaning. Case law may hash this out.

Example

If Newbridge Cutlery is well-known in Ireland, could it be protected as a mark in the United States?

Explanation

A geographic term can be distinctive if it is not merely descriptive, where consumers know the term so well that it has become associated with one particular seller. For U.S. trademark protection, whether a geographic term is sufficiently well known for protection depends on how well known it is in the United States, not its country of origin.[12] So the component of the mark constituting the name of an obscure (to consumers in the United States) town (as in Newbridge Cutlery) was barred from trademark protection as a primarily geographically descriptive mark, even if abroad the term was better known.

---

12. *In re* Newbridge Cutlery Co., 776 F.3d 854, 862 (Fed. Cir. 2015).

Mark Suggesting False Connection

The Lanham Act bars registration of marks that "falsely suggest a connection with persons, living or dead, institutions, beliefs, or national symbols." 15 U.S.C. §1052(a). As with misdescriptive geographic marks, there need be no showing that the misrepresentation is material to consumers. UNIVERSITY OF NOTRE DAME used on cheese is not a protectable mark if there is in fact no connection with the university. This is true even if consumers do not deem such a connection material in deciding to buy the cheese. The rule serves to protect the reputation interests of persons and institutions, as opposed to consumer protection. But the rule only applies if the symbol is "unmistakably associated" with a particular personality or institution. The use of just NOTRE DAME for cheese does not falsely suggest a connection with the University of Notre Dame because there are a number of other institutions named Notre Dame. *See Univ. of Notre Dame du Lac v. J.C. Gourmet Food Imports,* 703 F.2d 1372 (Fed. Cir. 1983).

Government Symbols

The Lanham Act also denies trademark registration to matter that "consists of or comprises the flag or coat of arms or other insignia of the United States, or of any State or municipality, or of any foreign nation, or any simulation thereof." 15 U.S.C. §1052(b). This provision is narrowly construed. It did not bar marks portraying the Capitol Building, the Statue of Liberty, or the initials USMC. *See* J. Thomas McCarthy, *Trademarks and Unfair Competition,* §19:78 (3d ed. 1992). Nor does the bar apply to a mark that merely makes incidental use of a flag as one component of the mark. Many marks incorporate the Stars and Stripes in various ways.

Names or Likenesses of Individuals

The Lanham Act denies trademark registration to matter that "consists of or comprises a name, portrait, or signature identifying a particular living individual except by his written consent." 15 U.S.C. §1052(c). The bar does not apply to all uses of names, signatures, and the like. Rather, it covers only uses that potential buyers will link to specific people because the name is so well known or the person is so closely associated with the relevant type of goods or services.

Examples

1. *Not identical.* MATTER OF PRINCIPLE is a trademark used quite successfully to sell woolen blankets and rugs nationwide. Eric Entrepreneur decides to sell his own line of woolen blankets and rugs. To get off to a flying start, he chooses a trademark that he hopes will attract some of the good-will attached to Matter of Principle products. Eric begins selling woolen blankets, rugs, and sweaters using the mark MATTER OF PRINCIPAL. As Eric points out, he is not using the same mark. His mark is spelled differently and has a different meaning. Is MATTER OF PRINCIPAL a protectable mark for Eric's woolen products?

2. *The sincerest form of flattery.* Vickie Venture visits an electronics trade show. She sees a digital camera sold under the trademark SALLY SCALLYWAG. The camera is a high-end model marketed only to professional photographers for aerial photography. Vickie likes the sound of the mark. She subsequently adopts it for use on her line of children's pogo sticks. Few consumers have ever seen the mark before, and none would think that it signifies any association or sponsorship with the other mark. Is SALLY SCALLYWAG a protectable mark for Vickie's pogo sticks?

3. *Knock-offs.* Tink invents a new form of yo-yo that uses a square block of wood and two strings. Tink's marvelous new yo-yo is easy to use and capable of performing wondrous tricks. Its double-string square block design gives it special characteristics that allow the user to channel the forces of friction and inertia to her advantage. The design is also strikingly different from other yo-yos. Tink sells millions of the yo-yos to eager buyers. Tink's yo-yo becomes a widely recognized artifact of popular culture. Tink is famous as the inventor and designer of the new form of yo-yo.

   Tink neglected to patent his yo-yo design. Now that the design has been in public use for several years, Tink can no longer seek a patent. Megabig Corp. begins manufacturing and selling yo-yos, meticulously following Tink's design. Tink tries to use trademark law to shut down Megabig's activity. He argues that the design of the yo-yo is a trademark for Tink's yo-yo. Tink can show that the design has acquired secondary meaning — that the primary significance of the design to consumers is an indication of source because the design is so closely associated with Tink. Does Tink have a protectable mark in the double-string square block design of the yo-yo?

4. *Curious purple.* Bespoke designs and builds racing bikes. Bespoke's bikes are works of great craftsmanship, highly sought after by knowledgeable buyers. Bespoke's bike design was quite an advance in bike technology, and she holds several utility patents on the ultralight, ultra-aerodynamic

design. Bespoke is also somewhat eccentric. She insists on having all her bikes painted purple. The color purple serves no purpose. It does not make the bikes go faster or make them safer (in fact, red or pink would be more visible). It does not make them more attractive. Buyers prefer other colors but take purple to get the fine machines. Over the years, Bespoke's bikes become very well known. They are ridden by the winners of several prominent races. They also are featured in a number of movies and TV shows. The public learns to associate purple with Bespoke's bikes. Another bike maker starts to use the identical shade of purple on its bikes. Bespoke claims trade dress protection in purple used on high-end racing bikes. The rival responds that Bespoke's patented bikes are clearly functional and therefore not protectable under trademark law. Can Bespoke claim trade dress protection for purple used on her bikes?

5. *White after Labor Day.* Feral Express, a leading package delivery service, dresses all of its delivery people in white uniforms. The uniforms are crisp, clean, and distinctive among the typical delivery environment of business-clad people. They also have several useful features. The white color reflects heat, sparing the delivery people a little in the sweltering financial district streets in which they often work. The bright white uniform also stands out quickly, allowing receptionists to spot deliveries quickly. Likewise, when on foot the delivery people are more visible to traffic, increasing their safety. Feral Express is well known and delivers so many packages that the public learns to associate the white uniforms with Feral's delivery services. Does Feral Express have protectable trade dress in the color white used to identify delivery services?

6. *Me first.* Waxmak makes and sells products for cleaning automobiles. Waxmak plasters the slogan "The First Name in Car Care" on all of its products. Roosevelt, a competitor, starts using the slogan "Number One in Auto Service" on its own products. Waxmak sues, claiming infringement of the trademark THE FIRST NAME IN CAR CARE. Roosevelt contends that the mark is not protectable on the grounds that it is deceptive. Waxmak is not the market leader. To the contrary, Waxmak sells only 10 percent of the products sold, whereas Roosevelt accounts for over half. Waxmak counters by showing that consumers do not interpret its mark to be a claim to be the best seller. Despite Waxmak's small market share, consumers readily recognize the mark and regard it primarily as indicating that the product comes from Waxmak and secondarily as praise of the products. Consumers do not interpret it as a claim of market leadership. Does Waxmak have a protectable mark in its slogan?

7. *Not a factor.* Vineyard sells a very popular wine under the trademark CHESTER SAFFRON. The primary meaning to consumers of the mark is a

source indicator. Consumers love Chester Saffron wine. Consumers also believe that one of the ingredients of the wine is saffron. No saffron is actually used in making the wine, but that is immaterial to consumers. They would buy the wine just the same. Is CHESTER SAFFRON a protectable trademark for the wine?

8. *Look and feel.* ADDERALL is Shire Pharmaceuticals' trademark for a drug to treat attention deficit hyperactivity disorder. Adderall is well known among patients and their physicians, who readily recognize the pills by shape and color. The drug is not patented, so Barr Pharmaceutical makes and sells a generic version. Barr's pills also have a similar, but not identical, look. Barr argues that it should be able to copy the shape of the pills and the color coding used to distinguish pills of different doses. Barr argues that it does so not to confuse consumers, but rather to avoid confusing them. Patients, Barr shows, rely on the shape of the pill and color coding to take the correct dosage. Patients are also more willing to take a generic version of the drug if the shapes and colors are familiar. For ADHD patients, these factors weigh heavily because their condition may reduce attention to other information and because they often have to adjust their dosage. Does Shire have trade dress protection in the color and shape of its pills?

Explanations

1. MATTER OF PRINCIPAL is not a protectable mark for Eric's woolen products. It is not protectable if its use is likely to cause confusion with an existing mark. There is already a mark, MATTER OF PRINCIPLE, used for similar products. The two marks are not identical, but they are not required to be so. Rather, the determination considers such factors as the strength of the plaintiff's mark, the degree of similarity between the marks, the proximity of the products in the marketplace, actual confusion, defendant's good faith in adopting its own mark, the quality of defendant's product, and the care and sophistication of the relevant consumers. We have no information about some of the factors, such as actual confusion and Eric's intent. But the marks are very similar and are used on very similar goods. The other mark is already in successful use nationwide. So likelihood of confusion is extremely probable here, and Eric's mark is not entitled to protected trademark status.

2. SALLY SCALLYWAG is a protectable mark for Vickie's pogo sticks. It is identical to a mark that is already in use. But likelihood of confusion requires examining all relevant factors to determine if consumers are likely to be confused about the source. Although the marks are identical, they are used on very disparate goods in disparate markets. If there was a likelihood that consumers would assume that the first SALLY SCALLYWAG mark

owner had sponsored the second use, there might be likelihood of confusion even with different markets. But that possibility has been ruled out here. So the previous use of an identical mark does not bar its use for other goods or services when there is no likelihood of confusion.

3. Tink does not have a protectable mark in the double-string square-block design of the yo-yo. The design is unprotectable as a trademark because it is functional. One way a mark can be functional is if it is essential to the use or purpose of the device. The design meets that test because the design is what enables the yo-yo to work the way it does. The fact that the design is so well known and so closely associated with Tink does not make it protectable. Functional matter cannot be a trademark, even if it has acquired secondary meaning. The theory is that functional aspects should not be given patent-like protection through trademark law.

4. Bespoke can claim trade dress protection for purple used on her bikes. The engineering design of the bikes is functional matter, unprotectable as trade dress. But the use of the color purple is not functional in this case. There are three ways for matter to be functional: (1) it is essential to the use or purpose of the device; (2) it affects the cost or quality of the device; or (3) its exclusive use by one seller puts competitors at a significant nonreputation-related disadvantage. None of those apply here. The color is not essential to the use of the bikes; they could be painted any color and work just as well. The color does not affect the cost of the bikes because paint of other colors would not be more expensive. Its use by Bespoke does not put other sellers at a significant nonreputation-related disadvantage. The use of purple does give Bespoke an advantage. Because Bespoke's bikes have been so successful and are associated with the color purple, consumers may prefer purple bikes, thinking they come from Bespoke. This advantage is a reputation-related advantage—exactly the sort of advantage trademark law seeks to encourage.

5. Feral Express does not have protectable trade dress in the color white used to identify delivery services. Color alone may qualify as a mark if it has acquired secondary meaning. Feral's use of the color white has acquired secondary meaning because the primary significance to the public of white in context is an indicator of source. The public readily recognizes the white uniforms as those of Feral. But even a distinctive mark is not protectable if it is functional. The color white is functional here under two of the types of functionality. Its use affects the quality of the services because the use of white makes the delivery people more visible, making deliveries faster and more reliable (because of the increased safety). Its use by only one seller also puts other sellers at a disadvantage because they have hotter, slower, and more-likely-to-be-run-over delivery people. So the color white is not protectable as trade dress, despite the showing of secondary meaning.

6. Waxmak does have a protectable mark in the slogan "The First Name in Car Care." The slogan may not be literally true, but that does not render it deceptive. Consumers do not regard it as describing the product as the market leader, so it is not deceptive (or deceptively misdescriptive or even misdescriptive). Rather, they interpret it as praising the product, which makes it a laudatory term. Laudatory terms are treated as descriptive, protectable if they have acquired secondary meaning. Consumers regard the slogan primarily as an indication of source, so it has the requisite secondary meaning. So the slogan is a protectable mark—it has acquired distinctiveness and is not barred by any of the categorical bars, such as deceptiveness. Cf. *The Hoover Co. v. Royal Appliance Mfg.*, 238 F.3d 1357 (Fed. Cir. 2001).

7. CHESTER SAFFRON is a protectable mark. Consumers interpret it as describing the ingredients to include saffron. It does not have saffron, so the description is inaccurate. But consumers do not regard that as material. They would buy the wine anyway. So the term falls into the category of deceptively misdescriptive (protectable if it has acquired secondary meaning) as opposed to deceptive (nonprotectable, even with secondary meaning). The mark has acquired secondary meaning. Consumers frequently ask for it by name and regard it as a source identifier. So the mark is protectable.

8. The color and shape of the pills were held functional and nonprotectable (even with secondary meaning). Features such as the blue-and-orange colors of a drug tablet and its round shape might seem like purely aesthetic elements. But those features, with this particular drug, were functional. Trade dress protection would not allow competitors to use elements that patients use in calibrating dosage and that patients find reassuring. Note that the court relied on the fact that ADHD patients put particular reliance on those features, both because of their condition and because of the varying dosage. Functionality would not broadly make things appealing to consumers nonprotectable. Otherwise, consumer goodwill, one goal of trademark law, would become an impediment to trade dress protection. *Shire U.S., Inc. v. Barr Labs., Inc.*, 329 F.3d 348, 351 (3d Cir. 2003).

Obtaining Protection and Licensing: Using, Registering, Licensing, and Losing a Trademark

12

What must a business do to have a trademark in Meercat Fast Efficient Strep Diagnosis Kit? Use the mark. Trademark rights begin when the mark is used and last as long as the owner keeps using the mark. This is quite different from patent and copyright, which have set terms. Like the basic standard for trademark infringement (likelihood of confusion), trademark rights are keyed to the purpose of trademark law — use of the mark to distinguish the seller from others.

This chapter discusses the acquisition of trademark rights, registration of trademarks, and other aspects of ownership (such as priority between similar marks, duration, licensing, and loss of trademark rights).

A symbol becomes a mark on bona fide use of the symbol as a mark in commerce in connection with the relevant goods or services.[1] By contrast, copyright vests as soon as the work is fixed in a tangible form, whereas patent rights vest when the patent is issued by the patent office. Like copyright (and unlike patent), trademark rights do not depend on registration. Registration is permitted and has a number of advantages for the trademark owner. But a mark that meets the substantive standards for protection may be enforced whether registered or not.

---

1. Note that this could mean the first use of an inherently distinctive mark or, for a descriptive term, the first use once it has acquired distinctiveness.

TRADEMARK RIGHTS COME WITH LAWFUL USE OF THE SYMBOL AS A MARK

Trademark Searching

Before a seller uses her intended trademark, she should consider whether the symbol is protectable. If her intended mark is merely descriptive, then it would not be a mark until it becomes so well known that it acquires secondary meaning—and few marks ever become that well known. If her intended mark is generic, functional, deceptive, or otherwise nonprotectable, she could waste resources trying to accrue goodwill to a symbol that cannot be a mark. In addition to the categorical barriers, the mark might be in use already. A putative mark is not protectable if it is likely to cause confusion with a mark that was already in use. If someone else is already using a similar mark for similar goods or services (or if his mark dilutes a famous mark, even one for dissimilar goods or services), the existing mark has priority.

The most common problems for would-be trademark owners are (1) choosing a descriptive term and (2) choosing a symbol that is likely to cause confusion with an existing mark. The first arises because businesses like to choose product names that describe the product. That may make the product more appealing to customers—but it means that the product name will not qualify as a trademark. If trademark protection is desired (and it usually is), the name should be tweaked until it is no longer descriptive—or changed completely. The second problem—that the chosen symbol is likely to cause confusion with an existing mark—arises for many reasons. A business owner may wish to have the product sound like a popular product—but that could bar trademark protection and even be trademark infringement. Similarity also may arise by chance, by following trends, or by seeking similar allusions. If the intended mark is confusingly similar to an existing mark, it should be changed if trademark protection is desired. Remember that similarity alone does not bar protection. Rather, it requires similarity that is likely to confuse the relevant consumers.

A trademark search can disclose some potential problems. One can do a search of the federal registers and pending applications (unlike patent applications, trademark applications are not confidential).[2] But that will not disclose unregistered marks. Moreover, even a search of the register is not certain to uncover a similar registered mark (as opposed to an identical word mark). A searcher with "zephyr" in mind might not come up with "cipher," but the marks sound enough alike to infringe if other factors exist. Likewise, "alligator" and "crocodile" could be confusingly similar in meaning used

---

2. Searches can be made for free at http://www.uspto.gov.

on goods in the same market, but a word search for one might not disclose the other. If the mark is not simply a word (like "zephyr"), but a design or a sound, the search becomes even harder because most information location devices work best with text.

A number of commercial services offer more comprehensive searches. Such a search covers other likely sources that would disclose use of relevant marks, such as trade publications and databases of trademarks, domain names, and business names. A good trademark search greatly reduces the chances of using a mark that conflicts with an existing mark. Note also that even if the search discloses that someone is already using the mark ZEPHYR, that does not necessarily mean that our motorcycle maker should not use it. ZEPHYR is in fact a registered mark for tanning beds (among other things). Its use for motorcycles is not likely to create confusion (and the tanning bed mark is not a famous mark, so dilution is not a problem).

It may be getting harder to come up with a mark that is not already taken. A study found possible reduction in potential trademarks:[3]

> To give a sense of how many of the most frequently used words are thereby claimed, in 2015, 20,024 (23.2%) of the 86,408 most frequently used words in American English were claimed as single-word marks. These 20,024 words account for 74.3% of all word usage. Moreover, 816 of the 1,000 most frequently used words identically matched an active single-word mark, and 6,121 (61.2%) of the 10,000 most frequently used words did so (Table 1). The data also show a steady increase in the proportion of the U.S. population carrying a surname claimed as a single-word trademark (Figure 2). We estimate that at least 55 percent of Americans currently carry a surname that is already claimed as a single-word mark.

The depletion is affecting choice of marks: "Given these conditions, new applicants are increasingly resorting to suboptimal marks. The data indicate that applicants are applying less often for standard English words and common surnames and more often for more complex marks, as measured by character, syllable, and word count."

Acquisition of Trademark Rights

The symbol is not a mark until the owner makes a bona fide, lawful use of the mark in trade. The Lanham Act requires specific categories of uses to support a federal registration. 15 U.S.C. §1127. How the mark holder meets this requirement depends on whether she has a trademark or a service mark.

---

3. *See* Barton Beebe, Jeanne Fromer, *Comment on Possible Streamlined Version of Cancellation Proceedings on Grounds of Abandonment and Nonuse*, Docket No. PTO-T-2017-0012, discussing findings of Beebe & Fromer, *Are We Running Out of Trademarks? An Empirical Study of Trademark Depletion and Congestion* (forthcoming Harvard Law Review) (via Rebecca Tushnet, Rebecca Tushnet's 43(B)log).

A trademark must be on the goods when they are sold or transported. The trademark may be on the goods themselves or on the containers, associated displays, tags, or labels. If the nature of goods makes such use impracticable, use on associated documents suffices. Service marks must be used in displays or advertising, and the services covered must be rendered in commerce. If goods or services are sold before use of the mark, that does not forfeit subsequent ownership of the mark (as publication without copyright notice once put works into the public domain). Rather, it simply delays the time of ownership. Likewise, after ownership of the mark is established, sales without use of the mark do not forfeit the mark (unless the mark is abandoned). But reduced use of the mark could count against the owner as a factor in the infringement analysis.

The use must be a "bona fide use of a mark in the ordinary course of trade, and not made merely to reserve a right in a mark." 15 U.S.C. §1127. A token use of the mark is not sufficient to establish trademark rights. Courts require sufficient use to show a continuing effort to establish the mark as a source identifier. Because the uses of trademarks are so diverse, no set of requirements governs. Courts look to the totality of the circumstances. The use must also be lawful to qualify as bona fide.

The use must be "in commerce." The statute defines "commerce" to mean "all commerce which may lawfully be regulated by Congress." 15 U.S.C. §1127. The Supreme Court has interpreted the Commerce Clause powers very broadly (although some decisions in recent years have shown it has limits). Almost any use of a trademark that is commercial in nature is likely to qualify. In addition, even noncommercial uses that have an effect on interstate commerce would likely fall within the Commerce Clause powers. The requirement that the use be "in commerce" does not require that the mark owner make a profit, receive any revenue, or be a commercial entity. But the statute also requires that the use be "in the ordinary course of trade," which would require that the use have some commercial aspect (as opposed to merely an effect on commerce).

The use must be lawful. The mark Herbal Access was denied registration in 2016, for lack of "lawful use." Even in states that may permit marijuana sales, federal laws still prohibit it.[4] That was not changed, in the TTAB's view, when Congress prohibited use of funds to enforce prohibitions where states have legalized medical marijuana.[5]

Use alone is not sufficient to acquire trademark rights with symbols that are not inherently distinctive and become marks only by acquiring distinctiveness. Until the symbol has acquired secondary meaning, it is not used as a mark, and hence ownership rights do not arise.

---

4. In re Morgan Brown, 119 U.S.P.Q.2d 1350 (TTAB 2016).

5. In re PharmaCann LLC, 123 U.S.P.Q.2d 1122 (TTAB 2017).

Examples

1. *Drink in a box.* Startup company is planning to sell water in little cardboard boxes, similar to juice boxes already sold for children. They are choosing a potential trademark. The following marks are already in use: POLAND SPRINGS, somewhat well known for adult-sized plastic water bottles. SESAME STREET for juice boxes (and a famous mark for various children's products). Which of the following would be protected if used as a mark by our startup?
   a. TASTY WATER
   b. POLAND SPRINGS
   c. SESAME AVENUE
   d. DOCTOR DALLY (a trademark search reveals no use of any similar symbol)

2. *Take a look.* Reluctant Rolf is on the verge of putting a new high-caffeine yogurt on the market. He has chosen the trademark ROLLEMCOLD. Rolf's attorney suggests that Rolf have a trademark search done before he starts using the mark. Rolf responds that a search is unnecessary. He devised the mark from combining elements from the names of his family members. No one else is likely to use such an odd new word. Because Rolf can show he made it up, he further reasons, no one can accuse him of copying somebody else's mark. Would Rolf benefit from a trademark search?

3. *Freedom of information.* Clever Cassie is likewise putting a new product on the market. She plans to sell fingernail polish with the mark CLAIMANT. Cassie uses the search engine on the U.S. Patent and Trademark Office (USPTO) Web site to search for confusingly similar marks. She searches for "claimant" and as many words with similar spelling, sound, meaning, or connotations that she can think of. She is satisfied that her use of CLAIMANT is not likely to cause confusion with any registered mark. Has Cassie done a sufficient search?

4. *It's not the thought that counts.* Better Batter Co.'s advertising campaign for Baffin, a new brand of frozen waffles, appears in the media. The first ads seek to arouse curiosity, stating simply "Baffin: your mornings will never be the same." Subsequent ads reveal Baffin to be a brand name for frozen waffles and depict the great pleasure consumers will take in toasting and eating the waffles. The campaign is very successful. Consumer surveys show broad public awareness of Baffin as a brand name for waffles, even though not a single Baffin waffle has even been sold or shipped yet. Is BAFFIN an enforceable trademark for waffles?

5. *Plain presentation.* Palmspring, an electronics maker, is in the final stages of bringing a new handheld computer to market. Palmspring has worked through many difficult technical, manufacturing, and marketing issues. It has produced and tested thousands of the new models, and even shipped

them to its retail outlets. The only thing Palmspring has not decided is the trademark for the new model. Consequently, it has shipped the computers in plain boxes that contain the computer and an instruction manual. Its delay actually helps the marketing of the model because considerable curiosity builds among potential buyers about what the model will be called and when it will go on sale. Finally, Palmspring decides to go with the trademark SANTIAGO. The stores put big signs saying SANTIAGO over the bins containing the plain boxes. Over the next week, all the models are sold and Palmspring starts producing more. The success of the new Santiago model is the talk of the handheld computer industry. Is SANTIAGO a federally protected trademark on handheld computers for Palmspring?

6. *Different standard.* Gogedder opens a new electronics repair and servicing business. Gogedder adopts the service mark FOOLOO REPAIRS. She opens shops for business in several states, placing large signs on the front and inside of the stores proclaiming Fooloo Repairs. She also runs ads in the local paper, identifying Fooloo Repairs as a new source of electronics repair and maintenance services and extolling the expertise of her staff. Fooloo does not appear on the staff uniforms, on the equipment used, or on the paperwork. Has Gogedder made sufficient use of the service mark to acquire trademark rights?

7. *Mere formality.* Custard Corp. designs and builds a new video game console. Custard plans to build and ship several million units. It decides to use the trademark CEMETERY LODGE. To establish trademark rights, Custard prints CEMETERY LODGE on a box, puts one game console in, and ships it to Retailer, who buys it for the expected wholesale price of $200. Has Custard made sufficient use of the mark to establish trademark rights? What if Custard had sold one console each to several dozen retailers to stir up interest in the new console?

8. *Secondary source.* Corners sells air conditioners to homeowners, taking orders through a Web site and over the phone (usually as a result of direct mail advertising). He ships the air conditioners to buyers in a number of states. Corners uses the mark FRIGATE BIRD on the air conditioners themselves, as well as on all his promotional and shipping material. Corners does not manufacture the air conditioners. In fact, he has a friend who is a dispatcher in the shipping department of an air conditioner maker. The friend simply steals as many units as Corners needs to fill his orders. The two remove all identifying marks from the machines and put the FRIGATE BIRD mark on each one sold and shipped. Has Corners made sufficient use to establish trademark rights in FRIGATE BIRD on air conditioners?

9. *Butterfly's wings.* Panacea provides chiropractic services in Littletown, using the service mark UNDER THE BRIDGES. A sign outside her office uses the mark, together with "Chiropractic Services." Panacea also uses the mark

in her marketing, which consists of running small ads run each month in the local papers and in some small papers in a nearby state and handing out fliers occasionally on Main Street. Panacea always treats her clients in her office in Littletown. Over the years, her reputation spreads. A number of clients travel from other states to see her, usually staying overnight at a local hotel. They arrange appointments by calling her or sending e-mails. Has Panacea made sufficient use of the service mark in commerce to qualify for federal protection?

10. *Enough.* A church sells a couple of hats bearing the trademark ADD A ZERO at a bake sale. Sufficient to establish trademark rights?

Explanations

1. a. TASTY WATER is merely descriptive, so would not be protected. If Startup used it anyway, and it became so well known that consumers interpreted TASTY WATER to denote Startup's product, then it would have acquired distinctiveness—and would be a protected mark. But very few sellers are that successful. A wiser move would be to choose an inherently distinctive mark, which would be protected upon use.

   b. POLAND SPRINGS would be likely to cause confusion with the existing mark, POLAND SPRINGS, for adult-size plastic bottles. The marks are identical and the products very close.

   c. SESAME AVENUE would probably be likely to cause confusion with the famous SESAME STREET mark. Even if SESAME STREET is not yet used on drinking water, it is used on juice boxes and is a famous mark for children's products. One might try to avoid confusion by using very different product design (different script, no cartoon characters, even a disclaimer), but a much wiser course would be to steer clear of the mark by choosing another.

   d. DOCTOR DALLY looks like an inherently distinctive mark and not likely to cause confusion with any existing mark. Startup can use it (and cross their fingers that a confusingly similar mark does not pop up—trademark searching is not an exact science).

2. Rolf might benefit from a trademark search, but it is not clear on these facts. Rolf's putative mark, ROLLEMCOLD, is not protectable as a mark if it is likely to cause confusion with a prior mark already in use. The facts that Rolf devised the mark and did not copy from anyone else do not protect his mark if another mark already has priority. His mark could be barred by a sufficiently similar mark, not just an identical one. It could also be barred by a mark used on goods or services other than the line of goods he will sell, provided the various factors show a likelihood of confusion. The chances do appear relatively small. The cost of a trademark search is relatively modest, however, so it may be worth it to Rolf to reduce the

possibility that he will expend resources on bringing the product to mark under the Rollemcold name and thereafter find another mark owner claiming priority. Rolf could do a search himself by using Internet search engines and his own imagination and knowledge of the relevant markets. Having said that, having a trademark search done is no guaranty of validity because even a good trademark search may miss a mark that is sufficiently similar (in the relevant marketplace context) to confuse. Rolf is simply faced with a question of weighing the costs and benefits of conducting a search.

3. Cassie may have determined that there is a very low chance that her mark is likely to cause confusion with any federally registered mark. But her mark will be invalid to the extent it is likely to cause confusion with a mark in prior use, whether that mark was registered or not (subject to the geographic limitations discussed below for unregistered marks). If Cassie wants to be sure that the risk of a prior mark is sufficiently low, she should search for unregistered marks that would be confusingly similar in the marketplace. She or a search service could search the Internet, databases of unregistered marks and trade names, trade publications, or any other likely source. A search of the trademark register alone discloses only registered marks.

4. Baffin is not yet a federally registrable trademark for waffles. Trademark rights depend on adoption and use. The Baffin mark has been used widely in advertising, but the use required under the Lanham Act requires the mark to be used on the goods themselves or on the containers, associated displays, tags, or labels (or on associated documents if such use is impracticable) when the goods are sold or transported in commerce. Such a use has not been made yet, so Baffin has yet to become a protected trademark. Note, however, that such "analogous use" could help the owner of the Baffin mark in a priority dispute, as discussed below. Moreover, if a competitor made use of a symbol confusingly similar to Baffin (in the context of the marketplace), Better Batter Co. might be able to enforce rights under false designation of origin (discussed in the infringement chapter). But Baffin is not yet entitled to the benefits of registration.

5. The Santiago mark has been used by Palmspring in the necessary manner to support a federal registration. The mark must be used on the goods themselves or on the containers, associated displays, tags, or labels (or on associated documents if such use is impracticable) when the goods are sold or transported in commerce. The mark was not actually printed on the goods, packaging, or labels. But it was used on big signs over the bins containing the goods that were sold in commerce. The mark need not be actually affixed to the goods for federal trademark rights to attach.

6. The Fooloo Repairs service mark has been used in the manner necessary to confer federal trademark protection (more precisely, to qualify for federal registration). Service mark protection requires that the mark be

used in displays or advertising and that the services be rendered in commerce. Gogedder used the mark in both displays and advertising, and she has rendered services in commerce.

7. Custard has not made sufficient use of the trademark to establish federal trademark rights. The use must be a bona fide use in trade, not done merely to reserve rights in a mark. Rather, the use must show a continuing effort to establish the mark as a source identifier. Using the mark on a single box of a video game console and transporting the box simply to establish trademark rights does not qualify as a bona fide use in trade. Rather, it is a token use, insufficient to establish rights.

If Custard sold one console each to several dozen retailers to stir up interest in the new console, the question would be closer. Courts look at the totality of the circumstances to determine if the use is sufficient. The number of units sold here was relatively small. But the purpose was to stir up sales, not to simply make a token use for trademark purposes. The use appears to be in the ordinary course of business and was made to a substantial number of buyers. On balance, a court likely would find the use sufficient, especially if it was followed by continued efforts to use the mark.

8. Corners has not made the requisite use of the Frigate Bird mark to establish trademark rights. The use must be a bona fide use in trade. An unlawful use is not a bona fide use. The use here was part of a scheme to traffic in stolen goods. Such a use does not qualify as bona fide.

9. Panacea has made sufficient use of the service mark in commerce to qualify for federal protection. Both trademarks and service marks must be used in commerce to qualify for federal protection. The Lanham Act defines "commerce" to include commerce to the extent that Congress has the power to regulate it. Panacea's use easily meets the requisite effect on interstate commerce. Her marketing and her services clearly affect interstate commerce. She advertises in other states. Clients travel from other states to see her and stay in the local hotel. Such an effect is sufficient to fall within the broad limits on the commerce power.

10. The court held that "the Church's sale of two 'ADD A ZERO'-marked hats to an out-of-state resident is within the powers of Congress under the Commerce Clause and, therefore, constitutes 'use in commerce' under the Lanham Act," which was sufficient to support registration of the ADD A ZERO mark.[6] The court refused to adopt a *de minimis* test, on the grounds that Lanham Act registration applied to the extent of Congress's Commerce Clause powers, and that sales to an out of state resident were comfortably within the powers of Congress to regulate interstate commerce.[7]

---

6. 2016 U.S. App. LEXIS 20382 at 15.
7. Christian Faith Fellowship Church v. Adidas AG, 841 F.3d 986 (Fed. Cir. 2016).

REGISTRATION

Registration Process

Trademark rights do not depend on registration. The maker of Zephyr motorcycles need not register the ZEPHYR mark to own it as a trademark or to sue others who infringe the mark. But federal registration offers a number of advantages:

1. Filing of the application (provided the mark is subsequently registered) is considered constructive use, nationwide in effect, for purposes of priority against similar marks. 15 U.S.C. §1057(c).
2. The certificate of registration is "prima facie evidence of the validity of the registered mark and of registration of the mark." 15 U.S.C. §1057(b).
3. The potential remedies for infringement are greater. 15 U.S.C. §1111.
4. The validity of registered marks can become "incontestable" after five years of continuous use. 15 U.S.C. §1065.
5. Registration is constructive notice of claim of ownership. 15 U.S.C. §1072.
6. Both registered and unregistered marks have protection against unauthorized importation, but the protection for registered marks is somewhat broader.
7. The mark owner may use a trademark notice, such as the ® symbol, with the mark (which, like a copyright notice or patent marking, serves as a warning to others), 15 U.S.C. §1111, although TM may be used with unregistered marks. Although trademark rights in the U.S. do not depend on registration, U.S. trademark holders are more likely to use ® and TM than in countries where marks become marks by registration, such as Ireland (although even there unregistered marks are protected by the tort of "passing off").
8. The mark will show up in trademark searches by others.

The statute permits two types of applications for U.S. marks: use applications and intent-to-use applications.[8] A use application seeks to register a mark that is already in use. An intent-to-use application may be filed by one with a bona fide intention to use the mark in commerce (to obtain registration, the applicant must subsequently use the mark in commerce).

---

8. The statute also provides for registration of foreign marks when the owner has a bona fide intent to use the mark in the United States. 15 U.S.C. §1126 (known as section 44 registrations). The enforceability of the mark, however, is subject to the same standards as U.S. marks. See 15 U.S.C. §1126(e) (providing that marks may be "registered on the principal register if eligible, otherwise on the supplemental register").

15 U.S.C. §1051(b). A valid intent-to-use application requires bona fide intent to use. Such applications may not be used simply to reserve rights in a symbol (in essence, to retain the option to use a mark). The intent-to-use application does not make the intended mark enforceable—it only becomes enforceable on actual use. But, as discussed in the next section, the intent-to-use filing date may be used as the priority date against competing claimants' trademarks. Accordingly, when a seller plans to use a mark, she no longer needs to use it as soon as possible to establish priority.

The statute also provides for two registers: the principal register and the supplemental register. The principal register is for marks that meet the requirements of protection discussed in the last chapter. The supplemental register, broadly stated, is for marks that are capable of identifying the source of goods or services but that do not meet the requirements for registration on the principal register. 15 U.S.C. §1091.[9] Most often, these are descriptive marks that have not attained secondary meaning. 15 U.S.C. §§1091 and 1052(e)(1)(2).[10] Marks unregistrable for most other reasons (such as deceptive or functional marks or marks likely to cause confusion with existing marks) are not eligible for the supplemental register. In general, the advantages of registration do not apply to marks on the supplemental register. Supplemental registration does give constructive notice (but does not establish constructive use for priority), allows the mark owner to use the ® symbol, and provides federal jurisdiction for an infringement lawsuit (although the mark may well not be enforceable). But the primary reason for the supplemental register lies in international trademark practice. Some jurisdictions may allow registration of descriptive marks (even without secondary meaning) but allow registration of foreign marks only if they are registered in their home country. The supplemental register allows a mark to be registered in the United States so it can be registered abroad. For sake of brevity, this book generally uses "registration" and "register" to refer to the principal register.

The applicant must submit the fee, an application and a verified statement, and requisite specimens or facsimiles of the mark as used. 15 U.S.C. §1051. The application, if based on use, includes specification of

> the applicant's domicile and citizenship, the date of the applicant's first use of the mark, the date of the applicant's first use of the mark in commerce, the goods [or services] in connection with which the mark is used, and a drawing of the mark [block capitals suffice for a word mark].

15 U.S.C. §1051(a)(2). The verified statement must specify the following:

---

9. Such marks could include descriptive marks, deceptively misdescriptive marks, and geographically descriptive marks.

10. Registration on the supplemental registration, however, does not constitute an admission that the mark has not acquired distinctiveness.

(A) the person making the verification believes that he or she, or the juristic person in whose behalf he or she makes the verification, to be the owner of the mark sought to be registered;

(B) to the best of the verifier's knowledge and belief, the facts recited in the application are accurate;

(C) the mark is in use in commerce; and

(D) to the best of the verifier's knowledge and belief, no other person has the right to use such mark in commerce either in the identical form thereof or in such near resemblance thereto as to be likely, when used on or in connection with the goods of such other person, to cause confusion, or to cause mistake.

15 U.S.C. §1051(a)(3). As discussed in the priority section below, a similar mark may be used on similar goods or services by sellers operating in different geographic areas. The statute provides that the USPTO may issue concurrent registrations. A party may apply for concurrent registration by disclosing the relevant facts, such as the nature of the goods and services and the scope of the relevant concurrent uses.

An intent-to-use application has the same general requirements, with relevant changes. The applicant verifies not that she owns the mark but that she is entitled to use it because before use there is no enforceable mark to own. She states a bona fide intention to use, rather than a date of first use. For the mark to be registered, the intent-to-use applicant must subsequently file a verified statement that the mark is in use in commerce. (The USPTO may allow the applicant up to three years to do this.)

Once the USPTO receives the application and fee, the application is referred to an examining attorney. 15 U.S.C. §1062. The examining attorney determines whether the mark is registrable (or, for intent-to-use applications, would be registrable on use), looking to the requirements set forth in the last chapter. The USPTO may require the applicant to disclaim an unregistrable component of a mark that is otherwise registrable. 15 U.S.C. §1056. The USPTO might require a kiwi fruit seller seeking to register MONOLITH KIWI FRUIT to disclaim any rights in the generic term "kiwi fruit." The mark holder could seek to enforce the mark against subsequent sellers who used the term "monolith" (or similar terms) but not ones that use the term "kiwi fruit."

If the examining attorney refuses registration, he must advise the applicant of the reason. The most common reasons for refusal are that the mark is likely to cause confusion with an existing mark or that the mark is merely descriptive. But refusals may also issue for other grounds: that the mark is generic, functional, or deceptive, and so on. The applicant is entitled to reply or amend the application. The applicant may abandon the application, either directly or by failing to reply for six months. If the mark is similar to a mark already registered or subject to an application, the USPTO may declare an interference proceeding (just as patent priority disputes may be subject to interference proceedings).

If the examining attorney determines the mark is registrable, the mark is published in the *Official Gazette of the Patent and Trademark Office*. Anyone "who believes that he would be damaged by the registration of a mark" may file an opposition in the USPTO within 30 days of publication. 15 U.S.C. §1063. To bring an opposition, an opposer must be more than a "mere intermeddler" or one who purports to represent the public interest: she must have a "real interest" in the outcome. *See, e.g., Ritchie v. Simpson,* 170 F.3d 1092 (Fed. Cir. 1999). But the opposer need not be a market competitor or the owner of a similar mark. The "real interest" requirement has been read broadly provided the opposer has a "direct and personal stake" in the outcome. There was standing to bring an opposition to the registration by O.J. Simpson (an alleged spouse murderer) of the marks O.J. Simpson, O.J., and The Juice, where the opposer was a "family man." *See Ritchie, supra.*

Opposition is not the only procedure available to resist registration. After registration of a mark, a party who believes she is damaged by the registration may bring a cancellation proceeding. 15 U.S.C. §1064. If the proceeding is brought within five years of registration, any grounds for nonregistrability may be alleged. If more than five years after registration, the grounds are limited. In particular, after five years, a cancellation proceeding cannot be based on a claim that the mark is merely descriptive or that the mark is confusingly similar to a prior mark. But cancellation after five years may be based on the grounds that the mark is generic, functional, was abandoned (or, for certification marks, was not properly used), was registered fraudulently, or was "deceptive." 15 U.S.C. §1064.

If the examining attorney issues a final refusal of an application, the applicant may appeal to the Trademark Trial and Appeal Board (TTAB). Likewise, the results of interferences, oppositions, applications for concurrent use, and cancellation proceedings may be appealed to the TTAB. A party may appeal an adverse decision of the TTAB to federal court[11] but must choose whether to appeal to federal district court or the federal appellate court (the Federal Circuit, the same court that hears appeals in patent cases). If the appeal goes to the federal district court, the appeal is de novo, meaning that the court decides all issues of law and fact anew without deferring to the record or reasoning of the TTAB (although the parties may agree to incorporate the TTAB record into the federal district court action). If the appellant chooses to go to the Federal Circuit,[12] that appellate court reviews the decision on the record before the TTAB. So in deciding where to appeal, the party must decide whether he wants to start from scratch

---

11. These appeal rules apply to decisions of the TTAB and to other decisions made by the director of the USPTO, such as renewals of registration.

12. If there are multiple parties and one appeals to the Federal Circuit, other parties may choose to move the case to the federal trial court.

before a trial court or to go directly to an appellate court for a limited review of specific legal issues.

If the mark is registered, registration remains effective for ten years (provided that required affidavits showing current use are filed after six years). 15 U.S.C. §1058. The registration may be renewed every ten years, without a time limitation. Moreover, even if the owner allows the registration to lapse or the mark is not registered at all, an unregistered mark is enforceable, also without any time limit. Although there is no time limit on the duration of a mark, there are other limits. Just as acquiring trademark rights depends on using the mark as a source indicator, so do continued rights. As discussed below, trademark rights may be lost through abandonment.

First Amendment Protection of Expression in Registration of Marks

The Lanham Act denies registration of marks that may disparage "persons, living or dead, institutions, beliefs, or national symbols, or bring them into contempt, or disrepute." 15 U.S.C. §1052(a). There are few cases on the standard for "disparaging" matter. In the leading case, *Blackhorse v. Pro-Football, Inc.*, No. 92046185 (T.T.A.B. June 18, 2014), the TTAB held that WASHINGTON REDSKINS mark was disparaging. When the term referenced a group, its meaning was to be judged not from the standpoint of the public at large (as with scandalousness), but rather from the point of view of the group referenced. On the basis of a variety of evidence submitted by both sides (dictionaries, consumer surveys, historical documents, expert testimony, and other sources), the TTAB concluded that the derogatory connotation of the word "redskin" in connection with Native Americans extended to its use by the professional football team at the time of registration. The TTAB canceled the mark.

While the Redskins appeal was still pending, the Supreme Court held in another case that the trademark statute's prohibition against registering disparaging marks was invalid, as an unconstitutional limit on free speech. A rock band composed of Asian musicians had adopted the mark THE SLANTS, appropriating the slur against Asians for their own. The USPTO rejected the registration as a disparaging term. The Supreme Court ultimately held that the rule against disparaging marks is an overbroad limitation on free speech, unrelated to the goals of trademark protection.[13] The Court also rejected

---

13. It is claimed that the disparagement clause serves two interests. The first is phrased in a variety of ways in the briefs. Echoing language in one of the opinions below, the Government asserts an interest in preventing "'underrepresented groups'" from being "'bombarded with demeaning messages in commercial advertising'" . . . But no matter how the point is phrased, its unmistakable thrust is this: The Government has an interest in preventing speech expressing ideas that offend. And, as we have explained, that idea strikes at the heart of the First Amendment. Speech that demeans on the basis of race, ethnicity, gender, religion, age, disability, or any other similar ground is hateful; but the proudest boast of our free speech jurisprudence is that we protect the freedom to express "the

such arguments as that registration of a mark is government speech, which the government has considerable freedom to regulate.[14]

Under this case, the WASHINGTON REDSKINS MARK is no longer barred from registration. In addition, the prohibitions against registration of immoral and deceptive matter and marks that bring persons, institutions, or beliefs into contempt or disrepute, are all certainly on shaky ground. The Federal Circuit soon held that, under *Tam*, the Lanham Act's similar bar against registration of "immoral or scandalous" marks was unconstitutional.15 The mark FUCT was therefore registrable, even if it was immoral or scandalous. The cause of action for dilution, especially in its tarnishment variation, has also come into question.[16]

Tam may also have impact in the opposite direction. The "more interesting question is whether the court's First Amendment analysis allows free speech advocates to argue that certain types of subject matter should not be registered or protected as a trademark to preserve the public domain and promote the free flow of commercial expression. . . . Legislatures and courts should consider whether granting trademark rights in inherently valuable descriptive words, product attributes or hand gestures" is unconstitutional. Lisa Ramsey, *Symposium: Increasing First Amendment scrutiny of trademark law after* Matal v. Tam, SCOTUS blog (June 20, 2017).

Incontestability

"Incontestability" is akin to the five-year limit on grounds for cancellation. After a registered mark has been in continuous use for five consecutive years after registration, the mark owner may file an affidavit with the USPTO. The registrant's right to use such registered mark in commerce for the relevant goods or services becomes "incontestable." 15 U.S.C. §1065. Whether the owner of the incontestable mark is plaintiff or defendant, the other party in litigation may not challenge the validity of the mark, its registration, and ownership. 15 U.S.C. §1115(b); *Park 'n' Fly v. Dollar Park & Fly*,

---

thought that we hate." . . . The second interest asserted is protecting the orderly flow of commerce . . . A simple answer to this argument is that the disparagement clause is not "narrowly drawn" to drive out trademarks that support invidious discrimination. The clause reaches any trademark that disparages *any person, group, or institution.*

Matal v. Tam, 137 S. Ct. 1744, 1764-1765 (2017).
14. Matal v. Tam, 137 S. Ct. 1744, 1757 (2017) (rejecting arguments "(1) that **trademarks** are government speech, not private speech, (2) that **trademarks** are a form of government subsidy, and (3) that the constitutionality of the disparagement clause should be tested under a new 'government-program' doctrine").
15. In re Brunetti, 877 F.3d 1330 (Fed. Cir. 2017).
16. Rebecca Tushnet, *Slightly cooler take on Tam* (June 21, 2017), Rebecca Tushnet, Rebecca Tushnet's 43(B)log).

469 U.S. 189 (1985). The mark owner must still prove infringement (if alleged) and remains subject to a list of defenses and other defects:

(1) fraudulent registration;

(2) abandonment;

(3) use of the mark to "misrepresent the source of the goods or services on or in connection with which the mark is used";

(4) fair use of the mark as an individual's name or as a descriptive term to "describe the goods or services of such party, or their geographic origin";

(5) the rights of a junior user of a mark subsequently registered by a senior user, as discussed above;

(6) use of the mark to violate the antitrust laws;

(7) that the mark is functional; or

(8) equitable principles, including laches, estoppel, and acquiescence.

15 U.S.C. §1115(b).

In practical terms, the most common advantage of incontestability is that the owner no longer needs to show secondary meaning (where the mark is arguably descriptive or otherwise may require secondary meaning). Accordingly, where competitors are concerned about others' use of descriptive terms, they must act within five years.

Examples

1. *To file or not to file.* Reluctant Rolf has used the trademark ROLLEMCOLD on high-caffeine yogurt for over a month, shipping thousands of crates all over the country. Sales are growing rapidly. Rolf's attorney suggests that Rolf register the trademark ROLLEMCOLD. But Rolf balks when she explains that, by using the mark on the goods when they were shipped and sold, Rolf has already established trademark rights. Why bother to go to the time and trouble of registering the mark, Rolf wonders, if I already have an enforceable trademark?

2. *Not so quick.* Impetuous Irma has filed an intent-to-use application for the service mark CHICKEN COOP, which she intends to use to identify her investment advice services. Irma has not yet rendered services to clients, but she is rapidly arranging for the launch of her business in a few months. Does Irma have a protectable service mark in CHICKEN COOP used for investment advice services? What if Irma had rendered services in commerce and used the mark in widespread advertising but had not been granted a registration?

3. *Reserve squad.* Palmspring makes and sells a little green and white computer. Palmspring markets it under the brand name Little Green and White Computer. The model is not very popular and sells only a few

hundred a year, which is a tiny fraction of the overall market. Palmspring does some modest advertising, clearly using its name Little Green and White Computer as an indicator of source. On the containers of the computers and on associated displays, Palmspring puts "Little Green and White Computer® — not as big or blue as other computers, but smarter and handier." A competitor notices the use of the ®, indicating that Little Green and White Computer is a registered trademark. The competitor wonders whether that can be true. The mark is clearly a descriptive mark. Descriptive marks are protectable if they have acquired secondary meaning, but Little Green and White Computer has come nowhere near the level of public awareness necessary for secondary meaning. Could Little Green and White Computer be a registered mark for Palmspring's little green and white computer?

4. *Disclaimer.* Shod seeks to register the mark Nuzzling Hiking Boots, which he has been using on the hiking boots he sells. The USPTO examining attorney indicates that she will determine the mark is registrable provided that Shod disclaims the term "hiking boots." Shod is greatly affronted at the suggestion that his products do not qualify as hiking boots. He is ready to submit affidavits from any number of hikers who will attest that Shod's shoes are not just hiking boots, but are some of the best hiking boots around. Is it appropriate for Shod to disclaim the Hiking Boots component of the mark?

5. *Concession.* Pillow Maker files an application to register the mark Nozama Pure Goose Down, which it uses on pillows. The USPTO examining attorney learns that the pillows are not in fact made with pure goose down but rather with plastic filler. He refuses registration on the basis that the mark is deceptive. Pillow Maker concedes that the Pure Goose Down component is deceptive and offers to disclaim trademark protection in that phrase to obtain registration of the mark. Is allowing registration subject to the disclaimer appropriate?

6. *Supermark?* Six years ago, Mercedes obtained registration of the mark Toddler Too, which she uses on running strollers. She has been using the mark continuously for almost ten years but still enjoys only a tiny market share among her competitors. She notices that a competitor has recently begun using the mark Toddler Shuttle on its running strollers. Mercedes files a trademark infringement action. The competitor argues that Toddler Too is not a valid mark because it is merely descriptive and has not acquired secondary meaning. Mercedes contends that because the mark is incontestable, the court must simply find infringement and determine the appropriate remedy. Is either one correct?

7. *Marks in the bank?* Naming Service is a consultant in the business of helping businesses choose symbols to use as trademarks. Naming Service's

creativity runs ahead of its clientele. It has devised a number of marks that it thinks are exceptionally creative for various goods and services. It decides to file intent-to-use applications for each of the marks and then to find clients in the relevant markets, convince them of the value of the marks, and assign the applications, for a price. Are the intent-to-use applications valid?

Explanations

1. Registration is not necessary to have trademark rights. But, as the text lists, registration does have several advantages for the mark owner. Perhaps the most relevant for a new product like Rolf's is nationwide priority. Rather than requiring Rolf to establish use in every market, registration is deemed constructive use nationwide, giving priority over marks that go into use on later dates.

2. Filing an intent-to-use application does not make the mark an enforceable trademark. Rather, bona fide use in trade establishes trademark rights. So Irma could not enforce her mark against alleged infringers. But the intent-to-use application will establish a priority date for her. Provided that she uses the date within the necessary time period, she will have nationwide priority based on her filing date. If she had used the mark after filing, she would be able to seek registration and then rely on the original priority date.

3. Little Green and White Computer is a descriptive mark that has not acquired secondary meaning, and hence it is not a protected trademark. But it may have been registered—not on the principal register but on the supplemental register. A mark that is capable of becoming distinctive may be registered on the supplemental register. It is not entitled to the same benefits as those on the principal register. Most important, an action for infringement of a registered mark can be brought only for marks on the principal register. But the owner may use the ® sign to indicate the mark is registered.

4. It is appropriate for Shod to disclaim the Hiking Boots component of the mark. Disclaimer means only that the applicant acknowledges that the disclaimed component is not registrable as a trademark. "Hiking boots" is a generic term, not protectable as a trademark. The mark as a whole, Nuzzling Hiking Boots, is an inherently distinctive mark. But for Shod to receive a registration, the USPTO may require him to acknowledge that he has no rights against others that use the term "hiking boots."

5. Allowing registration subject to a disclaimer of the Pure Goose Down component is not appropriate. Whether the mark is registrable depends

on the mark as a whole. If a component of the mark is not distinctive, for example, because it is generic or descriptive, the mark as a whole may nevertheless be distinctive. WET WUGGAWUGGA is a distinctive mark for bottled water despite the generic component WET. But with deceptive marks, a deceptive component is likely to make the entire mark deceptive. NOZAMA PURE GOOSE DOWN appears to be deceptive, giving consumers false material information about the product. A disclaimer filed with the USPTO would hardly dispel the false impression given to consumers. So disclaimers may not always be used to overcome problems with components of a mark.

6. Neither Mercedes nor her competitor is correct. The mark TODDLER TOO has acquired incontestable status. That protects it from attacks on validity based on such grounds as descriptiveness. So incontestability does bar competitor's argument that the mark is merely descriptive. But incontestability does not mean that the plaintiff automatically wins the lawsuit. Rather, it only bars challenges to ownership or validity on the listed grounds. The plaintiff is still required to prove infringement by defendant and is subject to the lengthy list of defenses.

7. The intent-to-use applications are not valid. An intent-to-use application must be based on a bona fide intent to use the mark. An application made merely to reserve rights in a mark does not have the requisite intent. Naming Service does not have the intent to use the marks. Rather, it intends to reserve rights in the marks, then sell them to businesses that would use them. Naming Service might argue that it does intend to use the marks in the sense that it intends to sell the marks. But anyone who reserves rights in a mark does so with a similar intent to use the mark, if the opportunity arises. So a more specific intent to actually make a trademark use of the mark is required to support a valid intent to use filing.

OWNERSHIP

Determining the Owner

The owner of the mark is the person who controls the first use of the mark for the relevant goods or services. 15 U.S.C. §1055. In most cases, it is clear who controls use of the mark. An employer generally controls, even though employees or independent contractors literally use the mark. In addition, parties may specify rights to trademarks in a contract. But sometimes, when multiple parties are involved in a venture without clarifying their respective rights, ownership of the mark may be in question.

Priority Between Confusingly Similar Marks
Priority Based on Use

The same mark cannot be used on the same type of goods or services in the same market by different sources because the mark then does not serve as a source identifier. Even if the marks are slightly different or the relevant goods and services are different, other factors may make the marks so confusingly similar that concurrent use is not appropriate. MARIJUANAVILLE was denied registration as confusingly similar to Jimmy Buffet's established MARGARITAVILLE, where both created highly similar commercial impressions of a "chemically induced mental paradise." In case of such a conflict, priority goes to the first mark to be used—but in a different sense of "used" than discussed above. To establish trademark rights, the owner must have made *actual* use of the mark in commerce. But in determining priority of use (between competing owners), the first use may be actual use, constructive use, or analogous use.

Actual use is the use required to support an application for registration. So if the applicant has made sufficient use to support a registration, the date of use will serve as her priority date. Note that the priority date is the date of use, not any subsequent date of filing an application for registration. Registration is not required to establish priority.

Constructive use is established by the date of an intent-to-use application provided it results in subsequent registration on filing of a statement of actual use. Although subsequent use is required before the mark is actually registered, the date of filing the application serves as the priority date. Only a valid intent-to-use application, however, may serve to establish such a priority date. The applicant must have had a "bona fide intention, under circumstances showing the good faith of such person, to use a trademark in commerce." 15 U.S.C. §1051(b)(1). Likewise, the applicant must attest that no one else has the right to use the same or similar mark on similar goods or services. An application filed without disclosing knowledge of a similar mark likewise could fail to establish priority. Finally, the general requirement of "good faith" could invalidate a filing done for anticompetitive reasons or as part of a plan to realize value from a mark not from its use but from its sale to someone with a similar mark.

"Analogous use" is a judicial doctrine under which priority is established by acts that, although not of the character required to support registration based on use, are deemed sufficient to establish the mark as an indicator of source to the public. Before the mark owner used the mark on goods that were sold or transported, she may have used the mark in advertising, trade publications, or other marketing. Such analogous use must be sufficiently widespread to create an association in the relevant market between the mark and the relevant source of goods or services. Although analogous use may serve as a substitute for actual use, the required showing is higher.

A wrinkle on priority arises when the mark in question is descriptive. Descriptive marks are protectable only when they acquire secondary meaning, so priority is established not by use of a descriptive term but rather by use of the term as a mark, which requires that it attain secondary meaning.

Geographic Limitations

The common law rule is that the use of a mark establishes trademark rights and gives priority to the mark owner, but only in the geographic area in which the mark is actually used. For example, if one merchant sells grapes under the ISEEYOU mark only in California and one merchant sells grapes under the ISEEYOU mark only in New York, each owns rights to use the mark in their respective markets and have priority over the other. The Lanham Act establishes nationwide priority for registered marks but also provides that unregistered marks retain priority in their geographic area of use. The junior user must use her mark without knowledge of prior use by the senior user.[17] So if the California grape seller registers the ISEEYOU mark, she has priority everywhere in the United States except in New York. But courts have interpreted the rule to mean that the registered mark has priority only when there is an actual conflict. *See National Association for Healthcare Communications v. Central Arkansas Area Agency on Aging*, 257 F.3d 732 (8th Cir. 2001) (quoting and citing earlier case law). So if the New York seller begins to sell her grapes in Illinois, the California seller (despite her nationwide priority) cannot enjoin the sales until the California seller enters, or has a concrete plan to enter, the Illinois market. Such geographic limitations are less important today because marketing is more likely to be nationwide in effect.

Assignment

A trademark serves to tell consumers the source of the goods or services. If the trademark is sold to another seller who provides completely different goods and services, consumers might be misled. Likewise, if the trademark owner licenses the mark to numerous sellers who have different standards for the relevant goods or services, the trademark fails to serve its function. Accordingly, if a trademark is sold, it must be sold with the associated goodwill of the business. 15 U.S.C. §1060. The buyer need not acquire

---

17. Section 1115(b)(5) provides a defense to infringement when the junior mark "was adopted without knowledge of the registrant's prior use and has been continuously used by such party or those in privity with him from a date prior [to the senior user's registration]."

the seller's inventory, equipment, customer lists, and employee contracts. Rather, courts look to whether the transferee will deliver substantially the same product to consumers, such that use of the mark by the transferee will not mislead consumers. An assignment was void when a mark used for a "pepper-flavored soft drink" was used by the transferee to sell a "cola-flavored soft drink." *See Pepsico v. The Grapette Co.*, 416 F.2d 285 (8th Cir. 1969). The consequences of an invalid assignment or license vary. A court might simply hold that the assignment was invalid—so the assignee could not enforce the mark, but the original owner would still own it. But, as discussed below, it can cause abandonment of the mark.

An assignment is not valid unless it is in a signed writing. Recording the assignment with the USPTO is not required, but unless the assignment is recorded, it will not be effective against a competing, subsequent assignee. 15 U.S.C. §1060. The rules on assignments raise special issues for lenders who take trademark rights as collateral. Whether the security interest is effective at all is not clear because it could be treated as an invalid assignment in gross. Whether recording a security interest perfects the security interest (or whether a state UCC filing must be made) is also an open question.

Abandonment and Loss of Rights

A trademark may be abandoned in several ways: if the owner discontinues use with intent not to resume use, if the mark becomes the generic name for the relevant goods or services, or if the mark otherwise uses its significance as a mark. 15 U.S.C. §1127. The key inquiry is whether there is intent to abandon. Even active discussions about further use of the mark, without actual use, may suffice to negate intent to abandon. *See Zelinski v. Columbia 300*, 335 F.3d 633 (7th Cir. 2003).

Use Discontinued with Intent Not to Resume Use

If someone accidentally drops her watch in the pond, she has not abandoned it. She still owns it. But if she tosses it in the pond intending to get rid of it, she has abandoned it. Intent likewise governs the first category of trademark abandonment. A mark is abandoned if the owner discontinues use with no intent to resume use. Failure to use alone is not abandonment. Rather, there must also be intent not to resume use. Because intent is a mental state, courts look to all the relevant facts and circumstances to determine whether the requisite intent is present.

The statute provides that nonuse for three consecutive years is prima facie evidence of abandonment. Token use or mere use of the mark in promotional activity is insufficient to constitute use to avoid the presumption of abandonment. But, in contrast to the requirements to establish incontestability, the use need not be continuous or meet the requirements of "use" necessary to initially establish trademark rights.

A mark owner who has not used the mark for three or more years nevertheless may rebut the presumption with evidence of continuing intent to use. He must have more than a vague intent to resume use. Rather, he must have a specific plan to use the mark in the reasonably foreseeable future. The intent to resume use may be subject to some contingencies. There may be actual intent to resume use, even if the plan is dependent on finding financing, doing marketing research, or other factors. But an owner cannot simply warehouse a mark with a vague plan to use it again some day. For example, CBS discontinued the use of the AMOS AND ANDY mark because it was associated with a television show that featured offensively stereotyped characters. CBS had no definite plan to resume use of the mark but wished to retain ownership in case changing social attitudes permitted further exploitation. Such a vague, contingent intent was insufficient to avoid abandonment. *See Silverman v. CBS*, 870 F.2d 40 (2d Cir. 1989). A dot-com company used the mark "Android Data" for e-commerce software but stopped operating in 2002. It thereby abandoned the mark and so was unable to recover against Google for its famous use of the mark 14 years later. *Specht v. Google Inc.*, 747 F.3d 929 (7th Cir. 2014).

Loss of Rights Through Mark Becoming Generic

A trademark owner wants her goods or services to be the first choice of every consumer. But she does not want the primary significance of the trademark to become the standard term for the goods or services because that destroys her trademark rights. When the public comes to interpret the term not as a source identifier but as a name for a category of goods or services, the term becomes generic and nonprotectable as a mark. The primary significance may be shown by such evidence as consumer surveys and use of the term in publications.

To avoid a mark becoming generic, mark holders often take steps to discourage use of the mark in a generic fashion. Owners of well-known marks remind users to refer to "photocopies," not "Xeroxes," and to "paper tissue," not "Kleenex." But the test for generic status is the public's perception of the mark. Whether the mark owner has been diligent is not decisive.

Other Ways to Lose Significance as a Mark

The basic purpose of a mark is to distinguish the goods or services from those of others and to indicate the source of the goods. A mark can lose its significance as a mark in several ways.

As discussed above, a trademark may be assigned only with the associated goodwill. If the owner of the BARNET FAIR mark simply sells it to another hair product seller who uses the mark on products of completely different qualities, the mark loses its significance as a mark.

The mark might also lose its significance through uncontrolled ("naked") licensing. If the trademark owner licenses her mark to other sellers without controlling their products, the source-indicating function of the mark is defeated. The theory is that consumer buys Barnet Fair hair products because of her experience with goods sold under the mark or the reputation of the seller. If the mark owner simply sells the right to use the BARNET FAIR mark to other sellers of hair products, consumer's expectations are defeated. A mark was held abandoned when the owner entered in to an agreement that allowed the licensee to use the mark on any of its products, with the mark owner retaining no power to control the quality of the products. *See Stanfield v. Osborne Industries*, 52 F.3d 867 (10th Cir. 1995). A contractual right to police the goods is not absolutely necessary. If the mark owner can reasonably rely on the licensee to adhere to its quality standards (for example, because of their past relationship or the licensee's record in similar transactions), neither contractual control nor active policing by the mark owner may be necessary. *See Taco Cabana International v. Two Pesos*, 932 F.2d 1113, 1121 (5th Cir. 1991). Over the years, courts have become less stringent in applying this rule. As long as the mark owner retains a contractual right to control the quality, actual policing of the licensee's product may not be required. But if a party freely allows others to use a symbol with no controls, the symbol will lose its source-distinguishing function and no longer be a protected trademark. *See FreecycleSunnyvale v. Freecycle Network*, 626 F.3d 509 (9th Cir. 2010).

As long as the mark owner controls the use of the mark and ensures the public is not deceived, the licensee's use actually works to the benefit of the mark owner—strengthening the mark by increasing its association with the relevant goods or services.

The mark owner may lose her rights not only by failing to police the activities of her licensees. If she permits widespread infringement to occur, there likewise can be abandonment. If the mark is used by both legitimate sellers and by bootleggers, it no longer serves to indicate a single source of the goods or services.

An assignment in gross, or naked, licensing or failure to enforce the mark does not automatically mean abandonment. The better view is that one must also show that the failure in question has in fact led to the mark losing its significance as an indicator or source. *See Exxon Corp. v. Oxxford Clothes*, 109 F.3d 1070 (5th Cir. 1997).

Examples

1. *Break-up.* MARNIA is the trademark used for a computer game that is sold in retail outlets and through Web site downloads. Marnia was written by Hanna Hack, an employee of Vertible Games. Hanna also thought of the name Marnia for the game. After Hanna wrote the game, Vertible had other employees test and market the program. After Marnia becomes a huge hit, Hanna seeks a better salary and a share of the profits. When Vertible refuses, Hanna decides to leave and form her own game company. She also informs Vertible that she is taking the trademark MARNIA with her. She wrote the game and named it, so she owns the name, Hanna tells Vertible. Is she correct?

2. *Unregistered.* East Hill Bunnies has been selling a popular line of chocolate bunnies for decades under the trademark FUNNY BORO. The bunnies are sold throughout the country in retail outlets and through catalog sales. East Hill has never registered the trademark. Three years ago, Chocka Corp. began selling chocolate bunnies with the trademark FUNNY BURROW. Chocka Corp. applied for and received a federal registration for the mark FUNNY BURROW used on chocolate bunnies. East Hill did not file an opposition when the mark was published in the trademark gazette. Chocka Corp. now informs East Hill that it will sue for infringement if East Hill does not cease and desist from using the FUNNY BORO mark. Which of the competing claimants has priority?

3. *Taken?* Artisan makes custom precision instruments for scientific laboratories using the trademark SALT FLATS. One day, Artisan receives a cease-and-desist letter from Fertilizer Corp. Fertilizer has used the mark SALT FLATS on bags of manure for decades, although it has remained an obscure mark. Fertilizer obtained a federal registration in 1991 (before Artisan began using the mark) and has kept the registration in place. Fertilizer claims it has nationwide priority in the mark and that Artisan must either license the use of the mark or stop using it. Does Fertilizer have priority?

4. *Discovering the other Freya.* Bookseller starts selling books over the Internet using the service mark FREYA.COM and rapidly becomes world famous as a source of bookselling services. Bookseller registers the service mark FREYA.COM. Then another FREYA BOOKS comes to light, the unregistered service mark of a local feminist bookstore in St. Paul. Freya Books had been operating for years before Bookseller used its FREYA.COM mark or filed a registration, but Freya Books never applied for a federal registration. Who has priority?

5. *Handshake deal.* Casper runs a successful bookbinding business. Casper uses several marks for various services, including TIZER for making custom leather covers for first editions. Casper obtained a federal registration for

the T ɪᴢᴇʀ mark, which still remains valid. Prosper, a long-time employee of Casper, has long worked in the department that renders services under the T ɪᴢᴇʀ mark. Casper and Prosper negotiate an agreement under which Prosper will buy the rights to the T ɪᴢᴇʀ mark and associated goodwill and, in return, Casper receives a percentage of Prosper's revenue. The two shake hands and assure each other that they have a binding deal, with the transfer of rights effective immediately. Prosper then rents his own workshop and starts buying equipment. Casper then phones and informs Prosper that Casper has decided not to go through with the deal. Prosper threatens to sue for infringement if Casper continues to use the T ɪᴢᴇʀ mark, on the grounds that the mark now belongs to Prosper. Does the mark belong to Prosper? What if they had signed an agreement but had not recorded the assignment with the USPTO?

6. *Change of mind.* Salamander Manufacturing makes and distributes a number of products for construction. Among other things, Salamander has long used the trademark Yᴀʀᴅᴀɴɢ to sell bricks and mortar. Salamander's visionary CEO convinces the board to gradually get out of production and to use its distribution expertise to operate an electronic marketplace for construction materials. As a signal to both investors and competitors that Salamander intends to put real resources into its new venture, Salamander announces that it will discontinue production of several product lines, including bricks and mortar. Salamander announces that it has permanently ended use of the Yᴀʀᴅᴀɴɢ mark. It sells the production facilities used to make the relevant goods, gives away all of its remaining inventory, and assigns the staff permanently to new duties. The CEO feels such decisive action will look to the future rather than to its outmoded past activities. Two years later, with its electronic marketplace floundering, Salamander decides to resume its discontinued lines. It learns that in the interim another company has begun using Yᴀʀᴅᴀɴɢ on bricks and mortar. Salamander contends that the rights to use the mark still belong to it because it had only stopped use for two years. Has Salamander abandoned the mark?

7. *Living off the royalties.* The furniture sold under the trademark Gɴᴇʟʟ is widely recognized by consumers as meeting the highest standards of materials and workmanship. But consumers also recognize that Gnell furniture has the highest prices, reflecting the costs of its materials and highly skilled workers. Gnell's sales decrease from year to year as competitors are able to produce furniture that is only slightly inferior but much less expensive. Ernest, the owner of the Gɴᴇʟʟ mark, is unable to show a profit. Ernest decides to cash in on the goodwill of the Gɴᴇʟʟ mark. Ernest permits any other furniture maker to use the Gɴᴇʟʟ mark with no restrictions, provided that a certain percentage of the sales revenue is paid to

Ernest. Numerous furniture makers jump at the deal, and soon the GNELL mark appears on all kinds of furniture. Some makers start to use the GNELL mark without permission, and Ernest sues for infringement. Does Ernest have an enforceable trademark?

8. *Laissez-faire.* A bar claimed trademark protection in the name BUSHWACKER for a cocktail, but did complain despite notice for years that other bars made similar use of the name. To gain customers, can the bar stop the others from using the name?

9. *Luck of the Irish.* Every pub in Ireland seems to have "Guinness" prominently displayed. Guinness beer, its said, tastes a little different after export to the United States. Does the difference in the end product mean Guinness have lost trademark rights?

Explanations

1. Vertible Games, not Hanna, owns the rights to the mark. Ownership does not depend on who devised the mark, who had the idea to use it, who made the underlying product, or who actually made the hands-on use of the mark. The owner is the one who controls the use of the mark. The use of the MARNIA mark was controlled by Vertible, who directed its employees to test and market the program.

2. East Hill has priority. Priority goes to the first user of the mark. Such use may be actual use, constructive use (filing a federal trademark application gives nationwide constructive use for priority purposes), or analogous use (uses that do not support a use application but are sufficient to establish the mark in the public mind). Registration is not necessary to establish priority; it is rather one means to establish a priority date. East Hill had established nationwide priority by its nationwide actual use. Chocka Corp.'s uses (both actual and constructive) came later, so Chocka loses a priority dispute. The failure to oppose registration also does not play a role.

3. Fertilizer does not have priority over Artisan. Priority is only an issue if the marks are confusingly similar. The marks are identical word marks but are used on very disparate goods: precision instruments for scientific laboratories versus bags of manure. Fertilizer has priority for the SALT FLATS mark used on manure, but that does not bar use of SALT FLATS for precision instruments for scientific laboratories because there is no likelihood of confusion.

4. They both have priority, in a sense. The initial issue is whether there is a likelihood of confusion. The marks are very similar: FREYA BOOKS and

FREYA.COM. One could argue that the difference in the marks, together with the difference in the relevant services—bookstore services versus online book sales—makes confusion unlikely. But (and a fuller discussion would consider more facts under all the likelihood of confusion factors) confusion does seem likely here. Assuming that there is a conflict, priority depends on priority of use. Freya Books has priority based on first use through its long-standing actual use of the mark. But priority based on actual use is limited to the geographic area of such use. The mark's use is limited to St. Paul, so Freya Books has priority there. Freya.com made subsequent actual use in other areas and then made nationwide constructive use by obtaining a federal registration. So Freya.com has priority nationwide except for in the Freya Books zone of use in St. Paul. How Freya.com could limit its usage not to fall within Freya Books' zone remains a thorny question.[18]

5. A valid assignment requires a signed writing. So Prosper cannot enforce the agreement. If they had signed a written agreement but not recorded with the USPTO, the result would be different. Recordation is not necessary for validity of the agreement, rather for enforceability against subsequent parties. So Prosper could have enforced a signed but unrecorded agreement.

6. Salamander did abandon the YARDANG mark. If the owner discontinues use with intent not to resume use, the mark is abandoned. Salamander unambiguously announced that it was ceasing use of the mark and did in fact cease use. It further showed its intent by selling the relevant production facilities and otherwise halting use of the mark. Abandonment does not require a three-year period of nonuse. Rather, a three-year period of nonuse creates a presumption that the owner has abandoned the mark. But no such presumption is necessary here. The owner affirmatively and clearly abandoned the mark.

7. Ernest no longer has enforceable mark in GNELL. He licensed the mark without maintaining control over its use. As a result, the use became so widespread that GNELL lost its significance as a trademark: it no longer acted as an indicator of one source because it appeared on all kinds of furniture. Consequently, Ernest abandoned the mark.

8. To maintain trademark protection, the trademark owner must take any steps necessary to ensure that the mark remains distinctive. Some enforcement may be necessary to avoid abandonment. When the bar belatedly asserted exclusive trademark rights, the court declined to permit

---

18. This example is drawn from a case between Amazon.com and Amazon Bookstore, which was reportedly settled.

the "Rip Van Winkle" method of enforcement.[19] The term was not a trademark, because it was not associated with a single source of the drink.

9. Abandonment by losing significance of source takes more than a slight variation in product. By noting that Guinness beer tastes differently in the US, people are at the same time reinforcing the strength of the mark, by showing that they recognize a single source for the beer.

---

19. Sandshaker Lounge & Package Store LLC v. Quietwater Entm't Inc., 2015 U.S. App. LEXIS 4419 (11th Cir. Mar. 19, 2015).

Infringement and Related Rights Under Trademark Law

13

The key to trademark infringement is the standard: whether use of a symbol is likely to cause confusion or deception with a valid trademark. MEERCAT strep test would be infringed by MEERCAT used for another's' strep test and probably by MEERCAT for another's' strep treatment but not for MEERCAT used for bicycles. The scope of protection is linked to the purpose of trademark law.

The Lanham Act provides several related causes of action: It imposes liability for unauthorized use of a trademark or other false designation of origin that is likely to cause confusion among relevant consumers; for false advertising that causes commercial, competitive injury; and for dilution of famous marks. The Lanham Act also imposes liability if someone acting in bad faith registers, traffics, or uses an Internet domain name that is identical or similar to a trademark.

TRADEMARK INFRINGEMENT

The elements of an action for infringement of a mark can be listed as follows:

(1) ownership of a valid mark
(2) the alleged infringer used
(3) in commerce
(4) the mark or a similar symbol

(5) in connection with the sale, offering for sale, distribution, or advertising of goods or services

(6) the use caused likelihood of confusion, mistake, or deception.

15 U.S.C. §1114, 1125.[1] The elements for infringement of an unregistered mark are essentially the same, as discussed in the next section. Registration, however, gives a trademark owner several procedural advantages, as listed in the previous chapter.

Note what is *not* required to prove infringement: intent (no need to show deceptive intent, intent to benefit from the value of the mark, bad faith, or even knowledge of the existence of the mark); copying (independent creation is no defense, so even if the infringer devises her own mark with absolutely no knowledge of the infringed mark, that is no defense); identity of mark or of goods and services (there may be infringement even if the symbol used or the relevant goods or services are different, as long as there is a likelihood of confusion); profits or even revenue (the infringer need not make any money from her activity).

Ownership of a Valid Mark

There is no infringement if the mark is invalid (for example, because it is functional or descriptive without secondary meaning). Although registration gives a presumption of validity, defendants may challenge the validity of the mark. If the mark has acquired "incontestable" status, the grounds for challenging validity are limited. A mark need not be registered to be valid and enforceable.

The Alleged Infringer Used

The meaning of "use" here is different than the use necessary to establish trademark rights. The use need not be on the goods, containers, displays, tags, or labels. Rather, much broader categories of use are potentially covered. The statute does not expressly require that use of the mark (or something similar) be used as a trademark (used to indicate the source of goods or services). But unless the mark is used to indicate source, there usually is not the requisite likelihood of confusion. One approach is to require use of the symbol as a mark, which simplifies the analysis, by avoiding the multifactor likelihood of confusion analysis discussed below. Another approach is that any use in commerce may potentially infringe, and to resolve the issue by applying the likelihood of confusion analysis. *Compare Sensient Technologies*

---

1. The Lanham Act also imposes liability for counterfeiting of marks and unauthorized importation of goods bearing the mark, which this chapter does not cover.

Corp. v. Sensory Effects Flavor Co., 613 F.3d 754 (8th Cir. 2010) (holding use of a competitor's mark in news releases and non-sales presentations was not a use in commerce) and Rescuecom Corp. v. Google, Inc., 562 F.3d 123 (2d Cir. 2009) (holding that sale of trademarks in keyword advertising was use of the mark for the purposes of trademark law and remanding for determination of whether use was likely to cause confusion.

Example

Ill use? Was there infringement in using the mark "NAACP" in an online article criticizing the NAACP?

Explanation

Use in social criticism and commentary is not use in connection with the sale of goods or services, as required for trademark infringement, the court held, even if the site solicited donations.[2] A Web search for "NAACP" might lead to the page, but that was not the consumer confusion that the Lanham Act guards against.

In Commerce

The requirement that the use be "in commerce" applies as broadly as Congress's power to regulate commerce. As broadly as the Commerce Clause is construed, almost any commercial use in the United States is likely to qualify. Even noncommercial uses with the requisite effect on commerce can qualify. Uses outside the United States may qualify provided there is the requisite effect on U.S. commerce. A foreign casino operator's promotional activity in the United States, done to advertise its foreign holdings, was sufficient. See International Bancorp v. Societe Des Bains De Mer Et Du Cercle Des Etrangers a Monaco, 329 F.3d 359 (4th Cir. 2003).

Example

Hallatt bought Trader Joe's goods in the United States and resold them using the Trader Joe's trademark at "Pirate Joe's" in Canada, without adhering to quality controls. Could Trader Joe's recover for trademark infringement?

---

2. Radiance Found., Inc. v. NAACP, 786 F.3d 316 (4th Cir. 2015).

Explanation

There was sufficient effect on United States commerce to bring a trademark infringement action under the Lanham Act, *Trader Joe's Co. v. Hallatt*, 835 F.3d 960 (9th Cir. 2016). Pirate Joe's then actually changed its name to Irate Joe's.

The Mark or a Similar Symbol

There is no infringement without use of a mark (or something similar). For example, use of a trade name is not trademark infringement (unless the trade name is also a mark). Making fraudulent statements related to a trademarked product is not trademark infringement (although there may be other grounds for liability). But infringement does not require use of the mark itself. Use of a symbol that is confusingly similar to the mark may be infringement. So the seller of knock-off Gucci products cannot protect herself by labeling them GUCI or GUCCCI. But not all similar marks will infringe. Use of GOOCHIE, a court might hold, will not confuse consumers but rather amuse them (and leave them knowing that the products do not come from Gucci).

In Connection with Marketing of Goods or Services

The infringing use must be made "in connection with the sale, offering for sale, distribution, or advertising of goods or services." The use need not be on the goods, related packaging, or documents. It could be in advertising, in a sign in a window, in a direct marketing letter, or many other forms. Nor need the use be in connection with the same category of goods or services for which the mark is used. If YCLEPT is a trademark for tractors, it might be infringed by unauthorized use in connection with servicing tractors or in connection with SUVs, provided that the requisite likelihood of confusion is met. If YCLEPT is used for bonbons, probably no likelihood of confusion exists.

There must, however, be a nexus to the sale or marketing of some goods or services, even if not in the same category as the mark. If in idle conversation, Smart Aleck makes any number of deceitful and confusing remarks about Coca-Cola, he does not infringe the mark. The Libertarian Party of Washington State alleged that the State of Washington infringed the party's mark by using it on election ballots in a manner objected to by the party. But the court held that the Libertarian Party "has not plausibly alleged that the state uses party labels on the ballot to perform a service in competition with the Libertarian Party." *Washington State Republican Party v. Washington State Grange,*

676 F.3d 784 (9th Cir. 2012). If another party called itself the Washington Stage Libertarian Party, that might infringe the mark of the Libertarian Party of Washington State. But the Libertarian Party of Washington State does not have a general right to control how others use its mark, only a right to prevent commercial uses of the symbol as a mark.

Likelihood of Confusion

The use must be "likely to cause confusion, or to cause mistake, or to deceive." The use need not actually deceive others or cause actual mistakes. It is sufficient if the use is likely to cause confusion. "Likelihood of confusion" is a standard that lies at the core of trademark law. The "property" that a trademark owner has is the right to exclude others from using symbols that are likely to cause confusion as to the source of goods or services. If a business owns the trademark GORDON'S ROCKS for socks, the business does not own the phrase "Gordon's rocks." It rather has the right to exclude others from using GORDON'S ROCKS or similar symbols in a way that is likely to cause confusion in the relevant market.

Necessary Showing of Confusion

Infringement requires a "likelihood of confusion." Courts construe that to require probability of confusion, not just a mere possibility. The likelihood of confusion is judged from the point of view of the reasonably prudent purchaser.

In the classic trademark infringement case, there is a likelihood that consumers will buy defendant's goods or services, while being confused or misled about the source of the goods, due to defendant's use of plaintiff's mark. Seller uses COCA-COLA (or COCA-KOLA) in selling her homemade cola, causing a likelihood of confusion among buyers familiar with the COCA-COLA mark. So in most cases, the question is whether two products in the same or related markets have confusingly similar marks, such as whether TWEEDLEDUM used on umbrellas is confusingly similar to TWEEDLEDUM used on rain gear.

But likelihood of confusion arises in other settings. Courts have held that actionable likelihood of confusion can spring from implicit sponsorship, can occur at times before or after the sale, can confuse someone other the purchaser, and can work in reverse.

Implied Endorsement

The confusion must relate to the source of the goods or services, but "source" can be broadly understood (as with use of the mark by the owner to indicate source). Courts now generally accept an implied endorsement cause of action. The confusion may not be that the mark owner actually made, sold, or distributed the goods or services but rather that the mark owner endorsed them. As some have noted, this doctrine can become a self-fulfilling prophecy. If a consumer sees a mark used in marketing goods or services, she may consider whether the mark owner has authorized the use. If she assumes that every legal use of a mark requires permission of the mark owner, she would likely assume that almost any use of the mark was endorsed by the mark owner. If she thinks permission is generally not required, she would likely assume that permission was not requested.

Not all uses of marks require authorization, even if the mark is famous. See Stacey L. Dogan & Mark A. Lemley, *The Merchandising Right: Fragile Theory or Fait Accompli?*, 54 Emory L.J. 461 (2005). Rather, infringement requires that the use is likely to cause confusion. So use of a mark on products (from T-shirts to video games to artwork) may be infringement—but only where it is used as a mark and is likely to cause confusion.

Initial Interest Confusion

The "initial interest confusion" doctrine finds liability when defendant's use of the mark may attract the attention of potential consumers looking for the products associated with the mark, even though the confusion is dispelled before a sale is made. Suppose a camera store runs an ad falsely proclaiming that Kodak cameras will be on sale. When consumers arrive at the store, they find no Kodak cameras available, but other cameras are. Consumers buy the non-Kodak cameras, not because they think they are Kodak cameras but because that is the easiest route to take, having expended the time and trouble to get to the camera store. Broadly applied, initial interest confusion could apply to many uses of a mark to get attention. Some courts accordingly limit application of the doctrine, such as to use of a mark by a competitor or to uses that require a consumer to invest time or other resources before the confusion is dispelled (such as traveling to the store). There was actionable confusion when telephone salespeople initially used the mark of a competitor in making "cold calls": By the time the confusion was cleared up, the customer had already gone most of the way toward the purchase and so would be unlikely to start the process again. See *Mobil Oil Corp. v. Pegasus Petroleum Corp.*, 818 F.2d 254 (2d Cir. 1987).

Post-Sale Confusion

Liability has also been applied when the likely confusion occurs after the sale, and the party confused is not the buyer. Suppose a seller sells knock-off Rolex watches under a big sign saying, "These are not genuine Rolex watches—but they are only one-tenth the price!!!!" There is no likelihood of confusion among buyers at the seller's store because they see the sign before they see the watches with the bogus ROLEX mark. But when buyers later wear the watches, there is a likelihood others will be confused as to whether Rolex is the source of the watches.

Reverse Confusion

"Reverse confusion" has also been held to be actionable. Here, defendant's use of the mark does not make consumers think that defendant is selling plaintiff's goods. Rather, use of a well-known junior mark confuses consumers into thinking that the senior mark is actually an infringer. MIRACLESUIT was a well-established, if not very well-known, mark for swimwear. The owners of the well-known MIRACLE BRA mark for lingerie began using that mark for swimwear. There is no direct confusion because consumers do not think that Miracle Bra suits came from the maker of Miraclesuit (because Miraclesuit was little known and Miracle Bra was famous). But there is reverse confusion, the danger that consumers now think that Miraclesuit is just a knock-off of the Miracle Bra swimsuit. But in the swimsuit market, the first user, Miraclesuit, has priority. Accordingly, there is liability for reverse confusion.

Factors for Determining Likelihood of Confusion

Courts apply a number of factors for determining whether there is a likelihood of confusion. The statute does not provide a list of factors, so courts have used a list derived from the Restatement (First) of Torts (and later, the Restatement (Third) of Unfair Competition). The various federal circuits apply slightly different lists as set forth in their respective leading cases, under such names as the *Polaroid* factors, *Squirtco* factors, *Roto-Rooter* factors, *Beer-Nuts* factors, *Elvis Presley* factors, and *Sleekcraft* factors. But all courts hold that the list is only a guide and is not an exhaustive list, so courts can consider any relevant evidence. The factors:

- Strength of the plaintiff's mark (commercial strength and distinctiveness)
- Degree of similarity between the marks
- Proximity of the products in the marketplace
- Likelihood that the prior owner will bridge the gap
- Actual confusion
- Defendant's good faith in adopting its own mark
- Quality of defendant's product
- Care and sophistication of the relevant consumers

Strength of the Plaintiff's Mark

The strength of the mark refers to its distinctiveness (along the spectrum of generic—descriptive—suggestive—arbitrary/fanciful) and to its commercial strength (how strong it is in the relevant market). The more distinctive the mark, the more likely its use by others would confuse potential buyers. Accordingly, the more distinctive the mark, the stronger it is. Inherently distinctive marks are the strongest; descriptive marks are deemed weaker. First, a distinctive mark is likely to be closely associated with the owner because, by hypothesis, it is not typically used in the relevant market (otherwise it would be descriptive). Suppose a massage therapy service uses the suggestive, distinctive mark UPPSALA. If a competitor used the mark, confusion seems likely. But suppose the massage therapy service's mark is the descriptive mark SOOTHING (which would require that it had achieved secondary meaning within the relevant market). If another service uses the word "soothing" in promotional materials, it might cause confusion or might be read in its descriptive sense. Second, if a mark is distinctive, symbols similar to the mark are more likely to be seen as associated with the mark. If a competitor of Uppsala uses the term "Oopsala," it likely would still be associated with the UPPSALA mark. But if a competitor of Soothing used SEETHING as a mark, that is less likely to cause confusion as to source (although it might cause just plain confusion, which is not actionable).

A mark is not strong just because it is "incontestable." Incontestable status means that the *validity* of the mark may not be challenged on the basis that it is merely descriptive (or related reasons). A mark becomes incontestable simply because no one successfully challenged the validity of the mark for the requisite five years. But the mark nevertheless may be descriptive and therefore relatively weak.

The second aspect of strength of the mark is its commercial strength. Commercial strength refers to such factors as number of customers, recognition level among prospective buyers, market share, and duration of use. The strength of the mark may be decreased if the mark owner has not enforced the mark, leading to other products bearing confusingly similar marks. The greater the commercial strength of the mark, the more likely that use of a similar mark will confuse consumers. Contrariwise, if plaintiff's mark is barely known among the public, even use of the identical mark might not cause any confusion. Note that a mark that is descriptive (and therefore weak under the first factor) must have acquired secondary meaning to be protected; it has some commercial strength and may be so well known that overall it is a strong mark.

Degree of Similarity Between the Marks

Infringement does not require use of plaintiff's mark; use of a similar mark may suffice. But the greater the similarity, the more likely that consumers will be confused. Courts look to the "sight, sound, and meaning" of the two marks in assessing similarity (although this may have to be adjusted for such marks as fragrances). If a mark is FISH, then similar marks could be FIISH (similar on sight), PHYTCH (sound), or TRAWL (meaning)—or a picture of a fish (meaning again).

Courts consider the marks as they appear in the marketplace. The placement of the marks, colors, typeface, and other design elements may affect the likelihood of confusion. Factors beyond the mark itself, such as the use of additional trademarks, may tend to dispel possible confusion. The prominent use of the maker of the product may dispel any confusion as to source. Likewise, even close similarity may be negated by sufficiently prominent disclaimers.

Proximity of the Products in the Marketplace

The more similar the goods and services (or their marketing), the more likely the confusion. Infringement does not require use by a competitor or even by someone who sells related goods and services. But use of UPPSALA by a competing massage service is more likely to cause confusion than use by a seller of model cars. Courts look to the actual nature of the goods and services (are parties selling the same thing?), channels of marketing (do they sell through the same media?), market segments (do they target the same buyers?), geographical trading area, and any other ways in which the relevant products do or do not share a market. "Proximity" can be quite literal—the products might sit near each other on store shelves. But it may also come through other modes of marketing. If the products are different in nature but are marketed through similar channels, confusion is more likely. If the goods are in a different market but are in a category that is closely related to the plaintiff's goods, consumers may still be likely to infer that the goods are produced or endorsed by the mark owner.

Likelihood That the Prior Owner Will Bridge the Gap

If plaintiff and defendant sell to different markets, plaintiff nevertheless may have the right to sell in the other market. If plaintiff has priority in that market (as discussed above) or sells in a very similar market, courts recognize a right of natural expansion where the plaintiff might be reasonably expected to expand.

Actual Confusion

Infringement does not require a showing that consumers are actually confused or deceived. But a showing of actual confusion is good evidence that confusion is likely. But note that a showing of actual confusion is not decisive. The test is whether confusion among the relevant purchasing public is likely. Accordingly, a showing of actual confusion among a small segment of the public or confusion among persons other than the relevant buyers may not be given much weight. Indeed, if the relevant market is consumers nationwide and plaintiff can muster only a few that are actually confused, the court may make the opposite inference.

Defendant's Good Faith in Adopting Its Own Mark

Defendant may have used plaintiff's mark (or a similar mark) intending to confuse or mislead consumers. But not all copying is bad faith. Defendant may have sought to use nonprotected aspects of plaintiff's mark (such as nonsource identifying or descriptive or functional matter). With trade dress in particular, it is difficult to determine which aspects are protected.

Good faith is not a defense. Even if defendant used a similar (not identical) mark, for good reason and without knowledge of plaintiff's mark (or even reason to know about it), there can still be a likelihood of confusion. But such factors are likely to weigh against infringement.

Quality of Defendant's Product

It is no defense for defendant to show that her product was just as good, or better, than the mark owner's product. The quality of defendant's product is relevant only if it affects the likelihood of confusion. If defendant's product is obviously different from plaintiff's, confusion is less likely.

Care and Sophistication of the Relevant Consumers

Careful, sophisticated buyers are less likely to be confused or misled. Accordingly, the analysis considers how the typical buyer is likely to behave. Someone purchasing a big-ticket item is likely to spend a lot of time considering the purchase. Other purchases may be made on impulse. The impulse buyer may be more easily confused or misled. Likewise, some markets have more sophisticated buyers.

Defenses

A range of defenses apply in an action for infringement of registered marks and for violations of Lanham Act §43(a) (discussed below). Invalidity of the mark is often raised by defendant. If the mark is unregistered, or is registered but has not become incontestable, the defendant may raise any of the grounds for protection discussed earlier. If a registered mark has become incontestable, the defendant cannot argue that the mark is invalid because it is merely descriptive (or deceptively misdescriptive, primarily geographically descriptive, or is merely a surname). See 15 U.S.C. §1065 (providing that incontestable mark remains subject to cancellation for any of the grounds in §1064(3) and (5) and subject to marks with priority). But most of the other grounds for invalidity may still be raised (such as that the mark is immoral, deceptive, or scandalous). All marks (incontestable or not) are subject to the following defenses:

(1) fraudulent registration;
(2) abandonment;
(3) use of the mark to "misrepresent the source of the goods or services on or in connection with which the mark is used";
(4) fair use of the mark by defendant, as an individual's name or as a descriptive term to "describe the goods or services of such party, or their geographic origin";

(5) the rights of a junior user of a mark subsequently registered by a senior user, as discussed above;

(6) use of the mark to violate the antitrust laws;

(7) that the mark is functional; or

(8) equitable principles, including laches, estoppel, and acquiescence.

15 U.S.C. §1115(b).

If defendant establishes the fair use defense, then there is no infringement, even if there is a likelihood of confusion. *KP Permanent Make-Up, Inc. v. Lasting Impression I, Inc.*, 125 S. Ct. 542, 546 (2004). *KP Permanent* rejected cases holding that the fair use defense required showing that there was not a likelihood of confusion. The Court reasoned that it would make little sense to have a defense requiring a showing of good faith and no confusion, where simply showing no confusion would negate the plaintiff's case. So some likelihood of consumer confusion is compatible with fair use.

But evidence of a likelihood of confusion remains relevant, as the Court noted. It tends to show that the defendant acted in bad faith and that the defendant did not use the mark in its descriptive sense, both of which would weigh against fair use. So the net effect of *KP Permanent* is to leave the burden on plaintiff to show likelihood of confusion and to rebut any fair use defense.

"First sale" may also provide a defense. Someone who has purchased a trademarked product may use it. But first sale has definite limits. In *Au-Tomotive Gold Inc. v. Volkswagen of America*, 603 F.3d 1133 (9th Cir. 2010), defendants bought genuine Volkswagen badges and put them on cars not produced by Volkswagen. First sale does not authorize such a use, and there was the requisite likelihood of confusion for infringement. Consumers could be confused, thinking that the cars were produced by or endorsed by Volkswagen. Likewise, a party that resells trademarked goods may infringe if the goods do not have the same quality or warranties as when sold new.

Courts have formulated other defenses. For example, some courts apply the "nominative use" defense when the mark has been used to refer to the goods or service in question. Establishing the defense requires showing three elements:

(1) the product or service in question is not readily identifiable without use of the trademark;

(2) only so much of the mark or marks is used as is reasonably necessary to identify the product or service; and

(3) the user does nothing that suggests, in conjunction with the mark, sponsorship or endorsement by the trademark holder.

Courts have also applied a "parody" defense, holding that a use of the mark that qualifies as a parody is not infringement. Like the nominative use defense, the parody defense could be seen as a per se rule for application of the likelihood of confusion test: A nominative use or a true parodic use does not create the requisite likelihood of confusion.

American Needle v. National Football League, 130 S. Ct. 2201 (2010) addressed the issue, to what extent competitors may band together in using trademarks to exclude other potential competitors. The Supreme Court analyzed the question of when a rights holder is, for antitrust purposes, negotiating with others or with itself. The question was whether the teams of the National Football League were a single entity or competitors, potentially liable under antitrust laws for concerted action in trademark licensing. The Court held that even if the teams have to cooperate to produce football games, "the teams compete with one another, not only on the playing field, but to attract fans, for gate receipts and for contracts with managerial and playing personnel." For competitors to band together the control the market for licensing their trademarks therefore was a potential antitrust violation. The ruling has considerable impact beyond sports licensing. In many industries, competitors have to cooperate, such as forming committees to set industry technology standards. *American Needle* may play a role in separating permissible cooperation from exclusionary practices.

Free expression rights may provide a defense. The First Amendment may protect mark owners' rights to register, but it may also protect others' rights to use the mark for expression. A NORML student group had First Amendment rights to use the trademark of Iowa State University on T-shirts advocating the legalization of marijuana. The university could not establish that use of the mark was government speech, over which it would have greater control.[3] Other expressive uses may likewise be protected. Empire Distribution, a record label whose products include hip hop, rap, and R&B, claimed infringement by Fox for its fictional series "Empire, which portrays a fictional hip hop music label."[4] The Ninth Circuit held the use protected, applying the *Rogers* test. "Under the *Rogers* test, the title of an expressive work does not violate the Lanham Act 'unless the title has no artistic relevance to the underlying work whatsoever, or, if it has some artistic relevance, unless the title explicitly misleads as to the source or the content of the work.'"[5]

---

3. Gerlich v. Leath, 847 F.3d 1005, 1015 (8th Cir. 2017). ISU allows approximately 800 student organizations to use its trademarks. Defendants repeatedly stated in their testimony and other record evidence that the university did not intend to communicate any message to the public by licensing ISU trademarks to student groups. Indeed, the university licenses its trademarks to groups that have opposite viewpoints from one another like the Iowa State Democrats and the ISU College Republicans.

4. Twentieth Century Fox TV v. Empire Distribution, Inc., 875 F.3d 1192, 1195 (9th Cir. 2017).

5. Twentieth Century Fox TV v. Empire Distribution, Inc., 875 F.3d 1192, 1196 (9th Cir. 2017).

Examples

1. *Unmarked.* Optig sells sunglasses, using the federally registered trademark WESTMAN. The sunglasses are sold through various types of retail outlets. Optig advertises extensively in newspapers and magazines, prominently using the WESTMAN mark. Westman sunglasses are well known among consumers and are one of the better sellers on the market. Pyritt runs ads in several newspapers, offering Westman sunglasses at a great price. Pyritt takes hundreds of phone orders. Pyritt does not ship genuine Westman sunglasses but rather shoddily made glasses bought at a flea market that do not even bear the WESTMAN mark. Optig sues Pyritt for trademark infringement. Pyritt argues that it did not infringe because it did not use the mark on the goods, containers, packaging, labels, or associated documents. Did Pyritt make the necessary use for infringement?

2. *No goods.* Feit, another sharp operator, seeks to make money from the demand for Westman sunglasses. Feit sets up a Web site that offers Westman glasses for an excellent price, along with a ten-year warranty and insurance against loss. Feit receives hundreds of orders but does not ship the buyers anything. He simply banks the money and goes on to his next venture. When Optig sues for infringement, Feit argues that he has not made the requisite use of the trademark because he did not ship any purported Westman sunglasses. Has Feit made the requisite use of the mark for infringement?

3. *Local practice.* Panacea offers chiropractic services in Littletown, using the service mark MAGNET, which appears on signs outside and inside her office. She always treats her clients at her office on Main Street. She engages in modest marketing using the MAGNET mark, running small ads each month in a local paper and some papers in other states, distributing flyers on Main Street, and supporting the local Chamber of Commerce. Her reputation has spread over the years. About 40 of her clients travel from neighboring states to receive treatment, usually staying at a nearby motel. Another local chiropractor opens up an office near her and adopts the MAGNET mark. The newcomer advertises in the local paper and also in papers in the cities in which Panacea's out-of-town clients live; these ads offer the non-Littletownians a special travel and treatment package. When sued for infringement, the MAGNET chiropractor contends that there is an insufficient link to interstate commerce to support a federal infringement action. Did the second chiropractor use MAGNET in interstate commerce?

4. *Message board.* Dylan purchases a set of Jake tires. Dylan gets several flat tires over the next year, which he blames on the lousy quality of the tires. Dylan unsuccessfully seeks a refund, along with expenses, from Goodday, the owner of the JAKE trademark. Dylan, who lives on a busy road, puts

483

a billboard in his front yard reading, "Jᴀᴋᴇ tires STINK." Goodday sues Dylan for infringement of the Jᴀᴋᴇ mark. Has Dylan infringed the Jᴀᴋᴇ mark?

5. *Race day.* Wᴏʀᴄᴇsᴛᴇʀ Mᴀʀᴀᴛʜᴏɴ is a service mark for the well-known race of the same name. The mark is owned by the Worcester Athletic Club, known as W.A.C., which administers the race. The race has taken place annually for over a century and draws thousands of runners from all over the globe. The race course winds in and around the small city of Worcester, following public streets and cutting through a public park.

   One year, W.A.C. brings infringement actions against two local businesses. WUCK, the local television station, televised the race live, using cameras placed in various public places along the route. In the week leading up to the race, WUCK ran promotional messages saying, "Join us for coverage of the Worcester Marathon." During the race, the announcers used "Worcester Marathon" many times to refer to the day's race, to previous races, and to the reputation and history of the race. At each commercial break, a visual appeared reading, "Worcester Marathon Coverage." W.A.C.'s other infringement action was brought against Petticoat, a T-shirt merchant. Petticoat's employees were in various public spots on race day, selling T-shirts emblazoned "Official Worcester Marathon Shirt." The W.A.C. had not granted official status to the shirts. Indeed, the W.A.C. did not license any T-shirts, although it was planning to do so in the coming years, to follow common practice among marathon organizers. Did either WUCK or Petticoat infringe the Wᴏʀᴄᴇsᴛᴇʀ Mᴀʀᴀᴛʜᴏɴ mark?

6. *The mouse that roared.* A small business in California has organized promotional events for toy sellers since 1980, using the service mark Sᴄʀᴇᴀᴍᴡᴇʀᴋs. Recently, the producers of several famous children's movies formed their own animation studio. They began using the mark Sᴄʀᴇᴀᴍᴡᴏʀᴋs as a service mark for animated films for children and as a trademark for toys springing from those films. Like most people, they had never heard of Screamwerks. Screamwerks was known only among some people in the toy promotion area and was not too well known there either. Although the services rendered in connection with Screamwerks were reliable and professional, they did not draw much attention even at the events they organized. The focus was on the toys promoted. Screamworks, by contrast, became instantly famous because of the past success of its famous founders. The owners of the Sᴄʀᴇᴀᴍᴡᴇʀᴋs mark sued Screamworks for infringement. Screamworks was shocked, proclaiming that it was ridiculous that there would be any confusion about whether the multimillion-dollar movies of Screamworks were the work of Screamwerks, a little toy expo organizing outfit. Is the requisite likelihood of confusion present here?

7. *Honest fakes.* Myvatn stereos are well known, with both cachet and snob appeal. Both the technical performance and aesthetic design are widely praised. Lectra runs an ad in an audiophile magazine, offering Myvatn stereo equipment and personalized installation. She gets quite a few responses. With each prospective buyer, Lectra's representative visits the home, selects a model that matches the acoustics and the decor, and demonstrates it. If the customer is interested, the salesperson then tells him that the stereo he sees and hears is an ersatz Myvatn, made by subcontractors of Lectra and bearing an unauthorized MYVATN mark. The salesperson tells the buyer that the stereo is just as good as a genuine Myvatn, which is essentially true. Only an expert could tell one of Lectra's knockoffs from the genuine article. The buyer's visitors will not know the difference. Only the buyer will know—just as the buyer will know that she saved several hundred dollars. Sued for infringement, Lectra argues that any confusion or deceit was dispelled by the frank disclosure and by supplying goods of matching quality. Has Lectra infringed the MYVATN mark?

8. *Micro Nauts v. Micronauts.* Vasa Products, using the unregistered mark MICRO NAUTS, has for many years sold highly realistic miniature recreations of naval war vessels. The vessels are bought for use in historical war gaming. They are high-quality products that sell for premium prices. War gamers are hobbyists who enact elaborate versions of historical events, with various gamers assuming key roles. Micro Nauts are sold primarily in small hobby shops dotted around the country and sometimes in toy stores that carry hobbyist items. They are not a very big seller, by standards of recreational consumer products, but sell reliably year after year. In the hobbyist market, the mark is rather well known and immediately understood to refer to Vasa Products as the source of the vessels. To nonhobbyists, Micro Nauts are virtually unknown.

Micro Nauts are packaged in brown boxes with blocks of text explaining how accurately the models reflect the historical vessels. The mark MICRO NAUTS is prominently used in block letters. Micro Nauts are advertised in specialty publications that cater to hobbyists or to those interested in military history and also occasionally in toy trade publications. The ads, like the packaging, are full of information about Micro Naut products. War gamers range in age from teenagers to adults. They usually combine their hobby of war gaming with interest in the historical events they reenact. War gamers are quite knowledgeable about the products they buy and expect realistic depictions of the equipment.

The term "Micro" is frequently used to market toys, both hobby items and children's toys. Frice Toys begins to sell futuristic, space-oriented action figures designed for children ages 6 to 11. Frice had made a trademark search, which did not disclose the mark MICRO NAUTS. The toys are sold in bright red-and-white packages with the mark MICRONAUTS prominently used in large distorted letters, followed by several explanation marks. The packages have little text other than a few phrases such as "Astronaut Soldiers of the Future." The toys sell successfully in toy stores nationwide.

When Vasa learns of the use of MICRONAUTS, it becomes concerned about confusion between the two marks. It contacts Frice, who politely declines to stop using its mark on the grounds that it has invested considerable resources in marketing the toys. Vasa runs an advertisement in a toy trade publication that it had previously advertised in. The ad reads in its entirety: "Micro Nauts available at 10% discount from wholesale prices," together with a phone number. Vasa receives several calls, all from retailers seeking Micronauts. Vasa sues for infringement of the MICRO NAUTS mark. Is there a likelihood of confusion?

9. *Full of moons.* BLUE MOON is a registered mark for general restaurant services. Coors Brewing subsequently uses BLUE MOON as a mark for beer, using a somewhat different design but the same words. The Blue Moon restaurant chain claims infringement. Beer is often served in restaurants, they argue, so of course consumers are likely to be confused. Likelihood of confusion?

10. *Virgin territory.* Virgin Enterprises operates numerous businesses with the famous trade name VIRGIN, including an airline, large record stores, and an Internet information service. It uses the VIRGIN name on music recordings, computer games, books, luggage, and a variety of electronics products. It was on the verge of going into the cell phone business when it learned that a small operation had begun selling VIRGIN cell phones and cell phone services. Infringement or winning the race?

11. *Veuve Clicquot v. Veuve Royal.* VEUVE CLICQUOT is a famous mark for champagne. Would consumers be likely to confuse it with VEUVE ROYALE, used on a new sparkling wine?

12. *Previously driven.* Refurbisher sells used golf balls. Refurbisher buys them from enterprising collectors (including scuba divers), cleans them up with chemicals so they look good as new, reapplies the original trademark, and sells them. Refurbisher does not want to be sued for trademark infringement but wants to tell consumers that these are indeed brand-name golf balls. Can Refurbisher use the trademark without infringing and without burying it in paragraphs of explanatory text?

13. *Fair use.* Spider puts the term Coca-Cola dozens of times into the text of his Web site. When consumers search for "Coca-Cola," Spider hopes, his Web site will appear in their results. Consumers are often initially confused, investing considerable time viewing Spider's site before realizing (if at all) that Spider is not affiliated with Coca-Cola. Sued for infringement, Spider argues fair use. The text, although buried, does describe Coca-Cola, if rather repetitively. Would fair use apply?

14. *Confused computers.* Bug also uses the term Coca-Cola in the text of her Web site but only in portions that are not visible to humans. She hopes that the uses will be detected by software that searches and indexes Web pages. In fact, her page is listed in various indexes and databases. She has certainly deceived some computers, in the sense that software designed to create links to pages associated with various trademarks has linked her page to Coca-Cola. There is no showing yet that her use is likely to confuse a human. Trademark infringement?

15. *Merchandising right?* The late Andy Warhol painted CAMPBELL SOUP cans. CAMPBELL SOUP is a famous mark for various types of soup. Warhol's paintings, prominently featuring the familiar soup cans, sell for several millions times the price of a can of soup. Seeking a share, Campbell files for trademark infringement. There is no showing that consumers are likely to believe that Campbell has sponsored or endorsed Warhol's activity. Rather, consumers view the paintings as implicitly commenting on consumer society. Campbell argues that Warhol's estate is profiting from the renown of Campbell's mark and is infringing. Is Warhol liable? Should he be?

16. *Louis Vuitton v. Chewy Vuiton.* Haute Diggity Dog sells Chewy Vuiton, a humorous chew toy imitating the famous Louis Vuitton line of handbags. Is this trademark infringement?

Explanations

1. Pyritt did make the necessary use of the mark for infringement. The use required for infringement is broader than the type of use necessary to support registration of the mark. Infringement does not require use on the good, containers, packaging, labels, or associated documents. Rather, a use in commerce in connection with the sale, offering for sale, distribution, or advertising of goods or services is sufficient. In short, Pyritt used Optig's mark to mislead, not just confuse, consumers about the source of goods. Because a likelihood of confusion is all that is needed for infringement, Pyritt is liable here.

2. Feit has made the requisite use necessary for infringement. Here again, the use necessary for infringement is more broadly defined than the use necessary to support a registration. To register the mark, the owner must have sold or transported the goods or rendered the services. But to infringe, it is sufficient to use the mark (or similar symbol) to offer the goods or services for sale. Feit did so, even if Feit had no intention of actually delivering goods. Feit infringed the mark.

3. Infringement must be use of the mark (or similar symbol) in commerce. Commerce is defined to extend to the limits of Congress's power to regulate under the Commerce Clause. The newcomer advertises in out-of-state

papers, offers travel and treatment packages, and causes patients to travel in interstate commerce for treatment. Such activity takes the newcomer well within Congress's power to regulate commerce. Indeed, courts have often held that a business that is engaged in only local commercial activities often has the necessary nexus to interstate commerce. Almost any business will buy supplies that traveled in interstate commerce or otherwise indirectly but substantially affect interstate commerce.

4. Dylan has not infringed the JAKE mark. Infringement must be use of the mark in connection with selling or marketing goods or services. Dylan was not selling any goods or services, so his use of the mark on the billboard is not infringement. The trademark owner does not own the symbol in general but has a much more specific right — the right to exclude others from using it in trade in a way that is likely to confuse consumers about the source of goods or services.

5. WUCK probably did not infringe the WORCESTER MARATHON mark; Petticoat probably did infringe. Cf. *Boston Athletic Assn. v. Sullivan*, 867 F.2d 22 (1st Cir. 1989); *WCVB-TV v. Boston Athletic Assn.*, 926 F.2d 42 (1st Cir. 1991). WUCK would be protected by the nominative use defense. WUCK used "Worcester Marathon" to identify the race, did so in a way reasonably necessary to do so, and did not suggest sponsorship or endorsement by the W.A.C. In a jurisdiction that has not recognized the nominative use defense, the result would be the same because WUCK's use did not create a likelihood of confusion. Its services are so different than the services of the W.A.C. that consumers would be unlikely to think that WUCK was run by the W.A.C. or vice versa. Nor was there a likelihood of confusion about W.A.C. authorizing WUCK's use when WUCK clearly identified its sponsors and disclaimed authorization from W.A.C.

Petticoat, on the other hand, used the WORCESTER MARATHON mark in a way that was definitely likely to cause the requisite likelihood of confusion (indeed, would reach the higher level of deception). The relevant factors weigh heavily in favor of a likelihood of confusion in the context in which the mark was used: marathon race day. Plaintiff's mark would be strong (immediately recognized) and used in a context intended to cause confusion as to sponsorship by the use of "Official T-Shirt." The goods and services were quite different but nevertheless were quite close in the context of the actual use: sale of T-shirts near the race course on race day. The W.A.C. was likely to bridge the gap and go into the T-shirt business. There was actual confusion among consumers, who mistakenly thought the shirts were authorized by the W.A.C. Defendant used the mark in bad faith with an intent to deceive consumers. Even when the relevant products are quite different, infringement may be quite clear.

6. Screamworks may well be correct, that consumers are unlikely to be confused into thinking that the famous new studio Screamworks is marketing

the products of the small event organizer Screamwerks. But the requisite likelihood of confusion may be met here on the theory of reverse confusion—that the relevant public will be confused about whether Screamwerks is trying to trade on the renown of the SCREAMWORKS mark. The marks are very similar. They are also quite distinctive, which would increase the likelihood of confusion with such great degree of similarity. The products are different—animated kids' movies as opposed to staging toy expos—but related enough that the relevant public might expect there to be a relationship. Kids movies often spawn licensing agreements for toys, a closely related market to the toy expo services provided by Screamwerks. There appears to be no actual likelihood that the owner would bridge the gap, but that factor is less relevant in a reverse confusion case. Defendants had good faith in adopting their mark, which would weigh against a finding of confusion. But they declined to use disclaimers after learning of the prior use of SCREAMWERKS. The ultimate balance of the factors is hardly clear-cut here, but the stronger case seems to be that the use of the SCREAMWORKS mark would cause a likelihood of confusion as to the source of Screamwerks's services (as opposed to the normal case, where the confusion goes to the source of the defendant's goods or services). Cf. *Dreamwerks Prod. v. SKG Studio*, 142 F.3d 1127 (9th Cir. 1998).

7. Lectra has infringed the MYVATN mark. Two theories would apply here—initial interest confusion and postsale confusion. Lectra intentionally used the MYVATN mark to attract buyers looking for Myvatn goods. Both doctrines have been questioned by commentators when applied too broadly because they could interfere with legitimate uses in marketing of marks for such purposes as comparative advertising, parody, or social commentary. But this case seems an appropriate application—intentional use of the mark by a competitor to take advantage of the goodwill associated with the mark, in a way that causes consumers to invest time before the confusion is dispelled and also causes consumers themselves to deliberately confuse others about the source of the goods. Lectra allowed the confusion to continue while the prospective buyer invested time in learning more about Lectra's goods and became interested enough to purchase them. Then Lectra intentionally took advantage of the fact that others would be fooled by the postsale use of the mark, enabling Lectra effectively to sell some of the goodwill attached to the MYVATN mark.

8. Although the case involves very similar marks used on related products, there is probably not the requisite likelihood of confusion for infringement. Cf. *Scott v. Mego Intl.*, 519 F. Supp. 1118 (D. Minn. 1981). To take the relevant factors one by one:
   a. Strength of the mark: MICRO NAUTS is not a strong mark in the broad market for recreational products but is strong within the narrower

market for hobbyist items. It is not inherently distinctive. Rather, it is on the border between descriptive and suggestive. The term appears literally descriptive of miniature nautical vessels but is sufficiently abbreviated that a court might deem it suggestive. It has acquired distinctiveness within the hobbyist market but not elsewhere. Likewise, its commercial strength is small in the toy market overall but strong in the hobbyist market.

b. The degree of similarity between the marks: The literal terms are very similar. Identical in sound and almost identical in spelling, with only an extra space in Micro Nauts. But similarity is judged in the marketplace context. The packaging of the products is very different as is the packaging's typeface.

c. The proximity of the products in the marketplace: Both products are war-related recreational products. But the products are used by groups of purchasers for different reasons. A hobbyist is unlikely to purchase a toy astronaut for her participation in a recreation of the battle of Trafalgar. Nor are the markets so closely related that the mark's use should be protected to allow for natural expansion.

Micro Nauts are sold primarily through hobbyist stores. They are advertised in special-interest publications to hobbyists. Micronauts are sold through distributors to toy stores, through marketing directed at children.

d. Actual confusion: Some potential buyers evidently are actually confused by Vasa's advertisement. Actual confusion is normally probative of likelihood of confusion. But the actual confusion here occurs in a context quite different from the relevant marketplace. The ad is run outside the plaintiff's primary marketing channels and simply uses the term "Micro Nauts," stripped of its usual context and any other identifying information. The response of buyers seeking Micronauts is therefore little evidence of confusion between the two sources.

e. Degree of care exercised by consumer: War gamers are likely to be sophisticated about the products. Although they may not be sophisticated about trademark law, they are likely to know that Napoleon did not have any astronauts in his navy.

f. Defendant's intent: The defendant made a trademark search before using Micronauts. Although it continued the use after learning of Micro Nauts, it did so in good faith. There is no showing that it had intent to pass its goods off as Micro Nauts.

Consideration of all the factors led to the conclusion that there is not the requisite likelihood of confusion. Almost every factor supports an inference that the use of the Micronaut mark on futuristic toy soldiers is not likely to cause confusion as to the source of either of the products.

9. There probably would be no likelihood of confusion and hence no infringement. Cf. *In re Coors Brewing Co.*, 343 F.3d 1340, 1347 (Fed. Cir. 2003) (reversing USPTO denial of registration on likelihood of confusion grounds). The word component of the marks is identical, but the designs are somewhat different. The businesses are somewhat related because restaurants often serve beer, and some restaurants even serve their own house brand of beer. There might be likelihood of confusion if BLUE MOON were registered specifically for brewpubs. But there is a huge number of restaurants in the country. If no one could use a symbol for food or drink that was already the name of some restaurant somewhere, the costs would be great. "Blue moon" is also a phrase with many preexisting uses ("once in a blue moon," the song "Blue Moon," etc.). So a consumer is less likely to associate its use on beer with the use by a restaurant.

10. The smaller VIRGIN was held to infringe. *See Virgin Enters. v. Nawab*, 335 F.3d 141, 150-151 (2d Cir. 2003). Although it was the first to use VIRGIN for telecommunications goods and services, the use was likely to confuse consumers. VIRGIN was a very strong mark (both inherently distinctive and commercially strong). It was used to sell products in neighboring markets (electronics devices) to similar consumers. In particular, one factor in the likelihood of confusion analysis is the likelihood of bridging the gap, and that was high here because VIRGIN had been used on an increasing number of goods and services that made it likely it would be used on cell phones. All considered, consumers would be likely to confuse the marks.

    By contrast, a servicer of Apple computers in Galway called iPear (a pun on I Repair), has apparently not been taken to task by Apple. Perhaps Apple does not deem it confusing, or perhaps Apple is less stringent overseas.

11. The court held that U.S. consumers would likely be confused. The products are very similar, the markets' placement rather similar. The symbols are quite different—if one speaks French. Champagne may be bought by oenophiles and Francophiles but also by many consumers for special occasions. The typical consumer of wine is likely not to speak French and likely to confuse VEUVE ROYALE with the famous VEUVE CLICQUOT. The consumer is likely to remember the distinctive component VEUVE and to miss the distinction with the second part of the mark in another language. In addition, "Veuve" is French for widow and so is not a descriptive term for wine that competitors need to use. *See Palm Bay Imps., Inc. v. Veuve Clicquot Ponsardin Maison Fondee En 1772*, 396 F.3d 1369 (Fed. Cir. 2005).

12. If Refurbisher simply sold the balls with the trademarks, it would likely be infringement. Consumers would likely be confused (or deceived), thinking that the golf balls were new. But disclaimers can negate possible

confusion. Refurbisher should unmistakably label the balls as USED, prominently on the packaging. *See Nitro Leisure Prods. v. Acushnet Co.*, 341 F.3d 1356 (Fed. Cir. 2003).

13. Fair use requires good faith. Defendant will not qualify where the use was done solely to benefit from the mark's good will. *See Horphag Research, Ltd. v. Pellegrini*, 328 F.3d 1036 (9th Cir. 2003).

14. Computer confusion is not consumer confusion. Trademark infringement is use of a symbol that is likely to confuse consumers. To date, only confusion among humans is actionable under the Lanham Act. So Bug would not be liable. Unlike the last example, her manipulation of software is not shown to cause likely confusion among people. *See Playtex Prods. v. Georgia-Pacific Corp.*, 390 F.3d 158, 166 (2d Cir. 2004) ("Plaintiff makes much of the fact that the search function of the Web site www. drugstore.com associates 'Moist-Ones' with 'Wet Ones.' We agree with the district court, however, that 'the fact that the computer associates "moist ones" with "Wet ones" reflects little, if anything, about whether consumers are actually confused.' ").

15. There is no general right to sell merchandise bearing a famous mark. Rather, the mark owner has the right to prevent uses of the mark that are likely to confuse consumers. Warhol's paintings are not likely to confuse consumers, so there is no trademark infringement.

   Should trademark law be expanded so that a mark owner is entitled to control all commercial uses of a mark? Reasonable minds might differ, but the underlying reasons for trademark law would not support such a right. Trademarks facilitate commerce by allowing purchasers to readily distinguish one seller from another. Protection against nonconfusing and nondiluting uses is not supported by that basic rationale. Trademark also gives an incentive to build goodwill by protecting the mark owner against uses of the mark that are likely to confuse potential customers. One might argue that a general merchandising right is consistent with that policy by creating additional incentives to make a mark favored by consumers. On the other hand, many incentives already exist to create goodwill, so that incentive would likely not lead to additional investment. Moreover, additional trademark protection would have costs, by limiting the offerings of other sellers, not to mention the costs of limiting expression.

16. Not sufficient likelihood of confusion or deception, so no infringement. *LouisVuitton Malletier S.A. v. Haute Diggity Dog, LLC*, 507 F.3d 253 (4th Cir. 2007). Several factors seem to point to likelihood of confusion: plaintiff's mark is strong, the marks are quite similar, and defendant deliberately used the mark. But here defendant's use does not lure customers through confusion but rather amuses them through a reference to plaintiff's mark. For the parody to succeed, defendant's use must be similar enough to evoke

the original in the mind of the consumer. A successful parody "distinguishes itself and, because of the implicit message communicated by the parody, allows the consumer to appreciate it." A parody use of a mark is an intentional use of another's mark but not to confuse: "the intent is to do just the opposite — to evoke a humorous, satirical association that distinguishes the products."

Secondary Liability

Secondary liability is of primary importance in applying intellectual property to Internet issues. Infringers may be numerous and hard to track down. But thousands of infringers may use a single online service provider, such as YouTube or eBay. So online service providers make a juicy target for rights holders. The Second Circuit, however, held that eBay was not liable for users' sales of knockoff Tiffany products. *Tiffany v. eBay*, 600 F.3d 93 (2d Cir. 2010). It held that for "contributory trademark infringement liability to lie, a service provider must have more than a general knowledge or reason to know that its service is being used to sell counterfeit goods. Some contemporary knowledge of which particular listings are infringing or will infringe in the future is necessary."

To move beyond trademark infringement, under the "apparent manufacturer" doctrine, the trademark owner may be liable for injuries caused by goods bearing its licensed mark, provided it participated substantially in the design, manufacture, or distribution of the products. Otis Elevator Company was liable for injuries caused by an escalator made by an overseas joint venture, where Otis Elevator provided its marks and technology under a license. *See Lou v. Otis Elevator Co.*, 77 Mass. App. Ct. 571 (2010). In an era when licensing transactions are increasingly common, trademark owners frequently rely on manufacturers who can produce the goods at lower costs, sometimes in other jurisdictions.

Examples

1. *Enabler.* Frontline processes credit card transactions for merchants. Frontline knows that some of its merchants sell counterfeit Gucci products. In order to reduce complaints from credit card customers, Frontline suggests to the merchants that they have purchasers check a box recognizing that they were buying replicas. Is Frontline liable to Gucci?

2. *Is an app store like a swap meet?* Some owners of swap meets have been held secondarily liable for trademark infringement by sellers at the meet, where the owners are aware of widespread infringement.[6] Can the owner of

---

6. *See, e.g.,* Fonovisa, Inc. v. Cherry Auction, Inc., 76 F.3d 259 (9th Cir. 1996).

the app Free Kick Master mark recover from Apple, Google, and Amazon, simply by showing that infringing apps could be found on their sites?

Explanations

1. Frontline may not be selling knock-off Gucci products, but it is secondarily liable because it knowingly served high-risk clients and helped them to infringe. *Gucci America, Inc. v. Frontline Processing Corp.*, 721 F. Supp. 2d 228 (S.D.N.Y. 2010).

2. Unlike the swap meet cases, there is no showing that defendants had knowledge of the infringing activity. *Free Kick Master LLC v. Apple Inc.*, 2016 U.S. Dist. LEXIS 25478 (N.D. Cal. Feb. 29, 2016). The common law standard for secondary liability in trademark hinges on the extent of knowledge, as it is in copyright and patent.

SECTION 43(A): "FALSE DESIGNATIONS OF ORIGIN AND FALSE DESCRIPTIONS FORBIDDEN"

Lanham Act §43(a), as it is known, provides broad tools for claims of unfair competition against a person's goods, services, or commercial activities.[7] Courts have understood it to grant a number of theories of liability, conventionally grouped into two broad categories: false designation of origin and false advertising.

False Designation of Origin

Section 43(a)(1) provides a cause of action for use of symbols or false designation that are likely to cause confusion about the "origin, sponsorship, or approval" of goods, services, or commercial activities. Like infringement of a registered mark, §43(a)(1) provides liability for use of a symbol that may cause confusion about the source of goods or services. But while infringement of a registered mark requires that defendant use a registered mark in a way that is likely to cause confusion about the source of goods or services, courts have construed the false designation theory to be broader in several ways.

---

7. Section 43 of the Lanham Act appears in the U.S. Code at 15 U.S.C. §1125. Trademark lawyers often refer to sections of the Lanham Act by their section numbers in the original act as opposed to the numbers in the U.S. Code. The definitions, for example, are in Lanham Act §45, also known as 15 U.S.C. §1127.

Infringement of Unregistered Mark

A common use of §43(a)(1) is to bring an action for infringement of an unregistered mark. As frequently noted, registration is not required for protection. But if the mark is unregistered, the plaintiff does not get the various advantages of registration discussed earlier (presumption of the mark's validity, constructive notice, constructive use, incontestability of validity after the requisite five years of continuous use and the filing of the affidavit). But in other respects, the case is treated largely the same as an action for infringement of a registered mark. The basic standard is likelihood of confusion, and an unregistered mark nevertheless can be a very strong mark.

The Supreme Court has stated that the general standards for protection of unregistered marks are the same as those for registered marks. An open question is whether there are some specific differences—marks that are not registrable but nonetheless protected against infringement. If a mark is cancelled because it is scandalous, the mark owner might try to enforce it as an unregistered mark. But there are strong policy reasons behind each of the bars to registration, which apply equally to enforcing the mark. So the better view is that an unregistrable mark probably is not enforceable by way of an infringement action. A court could hold that the owner lacks standing because it lacks the sufficient protectable interest in the symbol. A court could also apply such equitable defenses as unclean hands. As discussed below, however, deceptive use of an unregistrable mark may nonetheless give rise to liability under the other §43(a)(1) theory—false advertising—if additional requirements are met.

Trade Names and Other Nonmark Indications of Source

The infringement cause of action applies only to use of marks. But one could use a trade name or other nonmark symbol in a way that would confuse consumers. Courts have held that such use falls within the broad language of §43(a). Likewise, false claims to have made the goods could violate §43(a).

The "origin" of goods and services cannot be read too broadly. *Dastar Corp. v. Twentieth Century Fox Film Corp.*, 123 S. Ct. 2041, 2047-2049 (2003), carefully maintained a distinction between copyright and trademark protection. Plaintiff's copyrights in documentaries had expired. Defendants republished the works, after removing credits to the original producers. *Dastar* rejected the claim that such action misrepresented the origin of the videos. Such a broad reading of origin would effectively give copyrighted works unlimited terms. "Origin" referred to where goods were manufactured as opposed to the intellectual creator of the goods. *Dastar* limits trademark false attribution claims as a proxy for copyright protection. Under *Dastar*, a textbook author had no §43(a) claim, where she alleged that omitting her name as a coauthor of the third edition of a book falsely described the origin of the book, by crediting her coauthors with her work. *See Zyla v. Wadsworth*, 360 F.3d 243 (1st Cir. 2004).

Examples

1. *Croaky.* A vendor of karaoke tracks sued bars that used copies of those tracks made without the vendor's permission. The vendor did not claim copyright in the karaoke tracks, but alleged trademark infringement, because its trademark would appear to users when the tracks were played. Infringement?

2. *Character.* X One X Productions offered licenses for well-known phrases and character images from such works as *Gone with the Wind*, *The Wizard of Oz*, and *Tom and Jerry* cartoons, to the discernment of Warner Brothers, who owned the relevant copyrights. In addition to copyright claims, Warner Brothers brought trademark claims. The phrases and character images had been used for trademark purposes and registered as trademarks. X One X argued under *Dastar* that the trademark claims were not permissible, as an attempt to use trademark for what were copyright claims. Trademark infringement?

Explanations

1. The court rejected the claim, reasoning along the lines of *Dastar* that consumers would not be confused about who produced the tracks, rather that the trademark claim sought the equivalent of copyright, the exclusive right to perform the works in public. *Phoenix Entertainment Partners, LLC. v. Rumsey*, 829 F.3d 817 (7th Cir. 2016).

2. Unlike *Dastar*, the relevant symbols had been used as trademarks. An element from a copyrighted movie may be used as a mark and then will be protected by trademark. *Warner Bros. Entertainment, Inc. v. X One X Productions*, 840 F3d 971 (8th Cir. 2016).

Misrepresentations Concerning Commercial Activities

Infringement of a registered mark requires use of the mark in connection with sale or marketing of "goods or services." Section 43(a) is broader, encompassing false designation of origin or false advertising in connection with "goods, services, or *commercial activities*" (emphasis added). Section 43(a) goes well beyond the core concern of trademark (reliable identification of the source of goods or services) to liability for many other categories of commercial misrepresentations. For example, §43(a)(1) can serve to protect authors against misattribution. There can be misattribution liability for presenting someone else's work as one's own (akin to plagiarism) or for inaccurately attributing work to someone else (such as by presenting a distorted version of their work). *See, e.g., Gilliam v. ABC*, 538 F.2d 14 (2d Cir. 1976).

False Advertising

The breadth of false advertising liability under §43(a)(2) goes well beyond trademark infringement by imposing liability on one that "in commercial advertising or promotion, misrepresents the nature, characteristics, qualities, or geographic origin of his or her or another person's goods, services, or commercial activities." 15 U.S.C. §1125. Courts do not require literal falsity. Explicit or implied misrepresentations suffice. But mere statements of opinion do not give rise to liability.

Suppose throat lozenges are sold under the mark Gutenberg. A competitor, the seller of Baddenberg throat lozenges, could be liable for several types of false advertising:

- False statements about Gutenberg lozenges: Competitor falsely states in an ad that Gutenberg lozenges contain hamster hair.
- False statements about Baddenberg lozenges: Competitor falsely states that Baddenberg lozenges are a cure for the common cold. Even if no mention of Gutenberg is made, it could damage Gutenberg by siphoning away sales.
- False statements in comparative advertising: The Baddenberg seller falsely states that her lozenges have 50 percent more Vitamin C than Gutenberg lozenges.
- False statements about commercial activities, a potentially broad category: Baddenberg falsely states that Gutenberg lozenges are made using child labor.

Titles and Artistic Freedom

A particular type of mark may be the title of a work. But giving one author trademark protection in the title of a work may prevent artistically valuable uses of the same title. Courts have framed three different tests to balance the interests in consumer protection and artistic freedom: (a) the "likelihood of confusion" test; (b) the "alternative avenues" test; and (c) the *Rogers v. Grimaldi* test. *See Parks v. LaFace Records*, 329 F.3d 437, 448 (6th Cir. 2003), *citing Rogers v. Grimaldi*, 875 F.2d 994 (2d Cir. 1989). The first test relies on various factors in the likelihood of confusion test to balance freedom of expression and trademark rights. If the defendant has engaged in speech that is likely to confuse consumers, then her speech need not be protected. The second test adds a safety valve for phrases that other artists need to use: "[A] title of an expressive work will not be protected from a false advertising claim if there are sufficient alternative means for an artist to convey his or her idea." Under the third test, "a title will be protected unless it has 'no artistic relevance' to the underlying work or, if there is artistic relevance, the title 'explicitly misleads as to the source or the content of the work.' "

This rule was applied to protect a video game that depicted a "gentleman's club" called Pig Pen, allegedly infringing the Play Pen mark. *See E.S.S. Ent. 2000, Inc. v. Rock Star Videos, Inc.,* 2008 U.S. App. LEXIS 23294 (9th Cir. 2008). The use of similar name and trade dress was protected under the First Amendment because it was artistically relevant and did not explicitly mislead as to source.

Standing for §43(a) Actions

Section 43(a) provides that a violator "shall be liable in a civil action by any person who believes that he or she is or is likely to be damaged by such act." Literally read, it could impose liability for almost any kind of false commercial advertising. A consumer could bring an action alleging that he was deceived by seller's advertising. But courts have read significant limitations into the breadth of the statute, rather than extending it to "any person" claiming false designation or false advertising by another. Reasoning that §43(a) is an unfair competition law, many courts have interpreted it to apply only to commercial parties with the potential for commercial injury. For a false designation claim, the plaintiff must have a protectable interest in the relevant designation. For a false advertising claim, the plaintiff must be a competitor that suffered a competitive injury. A consumer plaintiff would lack standing (not being a commercial party). Likewise, a business could lack standing if it did not allege commercial injury.

Examples

1. *Stolen name.* For decades, Lobal Crossing has manufactured and sold a number of strong-selling and widely praised models of medical instruments. Lobal ships its instruments under various trademarks, such as Waliton and Scalrex. But it has never used its own trade name, Lobal Crossing, as a trademark. It does not put the name on the goods it manufactures except in insignificant places that purchasers are unlikely to notice. But those knowledgeable in the industry readily recognize the Lobal Crossing name and give it considerable respect. Cutter, a disreputable operator, has a large number of medical instruments made. The instruments are quite shoddy due to Cutter's complete disregard for quality. Cutter manages to sell the instruments to medical supply outlets, primarily because Cutter places "Produced by Lobal Crossing" in large letters on every box. Sued by Lobal Crossing under the Lanham Act, Cutter contends that it is

not liable under the trademark statute because "Lobal Crossing" is not a trademark. Does the Lanham Act offer any protection to Lobal Crossing here?

2. *Similar description.* Handmade Glasses, a small maker of eyewear, begins to sell a new line of titanium frames. Titanium frames have become quite popular among consumers, who often ask opticians specifically for "titanium frames." The term is used frequently in the trade literature to refer to that segment of the frame manufacturing industry. Handmade Glasses decides to use the mark TITANIUM FRAMES on its new models. Its attorney advises Handmade that the term is not registrable or protectable as a mark because it is a generic term for a product. Handmade nevertheless uses the term on its glasses. When another competitor uses the same term on its own titanium frames, Handmade sues under §43(a), claiming infringement of its unregistered mark. Does §43(a) provide a cause of action for Handmade? Suppose the competitor's frames are actually aluminum, but it calls them titanium frames because consumers vastly prefer to buy titanium frames. Does §43(a) offer a cause of action to Handmade? Does §43(a) offer a cause of action to a consumer who purchases the bogus frames?

3. *Name change.* Laura Olivia lands a supporting role in the film *Troilus Unbound.* The job is her first of any note. Laura spends several months in rehearsal and filming. As the filming progresses, the cast and crew become increasingly enthusiastic, feeling that the film will be a great success. Laura attends the premiere with high hopes. The film exceeds her expectations. Her joy is deflated when the credits role because her work is attributed to "Sue Denim." The producers explain to Laura that they made the change for marketing reasons and because the director had been irked by Laura's conduct during filming. Does §43(a) offer Laura a cause of action?

4. *Bold claim.* Herbal Products sells an organic remedy for indigestion. In its advertising, Herbal Products states that the product "reduces stomach acids by 25%." Herbal Products has never done any testing to determine whether the claim is true. A competitor sues for false advertising under §43(a). The competitor does not perform the lengthy and expensive human trials that are necessary to prove or disprove the claim. An expert testifies that the claim is not supported by any scientific evidence but is not impossible. Is Herbal Products liable for false advertising?

5. *Credit where credit not due.* Stefan Ray writes best-selling detective novels and often directs the hit movies made from the novels. His name as author and director draws fans to his works without them even needing to know the basic plot of the book or cast of the movie. He sells the movie rights to his latest book, *Unfair Competition,* to Psudio Studio. Stefan also signs on to direct the movie for Psudio. Psudio's staff makes the preparations

for filming. A scriptwriter writes a script from the book, locations are chosen, and actors are signed up. Shortly before filming begins, however, Psudio and Ray have a falling out. Ray is especially displeased with the script, which makes a number of changes in the plot and dialogue, tacking on an implausible happy ending. The parties agree to terminate his contract to direct the movie. Psudio signs another director, who completes the movie within a few months. In the month before the planned nationwide opening of the movie, Psudio runs newspaper ads describing the movie as "a Stefan Ray film" and "based on *Unfair Competition* by Stefan Ray." Evidence shows that consumers understand the phrase "a Stefan Ray film" to mean a film made by Stefan Ray, in the sense of directed by or produced by Ray. Consumers are also familiar with the phrase "based on" and understand that films based on books or even historic events often vary in many respects from the underlying base. Ray files an action under §43(a), seeking an injunction against both uses of his name, claiming false designation and false advertising. Does the advertising violate §43(a)?

6. *Calumny.* The Boules own a number of paintings attributed to artist Lazar Khidekel. ARTnews, an influential periodical, prints a story, questioning whether Khidekel created the paintings. Collectors are now much less willing to buy the paintings. The Boules sue ARTnews under §43(a), alleging ARTnews misrepresented the characteristics of the Boules' goods. Is §43(a) applicable?

7. *Stolen ideas.* Software company HAL copies various noncopyrightable elements of software sold by GUS and uses the material in its own products. GUS sues HAL, alleging a §43(a) violation, for false designation of origin. GUS alleges that HAL is taking credit for elements created by GUS and falsely putting its name on them. Is GUS liable?

Explanations

1. Section 43(a) of the Lanham Act does impose liability on Cutter here, even though "Lobal Crossing" has never been used as a trademark. Cutter's deceptive use of the phrase "Produced by Lobal Crossing" makes Cutter liable under both §43(a) theories, false designation of origin and false advertising. A false designation claim need not involve use of a trademark—false use of a trade name as the source of goods qualifies. The false advertising liability is clear-cut. Cutter makes false statements in advertising that cause direct competitive injury to Lobal Crossing.

2. If Handmade Glasses uses the generic term "titanium frames" as a brand name on its product, it has no claim under §43(a) simply because another competitor uses the phrase on its frames. A generic term is not

protectable as a mark, so Handmade cannot claim infringement of an unregistered mark, one form of false designation. To put it another way, Handmade lacks standing to bring a claim because it does not have a protectable interest in the relevant designation.

If the competitor falsely uses the term "titanium frames," Handmade has standing. It does not have standing to bring a false designation claim, but it does have standing to bring a false advertising claim. Handmade is a competitor that suffered a competitive injury.

A consumer who bought the mislabeled frames does not have standing to bring a false advertising claim, even if she can show she relied on the misrepresentation. Most courts have limited standing in such §43(a) actions to competitors.

3. Section 43(a) does offer a cause of action to Laura for false designation of origin. The producers falsely attributed her services to a fictional person. Laura has the requisite protectable interest in her name as identifying the source of her services (even if her name does not qualify as a service mark).

4. A court likely would hold Herbal Products liable for false advertising, even absent conclusive evidence that the representation was false. As in other areas, falsity under §43(a) is not a matter of pure logic. Claims that are misleading have been held to meet the falsity requirement. Consumers would likely interpret the claim to mean that Herbal has done the testing necessary to support the truth of its claim. To the contrary, the claim is unsubstantiated. Hence, the claim misleads the public about the amount of evidence to support it and is therefore misleading.

5. Psudio's advertising makes two separate representations: "a Stefan Ray film" and "based on *Unfair Competition* by Stefan Ray." The first is misleading because Stefan Ray withdrew early in the making of the film and objected to the planned production. So consumers, familiar with Ray's other works as film director, receive a false impression about the role Ray plays in this film. The other claim, "based on *Unfair Competition* by Stefan Ray," is not misleading. Although the film is different than the book and different than the film the book's author would have made, such differences are commonly seen when films are "based on" books or events. So consumers are not given an inaccurate impression about the product for sale.

6. Section 43(a) would not apply. It applies only to misrepresentations "in commercial advertising or promotion." Absent unusual fact, an article in a newspaper is not advertising or promotion. *See, e.g., Boule v. Hutton,* 328 F.3d 84 (2d Cir. 2003). Section 43(a) does not go beyond unfair competition to create a general cause of action for commercial defamation.

7. Under *Dastar*, GUS is not liable. *Dastar* prevents using a false attribution claim to gain copyright-like control over noncopyrighted material: "GUS has not accused HAL of taking tangible copies of its software, removing its trademarks, and selling them as its own. Rather, GUS asserts that HAL copied the ideas, concepts, structures, and sequences embodied in its copyrighted work. In sum and substance, GUS's claim is simply a claim that HAL has infringed its copyright in LOPEZ COBOL." *General Universal Systems v. Lee*, 379 F.3d 131, 149 (5th Cir. 2004).

REMEDIES FOR INFRINGEMENT, FALSE DESIGNATION, OR FALSE ADVERTISING

Trademark infringement (whether the mark is registered or not) and violations of §43 can give rise to a broad set of remedies: injunctions, monetary remedies, destruction of infringing articles, and cancellation of registration of marks. 15 U.S.C. §§1116-1119.

Preliminary and final injunctions are available, subject to the usual procedural requirements for injunctive relief, as well as certain requirements set forth in the trademark statute. The injunction could simply prohibit continuation of the infringing activity. Courts may also fashion injunctions to allow the defendant to continue its activity while providing safeguards against further infringement or curing existing confusion. The court may require the defendant to provide disclaimers, provide customers with accurate information, or run corrective advertising. Such orders must not be so broad as to violate the First Amendment. *See TrafficSchool.com, Inc. v. Edriver Inc.*, 653 F.3d 820 (9th Cir. 2011) (ordering an infringing Web site to display a full-screen disclaimer to all future users may be so overbroad as to infringe First Amendment).

In trademark, courts may be reluctant to grant injunctions where the mark owner has dallied in enforcement. The holder of the FyreTV mark for streaming video services filed a trademark infringement action about two weeks after Amazon began using the mark, Amazon Fire TV.[8] The plaintiff then did little for five months, and then filed a motion for a preliminary injunction. The Eleventh Circuit affirmed denial of the injunction, because the unexplained delay showed that the plaintiff was not at risk of imminent irreparable harm, a necessary showing.

The statute also specifically authorizes an order that articles bearing infringing marks be "delivered up and destroyed." 15 U.S.C. §1118.

---

8. See Wreal, Ltd. Liab. Co. v. Amazon.com, 840 F.3d 1244 (11th Cir. 2016).

Monetary remedies are available for infringement of registered marks or violations of §43(a) (including infringement of unregistered marks) and §43(d) (cybersquatting); monetary remedies are available for only willful violations of §43(c) (dilution). A range of monetary remedies is available, "subject to the principles of equity," to recover (1) defendant's profits, (2) any damages sustained by plaintiff, and (3) the costs of the action. The court may also award treble damages if necessary for adequate compensation. 15 U.S.C. §1117. Courts have struggled to define the line between trebling damages as a punitive measure and as compensation. Attorneys' fees may also be awarded to the prevailing party in exceptional cases. 15 U.S.C. §1118(a).

The right to damages is subject to certain limitations. If no notice was used and defendant did not have actual notice of the mark, damages may be barred. 15 U.S.C. §1111. The statute also limits the remedies available against in the case of innocent infringement by printers and publishers. 15 U.S.C. §1118(a).

Example

Hail a taxi. Uber Promotions, a seller of party bus services in Gainesville, Florida, won a trademark infringement suit against Uber Technologies ("a nationally known taxi-like service"). Notably, Uber Promotions relied only on its common law priority based on local use, and had not made a federal registration. Should the court grant a statewide injunction against using Uber?

Explanation

Such an injunction would be far too broad. As the court put it, "a preliminary injunction should not serve as a bazooka in the hands of a squirrel."

DILUTION

Uses that do not infringe a famous mark (because there is no likelihood of confusion) may still be prevented if they are likely to dilute the mark by blurring or by tarnishment. Dilution protects the distinctiveness of a famous mark. The more distinctive a mark, the greater power the mark owner has to enforce it. Beyond legal rights, the more distinctive and well known the mark is, the greater value it has as an asset. As discussed above, the distinctiveness of a mark can change over time. An inherently distinctive mark can even become generic. The power to police infringement of the mark does not give the mark owner power to prevent many uses that might decrease the distinctiveness of the mark.

The classic example is KODAK (although KODAK is now losing its fame). Used as a mark for photographic goods and services, KODAK was a very strong mark. It was well known and, as an invented word, is generally known only in association with the Eastman Kodak Co., the manufacturer and seller of photographic goods and services. In any context, the word "Kodak" brings to mind Kodak goods and services. That could change. Suppose sellers of unrelated goods and services start using KODAK to sell bicycles, massages, or fingernail polish. A court might hold there was no infringement of the mark because there is no likelihood of confusion. It is hard to confuse a bicycle with a camera. If Kodak could not prevent the use of the well-liked name KODAK by sellers of all stripes, before too long it might be used on all kinds of goods and services. If that were the case, KODAK would no longer instantly signal the single source it once did. Rather, the goodwill created by Kodak would be reduced.

Dilution is intended to reach noninfringing uses that cause such perceived harm. Using KODAK on bicycles may not be infringement (because it does not confuse consumers as to source) but might support dilution liability.

Dilution protection was strengthened by the Trademark Dilution Revision Act of 2006. The Supreme Court had held that dilution liability required showing "actual dilution." *Moseley v. V Secret Catalogue* 537 U.S. 418 (2003). Congress subsequently lowered the standard to a "likelihood of dilution." The owner of a distinctive famous mark is entitled to an injunction against a use that "is likely to cause dilution by blurring or dilution by tarnishment of the famous mark." 15 U.S.C. §1125(c)(1).

"Blurring" is defined as "association arising from the similarity between a mark or trade name and a famous mark that impairs the distinctiveness of the famous mark." 15 U.S.C. §1125(c)(2)(B). In determining whether a mark or trade name is likely to cause dilution by blurring, the court may consider all relevant factors, including the following:

(i) The degree of similarity between the mark or trade name and the famous mark.

(ii) The degree of inherent or acquired distinctiveness of the famous mark.

(iii) The extent to which the owner of the famous mark is engaging in substantially exclusive use of the mark.

(iv) The degree of recognition of the famous mark.

(v) Whether the user of the mark or trade name intended to create an association with the famous mark.

(vi) Any actual association between the mark or trade name and the famous mark.

15 U.S.C. §1125(c)(2)(B).

One of the factors is quite different from the likelihood of confusion factors. Courts are to consider "The extent to which the owner of the famous mark is engaging in substantially exclusive use of the mark." If a mark is not just famous but unique, then other uses of that mark are, all things being equal, more likely to cause dilution.

The statute defines "dilution by tarnishment" as "association arising from the similarity between a mark or trade name and a famous mark that harms the reputation of the famous mark." 15 U.S.C. §1125(c)(2)(B). Dilution may be used to protect the reputational value of a mark: not just its distinctiveness but also its connotations. For famous mark holders, this may prove to be a more valuable tool than the core protection against dilution by blurring. Blurring threatens only harm at the margin of the mark's commercial value by possibly reducing its ability to trigger an association with some consumers. But tarnishment, in theory at least, threatens to change the very meaning of the mark itself by loading disreputable meaning to the mark's associations.

Only famous marks are entitled to protection against dilution. The statute provides that "a mark is famous if it is widely recognized by the general consuming public of the United States as a designation of source of the goods or services of the mark's owner." 15 U.S.C. §1125(c)(2)(A). The statute further provides a list of factors for considering in deciding whether a mark is famous.

> In determining whether a mark possesses the requisite degree of recognition, the court may consider all relevant factors, including the following
>
> (i) The duration, extent, and geographic reach of advertising and publicity of the mark, whether advertised or publicized by the owner or third parties.
>
> (ii) The amount, volume, and geographic extent of sales of goods or services offered under the mark.
>
> (iii) The extent of actual recognition of the mark.
>
> (iv) Whether the mark was registered.

15 U.S.C. §1125(c)(2)(A).

True nationwide fame is required, as opposed to renown within a geographical area or product market or among a set of consumers. So dilution protection is limited to a small subset of trademarks. It is insufficient if a mark is well known within one part of the country (such as certain grocery stores) or within a particular field of endeavor (such as a premium producer of luxury products well known only to the affluent or more specialized products like sporting goods) or has been the subject of massive marketing efforts, unless they have succeeded in unusual fashion.

The statute also provides exceptions that protect freedom of expression and competition. Dilution does not apply to

> [a]ny fair use, including a nominative or descriptive fair use, or facilitation of such fair use, of a famous mark by another person other than as a designation of source for the person's own goods or services, including use in connection with—

  (i) advertising or promotion that permits consumers to compare goods or services; or

  (ii) identifying and parodying, criticizing, or commenting upon the famous mark owner or the goods or services of the famous mark owner.

15 U.S.C. §1125(c)(3)(A). In addition, the statute provides there is no dilution by "[a]ny noncommercial use of a mark."

So although dilution protects against "tarnishment," it hedges by protecting speech. Others may still talk about the mark and its owner freely. Dilution requires more than badmouthing the mark owner or the relevant product. Rather, the use must trigger an *association* that harms the reputation of the famous mark. Such use could be use on products of poor quality or of questionable use.

The 2006 Act also rejected cases that had restricted dilution protection to marks that were inherently distinctive, as opposed to marks that had acquired distinctiveness. Some courts had reasoned that dilution should not lie where a term also had a descriptive sense, even if the symbol had acquired distinctiveness by becoming widely known among the relevant set of consumers. The statute now provides to the contrary that "the owner of a famous mark that is distinctive, inherently or through acquired distinctiveness" is entitled to protection against dilution of the mark. 15 U.S.C. §1125(c)(1). MICROSOFT, COCA-COLA, and other famous marks with a descriptive meaning are entitled to protection against dilution. Courts have applied dilution broadly. *See* VISA *International Service Association v. JSL Corp.*, 610 F.3d 1088 (9th Cir. 2010) (holding that the use of the mark eVisa for an English-language tutoring service would dilute the famous mark Visa for credit card services); *Starbucks Corp. v. Wolfe's Borough Coffee, Inc.*, 588 F.3d 97 (2d Cir. 2009) (Charbucks diluted Starbucks, despite far different graphics); *Super Duper, Inc. v. Mattel, Inc.*, 382 Fed. Appx. 308 (4th Cir. 2010) (SEE IT! SAY IT! used by a family-owned educational products company diluted Mattel's popular SEE 'N SAY game).

Examples

1. *Bugs.* Nails has operated several hardware stores in Camtown for many years using the federally registered service mark MUGBUG HARDWARE. A local farmer starts selling produce from a roadside stand under the sign "Mugbug Veggies." Could Nails bring an action under the federal trademark statute for dilution of the MUGBUG HARDWARE mark?

2. *The diluted beer blues.* Mershey sells a famous brand of beer, Delta. The beer is the only one sold in bright blue bottles. The bright blue color has become so well known to consumers that its primary significance in the beer context is an indication of source. Mershey's national advertising reinforces the link between the color blue and Mershey as a source of beer. Accordingly, the color blue has become quite famous as a mark for

Mershey's beer. Mershey has registered the mark blue as a color used as trade dress on beer bottles. Mershey learns that a large shoemaker has begun selling a line of running shoes in exactly the same shade of blue as Mershey's beer bottles. Mershey does not think that there is the requisite likelihood of confusion to support an infringement action. But Mershey becomes concerned that the use of the color will decrease the distinctiveness of the Mershey mark. Could Mershey bring a successful action under the federal dilution provision?

3. *New name.* Fast Food Chain introduces a new sandwich under the trademark Vivoog. The sandwich rapidly becomes famous nationwide. Fast Food Chain learns that a chain of retail stores in North Dakota has been using the Vivoog mark for several years. Fast Food Chain sends them a cease-and-desist letter, claiming that further use would dilute the famous Vivoog mark for sandwiches. Could the North Dakota stores using Vivoog be subject to an injunction for dilution?

Explanations

1. The federal dilution statute does not apply because Mugbug is not a famous mark. It is insufficient to be famous regionally or in a niche market.

2. Dilution could apply here. Dilution applies to all famous marks, whether inherently distinctive or with acquired distinctiveness. Mershey's mark is not inherently distinctive because color alone used as a mark cannot be inherently distinctive. Rather, color alone may acquire distinctiveness—as Mershey's use of blue has. But a finding of dilution appears unlikely here. It seems unlikely that the use of the color blue on a running shoe would dilute the distinctiveness of the color blue used as a mark on beer bottles.

3. There is only dilution liability for use that begins after the mark becomes famous, so the North Dakota retail chain is not liable. If anything, it has a reverse confusion trademark infringement claim against Fast Food Chain, but the markets here are so different that the requisite likelihood of confusion probably would not obtain.

"CYBERSQUATTING": ACPA AND UDRP

As the Internet became of commercial interest, many disputes arose over what has been dubbed "cybersquatting." Suppose XYZ Manufacturing is a business that has been around for decades, using its name as both a trade name and a trademark. It realizes that potential customers and others interested in the company may type *www.xyzmanufacturing.com* into their browser to find information or to try to purchase products from XYZ. XYZ then attempts to register the domain name *www.xyzmanufacturing.com* but finds it has already been registered by Cy Skwatr. XYZ contacts Cy, who offers to sell the domain name for a handsome price. Or perhaps XYZ finds there is already a Web page at *www.xyzmanufacturing.com*, which states that *www.xyz manufacturing.com* is for sale.

One could argue that such transactions are simply a healthy example of a free market in action. Cy is like a prospector, author, or inventor who first locates some valuable property. If XYZ is a higher valued use, XYZ should buy it from Cy. Others might see Cy's activity as free-riding. But the legal basis for XYZ's claim is hardly clear. In particular, even if XYZ MANUFACTURING is a registered trademark, Cy's activity might not meet the elements of trademark infringement. If he merely registers the domain name, there might not be a "use" of the mark. If he put up a Web page, that might not qualify as a use in connection with offering goods or services. And his activity might infuriate XYZ but seems unlikely to confuse consumers as to the source of goods or services, especially if he either put up no page or put up a page with ample disclaimers.

Various legal theories, ranging from extortion to unjust enrichment, have been discussed by commentators and courts. *Panavision v. Toeppen*, 141 F.3d 1316 (9th Cir. 1998), held that the owner of *www.panavision.com* was liable for dilution and ordered him to transfer the mark to Panavision. But under the Lanham Act, dilution protects only famous marks, so many trademark holders could not use dilution. At the same time, there was recognition that there are perfectly valid reasons for someone to register and use a domain name, even if it is exactly the same as a trademark.

The scope of the problem is diminishing somewhat as domain names become less important as identifiers (instead acting simply as addresses). A sophisticated Internet user looking for the Web site of the Acme Potato Co. is now less likely to simply type *www.acmepotatocompany.com* into the browser's window for addresses. She is more likely to use a search engine to find the Web site. But domain name battles continue nevertheless.

In 1999, Congress passed the Anticybersquatting Consumer Protection Act (ACPA), which gives trademark owners a cause of action against anyone who has a bad faith intent to profit from a protected mark and "registers, traffics in, or uses a domain name" that is identical or confusingly similar to a distinctive mark or dilutive of a famous mark. 15 U.S.C. §1125(d). Liability depends on showing bad faith. The statute gives a lengthy but non-exclusive list of factors to consider in determining whether defendant acted in bad faith. If liability is found, remedies include transfer of the domain name to the plaintiff, along with a range of remedies for infringement, such as damages, injunctions, and attorneys' fees.

An alternative to the ACPA is the UDRP—the Uniform Domain Name Dispute Resolution Policy, administered under the auspices of the Internet Corporation for Assigned Names and Numbers (ICANN). Domain name registrants generally must agree in their registration agreements to be subject to the UDRP. If a dispute over the domain name arises, either party may elect to take the matter to a UDRP proceeding, an administrative dispute resolution proceeding. The UDRP proceeding is essentially an arbitration proceeding that determines whether a claimant or the registrant is entitled to the domain name. In some ways, the UDRP is an inexpensive and quicker alternative to litigation under the ACPA, where a trademark owner seeks to get a domain name for a registrant. Both the UDRP and ACPA turn on whether the registrant acted in bad faith. But there are a number of differences. Liability under the ACPA requires an intent to profit, whereas the UDRP looks to a lack of right or legitimate interest in the mark. The scope of marks and domain names covered by the two differ somewhat. The remedy available under the UDRP is to get the domain name; other remedies, such as damages and attorneys' fees, normally are not available. To succeed, the claimant must show the registrant registered *and used* the domain name in bad faith (as opposed to the ACPA, where the plaintiff may succeed by showing bad faith registration or trafficking or use of the domain name).

Good faith can give way to bad faith. Newport News, a women's clothing line, pursued an arbitration proceeding, seeking the domain, Newportnews.com, which was used for news in the Newport area. The arbitration panel found no bad faith, given the dissimilarity between the two markets (clothing and news). In following years, Newportnews.com, while offering to sell the domain to Newport News, shifted its focus from news to women's clothing. The court found bad faith and awarded damages and attorney's fees. *Newport News* shows that winning the right to retain a domain does not give carte blanche for use of that domain. *See Newport News Holdings Corp. v. Virtual City Vision Inc.*, 650 F.3d 423 (4th Cir. 2011).

Trademark law and the UDRP are not necessarily mutually exclusive alternatives. Courts have held that the loser in a UDRP hearing is not foreclosed from bringing an ACPA action. However, the unsuccessful party in trademark litigation can be precluded from bringing a subsequent UDRP proceeding.

Examples

1. *Bad faith?* An automobile broker used "Lexus" in its domain names, buy-a-lexus.com and buyorleaselexus.com. The broker was not a Toyota dealer but dealt in Toyotas along with other automobiles. Would the broker be subject to losing its domains under the UDRP or to liability under the ACPA?

2. *Shift.* An employee of a clothing merchant registered a domain name, www.eq-Italy.com, for the company. The company used the site with

increasing success over the years. The employee and the company then parted ways. Not long after, any visitor to www.eq-Italy.com saw only a notice referring "all fashion-related questions" to the employee's e-mail address. The employee demanded a considerable sum to hand over the domain. The employee argued that he registered the domain in good faith and so is not liable. Is he?

Explanations

1. The dealer would not be liable because it used the domains in good faith, in a legitimate manner to describe its goods. *See Toyota Motor Sales U.S.A. Inc. v. Tabari*, 610 F.3d 1171 (9th Cir. 2010).

2. The Ninth Circuit held that the employee used the domain in bad faith. *See DSPT International Inc. v. Nahum*, 624 F.3d 1213 (9th Cir. 2010). He had registered it in good faith and had never used it to deceive potential customers. But bad faith goes beyond such classic cybersquatting to encompass other abusive practices. *Toyota* and *DSPT* together provide considerable guidance on how courts will unpack the broad standard of "bad faith."

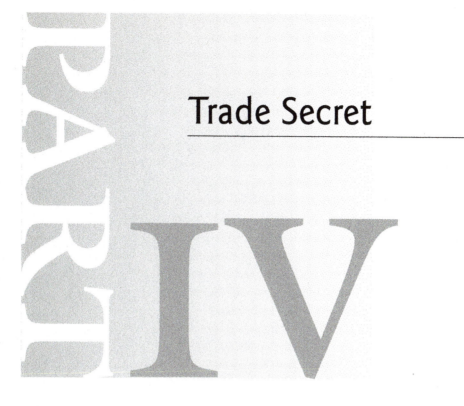

Trade Secret

PART IV

Trade Secret Subject Matter: Information with Economic Value from Not Being Generally Known

Wonka Confections guards its secret formula for chocolate. The formula is valuable because Wonka uses it to make especially delicious chocolate, envied by competitors. Wonka's formula is not protected by copyright (which does not protect functional matter), patent (because Wonka has not applied for a patent, and if the formula has been in commercial use for more than a year, any patent rights are now lost) or trademark (the formula is not a source-identifying symbol). Wonka does not have exclusive rights in the formula. Wonka, however, does have a different sort of legal protection—trade secret. Anyone who uses improper means to get or use the formula would be liable to Wonka. To keep protection, Wonka must keep the formula secret. If Wonka publishes the formula, if chemists manage to figure out the formula from Wonka's product, or even if a Wonka employee wrongfully makes it public, the formula will no longer be a trade secret.

A trade secret is information that has economic value from not being known to or readily ascertainable by those who could gain value from its use or disclosure and is the subject of reasonable security measures—in short, information that is economically valuable because it is kept secret. Some examples of information that have been protected as trade secrets are customer lists; manufacturing methods; chemical processes, formulas, and related equipment; computer program code; marketing data and strategies; blueprints for machines; geological data gained from surveys; and genetic information.

Like other forms of intellectual property, trade secret law provides an incentive for productive activity. But trade secret protection is different from copyright, patents, and trademarks, which grant exclusive rights in various categories of information (works, inventions, and marks). Such exclusive rights allow the owner to disclose or use the information in public with legal protection against others who use the information. By contrast, trade secret law does not grant a set of exclusive rights. Rather, it protects against wrongful access to information. If a business uses reasonable means to keep valuable information secret, the business may recover from anyone who improperly discloses, gains access to, or uses that information. The trade secret owner can use the information in secret, with legal protection only against anyone who improperly acquires, uses, or discloses the information.

Until 2016, there was no general federal trade secret statute.[1] Rather, trade secret law was generally state law.[2] With adoption by 47.5 states, the Uniform Trade Secret Act (UTSA) is the standard body of trade secret law, "47.5" because North Carolina has adopted much of the UTSA. Massachusetts and New York have not adopted the UTSA, but give similar protection under other law. Before the UTSA, states generally followed the Restatement of Torts.[3] The UTSA was drafted with the Restatement very much in mind, but there are some key differences. The enacted version and judicial interpretation of the UTSA may also differ from state to state. Even the general nature of trade secret law is disputed. Authorities differ on whether trade secret law is tort law, property law or a doctrinal mongrel. Whether trade secret law is seen as tort law or property law may subtly influence its application.

In 2016, Congress enacted the Defend Trade Secrets Act (DTSA), which broadened the Espionage Act of 1996 into a general federal trade secret act, providing for a civil cause of action and for a wide range of remedies. The DTSA is largely modelled on the UTSA, including the definition of misappropriation. The definition of a protected trade secret is also substantially similar, if anything broader because it exhaustively lists many types of information. The DTSA adopted the definition under the Economic Espionage Act, which tracks the UTSA definition, but also adds several categories of information (plans, designs, prototypes, procedures, or codes), and makes

---

1. Federal law does provide some criminal liability for trade secret infringement. *See* Economic Espionage Act, 18 U.S.C. §§1831-1839. The Computer Fraud and Abuse Act may impose liability for misappropriation involving unauthorized access to computers (which has been read to apply to unauthorized activity by employees). The Digital Millennium Copyright Act (DMCA) (discussed in the copyright chapters) protects some trade secrets (among other things) and also potentially reaches activity that might have been permissible reverse engineering under trade secret law. Trade secret owners may also use proceedings in the International Trade Commission to bar importations of products made using their trade secrets. *See TianRui Group Co. v. International Trade Commission*, No. 2010-1395 (Fed. Cir. 2011).

2. On the origins and the state of the art of trade secret law, *see* Roger M. Milgrim, *Milgrim on Trade Secrets* (Supp. 2002).

3. As of 1995, the *Restatement* (Third) of Unfair Competition also seeks to restate the common law of trade secrets.

clear that the protected secret may be stored in any form: "whether tangible or intangible, and whether or how stored, compiled, or memorialized physically, electronically, graphically, photographically, or in writing." The DTSA will affect trade secret practice. First, the DTSA provides a federal cause of action and nonexclusive federal jurisdiction over trade secret cases.[4] Jurisdiction extends to the limits of Congress's Commerce Clause powers.[5] Almost all trade secret cases have a commercial element, so federal jurisdiction will generally be available. The DTSA provides double damages for willful misappropriation and *ex parte* seizures with a strong showing of need. The Act makes clear that trade secrets may be protected from disclosure in litigation, such as through protective orders. The Act also provides certain safeguards, such as limits on remedies that would prevent someone practicing their profession and protections for whistleblowers. The DTSA also provides that an injunction may not issue "merely on the information the person knows," rather requiring a showing of threatened misappropriation, thereby rejecting the doctrine of "inevitable disclosure."[6] The DTSA, unlike patent and copyright, does not preempt state law.

The role of trade secret law is often contrasted with patents. In some cases, a business must choose between patent protection (disclose the information to the world in exchange for exclusive rights for a period of time) or trade secret protection (keep it secret and have trade secret protection as long as it remains a valuable secret). In some cases, there is no choice. Sometimes patent protection is unavailable. Much valuable but nonpatentable information (such as products or processes that are not sufficiently novel or nonobvious to patent, compilations of data such as customer lists, or ideas) can be protected as trade secrets. Likewise, some valuable information (such as the design of a product or a method of doing business that would be observable by others) cannot be utilized as a trade secret because use of the information will make it known to others. If there is a choice between seeking a patent and keeping the information secret, several factors affect the likely costs and benefits. *See* Andrew Beckerman-Rodau, *The Choice Between Patent Protection and Trade Secret Protection: A Legal and Business Decision*, 84 J. Pat. & Trademark Off. Socy., 371 (2002). Patent rights are broader but require meeting the substantive and procedural requirements of the patent process. Patents can also be very expensive to enforce. By contrast, the trade secret owner does not file a trade secret application or registration with any government office. To the contrary, she keeps the information secret. Nor does she face the various time constraints of patent law. There are no deadlines for acquiring protection (like the requirements of novelty

---

4. 18 U.S.C. §1836(b)(1). "Private Civil Actions. An owner of a trade secret that is misappropriated may bring a civil action under this subsection if the trade secret is related to a product or service used in, or intended for use in, interstate or foreign commerce."
5. *Id.*
6. 18 U.S.C. §1836(b)(3)(A)(I)–(II).

and statutory bars). Nor does a trade secret expire after a term of years. But the fact that no registration process is involved does not mean that obtaining trade secret protection is easy. It may require much broader efforts by instituting an entire program to create and administer reasonable measures to keep the information secret, while at the same time permitting access to employees and others to exploit the information. *See* Jerry Cohen & Alan S. Gutterman, *Trade Secrets: Protection and Exploitation* (1998). The trade secret is protected only as long as it has economic value, remains secret (which may be difficult if competitors can reverse engineer the information or develop the information independently or if use of the information requires disclosing it to numerous people), and reasonable security measures are taken.

Information licensing intersects with several branches of intellectual property law. Where copyright does not protect a database, a party may think of trade secret. But trade secret has its own requirements. Parties may claim information as a trade secret because it is valuable to them, without a showing that they have taken the steps necessary to secure trade secret protection. There was no trade secret for a database consisting primarily of information available to the public, without any showing that the defendant had hacked or copied information that was not from the public sources.[7] Database owners may often license access to the information in a database. That may create contractual obligations on the part of licensees, but does not, of itself, confer trade secret status on the information. Trade secret did not protect a database consisting primarily of information available to the public from the state.[8] So the contractual protections will not give the information trade secret status, meaning that parties not bound by the contract are free to acquire and use the information. A party cannot simply proclaim information to be proprietary and make it illegal for others to use the information, unless they are bound by a contract or other legal duty.

Atlantic Research Marketing Systems v. Troy, No. 2011-1002 (Fed. Cir., October 6, 2011) presented a logic problem reminiscent of Raymond Smullyan, with considerable practical implications for the overlap between patent and trade secret protection.[9] Atlantic Research patented a free-floating handguard for military rifles, which allowed devices like laser targeting systems to be attached to the rifle without the hazards of direct attachment to the rifle barrel. Atlantic Research sued a former employee for selling a competing rifle, which featured a free-floating handguard with a single clamp. Atlantic Research claimed both patent infringement (on the theory that the single-clamp handguard fell within the scope of its patent) and trade secret misappropriation (on the theory that the single-clamp handguard was a trade secret, subject to the

---

7. Infogroup, Inc. v. Database LLC, 95 F. Supp. 3d 1170 (D. Neb. 2015).
8. Id.
9. *See, e.g.,* Raymond Smullyan, *What Is the Name of This Book?* (1978).

employee's nondisclosure agreement). In short, Atlantic contended that it had published the single-clamp invention and that it had maintained the single-clamp invention as a trade secret. The defendant made symmetrically inconsistent arguments, that the patent had disclosed the single-clamp invention and that the patent failed to sufficiently disclose the single-clamp invention. As the court wryly put it, "These conflicting positions left little room for either party to prevail on both claims." The court held that the invention was not sufficiently disclosed to be covered by the patent but by the same token could qualify as a trade secret. The practical impact of the case is that it supports the use of both patent and trade secret protection for related technology.

TYPICAL TRADE SECRET CASES

The following examples give several typical trade secret disputes. The vast majority of trade secret actions are brought by businesses, although the law (as discussed below) is now broad enough that some types of noncommercial information are potential trade secrets.

Business vs. Former Employee

This is perhaps the most common trade secret case. Employee leaves her employment with Employer (sometimes together with several colleagues) and starts her own business or works for a competitor of Employer. Employer files a trade secret action, arguing that Employee is using Employer's trade secrets (such things as customer lists, manufacturing processes, business plans, or methods). Employee likely counters with one of two arguments: (1) that the information at issue was not a trade secret of Employer (because it was information Employee knew independently, was already generally known in the industry, was readily available from public sources, or was not sufficiently protected because Employer did not take reasonable measures to keep the information secret) or (2) that Employee had no duty of confidentiality (she signed no confidentiality agreement and was not in a position in which confidentiality would be implied), so her disclosure and use of the information is not wrongful.

Employer vs. Next Employer

Like the last example, except the defendant is the business that "raided" Employer and hired away Employee to gain access to the trade secrets that she knew.

Business vs. Former Partner or Former Potential Partner

Disputes over rights to information frequently arise after relationships between businesses end. Business may have a supplier, joint venture party, investor, or simply another business that negotiated a potential transaction that fell through. Information was disclosed (so the supplier knew what chemicals to supply, so the joint venture party could have information to do its part of the project, so investor knew the value of the business, or in negotiation, so the parties could each decide if they wanted to go forward). When the relationship ends, the other party continues in the same industry, and Business alleges that it is using trade secrets acquired from Business in its new activity.

Inventor or Author vs. Business

A number of trade secret cases arise in this setting: An individual discloses an idea to Business (for example, a manufacturing process or a movie idea). Individual subsequently claims that Business has used the idea without compensation. Among other theories (such as contract or implied contract), Individual argues that Business has misappropriated his trade secret. Business's likely defenses are that Business did not use the idea (rather, used a different idea or developed the same idea independently), that the idea was not a trade secret (rather, was already generally known or easily developed), or that Business did not misappropriate the idea (rather, Individual freely disclosed it without an explicit or implicit expectation of confidentiality or compensation).

Business vs. Competitor

Business files a trade secret action against a competitor, accusing it of using improper means to gain access to Business's trade secret. Alleged improper means might include bribery of employees, theft of documents, unauthorized access to Business's computer network, or deceitful means to gain information (pretending to be a potential investor or employee). Borderline cases have included the use of aerial photography and old-fashioned dumpster diving for documents.

Business vs. Person Who Makes Information Public

Business finds that sensitive information has been made public by an employee or someone else who gains access to the information. It might be details of business transactions, the computer code intended to guard against copying of the products that Business sells, information from a confidential investigation of possible wrongdoing by Business, or publication of documents normally only shown to clients of Business. When the defendant is not using the information in a business of her own, whether the information is a trade secret (as opposed to other types of confidential information) is likely to be an issue. Whether the acquisition or disclosure was improper may also be an issue. In addition to the usual trade secret law issues, there may be First Amendment considerations.

Business vs. Agency or Court

Whether information qualifies as a trade secret may be litigated in contexts other than Business trying to enforce its rights against misappropriators. Rather, Business may claim information is a trade secret to prevent its disclosure by a governmental agency, through discovery in litigation, or in other contexts. If the information is disclosed to the public, it is no longer a secret.

SUBJECT MATTER OF TRADE SECRET PROTECTION

The UTSA defines "trade secret" as follows:

> "Trade secret" means information, including a formula, pattern, compilation, program, device, method, technique, or process, that:
> (i) derives independent economic value, actual or potential, from not being generally known to, and not being readily ascertainable by proper means by, other persons who can obtain economic value from its disclosure or use, and
> (ii) is the subject of efforts that are reasonable under the circumstances to maintain its secrecy.

UTSA §1(4).

Trade Secret Must Be Information

The UTSA defines trade secrets to be "information, including a formula, pattern, compilation, program, device, method, technique, or process." UTSA §1(4). This gives a nonexclusive list of categories of potential trade secrets. A "Treasure Map" drawn by a geologist showing the likely location of a large natural gas field was a trade secret. *Lamont v. Vaquillas Energy Lopeno Ltd., LLP*, 421 S.W.3d 198 (Tex. App. 2013). Although information need not necessarily fall into one of the categories to be protected, the UTSA list covers the vast majority of reported cases.

Formula

A chemical formula is a common sort of trade secret, appearing in numerous reported cases. But a formula could cover many other expressions, such as a recipe or an algorithm.

Pattern

"Pattern" appears most often in trade secret cases to refer to the drawings necessary to make a machine or manufacture.

Compilation

If Datagather compiles a database of useful information, she can expect little protection from copyright because facts are not original. The information itself is not copyrightable, although the selection and arrangement may be. But a compilation of facts can be protected as a trade secret. Even if the facts themselves are publicly accessible, "a unique compilation of that information, which adds value to the information" may qualify as a trade secret. *Capital Asset Research v. Finnegan*, 160 F.3d 683 (11th Cir. 1998). Compilations such as customer lists, marketing data, and geological information are indeed frequently litigated, but information that is available to the public in the same form is not protectable.

Trade secret law grows in importance in the age of data (and the nonpatentability of natural DNA sequences). A valuable database of deer DNA was protected by an injunction:

> NADR's member list, deer genetic information, and deer lineages are its trade secrets. NADR expended significant time and effort in creating its Registry. Cassidy and Lyon each recognized that no other deer registry has as many as 230,000 animals. Further, NADR took significant steps to keep its biological materials, genetic information, genotype analysis data, and membership directory secret. NADR's efforts have been memorialized in three contracts it had with DNAS and in the previous agreements of the North American Deer Farmers Association and Texas Deer Association.[10]

Program

Computer programs can be trade secrets. If the program resides on the owner's network, keeping it secret is mainly a matter of limiting access. But

---

10. N. Am. Deer Registry, Inc. v. DNA Solutions., Inc., 2017 U.S. Dist. LEXIS 84687, at *20-21 (E.D. Tex. June 2, 2017).

even computer programs that are publicly distributed to customers may be distributed only in a machine language form that is difficult at best to read by hand. So a business may claim a trade secret in the source code version that it does not distribute.

Device

The design of a machine or manufacture could qualify as a device. The idea must be sufficiently concrete to have value. The idea of a time machine could not be a trade secret. The design of a functional time machine would be.

Method, Technique, or Process

A way of doing something can be very valuable information. Manufacturing processes, business methods, techniques for treating materials, and other processes are common trade secrets. A business that has a better way of doing something may have an advantage over its competitors. It can maintain that advantage by keeping the process to itself as a trade secret.

"Method, technique, or process" can include "know-how"—a vague category, "the cumulative knowledge and experience" necessary to operate a particular process or machine. An important subject matter area that is deemed not to be "know-how" is the general professional skill and knowledge of an employee. Suppose an employer trains employee (either explicitly or through on-the-job-learning). Identifiable information disclosed to the employee may qualify as trade secrets. But the overall increase in the employee's knowledge level cannot be captured by trade secret law: An employee's "aptitude, his skill, his dexterity, his manual and mental ability, and such other subjective knowledge as he obtains while in the course of his employment, are not the property of his employer and the right to use and expand these powers remains his property." *Pittsburgh Cut Wire v. Sufrin*, 350 Pa. 31 (1944).

Information Must Have Value

Courts look to a number of factors to determine if information has value:

- *Value to plaintiff's business*
- *Expert testimony*
- *Costs of developing the information:* Sunken costs may be water under the bridge, but if the information costs money to develop, that shows someone was willing to pay for it (namely plaintiff).
- *Licensing by others:* The willingness of others to pay fees for access to the information (either directly or for products or processes dependent on the information) is concrete evidence of value.

- *Costs of security:* The willingness of plaintiff to expend resources to keep the information secret is evidence of its value as a trade secret.
- *Improper acquisition:* The fact that defendant was willing to breach commercial ethics (and perhaps also expend some resources in so doing) indicates that defendant also believed the information had value.
- *Improper use:* The fact that defendant chose to use the information likewise shows that it has some value.
- *Costs for others to develop the information:* Even if plaintiff acquired the information by accident or gift, it may be valuable for others who are not so lucky.

There may be other relevant factors in individual cases.

Trade Secret Must Have "Economic" Value

Under the UTSA, information qualifies as a trade secret only if it has independent economic value. This sets a limit but a broad one. The breadth can best be shown by comparison to the Restatement definition, which takes a more narrow view of trade secret law as an unfair competition doctrine:

> A trade secret may consist of any formula, pattern, device or compilation of information which is used in one's business, and which gives him an opportunity to obtain an advantage over competitors who do not know or use it.

Restatement (First) of Torts §757 cmt. b.

The Restatement definition contains several limitations that the UTSA chose not to adopt. The Restatement would cover such common trade secrets as customer lists, manufacturing processes, plans for machines, chemical formulas, and marketing data. But the UTSA definition, requiring only "economic value," is broader in several respects:

Information Not in Continuous Use

A trade secret could be a one-time event, such as information relating to a corporate merger.

Information Not in Positive Use

"The definition includes information that has commercial value from a negative viewpoint, for example the results of lengthy and expensive research which proves that a certain process will not work could be of great value to a competitor." UTSA Comments to §1.

Information Not in Use in a Business

The category of information with economic value is broader than "in use in business." An investor buying for his retirement fund might not be deemed to be "in business," but valuable information he creates through research and analysis could be a trade secret. A church might not be a business, but its closely guarded information might have economic value in attracting adherents or donations.

Information Not Yet in Use

The UTSA includes information with economic value, "actual or potential." The information need not be in use. Information may still have demonstrable value even if it is still the subject of research or development and has not yet been commercialized.

Information That Does Not Give a Competitive Advantage

Under the Restatement, information must offer a competitive advantage. By not using this limitation, the UTSA is broader in two ways. First, the information need only be valuable; it need not be better than whatever the competitors use. Second, and more important, the information need not be valuable to competitors; it could be valuable if there is any class of users that could exploit it. Trade secret liability under the UTSA goes well beyond unfair *competition* to other wrongful exploitation of information.

The UTSA dispenses with many of the limitations of the Restatement, broadening the potential scope of trade secret law. The major limitation left is the requirement that the value be "economic." Accordingly, trade secret law is not a general tool to enforce duties of confidentiality. Lawyers may know secrets of their clients, AA members of their fellow members, spouses of each other. But many of those secrets do not have economic value as used in the UTSA. How broad the category of "economic" value remains to be seen as the case law develops.

Economic Value Must Be "From Not Being Generally Known"

The information cannot qualify as a trade secret unless it is not generally known, or readily ascertainable by, those who could economically exploit it. Trade secret does not require absolute secrecy. Even if more than one competitor in an industry knows the information, it may qualify as a trade secret provided it is not *generally* known. *See* UTSA Comments to §1.

The information need not be known among the public to be unprotectable as a trade secret. Rather, the relevant group is that which "can obtain economic value from its disclosure or use." The standard method of powering the space shuttle is not generally known, but it is generally known to rocket scientists. So a rocket scientist could not protect it as a trade secret. Conversely, information may be known in one field but not in another. Someone who engages in a form of information arbitrage (buying low in one area, selling high in another) could potentially have a trade secret. But the showing would be high. The group that knew the information would have to be unable to benefit from it economically.

Generally known information is not a trade secret. A business may have information that it deems valuable and confidential. It may take various measures to maintain that confidentiality. But unless the information has economic value to others from its disclosure or use, it cannot be a trade secret. A common manufacturing method might be valuable to a steel maker in the sense that the steel maker uses the method every day. But if the method is generally known in the industry, it lacks value in the trade secret sense.

The court must not disregard the forest for the trees. A trade secret may be a compilation or collection of public information. Even if all the individual elements are not secrets, the way that plaintiff has put them together may create independent value. *See Harvey Barnett Inc. v. Shidler*, 338 F.3d 1125 (10th Cir. 2003) (compilation of known elements concerning infant swim classes may be trade secret).

The broad "economic value" standard still requires specificity. Courts require that a trade secret plaintiff be able to specify the allegedly misappropriated information. It is not enough for plaintiff to show that a trusted employee, with long-standing access to the business's most confidential information, has left and joined a competitor. For a trade secret remedy, the plaintiff must be able to show specific confidential information. The value requirement is consistent with this rule.

Even if the holder does not plan to commercialize the information, it still may have the requisite "actual or potential" value. A nonprofit organization that guards valuable demographic or personal information could have a trade secret even if it does not seek to make money from direct marketing firms.

Information Must Not Be "Readily Ascertainable" by Others

Even if competitors do not have actual knowledge of the information, it is not a trade secret if it is "readily ascertainable." The UTSA is more restrictive here than the Restatement, which required actual knowledge (as do some enactments of the UTSA). This qualification jibes well with the requirement of actual value. If information is readily ascertainable, it cannot be too valuable. The UTSA Comments provide examples of information that is readily ascertainable. Information is readily ascertainable if it can be found easily in published sources such as trade journals or reference books. Information about a product often may be discerned by examining the product. Likewise, a business's customer list would be readily ascertainable if the customers readily identified themselves to competitors or could be quickly identified through public sources.

"Readily ascertainable" means easy and relatively cheap. If a competitor would have to hire experts to conduct lengthy, expensive work to duplicate the information, it is not "readily ascertainable." To the contrary, such costs of duplication tend to show that the information indeed has value. The information must also be readily ascertainable "by proper means." It might be quick and relatively cheap to bribe the right employee or burgle an office, but that does not make the information "readily ascertainable." If improper means must be used to acquire the information, it is not deemed readily ascertainable.

Examples

1. *Man bites dog.* The most common trade secret case is a business contending that a former employee (and/or her new employer) has misappropriated the business's trade secrets. Could a trade secret action involve a former employee contending that her former employer has misappropriated the employee's trade secret?

2. *Cache.* Tycoon owns an invaluable ancient Roman coin. Tycoon occasionally allows the coin to be exhibited at museums but generally prefers to leave it sitting locked in a special vault in his basement. The image from the face of the coin is used to advertise the wares of Tycoon's textile factory, so it is closely associated with the business by buyers. One evening, Katz breaks into the home while Tycoon is away, busts open the vault, and steals the coin. Tycoon contends that Katz has misappropriated a trade secret. Was the invaluable coin, locked in a vault, a trade secret?

3. *Ratchet.* Kensington Manufacturing is able to produce concentrated kiwi juice more efficiently than any of its competitors. Kensington's advantage lies in the special design of its pulping machines. The machines use a special double-helix kiwi shredder, which permits the machines to perform faster and more reliably than other pulping machines. Kensington has not patented the shredders but has very carefully limited access to them, so no competitor has been able to copy the design. A Kensington employee, however, steals one of the shredders while it was taken out for maintenance, despite stringent security measures. The employee sells

it to Brainerd Juice, a competitor. Kensington sues for trade secret misappropriation. Brainerd and the employee contend that no information was taken and hence no trade secret was misappropriated. Could selling a piece of metal be misappropriation of a trade secret?

4. *Process of elimination.* Farmajohn, a biotech firm, is searching for a cure for toesles, a painful foot condition. Widely known research indicates a strong probability that some chemical in the volgon group (a group of over 500 related compounds) may prove effective. Farmajohn, in six years of extensive research, has tested some 400 members of the volgon group without success. Farmajohn is continuing with its testing among the other 100 compounds. It is likely (although not certain) that at least one will lead to a marketable treatment. Farmajohn has maintained strict secrecy about the result of its testing, although it is known that Farmajohn has long been working in the area.

Sevenmill, another biotech firm, has recently begun similar research. Suspecting that Farmajohn is ahead, Sevenmill burglarizes Farmajohn's offices and makes off with the lab records. Sevenmill is disappointed to find that it was not able to get information about a positive result. Sevenmill is even more disappointed when it is sued for misappropriation of trade secrets. Sevenmill contends that it has not taken valuable information but only information about negative tests. Does the failure to find a positive result in six years of testing qualify as information with economic value and as a potential trade secret?

5. *Trash value.* Film Star has a personal assistant, PA, who has signed a confidentiality agreement. PA nevertheless sells Film Star's address book to Tabloid. Film Star uses the addresses strictly for social purposes, not for any career or business uses. Indeed, because it contains a number of dubious characters and because of a desire for privacy, Film Star never discloses the information contained in her address book. She is greatly pained by the disclosure. Film Star sues for trade secret misappropriation. Defendants PA and Tabloid argue that no trade secret exists because the information does not have economic value to Film Star.

6. *Peace of mind.* Funeral Services decides that a profitable line of business is to offer prepaid funerals. A potential customer pays a fixed fee and then knows that her future services are arranged for. The idea is one that has been widely discussed in the industry, but no business has yet invested in the necessary marketing and other changes to the normal way of doing business. Funeral Services, however, has a go-getter marketing director who has raised the necessary enthusiasm at the firm to introduce the new line of business. Funeral Services maintains strict security about its plans to offer prepaid funerals. Just before the new plan takes effect, the marketing director quits and goes to work for a competitor, who immediately rolls out a prepaid funeral plan. Meanwhile, absent the person

who had been the driving force, Funeral Services loses momentum and drops its plans. Funeral Services learns that the marketing director had for months been persuading the competitor to go into the prepaid business (although she had not passed on any information about Funeral Service's plans). Funeral Services wishes to sue for misappropriation of a trade secret. Was a trade secret taken?

7. *Outside reading.* Molar Engineering is a specialty journal for bioengineers working in the area of orthodontics. One subscriber is Fuzzy, a researcher at a dental institute. His wife Wuzzy works for an archeological reconstruction firm. One night, suffering from insomnia, Wuzzy leafs through an issue of *Molar Engineering.* She happens to run across a description of an obscure dental reconstruction process, which she instantly realizes could be used in restoring antique ceramics. She brings the article to work, and the workers in her department begin using the process with great success. No ceramics restorer would have thought to consult such a source for guidance. Because the process gives the firm an advantage over competitors, the firm maintains strict secrecy about the process. One technician, envious of a big bonus given to Wuzzy, sells the information to a competitor. In the ensuing trade secret case, the defendants contend that the process is not a trade secret because it had been published in a journal. Could a published process be a trade secret?

8. *A list.* Business keeps a mailing list of all the residents in Business's area. It is well known that the list is available for a $10 fee at the town hall. Although the list is inexpensive, it is an indispensable part of Business's marketing operations. Business keeps its copy under lock and key. It also keeps a backup copy in a secure location. Does the list have the necessary economic value to qualify for trade secret protection?

9. *Life list.* Mail Order has various specialized lists, all compiled from publicly available sources. It has lists of traveling bird watchers, of registered Democrats who own cats, of former high-school track stars, of wealthy amateur astronomers. Obtaining the lists is costly because skilled researchers have to comb through mountains of public data. But clients of Mail Order pay hefty licensing fees to have mailings sent. Mail Order does not permit its clients access to the lists; rather it sends the mailings out itself. Mail Order keeps the lists subject to stringent security measures. Competitor obtains the lists through trespass and trickery. Competitor argues that the lists are not protected trade secrets; rather, the information is available from public sources and hence readily ascertainable. Is the information readily ascertainable?

10. *Shortcut.* Soda Jerk sells a popular soft drink, Waterberry. It carefully guards the formula for Waterberry. An employee of Soda Jerk, however, obtains the formula from the safe and sells it to a competitor.

When Soda Jerk seeks to recover from the employee and the competitor for misappropriation, they present expert evidence that a team of skilled chemists, working with considerable resources over several months, could have reverse engineered the formula. Accordingly, they argue, the formula is readily ascertainable and not a trade secret. Is the formula readily ascertainable?

11. *Bit of luck.* Tist, a chemist, works for Steely Wheel, a chemical manufacturer. One day, Tist mistakenly sets the pressure for a magnoodium process at ten times the normal pressure used in standard industry procedure. Contrary to all the research on the subject, the new setting causes the process to produce a highly purified form of magnoodium. Tist bashfully informs the chief of engineering, and soon Steely Wheel is selling the purest magnoodium on the market. Steely Wheel maintains strict security about its new high-pressure process. Competitors are dumbfounded at the new product and spend several years fruitlessly trying to independently match the purity of Steely Wheel's product. Nothing in the relevant published research is helpful to the competitors. A competitor devises an elaborate scheme to get the process. The competitor manages to get a spy, the competitor's best chemist, hired by Steely Wheel. The spy spends two years gaining the trust of his new employers and manages to get assigned to the magnoodium department (which has several vacancies, caused by the competitor hiring away chemists for large salaries). Finally, the spy is entrusted with the details of the high-pressure process. The competitor subsequently argues that there is no trade secret because Steely Wheel discovered the information purely by accident. Is the high-pressure process a trade secret?

12. *Inside track.* Learning Curve Toys develops a concept for a noise-producing toy railroad track. The track has cross-cuts and changes in its surface that make it look, feel, and sound different than generic tracks. Learning Curve meets with Playwood Toys to discuss the potential new product. Playwood agrees not to use or disclose Learning Curve's idea. The parties do not carry through any further plans. Playwood next sells "Clickety-Clack Track," which incorporate Learning Curve's concept. Sales skyrocket. Sued for trade secret infringement, Playwood argues that a noisy railroad track cannot be a trade secret. Can it?

13. *Clean secret.* TeleChem, like others in the technology business, uses a "clean room" for sensitive tasks. TeleChem constructs its room in secrecy. It puts the room together out of elements already known in the industry. But TeleChem invests a great deal of money designing and constructing a combination of those elements that is not generally known. Competitors know that TeleChem's clean room operates very efficiently but cannot figure out the room's details by examining TeleChem's product. TeleChem discloses the details of the clean room, in confidence, to a

joint venture partner. After the joint venture goes on the rocks, the partner seeks to continue using the information. There is no trade secret in a clean room, the partner argues: Clean rooms are common in the industry, and every element of TeleChem's room is found in other rooms. Does TeleChem have a trade secret in its clean room?

14. *Public knowledge?* Tewari filed a patent application on a zero-oxygen meat-packing method. Tewari disclosed to a potential partner know-how about implementing the method, subject to a nondisclosure agreement. The joint venture ran asunder, but the other party used the information from Tewari. Sued for trade secret misappropriation, the defendant argued that all the information could be garnered from the published patent application, even if it took Tewari's information to know how to use the method. Trade secret?

15. *Posted.* Can a SyncSort UNIX command language remain a trade secret if its Reference Guide has been posted on an open Web site?

16. *Valuable.* Could the list of followers on a Twitter account be a trade secret?

17. *Open secret.* Nationwide Mutual collects agency agreement and other useful documents available to insurance agents and puts them in an electronic database. A departing agent copies the database. Was the database a trade secret?

18. *Public?* A physician analyzes published scientific research and public databases of nutritional information. She distills all the information into charts and tables and uses the information to formulate a dietary supplement. The information is disclosed to potential investors, who sign nondisclosure agreements. An investor secretly records a session and uses the information to formulate a competing product. The investor argues there is no trade secret because the product was based on public information. Trade secret?

19. *None of your beeswax.* Could a database of beehive foraging locations in western Nebraska qualify as a trade secret?

20. *ID.* Tucson Embedded Systems sought to engage Turbine Powered Technology to build engine control systems to control turbine engines for use with generators at oil and gas wells. Tucson Embedded Systems gave Turbine Powered Technology access to their equipment and various facilities as part of the development process. Tucson Embedded Systems claimed the defendant used that access to misappropriate trade secrets. Tucson Embedded Systems did not identify specific information used, rather just generally listed types of information that defendants had access to and general purposes that information could serve, such as for "retrofitting" and "modifying" an aircraft engine for use as generator. Trade secret misappropriation?

Explanations

1. There are a number of reported cases in this category. Suppose Engineer develops a valuable manufacturing process before taking a job with Business. She gets a job at Business, after agreeing that Business may use her trade secret. The parties continue to use the process as a trade secret for some time. Engineer decides to leave her job to start her own business. She informs Business that it may no longer use the process, but Business continues to use it. Employee might then contend that, by continuing to use her process without permission, Business is misappropriating Employee's trade secret.

2. A trade secret must be information of some kind. Tycoon's coin is not information and is not valuable for any information it embodies. So taking the coin is not misappropriation of a trade secret. A historic artifact could conceivably embody a trade secret. An antique naval report listing the location of a shipwreck might be a valuable trade secret to one in the business of salvaging historic wrecks.

3. A piece of metal could embody a trade secret. The design of a machine could, as here, be a trade secret. It would even fall into one of the specific categories listed in the UTSA, as a device. The design derives economic value from not being known to others in the business because the design allows Kensington to produce kiwi juice more efficiently. By selling one of the shredders, the employee sold a copy of the design to Brainerd.

4. The testing results in this case do qualify as a trade secret under the UTSA definition. The negative results from testing 400 of the 500 candidates is information that has economic value from being unknown to others that could obtain economic value from its use. Because Farmajohn knows that those 400 compounds have produced negative results, it need not test them any more and may concentrate its further testing on the other 100 compounds. A competitor without that information would not know which of the 500 compounds were likely candidates and could spend years eliminating the same 400, if it tested in the same order.

    Under the narrower Restatement definition of trade secret, the information might not qualify. The Restatement requires that the information be in "continuous use in business." If this is understood to mean that the information must be used in a positive way (such as using a secret process to make steel or using a secret customer list to market a product), the negative information does not qualify as a trade secret.

5. This example tests the limits of the UTSA definition of trade secrets. The information's actual value to Film Star is not to make money or to run a

business. Film Star uses the information purely for social purposes. But the definition of trade secret might be broad enough to include the list of addresses. The definition does not require that the information be valuable to the owner, rather that it have actual or potential economic value from not being known to those who could get value by disclosing or using it. As evidenced by the price paid for it, the information was indeed valuable to those who could use it, such as Tabloid. But much private information might be valuable in that broad sense, in that someone else might be willing to pay to acquire it. A court might likely reason that trade secret law exists to encourage the production of information that was valuable to producer, not all private information. A broader reading would transform the UTSA into a form of privacy protection.

6. No trade secret was taken. The idea of prepaid funerals was generally known to those in the industry, so it was not a trade secret. The marketing director did not pass on any other information about Funeral Service's plans. By hiring away a key employee, the competitor may have gotten a competitive advantage but did not do so by acquiring protected information.

7. The information was a trade secret, even though it had been published. To qualify as a trade secret, the information need not be perfectly secret. Rather, it must not be generally known to, or reasonably ascertainable by, those who could gain economic value from using or disclosing it. The use of the dental process for restoring ceramics was unknown among ceramics restorers. Nor was it readily ascertainable to them, even though it had been published. The information was published in a specialty journal that none of them (other than Wuzzy) was likely to read and would not have been consulted if they were attempting to find improved techniques. So the information had the requisite value to qualify as a trade secret.

8. The list is not a trade secret. Information that is readily ascertainable by the relevant parties lacks the necessary secrecy. Any business that wished to could easily obtain the list for a $10 fee, so it is not a trade secret. Not all useful information has the sort of value required for trade secrecy protection. Indeed, there would be little point in providing protection for information that is readily available elsewhere.

9. The information is not readily ascertainable by others. For information to be readily ascertainable, others must be able to get the information by proper means in a relatively inexpensive and speedy way. Here, to compile the lists, it is necessary for Mail Order to have teams of researchers comb through publicly available sources to select and arrange the special lists. Accordingly, even though the lists are compiled from public sources, the lists themselves are not readily ascertainable.

10. The information is not readily ascertainable by others. Information that can be obtained through reverse engineering is not necessarily readily ascertainable. Only if reverse engineering the process is relatively simple and cheap is the information considered readily ascertainable. It would have to be analogous to simply looking up the information in a publicly available reference work. If it requires considerable work by a team of skilled chemists, it is likely not readily ascertainable. A competitor may still reverse engineer the process (because, as discussed later, such means are not misappropriation). But the competitor may not acquire the information by improper means, such as bribery.

11. The high-pressure process does have the necessary economic value for trade secret protection, even if it was discovered by accident. The cost of producing the information is only one factor in deciding if it has value. Other relevant factors here include value to the business, costs of security, improper acquisition, and costs for others to develop. Even if we assume the information cost nothing to produce, all the other factors support a finding of value. Steely Wheel uses the process to sell a market-leading product. Steely Wheel spends a lot on security measures. It is very costly for others to figure out the process. The competitor resorts to a lengthy espionage campaign to get the information. All those factors show that the process does have value from not being known or readily ascertainable to those that could get economic value from using or disclosing it.

12. The concept for a noise-producing toy railroad track was held to be a trade secret. *See Learning Curve Toys, Inc. v. PlayWood Toys, Inc.*, 342 F.3d 714, 722 (7th Cir. 2003). A trade secret must be information with economic value due to not being generally known to others in the business. This concept enabled the production of a product with features new to the business and that allowed the seller to distinguish itself from other generic tracks. It had a different look, sound, and feel. The concept was not generally known but instead was kept with the small business and disclosed only under a confidentiality agreement. This also indicated that Learning Curve believed the concept had value. To use the information, Playwood breached an agreement, indicating Playwood considered the idea valuable. Sales skyrocketed, further indicating the concept's value to others.

13. TeleChem does have a trade secret in its clean room. "While the general concept of a clean room is not protected, clean rooms may differ in the details of their construction and efficiency, and it is those details that

can provide a competitive advantage and are protected." *Neo Gen Screening, Inc. v. TeleChem Intl., Inc.*, 69 Fed. Appx. 550, 555 (3d Cir. 2003). Several factors support this conclusion: TeleChem invested both in constructing the clean room and keeping it secret. It required a confidentiality agreement. The clean room operated very efficiently. Competitors could not figure out the details of the room and not copy its efficiency-enhancing features. The information had economic value from not being known or generally ascertainable by others.

14. Yes. Even if the individual elements were public information, the knowledge of how to combine those elements could remain a protected trade secret. *See Tewari De-Ox Systems Inc. v. Mountain States/Rosen LLC*, 637 F.3d 604 (5th Cir., 2011).

15. Yes, if it is taken down quickly enough, so that it does not become readily available to competitors. *SyncSort Incorporated v. Innovative Routines, International, Inc.*, Civ. No. 04-3623 (WHW).

16. Yes, provided it met the requirements for trade secret protection (value from secrecy, protected by reasonable security measures). That means that wrongful retention of the account and the list of followers by a departing employee could be misappropriation. *See PhoneDog v. Kravitz*, No. 11-3474 (N.D. Cal., November 11, 2011).

17. A trade secret must be information not readily available to others. Compiling a valuable database does not a trade secret make, where the same information is publicly available, albeit on paper. *Nationwide Mutual Insurance Co. v. Mortensen*, 606 F.3d 22 (2d Cir. 2010) The database in *Nationwide Mutual Insurance* was valuable to the business, especially because it was in electronic form. An electronic base is quicker to search, easier to organize, and can serve the business in many ways. The value to the business did not derive from the customer information being secret. To the contrary, the same information was available from public sources. Simply adapting old methods to new technologies does not vest them with legal protection.

18. The underlying information was publicly available, but the information developed from it was nonpublic, valuable information subject to reasonable security measures. It would be protected as a trade secret. *Daniels Health Sciences, L.L.C. v. Vascular Health Sciences, L.L.C.*, 710 F.3d 579 (5th Cir. 2013).

19. The court held that the locations of the beehives could be ascertained by others, by searching the Internet or by searching by driving a car around

western Nebraska. But information may be a trade secret if it is not readily ascertainable by others, and there is a difference between "readily
ascertainable and that which is *realistically* ascertainable."[11]

20. The court held that to claim trade secret protection, information must be
more specifically described than such "catch-all" phrases.

---

11. *See* Gabriel M. Ramsey, Jacob M. Heath and Kayvan Ghaffari, *The Location of Old McDonald's
Beehives Are Trade Secrets: Database Showing "Realistically" Ascertainable Locations Entitled to Protection*
(Oct. 24, 2016), http://blogs.orrick.com/trade-secrets-watch/2016/10/24/the-location-
of-ol-mcdonalds-beehives-are-trade-secrets-realistically-ascertainable-beehive-locations-on-
observable-property-warrant-trade-secret-protection/#more-2018.

Getting Protection Through Reasonable Security Measures and Losing Protection Through Public Disclosure

Economic value alone does not make information a trade secret. A manufacturing process, chemical formula, or database of marketing information may all meet the first requirement—economic value from not being generally known to those who could exploit the information—but none qualifies as a trade secret unless the owner can also show the second requirement—reasonable security measures. The owner must show that the information "is the subject of efforts that are reasonable under the circumstances to maintain its secrecy." UTSA §1.

Reasonable security measures are an independent requirement for trade secret status. But courts also consider security measures in other aspects of the case. The use of security measures can show the information has economic value (costly measures imply value); can support an inference of improper misappropriation, when no direct evidence of improper means is shown (the greater the security, the less likely the information reached the defendant through inadvertent disclosure); and can show damages (tend to show that the loss of information indeed caused damages). But it is important to remember that reasonable security measures alone do not make a trade secret. If the information lacks economic value, is generally known to those who can exploit it, or is reasonably ascertainable from public sources, the information is not a trade secret no matter how great the security measures are.

A common theme in trade secret case law is locking the barn door after the horse has been taken. There is no legal protection for valuable information if the owner has not taken reasonable security measures. The features and functions of software, discernible from output available to clients without security restrictions, did not constitute trade secrets.[1] By contrast, even if software is distributed, it may come from source code that is kept confidential and so remains a trade secret.[2]

Mere pretense of security will not give trade secret protection. Where a party licensed information, a database of media events, under terms that promoted public availability by encouraging disclosure of events to the public, the party could not demonstrate the necessary reasonable security measures for trade secret protection.[3] A contract that imposes restrictions on disclosure, but also has provisions permitting disclosure, will not create trade secret protection.[4] Often, only after a party realizes that it should have protected information against disclosure does it seek to use litigation to achieve that goal, but its initial failure to put reasonable security measures in place means that in litigation its trade secret claims will not succeed.

REASONABLENESS OF SECURITY MEASURES

The owner is not required to take extraordinary measures to keep the information secret. Just as only relative secrecy is required for the first prong, so only reasonable measures, not ironclad measures, are required. Rather, courts grant parties considerable latitude in deciding what level of security is reasonable. Cases finding insufficient security are usually cases in which the security was demonstrably lax. The UTSA comments echo this approach:

> [R]easonable efforts to maintain secrecy have been held to include advising employees of the existence of a trade secret, limiting access to a trade secret on "need to know basis," and controlling plant access. On the other hand, public disclosure of information through display, trade journal publications, advertising, or other carelessness can preclude protection.

UTSA Comments to §1.

---

1. *Warehouse Solutions, Inc. v. Integrated Logistics, LLC*, 2015 U.S. App. LEXIS 7633 (11th Cir. May 8, 2015).
2. *Warehouse Solutions, Inc. v. Integrated Logistics, LLC*, 2015 U.S. App. LEXIS 7633 (11th Cir. May 8, 2015).
3. *Events Media Network, Inc. v. Weather Channel Interactive, Inc.*, 2015 U.S. Dist. LEXIS 12497, *26 (D.N.J. Feb. 3, 2015) ("Finally, while the 2006 Agreement did contain a restriction on TWC's right to use the Information, or portions of it, in programs other than event or attraction listings, it is clear that this language also anticipates that such use could be permitted under the terms of the contract, and the following sentence even concedes that '[t]o the extent any such use has been made of the Information . . . [EMNI] consents to the continued use of such Information for such purpose.' (*Id.* ¶ 3.) Such a provision hardly indicates that Plaintiff was concerned that the Event and Attraction Data, or any portion thereof, remain confidential indefinitely.'").
4. *Id.*

Courts may consider any relevant facts or circumstances in determining whether reasonable security measures were in place, looking to both the costs and benefits of security measures. Some of the relevant factors, drawn from cases and commentary, follow.

Value of the Information

The more valuable the information, the greater the resources it is reasonable to expend guarding it. Courts do not necessarily require parties to spend as much guarding the information as is optimal. But reasonableness might require someone to spend more to guard highly valuable information than they would spend on less valuable information.

Need to Disclose the Information to Employees and Others to Exploit It

If the information is a manufacturing process or customer list, a number of employees may need access to perform their duties. Likewise, if the information is a chemical formula or blueprint for a machine, it may be necessary to disclose it to a supplier or to someone who builds or services the machine. Reasonableness might require measures to ensure the trustworthiness of employees or suppliers before disclosure.

Limits on Disclosure of the Information

Courts consider whether the information was disclosed only when necessary to further business purposes and whether the advantages of disclosure outweighed possible risks of further disclosures.

Means Taken to Maintain Confidentiality When Disclosure Is Made

Courts consider whether the information was disclosed only when the recipient was first required to sign a nondisclosure or confidentiality agreement (which impose limits on disclosure and use of information).

Physical Limitations on Access

Reasonableness may require that areas in which the information was being used or stored were made physically inaccessible to others (by fences, locked doors, or remote location), that plants or manufacturing areas were made secure (restricting access to employees or other visitors with reasons for access, checking bags), and that information was kept in locked files. Computer networks may require similar security measures, both physical and coded barriers to access.

Keeping Track of Copies of the Information and Keeping Records of Those with Access

Courts consider whether the business knew who had access to the information, when they had access, and why. They consider whether the business knew where copies of the information were (for example, by requiring engineers to sign when removing and returning confidential drawings) or whether the extent of disclosure was unknown. Computer networks, again, raise a host of issues, given the ease of duplicating and distributing information and the stubborn tendency of old files to stick around.

Whether Employees and Others Were Informed of Restrictions

Employees and others may be notified of the restrictions on information. Such notice could include employee rules, no trespassing signs, "confidential" stamps on appropriate documents, and statements affirming that any disclosures to outsiders were made in confidence. Such notices make clear that information is protected. With some types of information, employees might be expected to know it was confidential. But without explicit notice, other information might seem ordinary. Unless an employee knows that information is deemed confidential, she might share it through informal contacts with peers at other firms, through publication, or other means. The notices also act as a warning that the trade secret owner will take legal measures to enforce his rights.

Industry Standards and Ethics

A showing of reasonableness may be supported by conformity to industry standards. The level of security varies from industry to industry. Defense contractors, for instance, are likely to have sophisticated security programs—not just because of trade secrets but because much of their information is classified. Other industries are likely to have high security levels because of common knowledge of the value of categories of information. Other industries, in which competitors have not historically sought each other's information, are likely to have lower levels of security. IP rights may depend on local practices, as in a trade secret case brought by a Sarasota boatbuilder. The information at issue—suppliers' names and production costs—were readily determined due to local industry practices, and so did not qualify as trade secrets.[5] Boatyards are often adjacent, enabling employees to mix. And perhaps (see *Margaritaville* discussion above) people may be sociable and less concerned with legalities.

Whether an Overall Security Program Is in Place

Beyond taking specific security measures, courts consider whether the business had an overall program designed to keep the information secret. The implementation of a program is usually strong support of reasonable security measures.

Costs of Security Measures

Security can be very costly. Paying security guards, hiring consultants, buying special software, and running training seminars are just the start. Security measures can have great indirect costs. Restrictions on information may both increase the cost of using the information and reduce the chance employees will make productive use of it. Employees may be less happy (and therefore less productive or more likely to leave) if security measures feel restrictive with respect to their movements, activities, and communications with their peers. A researcher who solves a problem is likely to tell her peers, not keep it secret. Moreover, restricting the flow of information can make employees less productive. If employees have to be careful what they tell others, they may likely receive less information from others as well. Restrictions on the information may also keep it from those who think of better ways to exploit it.

APPLICATION OF THE FACTORS

Determining whether security measures were reasonable "under the circumstances" is necessarily a fact-bound, case-specific assessment. Courts look to all relevant factors. Perhaps the factor with the greatest weight is whether the owner had an overall security program and substantially complied with

---

5. Yellowfin Yachts, Inc. v. Barker Boatworks, LLC, 2017 U.S. Dist. LEXIS 21745, *29 (M.D. Fla. Feb. 16, 2017). Yellowfin alleges that Kevin Barker, who downloaded several hundred files from Yellowfin's main server on his last day at Yellowfin, misappropriated secret supplier and customer information. But a supplier's identity is well-known, and Barker Boatworks lacks the size and history to secure a discount from a supplier. And Barker learned Yellowfin's production costs in the ordinary course of business at Yellowfin. No reasonable jury could conclude that the supplier information is a trade secret.

the program plan. When an overall program is in place, courts frequently find sufficient security, even when particular actions do not take security into consideration. For example, the owner may have disclosed the secret in negotiations without first getting a signed nondisclosure agreement or even without indicating that disclosure was made with the expectation of confidentiality. Likewise, access to the information may have been given unnecessarily to some employees or outside business contacts. Inadvertent disclosures do not necessarily show lack of reasonable security measures. When the business is taking reasonable measures, its employees may make isolated mistakes without nullifying the reasonableness of the program.

Courts also do not require that access to the information be made as minimal as possible. Rather, courts look to both the extent of the disclosures (whether there was an attempt to limit access to those who needed the information to serve business purposes of the trade secret holder) and whether access was conditioned on confidentiality. Duplicative security measures need not be taken. If drawings are disclosed subject to a confidentiality agreement, the failure to stamp the drawings "confidential" does not render the security inadequate.

Restricting access to the information may be necessary, but it is also costly. The more access that employees and outside business contacts have to the information, the more likely it is to be improperly disclosed or used. But restrictions on the information have costs beyond simply administrative and security costs. The more knowledge employees and outside business contacts have about the information, the more likely it is also that they will contribute to the value of the information—by suggesting more ways to exploit it, more efficient ways to use it, or more valuable alternatives. So in deciding how broadly to grant access, a business has to weigh many possible risks (of wrongful loss), costs (security measures, lost opportunities, the work environment itself), and benefits. Courts are reluctant to second-guess such decisions provided they fall within a broad range of reasonableness.

Limited disclosures do not deem the overall security unreasonable, even if they could have been easily avoided. Someone who improperly acquires information cannot escape by combing the plaintiff's history to find a few disclosures or by pointing to some questionable security practices, if the overall program is reasonable.

CONTRACTUAL MEASURES USED IN CONNECTION WITH TRADE SECRETS

Under many circumstances, someone receiving trade secret information (be it an employee, supplier, consultant, joint venture partner, or other) takes it subject to an implicit obligation not to disclose. But using explicit contractual measures—putting it in writing—has several advantages for the aspiring trade secret owner. The fact that the owner seeks explicit agreements of confidentiality is good evidence of reasonable security measures, noted in numerous cases. Explicit agreements are also more predictable than relying on implicit duties, which always depend on the specific facts. The formality of a contract (especially if reinforced with periodic reminders) also makes clear to the recipient that confidentiality is expected and warns of possible consequences if it is not honored. Likewise, others may be put on notice of the trade secret status. Contracts also make available a breach of contract action as well as trade secret liability (and the contract may be construed to protect information that does not qualify as a trade secret).

So contractual measures aid in practical terms (by reducing the chance of disclosure) and legal terms (by increasing the chances of a remedy for disclosure). Like security measures generally, contractual arrangements have costs: drafting, administering, enforcing, as well as the possible negative effects on the workplace atmosphere or atmosphere of trust in relationships. In addition, if not all recipients sign nondisclosure agreements, that may imply that other recipients are not subject to implicit obligations of nondisclosure.

Employee Contracts

Employees are the biggest risk for most trade secret holders. Most trade secret cases involve former employees—from meritorious cases arising out of misappropriation to bad faith cases attempting to squelch proper competition. Clear and reasonable employee contracts serve to clarify restrictions on information, give strong notice to employees of the confidential status, and provide a basis for a subsequent remedy. But excessive restrictions have great costs, impinging on the employee's ability to find further employment, creating oppressive work environments, and acting as *in terrorem* measures, especially if employees are not assisted by knowledgeable counsel. So courts have placed a number of limits on the enforceability of such contracts.

Confidentiality/Nondisclosure Agreements

A confidentiality agreement or nondisclosure agreement places a clear, explicit duty on the employee not to disclose or improperly use the described information. In some settings, contract law may enforce agreements not to disclose information that does not qualify as a trade secret, so contracts can supplement trade secret law. But there are some hazards for employers. Contracts require consideration for enforcement. If an employer institutes a program and requires present employees to sign on, courts have held that there is no consideration for the nondisclosure agreement. Drafting raises many issues. An agreement simply not to disclose "trade secrets" begs the question of what specific information is protected. If certain specified items or categories are described, omitted categories may be deemed non-confidential. If the drafter tries to address that hazard by including every potentially applicable category she can think of, it may not pass the relevant standards for enforceability under contract law of the jurisdiction. A clause that purports to restrict information that the employee knew before his employment or that is generally known in the industry may not be enforceable.

Covenants Not to Compete

As another means for preventing disclosure or use of trade secrets, an employer may seek agreement that, if employee leaves the firm, she will not work for competitors for a certain time. This eliminates the need for monitoring (or proof, in litigation) to see if the employee is using the information in her new position. But such agreements run counter to strong policies—freedom to follow one's profession and limits on anti-competitive agreements. Accordingly, noncompete agreements by individual employees are unenforceable in some jurisdictions. California law, for example, strongly favors mobility of employees (and the resulting rapid interchange of know-how within the industry) and provides that noncompetition agreements are invalid unless they fall within narrow statutory exceptions, such as the sale of a business. *Edwards v. Arthur Andersen LLP*, 44 Cal. 4th 937 (Cal. 2008) (rejecting "narrow restraint" exception).

But most jurisdictions will enforce noncompete agreements, provided they are reasonable (although courts differ on whether an overly broad agreement will be void or be enforced to a reasonable extent). A noncompete agreement with worldwide scope and application to an entire industry was too broad to enforce.[6] A commonly used test of reasonableness looks to three factors:

One, is the restraint no greater than necessary to protect the legitimate business interests of the employer? Legitimate business interests include protecting against use of trade secrets and protecting against transfer of goodwill of the employer. A desire simply to keep a highly skilled employee from working for a competitor does not support a restriction. The reasonableness of the limitations is judged in light of time, geography, scope of activity, and any other limitation. If the employee has access to information valuable only in electronics, a clause that precludes him from working in any field is unreasonable, even if it has time and geography limitations. A microchip engineer would be free to go work as a farmer, even if there was an agreement not to work at all for a year.

---

6. NanoMech, Inc. v. Suresh, 777 F.3d 1020, 1025 (8th Cir. 2015).

Two, is the restraint unduly harsh and oppressive in curtailing the employee's legitimate efforts to earn a livelihood? An employee cannot assign away her future ability to work to secure a job. Because noncompete agreements are rather broad means to protect trade secrets and other legitimate employer interests, they must be drafted carefully to permit the employee to continue working in her field or line of professional development.

Three, is the restraint contrary to sound public policy? The court has broad scope to consider the effects on third parties. A noncompete clause that has adverse consequences for third parties or is contrary to public policy may not be enforced, even if very narrow in scope.

If a noncompete clause is too broad, some courts will not enforce it at all. Others may use the "blue-pencil" rule and enforce it to a reasonable extent.

Example

Race for the cure. Dr. Warren, a cancer researcher at the University of Iowa, also works one day a week at the University's Cancer Care clinic. He has signed an agreement that, if he leaves the University, he will not practice for two years within 50 miles of the university. He does leave and takes a job with Iowa Blood and Cancer Care in Cedar Rapids, which is within 50 miles. He does not take any patients with him. Studies show the area is underserved in that practice area. Can the University get an injunction against him?

Explanation

The court declined to grant an injunction. *See Bd. of Regents v. Warren*, No. 8-620 (Iowa Ct. App. 2008). Fifty miles and two years might be reasonable. But there was no showing that enforcing the agreement was necessary to protect the employer, where the employee had practiced just one day a week and took no patients. Permitting him to treat cancer patients would be in the public interest. The area is underserved, which might increase demand for the university's cancer practice but more importantly shows the public interest in permitting the doctor to practice.

Assignment of Inventions Clauses

As noted below, courts generally deem trade secrets developed within the scope of employment to belong to the employer. But putting it in writing serves to clarify rights and to make parties conscious of the claim to ownership. So an employee agreement may make explicit that information (be it patentable, trade secret, or other "proprietary" information) belongs to the employer. The contract may also contain an explicit obligation to turn over copies of the information (lab books, computer files, genetically

543

engineered hamsters, and so on). The parties less frequently agree that the employee will have sole or joint rights to information that she develops.

Holdover/Trailer Clauses

A holdover clause requires assignments of inventions or other information developed after the employee leaves. The rationale is that the employee is simply using the information acquired during his employment. Such clauses are more closely scrutinized than clauses applicable during the employment period. Courts look to similar principles as when considering noncompete clauses but apply them even more strictly because only such employer interests as trade secrets, not goodwill, are at issue. Careful drafting of clauses can result in enforceability, such as stating that they apply only to inventions that "result from and relate to" the previous employment. But, of course, that makes it harder to prove that the invention falls within the scope of the clause.

Keep Employees Happy — An Ounce of Prevention

Most trade secret cases involve former employees. So one way to protect trade secrets is to have fewer former employees by keeping them. The working environment can be improved with reasonable policies, measures to promote communication, and other means to promote employee welfare. Firms also attempt to provide incentives to employees through bonuses, stock options, or compensation related to specific work. Such measures not only may serve to keep employees happy but also may increase the value of information produced (and make it more likely to be utilized). Such programs, of course, have costs beyond the costs of options and bonuses. Some employees may resent special compensation given to others. Incentive programs can also create nonproductive incentives. Suppose an employee receives compensation based on the company's use of a trade secret software she developed. If she happens to learn of superior software that is commercially available, she may not bring that to the attention of management.

Regulations

Comprehensive regulations for employees (made part of their employment contract) and others can provide the structure of a trade secret program and inform relevant parties of the conduct expected from them. Courts frequently have looked to existence of relevant regulation in assessing whether reasonable security measures were taken. As written documents, regulations provide concrete evidence of security measures.

Outsider Contracts

Contracts with persons outside the business may take a number of forms: from complicated, long-term joint venture agreements to nondisclosure agreement signed by a visitor before a brief presentation. A joint venture agreement may address many aspects of trade secrets. In addition to nondisclosure agreements, the agreement may impose other security obligations on the parties, give warranties about the origins of information, and provide limits about other uses of the information and a number of other matters. One key issue is ownership. The agreement should be clear about who owns what information (or as clear as reasonably possible because even describing the relevant information may be a challenge). Suppose Elmo and Ernie are entering into a joint venture to exploit Elmo's secret radish-irradiating process. The agreement could provide that Elmo continues to own the information; that Elmo contributes it to the joint venture and both own it; that Elmo sells the information to Ernie (or many other variations). The key is for the parties to clearly address the matter—to clarify their expectations and, in the event the venture is terminated, to determine ownership.

Confidentiality/Nondisclosure Agreements

As with employees, contracts may be used to secure an obligation not to disclose or use information. An important practical point is that many commercial parties may refuse to sign such agreements. An inventor looking for financing or a writer trying to sell a screenplay may be reluctant to disclose it unless the other party signs a nondisclosure agreement, agreeing not to disclose or use the information. She may think that Venture Capitalist or Movie Studio has nothing to lose, other than an hour's time, in listening to her idea in confidence. But Venture Capitalist or Movie Studio may wish to retain complete freedom to finance other inventors in the area or produce other movies without risk of a lawsuit. Commentators have noted that even negotiating over a nondisclosure clause is problematic: The buyer does not know exactly what is for sale (otherwise she would already have the information that is for sale), and the seller cannot disclose it without in effect handing over what she is seeking to sell.

Cross-Licenses

Trade secret information may be more valuable if used with other information. The other information could be another's trade secret or another's patented process or product. A cross-license provides means for two parties to combine forces and increase the value of their respective information. *A* and *B* simply agree that they may utilize each other's information without an infringement claim. Cross-licenses appear in many settings. A joint venture may turn on cross-licenses. Litigation between competitors often includes cross-licenses in settlement agreements. But, as with other contracts with competitors, cross-licenses may have anticompetitive effects. *A* and *B* might enter into a cross-license not to increase productivity but to carve up the relevant market between them. Accordingly, as with other contractual measures discussed here, antitrust concerns may be relevant.

Grant-Back Clauses

A party who allows another to use a trade secret may seek a grant-back clause. Suppose Chemist licenses his trade secret process to Manufacturer rather than going into production himself. If Manufacturer improves the process, the grant-back clause requires Manufacturer to assign the rights to the improvement back to Chemist. The grant-back clause could require Manufacturer to assign all ownership of the improvements (so Chemist would own the information as a new trade secret or have patent rights) or require Manufacturer to grant back a nonexclusive license, which would allow both Manufacturer and Chemist to use the new information.

Enforceability Issues

The same sorts of agreements that protect trade secrets can also be used to restrain competition. Two industry leaders with a cross-license can exclude competitors. A patent licensor can require grant-backs of rights in potentially competing technology. So antitrust concerns may figure prominently in enforceability of such agreements. Beyond antitrust, ordinary contract issues frequently arise, especially if one party relies on contract to get rights with respect to information that turns out to be available from other sources or that becomes public knowledge during the pendency of the contract.

OWNERSHIP

The UTSA does not specifically address the ownership of a trade secret. Because trade secret law does not grant exclusive rights, a dispute over ownership generally arises when two parties with access to valuable information each claim that use by the other constitutes misappropriation of the trade secret. So the issue becomes whether one of the parties acquired the information "under circumstances giving rise to a duty to maintain its secrecy or limit its use." UTSA §1(2).

The issue arises most often between an employer and a former employee or between two parties who have terminated a common enterprise (a joint venture, research project, or a buyer/supplier or other contractual relationship).

In the employment context, there is usually no issue if the parties have contractually agreed to the assignment of rights. Likewise, if the employer disclosed the information to the employee, the employer continues to own any trade secret rights. Ownership becomes an issue when the employee generates the information (for example, writes a program, develops a process, or compiles a customer list). When the parties have not addressed the issue by contract, courts have looked to the other areas of law governing ownership of employee-created information. Some courts apply a rule similar to the work-for-hire doctrine of copyright law, which grants the employer all rights to works created within the scope of employment. Other courts have taken a more nuanced approach, analogous to the patent law rules. Rather than simply asking if the information was developed within the scope of employment, the court looks to the reasons the employee was hired. If the employee was specifically hired to develop the information, the trade secret rights belong to the employer. If the information was developed by the employee simply using her own skill without particular direction by the employer, the employee is not foreclosed from using it for her own benefit. Whether to follow copyright or patent law may depend on whether the underlying information is copyrightable or patentable. As courts have noted, using a similar rule avoids one party having the copyright or patent right, while the other party has the trade secret rights.

Note that in such a setting, the choice is usually not whether the former employee or the employer owns the trade secret. Rather, it is whether only the employer may use the trade secret or whether both the employer and the former employee may use it. But if the employee had imposed conditions on disclosure and use before disclosing the information to the employer, then the third alternative (former employee is sole owner) would arise.

When the dispute is between two businesses that worked together, the court seeks to determine if the parties explicitly or implicitly allocated ownership of the trade secrets, with particular attention to whether one party actually developed the information.

In both employer-employee and joint venture cases, a court could decide that neither party exclusively owns the trade secret but that they are joint owners. Reported joint ownership trade secret cases are rare. Commentators have noted several unsettled issues: how joint ownership arises, whether joint owners have a duty to account to each other for profits, whether one joint owner may make the information public, whether permission from both is necessary to secure a license, and who owns trade secret information developed by an independent contractor. *See* Jerry Cohen & Alan S. Gutterman, *Trade Secrets: Protection and Exploitation* (1998).

In addition to joint owners, there may be independent owners who share the same information as trade secrets. Two businesses could discover the same information through independent research or compilation of data. Alternatively, one could gain the information by examining the other's product. Suppose Horseshoe Maker uses a trade secret process to manufacture horseshoes. A competitor buys one and, through a lengthy and technically demanding process, manages to reverse engineer the process. The process, although now known to two entities, is still not generally known in the industry, so Horseshoe Maker's trade secret is not terminated. Competitor has properly acquired the information and, by taking reasonable security measures, may also protect it as a trade secret and exploit it in manufacturing or licensing. *See* UTSA Comments to §1.

TERMINATION OF THE TRADE SECRET BY PUBLIC DISCLOSURE

Information is not a trade secret unless it is not "generally known to, and not being readily ascertainable by proper means by, other persons who can obtain economic value from its disclosure or use." UTSA §1(4). Accordingly, information may lose its trade secret status on public disclosure, which makes the information generally known or accessible to those who could exploit the information. Disclosure of the trade secret can enter the trade secret analysis: Disclosure can make the information generally known (and hence not a trade secret); disclosure can show that the owner failed to take reasonable security measures (and hence the information was not a trade secret, even if the disclosure did not make the information publicly known); disclosure or use in breach of a duty of confidentiality is misappropriation; using improper means to induce disclosure is misappropriation; receiving a voluntary disclosure is receipt by proper means (and hence not misappropriation); and disclosure after misappropriation can destroy the trade secret (and hence destroy the need for an injunction).

Here we discuss disclosure as terminating the trade secret. Not every disclosure terminates the trade secret. To the contrary, a trade secret is frequently disclosed to employees and to outside parties (such as suppliers, licensees, and joint venture partners). Disclosure, however, can terminate the trade secret if the information no longer meets the definition of secret because it is generally known or readily ascertainable. Such "public disclosure" terminates the trade secret. Public disclosure can occur in many ways. Disclosure may be by the trade secret owner intentionally (such as by publishing the information or selling a product that reveals the information) or accidentally (such as by mistakenly including the information in a publication). Disclosure may be by another party (who may have received the information from the trade secret owner or developed it independently). Note that it is irrelevant whether the disclosure was reasonable, accidental, obtained by fraudulent means, or in a breach of a duty of confidentiality. If the information becomes sufficiently public, it is no longer a trade secret. Disclosure by an employee (breaching a confidentiality duty) or a competitor (after stealing the secret) still destroys the trade secret no matter how diligent that trade secret owner has been (although a court may stretch in such a case to find that the information has not become sufficiently public).

Disclosure does not destroy the secret unless it makes the information sufficiently public. Disclosure to a good number of people in the relevant trade may not destroy the trade secret, especially if made pursuant to restrictions. Likewise, temporarily making the information available to the public may not destroy secrecy. If the information is included in a court filing or other source available to the public but is not actually known to or readily ascertainable by the relevant public, the trade secret is not destroyed.

Governments frequently require disclosure of information. A trade secret owner might think that mandatory disclosure to a governmental body should not destroy the trade secret. But just as wrongful public disclosure still terminates the trade secret, so can compelled disclosure, provided that it makes the secret sufficiently known. When a governmental body seeks information, the trade secret owner may first seek to avoid disclosure and then seek to make disclosure on terms that maintain the secrecy of the trade secret. In some cases, mandatory disclosure may be deemed a taking of property requiring compensation.

Parties subject to federal regulation may have to submit valuable information. If others seek that information with Freedom of Information requests, the government may withhold "trade secrets and commercial or financial information obtained from a person and privileged or confidential." 5 U.S.C. §552(b)(4). However, where design specifications dating from the 1930s for the Fairchild F-45 airplane had been disclosed in decades past, the manufacturer was no longer able to prevent disclosure under the Freedom of Information Act. See *Taylor v. Babbitt*, 760 F. Supp. 2d 80 (D.D.C. 2011). So an airplane enthusiast, who owned one of the few remaining Fairchild F-45s, was entitled to obtain its design specifications. By contrast, a competitor was not entitled, under the Freedom of Information Act, to receive commercial information that a trademark owner disclosed to the customs bureau with respect to goods seized at ports of entry. See *Watkins v. Bureau of Customs and Border Protection*, 643 F.3d 1189 (9th Cir. 2011).

Examples

1. *No reasonable security measures, no trade secret.* Over many years, Zonatherm compiles a large database of actual and potential customers. Zonatherm visits trade shows, studies industry publications, visits businesses, and takes dozens of people out to lunch. The customer list database is central to Zonatherm's business because its sales people rely on it. The customer list exists on the computers of the sales people and on many printed hard copies. When a sales person leaves the company, the list is deleted from her computer. But Zonatherm makes no effort to keep track of paper copies, to restrict their distribution, or to prevent their copying. Nor does Zonatherm require its employees to sign agreements limiting use of the customer lists.

   After an employee leaves for a competitor, taking a copy of the customer list, Zonatherm sues for trade secret infringement, arguing that the employee is taking the crown jewel of the company. Trade secret misappropriation?

2. *Shutting the barn door.* Equine Industries develops a new formula for nutritional supplements for horses. Equine takes a lackadaisical approach to keeping this valuable information secret and allows suppliers, visitors, and others free access to the information. Sure enough, many people throughout the industry soon know the formula. Equine knows at present it cannot sue anyone for trade secret infringement. Equine did not take the reasonable security measures necessary for protection. But Equine decides to introduce a rigorous security program that stringently limits access to the formula. Is the formula then a protected trade secret for Equine?

3. *Thanks for the tip.* Al Chemist, an amateur scientist, develops a valuable spintronics process in his basement lab. He describes the process in a scholarly paper, which he submits to numerous peer-reviewed academic engineering journals but is summarily rejected by each one in turn. Every journal but one simply tossed the manuscript in the trash. Editors were skeptical about the ability of a basement hobbyist to do significant work in the field and were reluctant to wade through Al's idiosyncratic mix of prose and mathematics. To add injury to insult, Al discovers that Lucky Jim, the only editor to read the paper, is using the process in his high-tech manufacturing company. The custom in the relevant academic field is for submitted papers to be freely circulated among those interested, both for peer review and to disseminate knowledge. Other than Al and Lucky Jim, no one knew the process. Has Lucky Jim used a trade secret belonging to Al?

4. *Old wine in new bottles.* Winoceros sells Chablis in distinctive, rectangular bottles. The bottles are well received, greatly boosting Winoceros's sales. Competitors start to copy the bottle's rectangular design. Winoceros argues that such copying constitutes misappropriation of its trade secret bottle design. Winoceros concedes that it took absolutely no measures to

keep the bottle design secret. But it argues that this was entirely reasonable because sale of the wine to the public discloses the bottle's shape anyway. Therefore, it argues, it took a reasonable level of security measures and therefore has a trade secret. Does Winoceros have a trade secret in the design of the bottle?

5. *Leaving the barn door open.* Laxco uses a unique manufacturing process for making rubber bungee cords. Laxco is aware that the process is the best in the industry and that competitors would be glad to know of it. Nevertheless, Laxco does not take any measures to keep the process secret. Its employees are not told to limit disclosure. Laxco gives plant tours to tourists and allows visitors to view activity that discloses the process to a knowledgeable eye. The plant and offices are often left unlocked, and information about the process is left where almost anyone could discover it. Through pure luck, Laxco's process does not become known to others in the industry. Its employees do not go to work for competitors, either staying at Laxco or moving to other industries. Companies in the bungee industry do spend considerable resources to gain information about successful products. In response, most companies maintain security programs to guard their information. Competitors, unaware of Laxco's low level of security, do not attempt to find out the information. A Laxco employee who offers to sell the information to several competitors is too inarticulate to convince them of the information's value. One Laxco engineer is even given permission by Laxco to describe the process in a trade monthly but is too lazy to write the article. So the information remains known, within the industry, only to Laxco. After many years, Laxco's luck runs out. A former employee starts her own company and begins to use the process herself. Laxco sues for misappropriation. Is the information, known within the industry only to Laxco and the former employee, a trade secret?

6. *Sticky situation.* BZZZ Honey uses a special recipe to make its honey-chocolate cookies. The special-tasting cookies sell like hotcakes. BZZZ takes a number of measures to maintain the security of the information. Employees are clearly informed that the recipe is strictly confidential and is not to be disclosed or used outside BZZZ in any way. The plant is fenced off, with entry only through guarded entryways. Visitors are logged in and out and escorted at all times. The batter-mixing machines, where the recipe is used, are in a remote area of the plant.

But the security program could be improved in several ways. Employees are not permitted to remove objects, but guards do not check bags for contraband. Employees are permitted access to the Internet during work hours, which could be used to e-mail the recipe out. High-level staff sign confidentiality agreements, but many hourly employees with access to the information are not made to sign agreements, although they are informed that the recipe is "proprietary and confidential." Paper copies of the recipe are kept in a locked file but not stamped "Confidential."

The recipe remains known only within BZZZ until ZMMM Cookies offers a huge bribe to the chief of baking, who discloses the recipe in violation of confidentiality agreement. In the subsequent litigation, BZZZ claims both breach of contract and misappropriation of trade secrets. With respect to the trade secret count, ZMMM and the chief of baking argue that the recipe is not a trade secret because BZZZ failed to take reasonable security measures. Has BZZZ failed take reasonable security measures?

7. *Strings attached.* Varia works as a software engineer for Sheets Software, which produces navigation software used in airplanes and boats. Varia is to work as a member of the team developing a navigation program for automobiles. Sheets has invested a great deal in developing the new product and hopes to gradually use the navigation software to win a place in the growing market for use of communications and software in automobiles. Sheets requires Varia to sign a covenant not to compete in which she agrees that if she terminates her employment at Sheets, she will not work for any other software company in the United States for a period of five years. Varia works for Sheets for two years. She produces a lot of code for Sheets, which is incorporated into the automobile software project. Varia is not a member of the planning staff, so she does not have access to Sheet's secret marketing plans or key technical information. However, the experience she has at Sheets makes her very valuable both to Sheets and any other company that was starting a similar project. Varia leaves to take a higher-paid job at Transhuron Software, a developer of video games. Little of the specific knowledge that Varia acquired at Sheets helps Transhuron, but Transhuron would greatly benefit from Varia's increased technical skills judgment. Can Sheets enforce the covenant not to compete and prevent from working for Transhuron?

8. *Assignment of inventions.* Rosebud Botanicals produces roses and tulips for the consumer market. Rosebud has produced several popular varieties of roses, which it sells to wholesalers. Christo is Rosebud's head of gardening. His duties include tending to the gardens, ordering supplies, and dealing with suppliers. The accounting department is in charge of developing the software that performs many of the inventory functions. Christo uses the software as part of his work and believes the software leaves much to be desired. He makes numerous suggestions for improvement but is told repeatedly that software is not part of his job and to leave it to the specialists. Irked, Christo works for months in his spare time at home to write a new software package. He brings a copy to work and demonstrates to Rosebud how much better it is than the present software. By improving many functions, the software will make the business run more efficiently and enable it to increase its business considerably. By using the software without disclosing its code to

others, Rosebud could gain a considerable advantage over competitors. Christo offers to sell Rosebud the rights to use the software. Rosebud responds that it is entitled to use the software written by Christo, an employee, and threatens to sue him for trade secret misappropriation if he discloses the code to others. Assuming the software code qualifies as a trade secret, who owns the rights to the trade secret, Rosebud or Christo?

9. *Out of the bag.* Kadio Genetics isolates a gene in the whiffle plant responsible for producing the highly sought after whiffle sap, which effectively repels fruit flies. By transplanting the gene into wheat, Kadio is able to mass produce whiffle sap, which can be used as a nontoxic fruit fly repellent in agriculture. Kadio makes huge revenue licensing its information about the relevant genetic sequence. Kadio is careful to limit the information. It discloses the information only to trusted employees and licensees, subject to nondisclosure agreements and regulations strictly limiting further disclosure and use of the information. Kadio guards the computers on which the code is stored, keeping the information from being put on networks linked to the outside world. All employees are checked every morning to make sure they are not carrying out a disk with the code. Whick, the Kadio scientist who isolated the gene, is frustrated at being refused permission to publish her achievement in scientific journals. She ingeniously manages to encode the information on magnetic tape wrapped around her shoelace. She next publishes the code by e-mailing a discussion list of biologists. Soon, thousands of copies of the code are all over the world. Anyone who wishes for a copy can quickly get one from any of numerous sources. Several companies indicate that they will soon be moving into whiffle sap production. Kadio announces publicly that it will sue any such producer for wrongfully using its trade secret because Whick disclosed it in violation of her employment contract. Does Kadio have trade secret rights in the code?

10. *Posted.* A five-volume history of the Python Corp. is written by its long-standing librarian, Roswell. Roswell meticulously researches the corporate records and produces a detailed description of every major transaction of Python over the last 50 years, complete with descriptions of the various corporate and tax law devices employed. Roswell documents the success of Python with reams of financial information. Roswell also includes an appendix listing all of Python's current clients. Roswell is assigned to verify the addresses on the list and is strictly told not to make any copies of the information. Because Roswell has dealt with confidential information reliably for three decades, Roswell is not closely supervised while dealing with the list. Several dozen copies of the history are printed. Five copies are donated to local public libraries, which list them in their catalogs and put them on shelves, open to the public. Not a single potential reader goes farther than looking at the cover of the books.

Several months later, Roswell mentions to the chief of marketing the use of the client list as an appendix. The chief of marketing is horrified. Python's client list is a carefully guarded secret, available only to employees with demonstrated need for access and subject to various security measures. Every copy of the biography is quickly retrieved and stored in the company safe. Several months later, by coincidence, a marketing employee sells a copy of the list to a competitor. The competitor later argues that the list lost its trade secret status because it was published. Is the trade secret terminated by public disclosure?

11. *Trusting to a fault?* Lopez develops a version of the computer programming language, COBOL. Lopez takes a number of security measures: carefully guarding the code, limiting its distribution, avoiding disclosing information that would allow reverse engineering, and requiring employees to sign confidentiality agreements. Parkin and Lopez agree to a joint venture to commercialize LOPEZ COBOL. Lopez allows Parkin to copy LOPEZ COBOL onto a personal computer and take it with him to Arizona. The business relationship falters. When Lopez claims trade secret protection in LOPEZ COBOL, Parkin responds that Lopez has failed to take reasonable security measures because Lopez allowed Parkin to take a copy to another state. Has Lopez failed to take reasonable security measures?

12. *Open source.* Ivan developed a Web site for his employer, Dynamicscales.com, the largest online retail store. Information available on the Web site included product information for dozens of industry items, as well as a list of potentially valuable domain names. The Web site was not password protected or encrypted. Rather, the availability of useful industry information was a drawing card for potential clients.

Ivan left Dynamicscales.com and formed his own online retail store. His former boss, Victoria, was shocked to find that Ivan's new site included the vast trove of information that Dynamicscales.com had labored to collect. Victoria can prove that the information was very valuable to both potential clients and to businesses in the scale business. Has Ivan misappropriated trade secrets of Dynamicscales.com?

Explanations

1. No misappropriation because no trade secret. To have a trade secret, Zonatherm must show both economic value of the information (from not being generally known or readily ascertainable) *and* reasonable security measures. It failed to take any security measures with respect to the paper copies of the customer lists, which was clearly unreasonable in light of their value to Zonatherm and competitors. Without reasonable security measures, Zonatherm has no trade secret protection, despite the value of the information and the great expenses of acquiring it.

2. It is too late to make the formula a trade secret. The two requirements for trade secret status are economic value (from not being generally known or readily ascertainable) and reasonable security measures. Equine now is using stringent security measures. But it cannot meet the other requirement because the information has become generally known. Reasonable security measures alone cannot make information a trade secret if the information is not secret. Nor does it make much sense to give the information legal protection against misappropriation. If it is generally known, it is unnecessary to use improper means to acquire it.

3. The information is not a trade secret. It meets the first requirement for protection, economic value from not being generally known. But Al did not take reasonable security measures, the second requirement. To the contrary, he sought public disclosure of the process and disclosed it to numerous parties without any restrictions on further disclosure. These parties might be expected to disseminate the information further. He did not act unreasonably in a general sense (rather, he sought to further knowledge), but he did not take the steps necessary to secure trade secret protection. In addition, the information likely is not sufficiently secret for protection. This example illustrates a cost of trade secret protection, both to individuals and society. To gain trade secret protection, the owner must take measures to keep it secret — even if he would prefer to disclose it to the public and even if such disclosure would be socially beneficial. Countervailing benefits would obtain if individuals are more likely to produce useful information because of the benefits of trade secret protection and if the information eventually was disclosed to the public.

4. A specious argument, here to emphasize a basic point: If the information is generally known, there is no trade secret. No matter whether the security measures are reasonable or not, security measures alone cannot create trade secret protection if the information is not secret. Some valuable information, by its nature, is difficult to keep secret if utilized. Product design is the paramount example. It is difficult to sell something while keeping it secret (as opposed to keeping secret the process for making it or the ingredients).

5. The information is not a trade secret, even though it remained secret despite the lax security. Reasonable security measures are an independent requirement for trade secret protection. Laxco took no security measures at all, allowing free access to the information and not cautioning its employees to limit disclosure. Laxco might argue that its measures were reasonable, as shown by the fact that they were sufficient to keep the information secret. Courts have held relatively low levels of security to be reasonable when the general industry practice is to have low security and when competitors rarely seek each other's trade secrets. But here, Laxco took no security measures at all, which was unreasonable if Laxco

wished to keep the information unknown. The information remained secret only by accident. So Laxco cannot successfully claim trade secret protection for information it did not itself try to protect.

6. A court likely would hold that BZZZ has taken reasonable security measures. BZZZ has a broad security program in place, clearly identifies the confidential information, and takes several measures to prevent its disclosure outside BZZZ. BZZZ does not take several other relatively cheap measures that may have increased the level of security. But courts grant considerable latitude to parties in deciding whether security measures are reasonable. When a bona fide program is in place, and especially when the information is not disclosed through a lapse in security, courts are likely to hold that reasonable security measures were taken.

7. Sheets cannot enforce the agreement and prevent Varia from working at Transhuron, even though the literal terms of the agreement signed by Varia prevent her from taking the Transhuron job. The law on enforcing such agreements varies from state to state. We do not know what state's law governs this agreement, but no jurisdiction would enforce such an agreement in this case. Some jurisdictions refuse to enforce covenants not to compete at all. In such a state, the agreement would be unenforceable without any further analysis. Other agreements enforce only reasonable covenants not to compete, looking to such factors as the following:

    (1) Is the restraint no greater than necessary to protect the legitimate business interests of the employer?

    (2) Is the restraint unduly harsh and oppressive in curtailing the employee's legitimate efforts to earn a livelihood?

    (3) Is the restraint contrary to sound public policy?

    The agreement in this case is far too broad to be reasonable under such factors. It is far broader than necessary to protect the employer because it prevents Varia from working for any software company for five years, rather than restricting the bar to companies that are competitors of Sheets. It is unduly harsh from Varia's standpoint because it bars her from using her skills in her primary field for five years. From a public policy standpoint, it is not reasonable to unnecessarily keep a productive software engineer barred from working for software companies for five years. The agreement is clearly too broad to be reasonable. Some jurisdictions do not enforce overly broad covenants not to compete; other jurisdictions may enforce them to a reasonable extent. But Varia's new job falls outside reasonable restrictions. She is going to work for a company not competing with Sheets, and she is not going to use any of the specific information she learned from Sheets. Rather she is simply using her professional skills. So in any jurisdiction, the agreement cannot bar Varia from the new employment.

8. A court likely would hold that Christo owns the trade secret rights to the software. Some courts would apply a rule similar to the rule governing ownership of copyrighted material. Under this approach, the rights belong to the employer if the information is developed by an employee within the scope of the employment. Christo is an employee, but he developed the code outside the scope of his employment. His duties include tending to the gardens, ordering supplies, and dealing with suppliers. He used inventory software but was clearly told not to get involved with developing the software. He developed the software at home on his own time. So under the work-for-hire approach, the trade secret rights belong to Christo. Applying such a rule is especially apt here because the trade secret rights and copyright belong to the same person, a more efficient allocation.

    Some courts follow an approach borrowed from patent law, asking whether the employee was hired to develop the information in question. The result is the same under this approach. Christo was employed to perform gardening duties, not software development.

9. Kadio no longer has a trade secret in the information. It meets one requirement for protection, reasonable security measures. It had an extensive program in place to protect the information. The information was disclosed despite those measures but that does not show they were unreasonable. Rather, a scientist used an ingenious method to get past the restrictions.

    But Kadio no longer meets the other requirement, that the information have economic value from not being generally known to those who could get economic value from its use or disclosure. As a result of the public disclosure by Whick, the information is now generally known and easily ascertainable by those who do not know it. The fact that it has become known through apparently wrongful disclosure does not change the fact that the information is generally known. Under the UTSA, the information is no longer a trade secret. Some courts have taken a different approach and tried to enjoin use of trade secret information that has been publicly disclosed. But such attempts are limited to cases in which there was a public disclosure that was somehow limited. Even that approach makes little sense here because the public disclosure is so widespread.

10. The trade secret here is not terminated. It was made available to the public for a short time, despite reasonable security measures. Python retrieved every copy as soon as it was aware of the dissemination. The limited availability did not result in the information becoming known to others. Provided reasonable security has been taken, a disclosure destroys trade secret status only if it actually causes the information to become generally known or readily ascertainable. The information is now clearly not generally known or readily ascertainable, so it is a trade secret.

11. Lopez did not fail to take reasonable security measures. *See General Universal Sys. v. Lee*, 379 F.3d 131 (5th Cir. 2004). Absolute secrecy and perfect security are not required. Rather, reasonable disclosure is not inconsistent with reasonable security. Here, the information was disclosed to a joint venture partner. Such disclosure is reasonable, especially where the very purpose of the joint venture is to exploit the value of the information. Otherwise, joint ventures could never have trade secret protection.

12. Ivan is not liable for misappropriation because the information was not a trade secret. *See Paramanandam v. Herrmann*, 827 N.E.2d 1173 (Ind. Ct. App. 2005). To be a trade secret, there must be both economic value (as a result of not being generally known in the business) and reasonable security measures. Dyanamicscales.com took no security measures but instead left the information freely available on the Web site.

16

Misappropriation and Remedies

The basic cause of action in trade secret law is "misappropriation," not "infringement." This terminology emphasizes the nature of the wrong, which is not infringing another's exclusive right but rather improperly gaining or exploiting access to information.

MISAPPROPRIATION DEFINED AND ILLUSTRATED

Definition of Misappropriation

Misappropriation means improperly acquiring, disclosing, or using a trade secret. But because the trade secret owner does not have exclusive rights to the information, the definition of misappropriation is complex. The Uniform Trade Secret Act (UTSA) definition seeks to exclude the many proper uses that others may make of the information while capturing the many ways in which improper acquisition, disclosure, or use can occur. According to the UTSA, "misappropriation" means:

> (i) acquisition of a trade secret of another by a person who knows or has reason to know that the trade secret was acquired by improper means; or
> (ii) disclosure or use of a trade secret of another without express or implied consent by a person who
> (A) used improper means to acquire knowledge of the trade secret; or

(B) at the time of disclosure or use, knew or had reason to know that his knowledge of the trade secret was

(I) derived from or through a person who had utilized improper means to acquire it;

(II) acquired under circumstances giving rise to a duty to maintain its secrecy or limit its use; or

(III) derived from or through a person who owed a duty to the person seeking relief to maintain its secrecy or limit its use; or

(C) before a material change of his position, knew or had reason to know that it was a trade secret and that knowledge of it had been acquired by accident or mistake.

UTSA §1(2).

Variations on a Theme: Examples of Misappropriation

Suppose that Business has a trade secret, a process for making computer chips. Misappropriation of the trade secret could occur in several different ways.

(1) *Acquiring with reason to know of improper means:* Competitor learns the process by bribing an employee of Business or buys it from Shady, knowing Shady bribed an employee of Business.

(2) *Improper disclosure or use, where:*

(A) *Acquired using improper means:* Competitor bribes an employee of Business and then uses the process to make computer chips or sells (that is, discloses) the process to another business.

(B) Disclosed or used, with reason to know that:

(i) *Information was acquired wrongfully:* Competitor, who acquired the process by bribing an employee of Business, boastfully discloses it to Chemist. Chemist is liable if she discloses it or uses it, even though she did not acquire it wrongfully. She has reason to know it was acquired improperly.

(ii) *Information was acquired through a breach of confidentiality:* Employee approaches Competitor and voluntarily discloses the process, without any prompting or payment from Competitor. Employee does so under circumstances such that Competitor knows or should know that the process is a trade secret. Even if Competitor does not acquire the secret improperly, Competitor is liable for misappropriation if it uses or discloses the secret.

(iii) *Information was acquired subject to an obligation of confidence:* Employee acquires a trade secret subject to an explicit or implicit duty of confidentiality but nevertheless discloses the secret or uses it without the employer's permission. Or Business discloses the process to Contractor, who is building a new plant for Business, after Contractor agrees to maintain confidentiality. Contractor nevertheless sells the process to Competitor or uses it. Both Employee and Contractor acquire the secret properly (Business itself disclosed it to them) but breach an obligation of confidentiality.

(C) *Using or disclosing trade secret acquired by mistake:* Business mails a letter containing the trade secret. Through a clerical mistake, the letter is sent not to Business's chemicals division but rather to a competitor with a similar name. The competitor did not acquire the secret through either improper means or breach of a duty of confidentiality. But if the competitor should know it received the information by mistake but nevertheless uses the process, it misappropriates the trade secret.

Examples of Cases That Do Not Constitute Misappropriation

Many uses or disclosures of information do not constitute misappropriation, as the following four examples demonstrate.

(1) Business uses a special formula in making its treats for toddlers. Business regards the formula as valuable confidential information but does not take reasonable means to keep it secret. An employee sees a memo describing the formula lying unattended on a desk, takes it, and sells the formula to a competitor. Even assuming that employee improperly disclosed the formula and Competitor improperly acquired it, neither is liable for misappropriation. Unless reasonable security measures are taken, there is no trade secret and hence no misappropriation.

(2) Assume the same facts as in the previous paragraph, but in addition suppose that the employee heretofore had been honest and reliable. The employee also needed to know the formula to perform her job. So this probably would have occurred even if reasonable security measures had been taken. Nevertheless, if reasonable security measures are not taken, there is no trade secret to misappropriate. The lack of security need not cause the disclosure.

(3) Business uses a special machine to make fishing hooks. Business lets customers and even competitors know that it uses the special machine but carefully restricts access to avoid anyone making a similar machine. Business obtains a patent on the machine, which describes the machine thoroughly, as required. Competitor has an employee impersonate a government inspector to gain access to the machine, and Competitor makes its own machine from the

impersonator's report. Although Competitor used improper means to acquire the information, once again there is no trade secret (because the information is readily available in a published patent), so there is no misappropriation. A different result obtains if the patent application was still pending and being kept confidential by the U.S. Patent and Trademark Office (USPTO).

(4) Business has a valuable database of marketing information and guards access to the information carefully. Competitor closely studies Business's operations, relying on publicly available information. Competitor manages to duplicate the database. Competitor has acquired information that is Business's trade secret but has not done so improperly. Accordingly, there is no misappropriation.

To illustrate the commercial nature of trade secret law: scientists often do not have a legal claim for behavior that might violate academic principles. A physicist alleged that a colleague and a former graduate student of the plaintiff physicist misappropriated valuable information, namely a "4-level 2-electron atomic model with Pauli Exclusion Principle for simulating the dynamics of active media in a photonic device." The trade secret claim did not succeed because the information was not secret, having been published in a conference proceeding and a master's thesis. The plaintiff argued that misappropriation was applicable because the defendants did not give proper attribution for the idea. Lack of attribution may constitute plagiarism or violate scientific ethics. But publicly available information is not a trade secret, irrespective if the defendant inaccurately claims to have originated the information. *See Ho v. Taflove*, 648 F.3d 489 (7th Cir. 2011).

To have trade secret protection, a party must keep the information secret. In licensing, this may create tension between exploiting and marketing the information, which may require disclosing it, and securing trade secret protection, which requires secrecy. Where a party had authorized access to view software demonstrations, without a nondisclosure agreement, and later produced software with similar functions, there would be insufficient evidence that the party must have used trade secrets used in coding the software.[1]

Duty to Maintain Secrecy or Limit Use

A key concept in misappropriation analysis is the existence of a duty to maintain secrecy or limit use. A duty to maintain secrecy or limit the use of information may arise from an explicit agreement (such as an employee confidentiality agreement or a nondisclosure agreement signed by a joint venturer). A duty to maintain secrecy may also arise out of an existing confidential relationship in which one person "trusts in and relies upon another, whether the relation is a moral, social, domestic, or merely personal one."

---

1. Spear Mktg., Inc. v. BancorpSouth Bank, 2014 U.S. Dist. LEXIS 79319 (N.D. Tex. 2014).

Expansion Plus v. Brown-Forman Corp., 132 F.3d 1083, 1085 (5th Cir. 1998) (citations and quotation marks omitted). Fiduciaries and many employees fit into this category. But the relationship must have the necessary trust and reliance to impose a duty.

Even without an explicit agreement or a confidential relationship, an implicit duty of nondisclosure with respect to the specific information may arise implicitly from the surrounding circumstances. To determine whether there is an implied duty of confidence, courts are guided by the Restatement:

> [T]he proprietor of a trade secret may not unilaterally create a confidential relationship without the knowledge or consent of the party to whom he discloses the secret. No particular form of notice is necessary, however; the question is whether the recipient of the information knew or should have known that the disclosure was made in confidence.

Restatement (First) of Torts §757(b). There was no duty of confidentiality when an inventor submitted an idea for combining two tools on the tool manufacturer's suggestion form, was not involved in business negotiations with the manufacturer, and did not indicate that the submission was made in confidence. *See Smith v. Snap-On Tools Corp.*, 833 F.2d 578 (5th Cir. 1988). By contrast, there was an implied duty of confidentiality when a manufacturer actively solicited disclosure of a valuable manufacturing process during negotiation of the sale of a business (whose value derived in part from the trade secret). *Phillips v. Frey*, 20 F.3d 623 (5th Cir. 1994).

MODES OF MISAPPROPRIATION

There are several modes of misappropriation: improper disclosure, use, or acquisition. With respect to any, the plaintiff must always be able to identify the specific information that qualifies as a trade secret.

Improper Disclosure

Improper disclosure may be misappropriation. The value of a trade secret depends on secrecy, so disclosure threatens the very existence of the trade secret. Likewise, the value depends on the secret being unknown to others in the field, so even a limited disclosure harms the owner. Accordingly, the disclosure necessarily for misappropriation need not be the disclosure to the public that destroys a trade secret—it can be a disclosure that informs a single person.

Improper Use

Use of a trade secret may, if improper, be misappropriation (for example, when obtained through improper means, through breach of a duty of confidentiality or even if through perfectly innocent means such as accident or mistake).

The most common use of the information is using it in the manner that the trade secret owner uses it: A former employee markets products of her new employer using the trade secret customer list from her last employer; competitor uses a manufacturing process acquired by burglary or bribery. But other means of exploiting the information also qualify as use. The employee could use the customer list in a new manner (to market different products or to approach the people on the list not as buyers but as potential investors). Even if the employee added more names or other information to the list, use of the new list could still constitute misappropriation of the original list. Similarly, a modified manufacturing process could still use the original process.

Under the UTSA, the definition of trade secret goes well beyond information that gives a competitive advantage. Some courts reason that "use" necessary for misappropriation must be for "competitive reasons." But other cases have implicitly rejected this limitation, in applying "use" to reach a number of uses not competitive with the trade secret owner. Such a reading is more consistent with the literal language and policy of the UTSA.

A common issue is whether a former employee is (improperly) using trade secrets or (properly) using the experience, knowledge, or skills acquired during his employment. No clear distinction exists. Rather, courts require the employer to identify specific items of information that are being used. Some courts have also attempted to draw the line by requiring tangible evidence. Under this "memory" rule, there is no misappropriation unless the employee takes a physical embodiment of the information (a computer disk, a printed list, an embodiment of the device). But the majority of courts have rejected this approach, holding that trade secret information may be memorized. *See, e.g., Al Minor & Assocs. v. Martin,* 117 Ohio St. 3d 58, 59 (Ohio 2008). Otherwise, employers would have to resort to inefficient measures, such as limiting the access to customer lists even where valid business purposes are undercut.

Example

GlobeRanger, a government contractor, alleged that Software AG misappropriated trade secrets by studying the GlobeRanger's software code developed its own software. Both contractors were working on the same project to develop RFID technology for the Navy.[2] Software AG had access to the code of GlobeRanger, subject to confidentiality agreements, as part of its

---

2. GlobeRanger Corp. v. Software AG US of Am., 836 F.3d 477, 482 (5th Cir. 2016).

work. Software AG employed that access to develop its own software, which the Navy then chose over GlobeRanger for a bigger project.[3] The Software AG argued that it did not misappropriated the code, because it had authority to access it and did not "use" the code in the sense of running the code, rather only studied it. Misappropriation?

Explanation

Software AG did "use" the software in the senses of misappropriation: not by using it to manage inventory, but by using it as a model for developing its inventory management software.[4] The case also illustrates the latitude that courts have in trade secret cases to assess damages, due to the uncertain nature of valuing trade secrets. Damages were properly awarded based on GlobeRanger's cost of developing the information, not limited to the cost that Software AG saved by not developing the information itself.[5]

Improper Acquisition

Improper acquisition alone gives rise to liability. One might argue that if no use or disclosure is made, there are no damages. But the trade secret depends on secrecy, so the mere fact that defendant has acquired it damages the value of the secret. Imposing liability makes it clear that the court can then enjoin use or disclosure, in addition to granting damages (if any).

> The UTSA gives several examples of what constitutes "improper means": "Improper means" includes theft, bribery, misrepresentation, breach or inducement of a breach of a duty to maintain secrecy, or espionage through electronic or other means.

UTSA §1(1). Criminal activity done to acquire a trade secret (burglary, extortion, illegal wiretapping) is clearly improper acquisition. But courts, following the Restatement, find improper means when defendant's actions, even though legal, "fall below the generally accepted standards of commercial morality and reasonable conduct." In the leading case, *E. I. du Pont de Nemours & Co. v. Christopher*, 431 F.2d 1012 (5th Cir. 1970), defendants flew over a construction site to take photos of a plant's layout to learn the trade secret manufacturing process used there. Although such conduct was not criminal, it was deemed improper means.

---

3. *GlobeRanger*, 836 F.3d at 482.
4. *GlobeRanger*, 836 F.3d at 497-499.
5. *GlobeRanger*, 836 F.3d at 501.

Other decisions likewise have found liability for conduct that was not otherwise illegal. Improper means were found when a telecommunications company copied the code of a program from a memory card by falsely telling the possessor of a card that they wanted to put the card into a computer to test it. *See Alcatel USA v. DGI Techs.*, 166 F.3d 772 (5th Cir. 1999). Improper means were also found to include sifting through the garbage of a competitor looking for discarded copies of confidential information. Such decisions often link the issue of improper means to that of reasonable security measures. When the owner of the information has taken reasonable means to keep the information secure, efforts to circumvent those means are likely to be held improper, even if not criminal. This does give rise to a risk of circularity in the analysis. For example, as some have noted, there may have been relatively inexpensive means to frustrate the aerial photographers or dumpster divers, such as covering or disguising the construction layout or shredding documents.

Many means of acquiring trade secrets are not improper. Simply asking an inventor about her invention and asking for a prototype are not improper means. *See Hurst v. Hughes Tool Co.*, 634 F.2d 895 (5th Cir. 1981).

The comments to the UTSA list various proper means to acquire information:

1. discovery by independent invention;
2. discovery by reverse engineering, that is, by starting with the known product and working backward to find the method by which it was developed (the acquisition of the known product, of course, must also be by a fair and honest means, such as purchase of the item on the open market, for reverse engineering to be lawful);
3. discovery under a license from the owner of the trade secret;
4. observation of the item in public use or on public display;
5. obtaining the trade secret from published literature.

UTSA Comments to §1.

Not all efforts directed specifically to discover trade secret information are prohibited. Suppose Paint Maker sells an especially durable house paint. The ingredients and manufacturing process are closely guarded secrets, and simply observing the paint does not disclose the information. Trade secret law does not bar competitors from expending huge efforts in research directed at duplicating the paint, either independently or through reverse engineering. Likewise, it is not misappropriation to canvas the world's paint experts and scientific journals to duplicate the paint.

Why is it "improper means" to scrutinize property with aerial photography but "proper means" to scrutinize a product through reverse engineering? Authorities have suggested that the difference lies in the incentives provided. The underlying policy of trade secret law is to encourage productive activity and discourage activity that simply aims to get others' valuable information on the cheap. Reverse engineering is something of a mix. Its purpose is to duplicate information, but the means used require skills in developing information and the source is property made available to the public.

Reverse engineering will be misappropriation, if unfair means are used. The information must be developed in a truly independent manner. Where the team performing reverse engineering on the product included a former employee of the trade secret holder (one with knowledge of the relevant information), the reverse engineering was not sufficiently independent to avoid misappropriation liability. *See Faiveley Transp. Malmo AB v. Wabtec Corp.*, 572 F. Supp. 2d 400 (S.D.N.Y. 2008).

REMEDIES

Remedies for misappropriation of a trade secret include injunctions, damages, and other proper relief.

Injunctions

The UTSA provides for the entry of injunctions for actual or threatened misappropriation. UTSA §2(a). At one time, courts were split on whether an injunction should be perpetual or should last only until the information had become public. The perpetual injunction approach was seen as a deterrent to wrongful competition. The injunction-until-public approach rested on the policy of remedies as compensation; the injunction should put the parties in approximately the same position they would have been absent the misappropriation. Allowing perpetual relief against the use of public information was seen as anticompetitive (subverting the general purpose of trade secret law). The UTSA (and so the great majority of states) now favors temporary injunctions. In addition to negative injunctions against further use or disclosure, the court may order positive injunctions for return of copies of the information or destruction of products. An injunction may be appropriate for the plaintiff to recover the "kick-start" advantage a competitor gained by using the plaintiff's former employees, in violation of agreements of confidentiality and agreements not to compete. *Litigation Management Inc. v. Bourgeois*, 2011 Ohio 2794 (Ohio Ct. App., 2011).[6] In such a case,

---

6. *See also Aspect Software, Inc. v. Barnett*, 787 F. Supp. 2d 118 (D. Mass. 2011) (where employee joined competitor in breach of covenant not to compete, injunction granted despite new employer's good-faith efforts to protect integrity of trade secret information); *IBM v. Visentin*, 11 Civ. 399 (LAP) (S.D.N.Y. Feb. 16, 2011), *aff'd*, No. 11-902-cv (2d Cir., Nov. 3, 2011) (Hewlett-Packard not subject to injunction under inevitable disclosure doctrine, where it took steps to keep employee from working in areas he covered previously at IBM).

monetary damages could be too difficult to assess and may not adequately restore the plaintiff.

If the information becomes public from another source or through legitimate reverse engineering of plaintiff's product, the rationale for the injunction is gone. Accordingly, the court may terminate the injunction, although it may continue it for a period appropriate to eliminate any advantage gained from the misappropriation. UTSA §2(a).

A difficult question arises when the information becomes public as a result of defendant's misappropriation. If defendant burgles an office to obtain a trade secret manufacturing formula and then not only uses it in defendant's operations but sells it to others, it seems unjust to deny an injunction against defendant on the grounds that the information is no longer secret. One approach is to grant a permanent injunction to prevent defendant from further profiting from its wrong. Another is simply to turn to damages as a remedy (as discussed below).

The UTSA recognizes that, in some circumstances, awarding an injunction is inequitable:

> In exceptional circumstances, an injunction may condition future use upon payment of a reasonable royalty for no longer than the period of time for which use could have been prohibited. Exceptional circumstances include, but are not limited to, a material and prejudicial change of position prior to acquiring knowledge or reason to know of misappropriation that renders a prohibitive injunction inequitable.

UTSA §2(b). Suppose Bike Maker unknowingly acquires a trade secret used in manufacturing bikes and invests in marketing and retooling, relying on its plan to use the process. Once Bike Maker has reason to know the information is a trade secret, further use is misappropriation. But, given Biker Maker's innocent reliance, the court may order the payment of a reasonable royalty rather than order an injunction. Even a knowing misappropriator may be allowed to continue to use the secret under other exceptional circumstances. For example, third parties may have come to rely on the use of the information.

The UTSA authorizes the court to enjoin actual or threatened misappropriation. The trade secret owner need not wait until misappropriation has occurred. Courts have even entered into injunctions when there was no showing of any wrongful disclosure, use, or acquisition — when, under the circumstances, disclosure or use was deemed "inevitable." If a competitor hires a key employee to a position that inevitably requires use of the previous employer's trade secrets, a court may order an injunction, even without a showing of any improper use or disclosure. Such situations are rare, and the injunction should be narrow.

Damages

Damages are also available. The plaintiff is entitled to recover its actual losses and to restitution of defendant's wrongful profits (but without counting the same damages twice). A court may also use other reasonable means of calculating damages, such as payment of a reasonable royalty.

Suppose Firm B acquires a trade secret of Firm A by bribing Employee and then makes a competing product, undercutting A in price. Firm A's damages could include (1) lost profits: the lost sales revenue, minus any costs saved if it cut back on production; (2) unjust enrichment: the bribe received by Employee and profits reaped by Firm B; and (3) reasonable royalty from Firm B, based on sales. But the court should ensure that the multiple categories do not result in the same loss being compensated more than once — such as counting the same lost sales as compensable lost profits to Firm A, as restitution of profits received by Firm B, and as sales subject to a royalty. All elements of damage are also subject to proof of causation. For example, Firm A would have to show that its lost sales or Firm B's additional sales flowed from the misappropriation, not from other factors such as other product qualities or marketing.

Damages are not restricted to lost profits, restitution of unjust enrichment, and royalty damages. Rather, any damages caused by the misappropriation may be compensable. For example, although trade secret is often seen as a variety of tort, it is not subject to the "economic loss" limitation applied in some areas of tort law. *See Bell Helicopter Textron v. Tridair Helicopters,* 982 F. Supp. 318 (D. Del. 1997). Damages could take many forms other than simply lost sales. Wrongful disclosure of an invention could make it public knowledge, leading to loss of the ability to obtain a patent. In such a case, damages properly include the value of the lost patent. *See Evans Cooling Systems v. General Motors Corp.,* 125 F.3d 1448 (Fed. Cir. 1997). But in all cases, only amounts that actually represent damages stemming from the misappropriation should be awarded.

Punitive Damages and Attorneys' Fees

In cases of willful and malicious misappropriation, the UTSA authorizes the court to award punitive damages up to twice the actual damages. The court may also award attorneys' fees in such cases. Attorneys' fees may also be awarded for bad faith claims of misappropriation or for bad faith in making or resisting a motion to terminate an injunction. Both defendants and plaintiffs are potentially liable for attorneys' fees, an important factor in litigation strategy.

Examples

1. *Disgruntled data dump.* Retail Empire employs Techster to administer their computer network and entrusts her with much confidential information, including control of several valuable electronic databases. One day Techster, aggrieved at perceived slights by management, uses her skills to erase every copy of several databases, which were the sole repository of much trade secret information. The databases are lost and impossible to reconstruct. Has Techster misappropriated the trade secrets?

2. *No honor among thieves.* Shady Electronics contacts an executive of Innovative Lites. They agree that the executive will pass on some of Innovative's trade secret machine drawings. Executive takes a large cash payment as an advance. He never delivers the drawings. Rather, he leaves his job at Innovative to retire to a tropical island. Is Shady liable for misappropriation?

3. *Wasted bribe.* Shady Systems bribes the chief of sales of Sunny Systems to obtain Sunny's customer list. Sunny strictly prohibits its salespeople from sharing the list with outsiders. The list, however, is easy to obtain from public sources. Sunny builds systems for use in environmental compliance, and all of Sunny's clients are required to disclose the source of their software with regulatory agencies. Sunny's customer list could be easily obtained from the agency's cross-indexed reports. Shady begins to use the customer list to solicit new clients. Is Shady liable for trade secret misappropriation?

4. *Accidental disclosure.* Food Shop purchases a secondhand computer from Restaurants Revisited, a secondhand dealer in the food services business. Food Shop is amused to find that the computer still contains all the files from its last owner, famous chef Kipper. Food Shop is then thrilled to find copies of all Kipper's recipes, which Kipper heretofore has kept to himself with strict security. Kipper had very carefully arranged for the files to be deleted before he sold the computer, but through an unforeseeable quirk in the process, the files survived. Food Shop makes some discrete inquiries and learns that Kipper had always treated the recipes as trade secrets and that Food Shop is now the only other party to have access to the recipes. Food Shop starts using the recipes for its own products. Kipper sues for trade secret infringement. Food Shop contends that there can be no liability because the information did not come through breach of a confidential relationship or through improper means. Assuming the recipes are trade secrets, is Food Shop liable for misappropriation?

5. *Time's up.* As an employee, Optician has access to a number of Eye Counter's trade secrets. Optician signs an employment contract that contains, among other things, the following two clauses:

1. *Disclosure of confidential information:* Optician agrees not to disclose or use any confidential information of Eye Counter for three years after termination of employment.

2. *Integration:* This writing shall contain the entire agreement between the parties.

Optician leaves Eye Counter to work for a competitor. Just over three years after that, Optician starts to disclose and use a number of valuable trade secrets of Eye Counter. Sued for misappropriation, Optician contends that the obligation of nondisclosure lasted only three years, as set forth in the contract. Eye Counter contends that, in addition to the contract, Optician received the information under an implicit obligation of confidentiality (as would employees generally), and such implicit obligations do not expire. Is Optician barred from using Eye Counter's trade secrets?

6. *Sign in, sign out.* Factory hires Machine Shop to make some machine tools. The two parties have often done business before. They deal with each other at arm's length, both being free to disclose details of their dealing to others. When Machine Shop's employee arrives at Factory to pick up the blueprints for the tools, Factory requires the employee to present identification, to sign a receipt, and to sign a log that indicates the time the blueprints were removed and the purpose. When blueprints are returned, the employee likewise must sign the log. Such procedures are standard in the industry, used for all blueprints. Whether blueprints are deemed confidential or not, such procedures are normally used because they keep track of the drawings for inventory purposes. Machine Shop makes the machine tools for Factory — but it also makes a number of others, which it sells. Such a practice is common in the industry, unless the parties specifically agree to limit use or disclosure. Has Machine Shop taken the blueprints under an obligation not to use or disclose them, beyond making the tools for Factory?

7. *Recall.* Salesman leaves his job selling tanker trucks for Business. To identify potential buyers, Salesman had often used the trade secret customer list of Business. In his new job, Salesman calls several of the customers whose names are on that lengthy list. Salesman did not take a copy of the list or even use his memory to remember the client's names. Rather, the names had been suggested to him by his new employer. The clients were well-known buyers of tanker trucks. Has Salesman misappropriated trade secrets of Business?

8. *Use?* Chembo signs a nondisclosure agreement as part of negotiations to license the use of a trade secret chemical process. Chembo agrees not to use the process unless a licensing agreement is reached. Negotiations fall through. Chembo's chemists then study the process and figure out ways to improve it. The chemists determine that the key to the process is the use of titanium, a novel approach in the field. The chemists develop a

new process, which also relies on titanium. Chembo uses the new process in its hair dye plant. It argues that it cannot be liable for misappropriation because it did not acquire the information by improper means (it was disclosed voluntarily, subject to nondisclosure agreement), disclose it (it was not disclosed outside Chembo), or use it (rather, it used the new process, concocted by its own chemists). Is Chembo liable for misappropriation?

9. *Using nothing.* Oxxon Oil employs researchers, who sign confidentiality agreements, to look for oil deposits. It is generally known that oil is likely to be found in the Gulf of Thomas, a huge body of water with special geological properties. Oxxon's secret research covers three-quarters of the gulf, in vain. Shale, one of the researchers, leaves Oxxon to work for Imaco Oil. Under Shale's lead, Imaco starts to search the other quarter of the gulf. Shale and Imaco argue that they did not use any information because the only information was the location of useless places to drill. Does Shale and Imaco use a trade secret of Oxxon?

10. *Robin Hood.* Health E sells Ognam, a nutritional supplement derived from mangoes. The process for preparing Ognam is a valuable trade secret, and Health E sells Ognam for far more than its costs. Coop bribes Health E's director of manufacturing to breach her contract and disclose the process to Coop. Coop then makes the process public and at the same time starts selling the supplement (prepared using the process) at bargain prices. Coop argues that it is not liable for misappropriation because the information is now publicly available and therefore not a trade secret. Has Coop misappropriated a trade secret?

11. *Long shot.* Turtle Park Bank has a lucrative private banking division. Its clients pay a modest percentage to get close personal attention for all their personal finance needs. Turtle maintains strict security over the identity of its clients, both for privacy reasons and because it knows other banks would dearly like to pitch their services to the clients. A competitor sets up a powerful telescope on the other side of Turtle Park. Despite being separated by the broad park, the competitor is able to see into the offices of Turtle Park Bank. After months of surveillance, looking at the computer screens and other things visible, the competitor manages to reconstruct the client list. After the competitor starts soliciting clients using the list, Turtle Park Bank sues for misappropriation. Assuming the client list is a trade secret, has the competitor used improper means to acquire it?

12. *Can can.* An existing concept in the industry is to have a window in a soda can, with a message inside that can be read only after the can is empty. After drinking the beverage, a consumer could decode the scrambled message inside. Penalty Kick develops "Magic Windows," a clever way to implement that concept. Penalty Kick discloses the design to concept

to Coca-Cola, in confidence. Coca-Cola did not sign on. Coca-Cola subsequently asked another firm to design a windowed can. However, Coca-Cola did not disclose any details of Penalty Kick's concept, rather the firm independently designed a windowed beverage container. Misappropriation?

13. *Idea protected?* Contour Design has the idea for a new product, an ergonomic roller as alternative to computer mouse. Before the product is even made, an employee passes the idea to a competitor. Misappropriation of a trade secret?

14. *Misappropriation?* A disgruntled employee deleted copies of the source code of the company's trade secret software, the company's crown jewel. Then, he deposited nonconfidential portions of the software as part of an attempt to register the software's copyright and threatened to withhold the software from the company. Misappropriation?

Explanations

1. Misappropriation requires improper disclosure, use, or acquisition. None of those are present here. Techster did not use the information. Rather, she deleted copies of the information (although perhaps one could make some kind of argument that use was required to perform the deletion, depending on the storage medium). Rather, Retail Empire must find some other tort or contract theory for recovery.

2. Shady is not liable for misappropriation. Improper acquisition, disclosure, or use has not yet occurred, so technically there is no misappropriation. Courts may also enjoin threatened misappropriation. But that is no longer present here because Shady no longer has access to the information.

3. Shady is not liable for trade secret misappropriation. The information is readily ascertainable, so it is not a trade secret. Even though Shady used improper means, Shady did not misappropriate a trade secret.

4. Food Shop is liable for misappropriation. One who acquires another's trade secret through accident can be liable for misappropriation if she uses or discloses it after having reason to know it was a trade secret. Food Shop did not improperly acquire the information. But Food Shop knew that it was through accident that it had acquired the recipes and that they were trade secrets. By using them, Food Shop became liable for misappropriation.

5. A court likely would hold that Optician is not barred from using the trade secrets. The parties agreed to a three-year term limiting use and

had an integration clause seeking to explicitly bar any other terms. Moreover, contracts limiting employees are generally construed against the employer. Accordingly, the only express limit on disclosure is the explicit three-year limit, leaving the employee free after three years of any confidentiality requirements. To read in an additional implied limitation is to give the employer more than the parties explicitly bargained for. Cf. *Expansion Plus v. Brown-Forman Corp.*, 132 F.3d 1083 (5th Cir. 1998). This case illustrates one of the hazards of using explicit agreements—matters not explicitly addressed may be deemed outside protection.

6. Machine Shop probably is under no duty limiting use or disclosure. Machine Shop used the blueprints. It has not signed a confidentiality agreement or nondisclosure agreement. It did not acquire the blueprints as a result of improper means, wrongful disclosure, or accident. It is only liable if it acquired the blueprints subject to an implied limitation on use and disclosure. There was no confidential relationship. Nor was there the necessary notice to impose a duty with respect to the transaction. There must be notice sufficient to inform a reasonable person that the disclosure was made in confidence. The only notice of such a limitation was the log and the receipts. However, such means alone gives notice of trade secret status when they are normal procedures in the industry for all blueprints, whether confidential or not. The Machine Shop did not take the information subject to a duty to limit use or disclosure.

7. Salesman is not liable for misappropriation. He did not use the list, either a copy or from memory. The names were on the list, but Salesman received them from another source. It would be a different matter if he called every customer on the lengthy list by using a copy or his memory.

8. Chembo is liable for misappropriation for using the information in violation of the duty not to use it. "Use" of the information does not mean only its normal use by the trade secret owner. Chembo did not use the process to make hair dye, but it used it to make its own process. The purpose of trade secret law is to guard the economic value of information, and Chembo exploited the economic value of the information as best it could. Cf. *Mangren Research & Dev. Corp. v. National Chem. Co.*, 87 F.3d 937 (7th Cir. 1996).

9. Oxxon and Shale do use the information, rendering them liable for misappropriation. The negative information that three-quarters of the gulf appear to be oil-free had economic value. It saved Imaco the cost of doing its own searching in such areas and greatly narrowed the region worth searching. So it used the information in deciding where to search.

10. Coop is liable for misappropriation. At the time that it acquired the information by improper means, the information had not become public. So it becomes liable for misappropriation. The fact that the information

subsequently became public does not wipe out the liability for Health E's lost profits. To the contrary, the loss of the trade secret counts as damages attributable to the misappropriation.

11. The line between proper and improper acquisition is far from settled, but the weight of authority probably would indicate a finding of improper means here. The spying seems to fall within the UTSA comments, as "espionage through electronic or other means." UTSA §1(1). The competitor's actions may not have violated any criminal statutes. The competitor did not burgle the offices or bribe any employees. The relevant standard, however, is higher: actions that fall below "the generally accepted standards of commercial morality and reasonable conduct." Aerial photography, searching through garbage cans, or nonfraudulent misrepresentations to third parties have all been held to constitute improper means. Such courts reason that permitting such acquisition of information would require trade secret holders to take unreasonably strict security measures. Telescopic surveillance into an office for a period of months seems to fall into the same category.

12. No misappropriation. *See Penalty Kick Mgmt. v. Coca-Cola Co.*, 318 F.3d 1284 (11th Cir. 2003). Penalty Kick did have a trade secret. Its design was valuable, and the value derived from not being generally known to others. Coca-Cola knew the trade secret and was subject to a duty of confidence. But Coca-Cola did not misappropriate the trade secret because it did not use or disclose it. Rather, it disclosed only publicly known information, and the design firm independently developed a product design.

13. Trade secret protection may attach to information before it has yielded any income. Trade secrets are usually information used in making or selling: manufacturing processes, customer lists, chip designs, software. The value is shown by an existing market for the goods or services. But if the information is valuable, protection may attach, early in the product cycle. A concept not yet made into a product (an ergonomic roller as alternative to computer mouse) had sufficient commercial value to be a trade secret. *See Contour Design, Inc. v. Chance Mold Steel Co.*, 2010 WL 174315 (D.N.H. Jan. 14, 2010). Start-ups and other entrepreneurial thinkers have some legal protection for valuable ideas.

14. Breach of contract, perhaps. But trade secret misappropriation requires wrongful acquisition, use, or disclosure of the trade secret. Deleting it, withholding it, and submitting partial copies in confidence to the Copyright Office fall outside those categories.

PART V

Three State Law Theories and Preemption

17

Three More State Law Theories and Federal Preemption

CONTRACT LAW AND IDEA SUBMISSIONS

Mere ideas are not protected by copyright, patent, or trademark law. The owner of a copyright has the exclusive right to make copies, distribute the work publicly, adapt it, display copies publicly, or perform the work publicly. But copyright protects only creative expression, not ideas (no matter how original and creative). Likewise, a patentee has the right to exclude others from using, making, offering to sell, selling, or importing the invention. But mere ideas are not patentable; the invention must be reduced to practice as a product or process. A trademark owner may exclude others from using her symbol in a manner that is likely to confuse consumers, but trademark law likewise does not protect ideas. A valuable idea could have sufficient potential commercial value to be a trade secret; but trade secret does not grant the owner exclusive rights in the idea. Rather, he has trade secret protection only if he keeps the idea secret, using reasonable security measures.

Contract law can be used, not to give exclusive rights against the world (like a copyright, patent, or trademark), but to impose an obligation on the recipient of the idea. The submitter could offer to disclose the idea to the studio, publisher, or manufacturer, subject to an agreement to share the proceeds of the movie, book, or toy. Contract law gives some partial protection for ideas, provided the parties so agree (implicitly or explicitly). An inventor might share her ideas with potential investors subject to a nondisclosure agreement, a contract by which the recipients of the information agree not to use it. More broadly, employees, investors, and others in a firm often sign contracts controlling their use of ideas: nondisclosure agreements, noncompete agreements, assignments of rights concerning works and inventions. That way, ideas may be circulated within the firm, with contract law giving some protection against the ideas being disclosed. *See* Oren Bar-Gill & Gideon Parchomovsky, *Intellectual Property and the Boundaries of the Firm* (2004) (suggesting that intellectual property law affects the optimal size of the firm because pre-patent innovation must be carried out within the boundaries of a single firm).

Here we will focus on the idea submission cases. The lack of protection for ideas can pose a problem for someone who has an idea she believes is valuable. Someone might have an idea for a movie, book, or children's toy. To exploit the idea, she might need to convince a movie studio, publisher, or manufacturer to produce the proposed item. But if she discloses an unprotected idea, the recipient could simply make the movie, book, or toy and sell it without paying her for it. If the idea is unprotected, the recipient does not need the creator's permission and is not obliged to pay her royalties.

In a typical idea submission case, the submitter alleges that she submitted a valuable idea that the recipient used without paying compensation required by an explicit or implicit obligation. Courts have many sources of law to apply to such fact patterns, including contract, unjust enrichment, fiduciary relations, property, and fraud. Here we discuss just some of the contract law rules that courts have employed in idea submission cases.

Courts apply several contract doctrines but with common threads. Courts may require that the idea be novel and concrete, that the parties have an express or implied agreement, and that the recipient have actually used the idea submitted. The standards for novelty and concreteness vary considerably. An idea may not be novel if the recipient already knew it, could easily have developed it herself, or could have gotten it elsewhere. A higher standard of novelty might require that the idea also be strikingly creative. Concreteness will not be met if the idea is too vague or preliminary to be of any specific use. A higher standard may require that the idea be developed into a commercialized form.

As discussed below, courts look to the requirements listed above in applying contract law doctrine to idea submission cases.

Was a Contract Formed?

Express Contract: Offer and Acceptance, Definiteness

The requirements of offer and acceptance provide several hurdles for a submitter to overcome to show a binding contract. Ideas are often submitted in a manner that does not amount to an offer to enter into a contract. The submitter may just send in the idea, send in the idea with a request for payment, or leave the question of compensation to the judgment of the recipient. If the idea is not concrete, an intended offer may be too vague to be the basis of a contract.

Even if the idea is submitted as part of a clear offer to enter into a contract, the recipient may clearly reject the offer. She may make an acceptance but one that varies the terms; without an acceptance that matches the offer, courts may hold no contract formed. The submitter may also claim that the recipient, by using the idea, accepted the offer by conduct. But when the idea was not novel or concrete, the court may hold that there was no acceptance by conduct. Suppose the nonoriginal idea was to make a film from a best-selling detective novel. If the recipient studio did indeed make the film, a court could hold that it nonetheless did not accept the contract by taking such an obvious course of action. The idea may also be too vague to have been accepted by conduct. Likewise, if the recipient's project is different from the idea submitted, there is no acceptance by conduct.

Consideration

If the idea submitted is not valuable (because it was not novel and concrete), the consideration necessary for a binding contract may not be shown. Consideration is a notoriously elusive doctrine in contract law. But when one party to the transaction gives nothing of value to the other, courts can use the requirement of consideration to hold that there was no binding contract, even if an express agreement was made.

Implied Contract

In many idea submission cases, there is no express offer and acceptance of a legally binding contract. In some circumstances, courts hold an implied agreement exists, as evidenced from the conduct of the parties and the surrounding circumstances. Courts look to such factors as industry custom, whether the recipient encouraged submission of the idea, previous dealings between the parties, any confidential relationship between the parties, the status and commercial sophistication of the parties, and the nature of the idea and the relevant business. A commonly used test is whether a reasonable person in the recipient's position would have considered that the idea was submitted subject to an implicit condition that use of the idea would require compensation.

Did the Defendant Use the Submitted Idea?

If the defendant does not use the submitted idea, there may be no obligation to pay, even if a binding contract was made. Suppose Writer and Studio agree that Writer will submit an idea for a movie to Studio, contingent on a fee and acknowledgment in the credits of the film. Writer's idea is a comedy based on the nineteenth-century comic novel *Diary of a Nobody*. But Studio already has such a project under way, with someone working on the screenplay and others choosing a cast. Because Studio did not get the idea from Writer, a court may hold it did not use Writer's idea, and there is no liability to pay. The result might be the same if Studio subsequently made a movie based on a nineteenth-century comic novel—but a different one than suggested.

If the idea submitted is not novel and concrete, it may also be difficult to show that defendant used the idea. If the idea is not novel, defendant may likely have gotten the same idea from another source. If the idea is vague or preliminary, it is difficult to show that defendant actually used that particular idea.

Did the Submitter Perform the Promised Contractual Obligation?

If the idea is not novel and concrete, the submitter may have failed to live up to her obligation under the contract. Suppose Consultant offers to sell a valuable new manufacturing process to Business, contingent on Business paying Consultant a percentage of revenue. After the agreement is made, Consultant submits a process that is already well known in the industry (and so not novel) or is very vague. Consultant's failure to produce an idea that matched its representations breaches the contract, relieving Business of the obligation to pay.

Avoiding Contractual Obligations

Some firms maintain policies to ensure that they are not deemed to have explicitly or implicitly agreed-to contracts with idea submitters. Venture capitalists frequently make clear that they will not sign nondisclosure agreements when they hear "pitches" of business ideas. Otherwise, a venture capitalist might turn down an investment in one company, then find itself unable to invest in others that have similar ideas. A movie studio, music company, or book publisher may have a policy of sending back unsolicited manuscripts or tapes without reading or hearing them, in order to avoid any possible obligation to the authors. It might also save some time—but pass on some opportunities. The fact that ideas are unprotected, in some cases, makes it more difficult for the creator of the idea to share it with others. But the alternative—ownership of abstract ideas—would result in much greater restrictions on the flow of ideas.

Examples

1. *No-brainer.* Tenzing successfully builds and sells ice axes for mountaineering under the brand name K1. Tenzing's sales have been increasing at 10 percent a year for the past six years. Edmund, an engineer and marketing consultant, reads an article in a finance magazine lauding Tenzing's operation. Edmund approaches Tenzing and offers to give him a suggestion that will increase Tenzing's sale by 10 percent, on the condition that Tenzing pays a hefty finder's fee. Tenzing agrees to the transaction. Edmund then says, "Just keep doing what you are doing. Success breeds success." Tenzing continues to operate his business without substantial changes, just as he had planned before speaking with Edmund. Tenzing's sales increase by 10 percent in the next year. Is Tenzing contractually bound to pay Edmund's hefty fee?

2. *Molehill?* Margaret, the CEO of Mortar Products, is concerned about whether her company is keeping up with the times. Mortar has made and sold essentially the same line of building supplies for over a decade. Mortar advertises regularly in trade magazines, featuring its slogan ("Good old dependable Mortar"), some endorsements by well-known builders, and rather prosaic listings of its products and their prices. Margaret and her management team are considering expanding into new product areas and introducing a new, snazzy advertising campaign. Margaret hires Lourdes Consulting Group to conduct a thorough marketing survey. The parties draw up a detailed contract, specifying the tasks Lourdes will perform (customer surveys, focus groups with leading buyers, benchmark comparisons with various companies, drafting of possible marketing campaigns). Lourdes and her associates spend several thousand hours compiling data and analyzing it. They draft a report detailing their findings and presenting a plan of action. In sum, the plan is for Margaret to avoid any substantial changes in the way the business is run. The present product lines are increasingly profitable. If Mortar were to expand into new product lines, it would be difficult to win market share, and the necessary investment in manufacturing and distribution facilities would be prohibitive. Even the marketing campaign should remain unchanged. The research shows great affection and trust among prospective buyers for the campaign. Margaret reads the report with great interest. She decides to follow the advice. She informs Lourdes, however, that she will not pay the fee because the report did not tell them to do anything they were not already doing. Is Margaret contractually obliged to pay the fee?

3. *Dear reader.* Phisto, a computer scientist, figures out an elegant way to write a short program that gets rid of advertising for Internet users. Phisto submits an article to a computer science journal detailing his method. He also posts the paper on his Web page. In the first footnote to the paper,

Phisto includes the following language: "Anyone who uses my method hereby agrees to pay me the modest fee of $365 per year, $1 a day for avoiding all those annoying ads." Such a condition is highly unusual in the area. Rather, the information in published academic articles is generally considered to be free for whatever uses readers find. Phisto's paper becomes widely circulated among software developers, many of whom use it to write programs putting the method to work. The programs are in turn widely distributed and are often included with Web browsers. Soon, millions of people are using programs that incorporate Phisto's method. Are they all obliged to pay Phisto $1 a day?

Explanations

1. Tenzing is not contractually bound to pay Edmund's hefty fee. A court would very likely hold that the idea was not sufficiently novel and concrete to support the creation of a binding obligation. Edmund's suggestion was completely obvious, based on no particular useful information. It may also be too vague to meet the concreteness requirement. Edmund's knowledge of Tenzing's operations was limited to reading a magazine article. So when Edmund advised him to continue his course of action, that advice had little specific content to it.

   A court might use the lack of novelty and concreteness to apply any of several doctrines. It might hold that Edmund did not provide the necessary consideration for a binding contract, that Edmund's offer was too vague to form a binding contract, or that Tenzing did not use Edmund's obvious idea (rather that Tenzing would have done the same thing without the suggestion).

2. Margaret is contractually obliged to pay the fee. This case involves both an idea submission and a contract for other services. Lourdes's performance of the various research services alone entitles her to at least compensation. In addition, the ideas submitted did not lack novelty and concreteness. Rather, they were well-supported arguments for choosing between various alternatives, for a specific business under specific circumstances. The plan of action could be described as obvious, but the suggestion was based on considerable research and analysis. Unlike the last case, the parties had a clearly drafted contract that specified their respective duties in detail. The suggestion had value because it was based on the research and analysis. Margaret clearly did use the idea (as well as the fruits of the research and analysis). Lourdes gave consideration—not just the suggestion but also the considerable resources used in compiling and analyzing data. So here, the court would hold that the various contract law requirements were met and that Margaret was obliged to pay for the specific, agreed-on services that she received.

3. Phisto is not entitled to payment from any of the people using his idea, neither the developers who wrote his method into their programs nor the users who used those programs. This case illustrates the fact that even if a novel is novel and concrete, submission of the idea to others who use it does not always entitle the submitter to compensation. Rather, there must be other circumstances to give rise to an express or implied obligation to pay for the idea. Phisto submitted his idea in a form that would make it part of the public knowledge without any obligation to pay on the part of others. He did include the legend "Anyone who uses my method hereby agrees to pay me the modest fee of $365 per year, $1 a day for avoiding all those annoying ads." Others did subsequently use the method. But a court would be unlikely to hold that this amounted to either an express or implied contract.

The circumstances of submission were not such to create an implied obligation. The method was published in an academic journal, in which writers and readers normally understood information to be free for use. The recipients had no confidential relationship with Phisto and had not encouraged him to submit commercially useful information. Indeed, most users did not have any direct contact with Phisto. No one made an express verbal acceptance of the contract. Nor would a court find acceptance by conduct. Once the method had been published, it was widely known information among the public. Use of public information does not constitute acceptance of a contract (the doctrines of consideration or offer and acceptance could be used here). Otherwise, Phisto would effectively have the right to exclude others from using his publicly known process.

MISAPPROPRIATION

The tort of misappropriation comes from *International News Service v. Associated Press*, 248 U.S. 215 (1918). AP and INS were two competing news services. AP, a cooperative of newspapers, expended considerable resources in gathering news and distributing news reports to its member newspapers throughout the United States. INS systematically obtained copies of the reports as quickly as possible and wired the information to its client newspapers. INS acted so quickly that its clients often received the reports as quickly as the local AP member newspaper.

The Court held that INS was liable for the tort of misappropriation, under federal common law, without defining the scope of the tort. A number of states later adopted the tort under state common law. Some cases interpreted the tort broadly, to grant a right against the taking of valuable information, where such taking seemed to violate business ethics. Other cases construed it very narrowly. The drafters of the Third Restatement of Unfair Competition even advocated the rejection of the misappropriation tort because it was ill-defined and covered material better left to other law such as copyright and patent.

The leading case now is *National Basketball Association v. Motorola*, 105 F.3d 841 (2d Cir. 1997). Motorola transmitted to its pager customers the latest information about NBA basketball games while the games were still in progress. The *NBA* court held that, to avoid preemption by the federal copyright act, the misappropriation tort survived under New York law in only a narrow version, applying where

1. a plaintiff generates or gathers information at a cost;
2. the information is time-sensitive;
3. a defendant's use of the information constitutes free-riding on the plaintiff's efforts;
4. the defendant is in direct competition with a product or service offered by the plaintiffs; and
5. the ability of other parties to free-ride on the efforts of the plaintiff or others would so reduce the incentive to produce the product or service that its existence or quality would be substantially threatened.

Motorola's conduct did not fall within such a narrowly defined tort. In particular, the fifth element was clearly not met. The existence of the NBA was not threatened by Motorola providing information over pagers, even if the NBA's ability to create a competing service was hampered.

Examples

1. *Database.* Info LLC compiles white pages telephone books. Info spends considerable resources in gathering the names, addresses, and telephone numbers of everyone in a town, arranging the information alphabetically by name, and printing and distributing the phone books. Info gives the books away, making money from selling advertisements in the books. Data LLC, a competitor, gets copies of the phone books by buying them from recipients. Data uses machines to disassemble the books and scan the information, at much less cost than Info needed to compile the information. Data publishes and sells its own phone books. Is Data liable for misappropriation under the NBA test?

2. *The edge.* Punter News is a news service for stock market traders. Punter has dozens of sources and long-standing relationships with many important people in the finance world. Punter is often the first news service to get wind of developments that will affect stock prices. Punter charges a very high fee for subscribers. In return, Punter sends news out to subscribers as quickly as possible, 24 hours a day, and makes special efforts to reach

subscribers wherever they are. The subscribers agree to use the information for their own trading purposes but not to share the information with others. One of Punter's subscribers is Levon Investing. Punter learns that Marta, an administrator at Levon, has used her access to Punter's reports to trade for her own account over the last several years. Marta has made many thousands of dollars in profits from this activity. Marta is aware that her use violates the terms on which the information is provided to Levon. Her conduct also violates her contract with Levon because it is contrary to Levon's employee regulations. Is Marta liable to Punter for the tort of misappropriation under the NBA test?

Explanations

1. Data is not liable for misappropriation under the NBA test. Most of the elements are met: Info gathered the information at a cost; Data's use probably constitutes free-riding because Data put little effort into getting the information; Data and Info are in direct competition. But there is no showing that Data meets the last element, that the ability of people to make such use of the information would drastically reduce the incentive to gather the information. And the second element is clearly not met. The information is not time-sensitive; to the contrary, the information in a phone book is intended to remain useful for a long period of time. So not all of the necessary elements are met here. The case illustrates the fact that NBA leaves only a very narrow tort of misappropriation.

2. Marta is not liable to Punter for misappropriation. One element is that the defendant be in direct competition with a product or service offered by the plaintiff. But Marta does not offer a product or service that competes with Punter. To the contrary, she is simply buying and selling stock, rather than selling products or services. Marta is breaching her contract with Levon and knows her use violates the terms on which the information is provided. But the misappropriation tort does not depend solely on the wrongfulness of the defendant's conduct. Rather, as formulated by NBA, it requires meeting several very specific limitations. Note that some earlier cases may have applied misappropriation here, reasoning that Marta used valuable commercial information in an unethical manner. But the trend, exemplified by NBA, is away from such a broad formulation.

RIGHT OF PUBLICITY

States are increasingly recognizing a right of publicity, an exclusive right to the commercial exploitation of one's identity. *See generally* J. Thomas

McCarthy, *The Rights of Publicity and Privacy* (2d ed. 1987 and Supp.). Several policies support such a right. A right of publicity can create an incentive for people to do things that make them well known and create a demand for uses of their identity. The right can also be seen as preventing free-riding on the goodwill of others and as enforcing a moral right to control the exploitation of one's identity. The right can serve a role similar to trademarks, to prevent consumer deception about an individual's association with goods and services. Historically, the right of publicity is often considered to be an extension of the right of privacy.

Other policy considerations weigh in the other direction. Like copyright, the right of publicity is a restraint on expression. Identities are material for speech, from entertainment to art to news reporting to gossip. The subject matter most interesting to people is people. To the extent that individuals control expression concerning them, avenues of expression are foreclosed. So a delicate balance is at stake.

The scope of the right of publicity varies considerably from state to state (and in many respects remains undefined). Some of the key issues in defining the extent of the right to publicity follow.

Whether the State Recognizes the Right of Publicity

Most states have adopted a right of publicity cause of action, through case law or statute. But a number of states have not. Generally, these states have not definitively rejected the cause of action. More often, the issue has not been decided by the highest court in the state.

Who Has a Right of Publicity

The right of publicity can be applied only when the individual has become well known. If an individual has not been the subject of publicity, one who uses her image for commercial purposes may not be undercutting uses that would have been made. The right could also be limited to its incentive rationale. If the right is an incentive to acts that gain acclaim, it could be limited to individuals who have earned fame through their achievements or professional efforts, as opposed to more accidental celebrities. But the general approach has been to extend the right to all individuals, even if there exists little public interest in a particular individual.

How Broadly the Protected Identity Is Defined

The right could be restricted to the use of one's name and likeness. The trend, however, is to recognize more broadly many ways in which individuals may be recognized. The right can apply to names, identifying phrases such as nicknames or catchphrases, voice, style of speaking, or visual likenesses broadly defined (such as a silhouette or even a robot dressed, coifed, and posed in a way to bring a particular celebrity to mind).

States agree that, whether the protected modes are broadly or narrowly defined, the characteristic at issue must be one that could identify the subject. If an anonymous individual has the name Carla Peirce, her right of publicity is not infringed if a character coincidentally named Carla Peirce is featured in advertisements because the public would not link the fictional Peirce with the real one. By contrast, it is less settled whether the likeness need be one that would be used by the public to actually identify the person. Suppose the face of an unknown person is used in a commercial, and the public has no idea who she is. Whether that invokes the right of publicity is a question unsettled in most jurisdictions.

How Broadly the Exclusive Right to Commercial Exploitation Is Defined

The right can be applied to uses of the subject's identity in advertising goods or services. But it could also be extended to a whole spectrum of commercial uses.

The Duration of the Right

The term of protection may be set in many ways: the time in which the subject is well known to the public; a given term of years; the lifetime of the subject; the lifetime of the subject plus a given term of years; or even a perpetual right that would pass from generation to generation.

Assignability

Depending on how the right is categorized may govern whether the right is an assignable piece of property or an inalienable right.

The Scope of Limitations to the Right

By definition, the right of publicity is a limitation on freedom of expression. Accordingly, some states have expressly recognized such exceptions as news reporting, commentaries, or parodies. When the right is understood very broadly, the First Amendment can also come into play as a restriction. The California Supreme Court has formulated a balancing test, holding

589

that the right of publicity is trumped by the First Amendment when "the work in question adds significant creative elements so as to be transformed into something more than a mere celebrity likeness or imitation." *Compare Comedy III Prods. v. Gary Saderup*, 25 Cal. 4th 387 (Cal. 2001) (right of publicity infringed by sale of T-shirts bearing mere likeness of Three Stooges, without transformative element) and *Winter v. DC Comics*, 30 Cal. 4th 881, 885 (Cal. 2003) (First Amendment prevents right of publicity action by blues musician brothers, where characters in comic book were based on brothers but were transformed into "villainous half-worm, half-human offspring").

The right can also be subject to limitations similar to those in copyright, such as first sale. If an item bearing a person's likeness were sold, then the owner would likely have the right to display or further distribute the item without infringing the right of publicity.

Examples

The states of Broadonia and Narrovania have each recently enacted statutes creating a right of publicity.

The Broadonia statute reads:

> Every person, living or dead, shall have the exclusive right to any commercial exploitation of her name, likeness, voice, signature, or any other symbol, representation or combination thereof that could identify her. Such right shall have the attributes of personal property and shall endure for the life of the individual plus fifty years. Anyone who infringes this right shall be liable for damages and attorneys' fees. Mere references to such person for literary, cultural, news reporting, critical, or entertainment purposes shall not fall within such right, where such reference does not have a commercial purpose.

The Narrovania statute reads:

> Every well-known person shall have the exclusive right to use her name or face, where the sole purpose of such use is to advertise goods or services. Such right shall not be assignable or survive the owner of the right.

1. *Bandwagon.* Eagle Iron wins several professional golf tournaments in a row and becomes nationally famous. Green Beer runs television advertisements that consist of close-ups of Eagle's face as she plays, while a voice in the background extols the relaxing powers of Green Beer ale. Eagle has not given permission for the use of her image. Is Green Beer liable under the law of Broadonia? Of Narrovania? Would the result be different if rather than a famous golfer, Green Beer had just used close-ups of the face of an obscure golf fan?

2. *Shape.* Eagle continues to have great success. Every time she wins a tournament, she raises her putter over her head in a distinctive celebratory

gesture. Instant Products begins to sell a T-shirt that bears only a simple photo of Eagle making her well-known gesture. The photo is of too poor quality to make the face recognizable, but most viewers of the photo instantly recognize Eagle as the only person who makes such a gesture standing on a golf green. Is Instant Products liable under the law of Broadonia? of Narrovania? Would the result be different if the photo were simply a stock photo of Eagle's face?

3. *Truer than life.* Widget is a character in Otter's new novel, *Look-In.* To get the book published, Otter sold the copyright to Bond for several thousand dollars. Widget, a college student struggling to find her identity, strikes a chord with students nationwide. Soon Agent authorizes an animated film to be made based on Otter's book. After the film is released, Agent sells a license to Carrie's Phone Cards to use the face of Widget, copied from the film, in phone card advertising. Otter, aghast at the commercialization of Widget, files an action to enjoin the advertising. Otter acknowledges that he has sold the copyright to the book but claims that, as the creator of Widget, he owns Widget's rights to publicity. Would Otter succeed under the Broadonia statute? The Narrovania statute?

Explanations

1. Green Beer is liable under both the Broadonia and Narrovania statutes. Eagle Iron's face is used prominently in television advertisements while beer is praised in the background. Under the Broadonia statute, that constitutes "commercial exploitation" of her likeness. Under the Narrovania statute, that constitutes the requisite use of her face, where the sole purpose is to advertise goods or services.

    If an obscure subject had been chosen, the result would be different under the Narrovania statute, which only applies to well-known persons. But the result would be the same under the Broadonia statute. The use of the individual's face constitutes commercial exploitation of her likeness when the entire commercial is made of close-ups of the individual's face. The Broadonia statute does not require that the public be able to actually identify the person whose likeness is used.

2. Instant Products may be liable under the Broadonia statute but is not under the Narrovania statute. The Narrovania statute does not apply because it applies only to uses of the subject's name or face. Here, the T-shirt does not use Eagle's name or face.

    The Broadonia statute requires "commercial exploitation" of a representation that would identify Eagle. The T-shirt does include the necessary identifying representation because the figure in the photo is readily identifiable as Eagle. The issue is whether using the representation on T-shirts qualifies as commercial exploitation of the identifying representation. Putting her figure on T-shirts and selling them may constitute the necessary commercial exploitation. But a court might reason that the statute is not intended to reach every commercial activity that invokes an individual. The statute does contain an exception for "mere references" for various purposes, provided there is no commercial purpose. The making and selling of T-shirts seems to have a commercial purpose and also does not fit clearly into one of the protected purposes. But "commercial exploitation" might be read to include only uses of the subject's identity in advertising or similar uses.

In addition, the use of the image on T-shirts is an expressive use and not "commercial speech," which receives limited First Amendment protection. So, although the case law is as yet unsettled, it may be unconstitutional to grant exclusive rights that would so restrict expression concerning individuals.

If the T-shirt used a stock photo of Eagle's face, the analysis would be similar under the Broadonia statute, although the argument for "commercial exploitation" might be a little stronger. Under the Narrovania statute, the issue would be closer. The photo of the face (unlike the photo of the gesturing figure) falls within the protected uses of name or face. But the Narrovania statute is limited to cases in which the sole purpose is to advertise goods or services. Here, the image appears on the goods themselves. So the image serves as the product itself—although it might also be used to advertise the product wherever the T-shirts are exhibited for sale. So, the *sole* purpose is not advertising, and the use would not fall inside the Narrovania statute.

3. Otter would not succeed under either statute. The question is whether a fictional person has a right of publicity. The Broadonia statute grants rights to "Every person, living or dead." The Narrovania statute grants rights to "Every well-known person" and provides that the right does not survive the subject. Both statutes appear to apply only to actual human beings as opposed to fictional persons (such as characters in works of fiction) or to strictly legal persons (such as like corporations). So there is no right to publicity with respect to Widget.

FEDERAL PREEMPTION OF STATE LAW AFFECTING INTELLECTUAL PROPERTY RIGHTS

The federal government and the states both have the power to regulate in the area of intellectual property. Under the Constitution, federal law is the supreme law of the land. To the extent that federal law preempts regulation in an area, state law is invalid. Courts apply three types of preemption:

1. *Explicit preemption:* A federal statute may expressly preempt state law in the relevant field, completely or partly.
2. *Field preemption:* If federal law occupies the entire field, there is no room for application of state law.
3. *Conflict preemption:* State law is preempted if
   a. it would be impossible to comply with both state and federal law, or
   b. state law stands in the way of accomplishment of the objectives of the federal law.

The federal trademark and trade secrets statute generally permit the states to continue trademark and trade secret regulation.[1] The preemptive reach of the copyright and patent statutes, however, is considerable.[2]

Copyright Preemption

Copying information potentially violates many types of state law, such as contract law (by using the information in violation of contractual limits or without paying agreed compensation), trade secret law (by obtaining the information through misappropriation of a trade secret), rights of publicity (by making commercial use of something that identifies an individual), unfair competition (by selling copied products), or the tort of misappropriation (by copying valuable information). The federal copyright act preempts some state regulation of rights against copying.

Explicit Preemption

The Copyright Act expressly preempts state law granting equivalent rights. 17 U.S.C. §301(a). Under §301, the Copyright Act exclusively governs all rights that

1. are equivalent to any of the §106 exclusive rights,

---

1. Some provisions of the Lanham Act do place specific limits on state regulation. *See* 15 U.S.C. §1125(c) (limiting application of state dilution law to federally registered marks); §1121(b) (limiting powers of states to require changes in federally registered marks). There could also be preemption if a state statute conflicted with the federal scheme, but cases have been rare. *See* Paul Heald, *Federal Intellectual Property Law and the Economics of Preemption,* 76 Iowa L. Rev. 959 (1991).
2. This chapter discusses federal/state preemption. Preemption could also occur between federal law and tribal law. In efforts to protect traditional knowledge and promote economic development, tribes increasingly consider regulation affecting intellectual property. Applicable preemption principles in federal Indian law are somewhat different than federal/state preemption. There can also be preemption of one federal statute by another. A number of cases have dealt with the interplay between the federal intellectual property statutes and each other, or with other federal law. *See, e.g., Dastar Corp. v. Twentieth Century Fox Film Corp.,* 123 S. Ct. 2041 (2003) (construing trademark statute narrowly to avoid giving copyright-like protection under trademark law).

2. are in works of authorship fixed in a tangible medium of expression, and

3. come within the scope of copyright as specified by §§102 and 103.

Section 301 does not preempt state rights that are not equivalent to federal copyright rights (such as state law governing ownership of a painting, as opposed to ownership of the copyright in the painting), state rights in unfixed works (such as a common law copyright in a dance that has not been fixed in a tangible form), or state rights that do not fall within the scope of copyright (such as rights to inherit the painting).

Courts generally have read "the scope of copyright" to include matter protected by copyright but also subject matter that the Copyright Act leaves unprotected. For example, ideas are excluded from copyright protection by §§102 and 103. Such subject matter falls within the scope of copyright, however, for preemption purposes, meaning states could not grant copyrights in ideas. The fact that the Copyright Act leaves subject matter unprotected does not mean that it is free for the states to grant rights in the subject matter. Rather, the effect is that the matter is left in the public domain, for copyright purposes. A state law that granted copyright protection in ideas would be preempted. The state remains free to grant rights in ideas if the rights are not equivalent to those in copyright.

Section 301 bars state rights that are "equivalent" to any of the §106 exclusive rights (the right to make copies, the right to adapt the work, the right to distribute the work to the public, the right to perform the work publicly, and the right to display the work publicly). To decide whether a right is equivalent, most courts use the "extra element" test. The court determines whether the state right would be infringed by an act that would potentially infringe a federal copyright or whether infringement of the state right required showing additional substantial elements. Suppose a state law prohibits making unauthorized copies of paintings. Anyone who makes an unauthorized copy violates both state and federal law. The rights are equivalent, and the state statute is preempted. Likewise, the Copyright Act preempts a state law unjust enrichment claim based on using a screenplay and novel to make a movie without compensation. Although "enrichment" is not an element of a copyright infringement action, the suit was essentially enforcing "the right of adaptation—i.e., the right to prepare or authorize preparation of a derivative work based on a novel or screenplay." *Briarpatch Ltd., L.P. v. Phoenix Pictures, Inc.*, 373 F.3d 296, 306 (2d Cir. 2004).

Suppose the state statute, by contrast, prohibits fraudulently selling unauthorized copies of paintings. The additional element of fraudulent intent is not required by copyright. The state right is not equivalent here and is not preempted.

Whether rights are equivalent is not always clear. Courts usually require that there be a substantial difference in the state right to avoid preemption. Suppose a state law prohibits unauthorized copying of paintings done for commercial gain. The element of commercial gain is not required for copyright infringement. But because that additional element makes little difference to the substance of the right, the state right is still substantially equivalent and therefore preempted. In considering equivalence, courts also consider which parties are subject to the right. For example, a contract may provide limitations on the use of information that are similar to the §106 rights. The recipient of information may agree that she will not make copies, distribute, or adapt the information. A leading decision held that such a contractual right is not equivalent to a right under copyright because it applies only to the contracting parties and is not an exclusive right against the rest of the world. *See ProCD v. Zeidenburg*, 86 F.3d 1447 (7th Cir. 1996). But commentators have argued that if the information is widely licensed subject to such restrictions (such as mass-market software), the restriction may be functionally equivalent to an exclusive right.

Finally, the federal statute preempts only rights in works fixed in tangible form. Before the 1976 Act, federal copyright applied primarily to published works, although some unpublished works could be copyrighted through registration. State copyright law generally applied to unpublished works. Congress changed that balance in the 1976 Act, expanding federal copyright protection to works as soon as they were fixed in a tangible form. The preemption provision likewise preempts state copyright law, except as to "unfixed" works—works not fixed in tangible form. As the legislative history notes, this leaves some (not many) works to state copyright law protection: "Examples would include choreography that has never been filmed or notated, an extemporaneous speech, 'original works of authorship' communicated solely through conversations or live broadcasts [that were not recorded], and a dramatic sketch or musical composition improvised or developed from memory and without being recorded or written down." House Report No. 94-1476.

Conflict Preemption

In addition to express preemption under §301, state law is subject to conflict preemption. The first type of conflict preemption (impossible to comply with both federal and state law) is rare with such subject matter. But the second type of conflict preemption (state law obstructs accomplishment of objectives of federal law) has been raised in several areas. Contracts often contain restrict uses that are permitted by copyright law.

Courts have regularly applied federal copyright rules to supplant contract law where state law conflicts with specific provisions of the Copyright Act. The requirements of a signed writing for a transfer of copyright ownership under §204 will control, even where the parties would have had an enforceable oral agreement under state law. Likewise, a party may exercise its rights under the Copyright Act to terminate a license or transfer of copyright, even if applicable state law would have made the agreement permanent.

Where the conflict is more abstract, courts to date have been less likely to apply preemption. Software licenses might contain clauses prohibiting reverse engineering, which otherwise would be fair use. Database licenses may prohibit copying or distribution of facts, which are not protected by law. Nondisclosure agreements likewise prohibit restrictions on noncopyrightable material, such as functional matter, facts, or ideas. Most cases have upheld contractual restrictions against preemption arguments. *See, e.g., ProCD, supra; Bowers v. Baystate Techs.*, 302 F.3d 1334, 1343 (Fed. Cir. 2002) (holding no preemption of "shrinkwrap" contract that prohibited any reverse engineering of the software covered by the agreement); *Davidson & Assocs. v. Jung*, 422 F.3d 630 (8th Cir. 2005) (same). But some courts have (similar to patent law, as discussed below)[3] limited enforceability of state law rights that appear to conflict with copyright policy. *See Vault Corp. v. Quaid Software Ltd.*, 847 F.2d 255 (5th Cir. 1988) (applying preemption to enforcement of software license terms when license effectively denied rights provided by §117 of the Copyright Act).

Case law is struggling with preemption in other areas. Suppose a photographer makes a photograph of some surfers. The photo is used in an advertising campaign with permission of the photographer, who owns the copyright. Do the surfers have a cause of action under the right of publicity, or are rights in use of the photo governed exclusively by federal copyright law? *Downing v. Abercrombie & Fitch*, 265 F.3d 994 (9th Cir. 2001) held that the surfers' rights of publicity were not preempted. As the right to publicity expands, such possible conflicts are likely to increase. Another type of conflict arises with respect to using copyrights as collateral for loans. Whether the creditor should protect her rights by filing in the copyright office or the state UCC office remains unsettled. *See World Auxiliary Power v. Silicon Valley Bank*, 303 F.3d 1120 (9th Cir. 2002) (holding that federal law preempted perfection of security interests in registered copyrights but not in unregistered copyrights).

Patent Preemption

The patent statute does not expressly preempt state law. Courts, however, have consistently given it preemptive effect. Most cases do not involve field preemption or the impossibility version of conflict preemption. Rather, the cases generally involve the issue of whether state law conflicts with the objectives of patent law. The leading Supreme Court cases have emphasized different objectives of patent law.

One line of cases has found preemption when state law simply prohibits copying and selling an unpatented product. *See Bonito Boats v. Thunder Craft Boats,*

---

3. One court expressly declined to apply patent restrictions in the copyright context. As discussed below, courts generally will not enforce a licensee's agreement not to challenge the validity of the patent. The court declined to apply a similar rule to copyright license in *Saturday Evening Post Co. v. Rumbleseat Press*, 816 F.2d 1191 (7th Cir. 1987).

489 U.S. 141 (1989); *Sears, Roebuck & Co. v. Stiffel*, 376 U.S. 225 (1964); *Compco Corp. v. Day-Brite Lighting*, 376 U.S. 234 (1964). *Sears* and *Compco* involved liability under unfair competition law for selling a product copied from a competitor's product. Both laws imposed liability without requiring a showing of deception or confusion among buyers about the source of the product. Rather, merely selling a copied product was prohibited, even though the product was unpatented. In *Bonito Boats*, a state statute prohibited the use of a molding process to copy boat hull designs (even if the designs were unpatented). This line of cases emphasized that the state law granted exclusive rights in publicly known functional products, without requiring compliance with the high standards of patent law (novelty, originality, and nonobviousness). In effect, an inventor could get state patent rights even if she could not meet the federal patent standards. Such laws were preempted by conflict with the patent statute.

In *Kewanee Oil v. Bicron Corp.*, 416 U.S. 470 (1974), the Court emphasized different objectives of the patent statute. The issue in *Kewanee* was whether federal patent law preempted state trade secret law. The *Kewanee* Court considered whether state trade secret protection interfered with the patent law policies of encouraging invention and of requiring disclosure of the invention in exchange for protection. The Court reasoned that there was no conflict with respect to incentives for invention because both trade secret law and patent law encouraged inventive activity. The Court also held that trade secret law did not interfere with the patent law policy of disclosure, even though trade secret protection depends on concealing, rather than disclosing, the information. The Court reasoned that the trade secret might be unpatentable, in which case it would not be disclosed to the U.S. Patent and Trademark Office (USPTO); might be of questionable patentability, in which case its disclosure would be of marginal value; and might be patentable, in which case the inventor would more likely seek the stronger rights of a patent than the more limited rights under trade secret protection.

A third line of cases has applied preemption when state law rights could interfere with specific patent law policies. A patent license clause agreeing not to challenge the validity of the patent was unenforceable because it undermined the strong federal policy against enforcing invalid patents. *See Lear v. Adkins*, 395 U.S. 653 (1969). An agreement to pay licensing royalties beyond the term of the patent was unenforceable because it effectively extended the term set by the statute. *See Brulotte v. Thys Co.*, 379 U.S. 29 (1964). By contrast, patent law did not preempt enforcement of an agreement to pay royalties for an unpatented invention, even when royalties were required if the patent application was denied. *See Aronson v. Quick Point Pencil*, 440 U.S. 257 (1979). The *Aronson* Court found no conflict with a specific patent law policy and considered enforcement of the agreement consistent with the general goals of encouraging inventive activity (including nonpatentable inventions) and disclosure (because the agreement helped the product be disclosed to the public).

Examples

1. *Fair's fair?* Ford Motor Company has a problem with noise, vibration, and harshness in its vehicles' air conditioners. Ultra-Precision works together with Ford to address the problem. The parties, however, do not have an express or implied contract. Ultra-Precision invents an improvement to the design of the air conditioners and suggests it to Ford. Ultra-Precision does not patent the invention, leaving it in the public domain. Ford Motor adopts Ultra-Precision's technical enhancement, but does not compensate Ultra-Precision. Ultra-Precision sues Ford for unjust enrichment. Is Ultra-Precision's state law claim for unjust enrichment preempted by the federal patent statute?

2. *Author's rights.* A new Broadonia statute provides that any poet has the exclusive right to sell copies of her poems or to read them in public once she has written the poem down or otherwise preserved it. Shakes, a poet, seeks to enforce his rights under the statute against a literary magazine that printed one of his poems without permission. The magazine contends that the Broadonia statute is preempted by the federal statute. Shakes responds that the Broadonia is not preempted because it is entirely consistent with the federal statute. Both grant rights to the authors of poems. Is the Broadonia statute preempted? Would it make a difference if the Broadonia statute applied only to poems that had not been written down or otherwise preserved in a stable form by the poet (that is, to poems saved only in the poet's mind)?

3. *Unauthorized biography.* Broadonia passes a statute granting each person the exclusive right to make or sell any book based on the person's life. Anyone making or selling a book about someone without permission is liable for a percentage of the receipts from the work. The statute expressly provides that it does not apply to copying of expression that is protected by copyright, rather only to use of facts or ideas involving the person. Is the statute preempted by federal law?

4. *Bio-rights.* In several publicized cases, biotech companies in Broadonia make huge profits based on biological material drawn from particular individuals, without sharing the profits with the individuals. For example, Gene was a subject in Zoomzyne's blood research program. With Gene's full knowledge and consent, Zoomzyne isolated certain cells in Gene's blood with unusual characteristics. Zoomzyne later patented an enzyme found in Gene's blood cells and now receives millions in licensing fees. Gene received only the free medical testing that Zoomzyne agreed to provide him. Reacting to such cases, Broadonia passes a statute providing that any individual has the right to exclude others from

making, using, or selling a product that is directly or indirectly drawn from her tissue. Is the Broadonia statute preempted by federal law?

5. *Broken promise.* Zosoft sells widely used software for processing digital images. In order to use the software, the user must click on YES to the click-wrap agreement. One clause of the agreement provides that the user agrees not to copy any aspect of Zosoft's software into other software. Myrtle buys a copy of the software and greatly admires how well the software works. Myrtle then develops her own digital imaging software for the commercial market, copying several functional aspects of Zosoft's software. Zosoft sues for breach of contract. Myrtle contends that enforcement of the contract is preempted by federal law. Is Zosoft's cause of action preempted?

6. *Characters are people, too.* Broadonia expands the scope of its right to publicity statute by granting a right of publicity to fictional characters in books, films, or other works. The Broadonia statute provides that there shall be a right of publicity for any fictional character, encompassing the exclusive right to make or distribute any work that contains the character. Such right belongs to the author of the work in which the fictional character first appears. Years ago, Downpike sold the copyright to her first novel, which features the hardboiled detective Annie Asphalt. The buyer of the copyright has just published a sequel to the novel and released a movie based on the novel, both featuring Annie Asphalt. Is Downpike's cause of action under the Broadonia statute preempted by federal law?

7. *Self-patent.* As described in a previous example, Phisto, a computer scientist, publishes an academic article disclosing the code to a useful computer program. The article includes the following language: "Anyone who uses my method hereby agrees to pay me the modest fee of $365 per year, $1 a day for avoiding all those annoying ads." Suppose that Broadonia, unlike other states, enforces such a restriction under contract law and requires royalties from anyone who uses the method. Broadonia enforces the restriction against anyone, without requiring a showing that the person agreed to the restriction or even that the person took the information under circumstances giving her notice of the restriction. Are such contract law rights preempted by federal law?

8. *Preemption of misappropriation?* Theflyonthewall.com collected investment recommendations made by major financial institutions and published the information before the financial institutions themselves made them public. Sued for state law misappropriation, Theflyontheall.com argued that the federal copyright statute preempted any state law liability. Does it?

9. *Zombie lawsuit?* Montz spoke with some TV producers to sell his "idea for a television show that would follow a team of paranormal investigators

conducting field investigations." They did not hire him. But later on, they produced *Ghost Hunters*, which Montz deemed to be an incarnation of his idea. Under California law, where a writer discloses a script idea to a producer, there may be an implied contract that the writer will be compensated if the idea is used. But the producers argued that federal law preempted a suit based simply on copying ideas. Federal copyright law permits copying of ideas, so state law cannot forbid it. Can Montz proceed?

10. *Following rights.* The California Resale Royalties Act required that when works of fine art are resold, 5 percent must go to the artist. Any conflict with federal copyright law?

11. *Offsides?* Former professional football players file suit, alleging that commercial use of footage from their playing days infringes their right of publicity. Preemption?

Explanations

1. Ultra-Precision's claim was preempted by the federal patent statute. *See Ultra-Precision Mfg. v. Ford Motor Co.*, 411 F.3d 1369 (Fed. Cir. 2005). Ultra-Precision is simply claiming that Ford benefited by using technology developed by Ultra-Precision and therefore must compensate Ultra-Precision. If state law granted such a right, it would grant patent-like protection. The result would be different if there were a contract between Ultra-Precision and Ford or if Ultra-Precision alleged that Ford misappropriated a trade secret of Ultra-Precision. But Ultra-Precision here is seeking patent-like protection without complying with the requirements set forth by federal patent law.

2. The Broadonia statute is preempted under §301 of the Copyright Act. It is unnecessary to consider conflict preemption or field preemption. The Copyright Act expressly preempts certain state rights such as this Broadonia statute. Under §301, the Copyright Act preempts any state right that is

   1. is equivalent to any of the §106 exclusive rights,
   2. is in works of authorship fixed in a tangible medium of expression, and
   3. comes within the scope of copyright as specified by §§102 and 103.

   The rights under the Broadonia statute meet all three requirements. The rights are equivalent to the §106 rights to distribute the work to the public and perform the work publicly. The rights are in a fixed work of authorship, having been written down or otherwise preserved. Poetry comes well within the scope of copyright.

The Broadonia statute would not be preempted if it applied only to poetry that the author had not preserved in tangible form. As listed above, §301 preemption applies only to works that are fixed in a tangible medium of expression. Field preemption and conflict preemption would also be inapplicable to unfixed works. Rather, states remain generally free to regulate copyright in unfixed works (a narrow category of works).

3. The Broadonia statute is preempted. It is not clear that §301 preemption applies. The Broadonia statute does grant a right equivalent to §106 rights (a right to make copies or distribute works to the public) that comes within the scope of copyright. But the right arguably is not based on a work of authorship that is fixed in tangible form; rather it is based only on intangible facts and ideas relating to the life of a person. One might conclude, however, that the statute gives the subject a copyright once the ideas have been fixed in the form of a book written by someone else. In any case, the statute surely is invalid under conflict preemption because it grants exclusive rights to make and distribute works using certain ideas and facts, exactly the sort of material that the Copyright Act seeks to keep in the public domain. It does not have any extra elements such as deception and so is equivalent to granting a copyright in ideas and facts.

4. The Broadonia statute probably would be preempted, due to its conflict with federal patent law. The Broadonia statute gives a set of exclusive rights that are equivalent to the rights of a patent holder. But it does not grant the rights to the inventor of the product or require that the person meet the standards for obtaining a patent (the substantive standards of novelty and nonobviousness, and the procedural standards of disclosure required in the patent application). Cf. *Moore v. Regents of University of California*, 51 Cal. 3d 120 (1990) (briefly suggesting preemption would be applicable). So the conflict with the balance set by federal patent law probably would lead to a conclusion of preemption. Note that contracts between individuals and researchers requiring a share in patent rights very likely would not be preempted.

5. This case gives an example of an area that is presently unsettled, the extent to which contract law may be used to obtain rights that copyright law does not grant. Contracts frequently protect information that is not protectable by copyright (such as facts, ideas, or functional matter) or reduce user rights granted by copyright (such as fair use or first sale rights). Courts generally have upheld such restrictions. When only a few parties are subject to the contract, such private agreements seem to have little conflict with copyright law — and indeed often further copyright law by enabling efficient licensing of copyrighted works. But, as both legal and technological licensing techniques continue to refine control

over information, there may be more cases in which (as in patent law) courts hold that contractual restrictions are unenforceable in light of federal copyright law policy (or other federal law, such as antitrust). So there is no clear answer to this case. Courts generally have upheld contractual restrictions that exceed the exclusive rights of copyright, but where the lines may be drawn awaits further development of the case law. A court conceivably could hold that enforcement of the agreement not to copy would effectively give exclusive rights in noncopyrightable, nonpatented product and is therefore preempted.

6. Downpike's state law cause of action would be preempted by the federal copyright statute. The Broadonia statute gives the author of a fictional works the exclusive right to make or distribute any work that contains the character. Such an exclusive right is equivalent to some of the exclusive rights of federal copyright law (the rights to make copies, to adapt the work, and to distribute copies). It would be preempted under §301 of the Copyright Act.

7. The state law rights granted to Phisto are preempted by federal patent law. Even though these rights are nominally granted under contract law, Broadonia is effectively granting a state law patent to Phisto. He has the right to exclude others from using his method without compensation. To obtain this right, he need merely publish the method with the quoted language demanding payment (as opposed to applying for a patent and meeting the substantive and procedural requirements for protection). Such a scheme conflicts with the balance set by federal patent law.

8. The court held that federal copyright law would preempt liability for simply copying information in this case, following the *NBA v. Motorola* case discussed above with respect to the tort of misappropriation. *Barclays Capital Inc. v. Theflyonthewall.com Inc.*, 99 U.S.P.Q.2d (BNA) 1247 (2d Cir. 2011). Federal copyright law allows copying of facts, nonoriginal expression, and other noncopyrightable elements. *Theflyonthewall.com* addresses the "ghostly presence" of *International News Service v. Associated Press*, 248 U.S. 215 (1918), under which misappropriation of "hot news" might supply a cause of action. The Second Circuit held that "hot news" might still survive where it was sufficiently different from the federal copyright law. But the tort would be very narrow. It would only apply where free-riding allowed the defendant to produce a product in direct competition for lower cost. But the plaintiffs here were financial institutions making the recommendations as part of a broader business providing financial services. They were not in direct competition with the seller of investment tips, and their entire business would not be at risk if the recommendations would be prematurely made public. Under *Theflyonthewall.com*, it will be difficult to impose liability simply for copying information (as

opposed to using improper means to obtain information, which will still be subject to liability under such theories as trade secret misappropriation or breach of contractual promises not to disclose information).

9. Copyright did not preempt the state law claim because it had an "an added element: an agreement to pay for use of the disclosed ideas." *Montz v. Pilgrim Films & Television Inc.*, 98 U.S.P.Q.2d (BNA) 1569 (9th Cir. 2011) (en banc).

10. The California law conflicted with federal copyright's first sale doctrine, which authorizes the owner of a copy (including the original) of a work to resell it, free of obligations to the copyright holder. "Because the CRRA disrupts Congress's efforts to balance the interests of copyright holders and downstream consumers, it must be preempted." *Estate of Graham v. Sotheby's, Inc.*, 178 F. Supp. 3d 974, 988 (C.D. Cal. 2016).

11. The court held that the federal copyright statute preempted state law right of publicity claims brought by former professional football players against NFL Films. *Dryer v. National Football League*, 814 F.3d 938 (8th Cir. 2016). The court reasoned that their claims would be the state law equivalent of copyright claims. The court distinguished the case where an announcer's voice had been used in advertising, because that was a commercial use of the identity, as opposed to the sort of expressive use that copyright protects. *Dryer* viewed the player's claims as analogous to claims brought by actors in a movie: "If [a] performer [in a copyrighted recording] later objects to the reproduction or performance of that recording in an expressive, non-advertising use, then the claim is one of copyright infringement, not of infringement of the right of publicity."[4]

Others might differ. Football players, unlike actors or musicians, are not performing a copyrighted work. Football games are not scripted, nor was this based on some claimed copyright in the choreography of the plays. Rather, the relevant copyright was in the game footage. The court placed weight on the fact that NFL Films had permission to make the films. But the players were not claiming to hold copyright in the films as authors, they were alleging that use of the films infringed their state law rights of publicity. A sounder way to resolve the case may have been an issue the court did reach, whether the First Amendment would bar such a broad interpretation of the state law right of publicity.

---

4. *Dryer v. NFL*, 814 F.3d at 943 (quoting, in parenthetical, J. Thomas McCarthy, *The Rights of Publicity and Privacy* §11.55 (2d ed. 2013)).

Index

Index